BIBLICAL
THEOLOGY

The God of the Christian Scriptures

✛

JOHN GOLDINGAY

IVP Academic

An imprint of InterVarsity Press
Downers Grove, Illinois

InterVarsity Press
P.O. Box 1400, Downers Grove, IL 60515-1426
ivpress.com
email@ivpress.com

©2016 by John Goldingay

*InterVarsity Press® is the book-publishing division of InterVarsity Christian Fellowship/USA®, a
movement of students and faculty active on campus at hundreds of universities, colleges and schools
of nursing in the United States of America, and a member movement of the International Fellowship
of Evangelical Students. For information about local and regional activities, visit intervarsity.org.*

All Scripture quotations, unless otherwise indicated, are the author's translation.

Cover design: Cindy Kiple
Interior design: Beth McGill
Images: ©Langfactor/iStockphoto

ISBN 978-0-8308-5153-9 (print)
ISBN 978-0-8308-7314-2 (digital)

Printed in the United States of America ∞

Library of Congress Cataloging-in-Publication Data

A catalog record for this book is available from the Library of Congress.

P	25	24	23	22	21	20	19	18	17	16	15	14	13	12	11	10	9	8	7	6	5	4	3	2	1
Y	34	33	32	31	30	29	28	27	26	25	24	23	22	21	20	19	18	17	16						

To no one has [the Lord] given power to proclaim his works,
and who can fathom his mighty deeds?
Who can measure his majestic power,
and who can go on to recount his mercies?
It is not possible to lessen or increase them,
nor is it possible to fathom the Lord's wonders.
When human beings have finished, they are just beginning,
and when they stop, they are still at a loss.

SIRACH 18:4-7

Mystery is the lifeblood of dogmatics.

BAVINCK, *REFORMED DOGMATICS* 2:29

(It's important to biblical theology, too.)

CONTENTS

PREFACE

When I was writing an *Old Testament Theology*,[1] a voice in my head told me that it should be a biblical theology. To consider the theological significance of the Old Testament in isolation was an odd exercise, given that the church acknowledges the two Testaments as its Scriptures. Admittedly, it's not as odd an exercise as treating the New Testament in isolation. The Old Testament Scriptures do not presuppose the New, and they are not incomprehensible without the New, and the idea of someone in the year 10 BC asking about the theological contents of the Old Testament as a whole is not an incoherent one (if I may sidestep questions about when the precise list of its books became settled). In contrast, the New Testament presupposes the scriptural status of those writings, and asking about the New Testament's theological implications in isolation from them is a dangerously incoherent enterprise.

I had no answer of principle to the voice in my head, only the tactical conviction (implicit in that point about the danger of New Testament theology) that it was important to focus on the Old Testament to counterbalance the usual practice of ignoring it theologically. But I recognized the force of the voice, and this book is my attempt to meet its point.

In writing, I followed a similar procedure to the one I used for my *Old Testament Theology*. I made a list of possible chapter headings on the basis of my hunches as to what headings might be needed, and then began to read the New Testament and to make notes under those headings.

By working in this way I wanted to give priority to my reading of the Scriptures themselves and to let them set the agenda for the work. Having written an *Old Testament Theology*, I wasn't confident I could think through

---

[1]3 vols. (Downers Grove, IL: InterVarsity Press; Milton Keynes, UK: Paternoster, 2003, 2006, 2009).

the Old Testament material afresh if I began there; it would be a rehash of previous work. Beginning with the New Testament gave me a different entry into the Old Testament material. In keeping with the way I went about the task, in presenting the material in this volume I often start with the New Testament, which has the advantage of starting where the church is, in its own greater involvement with the New Testament.

As well as studying the Scriptures, I read some commentaries and other works, and reshaped and developed the headings and the structure of the work as the data seemed to require it. On the way along, I added consideration of material from the Old Testament that linked with the various themes (and that did not), and did so more systematically when I had completed my initial work.

Beyond this preface and the introduction that follows, I do not discuss method or take up questions about the relationship between the Testaments. My most recent consideration of such questions turned into a book of its own, *Do We Need the New Testament?*[2] The present book presupposes positions laid out there. It does pay proportionately more attention to the New Testament than that other title might suggest or than you or I might have expected. This characteristic reflects the method of working that started from the New Testament; it also means that I don't substantially repeat the contents of the *Old Testament Theology* and that I'm not tempted to let this book get too long. Often I have simply indicated where a characteristically Old Testament theme fits, made a brief comment on it, and added some footnote references to material in the *Old Testament Theology*, though the three volumes of the latter include material that expands on almost every section of this book. I hold onto a silly hope that you might even be pushed into reading that work.

Biblical translations are my own unless otherwise indicated. In references such as "Ps 31:19 [MT 20]," the figures within the square bracket indicate the versification in printed Hebrew Bibles where this differs from the versification in English Bibles. In the New Testament, I usually translate the Greek word *christos* as "Anointed" rather than using the transliteration

---

[2]Downers Grove, IL: InterVarsity Press, 2015.

"Christ," which easily gives the impression that the word is a name,[3] and I translate the expression *huios tou anthrōpou* "Man" rather than "Son of man."[4] I generally use the word *congregation* rather than the word *church* and the word *believers* rather than the word *Christians*, which is hardly used in the New Testament; Jesus talks about discipling people, not making them Christians,[5] while in Paul, *believers* is the main word in this connection, "saints" (*hagioi*) being his other principal word—both Jews and pagans are called "unbelievers" (*apistoi*).[6] In speaking of the origin of biblical books such as Jeremiah or Matthew or Ephesians, I often refer to the authors of the entire books by the names traditionally associated with them, without meaning to imply that I necessarily have a view on the author's actual identity.

I have used the following abbreviations:

CD   Karl Barth, *Church Dogmatics*. 13 vols. Edinburgh: T&T Clark, 1936–1969

JBL   *Journal of Biblical Literature*

JPSV   Jewish Publication Society Version

JSNT   *Journal for the Study of the New Testament*

KJV   King James (Authorized) Version

LW   Luther's Works

MT   Masoretic Text, especially in references to the verse numbers in printed Hebrew Bibles when they differ from verse numbers in English Bibles

NIV   New International Version

NPNF   *A Select Library of the Nicene and Post-Nicene Fathers*. Reprint, Edinburgh: T&T Clark; Grand Rapids: Eerdmans, 1991

NRSV   New Revised Standard Version

NTS   *New Testament Studies*

---

[3]See the comments in N. T. Wright, *Paul and the Faithfulness of God* (Minneapolis: Fortress; London: SPCK, 2013), 835, though he does use the transliteration.

[4]See the paragraphs under "Man" in section 5.2 below; and Johnny Cash's "When the Man Comes Around."

[5]Cf. Barth, *CD* IV, 3:525.

[6]E. P. Sanders, *Paul and Palestinian Judaism* (London: SCM Press; Philadelphia: Fortress, 1977), 445, 452.

OTT   John Goldingay, *Old Testament Theology*. 3 vols. Downers Grove,
         IL: InterVarsity Press; Milton Keynes, UK: Paternoster, 2003, 2006,
         2009
TNIV   Today's New International Version

I am grateful to Thomas A. Bennett and to Kathleen Scott Goldingay for their careful reading and comments on a draft of this book, as of many others. I occasionally refer to them in footnotes, but their contribution is greater than these references imply. And I'm grateful to Anna Lo for compiling the indexes. It's also time I expressed my gratitude for the advice and support of Dan Reid, my editor at IVP, who has also given me such wise advice and support over quite some years. The last suggestion in connection with this volume was to tell you that I was making the last touches to its text as the Rose Parade made its way past our house on South Orange Grove Boulevard in Pasadena, California, on New Year's Day 2016.

INTRODUCTION

"Biblical theology" means different things to different people, and I am not concerned to argue that the expression should be used only in the sense that I attach to it; I will just make clear what I mean by the phrase. There is a collection of works that comprise the Scriptures for the Jewish community, which calls them the Torah, the Prophets and the Writings; it is the collection that Christians call the Old Testament, which I will henceforth usually refer to as the First Testament. There is a further collection that the church came to define, which Christians call the New Testament. The church regards these two collections as belonging together, and they are commonly printed as one volume. In this book, I am asking, "What understanding of God and the world and life emerges from these two Testaments?" It doesn't seem an outrageous question, even if seeking to answer it might be "an act of naïve hubris."[1] Even if it does seem outrageous, I've been asking it, and this book gives you my answer.

One reason why it has seemed a tricky question is that the two Testaments consist of writings that came into existence through the work of scores of people over the best part of a thousand years, over a wide area of the Middle East and the eastern Mediterranean. Yet they issued from what Christians see as a single story, about God's involvement with a particular people and about the way that involvement came to embrace other peoples. They comprise a collection of documents that relate aspects of that story, pass on insights about the God who orchestrated it, challenge people about the lives they lived in its context, issue warnings and promises about the future, record the prayer and praise that people addressed to God, and also incorporate letters, poems and observations about life. They resemble a

---

[1]Scott J. Hafemann's unease about his own attempt, *The God of Promise and the Life of Faith* (Wheaton, IL: Crossway, 2001), 19.

family photograph album or commonplace book or scrapbook or collection
of memorabilia, an anthology that tells a family history and gives us a picture
of the family in different periods.

They are thus not a "coherent tradition" like the work of Thomas Aquinas
or John Calvin but a "canonical bundle of overlapping testimonies from
radically different contexts to the one history of God with humanity which
culminates in Christ's death and resurrection. The Scriptures come to us in
the form of plural traditions." Indeed (as Nietzsche puts it), "the will to a
system is a lack of integrity."[2] But "in the agenda of a hermeneutics of doctrine . . . there is room for 'system' both as coherence . . . and as a provision
for boundary markers and identity markers in interaction with ongoing
history, experience, and hermeneutical life-worlds" even though "the notion
of a 'final system' is excluded."[3]

In the way the Scriptures themselves do theology, two forms are most
prominent. Both Testaments are dominated by a series of narratives, and
this characteristic reflects and points to a key feature of the Scriptures' theology. It is a theology that focuses on a story. It comprises an account of
particular things that God and human beings did in particular places and
times, and considerable reflection on these actions and events. Both Testaments also incorporate much material that is more discursive and analytic;
it consists of teaching that explicitly or implicitly deals with the implications of the events that the narratives relate. It thus covers theological
themes (the truth about God, Israel, the world, humanity and so on), and
the nature of a proper response to God (in worship, spirituality, ethics and
so on). In my *Old Testament Theology* the first volume took up the narrative
form, while the other two volumes took up the discursive and analytic form
(the First Testament also does theology by means of praise and prayer; I
did not try to emulate that approach). In this book the two forms interweave more. I begin with God's own being and go on to the world, humanity, the people of God and God's expectations. At the same time, I
move from creation to Israel to Jesus to the consummation of God's

---

[2]Miroslav Volf, *Exclusion and Embrace* (Nashville: Abingdon, 1996), 208-9, quoting from Friedrich
Nietzsche's opening "Maxims and Arrows" in *Twilight of the Idols and The Anti-Christ* (London
and New York: Penguin, 1968), 25.
[3]Anthony C. Thiselton, *The Hermeneutics of Doctrine* (Grand Rapids: Eerdmans, 2007), 141.

purpose. I begin with the discursive (God's person) and end with the narrative (God's triumph).

Definitions of biblical theology have distinguished between "the theology contained in the Bible" and "the theology that accords with the Bible."[4] My aim lies somewhere between these alternatives. Like Jerome, or Calvin or Barth, I do theology as the person I am in the time in which I write, which in my case means as an aging British priest, scholar and music freak living in Los Angeles in the twenty-first century. I formulate a biblical theology with the help of works by scholars such as Karl Barth, Richard Bauckham, Rudolf Bultmann, James Dunn, Richard Hays, E. P. Sanders and N. T. Wright, and fifty years ago I could not have written it in the way I do. Even more frighteningly, in fifty years' time it will need formulating differently.

I want to know what significance these Scriptures have in our time, and I want other people to see it, and this interest will poke through. "Ethics, while descriptive, is not detached; it reflects normatively,"[5] and the same is true of biblical theology. I do not always resist the temptation to note ways in which these Scriptures are significant for us or to try to think through questions they raise for us. But I don't want such interests to stop me seeing what they have to say in their own right. I am passionately concerned for them to affect our life here and now, and that fact cannot but impact the way I see biblical theology. Yet I am not intentionally seeking to state its nature in a way that mainly makes it a message for my context, and I do not pay much attention to questions that are more important in our context than they are in the Scriptures, such as race or violence or abortion or homosexuality or the rights of women or ecology. When a theology student in his first term heard that I was writing a biblical theology, he inferred that it was therefore a systematic theology. It isn't. Systematic theology works out the implications of the Scriptures in a way that makes sense in its author's own context, using the categories of thought that belong in that context. I don't disapprove of that enterprise, but I'm trying to avoid undertaking it.

---

[4]Gerhard Ebeling, *Word and Faith* (Philadelphia: Fortress; London: SCM Press, 1963), 79; cf. Brevard S. Childs, *Biblical Theology of the Old and New Testaments* (London: SCM Press, 1992; Minneapolis: Fortress, 1993), 3.

[5]Oliver O'Donovan, *Self, World, and Time* (Grand Rapids and Cambridge, UK: Eerdmans, 2013), 71.

My aim is not to identify a "common core" or "underlying unity" that
the biblical writings share; the nature of such a common core is inclined
to be thin.[6] I am seeking to identify the "building" that might be constructed from the materials that the writings offer, in a way that does
justice to them.[7] People and events are complicated, and after watching a
movie or listening to an album together, a group of people may come away
with different impressions and may have quite a heated discussion about
them. This volume is the impression I have as I come away from the Scriptures. When John Calvin wrote the *Institutes of the Christian Religion*, he
did so to provide an outline of the nature of biblical faith, to give people a
context within which they could then read the Scriptures. My hopes for
this volume will have been fulfilled if it helps people do so. It is an attempt
at a digest of the Scriptures. It is for the reader then to test the digest against
the Scriptures themselves.

I presuppose that these Scriptures do all belong to the same album. Most
Jewish readers of the New Testament would question this conviction, and
Christian readers may have an uneasy suspicion that they are right. For most
Jewish readers, the idea that Jesus fulfilled Israel's messianic hopes seems
implausible. For Christian readers, the compassionate Jesus of the Gospels
doesn't look like an embodiment of the wrathful God they associate with
the first three-quarters of their Scriptures.

Yet the writers of the documents that became the New Testament didn't feel
any tension over recognizing the God of the Jewish Scriptures as the Father of
Jesus, and I would say that there is no more "problem" about the relationship
between the content of First Testament faith and New Testament faith than
there is about the relationship among (say) Matthew, 1 Corinthians and

---

[6]Cf. the comments of Heikki Räisänen, "The New Testament in Theology," in *Companion Encyclopedia of Theology*, ed. Peter Byrne and Leslie Houlden (London and New York: Routledge,
1995), 122-41 (on 124), in relation to James D. G. Dunn, *Unity and Diversity in the New Testament*,
2nd ed. (London: SCM Press, 1990); cf. Anthony C. Thiselton, *Thiselton on Hermeneutics* (Grand
Rapids and Cambridge, UK: Eerdmans, 2006), 43.

[7]For these images, see, e.g., I. Howard Marshall, *New Testament Theology* (Downers Grove, IL;
Nottingham, UK: InterVarsity Press, 2004), 23-34, 710-26. I describe the constructive nature of
Old Testament theology in *Theological Diversity and the Authority of the Old Testament* (Grand
Rapids: Eerdmans, 1987; Carlisle, UK: Paternoster, 1995), 181-99. Compare also Childs, *Biblical
Theology of the Old and New Testaments*, 85, though I do not see the Old Testament as "witness
to Christ" in the way that he does; it is about God, not about Christ.

Revelation, or among Exodus, the Song of Songs and Joel.[8] The church's recognition of these two collections of Scriptures implies at least some prima facie plausibility about treating them together, and about asking what impression we have as we close the album. Reading the end of a story often makes us revisit the earlier part and see things whose significance we did not perceive the first time around. It doesn't make us read into the story things that weren't there, but it enables us to see things that we missed. On the other hand, the common Christian practice of fast-forwarding through the first three-quarters of the movie to get to the denouement means understanding neither Testament.

I do not attempt to demonstrate that biblical theology is true, or to question whether it is true. I aim to write a critical biblical theology in the sense that I seek to avoid reading into the Scriptures the categories and convictions of postbiblical Christian theology. Thus, while I accept the doctrine of the Trinity, as a set of inferences from the Scriptures issuing from the translation of biblical ideas into European philosophical categories some while after the New Testament, and while I say the Nicene Creed without mental reservation every Sunday, I do not assume that such later understandings of God as Trinity, or later understandings of the atonement, are present in the Scriptures themselves, and in this sense I am not writing an "ecclesial theology."[9]

But the choice between being historical, critical and academic or being ecclesial in that sense[10] is phony. I am betting that it is possible even for a Christian to ask the critical, historical and academic question, "Given the existence of the Scriptures, what understanding of reality emerges from them?" My conviction that their understanding of reality is true may lead to my skewing some aspects of them in order to make them say something I can accept, though it may also lead to my seeing other aspects more clearly than I might if I did not have that conviction in the back of my head.

---

[8]Compare Peter Balla's observation that Childs's view of the two Testaments as speaking in "dissident voices" exaggerates the difference between them (*Challenges to New Testament Theology* [Tübingen: Mohr, 1997], 230).

[9]I like Heikki Räisänen's characterization of Alan Richardson's *An Introduction to the Theology of the New Testament* (London: SCM Press; New York: Harper, 1958) as describing "the teachings of an Anglican Jesus" (Räisänen, *Beyond New Testament Theology* [London: SCM Press; Philadelphia: Trinity Press International, 1990], 53).

[10]The choice Räisänen postulates (*Beyond New Testament Theology*, xviii).

I have presented biblical theology as a logically feasible exercise. Does it matter? Does theology in general matter? It matters because the way we think matters, just because we are thinking beings. It matters because the way we think has an impact on the way we live, though the converse is also true. It then matters because both the way we think and the way we live are inclined to be shaped by the culture in which we live, and studying the Scriptures gives us something to think against, or something that thinks against us.

It is fine to come to the Scriptures with our questions and assumptions, which sometimes allow us to see things that people with other questions and assumptions would miss. But if we make our questions and assumptions the criteria for deciding whether the Scriptures are relevant or correct, we have absolutized ourselves, and we can never escape the limitations of our questions and assumptions. As Christians, at least, we owe it to ourselves (not to say God and the world) to test our thinking by the Scriptures rather than simply vice versa, and thus to expand the horizons of our thinking. Assumptions and convictions that come out of our cultural context commonly make the gospel message look stupid, and we have to think about whether it is indeed the gospel message that expresses real insight (1 Cor 1–2). On the other hand, anyone who likes thinking about theological questions has to keep remembering that knowledge puffs up, but love builds up (1 Cor 8:1).

1

GOD'S PERSON

✝

Alexander Pope declared that "the proper study of mankind is Man,"[1] which seemed a more secure enterprise than trying to study God. But "the proper study of God's elect is God."[2]

The word *God* is so familiar that it can seem to be a word of unequivocal meaning and reference, but in the ancient world it signified different things to different people, and in the modern world one cannot assume that people who use the word *God* mean by it the being or the kind of being that the Scriptures speak of.[3] The point is implicit when people ask, e.g., whether Muslims worship the same God as Christians. In connection with the First Testament, it is one reason for continuing to use the name Yahweh rather than replacing it by an ordinary word for "the Lord" or "God." It is as Yahweh that God is the one who created the cosmos, is ultimately sovereign over everything in the heavens and on the earth, has been revealingly, persistently and self-sacrificially involved with Israel in a way that embodies love but also toughness, is committed to bringing Israel and the world to their destiny in the

---

[1] So *An Essay on Man*, epistle II, line 2, in *The Complete Poetical Works of Alexander Pope* (Boston: Houghton Mifflin, 1903), 142.

[2] C. H. Spurgeon, "The Immutability of God," *The New Park Street Pulpit*, www.spurgeon.org /sermons/0001.htm; cf. James I. Packer, *Knowing God* (London: Hodder; Downers Grove, IL: InterVarsity Press, 1973), 13.

[3] Cf. Larry W. Hurtado, *God in New Testament Theology* (Nashville: Abingdon, 2010), 5-6; Richard B. Hays, "The God of Mercy Who Rescues Us from the Present Evil Age," in A. Andrew Das and Frank J. Matera, eds., *The Forgotten God*, Paul J. Achtemeier Festschrift (Louisville and London: Westminster John Knox, 2002), 123-43 (on 123).

acknowledgment of him, has embodied himself in Jesus, makes himself known in the Holy Spirit and will be God to eternity as he was God from eternity.[4]

One could see this identity emerging from Psalms 96–100. Yahweh created the entire cosmos and is to be acknowledged by all the nations and worshiped by all creation. He has established his sovereignty in the world and intends to rule its peoples fairly. Along with his own people, these other peoples have reason to rejoice in the prospect of that rule and in the burning up of his foes. His actions on Israel's behalf are expressions of a commitment and faithfulness that are significant for the whole world, and they are thus reason for the whole world to rejoice. He is good, and his commitment and faithfulness go on forever. Yahweh's deity is such that "gods" is only a courtesy title when applied to any other beings.

When God reveals the name Yahweh to Moses, he attaches to it the phrase 'ehyeh 'ăšer 'ehyeh (Ex 3:14), which suggests the promise that he will be "the God who is there"[5] in the sense that he will be present and active in different ways and different contexts in whatever ways these contexts require. He is thus the living God. That fact constitutes a starting point for thinking about God that marks a contrast over against lifeless gods and images (e.g., Jer 10:14; Acts 14:15), though the contrast with images should not make one sit light to the theological seriousness of the Scriptures' declarations that God has face, eyes, mouth, ears, nose, back, hand, finger and feet (to the "confusion of all spiritualisers").[6] God is a real person and is really alive.

In this chapter we will look at God's moral character (section 1.1) and at his metaphysical nature (section 1.2), then at his ways of expressing himself in the world, which come to be focused in talk of the Holy Spirit (section 1.3), and at his mind or message, which comes to be embodied in Jesus (section 1.4).

---

[4]Cf. Richard Bauckham's definition in "The Divinity of Jesus Christ in the Epistle to the Hebrews," in Bauckham et al., eds., *The Epistle to the Hebrews and Christian Theology* (Grand Rapids and Cambridge, UK: Eerdmans, 2009), 15-36 (on 16).

[5]The title of a book by Francis A. Schaeffer, *The God Who Is There* (London: Hodder; Chicago: InterVarsity Press, 1968), though I use the expression in a different way.

[6]Cf. Barth, *CD* II, 1:263, 266.

1.1 GOD'S CHARACTER

"The fruit of the Spirit is love, joy, peace, long-temperedness, generosity, goodness, faithfulness, gentleness, and restraint" (Gal 5:22-23). For such qualities to be the Spirit's fruit, one would expect them to be the Spirit's own qualities, and one would expect them to be the Spirit's qualities only if they are God's own qualities. And indeed they are. The Scriptures do describe God as loving, compassionate, gracious and forgiving, though they also describe God as capable of being wrathful and as not inclined simply to ignore our wrongdoing. So God acts in judgment, but the greater centrality of the first kind of characteristic in God means that he does so rather unwillingly. The combination of the two kinds of characteristics also points to the need for God to be flexible about the way he acts in different contexts.

Loving, Compassionate and Gracious

"God is love." This declaration cannot be reversed into "love is God"; "God is love" means "God is the One who loves."[7] His love finds expression and definition in sending his Son into the world "so that we might live though him," and also (in that connection) so that he might deal with the negative features about us, by being "the expiation for our failures" (1 Jn 4:8-10). If God's love thus issues in a concern to give us life, this fact constitutes a hint that God's original creation of life was an act of love. Humanity's waywardness then meant that God's love had to proceed to clean us up if we were to participate in his life. We were dead in our wrongdoing in the sense that we were doomed to death, after which there would be nothing worthwhile and possibly something very unpleasant. So whether or not we realized it we had no hope. It was then that God made us alive with Jesus "because of the great love with which he loved us" (Eph 2:4-5).

Among the corollaries of God's love (in Eph 2:4-8) are, first, that the act of love in sending Jesus was an expression of God's being "rich in mercy" toward people who would otherwise be on the way to experiencing God's wrath, and who indeed are already experiencing it. Mercy (*eleos*) is the Septuagint's equivalent of the First Testament's distinctive word for steadfast love or commitment (*ḥesed*); in substance, the distinctive New Testament word for love (*agapē*) is equivalent to that First Testament word. In mercy

---

[7]Cf. Barth, *CD* II, 1:272, 276.

and in such love God thus takes action that makes it unnecessary for him to continue showing wrath to people.

A second corollary of God's love is that God is rich in grace. "By grace you have been rescued" from that wrath, and raised up with Jesus "so that [God] might demonstrate the extraordinary riches of his grace"; because "it is by grace that you have been rescued." In substance grace (*charis*) is arguably another equivalent to that First Testament word for commitment, though in more straightforward linguistic terms the First Testament has its own word for grace (*ḥēn*). Paul's use of *charis* combines the Hebrew ideas of *ḥēn* and *ḥesed*, since *ḥēn* suggests something more occasional that is shown by a superior to an inferior, while *ḥesed* suggests an ongoing commitment.[8]

Third, God's action of love is an expression of God's generous goodness (*chrēstotēs*)—a word used in the Septuagint to refer to the quality of goodness in God (e.g., Pss 25:7; 31:19 [MT 31:20]; 34:8 [MT 9]). Fortunately for us, God is generous rather than fair (Mt 20:1-16), like a landowner who behaves like a strange "patron," foolish, prodigal and disturbing.[9]

The words in Ephesians that describe the outworking of love fit with the Scriptures' first great systematic statement of who God is, which comes from God's own lips as an act of reassurance and challenge when Israel has been involved in gross unfaithfulness to him:

> Yahweh, God compassionate and gracious, long-tempered and big in commitment and steadfastness, keeping commitment for thousands, carrying waywardness and rebellion and shortcoming, but he certainly does not acquit, attending to parents' waywardness upon children and upon grandchildren, upon thirds and fourths. (Ex 34:6-7)

There was nothing very new about this statement: such qualities are ones that are "shining in heaven and on earth."[10] Yet its importance is reflected in the way its expressions reappear elsewhere.[11] They recur most systematically on Moses' lips in addressing Yahweh in a subsequent similar context of Israel's rebellion against Yahweh (Num 14:18). They reappear again in Israel's

---

[8]James D. G. Dunn, *The Theology of Paul the Apostle* (Grand Rapids and Cambridge, UK: Eerdmans, 1998), 320-23.

[9]Jerome H. Neyrey, *Render to God* (Minneapolis: Fortress, 2004), 73.

[10]John Calvin, *Institutes of the Christian Religion* I.10, 2.

[11]See Michael P. Knowles, *The Unfolding Mystery of the Divine Name* (Downers Grove, IL: InterVarsity Press, 2012).

prayers, with an emphasis on their positive side (e.g., Neh 9:17; Pss 86:15; 103:8; 145:8; see also Joel 2:13, and with irony in Jon 4:2), and then in a fearful twist where the emphasis lies on the negative (Nah 1:2-3, with more irony). The positive side appears again in John's description of Jesus as "full of grace and truthfulness" (Jn 1:17); in other words, Jesus was the very embodiment of God as God described himself at Sinai. In substance, both sides appear when Paul declares that God's putting things right is revealed in the gospel, and that this revelation happens against the background of God's anger being revealed (Rom 1:17-18).

The declaration that God's love meant a willingness to remove our defilement (1 Jn 4:8-10) also concurs with that first great systematic description of God at Sinai, where one crucial expression of Yahweh's grace and truthfulness lies in carrying waywardness. Thus "it is God himself who atones for the sins of his people. . . . Atonement is not humanly possible. It is possible only for God. God atones by transmuting human guilt into divine suffering."[12] As a hymn puts it, God's love is the "love that will not let [Israel] go"; 1 Corinthians 13 and Song of Songs 8:6 are illustrated in Yahweh's involvement in Israel's history.[13]

Carrying Waywardness

Grace is the very essence of the being of God. . . . This is, of course, the secret of the forgiveness of sins. . . . [Forgiveness] meets us, not in spite of, but in and with all the holiness, righteousness and wisdom of God. . . . For God Himself is in it. He reveals His very essence in this streaming forth of grace. There is no higher divine being than that of the gracious God, there is no higher divine holiness than that which He shows in being merciful and forgiving sins. For in this action He interposes no less and no other than Himself for us.[14]

There is a cost for Yahweh in being involved with us. Paying the cost goes back to the Beginning. When human perversity reached its peak, Yahweh "regretted" having made human beings at all (Gen 6:6-7). While the word for "regret" (*nāḥam*) can denote having a change of mind about some intention, and having a change of mind need not have emotional connotations, that

---

[12]Jürgen Moltmann, *The Spirit of Life* (London: SCM Press; Minneapolis: Fortress, 1992), 134.
[13]Anthony C. Thiselton, *1 Corinthians* (Grand Rapids: Eerdmans, 2006), 234.
[14]Barth, *CD* II, 1:356.

Hebrew word for "regret" does regularly have emotional connotations, and when applied to something that has already happened, it can hardly simply mean "have a change of mind." The expression denotes God's sadness about creation. In case there is any doubt, Genesis goes on to make the point explicit: "It hurt him to his heart" (Gen 6:6). A related noun has been used of the pain that motherhood will bring to Eve and that work will bring to Adam (Gen 3:16-17).

John follows up the description of Jesus as full of grace and truthfulness with an account of John the Baptizer's pointing to Jesus as the lamb of God who "carries" the world's sin (Jn 1:29). It is conventional to understand him to describe Jesus as "taking away" the world's sin, which he does, but the verb *airō* would more commonly suggest that he was "taking" or "carrying" the world's sin, which is the point Exodus makes.[15] At Sinai, it is the waywardness of Israel in particular that Yahweh implicitly speaks of carrying, but the way Yahweh's qualities are indeed "shining in heaven and earth" would imply that this carrying applies to the world as a whole. John the Baptizer makes that point explicit. The world is the *kosmos*, so his comment about carrying applies directly not so much or not only to each individual's sin but to the sin that characterizes the world as an entity, the world into which Jesus came, which was made through him, but which did not recognize him (Jn 1:9-10), the world that God almost destroyed but did not.

The expression "lamb of God" comes only here, and there is no lamb that "carries" or "takes away" sin in the First Testament, but there are passages either side of Exodus 34 with which these phrases resonate.[16] In Exodus 12 God prescribes the daubing of a lamb's blood on a family's door to protect it from the Destroyer acting in judgment on Egypt for its rebellion against God. In due course Jesus' death for the world's sin will come at the time when the Jewish community is reenacting that event, and Paul will declare that Jesus our Passover lamb has been sacrificed for us (1 Cor 5:7). The other side of Exodus 34, Yahweh lays down another aspect of the way God's grace

---

[15]Cf. the alternative translation in the English Revised Version and the American Standard Version. The Latin verb *tollō*, which underlies the *Agnus Dei*, traditionally used in the Eucharist and rendered "takes away" in English liturgies, would also more commonly suggest "take" or "carry." In Ex 34:7 the Septuagint uses *aphairōn*, which does imply "take away."

[16]Cf. Jon D. Levenson, *The Death and Resurrection of the Beloved Son* (New Haven, CT, and London: Yale University Press, 1993), 208-10.

and truthfulness will work itself out in connection with carrying or taking sin. It happens in the Expiation Day provision whereby a goat is to carry or take away all the people's wayward acts to an isolated place (Lev 16:22; the verb and the noun are the same as in Ex 34). Much later in the First Testament, following on a description of the glory embodied and revealed in Yahweh's victory over Babylon, there is also a description of a glory embodied and revealed in the persecution and martyrdom of Yahweh's servant, who "carries" people's weaknesses and failure (Is 52:10; 53:1, 4, 12). Indeed, "the glory of God [is] the basis of mercy."[17]

Thus, while the "cruciformity" of God finds physical expression in *the* cross,[18] it was the cruciform God who related to the world and to Israel over the centuries, and who continues to do so. The cross "attests to a God who does not look and act as a respectable God ought to look and act. God's ways are simply not our ways."[19] It has always been so, in the world's history and in Israel's. Not "although" but "'precisely because'" Christ Jesus was in the form of this God who had been involved with the world and with Israel, and "was equal with God, he emptied himself" (Phil 2:6).[20] "The enfleshment of the divine Logos is neither a renunciation of the divinity nor a concealing of it, but a particularly total revealing of it which could only occur as the Son of God, existing as the form of God, also takes on the form of servant."[21]

But Wrathful and Not Acquitting

Back at the Beginning, God was carrying waywardness in disallowing the possibility of destroying the entire world, in exempting Noah and his family from the destruction and in starting again. The exemption happened because Noah was an upright man. Was he simply an exception to the general waywardness of the world? The phrase "Noah found grace in Yahweh's eyes" (Gen 6:8) points in another direction. If it were Noah's uprightness that made God exempt him, it was hardly "grace" that Noah "found"; he deserved his exemption. Thus one of my first mentors, Alec Motyer, liked to speak in

---

[17]Scott J. Hafemann, *The God of Promise and the Life of Faith* (Wheaton, IL: Crossway, 2001), 88.

[18]See Michael J. Gorman, *Cruciformity* (Grand Rapids and Cambridge, UK: Eerdmans, 2001).

[19]Charles B. Cousar, *A Theology of the Cross* (Minneapolis: Fortress, 1990), 181.

[20]Michael J. Gorman, *Inhabiting the Cruciform God* (Grand Rapids and Cambridge, UK: Eerdmans, 2009), 29.

[21]Ray S. Anderson, *Historical Transcendence and the Reality of God* (Grand Rapids: Eerdmans, 1975), 167.

terms of grace finding Noah.[22] This understanding gains support from the way reference to Noah's uprightness follows on reference to God's grace rather than preceding it (Gen 6:9). It was God's reaching out to Noah that turned him into an upright man.

Either way, the aftermath of the flood does affirm that God carries the world's waywardness and does operate on the basis of grace. When God accepts a thanksgiving sacrifice from Noah, he declares that he will never again curse the earth, "because the inclination of the human mind is bad from its youth" (Gen 8:21). The magnificent illogic about the statement causes some translations to change "because" to "although." Yet Genesis uses the ordinary Hebrew word for "because" (*kî*) and makes a profound theological point. Humanity's incorrigible perversity means that God will just have to carry its waywardness if he is to persist with his project. Grace will have to be the basis on which he relates to the world. God seals the point with the Scriptures' first covenant (Gen 9:8-17), a covenant of grace. Each rainbow that shines after rain reminds God and humanity of this gracious commitment.

Yet God had all but destroyed the world. If "God is love," is it the case that "'love' describes all God's dealings with the temporal and contingent world"?[23] Do "these two words, 'grace' and 'love,' together sum up and most clearly characterize [Paul's] whole theology"?[24] Is judgment then a paradoxical expression of love? Is the wrath of the lamb (the lamb that let itself be killed) an expression of love, being a wrath that is always designed to lead people to repentance (cf. Rev 3:19), so that its goal is not destruction?[25] Wrath does commonly have that aim, but it may fail in its goal; not everyone repents (Rev 9:20-21; 16:9, 11). Revelation's references to wrath do not suggest something always designed to lead to repentance, and a refusal to repent opens one to more wrath (Rev 6:16-17; 11:18; 14:10, 19; 15:1, 7; 16:1, 19; 18:3; 19:5).

---

[22]Cf. J. A. Motyer, "Covenant and Promise," *Evangel: The British Evangelical Review* 1, no. 1 (1983): 2-4 (on 2). See further Carol M. Kaminski, *Was Noah Good?* (London and New York: T&T Clark, 2014).

[23]So Miroslav Volf, *Against the Tide* (Grand Rapids: Eerdmans, 2010), x. See further Volf, *Captive to the Word of God* (Grand Rapids and Cambridge, UK: Eerdmans, 2010), 133-50.

[24]So Dunn, *Theology of Paul the Apostle*, 320.

[25]Cf. Mathias Rissi, *The Future of the World* (London: SCM Press; Naperville, IL: Allenson, 1972), 13.

The opening chapters of Paul's exposition of his gospel in Romans give a prominent place to wrath. Indeed, in Romans Paul refers to wrath almost as often as to love. "With what earnestness Paul speaks of the wrath of God and how real this is for him."[26] It might still be said that "even where Paul uses scriptural allusions to underscore the message of God's judgment, the texts themselves whisper the countertheme of God's mercy," which "fits the character of Scripture's original witness and the goal towards which Paul's own argument ultimately drives." The point applies to his quotations from Isaiah 52, Psalm 51 and Psalm 143. Thus there is a "dialectical movement of judgment and grace that structures Paul's presentation of the gospel," which "is in fact a recapitulation of the judgment/grace paradigm that undergirds the whole witness of Scripture."[27]

But it is not a dialectical movement implying that God has "two souls in his breast"[28] (one of which finds expression in the First Testament, the other in the New Testament?). The balance between love and chastisement in Exodus 34:6-7 shows that the former has priority. One significance of the Sinai story as a whole (especially Ex 32–34) is that it offers an extensive narrative exposition of the way God has to live with the tension between mercy and chastisement.[29]

Actually, "few words suffer more inflation" than the word *love*.[30] Really, "one must speak of a mystery, when one begins to speak of God and of love."[31] Over against "the tempting definition that 'God is love,'"[32] the formula "God is . . . in his essence, his reality, holy, free, sovereign love" is more open in its possible implications.[33] The Synoptic Gospels don't refer to God's love.[34] Other New Testament writings more often say "God is faithful" (1 Cor 1:9;

---

[26]Herman Ridderbos, *Paul: An Outline of His Theology* (Grand Rapids: Eerdmans, 1975), 110.

[27]Richard B. Hays, *Echoes of Scripture in the Letters of Paul* (New Haven, CT, and London: Yale University Press, 1989), 44-52 (on 46, 47).

[28]Reinhard Feldmeier and Hermann Spieckermann, *God of the Living* (Waco, TX: Baylor University Press, 2011), 339. The phrase comes from Goethe, who puts on the lips of Faust in his poem "Faust."

[29]See further *OTT* 1:408-25; 2:156-70.

[30]Krister Stendahl, *Paul Among Jews and Gentiles and Other Essays* (Philadelphia: Fortress, 1976), 53.

[31]Eberhard Jüngel, "What Does It Mean to Say, 'God Is Love'?," in T. A. Hart and D. P. Thimell, eds., *Christ in Our Place*, J. Torrance Festschrift (Exeter, UK: Paternoster; Allison Park, PA: Pickwick, 1990), 264-312 (on 302).

[32]Barth, *CD* II, 1:275.

[33]Otto Weber, *Foundations of Dogmatics* (Grand Rapids: Eerdmans, 1981), 1:407.

[34]Cf. Barth, *CD* IV, 2:764.

10:13; 2 Cor 1:18) and "God is one" (Rom 3:30; Gal 3:20; Jas 2:19) than "God is love," and they also declare that "our God is a consuming fire" (Heb 12:29).

Unwilling Judgment

The point is well conveyed by the declaration that God "does not willingly afflict or grieve people" (Lam 3:33). More literally, he does not afflict or grieve people "from the heart" or "from the inner being." It is not that wrath is somehow an expression of love; rather, while love is indeed God's heart or inner being, God's being also incorporates wrath. It belongs somewhere nearer its periphery, but it can be called on when necessary. Ben Kingsley, having played Gandhi and then played a foul-mouthed brutal gangster in *Sexy Beast*, was asked how he managed to take two such different roles; he answered that he had to reach deep into other aspects of his person in order to locate the aspects of himself that could find expression in that second role. Yahweh does so in order to be wrathful and violent.

These characteristics are not foreign to him, and they are not his shadow side in the sense that they are unacceptable to him, but they do not represent what he is at heart. Judgment is his strange work; if it is in a sense alien to him, it does express something of which he is capable (Is 28:21). Anger is not God's preferred way of relating to the world. "Calvin is conscious of the fact that he can only stammer when speaking of both God's love and his wrath."[35] God can relate to the world in anger but prefers to avoid doing so. His preference is to mend relationships. World history and Israel's history as a whole evidence his restraint. They embody his desire to be at one rather than express anger. But he can do it.

One could get the impression from the lists of the fruit of the Spirit and the deeds of the lower nature (Gal 5:19-24) that jealousy and rage are inherently sinful, but both Testaments make clear that it is not so. They indicate that human beings and God can and should be jealous and angry from time to time. Emotions do not divide into good ones and bad ones; there are times for withholding some of that fruit of the Spirit and times for jealousy and anger. God has the entire range of emotions possessed by a person and can call on them when it is appropriate. God is not just nice. "A God that can be grasped, a God that can be conceptualized is not

---

[35]G. C. Berkouwer, *The Work of Christ* (Grand Rapids: Eerdmans, 1971), 269.

a God."[36] "Yahweh is beyond any representations except those of the Tanakh at its strongest. Yahweh's own complexities are infinite, labyrinthine, and permanently inexplicable. . . . Mischievous, inquisitive, jealous, and turbulent, Yahweh is fully as personal as a god can be."[37] "The opposite of love . . . *is not wrath but indifference*,"[38] and "the axiom of apathy, widely applied to the deity in ancient metaphysics," does not apply to the God of the Scriptures.[39] Yahweh "acts out" his anger and rejection (and his election).[40]

He does so not least by hiding: "You got angry with us" and "you hid your face from us" (Is 64:5, 7 [MT 4, 6]).[41] For this God, judgment is not only a possibility but a necessity: "Grace that forgives everything would be cheap and no sign of love but of indifference and apathy. True love does not know the category of permissible infidelity, but only of faithfulness or betrayal, and consequently of wrath, judgment—and forgiveness."[42]

"The real conflict which is present in the antithesis between wrath and grace must be endured. When doing theology, we are constantly faced with the temptation to avoid the theme of the wrath of God, in order to attain a harmonious image of God."[43] The way God can be alternately loving and wrathful is an aspect of the way a person's character comes out differently in different contexts.

The difference need not imply inconsistency; it's just that changing contexts call forth the expression of different facets of the character. Exodus 1–18 describes how Yahweh became a warrior when the Egyptians oppressed Israel. Exodus 32–34 relates how Yahweh let mercy rule over justice when Israel flouted his expectations. Isaiah describes how Yahweh got involved in international affairs when the Assyrian empire arose. Isaiah 40–55 describes how Yahweh promised to act as creator when Israel needed such

---

[36]Adam B. Seligman, *Modernity's Wager* (Princeton, NJ, and Oxford: Princeton University Press, 2000), 35.

[37]Harold Bloom, *Jesus and Yahweh* (New York: Riverhead, 2005), 131-32 (following up Seligman's observation), 138.

[38]Anthony C. Thiselton, *The Hermeneutics of Doctrine* (Grand Rapids: Eerdmans, 2007), 573.

[39]Feldmeier and Spieckermann, *God of the Living*, 361.

[40]Baruch A. Levine, *In Pursuit of Meaning* (Winona Lake, IN: Eisenbrauns, 2011), 1:365-84.

[41]Feldmeier and Spieckermann, *God of the Living*, 339-60.

[42]Ibid., 316.

[43]Halvor Moxnes, *Theology in Conflict* (Leiden: Brill, 1980), 287.

creative action. The Gospels relate how God embodied mercy and creativity in Jesus.

Flexible

So different contexts draw out different facets of what God is and what God can be. God is constant, consistent, unswerving and dependable. He consistently shows integrity to people of integrity but refractoriness to people who are crooked (Ps 18:25 [MT 26]). But his consistency doesn't mean God is rigid, which would be close to saying that he is dead. Nor does it mean he is inflexible. Kings who are not free to change their minds are stupid (Dan 6).

The First Testament often makes explicit that God can have a change of mind, in the short term. Two verbs can suggest this idea. One we have noted already, *nāḥam*, implies emotion and in other contexts can mean be sorry or find comfort. The other, *šûb*, suggests action; it literally means to turn. Translations can render either verb "repent," which gives a misleading impression in either connection. With regard to having a change of mind, one might use the English words "relent" and "turn back" for the two verbs. Jonah and Jeremiah provide illuminating instances of them. When the king of Nineveh decrees that people must "turn back" from their wrong ways, he hopes that God may "turn back" and "relent" of his intention to destroy the city. The Ninevites do "turn back," and God "turns back" and "relents" (Jon 3:8-10). In Jeremiah 18:1-12 God lays down the principle involved, which also applies to Judah. If he announces the intention to destroy a nation and it "turns back" from its wrong ways, he will "relent"—but if he announces the intention to bless it and it does what is wrong, he will also "relent" of that intention. It's therefore possible for Moses to urge Yahweh to "turn back" from wrath and "relent" of the trouble he intends to bring on the people even though they deserve it; and Yahweh does so (Ex 32:12-14; cf. Num 14:11-20). Amos acts in the same way, though the sequence in Amos 7:1-9; 8:1-2 may imply that there comes a time when this possibility disappears.

Jonah, Jeremiah, Moses and Amos are evidently not worried about the possibility that Yahweh's having a change of mind might compromise his sovereignty or insight or control of events. They are more impressed by the positive insight about Yahweh, which Jonah frowns upon: the trouble with Yahweh is that he is always inclined to give in to grace, compassion and love

(Jon 4:2). It is good news that Yahweh is flexible in this way. The Prophets know that God's ultimate purpose is not imperiled but furthered by such flexibility. It does not mean God is inconsistent. It means God is reliably faithful—loving, compassionate and gracious. God's life does not change, God's character does not change, God's truth does not change, God's ways do not change, God's purpose does not change and God's Son does not change.[44] But precisely in order to maintain that consistent integrity, God does sometimes say one thing but then do another as a result of the response his declarations receive.

Sometimes, then, God simply says what is going to happen and it happens. Sometimes God acts in interaction with human decisions. Sometimes the sequence is broken without any indication that anyone repented. Yahweh declares that Nebuchadnezzar will destroy Tyre but later notes that Nebuchadnezzar has been unable to do so, and therefore tells him he can have Egypt instead (Ezek 26–28; 29:17-20). There have been occasions when Yahweh could use Assyria, Babylon and Persia as his agent in bringing trouble or deliverance to Judah, but in Isaiah 63:1-6 he laments the fact that lately there has been no one available, so he is being driven to act himself. And further, within the time period to which the book of Isaiah belongs there was no subsequent action that could count as the implementation of that undertaking. There were even occasions when God wrestled with Jacob and Jacob won (Gen 32:25-31) and when God tried to kill Moses and didn't succeed (Ex 4:24).

Not surprisingly, the flexibility implied by some sayings of Jesus that the Gospel writers know did not "come true" matches the portrait of God in his consistency-with-flexibility in the First Testament.

1.2 ONE GOD

Reflection on God's flexibility suggests a transition from considering God's moral character to considering his metaphysical attributes. While love and integrity require flexibility, flexibility may seem to compromise the metaphysical qualities that one expects to associate with deity, such as God's sovereignty and time-transcending nature. What is the nature of God's

---

[44]Packer, *Knowing God*, 68-72.

existence? What are God's properties? What type of being is God? First, God is one, though the Scriptures make clear that God's oneness is modulated by the fact that Jesus is (also) Lord. God is our heavenly Father, which suggests both commitment and transcendence. God is sovereign in the world; the Scriptures suggest various nuances on that fact in connection with the lesser sovereignty exercised by human beings, by the created world and by other supernatural beings. God is omni-temporal and capable of knowing whatever he wants to know, about what is past, present and future from a human perspective.

Yahweh Our God Yahweh One

"That the issue of 'monotheism' is a central issue for biblical theology hardly needs arguing."[45] Actually it does need arguing. The *Shema*ʿ (Deut 6:4) declares not "There is one God" but "Yahweh our God Yahweh one."[46] For the First Testament the key question is not how many gods there are or how united God is, but who is God. For Judaism, the key affirmation is that Yahweh is the one true God, the creator of the entire world and the judge of all.[47] For the New Testament the key question in this connection would then concern how Jesus' being Lord fits into what one may call mono-Yahwism. Both Testaments assume that there is only one being who can properly be called God, but it remains significant that the word *monotheism* was coined only in the seventeenth century.[48] In the Scriptures, the starting point for understanding God's being is not an analysis in terms of monotheism with

---

[45]So Richard Bauckham, *Jesus and the God of Israel* (Carlisle, UK: Paternoster, 2008; Grand Rapids: Eerdmans, 2009), 60. James D. G. Dunn sees monotheism as the first of the "four pillars of Second Temple Judaism" (*The Partings of the Ways* [London: SCM Press; Philadelphia: Trinity Press International, 1991], 19).

[46]Bauckham in effect grants this point; what he means by monotheism is "Jewish monotheism," the fact that "YHWH is the only true God" (*Jesus and the God of Israel*, 84). Similarly N. T. Wright declares that in "the Jewish, and nascent Christian, world" monotheism was one of the "major issues at stake," but he then explains that by monotheism he means "the belief that Israel's God was the God of all the earth" (*The Climax of the Covenant* [Edinburgh: T&T Clark, 1991; Minneapolis: Fortress, 1992], 122, 125).

[47]Cf. N. T. Wright, *Paul and the Faithfulness of God* (Minneapolis: Fortress; London: SPCK, 2013), 638.

[48]See Nathan MacDonald, *Deuteronomy and the Meaning of "Monotheism"* (Tübingen: Mohr, 2003), 5-52; MacDonald, "The Origin of 'Monotheism,'" in Wendy North and Loren T. Stuckenbruck, eds., *Early Jewish and Christian Monotheism* (London and New York: Continuum, 2004), 204-15; R. W. L. Moberly, "How Appropriate Is 'Monotheism' as a Category for Biblical Interpretation?," in the same volume, 216-34. Bloom in *Jesus and Yahweh*, 2-4, interestingly speculates as to the psychological reasons for the emergence of monotheism. On the relationship between

its concomitant definitions in terms of omnipotence, omniscience and omnipresence. It is the biblical portrait of Yahweh as the one God and as the God who has a name,[49] which reflects his being not an idea but a person.[50]

Yahweh feels strongly about any compromising of the fact that he alone is God, and he gets indignant about his people serving other so-called deities (Ex 20:5; 34:14). He declares himself to be jealous or "impassioned" (*qannā'*; JPSV). He has the feelings of someone whose husband or wife has been having an affair. The adjective also covers other kinds of strong feelings. Yahweh is passionately indignant about Jerusalem in its broken state (Zech 1:14; 8:2), and the passionate indignation of Yahweh Armies will see to the fulfillment of what he says he will do (e.g., Is 9:7 [MT 6]). It's therefore possible to appeal to Yahweh's passion when deliverance isn't arriving (Is 63:15). Indignant passion about the temple has consumed the person who prays Psalm 69:9 (MT 10), and it comes to be characteristic of Jesus (Jn 2:17). Yes, God is a person, with the passions of a person. Neither God nor Jesus is mild and gentle, or cool and theoretical. Passion is a better starting point than *apatheia* for thinking about God.[51]

Yahweh is indeed the only God. Even in its most far-reaching statements about Jesus' nature, the New Testament works within the framework of there being one God. Jesus is then "the expression of the one God."[52] God has one name, though several faces.[53]

The One God and the One Lord

Paul begins many of his letters with the greeting "Grace and peace from God the Father and from our Lord Jesus, the Anointed One" (1 Cor 1:3; 2 Cor 1:2; Gal 1:3; Eph 1:2; Phil 1:2; 2 Thess 1:2; Philemon; similar formulae appear in Rom 1:7; 1 Tim 1:2; 2 Tim 1:2; Tit 1:4; 2 Pet 1:2; 2 Jn 3). Paul expands on this collocation in declaring, "For us" there is "one God, the Father (from whom all things exist, and we exist toward him), and one Lord, Jesus the Anointed

---

monotheism and polytheism in the ancient world, see, e.g., Barbara N. Porter, ed., *One God or Many?* (Chebeague, ME: Casco Bay Assyriological Institute, 2000).

[49] Hans Küng, *Does God Exist?* (Garden City, NY: Doubleday; London: Collins, 1980), 621.

[50] Cf. Weber, *Foundations of Dogmatics*, 1:417.

[51] Cf. Jürgen Moltmann, *The Trinity and the Kingdom of God* (London: SCM Press; New York: Harper, 1981), 21-25.

[52] Dunn, *Partings of the Ways*, 245.

[53] Which fact (Thomas A. Bennett points out to me) is spelled out in the doctrine of the Trinity.

One (through whom all things exist, and we exist through him)" (1 Cor 8:6). The "for us" with which the declaration begins hardly implies that this affirmation about the Father and Jesus is merely a personal opinion held by people who believe in Jesus. It's an objective fact, which "we" are privileged to recognize, an objective fact that is indeed of key importance for Christian faith and that distinguishes "we" who acknowledge the truth about God and Jesus from people who don't.

The *Shema*ʿ stands in the background of this declaration. It takes its name from its opening bidding, "Listen," which leads into that key confession, "Yahweh our God Yahweh one." The Septuagint translates "the Lord our God [is] one Lord" or "the Lord our God—the Lord [is] one"; as with the Hebrew, it's hard to be sure where to put an "is." Paul has then glossed "God" with "the Father" and "Lord" with "Jesus, the Anointed One," and "in effect split the *Shema* between the one God and the one Lord."[54] He has thereby "redefined [the *Shema*ʿ] christologically, producing what we can only call a sort of christological monotheism."[55] He does not believe in two gods. He is "including Jesus in the unique identity of the one God affirmed in the Shemaʿ'" and "identifying Jesus as the 'Lord' whom the Shemaʿ affirms to be one," so that "the unique identity of the one God *consists of* the one God, the Father, *and* the one Lord." He "rewrites the Shemaʿ to include both God and Jesus in the unique divine identity."[56] So something radical happens when the Greek word for "Lord," the Septuagint's equivalent to Yahweh, is used to refer to Jesus.[57]

These considerations point to a central aspect of God's distinctive nature as the Scriptures describe him. "In the New Testament christology functions within theology, the divine significance of Christ is actually a subcategory of the doctrine of God, the divine identity of Jesus Christ is held firmly within the framework of the Christian (as well as Jewish) axiom that God is one." Paul puts it in terms of God in Jesus (he is a revelation of God's love and faithfulness), Matthew in terms of Jesus as God with us, John in terms of Jesus being equal with God (he is the one who reveals God), Revelation

---

[54]Dunn, *Theology of Paul the Apostle*, 268.
[55]Wright, *Climax of the Covenant*, 120.
[56]Bauckham, *Jesus and the God of Israel*, 101.
[57]Feldmeier and Spieckermann, *God of the Living*, 41.

in terms of Jesus sharing God's throne and God's worship.[58] It is thus possible both to declare that the New Testament simply reaffirms the understanding of God that emerges from the First Testament and reveals nothing new about God, and also that it radically redefines God.[59] The gospel expounded in the New Testament reexpresses First Testament affirmations about God; other versions of a gospel (even Jewish versions) do not do so.[60]

Fluidity

The New Testament seems not to fret about the logical difficulty involved in the paradoxical conviction that God is one and also that Jesus is divine. This conviction emerges inescapably from the biblical story, and it is wiser "to start from the biblical history, and therefore to make the unity of the three divine Persons the problem," rather than to start from the philosophical postulate of unity and then have a problem with the way the Scriptures talk.[61]

While commitment to the one God could coexist with a recognition and veneration of angels and spirits in both Testaments and in Judaism,[62] this recognition did not imply a loosening of the distinction between God and such entities, and New Testament talk about Jesus has more in common with Jewish thought about God than with Jewish talk of angels and spirits. "To put Jesus in the position . . . of a very high ranking angelic servant of God would not be to come close to a further step of assimilating him to God, because the absolute distinction between God and all other reality would still have to be crossed."[63]

The New Testament was helped rather by the fact that the articulation of Christian thinking about Jesus took place against the background of

---

[58]Cf. James D. G. Dunn, *The Christ and the Spirit* (Edinburgh: T&T Clark; Grand Rapids: Eerdmans, 1998), 1:377-87 (quotation from 378); also Larry W. Hurtado, *Lord Jesus Christ: Devotion to Jesus in Earliest Christianity* (Grand Rapids and Cambridge, UK: Eerdmans, 2003), e.g., 29-53; Hurtado, *How on Earth Did Jesus Become God?* (Grand Rapids and Cambridge, UK: Eerdmans, 2005), 31-55.

[59]Cf. Hurtado's survey of statements by New Testament scholars in his *God in New Testament Theology*, 10-25.

[60]Cf. Moxnes, *Theology in Conflict*.

[61]Moltmann, *Trinity and the Kingdom of God*, 149. Cf. Jürgen Moltmann, *History and the Triune God* (London: SCM Press, 1991; New York: Crossroad, 1992), 82.

[62]See, e.g., North and Stuckenbruck, *Early Jewish and Christian Monotheism*; Carey C. Newman et al., eds., *The Jewish Roots of Christological Monotheism* (Leiden and Boston: Brill, 1999).

[63]Richard Bauckham, *God Crucified* (Grand Rapids: Eerdmans, 1998), 28 (2nd rev. ed., *Jesus and the God of Israel*, 20).

Jewish thinking in terms of there being "two powers in heaven"—not a
dualistic understanding of a good power and an evil power, but the reality
of semiseparate expressions of God.[64] The First Testament itself combined its strong affirmations of Yahweh's sole deity with declarations such
as the description of God's insight as a personal being distinguishable
from God (Prov 8:22-31), which had been taken further in later Jewish
works such as the book of Wisdom and Sirach and is picked up by Paul
(e.g., Col 1-2).

Many Jewish thinkers might thus have been comfortable with understanding God's Insight as a quasi-person semi-independent of God, and
Paul could have been able to think in those terms before Jesus confronted
him. Whether he did so or not, given that Jesus is clearly a discrete person
distinct from God, the figure of God's Insight gave Paul a way of thinking
about Jesus' significance as a discrete person yet one who is at the same time
essentially one in nature with God in a way unlike any other human.[65] God
had his insight from the beginning and used it in creating the world, and
Jesus is the supreme embodiment of God's insight, especially though paradoxically in being executed (1 Cor 1:18-31). Jewish thinking could also think
of God's spirit or God's word as semiseparable from God, and the New Testament's way of speaking has more in common with this way of thinking,
too, than with the recognition of subordinate supernatural beings such as
angels and spirits.

Such fluidity in the Jewish Scriptures' understanding of God means that
the doctrine of the Trinity in itself need not raise problems for a Jew. The
reason why a Jew may be unable to be a Christian is that Judaism regards
Jesus as someone who falsely claimed to be the Anointed One.[66] He did not
fulfill Yahweh's promises concerning the Anointed One (which is one reason
why he needs to come back).

Conversely, the Christian recognition that God is Father, Son and Spirit
issues from the story of Jesus as God's Son as this story comes home through
the mediation of the Spirit in the congregation, not (for instance) from

---

[64]See Alan F. Segal, *Two Powers in Heaven* (Leiden: Brill, 1977).

[65]See, e.g., James D. G. Dunn, *Christology in the Making* (London: SCM Press; Philadelphia: Westminster, 1980; 2nd ed., London: SCM Press; Grand Rapids: Eerdmans, 1989), 163-212.

[66]So Benjamin Sommer, *The Bodies of God and the World of Ancient Israel* (Cambridge and New
York: Cambridge University Press, 2009), 132-37.

theoretical thinking or as an attempt to solve a problem.[67] Christians ended up believing in the complicated, mysterious and apparently illogical doctrine of the Trinity because for all its disadvantages, it was the best way of making sense of the account of God in the Scriptures.

Father . . .

In Paul's adaptation of the *Shema*ʿ, the description of God as Father denotes God's relationship to his people, and Luke's version of the prayer that Jesus gave his disciples begins with the simple invocation "Father" (Lk 11:2). This form of address to God sums up something of the New Testament's understanding of that relationship. The plain form of the word ("Father" rather than "our Father") suggests that behind the Greek word *patēr* is the Aramaic word ʾ*abbā*ʾ. Adopted into Hebrew, it was the ordinary word used by a child addressing its father, though rendering it "Daddy" dilutes its implications.[68] Against the background of understandings in the First Testament and in Judaism, being father suggests being the origin or source of life and thus being the one who grants an inheritance, being a figure of authority who deserves submission and obedience, and being one who loves and cares for his children.[69] A fatherly relationship to people is an instance of a patron-client relationship, one that involves a mutual commitment between two parties of unequal status.[70] A master and his servants, a king and his subjects, a father and his sons, are all instances of such relationships.

Israel knew that God was its Father, though the First Testament uses the image only rarely. A notable occurrence is God's declaration of intent to "bring my sons from afar and my daughters from the end of the earth" (Is 43:6). It is the only place in the Scriptures where God speaks of "my daughters," except for one New Testament passage that apparently takes it up (2 Cor 6:18). Israel's reticence in using the image usefully distinguished Israelite religion from Canaanite religion, which spoke of the senior god, El, as Father, and believed that El had sons and daughters. It also distinguished

---

[67]Thiselton, *Hermeneutics of Doctrine*, 452-53.

[68]Cf. Thomas A. Smail, *The Forgotten Father* (London: Hodder, 1980; Grand Rapids: Eerdmans, 1981), 39; James Barr, "*Abba* Isn't 'Daddy,'" *Journal of Theological Studies* 39 (1988): 28-47.

[69]Marianne Meye Thompson, *The God of the Gospel of John* (Grand Rapids and Cambridge, UK: Eerdmans, 2001), 58.

[70]See further, e.g., Neyrey, *Render to God*, 249-51.

Israelite religion from the Greek religion presupposed by Homer, where Zeus was "father of men and of gods."[71]

The New Testament does see God as having a fatherly relationship with all humanity and all creation: Aratus, a Hellenistic Greek poet, had described humanity as God's "offspring," and Paul agrees (Acts 17:28). God is the "Father of the lights, with whom there is no variation or shadow caused by turning" (Jas 1:17). The idea that there is a natural fatherly relationship between God and human beings is a common feature of religions.[72] But there are disadvantages to the idea that we are "naturally" God's children and that God is "naturally" our Father.[73] Talk about God as our Father is familiar, and it can be cheap. Israel did know that it belonged to Yahweh's family, but rather than speaking of Yahweh as its Father, it was more inclined to speak of Yahweh as its gō'ēl, the family member who is expected to be willing to make his resources available to deal with difficulties in the life of a relative in need, and thus to restore or redeem the person. It is another patron-client relationship; at its heart is family relationship, powerful intervention and effective restoration.[74]

Although Israelites were not inclined to address God as Father, they knew well that they could relate to God with the freedom of children, as the Psalms make clear, and the Judaism of Jesus' day thus prayed to God as Father. The awareness of Jews that there was a relationship of mutual love and commitment between God and Israel would mean that they need not have seen anything novel in the way Jesus spoke of God's fatherly relationship with them. It is against the background of this Jewish awareness that Jesus' talk of God as Father encourages his disciples to call on God as Father in connection with their urging God to bring in his reign and to protect them.[75]

Like the opening of other epistles, the beginning of Ephesians picks up the image of God as Father, but it takes it in a different direction and then nuances it: "Grace to you and peace from God our Father and the Lord Jesus

---

[71]E.g., Homer, *Iliad* 8.132.

[72]Cf. Friedrich Heiler, *Prayer* (London and New York: Oxford University Press, 1932), 59-60.

[73]Cf. Feldmeier and Spieckermann, *God of the Living*, 68-72.

[74]Cf. Christopher J. H. Wright, *The Mission of God* (Downers Grove, IL: InterVarsity Press; Nottingham, UK: Inter-Varsity Press, 2006), 267.

[75]Cf. Marianne Meye Thompson, *The Promise of the Father* (Louisville: Westminster John Knox, 2000), 34.

the Anointed One. Praised be the God and Father of our Lord Jesus, the Anointed One. . . . He destined us to be adopted as his children through Jesus the Anointed One" (Eph 1:2-5). God is the Father of Jesus, the Father of Israel and the Father of people who become Jesus' brothers and sisters. Whereas Canaanite talk of El as a Father with sons and daughters among the gods might have made Israel hesitant to speak of God as the Father of a Son in a metaphysical sense, in New Testament times early Christian writers evidently think it is now safe to do so.

Hebrews feels no need for hesitation: God who spoke to Israel in a variety of ways through the prophets finally spoke through a Son (Heb 1:1-2). In the Gospels, too, "Father" is more often a description of the relationship of God to Jesus than to the disciples, and it expresses the distinctiveness of that relationship. Ephesians 1:2-5 then points to a new insight about God as Father: the position of believers as God's sons and daughters is related to the fact that God the Father himself has a Son. We come to share in his position; we are adopted as children of his Father. Through Jesus, Gentiles alongside Jews have access to the Father and become members of his household (Eph 2:18-19).

To say that God is Father is not to say that God is male rather than female. Fatherhood is a metaphor, and metaphor involves overlap, not identity between one thing and another. We have to let other metaphors guide us in seeing how far a metaphor can be taken. The First Testament gives God more or less all body parts, but not genitals, though it does attribute to God breasts and a womb. Describing God as Father and giving God motherly characteristics ascribe to God some important characteristics of both forms of parenthood. Calling God "he" designates God as a person, not a thing; it does not designate God as male rather than female. Of course in a particular cultural context (e.g., that of the West in the twenty-first century) such descriptions may have other resonances, and we may need to be careful about how we use them in order to avoid giving the wrong impression.

. . . in the Heavens

In Matthew's version, the prayer that Jesus gave his disciples begins, "Our Father in the heavens" (Mt 6:9), and it thereby makes explicit that we are talking about no ordinary father. It's been suggested that Matthew's description of the Father makes for an unfavorable contrast with the First

Testament: in Genesis, "Yahweh is intimate with us, close by, while the Christian God the Father has retreated into the heavens."[76] While it's neat to have the contrast drawn this way around rather than to the First Testament's disfavor, describing the Father as in the heavens doesn't actually suggest withdrawal. The First Testament itself frequently describes Yahweh as in the heavens, but it doesn't imply that God is thereby not present and active on the earth. If anything, the description has the opposite implication (see e.g., 1 Sam 2:10; 1 Kings 8:30-49). From his position at the height of the city, the king can see what's happening in the city below and do something about it; from his position in the height of the heavens, God can see what's happening in the world below and do something about it (Ps 11:4). When Matthew uses phrases such as "kingdom of heaven" as opposed to "kingdom of God" (as the Greek phrases are traditionally rendered), he is following contemporary Jewish usage; Jesus himself may have employed both expressions.

While there is no implication of remoteness in referring to "the heavens" rather than "God," the expression "the heavens" is not explicitly personal. The phrase "Our Father in the heavens" thus actually reaffirms the personal nature of the one to whom we pray. We are not addressing the heavens but "our Father" who is there.[77]

Describing the Father as "in the heavens" does suggest transcendence, and it invites comparison with the description of God as holy. Arguably, holiness is a better starting point than love for articulating Jesus' own understanding of God,[78] and in the First Testament, "holy" is the most fundamental description of God, a term for God in his God-ness. In Isaiah 6 the seraphs proclaim, "Holy, holy, holy."[79] Yahweh is not merely once holy, and not merely holy to the power of two, but holy to the power of three.

Yet in Isaiah, Yahweh is not simply "the Holy One" but "the Holy One of Israel." The title indicates that the transcendent God has attached himself to

---

[76]Bloom, *Jesus and Yahweh*, 138.

[77]Cf. Alon Goshen-Gottstein, "God the Father in Rabbinic Judaism and Christianity," *Journal of Ecumenical Studies* 38 (2000–2001): 471-504 (on 477-79).

[78]Cf. Scot McKnight, *A New Vision for Israel* (Grand Rapids and Cambridge, UK: Eerdmans, 1999), 22.

[79]Or, since Isaiah elsewhere uses *qādôš* as a noun, "The Holy One, the Holy One, the Holy One!": so Levine, *In Pursuit of Meaning*, 1:332.

a particular people, and it simultaneously offers encouragement and pressure. The Holy One is committed to this people, but he also looks for a commitment from them, and he is to be expected to confront them when they fail in their commitment. To say that Yahweh is the Holy One of Israel, then, is to say that Yahweh is "incomparable, sovereign, beyond the unaided comprehension of humankind, unapproachable yet in the midst of his chosen people."[80]

While the New Testament can use the word *holy* to imply righteous or moral (e.g., 2 Cor 6:6; 1 Pet 1:15-16; Rev 22:11), it, too, can also use it to denote transcendent, or set apart, when it applies it to a city, angels, covenant or firstfruits (e.g., Mt 4:5; Mk 8:38; Lk 1:72; Rom 11:16), and not least in the expression "Holy Spirit." Perhaps those connotations of both commitment and confrontation might attach to the phrase "the Holy Spirit," and to Jesus' being "the holy one." When the living creatures take up the seraphs' cry (Rev 4:8) and proclaim God's holiness, they, too, are declaring that the one on the throne is the ultimate transcendent, supernatural, awe-inspiring God, and therefore not someone you can mess with. In Luke's version of the Lord's Prayer, the point emerges from the sequence, "Father, your name be acknowledged as holy." Addressing God as Father expresses his nearness; the jussive recognizes his holiness.[81]

Genesis does not call God "holy"; it does apply to the one God, Yahweh, the term *El*, notwithstanding the fact that other peoples called the top god El. The qualifiers added to that term help bring out truths about God. He is El Elyon, God on High, creator of the heavens and the earth (Gen 14:19). He is El Ro'i, God who sees me or God whom I have seen (Gen 16:13). He is El Shadday: etymologically, the term might have several meanings, but the only one that the First Testament takes up is "destroyer" (e.g., Is 13:6). He is El Olam (e.g., Gen 21:33), the one who has been God from ages past and will be God to ages future. The names are thus theologically significant, as is the fact that they compare with Canaanite names for the top God. Abraham's willingness to use the title

---

[80]John Rogerson, "What Is Holiness," in Stephen C. Barton, ed., *Holiness* (London and New York: T&T Clark, 2003), 3-21 (on 20). See further Philip Jenson, "Holiness in the Priestly Writings of the Old Testament," in that volume (93-121).

[81]Feldmeier and Spieckermann, *God of the Living*, 17.

God on High but his qualifying it by the name Yahweh (Gen 14:22) is doubly significant. Other peoples are not without true knowledge of God, but they need to have added to their knowledge the truth wrapped up in who Yahweh is.

Israel's ancestors' more distinctive way of describing God is as "the God of your father"—that is, "God of Abraham, God of Isaac, and God of Jacob" (Ex 3:6). These phrases suggest that God enters into a personal commitment to the ancestor who has responsibility for the family. He is the God who says "I am/will be with you" (Gen 26:24). Jesus' description of God as "our Father in the heavens" corresponds to the two sides to Israel's ancestors' description of God as El and as the God who related personally to these ancestors.

Sovereign

John's vision of heaven takes up the connotation of transcendence that attaches to holiness when he sees an awe-inspiring figure on a throne and hears voices issuing the same declaration as the seraphs: "Holy, holy, holy is the Lord God All-powerful, who was, and is, and is coming." Another set of voices declares, "You are worthy, our Lord and God, to receive glory, honor, and power, because you are the one who created all things, and by your will they came into being and were created" (Rev 4:8, 11). John's description of God as "Lord God All-powerful" recurs through the book, appearing for the last time in its closing vision of the new heaven and the new earth (Rev 21:22); "all-powerful" is an equivalent to the seraphs' own further description of the Holy One as "Yahweh Armies" (Is 6:3).[82] Power or sovereignty is an important characteristic of God.

In what sense do the Scriptures suggest that God is all-powerful or omnipotent or sovereign?[83] On some understandings of sovereignty, if God is sovereign, then many events in the world are puzzling. It's often impossible to see rhyme or reason behind things that happen and things that don't happen. Because Yahweh is powerful, he is able to deliver his people (e.g., Pss 21:13 [MT 14]; 28:8), yet sometimes Yahweh lets his people be defeated, even when the defeat cannot be understood as a chastisement for

---

[82]In Isaiah the Septuagint has *kurios sabaōth*, but elsewhere (e.g., Amos 4:13) it uses the paraphrastic *pantokratōr*, the word Revelation uses.

[83]See further *OTT* 1:642-56; 2:59-84.

their faithlessness (e.g., Ps 44). When challenged, Yahweh responds by saying. "Sorry (except that he doesn't say 'Sorry'), but the world doesn't revolve around you. You just have to live with what's happened in light of the evidence that on the whole I'm not doing too bad a job of running the world" (Job 38–41). At the same time, for people who love God, he "makes all things work together for good" (Rom 8:28).[84] The test of God's sovereignty lies not in things that happen but in what he does with things after they happen.

Revelation associates God's power or sovereignty with the original creation and with the new heavens and the new earth, and other scriptural assertions of God's sovereignty and power make the same connection. This association suggests a starting point for understanding God's sovereignty and power. God's sovereignty means that God alone initiated the project that brought the world into existence and that God alone will bring it to its consummation. Further significant assertions of that sovereignty in Jesus' incarnation and resurrection also relate to the fulfillment of this purpose. So does Jesus' execution, which further nuances an understanding of God's sovereignty.

More broadly, God "intends to employ the potential for power at his universal and personal disposal for the maintenance and benevolent order of his world." In addition, "he is the sovereign Lord who comes to judge his people." In Revelation, "the discussion of the Almighty contradicts a present experienced as lacking salvation. It adheres to the confidence that God is capable and willing to establish his kingdom in the battle against powers hostile to God."[85]

God exercises his sovereignty in various ways: God's intentions, worldly events and human decisions interrelate in a number of ways. Life works on the basis of natural processes, the dynamics of wisdom and the dynamics of ethics. Yahweh makes life work, makes bad things happen to bad people, acts via this-worldly means, makes our experiences match our actions, works despite our plans, protects and delivers. Death puts down the oppressor. Yet the Scriptures also recognize that life does not always reflect these rules.

---

[84]It makes little difference if one renders the line "all things work together for good."
[85]Feldmeier and Spieckermann, *God of the Living*, 151, 157, 161, 195.

Working Indirectly

God's creation project involved his working via elements within creation. While God's creating begins by his using words that bring about their own fulfillment (Gen 1:3), many of God's subsequent words involve commissioning action by elements within creation. When fruit trees grow in Eden or when Eve gets pregnant, these events implement God's will; God's sovereignty works via them. Everything that takes place in the natural world is a working out of God's sovereignty. When a tree produces fruit, it is doing something quite "natural," but it is also being the means of God's providing us with food to eat. One can formulate more than one level of explanation of what happens, and the levels of explanation complement one another.

God uses human beings as his agents. When Tiglath-pileser, Sennacherib or Nebuchadnezzar invaded Judah, Yahweh had stirred up their spirit to get them to do so (e.g., 1 Chron 5:26). When Cyrus commissioned Judahites to go back to Jerusalem to rebuild the temple, Yahweh had stirred up his spirit to get him to do so (Ezra 1:1). It is not that they came because they felt impelled by Yahweh to do so. Although they might be prepared to refer to themselves as Yahweh's agents when it suited them, in other contexts they would speak of themselves as the servants of some other deity, and one may speculate that in their own minds they undertook their action because they wanted to extend and secure their empire. They were not seeking to act as Yahweh's agents, but they were so acting, like the fruit tree that unwittingly fulfills God's intent.

When Caiaphas says that it is expedient for Jesus to die rather than that the entire people perish, John comments that it was not of his own accord that he made this outstandingly profound remark; he was prophesying (Jn 11:49-52). Now in a sense he certainly made this comment of his own accord. He was not manipulated by God into saying something that didn't occur to him. But his words were open to another level of explanation as well as another level of interpretation.

In the exodus story, Yahweh acts via some midwives, via Moses' mother, via his sister and via the king's daughter, as well as via Moses himself, who knows he acts on Yahweh's commission (if he can be persuaded, and all he has to do is speak), and via Pharaoh (who thinks he is resisting Yahweh), and by means of signs and wonders in nature that are both frightening and beneficial (Ex 4–18). The interweaving of divine intent and human responsibility finds further expression in the way Exodus speaks of God's intention to harden Pharaoh's heart, of Pharaoh's heart being hard, and of Pharaoh hardening his heart, and in the way Jesus aims to get people to become more blind (Mk 4:10-12).

One might say that sometimes, at least, God does not make things happen for people but that God accompanies people as they act and experience things happening.[86] God and humanity work together, though the human beings may be unaware of what is happening. God does not operate like the pilot of a drone. So God's acts may precede or follow human acts, or may mysteriously work along with them. Esther undertakes her brave acts, and her story makes no mention of God, but its silence speaks loudly of God's mysterious involvement. Ruth insists on committing herself to Naomi and to Yahweh, and her story, too, makes hardly any reference to God's activity, yet it speaks loudly of it.

Not only do Esther and Ruth undertake their own brave acts; they find success through unexpected coincidences. In this respect, too, their stories make hardly any reference to God's activity, yet speak loudly of God acting sovereignly by means of these coincidences. Events in the world may unfold by their own dynamic, but at another level God is acting through them. By "chance" Ruth happens to glean in a particular field (Ruth 2:3), and the rest of the story depends on this chance. Both stories assume that Yahweh works via the chance occurrences they report. Whereas these stories do not speak in terms of Yahweh making the chances happen, that conviction does receive paradoxical expression when Abraham's servant asks Yahweh to make chance work out in a certain way (Gen 24:12). Only people such as Philistines speak of *either* Yahweh *or* chance (2 Sam 6:9).

Whereas Westerners are inclined to see it as a matter of chance whether someone cannot see or cannot have children, or whether rain does or does not fall, the Scriptures are more inclined to see God's involvement in these events. God may make infertility or blindness happen as a chastisement, or as an experience into which he intends to intervene in order to achieve something (e.g., 1 Sam 1:5-6; Jn 9:3). Yet there are also some afflictions or

---

[86]Cf. Barth, *CD* III, 3:90-154.

healings that just happen, because God made the world that way. There are
occasions when God brings healings and doctors might see nothing strange
or miraculous in them; God was using natural processes. And there are
other occasions when doctors might be able to give no explanation of how
the healing happened, and it may be because God has acted in a way that
did not involve regular processes—as when Peter prayed for Dorcas and she
came back from the dead (Acts 9:36-42).

Deliberate Sovereignty

If God can seem not powerful enough, he can also seem too powerful,
"forming light and creating dark, making well-being (*šālôm*) and creating
bad things (*raʿ*)" (Is 45:7).[87] Two aspects of that statement need to be clar-
ified. One is that light and dark can be images for blessing and trouble, and
this connotation fits in the context. The words describe situations in which
things are going well for people and situations when they are going badly,
when a people experiences catastrophe. The passage is not describing God
as creating moral evil.

The other is that it does not imply that all catastrophes and blessings issue
from Yahweh's sovereignty, at least not in the same sense. This particular
declaration is concerned to affirm that Jerusalem's recent destruction by
Nebuchadnezzar and its imminent restoration through Cyrus both came
from Yahweh. While not every destruction or restoration issues directly
from Yahweh, some do.

"Does something bad happen to a city and Yahweh has not acted?"
(Amos 3:6). At first, the question sounds like a particularly strong declaration of Yahweh's active sovereignty in every event. But Amos goes on, "The
sovereign Yahweh doesn't do a thing unless he has revealed his plan to his
servants the prophets" (Amos 3:7). That statement implies that he is talking
about the bad things that have been happening in Ephraim, not about everything that ever happens to any city, since most such events are not announced by prophets.

In principle, anything that happens in the world is an outworking of
God's sovereignty, in keeping with the at-first-sight reading of Amos 3:6.

---

[87]On "Yahweh as the source of evil," see, e.g., John Barton, *Ethics in Ancient Israel* (Oxford and
New York: Oxford University Press, 2014), 257-61.

There is a sense in which God is behind all of history. Yet there are events in which God acts with a more deliberate sovereignty in connection with his creation project. The distinction implies a related nuancing of the related idea of God's presence. Yahweh says to Moses, "I have come down to rescue them" (Ex 3:8), come down from the heavens to the earth like the king going down into the city. If we think only in terms of a permanent divine presence and a uniform divine sovereignty, we exclude the scriptural portrayal of divine absence and inactivity, which is able to look for God to come and act.[88]

When Cyrus was extending his empire, the Phoenicians were extending theirs across the Mediterranean. Both the Persians and the Phoenicians were doing what they did because they wanted to add to their sphere of influence and/or their power, yet the Phoenicians' action was not an expression of God's will and purpose in the way that the Persians' action was. Earlier, God had brought Israel from Egypt to Canaan, and also brought the Philistines from Kaphtor and the Arameans from Qir (Amos 9:7). Aside from any questions of special divine intervention in Israel's story, the movements of all these five peoples involved the exercise of the human will and constituted a working out of God's creation commission, yet the initiative of Cyrus and that move of Israel had significance as exercises of God's sovereignty that did not attach to the other three.

Historians do not generally need to talk in terms of divine intervention in order to explain what happens. It reflects the realities of human ambition, power and stupidity. Yet Yahweh is in a position to say to his people, "I said I would do it, and it happened." Such events have a place in God's overall intention to achieve something in the long term in and through Israel's story. God has a purpose for that story, and formulates short-term plans or intentions for Israel. He may also have intentions for Assyria or Ammon in their own right, but they don't have that same significance in God's wider purpose.

Sovereignty That Holds Back

Cyrus's example suggests a further nuancing of the idea of divine sovereignty. Cyrus was taking up the role of Yahweh's agent from the king of Babylon, who had himself taken it up from the king of Assyria. In each case their activity related to the fact that Israel had refused to accept God's sovereignty.

---

[88]See further section 1.3 below.

Subsequently, Jesus announces that God's reign is now here (Mk 1:15), which suggests that in some sense God's reign had not been here; God has not been exercising sovereignty, except in a self-denying sense.

When God asks Eve, "What is this that you have done?" and later asks a similar question of her son (Gen 3:13; 4:10), he implies that they have not fulfilled his will. God told Adam and Eve to do something different from what they did. God did not will their action. Although "the Lord doesn't wish any to perish but all to make room for repentance" (2 Pet 3:9), it seems that many do not come to repentance and do perish. In a sense God's sovereign will finds expression; in another sense it is frustrated.

For European thinking, absolute power has been the preeminent attribute of divinity.[89] Yet "no divine attribute is as controversial now as omnipotence."[90] Is God not powerful enough, apparently incapable of stopping evil in the world, or is he capable of doing so but not exercising that power? God's sovereignty involves a self-denying willingness for people to disobey. The all-powerful nature of God means that God can make things happen and can stop things happening; he could have stopped Eve taking the fruit from the tree, but he didn't do so. God had the capacity to send legions of angels to rescue Jesus (Mt 26:53), but he didn't do so.

Instead he let humanity do its worst, and in this way he did achieve something that he himself intended. He knew it was going to happen, he intended it to happen, and he overcame the consequences of humanity's doing its worst (Acts 2:23-24). The assumptions about divine and human action correspond to ones that apply to Sennacherib: the Assyrians invade Judah because God aroused them, but as far as they are concerned they do so in order to extend their empire, and they will pay the penalty for their action even though it fulfills God's will (Is 10:4-19).

The image of God as Father illumines the way God's sovereignty works out. God's sovereignty is like that of parents in relation to their young children. There is a sense in which parents have absolute sovereignty over these children and can require or compel them to do what the parents say at every point and prevent them from doing what the parents forbid. Parents

---

[89]Jürgen Moltmann, *God in Creation* (London: SCM Press; San Francisco: Harper, 1985), 26.
[90]Feldmeier and Spieckermann, *God of the Living*, 147.

thus have to accept some responsibility for anything that their children do—though the children also have their own responsibility.

In practice, parents are unlikely to exercise their sovereignty in a thoroughgoing way. At some points they likely set constraints for their children and enforce them. At other points they let the children make decisions and achieve their own aims through the decisions the children make. At yet other points they let the children make decisions and they clean up the mess afterwards. Sometimes they ask or tell the children to do something that the parents want done, and the children do it, and sometimes the children don't. Sometimes the parents may sow the seed of an idea in their children's minds, and it may produce fruit in the decisions the children make; so we might understand God's being behind Joseph's brothers' plotting, or Pharaoh's stubbornness, or Judas's act of betrayal. Sometimes the children may have ideas about what the family should do, and the parents may agree. Further, the parents' sovereignty doesn't mean they can compel their children to think in the way the parents do.

The desire of God the Father for his children to come to repentance means that he is prepared to wait almost forever, though not actually forever; and that it is possible for people to speed the coming of God's day (2 Pet 3:8-12).

God over Against . . .

There is one God. The Scriptures are not dualistic. There are not two realities such as good and evil that are both part of ultimate reality. But was darkness in existence before light (as Gen 1 implies), and were forces of disorder competing with forces of order from the Beginning? Is oneness a goal for the End rather than a feature of the Beginning?

One could say that the First Testament inclines to monism, the New Testament to dualism, but the verb *inclines* allows for not being dualistic about this comparison, which would be a parable for the nature of that duality itself.[91] In the First Testament, God is involved in this world and this age and is in some sense responsible for all events in the world, including the assaults of great imperial powers and the afflictions that individuals experience, and

---

[91]On this question, see, e.g., Stephen C. Barton, "Johannine Dualism and Contemporary Pluralism," in Richard Bauckham and Carl Mosser, eds., *The Gospel of John and Christian Theology* (Grand Rapids and Cambridge, UK: Eerdmans, 2008), 3-18.

this world is the one context in which human beings experience life. Yet on the edge of this picture is a recognition that there are dynamic powers resisting God's will, that death often works its will in a way that deprives people of fullness of life and/or prevents them reaching fullness of years, and that God's will does not come to achievement in this age but awaits "that day." Conversely, the New Testament can set God over against Satan, light over against darkness, this age over against the age to come, this world over against the heavenly world, and the church over against the world. Yet Satan's power is constrained and ultimately subordinate to God's; darkness does not quench light; this age is invaded by and destined to give way to the age to come; and the world has been overcome by Jesus.

In significant ways the Scriptures point to duality rather than dualism. God is distinct from us, but God becomes a human being, and human beings can be in God's presence. Life is distinct from death, but the dead can be resurrected, and death can invade life. The coming age is distinct from this age, but the coming age can have an effect on this age, and the person who belongs to this age can move on into the coming age (Jn 12:25). Good is distinct from evil, but human beings have elements of both. Humanity in God's image is distinct from humanity when that image has been defaced, but defaced humanity continues to embody that image.

Whereas Genesis 1 starts with darkness, John 1 has light present from the Beginning. Both Genesis and John see darkness as the backdrop against which they speak of light, and neither indicates where darkness came from, though both declare that God set about dispelling it and will complete that project. So neither points toward a cosmic or metaphysical dualism in which light and darkness always have been and always will be in conflict. Nor do they point to a cosmic or metaphysical monism in which only light has been there from the Beginning. Nor do they point to a monism in which the triumph of light belongs only to the End. They point toward a historical monism in which God has been ensuring since creation that light keeps asserting itself over darkness ("the darkness did not overcome it"), the focus of this assertion being the story of Israel that comes to its climax in the death and resurrection of Jesus.

Perhaps it is the coming of light that brings about the coming of darkness. Only when there is light does the darkness of darkness become apparent.

The more God shines light into the world, the more darkness seeks to overcome it. And it is precisely darkness's attempt to do so that brings about its own demise. By striving against the light, darkness brings about the victory of the light. It does it in Jesus' ministry as demonic powers come out into the open in resisting Jesus and get publicly defeated; it does it in bringing about the death of Jesus, which is the means of light triumphing; and it does it in the life of the infant church as its persecution is the stimulus to the church's spreading.

That God is one is important to Christian theology and philosophy, and it may therefore seem odd that the Scriptures themselves do not seem very interested in such an affirmation. Perhaps the reasons are contextual, as our need to affirm a metaphysical monism may reflect contextual considerations of our own. In the Scriptures' case, in the context of Middle Eastern thinking, the question did not arise, whereas it does arise in ours, in the context of European thinking. But the declarations in the Scriptures that Yahweh is the one God imply that there is only one God, and even their portrayal of the one God as in conflict with opposing forces and certain to overcome them may both suggest a critique of the pluralist instincts of our world, which presuppose no one unified truth or reality.[92]

Eternal

"I am the first and I am the last," Yahweh says (Is 44:6; 48:12). The claim recurs in Revelation. "'I am the A and the Z,' says the Lord God, the one who is, and who was, and who is coming, the all-powerful"; and at the other end of the book, "I am the A and the Z, the Beginning and the End" (Rev 1:8; 21:6; cf. Rev 1:4; 4:8). In turn, the expression "the one who is, and who was, and who is coming" reaffirms the words Yahweh addressed to Moses, "I am who I am" and/or "I will be what I will be," and "I am" (Ex 3:14). When the End comes, the elders will be able to turn this acknowledgment into "we give thanks to you, Lord God All-powerful, the one who is and who was, because you have taken your great power and begun to reign" (Rev 11:17).

Eternity is an idea with positive substance; it is not simply the negation of time. The affirmations in Isaiah and Revelation suggest not that God is

---

[92]Cf. Miroslav Volf, "Johannine Dualism and Contemporary Pluralism," in Bauckham and Mosser, *Gospel of John and Christian Theology*, 19-50 (on 27-29) = Volf, *Captive to the Word of God*, 100-103.

time-less but that he is omni-temporal. He is God throughout time. He is God *mē'ôlām 'ad-'ôlām,* from age to age (Ps 90:2). Perhaps there is a timeless realm beyond that of our world, and there God is timeless; the Scriptures do not reveal whether or not it is so. Perhaps there was a timeless reality before time, and perhaps there will be a timeless reality after time; again, the Scriptures do not indicate whether or not it is so. But within time, there is no time that is beyond God's being and reach. It is one reason why God is able to reveal to his servants "what must soon take place" (Rev 1:1). God knows that Abraham's descendants will live as serfs in a foreign country and will be ill-treated for four hundred years and that Pharaoh will not let Israel go unless he is forced to do so (Gen 15:13; Ex 3:19). The whole of time is existent to God. He is the dramatist to whose being the entire drama is present. What is future to people who play a part in the story is present to God.

There is another reason why God is able to make declarations about the future. He speaks as the one who can determine what will happen. While prophets predict the future, and God does so when speaking of things that human beings will do, God does not merely predict the future. More distinctively, he determines it, and it is on this basis that he is in a position to say what it holds (e.g., Gen 41:25, 32). Yahweh's capacity to announce some events because he determines them is a key reason for believing that he is God (Is 41:21-29). It is for this reason that "No one knows about that day or hour . . . not even the Son, only the Father" (Mk 13:32), and for this reason that God can reveal what *must* soon take place (e.g., Rev 1:1).

Yet alongside the fact that God is God throughout time is the fact that there is a "before" and an "after" for God. I have been present to the past seventy years or so, but not all at once, and perhaps something is similar for God. The Scriptures talk about God remembering the past and thinking about the future. God's remembering is a key expression of his love and compassion, though it is also potentially a threat because it might mean he will not acquit. Perhaps God can move between past, present and future. Further, the Scriptures often describe the future working out in a way that God does not anticipate. God can wonder about the future and say "perhaps" (e.g., Jer 26:3; Ezek 12:3). God can have his expectations disappointed (e.g., Is 5:1-7; 63:8-10; Jer 3:6-7, 19-20).

One might ask whether either observations about God knowing the future or observations about God being surprised should be taken metaphorically and anthropomorphically, but such suggestions may seem too close to demythologizing for comfort. They conform the Scriptures to our thinking rather than vice versa. Whether taken literally or anthropomorphically, they indicate the reality of God's sovereignty in relation to the future. On one hand, nothing catches God out in the sense that it constitutes something God cannot handle. On the other, God is involved in genuine interaction with people. God does have expectations of them but does not predetermine the results of his actions in a way that removes the reality of their responsibility to God and to life. People do truly respond to God, for good or ill, and God can be grieved and disappointed as well as gratified and thrilled by what they do.[93]

Knowledgeable

God knows what is going on in congregations (Rev 2:1–3:22): he knows about their activities, their perseverance and faithfulness, their affliction and their poverty, and also about their loss of their "first love" and their tolerance of false teaching. He knows the difference between people within the congregation who are faithful and people who are not. It is impossible to hide from God; "all things are bare and laid open to the eyes of the one to whom our account has to be given" (Heb 4:13). God has access to people's thoughts as well as their actions (e.g., 1 Chron 28:9; Ps 44:21 [MT 22]).

Whereas one might have assumed that omniscience is inherent in being God, the Scriptures often refer to God asking questions and apparently gaining information by doing so, as well as to God being surprised and disappointed. Some of these questions might be rhetorical; God may be acting like a parent who wants to give a child a chance to own up to something (e.g., Gen 3:13; 4:6). Some look more literal and designed to enable God to find something out. So it is with references to God testing people. God's testing of Abraham leads to the conclusion, "Now I know that you are in awe of God, and have not held back your son, your only one, from me" (Gen 22:12). God tests Israel in order to discover whether

---

[93]On the issues raised in these paragraphs, see further John Goldingay, "Does God Have Surprises?," in *Key Questions About Christian Faith* (Grand Rapids: Baker, 2010), 25-41.

it will do as he says (Ex 16:4; cf. Deut 8:2; Judg 2:22). God agrees to the testing of Job to establish that his reason for living in awe of God is not simply that it pays (Job 1:8-12). Sometimes God uses testing to establish the truth for himself; in Job's case, it is to prove the truth of what God is convinced of.

Psalm 139 is a striking confession concerning God's knowledge.

> Yahweh, you have examined me and known me:
>> you yourself have known my sitting and my rising,
>> you have discerned my intention, from far away.
> My walking and my reclining you have measured;
>> with all my ways you have become familiar.
> Because there is not a word on my tongue—
>> there, Yahweh, you have known it all.
> Behind and in front you have bound me,
>> and put your hand on me.
> Your knowledge is too extraordinary for me;
>> it has towered high, I cannot prevail over it. . . .
>
> I myself acknowledge you fully;
>> my frame was not concealed from you,
> When I was made in secret,
>> when I was embroidered in earth's depths.
> Your eyes saw me as an embryo,
>> and on your scroll were written, all of them,
> The days that were shaped,
>> when there was not one of them.
> So for me, how imposing were your intentions,
>> God, how huge is the sum of them! . . .
>
> Examine me, God, and know my mind;
>> test me and know my concerns.
> See if there is an idolatrous way in me
>> and lead me in the ancient way. (Ps 139:1-6, 14-17, 23-24)

The psalm makes clear that the knowledge of which it speaks is not knowledge inherent in God by virtue of his being omniscient but knowledge that God acquires. God looks, and thus knows. It is this process that enables God to perceive the length of the life that a person might live, on the basis (as we would put it) of information in the person's genes. For human beings, there is innate knowledge, and there is knowledge we acquire. The same is true of God. The difference between human beings and God is that there are no limits to the knowledge that God can acquire. God can look anywhere, and can (for instance) look into the human heart. God indeed looks, in order to see (Ps 33:13-15); here too, God does not know "automatically." The same applies to Jesus, who sometimes knows what someone is thinking but sometimes asks questions (Lk 7:39-47; 8:45).

As might be the case with statements about God's relationship with the future, perhaps the Scriptures' many statements about God coming to know things are metaphorical or anthropomorphic. Alternatively, the statement that God "knows all things" (1 Jn 3:20) may need to be understood contextually; it then refers to God's knowing all that he needs to know in order to render a fairer judgment than the one we make of ourselves.[94] Either way, we have to ask about the theological significance of each kind of statement. The statements about God coming to know things testify to the reality of God's interactions with us. God's supernatural knowledge does not turn his relationship with us into a sham. The statements about God possessing knowledge in relation to us, like a parent's vastly superior knowledge in relation to a child, give us security and also safeguard us from thinking that we can get away with things.

1.3 God's Spirit, Wind and Fire

If Yahweh is the all-powerful, time-transcendent, awe-inspiring God in the heavens, how is he involved in the ordinary world? Where and how can he be experienced, met, interacted with? "Our God is a consuming fire" (Heb 12:24): the direct presence and activity of God, the absolute and transcendent one, would surely be overwhelming for created humanity, like the power of electricity or the brightness of the sun, even without taking account of the complication introduced by sin.

When the Scriptures speak of the presence and activity of an aspect of God, such as God's spirit, face, insight, arm, hand, word or name, they denote a reality of God's presence and activity that is more manageable

---

[94]So C. Clifton Black, "The First, Second, and Third Letters of John," in Leander E. Keck et al., eds., *The New Interpreter's Bible* (Nashville: Abingdon, 1998), 12:363-469 (on the passage).

for humanity. Such ways of speaking also provide ways of conceptualizing Jesus' relationship with God and with the world. Jesus is the embodiment of God's spirit or insight or word or face or arm or hand or
splendor or name in the world. He is thus the embodiment of the whole
of God, because the whole of God is expressed in one of those aspects of
God. Such ways of speaking suggest how being overcome by God can be
like being overwhelmed by a supernatural force or being met by a supernatural person.

Face, Presence

To return to Psalm 139:

> Where could I go from your spirit,
>   where could I flee from your face?
> If I were to go up to the heavens,
>   you would be there.
> If I were to make Sheol my bed—
>   there you would be.
> Were I to take dawn's wings,
>   dwell on the far side of the sea,
> There, too, your hand could lead me away,
>   your right hand could take hold of me.
> Were I to say, "The darkness can certainly seize me,
>   light can be night around me,"
> Darkness, too, would not be too dark for you,
>   and night would be light like day;
>   darkness and light are the same. (Ps 139:7-12)

A neat feature of the psalm is its ambiguity about whether God's ability to
reach us anywhere is good news or bad news. A person who lives on the
basis of commitment to God can take it as good news, but some declarations
of Jeremiah warn other people against that reading.

> Am I a God nearby (Yahweh's declaration),
>   and not a God far away?
> If someone hides in hiding places,
>   don't I myself see him? . . .
> Don't I fill the heavens and the earth? (Jer 23:23-24)

The same warning issues when similar language recurs in Amos 9. Indeed, the context in Psalm 139 has the identical implication; I cannot hide from God's presence any more than from God's capacity to know what I'm doing.

There is a sense in which God is everywhere. Were it not for God's presence, the cosmos would lack the energy to exist. Yet the Scriptures put more emphasis on God's dynamic capacity to reach out everywhere than they put on God's omnipresence. Their understanding of God's presence parallels their understanding of God's power and God's knowledge. They speak more of God's capacity to do anything, know anything and be anywhere than of omnipotence, omniscience or omnipresence. The implication of the rhetorical questions in the psalm and in Jeremiah is that God can reach and find us wherever we are. It's both impossible to escape from God and impossible to be outside the realm where God can act on our behalf. Wherever Jesus' followers go to disciple all the nations, through all the days to the completion of the age, Jesus will be with them (Mt 28:16-20).

Such scriptures suggest some further nuancing of the idea of God's presence. "Where there are two or three gathered together for my name, I'm there in their midst," Jesus says to his disciples (Mt 18:20). "The Lord is with you," Gabriel says to Mary (Lk 1:28). "Be strong, stand firm, don't panic, don't be afraid, because Yahweh your God will be with you everywhere you go," Joshua says to the Israelites on the edge of Canaan (Josh 1:9). Yahweh had also already bidden the Israelites to make a sanctuary "so that I may dwell in their midst," and on its completion "Yahweh's splendor filled the dwelling" (Ex 25:8; 40:34). Subsequently "Yahweh's splendor filled Yahweh's house," and Solomon described it as a house "for you to live in forever" (1 Kings 8:10-13), though that hope was not fulfilled, because Yahweh's splendor later left the house (Ezek 9–10).

So God's presence can take several forms. The difference is not merely a matter of different degrees to which people feel God's presence; the Scriptures are less concerned than Western readers with the question of feeling God's presence. They focus more on the objective fact of God's presence. There is a general reality of God's presence through the entire cosmos that keeps it in being and holds it together. There is a concentrated and guaranteed presence of God in particular places that makes it possible for people to come to make offerings, pray and know that they will be seen and heard and that God will take notice. There is a dynamic and active presence of God that makes things happen out in the world.[95] None of these objective realities have to do with a *sense* of God being present.

Splendor, Name

In what sense did Yahweh's splendor (*kābôd*) fill his house? Talk of the splendor, glory or honor of God or of a human being is usually figurative. The heavens declare Yahweh's splendor; all the peoples are to see Yahweh's splendor; Yahweh's splendor is to be manifest in his return to Jerusalem and in Jerusalem's own restoration; Jesus manifests God's splendor; God's splendor is shown in his raising Jesus (Pss 19:1 [MT 2]; 97:6; Is 40:5; 60:1; Jn 1:14; 2:11; Rom 6:4; 2 Cor 4:4).

The First Testament includes no personal accounts of people who saw this splendor with their physical eyes and could describe it. Descriptions come either in the visions of prophets such as Ezekiel or in narratives such as those in Exodus, Kings and Chronicles that use such terms figuratively to give symbolic expression to the awe-inspiring significance of the awe-inspiring fact that the awe-inspiring God had once long ago truly come to live in the wilderness sanctuary and then in the temple. In the course of the temple's rebuilding, God promises to come to fill it with great splendor (Hag 2:1-9), and the account of its completion describes the joy with which the work is finished (Ezra 6:13-23), but the Scriptures don't speak of the splendor appearing at the temple's dedication in the way the Deuteronomists have Solomon speaking of it.

Deuteronomy's talk of the place where Yahweh puts his name (e.g., Deut 12:5, 11; 26:2) helps our understanding of God's presence in the sanctuary; the talk in terms of Yahweh's name is also taken up systematically by Solomon (1 Kings; 2 Chron 6) and elsewhere in Kings and Chronicles. A person's name stands for the person. It suggests the reality of the person, and it conjures up an awareness of the person. Further, if the name suggests something of the person's significance in addition to providing a label (as the name Yahweh does), it conjures up an awareness of the person in a more multifaceted way. Declaring the name "Yahweh" generates an awareness of the reality of Yahweh's presence among his people and of the

---

[95]See further *OTT* 1:385-408; 2:96-108.

significance of that presence. God's putting his name in the sanctuary means putting his real presence there (it's not just a human awareness). Israel's declaring the name encourages the human awareness (it's not just a theological fact).

God's being present to Israel in the wilderness dwelling and then in the Jerusalem temple generates huge enthusiasm for the temple, not least on the part of that majority of Israelites who were in no position to go there more than once or twice a year. While they knew that they could pray anywhere because Yahweh listened to prayer wherever they lived, and they knew that Yahweh could be present and active anywhere, they still valued being able to go to Yahweh's dwelling, as believers in Jesus who know that God is with them anywhere still appreciate being able to gather with other believers and knowing that Jesus is then in their midst in a special sense.

> How much loved is your fine dwelling,
>   Yahweh Armies.
> My whole being has yearned, it is spent
>   [with looking] for Yahweh's courtyards
> So that my heart and my body might resound
>   for the living God.
> Yes, a bird—it found a home,
>   a pigeon [found] itself a nest,
> Where it has put its young—your great altar,
>   Yahweh Armies, my King and my God.
> The blessings of the people who live in your house,
>   who can still praise you! . . .
>
> A day in your courtyards is better than a thousand [elsewhere];
>   I would choose being at the threshold of my God's house,
>   rather than dwelling in the tents of the faithless person. (Ps 84:1-4, 10)

There were advantages and drawbacks about God making a commitment to being present in the sanctuary. People knew they could go there and talk to God or show him things—as Hezekiah does with a threatening letter (2 Kings 19:14). But Yahweh notes two disadvantages when David first proposes building a temple in a fixed location (2 Sam 7). Like an image, a temple conveys a false impression of Yahweh's nature, given that Yahweh likes to be active and on the move, and it reverses the proper relationship between

Yahweh and David over house building. Solomon's dedication prayer recognizes the tension between the fact that Yahweh dwells in a thick cloud and the fact that he himself has built Yahweh a house (1 Kings 8:12-13). Yahweh makes the same point in speaking of the heavens as his throne and the earth as something to put his feet on (so how could people think of building him an earthly house?), while also being one who pays attention to people who are afflicted and crushed (Is 66:1-2; cf. Is 57:15).

Place and Presence

Psalm 84 indirectly recognizes the danger that people might think that the sanctuary was the only place where they could be in Yahweh's presence. It's fine for people living in Jerusalem but not for people who live many miles away. The psalm offers a neat reflection on this question in which it affirms the wonder of being in Yahweh's presence in the temple but also implies that one can relate to Yahweh elsewhere (cf. also Pss 16; 27; 42). The potential for anxiety that it reflects compares with the actual anxiety expressed in the Israelites' question, "Is Yahweh present in our midst or not?" (Ex 17:7; cf. Ex 34:9). One might see Yahweh's answer in his commission, "They are to make me a sanctuary so that I may dwell among them" (Ex 25:8). Although Israelites knew that Yahweh was accessible anywhere (Ps 145:18), "there was always a need for tangible, visible evidence of the divine presence."[96]

While the First Testament usually speaks simply of Yahweh himself being with Israel, it can also speak in terms of Yahweh "putting his holy spirit" among them and of his giving them a resting place "by Yahweh's spirit" (Is 63:7-14). Yahweh can say "I am with you" or "my spirit remains among you" (Hag 2:4-5); they are two ways of describing the same reality. Indeed, whether referring to God's presence as a general reality, a concentrated reality in particular places or a presence that makes things happen, in all three connections the Scriptures also speak in terms of God's spirit. The New Testament likewise can speak of God being with us but also of the Holy Spirit being with us. Thus both expressions refer to the same reality, but talk in terms of the Holy Spirit becomes a dominant way in which the New Testament

---

[96]Baruch A. Levine, "Temple Building in the Hebrew Bible," in Mark J. Boda and Jamie Novotny, eds., *From the Foundations to the Crenellations* (Münster: Ugarit-Verlag, 2010), 423-36 (on 425).

speaks of God's presence. So Genesis (for instance) relates many occasions when God spoke to people or gave them revelatory dreams; theologically one could say that it was always the Holy Spirit who was doing the speaking or revealing.

While rabbinic tradition spoke of the Holy Spirit as present in the first temple but not in the second, along with fire from heaven, the anointing oil, the covenant chest, and the Urim and Thummim,[97] the Qumran community believed that God's spirit was present in its midst, and there is little evidence that the Scriptures think in terms of God having withdrawn his spirit from Israel in later First Testament times. References to the absence of prophets (Ps 74:9; Lam 2:9) relate to particular situations when there is a "famine . . . in respect of hearing Yahweh's message" (Amos 8:11-12). Haggai's promise, just noted, does not suggest that the fall of Jerusalem and the exile meant God's presence had permanently withdrawn (cf. also Zech 4:6).[98] Second Temple writings such as Ezra, Nehemiah, Chronicles, Haggai and Zechariah assume the presence of God in Israel even though they also lament God's relative inactivity.

On the other hand, Joel 2:28-32 (MT 3:1-5) does promise a new outpouring of Yahweh's spirit. Joel's general picture of the community's troubled experience likely implies that people in his day were not aware of the presence and activity of God's spirit even in the way Isaiah 63 or Haggai suggest. Further, most explicit references to God's spirit's speaking and revealing in the First Testament involve people in leadership positions. The promise in Joel envisages not merely the restoration of how things had been but the arrival of something unprecedented in scope, and Acts 2 sees the Pentecost event as fulfilling this promise.

Without referring to Joel, Paul likewise sees "the promise of the Spirit" fulfilled in the life of congregations in Turkey. The spirit is a dynamic experienced reality that signifies the very presence of God and that inspires people to live godly lives and to pray and praise. The Spirit's coming fulfills God's promise to Abraham of blessing for the Gentiles (Gal 3:13-14). In other

---

[97]E.g., Babylonian Yoma 21b 48a; Song of Songs Rabbah VIII, 9.3 on Song 8:8.

[98]So Gordon D. Fee, *God's Empowering Presence* (Peabody, MA: Hendrickson, 1994), 7. His only evidence is Hag 2:3, which belongs to the time before the temple has been built (and two verses later Haggai reassures people that God's spirit remains among them).

words, Abraham's blessing and the Spirit are the same thing. The Spirit thus plays a crucial role in the experience of believers and in Paul's understanding of the gospel. And as well as indicating that God's promises have been fulfilled, the Spirit's activity constitutes a guarantee that they will be fulfilled.

Spirit and Truth

Jesus himself affirms the truth that Psalm 84 directly questions but indirectly affirms, that the presence of God is not a matter of the right place. A much-married Samaritan woman, needing to change the subject from one that embarrasses her, has implied another problem about the idea of God's presence being known in a specific place. How do you know which is the place? For instance, is it Jerusalem or Gerizim? While Jesus has already made clear in John that he cares passionately about the temple—his father lived there (Jn 2:12-17)—someone greater than the temple is here (Mt 12:6). In his conversation, for the time being he lets himself be sidetracked and says, "The time is coming (and it's now here) when the true worshipers will worship the Father in/by spirit and truth. . . . God is spirit, and people who worship him must worship in/by spirit and truth" (Jn 4:23-24).

The enigmatic nature of that statement[99] reflects the timing of the conversation (cf. Jn 7:39). "Spirit and truth" is a compound expression not so different from "spirit of truth" (Jn 14:17; 15:26; 16:13); it refers to worship "by/in the true/truthful Spirit." Worship will be offered by/in the Holy Spirit rather than in a particular place. "We worship by God's Spirit" (Phil 3:3).[100] Paul similarly takes up the Torah's language about God being present among his people (Lev 26:11-12) and declares that it applies to God's presence in the congregation: "you are God's temple and God's Spirit lives among you" (1 Cor 3:16-17; 2 Cor 6:16; applied to the individual in 1 Cor 6:19). In light of the key place of the temple as "the epicentre of the Jewish world, . . . the one place where the living God had chosen to put his name, . . . the place to which the nations would flock to see that glory and learn that name," the declaration that some little congregation is God's temple is breathtaking.[101]

---

[99]See Benny Thattayil, *In Spirit and Truth* (Louvain: Peeters, 2007).
[100]Though the verb here is *latreuō*, which can be translated "serve," and there is no preposition before *pneumati*.
[101]Wright, *Paul and the Faithfulness of God*, 355.

This move on God's part is also a return to the way things once were when the wind-like God was not fixed in a place, the situation that God always preferred to being tied to a building (see 2 Sam 7). Yet the church came to reinvent the idea of buildings that were "the house of God" or "the sanctuary." Whereas Psalm 84 overtly affirmed the temple but indirectly declared that God could be worshiped anywhere, the church turned the psalm's stance on its head. Although the church knew that it was the temple of the Holy Spirit and that worship in/by the Spirit was what counted, it came to associate God's presence with buildings and even came to call them churches (the word that was properly the name for the fellowship itself). Behind that development was the same human instinct that underlay the establishment in Israel of sanctuaries such as the "high places," the desire for a sacred space where one can have a conviction that one can meet with God.

One problem with the idea that we worship in/by the Holy Spirit is that we can't control when the Holy Spirit inspires such worship. We can't compel the coming of the Holy Spirit or fulfill conditions that will guarantee that coming. So we can maybe circumnavigate this difficulty by building sanctuaries. Whereas God had been unwilling to compromise with the human instinct to make images of God (cf. the comment in Acts 17:29), he had been willing to compromise over building a house of God, and maybe he is also willing to compromise over Christians building sanctuaries.[102]

But there is no temple in the new Jerusalem in Revelation, because God's presence occupies the entire city, the new world that embodies the new heavens and the new earth. You could almost say the city *is* a temple.[103]

Force, Wind and Fire

Although "I am with you" and "my spirit remains among you" refer to the same reality, the difference between the two expressions is significant. Both Hebrew *rûaḥ* and Greek *pneuma* can denote the dynamic of a person but can also refer to the wind. The image of the pouring out of the spirit from on high suggests that the spirit's coming is like the coming of a storm of rain.

---

[102]See further the comments under "Purity" and "Preserving a Realm of Sacredness" in section 7.1 below.

[103]So G. K. Beale, *The Temple and the Church's Mission* (Leicester, UK: Inter-Varsity Press; Downers Grove, IL: InterVarsity Press, 2004), e.g., 23-25 (though I would not say that the Jerusalem temple looks forward to that presence—rather, the vision of that presence looks backward to the temple for a way of picturing it).

A storm cannot be determined or controlled or manipulated by humanity.[104] *Spirit* is a word "to express and explain the mysteriousness of life experienced as something given and sustained from without," suggested by the power of the wind and the breath of life.[105] The Holy Spirit is "the stranger," "God beyond our control."[106]

"It is the mysterious and the overwhelming in human life which is derived from the Spirit of God"; a person hears words, sees visions or recognizes compulsions that are "given him from without."[107] Talk of God's spirit implies God's presence in an earth-shattering form. "Pneuma is the miraculous divine power that stands in absolute contrast to all that is human."[108] In speaking of God's spirit, Isaiah 63:7-14 thus recognizes that at the exodus and specifically at the Reed Sea Yahweh was with Israel in person and in power. In the context of the challenges of Haggai's day, Yahweh in person is with the Judahites, and Yahweh in power is with them. "The Spirit of God makes God's power knowable. The Spirit reveals the power of God in and on human beings and in and on their fellow-creatures." Whereas Western thinking sets "spirit" over against "body," *rûaḥ* suggests a force experienced in the world and in the body. In a further contrast, "the Spirit is not something numinous, but a power that changes real life relations."[109] People in the New Testament "understood—and assumed—the Spirit to be manifested in power, . . . so that the terms 'Spirit' and 'power' at times are used interchangeably" (e.g., Lk 1:35; 1 Cor 2:4).[110]

Like Isaiah 63:7-14, the Torah also connects *rûaḥ* with Israel's deliverance from the Egyptians at the Reed Sea (Ex 14:21; 15:8, 10), though translations usually assume that the word refers to the blast of the wind. In Judges Yahweh's spirit comes spectacularly on individuals in connection with their fighting to deliver his people, though this spirit is "not a spirit of war, but

---

[104]Michael Welker, *God the Spirit* (Minneapolis: Fortress, 1994), 138.

[105]Dunn, *Christ and the Spirit*, 2:vii.

[106]Eduard Schweizer, *The Holy Spirit* (Philadelphia: Fortress, 1980), 46, 127.

[107]Hermann Gunkel, *The Influence of the Holy Spirit* (Philadelphia: Fortress, 1979), 32, 33. Cf. John R. Levison, *Filled with the Spirit* (Grand Rapids and Cambridge, UK: Eerdmans, 2009), 3.

[108]Rudolf Bultmann, *Theology of the New Testament* (repr., Waco, TX: Baylor University Press, 2007), 1:153; cf. Thiselton, *Hermeneutics of Doctrine*, 416.

[109]Welker, *God the Spirit*, 2, 108.

[110]Fee, *God's Empowering Presence*, 35.

delivers out of distress and helplessness as a 'Spirit of righteousness and mercy.'"[111] But

> the Spirit of God is experienced as a power that not only brings deliverance in situations that appear to offer no way out, but also affords preservation in ongoing danger and distress. Even here the Spirit acts—albeit in a manner as yet unclear—as "comforter," as a power that lends steadfastness in affliction. The experience of being preserved in ongoing affliction is thoroughly ambiguous. Preservation in affliction means, after all, that human beings must persevere in a tormenting, intolerable situation.[112]

Indeed, perhaps the comfort the Spirit provides somehow issues from its unpredictability and our lack of control, and power.[113]

God regularly offers sustaining, not explanation. Further, "although God's Spirit unleashes unexpected forces and produces improbable results, this Spirit acts under the conditions of what is creaturely and finite. The services of imperfect, mortal human beings are enlisted by this Spirit, and they remain real human beings," as the stories of Jephtah and Samson illustrate. "The action of the Spirit is surrounded by that which is uncanny, ambiguous and dismaying." It "is by no means necessarily connected with joy and good fortune for the person who bears the Spirit and for this person's surroundings." On the other hand, throughout these stories the background is Israel's sins, so that the activity of God's spirit is designed to bring about the community's restoration and the forgiveness of sins, which resonates with the association in the third article of the creed among the Holy Spirit, the communion of saints and the forgiveness of sins.[114]

Person as Well as Force

The coming of God's spirit is disturbing for the person on whom God comes and for other people. It's not something that people seek or try to bring about, nor is it ever a private experience that is unnoticed by others or has no significance for others. It brings about a new capacity to act on behalf of one's people yet not a kind of confidence or sure conviction or sense of being in control. "In all cases of the Spirit's descent, the general

---

[111]Welker, *God the Spirit*, 55.
[112]Ibid., 65.
[113]I owe this idea to Thomas A. Bennett.
[114]Welker, *God the Spirit*, 55-56, 60, 62-65.

security of expectation is called into question," whether it was of defeat or continuing order.[115] God's spirit gripped David in an ongoing way (1 Sam 16:13), and we might think of this reality as the spirit "resting" on him, but the First Testament does not use that image,[116] and "rest" seems rather gentle an expression. While the verb that commonly means "rest" (*nûaḥ*) is used in connection with God's spirit in Numbers 11:25, this "resting" is temporary, and "alighting" is a more appropriate translation. Isaiah 11:2 similarly speaks of God's spirit resting in the sense of alighting on the shoot from Jesse's stump, and Acts 2:3 pictures the Holy Spirit alighting on the disciples. Perhaps it's more like an eagle's talons getting a grip of you.[117] In Isaiah 42; 61 God's spirit is simply "on" God's servant and "on" the prophet.

The spirit of God being "on" someone in Isaiah 11; 42; 61 means their being concerned for *mišpāṭ ûṣədāqâ*, for exercising authority in the right way. The promised shoot from Jesse's stump will take up David's role (2 Sam 8:15): "He will exercise authority in the right way for the poor, and reprove with uprightness for the lowly people in the country; he will strike the country with the club in his mouth, with the breath from his lips" (Is 11:4). God's servant will tell the world that God is bringing about *mišpāṭ*, the exercise of his authority in the world. The prophet who speaks in Isaiah 61 will tell oppressed Judah that God is doing so.

Both Testaments speak of God's spirit both as a person and as a phenomenon,[118] though the New Testament speaks more often in the first way while the First Testament speaks more often in the second way. Understanding the Holy Spirit would be less complicated if we didn't have to take account of both aspects, but both were aspects of the way people experienced the presence of God's spirit.

So the coming of the Spirit is like a flood or a fire overwhelming people; it's also like a person speaking to them or loving them. God's spirit is like wind or breath, as the New Testament word *pneuma* and the First Testament word *rûaḥ* suggest. God's spirit is also the spirit of a

---

[115]Ibid., 82.
[116]Against ibid., 109.
[117]I owe this comment to Kathleen Scott Goldingay.
[118]Cf. Bultmann, *Theology of the New Testament*, 1:155-56.

person, which as such brings the reality of the person. It makes one vividly aware of the person's presence, mysteriously within one's own spirit as well as operating from outside. The notion of the spirit as a force field[119] conveys effectively the spirit's nonpersonal nature, though not the spirit's personal nature.[120] The spirit also teaches and guides (Neh 9:20; Jn 14:25-26), meets opposition (Is 63:10; Acts 7:51), inspires prayer, praise and prophecy (Joel 2:28; Acts 2:17-18; Eph 6:18), appoints overseers (Acts 20:28), speaks (Acts 28:25), testifies (Rom 8:16), intercedes (Rom 8:26-27), investigates, knows and teaches (1 Cor 2:10-13), and can be lied to and grieved (Is 63:10; Acts 5:3; Eph 4:30). The spirit's presence needs to be a personal one if there is to be some equivalence between saying "I am with you" and saying "my spirit is with you." John 16 offers a particularly systematic portrait of the spirit as a person, who will convict, guide, speak, hear and glorify. It is because he is an entity with these personal capacities and not merely a thing that the spirit will be able to make up for the departure of Jesus himself (Jn 14:16-17). The spirit will mediate a personal presence.

The Testaments further complement each other in the way that the First Testament's talk of God's spirit in humanity commonly suggests an endowment given to humanity by dint of creation, while the New Testament rarely refers to this notion (e.g., 2 Cor 6:6-7; Acts 6:5, 10). What is the relationship between the spirit that God breathes into humanity by dint of birth and the spirit that brings about extraordinary effects? In the First Testament, the filling with God's spirit was not an endowment simply added on to what humans are by birth but a working out of the original endowment.[121] The New Testament commonly suggests an endowment that comes on people as a superadded gift through their coming to know Jesus,[122] though it much more often refers to God's spirit than to Jesus' spirit.[123] In addition the First Testament's promise of the spirit in Ezekiel 36–37 refers to the people as a whole, whereas Paul's use of its imagery and phraseology

---

[119]Welker, God the Spirit, 242.
[120]See, e.g., Timothy Harvie, "God as a Field of Force," Heythrop Journal 52 (2011): 250-59.
[121]Cf. Levison, Filled with the Spirit, 11-12, and what follows (14-105).
[122]Cf. ibid., 229-46.
[123]Fee, God's Empowering Presence, 835.

(e.g., Rom 5:3; 1 Thess 4:8) corresponds to that at Qumran in relating it more to the individual.[124]

1.4 GOD'S MIND AND MESSAGE

"In the beginning was the *logos*, and the *logos* was with God, and the *logos* was divine" (Jn 1:1). John opens his Gospel by thus taking up the opening words of the First Testament, "In the beginning, God created the heavens and the earth . . . and God said . . ." (Gen 1:1, 3). *Logos* means "word," and God created by speaking, which would suggest one sense in which the *logos* was there at the Beginning. The heavens were made "by Yahweh's word" (Ps 33:6). God's speech is by its very nature God's act. But *logos* means much more than "word." It means an idea, a principle, a mind. And it denotes the gospel message. Jesus is the embodiment of all these. He is the embodiment of God.

From the Beginning

God's first actual words in Genesis brought light into being. John, too, goes on to say that everything that came into being through the *logos* was life, "and the life was the light of human beings" (Jn 1:3-4). There is some rhyme and reason about the created world. The world is not simply the product of "the impersonal plus time plus chance."[125] It is the expression of a purpose; it has some meaning. In John's intellectual world, people could express that conviction by talking in terms of there being a *logos* in the world that goes back to its beginning—some logic, an idea, a thought, a principle, a rationale, a mind. In the Beginning was the mind.

While John starts by affirming that assumption, he does not subsequently take up this way of thinking. He uses the word *logos* more than any of the other Gospels, but it always denotes not a philosophical idea, nor an individual word, but something more like a statement or a message (e.g., Jn 2:22; 4:41, 50; 5:24). Acts uses the word *logos* even more than John, and there it characteristically refers to the gospel message (e.g., Acts 4:4, 29, 31; 6:2, 4, 7; 8:4; cf. Col 1:25; 3:16).[126]

---

[124]So Levison, *Filled with the Spirit*, 253-316.

[125]Francis A. Schaeffer, e.g., *He Is There and He Is Not Silent*, rev. ed. (Wheaton, IL: Tyndale House, 2001), 8.

[126]See further Dunn, *Christology in the Making*, 230-34, though he does not go on to interpret Jn 1 in light of this usage.

For many of John's readers, then, *logos* would suggest the message of the gospel; people went about preaching the *logos*, the *logos* of God or the *logos* of the Anointed One (John does not use the word "gospel" [*euangelion*], and Acts uses it only twice, in Acts 15:7; 20:24).[127] "In the Beginning was the Message," then. That connotation would suggest a connection between creation and the gospel. The gospel message went back to God's creation of the world, and went back before it. Jesus is "the sacrificial self-giving of God," but his being the lamb slain from the world's foundation (Rev 13:8) signals that being the sacrificial self-giver is an aspect of God's eternal being. "The temporal sacrifice which is the 'giving up' or 'sending' of the Son is not an act foreign to the deity, not an isolated intervention, because it springs from what God is in eternity."[128]

Thus the gospel message is age-old (as is reflected in the New Testament's instinctive reading back of Jesus' birth and death into the First Testament) and was written into the act of creation. God had always been the kind of person who would eventually become incarnate and would give himself to die for the world. In a sense there is nothing new about the gospel message. It goes back to the very Beginning. The gospel was always the message. The instinct and the principles inscribed in the gospel were inscribed into the way God created the world. The implication is not that creation itself is divine but that God's own power and love are declared in and through it. God's commitment is expressed in the heavens; his faithfulness reaches to the skies (Ps 36:5 [MT 6]). In later Jewish thinking, the Torah likewise went back to the Beginning.

> The Torah declares: "I was the working tool of the Holy One, blessed be He." In human practice, when a mortal king builds a palace, he builds it not with his own skill but with the skill of an architect. The architect moreover does not build it out of his head, but employs plans and diagrams to know how to arrange the chambers and the wicket doors. Thus God consulted the Torah and created the world. . . . The world and the fullness thereof were created only for the sake of the Torah. (Genesis Rabbah, on Gen 1:1)[129]

---

[127]Other occurrences of the word *gospel* in English translations represent the verb *euangelizomai*, "proclaim the gospel."

[128]Colin E. Gunton, *The Actuality of Atonement* (Edinburgh: T&T Clark; Grand Rapids: Eerdmans, 1989), 149; cf. Thomas A. Bennett, "The Cross as the Labor of God" (PhD diss., Fuller Theological Seminary, 2015), 14.

[129]*Midrash Rabbah: Genesis* (repr., London: Soncino, 1961), 1:1, 7. Cf. Frederick E. Greenspahn, "Jewish Theologies of Scripture," in Isaac Kalimi, ed., *Jewish Bible Theology* (Winona Lake, IN: Eisenbrauns, 2012), 13-29 (on 19).

John further declares, "He was with God in the beginning. All things came into being through him" (Jn 1:2). The mind or message was a person. Things thus become more mysterious for readers to whom the "word" suggests the gospel message, though not for readers to whom it suggests mind or rationale or idea. Jewish philosopher Philo of Alexandria, Jesus' contemporary, had taken the idea of a mind behind creation into the framework of his belief in a personal God. He saw the *logos* not only as God's mind, but as God's firstborn son, as his chief messenger and mediator in relating to the world.[130] So it would not be so hard to think of the mind as a "he."

The Mind, Insight and Speech Involved in the Making of the World

Many people listening to John 1 would pick up another scriptural allusion, to Proverbs 8:22-31 as well as to Genesis 1. Insight herself features there as a quasi-person.[131] She speaks of herself as coming into existence "in the beginning" and as being with God before God began to create anything. God's insight stood alongside God as if she was a separate person from God when God was making the world. So insight and reason and the gospel message were all intertwined at the creation of the heavens and the earth.

God brought the world into being, Proverbs 8 implies, by thinking hard, making a plan and speaking to implement the plan. God used insight in founding the earth, establishing the heavens and making it possible for rain to come from the heavens to the earth (Prov 3:19-20). Proverbs itself is making the point in order to get human beings to take insight seriously in the way they run their lives: "God used insight in making the world: wouldn't it be a good idea for you to follow God's example in the way you live your life?"

In this connection, Proverbs 8 has several models for understanding how Yahweh went about bringing the world into being. It involved making like a craft worker, founding like a builder, marking things out like an engineer and giving orders like a king—setting limits for the sea by means of a command that it should not transgress. Both active and verbal models also appear in Genesis 1-2. There God creates like an artist, makes like a craft worker, shapes like a potter, breathes like a paramedic, plants like a gardener

---

[130]Philo's comments on the subject come in the course of commentaries on Genesis and Exodus: e.g., *Concerning the Cherubim, Concerning the Confusion of Tongues* and *Concerning Dreams.*
[131]See the paragraphs headed "Fluidity" in section 1.2 above.

and also issues commands: "Light!" "A dome!" "Waters are to gather and land appear!" "Earth is to put forth vegetation!" "Be fruitful and multiply!" "Don't eat from that tree!"

God thus uses a number of forms of speech, which become easier to understand as the chapters unfold. The last two, the direct imperatives, are straightforward enough. The others are more challenging. Whom is God addressing? Are the waters and the earth to overhear these jussives and realize that they had better do what the jussives say? (The first, "be fruitful and multiply," also has nonhuman addressees.) Or is God addressing heavenly aides, who hasten to collect the waters and plant some trees? Or does God issue the jussive and then go on to make the thing happen, as is the case with the dome, and with earth bringing forth animate life? What about that initial "There is to be light"? The bareness of the sentence ("God said, 'Light!' And there was light") suggests that there is something powerful about God's very speaking. Words, after all, can be creative things. When a person has power, because of who they are or what they mean to us or the position they occupy, their words can make a monumental difference to a situation. They can make things happen. "When God speaks, there is no point in looking about for a related act."[132]

God's insight and God's speaking are thus important to the way the world was brought into being. They are also important to the way it stays in being, and in particular to the story of Israel. The Scriptures do not picture all the events in the world as working out in accordance with a master plan of God's (it would have to have been a very odd plan). They do speak of God making plans from time to time and implementing them, though they portray God doing so in interaction with the human beings who are crucial to the plan.

But we have to read only two or three pages into the Scriptures to discover that things do not work out in accordance with God's master plan. God's intentions indeed get implemented in interaction with the human beings who are part of the plan. The Scriptures do not say why this is so. It would have been possible, and more efficient, for God to make a plan and implement it without involving humanity—in fact, to do it by the divine fiat of which we read in Genesis 1. Perhaps God didn't act in this way because the

---

[132]Barth, *CD* I, 1:143.

plan itself involved creating a people who would take part in determining how the plan got fulfilled, and/or because God was interested in working out a relationship with such a people. Perhaps it was for such reasons that God was not interested in a plan that worked like clockwork or like a computer program. But this suggestion is a guess, not something the Scriptures tell us.

The Mind/Message Became Flesh

In the dramatic unfolding of the narrative, John's Gospel first introduces us to something, the mind or message, which becomes a person who is the embodiment of life and light, and then to John the Baptizer, who speaks about this person in a way that presupposes him to be a human person. Only later does it eventually make explicit that "the mind/message" who "became flesh and dwelt among us" was God's Son, who manifested the splendor that the Son of God would manifest (Jn 1:14). We are almost at the end of the narrative before John tells us his name (Jn 1:17).

Jesus is the very embodiment of that rational principle that underlies the universe, the very embodiment of insight. He is also the very embodiment of the message. The New Testament's message is not merely about some truths or even merely about a person. The message *is* a person; the person *is* the message. This message/messenger has always lived close to God, lived in close communication with God, channeled God's grace and power. Indeed he shares in God's being. When you meet him, you may eventually realize you have met God. He channels God in person. The messenger-message is divine (this translation may convey better John's point than the translation "he is God," which would imply he is the Father).

All this is not so very new. The message/messenger who did not appear like a bolt out of the blue but goes way back to the Beginning always lived close to God, in close communication with God, channeling God's grace and power. He/she/it always shared in God's very being. The message about grace and power was a divine message, and it thus expressed from the Beginning who God was. It was not a new message when Jesus began to embody and proclaim it. How could that be the case? If God is grace and power, how could God not always have been so, and how could God have been hiding these characteristics rather than making them manifest from the Beginning? It's not that people didn't know already the kind of person God is, but they have never seen God embodied before. Now they have seen; they have seen the magnificence. In the First Testament, God has a name; "the God of the New Testament has a name and a face."[133]

Conversely, Jesus did not come into existence when he was born as a human being. God always had his mind, his insight, his message. Having declared that the mind or message was not only by God's side but was divine, John adds that the mind or message became a human being: so the man called Jesus was the embodiment of the mind or message written into creation. This Son of God was the one through whom God made the worlds (in the sense of the ages—this world and the coming world), the one who carries all things by means of his powerful word (Heb 1:1-3). "By means of him all things were created, in the heavens and on the earth, things visible and invisible, whether thrones or powers or rulers or authorities—all things were created through him and with a view to him. He is before all things and in him all things have held together" (Col 1:16-17). Yes, there is something that holds creation together—or rather, there is someone who does so. Jesus shares in God's being and is the means of God's acting, from creation to the consummation of God's purpose (Heb 1:2-4).[134]

Most readers would know that Jesus was the one whose story John 1 was telling, and holding back the name a long time thus inverts one aspect of their relationship with the chapter. The fact that Jesus' being went back to the very creation was not the first fact about him that they would have realized, and in this sense it does not belong first in a chapter about him. Arguably, it belongs at the end, in the manner of Thomas's confession (Jn 20:28). But once people had realized that his being goes back to the very Beginning, this fact can appropriately come first.

The nature of Jesus' identity has a central place in John's Gospel as it has nowhere else.[135] Whereas Matthew begins by establishing Jesus' credentials

---

[133]Hans Küng, *Does God Exist?* (Garden City, NY: Doubleday; London: Collins, 1980), 690.

[134]The reference to creation in Heb 1:2 surely implies Jesus' preexistence: so Richard Bauckham in "Monotheism and Christology in Hebrew 1," in Wendy North and Loren T. Stuckenbruck, eds., *Early Jewish and Christian Monotheism* (London and New York: Continuum, 2004), 167-85 (on 184-85), arguing against Dunn, *Christology in the Making*, 208-9.

[135]See D. Moody Smith, *The Theology of the Gospel of John* (Cambridge and New York: Cambridge University Press, 1995), 21, and the chapter that follows.

as the Anointed One by describing his earthly origins, John goes way behind them. Matthew picks up Isaiah's declaration that after a great deliverance a girl will call her baby "Immanuel," which means "God is with us" (Mt 1:23). In light of Jesus' actual life one can see that he is God with us in a sense that Joseph could not have realized. While John makes clear his assumption that Jesus was a fully human being, and the point comes out incidentally from time to time, and while he writes so that people may come to believe that Jesus is the Anointed One (Jn 20:31), his concern goes further in aiming to help people come to believe that Jesus is the Son of God, not only in a kind of honorary sense but in his very being.

The "I Am"

In between the confessions at the beginning and end of John's Gospel, Jesus himself makes statements with similar implications to theirs. He had splendor with the Father before the world began (Jn 17:5). Indeed, "before Abraham came into being, I am" (Jn 8:58). He tells his disciples ahead of time things that will happen, "so that when it happens, you will believe that I am he" (Jn 13:19; cf. Jn 8:24-25; 18:5-8). "I am" is the equivalent in the Septuagint of *'ănî hû'*, "I am the One," a phrase that occurs on Yahweh's lips whereby he asserts his sole deity as the one who alone has the capacity to kill and bring to life (Deut 32:39), who alone has been making events happen in the world from the Beginning and will still be there at the End (Is 43:13; 46:4; 48:12), and who alone is sovereign and fulfilling intentions in events unfolding in Israel's lifetime (Is 41:4; 43:10). The phrase also recalls Yahweh's *'ehyeh* in Exodus 3:14 (in the Septuagint, *egō eimi ho ōn*).

Revelation goes even further in its affirmations of Jesus' deity.[136] In the traditional marriage service, people declare that they "worship" one another. Worship is not something confined to God; the context determines what kind of worship we are offering. Analogously, the New Testament's references to "worship" of Jesus need not imply that he is seen as divine, and the New Testament does not apply to Jesus some terms used in relation to God such as *latreuein* (liturgical worship), *ainein* (praise), *eucharistein* (thanksgiving), or

---

[136]Cf. J. D. G. Dunn, *Did the First Christians Worship Jesus?* (Louisville: Westminster John Knox; London: SPCK, 2010), 130.

proseuchesthai (prayer), nor do people offer sacrifices to Jesus. After his death and resurrection, worship and prayer are characteristically offered to God through Jesus in the Spirit.

Yet the songs addressed to him imply that he has a similar status to God. Because the slain lamb "bought [people] for God with his blood from every tribe, language, people, and nation, and made them a kingdom and priests for our God, and they will reign on the earth," he "is worthy to receive power, wealth, wisdom, strength, honor, glory, and praise. . . . To the one who sits on the throne and to the lamb be praise, honor, glory, and might, to the furthest ages" (Rev 5:9-13). It is the clearest indication of worship of Jesus as of God in the New Testament.[137] "Salvation was too closely connected with Jesus himself for Jesus to be bypassed in worship offered to God for it. . . . What Christ does, God does." Thus God is the coming one, as Christ is the coming one.[138] "I am the Alpha and the Omega, the First and the Last, the Beginning and the End," he himself says (Rev 22:13; cf. Rev 1:17): these phrases are God's own self-descriptions in the near contexts (Rev 1:8; 21:6). They, too, are taken up from Isaiah (Is 44:6; 48:12), where they are strong assertions that Yahweh alone is God. Jesus not merely does the kind of things that God does and acts on God's behalf and is closely associated with God in judgment; in his person he shares God's divine nature.

In Jesus people see God's magnificence (Jn 1:14). They see it in Jesus' face (2 Cor 4:6). It is a different experience from the seeing with the physical eye that is the privilege of people who saw Jesus during his lifetime or after his resurrection,[139] and a different sort of magnificence from the one they might have expected. The embodied message did not come with the dazzling splendor of a superstar. He is not arrayed like a professor processing into commencement exercises. He wears no morning suit. No paparazzi stalk him. His magnificence lies in being "full of grace and truthfulness." It is

---

[137]See Richard Bauckham, *The Climax of Prophecy* (Edinburgh: T&T Clark, 1993), 118-49. For further indications of such worship within the New Testament, see, e.g., Bauckham, *Jesus and the God of Israel*, 127-51; Hurtado, *How on Earth Did Jesus Become God?*

[138]Richard Bauckham, *The Theology of the Book of Revelation* (Cambridge and New York: Cambridge University Press, 1993), 62, 63.

[139]Cf. N. T. Wright, *The Resurrection of the Son of God* (London: SPCK; Minneapolis: Fortress, 2003), 384.

these characteristics that make him an adequate embodiment of God. They were the qualities God claimed in his self-description to Israel at Sinai. They are not ordinary qualities, and they are not very characteristic of the gods of Israel's world. Nor are they very characteristic of the God (or god, as it is not the real God) whom many Christians worship, who is either cozy and genial, or frightening and judgmental.

The First Testament's story all the way to Sinai and through the story as it proceeds is a message about a God who is grace and truthfulness. This message has now been embodied. "Anyone who has seen me has seen the Father" because "I am in the Father and the Father is in me. The words that I say to you" are "not from me"; rather, "the Father living within me does his deeds." So they can believe his words about his being in the Father and the Father being in him, or they can believe on the basis of the deeds (Jn 14:9-11).

"In his life, death and resurrection Jesus had accomplished the new exodus, had done in person what Israel's God had said he would do in person." Thus it was inevitable that his followers acknowledged him as the embodiment of God.[140]

The Eternal One Stayed for a While

In Exodus God commissioned people to build a sanctuary at the center of Israel's encampment where God would come to stay. When Jesus was born, the mind or message that had been in existence from the Beginning, that had been in the world from its beginning, became human and stayed around among people for a while so that they could see how glorious it was (Jn 1:14).

There is a nice paronomasia in the talk of Jesus staying a while, as the Greek word for "stay" (*skēnoō*) more literally means "camp," and further, it is similar to the Hebrew word for Yahweh's "staying" in that sanctuary (*šākan*), the verb that produces the postbiblical word for God's "glory" (*šəkînâ*). Israelites knew that they could go to the sanctuary and meet with God. Its splendor with its tapestry and ornamentation spoke of God's splendor or glory; indeed, God's glory filled that tent (Ex 40:34-35), as it later filled the temple. When Jesus came, he mediated that glory to people. As was the case in Exodus, the glory is the glory of one who is

---

[140]Wright, *Paul and the Faithfulness of God*, 655.

grace and truthfulness; indeed, the glory lies in that grace and truthfulness, as God's self-revelation has indicated. "I have revealed your
name to the people you gave me out of the world. . . . The words that you
gave me, I gave them" (Jn 17:6, 8). Jesus went about being Godlike, exercising power, forgiving people, healing people, staying faithful to people
despite their unreliability—and being straight with them and confrontational with them, like God. It is all part of being gracious and truthful.
He embodied God. So people saw his magnificence. The embodiment of
God's self-giving in a human life "could not have been expected, but nor
is it uncharacteristic. It is novel but appropriate to the identity of the
God of Israel."[141]

It fits with this dynamic that, paradoxically, one of the ways the tent-
sanctuary testified to God's magnificence was by having nothing that
attempted to picture God. Humanity has a natural need for something to
represent and mediate God physically, something to look at and touch. God
denied it, knowing that it could only be misleading. The real God is one who
acts and speaks, and a picture or image cannot represent the real God; it will
inevitably mislead (cf. Deut 4). The only icon biblical faith eventually generated was a book, the Torah, the Prophets and the Writings, which could
get much closer to representing the real God because it could record God's
words and actions and thus portray God as living, active and speaking. It
could record the message.

When the message eventually became a human being, it was a permanent development. Once it had happened, the message was embodied
forever, and when the embodied message went back to be with God, it remained embodied. But it stayed here only for a while. (I wonder why?
Imagine that Jesus had never gone back to be with the Father but had
simply stayed here forever. There is a novel to be written imagining what it
would have been like.)

For a while some people were able to see how magnificent it was. It could
represent God in person to people. Like father, like son, we say. If a person's
son comes to see you, then you know what the father is like. One cannot

---

[141]Bauckham, *God Crucified*, 74 (2nd ed., *Jesus and the God of Israel*, 55); cf. Graham A. Cole, *The
God Who Became Human* (Downers Grove, IL: InterVarsity Press; Nottingham, UK: Inter-
Varsity Press, 2013), 111.

press the analogy; in characteristics, children can be different from parents. But if the father is a human being, the son will be a human being; if the father is a lion, the son will be a lion. When you meet the offspring, you get a fair idea of the father. When you meet the embodied message, it's like meeting someone's son, and it tells you what the father is like. Indeed, you can think of him *as* the Son of the Father. It is a metaphor, with limited application. You cannot ask how this father begot this son or who the mother is in this arrangement. Its significance here is that a son represents the kind of entity that his father is.

In John 1 no sacrifice is involved in the Son becoming a human being. Elsewhere, sacrifice is implied. Jesus was rich; he became poor so that we might come to share his riches (2 Cor 8:9). He shared God's very nature, but he took the nature of a slave, and then humbled himself as far as death (Phil 2:6-11). He was in God's profile (*morphē*), but he didn't take the view that being the same kind of person as God was something to hang onto or use to his advantage. He was willing to take on a slave's profile. While the description of him as bearing God's image might refer to him as a man who then accepted impoverishment within his human life and did not make Adam's mistake,[142] it looks more like a description of the way he laid aside heavenly splendor in order to become an ordinary human being.[143] In being divine but prepared to become truly a human being, he was prepared to empty himself, to set aside the outwardly impressive aspect to deity in becoming human.

He was indeed then also prepared to set aside the outwardly impressive aspect to being a human being in submitting to a path that would lead to execution. "His death on the cross was and is the fulfilment of the incarnation of the Word and therefore the humiliation of the Son of God and exaltation of the Son of Man."[144] He simply poured himself out.[145] As a human being, he indeed represents a new start over against Adam. As "the last Adam" he reverses the disaster brought about by the first Adam (1 Cor 15:45; cf. Rom 5:12-19).[146] God then made his self-emptying a basis for

[142]Dunn, *Christology in the Making*, 2nd. ed., 113-25; also xviii-xx.
[143]See, e.g., Wright, *Climax of the Covenant*, 90-97.
[144]Barth, *CD* IV, 2:140-41.
[145]See Gerald F. Hawthorne, *Philippians* (Waco, TX: Word, 1983), 85-86.
[146]See, e.g., Dunn, *Christology in the Making*, 98-128.

installing him into the position proper to deity, for giving him the name above every name, so that every knee should bow to him and every tongue confess him Lord—still to the glory of God the Father (Phil 2:6-11).

"There can be no question of understanding how the condescension of God acts. We can only know and worship its actuality."[147]

The Son

In the First Testament the idea of God having a son is not used to suggest that a person is one in nature with God. God's son is a human person, to whom God is committed in a fatherly relationship. God's son is not an embodiment of God or of an aspect of God. But having been designated even during his earthly lifetime as the son of God in that First Testament sense, once Jesus has also been identified as an embodiment of God or of aspects of God, it would be a natural move to stretch the meaning of his being the son of God so that he is more like a birth son than an adopted son, and is thus one who shares his Father's nature (cf. Col 1:15; Heb 1). In John, in contrast to the other Gospels, Jesus frequently refers to himself as God's son. Once Jesus has been identified as the personal embodiment of God's insight and message, the fact that he is God's envoy and God's son could take on extra significance. For instance, it is as God's son that Jesus is the one through whom God created the world (Heb 1:2).

While Jews would not have seen anything very new in the way Jesus spoke of God's fatherly relationship with his people, they did not know that there was a relationship of love and commitment within God. Yet this fact would hardly be much of a surprise. They knew that love belongs to God, that "*ḥesed* is yours, Lord" (Ps 62:12 [MT 13]). They knew that God's goodness and love pursued them (Ps 23:6) in the manner of the divine aides who embodied God's presence and yet were somehow distinguishable from God, and therefore did not bring the threat that God's high-voltage presence could electrocute people whom they approached. They knew that God was a complex and mysterious person, capable of internal conversation.

It's an exaggeration to say that the New Testament brings "a radical deepening of the Old Testament doctrine of God," because "'Father' is now revealed

---

[147]Barth, *CD* I, 2:34.

to be more than an epithet—it is the personal name of God in which the form and content of his self-revelation as Father through Jesus Christ his Son are inseparable."[148] For one thing, "Father" is not a personal name but an epithet (Yahweh is God's personal name).[149] While it is an epithet that now makes a metaphysical and not just a metaphorical point, it's not clear that this development should be called a deepening; metaphors are at least as important as metaphysics. But Jesus' talk of the mutual love and commitment between Father and Son would take people's understanding of God and of God's fatherliness to a new level.

Like any son, Jesus is the same as his Father in nature. In this sense, he is equal with God. But like any son, he is subordinate to the Father. "The Father is greater than me" (Jn 14:28). The Father gives the orders; the Son obeys them (Jn 14:31). This subordination does not raise a question about Jesus' status; it helps to confirm it. At the end, he will hand over his sovereignty to God the Father and become subject to the one who subjected everything to him, so that God may be all in all (1 Cor 15:25-28).

The realities that the doctrine of the Trinity seeks to encapsulate are present within the New Testament: that God is one, and that people experienced God as Father, as Son, and as Spirit, who were distinct enough to be able to talk about each other.[150] The Son is divine yet is able to talk to the Father, but God is one. The Spirit has a personal nature, is of a similar nature to Jesus, but is distinct from God the Father and from Jesus. Yet God is one. The Christian recognition that God is Father, Son and Spirit issued from the congregation's experience of God's presence and activity.

We have noted that, while the New Testament does not presuppose that God is Trinity, the idea of Trinity is the only way the church has found to interrelate the data from the Scriptures in a form that does justice to them.[151] It can be illuminating to explore the implications of articulating the

---

[148]So Thomas F. Torrance, "The Christian Apprehension of God the Father," in Alvin F. Kimel, ed., *Speaking the Christian God* (Grand Rapids: Eerdmans; Leominster, UK: Gracewing, 1992), 120-43 (on 131); Marianne Meye Thompson includes several similar quotations in *Promise of the Father*, 10-15.

[149]Torrance does note that "Yahweh" is God's personal name in the First Testament.

[150]Cf. Fee, *God's Empowering Presence*, 828.

[151]Cf. the paragraphs under "Fluidity" in section 1.2 above.

implications of God's being Trinity, though it is also important to explore the implications of the Scriptures' own observations about the one God, the spirit, the wind, the face, the mind, the message and so on, and not lose these in reflecting on the implications of God's being Trinity that excite us in our cultural context.[152]

---

[152]Cf. John Goldingay, *Do We Need the New Testament?* (Downers Grove, IL: InterVarsity Press, 2015), 22.

2

GOD'S INSIGHT

✝

So the divine mind or message or insight was embodied in Jesus, and he was full of grace and truthfulness (Jn 1:1-18). God thus spoke through a Son (Heb 1:1-2); he was the embodiment of God's mind or message or insight. Hebrews also notes in this connection that God had already spoken through Prophets such as Isaiah. The Torah, the Prophets and the Writings were the earlier deposit of God's speaking and acting in Israel's life. The existence of the New Testament presupposes that God continued to speak through writers such as the authors of Hebrews and other New Testament documents. It also presupposes that God's speaking through the Son needed to be recorded for people who didn't hear that speaking—the Gospels being the deposit of that record. Some new covenant Scriptures thus came to join the Torah, the Prophets and the Writings.

The form, or rather forms,[1] of the double deposit are in part surprising (psalmody, musing and letters, as well as narrative, prophecy and instruction), though with hindsight one can infer some aspects of the rationale for its taking the forms that it does.[2] The Scriptures are of key importance because they offer access to God's acting and speaking in the key story of Israel that comes to a climax in God's acting and speaking through his Son, who became an Israelite. Thus both Testaments begin with lengthy narratives about how God acted, action that is decisive for the world and for his

---

[1]Cf. Paul Ricoeur's stress on the varied forms of discourse in the Scriptures in *Essays on Biblical Interpretation* (Philadelphia: Fortress, 1980; London: SPCK, 1981), 73-95.
[2]Cf. comments in the introduction to this volume.

people even when they are living outside the chronological frame of these narratives. Such people need to know about this story in order to live within it. Then the latter half of both Testaments is dominated by the spelling out of the story's implications for people's understanding of God and of themselves, and for the way they live.

Consideration of the nature of Christian faith as these Scriptures expound it clarifies why it is not so puzzling that God provoked or allowed his people to recognize Scriptures that have the form they do, rather than some other form, such as an apparently timeless collection of eternal principles or a series of love letters by someone to the woman he loves.

Assumptions that underlie these Scriptures confront assumptions often made in the Western world in the twenty-first century. The Scriptures constitute a metanarrative, in both senses of that word. They offer a metanarrative in the narrow sense, a story about God's activity in the world, in Israel and in Jesus that is key to an understanding of God and the world and life. They also imply a metanarrative in the looser sense, a set of insights into the nature of God and reality that is more than merely local. While our grasp of truth is partial and is skewed by our perspective and context, so that our account of the narrative will be local, there is such a thing as objective truth, there is a difference between truth and falsehood, and the Scriptures convey truth.

The people of God are always tempted to look at the world in the same way as other people. It is a regular purpose of the Scriptures to get them to look at things another way. The scriptural story seeks to encourage people to look at their own story in the context of the story of creation; the exodus; David; the exile; Ezra and Nehemiah; the Maccabees; Jesus' birth, ministry, death and resurrection; and the beginnings of the Jesus movement. Prophets and visionaries such as John in Revelation seek to get them to look at earthly realities in light of heavenly realities and to look at present realities in light of what God intends to do. Revelation does so by portraying an alternative symbolic universe.[3] This extraordinary, bewildering, complex, fantastic portrayal overpowers its audience in the manner of a fantasy movie. It takes people into a wholly other world that overwhelms the empirical world that

---

[3]Cf. Richard Bauckham, *The Theology of the Book of Revelation* (Cambridge and New York: Cambridge University Press, 1993), 10.

otherwise holds sway over them. Likewise it's tempting for the people of God to assume that they can work out for themselves how to worship God and how to pray, but both Revelation and the Psalms suggest otherwise.

In this chapter we consider the area commonly covered in theology under headings such as revelation, authority, inspiration and word of God, but the Scriptures themselves use these expressions in other ways, and "insight" or wisdom (*ḥokmâ, sophia*) is nearer to being their own word for it. We will consider the insight embodied in the world (section 2.1), and at the way God's insight is expressed in declarations or promises (section 2.2), in testimony or story (section 2.3), in imperatives and expectations (section 2.4), and in prayers and praises that inspire ours (section 2.5). The diversity in the forms by which God's insight finds expression, and then the diversity within those forms (e.g., different Prophets, different Gospels) reflects the complexity of reality (section 2.6). It implies a warning about biblical theology, about thinking that we can systematize it without losing the reality. Let the reader beware.

2.1 Embodied in the World

A surprising feature of the Scriptures is their including books that read like reflections on human experience and make no reference to God's special involvement with Israel (or even any reference to God). Their inclusion links with the assumption that God's insight is embodied in the world and in human experience for all to see, even if all do not see it. It is written into the nature of the world and into the way life works. That awareness extends to an awareness of the basics about God and the basics about right and wrong, which are hardwired into humanity.

Insight Written into Material Reality

While the Scriptures are the key deposit of God's sharing his insight, they do not portray themselves as the first such deposit. They themselves see God's insight as embodied in the world that God created before it was embodied in his dealings with Israel, in the incarnation and in the gospel message. "Insight calls, doesn't it?" (Prov 8:1). But why should it do so? Because it's "a call of God" that "echoes the creator's will for us as expressed in his creation."[4]

---

[4]Oliver O'Donovan, *Finding and Seeking* (Grand Rapids and Cambridge, UK: Eerdmans, 2014), 100.

Given that the mind or message embodied in Jesus goes back to creation, it's hardly surprising that it's expressed in the way God created things and in the results of that creative work. How could it be otherwise? The nature of the world reflects the nature of the mind or message.

The world itself is an embodiment of grace and truthfulness. It shines out with God's love and generosity toward people who ignore God as well as toward people who seek to live for God (cf. Mt 5:45). It manifests God's truthfulness and commitment, no matter how much the world is inclined to resist God. The eventual coming and dying of Jesus were the logical end term of the way God created the world and relates to it. The coming and dying ought not to have been so surprising, because the message/messenger was the one through whom God made everything. Hence "in created things lies the forgiveness of sins."[5] Creation was an act of grace.[6] "In the light of the cross of Christ, *creatio ex nihilo* [creation out of nothing] means forgiveness of sins through Christ's suffering."[7]

What came into being by means of the mind and message was life (Jn 1:3-4). The message itself tells of real life given to people who are nominally alive but whose lives often look like a living death and who are on their way to actual death. From the Beginning, the message or messenger was life-giving, so the scriptural message picks up the original message's inherent nature and aim and reestablishes it. Jesus brought illumination and life to people by speaking to them, and his words matched the way God brought life at the Beginning by speaking and by shining light. He said things that brought life to people. He had "the words of eternal life" (Jn 6:68). While people found many of his words tough, his words were also illuminating and life-giving.

That dynamic again matches the way things had been at the Beginning. God *said*, "There is to be *light*," and there was (Gen 1:3); and this light was life-giving. Where there is no light, there is no life; nothing can grow. So light is a natural image for blessing. When someone smiles, light emanates from their face in a life-giving way. When God smiles on the world, there is light,

---

[5]I owe this remark to my former colleague Charles Napier, who described it as a summary of the views of Martin Luther.

[6]Otto Weber, *Foundations of Dogmatics* (Grand Rapids: Eerdmans, 1981), 1:479-86, following Karl Barth, *CD* III, 1.

[7]Jürgen Moltmann, *God in Creation* (London: SCM Press; San Francisco: Harper, 1985), 91.

life and blessing. It was so from the Beginning. Until God spoke, there was only darkness; there could be no life. Once God spoke light into being, there could be life, and darkness was finished.

Human beings were then able to know something of God because "what can be known of God was manifest among them, because God made it manifest to them, because since the world's creation the invisible characteristics of God (both his eternal power and his deity) have been visible, being understood by means of the things that have been made" (Rom 1:19-20). Thus Jesus bids people learn from the created world. "Look at the birds in the heavens," he urges; "consider the flowers of the field, how they grow—they don't toil or spin" (Mt 6:26, 28). His parables, too, sometimes start from realities of nature (seeds, fig trees, wheat) or of human experience (a rich fool, a shepherd, a woman who lost a coin). He assumes that there are things to be learned from the way the world is and the way human experience is.[8]

Paul does also assume that creation's embodiment of God's power and deity did not really get people anywhere. When people are shown something, everything depends on what they do with it. But humanity did have this revelation available, and it still has it available. Perhaps Jesus' exhortation works better with believers than with unbelievers. Paul does not envisage arguing atheists into becoming theists on the basis of an argument from creation, or even providing believers with a way of justifying their belief to themselves on this basis. He does presuppose that everyone really knows that God is there, as naturally as they know that other people are there. God's power and deity are visible from the nature of the world. So are humanity's powerlessness and relative ordinariness. But Paul is also aware that there is a gap between what stares people in the face and how people respond to what they see. And by ignoring what they see, humanity became empty in their thinking, and even more powerless and ordinary.

Insight Written into How Life Works

The assumption that we can learn from the world and from human experience especially characterizes the works commonly called Wisdom books, Proverbs, Job and Ecclesiastes; the Song of Songs implies the same idea.

---

[8]On Jesus as a wisdom teacher, see, e.g., Karl Löning and Erich Zenger, *To Begin with, God Created* . . . (Collegeville, MN: Liturgical, 2000), 143-62.

Proverbs makes this assumption as it offers teaching about how things work out in life and thus about sensible behavior. It works empirically. The Song of Songs makes the same assumption about the relationship between a man and a woman; it also works empirically.

Further, Proverbs manifests an ecumenical instinct as it incorporates quotations from people such as Agur and Lemuel (Prov 30:1; 31:1); we don't know who they were, but they don't sound like Israelites. Less overtly, it includes a thirty-unit section (Prov 22:17–24:22) that compares with an older Egyptian thirty-unit document, the teaching of Amenemope. Maybe Amenemope and Proverbs are independent versions of common Middle Eastern insight and neither is directly dependent on the other. Either way, the link reflects Proverbs's assumption that we can learn from other people's experience of life and their reflection on it, as well as from our own experience within the people of God. God set life up to make sense if people use their God-given good sense, even when they are not aware of all that can be known about who God is. The book of Job tells a story about people who seem not to be Israelites and who live in Edom, another Middle Eastern culture known for the insight of its teaching about life.

In contrast to much so-called insight, ancient and modern, however, Job and Proverbs emphasize how God and ethics are inherent in the empirical reality that the books are considering. Into their observations about insight they incorporate reference to uprightness on one hand, and awe for God on the other (Job 28:28; Prov 1:1-7). After beginning with this interweaving, the main body of sayings in Proverbs illustrates the point as it moves randomly between empirical observations about how life works, comments about integrity in practice, and observations about Yahweh's involvement in ordinary life. In the chapters that follow that unexpected punch line to the poem about insight in Job 28, the book of Job likewise develops the two points that this punch line makes.

Taken in isolation, many individual sayings in Jesus' teaching or in Proverbs are unrealistic, but other sayings show the other side of the picture. In the Wisdom books, the general cast of the observations in Proverbs is complemented by the general cast of Job and Ecclesiastes. These works, too, argue on the basis of the insight embodied in the world and in experience but draw different inferences. The Song of Songs both enthuses over the relationship between two people in love and draws attention to the threats and anxieties built into the relationship. While human experience often suggests a link between doing right or doing wrong on one hand, and finding that things go well or badly in your life on the other, Ecclesiastes faces the fact that the link can break down.

People can learn much from the created world, but one of the things they learn is that it does not revolve around human need; it has an ecology of its own (Job 28; 38–39). Indeed, it seems that God has put into the human mind a longing to understand the nature of reality as a whole but has not opened up a way to satisfy that longing. We cannot understand the rationale for the way human experience alternates between birth and death, war and peace, and so on (Eccles 3:1-11). From the world and from life we can get partial insights and some clues about living a happy life in the context of the family, but we can't get the big picture. There is enough in the way the created world embodies God's faithfulness and commitment, and God's capacity to hold back evil, to make it possible for us to live our lives on the basis of trust in God, but that trust also involves living with mystery. Part of our happiness and our peace lies in being willing and able to do so.

So Job and Ecclesiastes agree with Proverbs that we should be able to look at life itself in order to see life and to know how to live life, but they argue with Proverbs about what we see when we look there. "Proverbs seems to say, 'These are the rules for life; try them and find that they will work.' Job and Ecclesiastes say, 'We did and they don't.'"[9] The book of Job "questions an answer, rather than answers a question,"[10] and so does Ecclesiastes. Indeed, the three books' commonalities of language could make readers miss the radical difference in their theologies.[11] While Proverbs focuses on the logic, predictability, propriety and rightness about the way life works, Job and Ecclesiastes focus on the illogic, unpredictability, impropriety and wrongness. They note both the importance and the limitations of what can be perceived in the world. Realities such as unexplained human suffering and irreversible injustice deserve to be acknowledged rather than evaded.

---

[9]David A. Hubbard, "The Wisdom Movement and Israel's Covenant Faith," *Tyndale Bulletin* 17 (1966): 3-34 (on 6).

[10]Elizabeth R. Moberly, *Suffering, Innocent and Guilty* (London: SPCK, 1978), 42; cf. Leslie C. Allen, *A Theological Approach to the Old Testament* (Eugene, OR: Wipf and Stock, 2014), 43.

[11]Cf. Tomáš Frydrych, *Living Under the Sun* (Leiden and Boston: Brill, 2002), 3-4.

At the same time, Job offers a range of insights that suggest partial understandings of suffering and of what it says about God's relationship with us. Our troubles can be a test of our integrity, or can be a result of our wrongdoing, or can be designed to draw us nearer to God; but they can simply be a mystery. The appropriate response to them may be protest and/or repentance and/or submission and/or the expectation that God will put things right in due course and/or acceptance of the limits to what we can understand, which make it more rather than less important to live life on the basis of trust in God. Further contemplation of the created world itself pushes us toward such trust and submission. Ecclesiastes, too, urges readers to acknowledge the limitations of human insight but takes for granted that we continue to live assuming the reality of both faithfulness and integrity on one hand and God's actuality on the other.

What's Right and What's Wrong

Comparable to the parallels between these Wisdom books and writings from sister cultures (and from totally unrelated cultures) are parallels between decrees in the Torah and statutes in the codes and policies of sister peoples (and of totally unrelated cultures). A classic example is the overlap with the code promulgated by Hammurabi in Babylon centuries before Moses' day. There are ways in which the Torah is arguably more elevated: it is more egalitarian, and a man who gets into economic trouble has seven years instead of only three years to work his way out of debt. But the two documents overlap in ethos and content, with the theological implication that other peoples are not lacking in the kind of awareness about right and wrong expressed in the Torah. People do not need to be told that murder or adultery is wrong. It is inscribed into the way they are created. Like their awareness of who God is, they can abandon this awareness and lose it. But what they have indeed then done is abandon an aspect of the way they were created.

Paul also assumes that as human beings people know something about the way God expects us to live our lives. "When Gentiles, who do not have the Torah, by nature do the things the Torah says, . . . they show they have the work of the Torah written in their inner beings" (Rom 2:14-15).

Paul's main aim here is to get his fellow Jews to face the question of whether they themselves have lived God's way and to face the implications of their not having done so, and it's not easy to be clear whom he has in mind in these verses. His words would apply to honorable pagans, people such as Mahatma Gandhi in our age. They would apply to ordinary people who are faithful in their marriages and who care for their children. They would apply to a Gentile such as Ruth who lived Yahweh's way and came to believe in Yahweh. They would apply to a Samaritan who knows what it is to be a neighbor.[12] They would apply to believers in Jesus who do not directly seek to live by the Torah but do so intuitively in some respects. While their diet (for instance) will not match the Torah's regulations, because these rules are not written into their inner beings, they show that other aspects of the Torah's expectations are indeed written there insofar as they are people who live by trust in God like Abraham, forgive people who wrong them like Joseph, and disobey immoral orders like the Hebrew midwives.

The Prophets likewise assume that the nations as a whole broadly know God's expectations of humanity. The Babylonian king is guilty for destroying his country and slaughtering his people, and Babylon itself is guilty for not showing compassion on Judah even when it is the agent of Yahweh's judgment (Is 14:20; 47:6). They should have known better. Amos makes the point clear in declaring that Yahweh will not revoke his wrath at local powers such as Syria, Philistia, Tyre, Edom, Ammon and Moab, for actions that we might call war crimes. These actions include treating other people as if they were land to be threshed, transporting peoples and ripping open pregnant women; Amos, too, mentions failure of compassion (Amos 1:3–2:3).

It is thus not inconceivable to expect the nations to operate on the basis of expectations expounded in the Sermon on the Mount, because these expectations, too, are based in the way God created us as human beings and communities. "Forgiveness is what happens when the victim of some hurtful action freely chooses to release the perpetrator of that action from the bondage of guilt, gives up his or her own feelings of ill will, and surrenders

---

[12]See Barth's exposition of the parable in *CD* I, 2:417-26.

any attempt to hurt or damage the perpetrator in return, thus clearing the way for reconciliation and restoration of relationship."[13] The love expressed in forgiveness is not satisfied with letting go; it wants the well-being of the wrongdoer, and it thus desires and works for a response, for reconciliation.[14] And sometimes nonbelievers are as ready as believers to recognize that fact. They show that by virtue of being human they do have such truths written into their awareness. It is therefore worth urging people and nations to do the right and selfless thing, even if it seems inappropriate or unwise to appeal to Jesus or to the Scriptures in doing so. We are appealing to what people really know just because they are human beings.

"But be he as pious as he will, he is and remains still for all such piety Adam's child, that is, an earthy man, under sin and death."[15]

2.2 Declaratory

As the Wisdom books recognize how creation and regular human experience leave us with limited understanding about some big questions, the story that unfolds in Genesis 1–11 ends in uncertainty about whether blessing or curse will win out in their wrestling for victory in the world's story. Perhaps a better way to put it is to recognize that the power and grace of God mean that blessing will win, but it is not clear how this victory will come about.

In Western culture, readers might infer that as human beings we had better commit ourselves to taking action to work for the victory of blessing and to find ways to encourage it. The Scriptures see that assumption as whistling in the wind. There is no basis for thinking it will work. We cannot do it. What is needed is some further action on God's part. Thus what follows Genesis 1–11 is God's declaration about action he intends to take. His declaration does involve commissioning some human action, but the importance of this human action is eclipsed by the undertakings God gives.

Making promises has a crucial place in the Scriptures' inventory of God's forms of speech. It is a vital way in which God speaks: vital for God, and

---

[13]See Christopher D. Marshall, *Beyond Retribution* (Grand Rapids and Cambridge, UK: Eerdmans, 2001), 264.

[14]Ibid., 17.

[15]Martin Luther, "Evangelium um vierten Sonntag nach Ostern: Joh. 16, 5-15," in *D. Martin Luthers Werke* (Weimarer Ausgabe) 21:352-80 (on 365); cf. Barth, *CD* I, 2:310.

vital for his people. It has a key role in the story that continues after Genesis 1–11. By their nature, promises are revelatory, and in the Scriptures such revelation is both personal and propositional. The revelation then requires a response; God's people are called to live by God's promises. Faith has to become trust. God's promises make it possible to understand events that constitute their fulfillment; at the same time, the fulfillment may well make it easier to understand the promise.

Promising

Instead of issuing more exhortations about what humanity needs to do, then, at the end of their opening exposition of world history the Scriptures present readers with God's promise about how God's purpose of blessing will find fulfillment. In the course of the scattering that issues from the last mistake in the story so far, one family leaves Babylon for the north and west, as part of the migratory activity of the day. They apparently intend to move to Canaan but stop and settle in Harran, on the border of modern Syria and Turkey (Gen 11). There Yahweh gets involved in the story, bidding Abraham to resume the journey and giving him a series of promises in this connection (Gen 12:1-3). They will become a great nation (an unlikely event because Abraham's wife cannot have children) in the country they had set out for (an unlikely event because the country is occupied by another people).

God's promise closes by speaking of the way all earth's peoples will be blessed through Abraham or will pray to be blessed like Abraham. He will do so well that other people will use his name in prayers for blessing ("May God bless us as he blessed Abraham's family"). While this element in the promise magnifies what God will do for Abraham personally, its context following Genesis 1–11 also points to its significance for the nations themselves. God will also do good to people who bless Abraham's family, but he will put down anyone who tries to put them down—in other words, God will protect Abraham's family. God later nuances the promises with a note that is implicit here, when he makes a covenant commitment "to be God for you and for your offspring after you" (Gen 17:7).

God's words in Genesis 1–11 interwove commands and promises, and the pattern continues in his words to Abraham. In due course Paul will describe his own vocation as the issuing of a summon to the nations to "the obedience of faith" (Rom 1:5; cf. Rom 16:26). Different translations have "faithful obedience" or "faith and obedience" or "obedience to the faith" or "obedient trust." Any of those expressions would describe what God has been seeking in vain from humanity and what he is now seeking from Abraham. Abraham needs to go where God says and to do so trusting in God's promises. He needs to trust in God's promises and to express that trust by going where God says.

While God's speech thus embraces both command and promise, there is one command and half a dozen promises, so the emphasis lies on the latter. Likewise, God later connects a challenge to be faithful and wholly committed to Yahweh with the promise about a covenant (Gen 17:1-2), but faithfulness and commitment are a response to who God is and to God's own faithfulness and commitment; they are not a qualification for it. When Paul affirms the priority of trust in God's promises over anything Abraham does (Rom 4), he notes that in the context of God's making that covenant promise it was too late for God to make an expectation of obedience into a condition of his covenant making. Paul argues on the basis of the chronological relationship between God's making promises and his issuing the requirement of circumcision (Gen 17:10), but he could have made it on the basis of the way God's earlier covenant promises to Noah work (Gen 9:1-17). These two covenants are "God's maps of times."[16] In connection with the Noah covenant, too, commands feature, but the promise that human life will continue on earth is simply a promise. The covenant has no conditions attached.

The actual word *promise* is a New Testament word (e.g., Rom 4). Hebrew does not have a word for "promise." It has a word for a vow or pledge (*neder*), a particularly solemn promise, but that word is not used of God's promises. God's "promise" is simply his "word," when he makes the promise to which Abraham gives the response of "trust" (Gen 15:6, taken up in Rom 4). God's yes means yes and his no means no (Mt 5:37; Jas 5:12). On the other hand, God does later swear an oath to keep his promise (Gen 22:16; cf. Gen 24:7; Heb 6:13-17), and the Scriptures subsequently refer a number of times to God's oaths as a basis for praise, trust and prayer (e.g., Deut 26:3, 15; 31:7).

---

[16]Jerome H. Neyrey, *Render to God* (Minneapolis: Fortress, 2004), 202.

Revelatory

In his promises, God reveals his intentions. Now the first talk of revelation in the Scriptures treats it as a personal phenomenon. God in person "revealed himself" to Jacob (Gen 35:7; *gālâ*) and "appeared" to Moses (e.g., Ex 3:16; *rāʾâ*). In the latter connection God revealed his name to Moses. The name itself points to a revelation of the person. It does so in two ways.[17] Anyone's name identifies them as a person. But further, sometimes a name says something about the person, and so it is with Yahweh, because the name is similar to forms of the verb "to be": Yahweh is "the God who is there" in the sense that he is there when his people need deliverance, there able to be and do what different situations require. While there were reasons why Jews stopped using the name Yahweh, much is lost by substituting the word *Lord* for the significant name that Yahweh revealed to his people.[18]

But in Genesis and Exodus God also gives important revelations about his intentions, and these intentions are key to his revelation to prophets and apostles: "We must call this thing that happened to them: Deus dixit [God has spoken]. What has engendered Scripture and what Scripture for its part attests has happened truly and definitively, once and once-for-all."[19] *The* Revelation, to John on Patmos, concerned "things that must happen soon" (Rev 1:1). Revelation involves the unveiling of things that would otherwise be unknown, the disclosure of what would otherwise be mystery. If faith is the substance of things hoped for and the evidence of things not seen (Heb 11:1), revelation is what provides the substance and the evidence, though it does not thereby empirically provide the reality itself—hence it requires faith as its response. Paul's letters, too, announce things that will happen and challenge congregations to live in light of them.

When Yahweh announces things that will happen, for instance in the Torah, Abraham or the Israelites in Egypt are challenged to live in light of them. Yahweh reveals to Pharaoh the plenty and the subsequent famine he is going to bring, so that Pharaoh can respond to the prospect appropriately (Gen 41:25).

---

[17]Cf. the paragraphs under "Splendor, Name," in section 1.3 above.

[18]See further the introductory paragraphs to chapter 1 above.

[19]Barth, *CD* I, 1:116. The expression "Deus dixit" comes from Herman Bavinck (e.g., *Reformed Dogmatics* [Grand Rapids: Baker, 2003], 1:582).

Yahweh could reveal these facts about the future because he is the one who brings them about. When he does so and the event then happens, he is able to say, "You see: now you have to acknowledge that I am Yahweh" (see, e.g., Is 41–44). The expression "acknowledge that I am Yahweh" sounds less odd in Hebrew than in English, though it still involves an ellipse. It is a noun clause, paralleling the *Shema*',[20] of which it is indeed a variant. What people more literally acknowledge is "That I Yahweh"—which means "that I Yahweh am God."

Whereas Luke and John describe the process whereby they composed their Gospels in terms that suggest nothing directly supernatural about how they wrote, the Prophets often speak in terms of something like dictation, which suggests that they speak in light of being given a supernatural revelation. At the beginning of Jesus' story, too, people prophesy as a result of the Holy Spirit's coming on them (e.g., Lk 1:41, 67), and the beginning of the story in Acts uses similar terms and associates this phenomenon with the promise in Joel 2:28-32 (see Acts 2). In the background is the way Judaism associates the spirit of God especially with prophecy, revelation and insight.[21]

A revelation provides understanding to the people who experience the event that follows, partly through the very fact that this event had been the subject of a revelation that came ahead of time rather than merely after it happened. The revelation provides evidence of the importance of the event, and the event provides evidence of the truth of the revelation. In turn, revelation-plus-event leads into praise expressed in testimony (e.g., Ex 15:1-21), which eventually receives written form (in this case, in Exodus) in a way that also expresses its significance for future generations. Scriptures such as Exodus thus pass on the revelation, the account of the event, the proclamation and the interpretation.

The sequence of revelation, event, and interpretive correlation of revelation and event is significant for all the items in the sequence. The

---

[20]See the paragraphs under "Yahweh Our God Yahweh One" in section 1.2 above.
[21]See, e.g., Archie Hui, "The Spirit of Prophecy and Pauline Pneumatology," *Tyndale Bulletin* 50 (1999): 93-115; Max Turner, *Power from on High*, corrected ed. (Sheffield: Sheffield Academic Press, 2000), esp. 81-165, 348-400. Turner notes this emphasis in John and Paul as well as in Luke-Acts: see *The Holy Spirit and Spiritual Gifts in the New Testament Church and Today*, rev. ed. (Carlisle, UK: Paternoster; Peabody, MA: Hendrickson, 1998), 57-135.

revelation gains its validation and significance through the event and the interpretation that follow. The event gains its significance through its association with the revelation and the interpretation. The praise expressed in the testimony has its basis in the event as a fulfillment of the promissory revelation. The interpretation gains its validation though its association with the revelation and the event, and it enables the testimony to continue to sound through the ages.

Trustworthy

While the Revelation to John focuses on events to come, it speaks of them in terms of witness. The notion of witness is paradoxical when applied to the future, since one can only witness to things that have happened (hence the oddness of common talk of the Old Testament as witness to Christ). The language reflects the fact that John has indeed "seen" these things that are future but that are actual because God has decided on them. Revelation begins by describing how God gave a revelation to Jesus; Jesus commissioned a supernatural messenger; the messenger gave the revelation to God's slave John on Patmos; he saw it; he witnessed to what he had seen, to the message from God and the witness of Jesus; someone wrote the prophecy down (by implication, it was John himself); a reader reads it out; and people listen to it and take it to heart (Rev 1:1-3).

It's "a revelation of Jesus, the Anointed One": that is, it comes from him, which fits with the way it spells out the implications of his earthly teaching concerning the End (Mk 13). Jesus is the faithful and true witness (Rev 1:5; 3:14). There is a chain of revelation: from God to Jesus to an angel to John to its readers to its hearers, with the object of their taking it to heart. Yet being able to understand this revelation requires the gift of the Spirit, without which people will not be able to receive the gift of the message (Jn 1). Faith or trust is necessary to the receiving of the Spirit (Gal 3), but the Spirit is necessary to the exercise of faith.

The question of faith or trust in God's word goes back to the Beginning. The issue then was whether Eve and Adam would trust the goodness of Yahweh's bidding or would rather believe the snake's questioning of it. While Abraham is initially remarkable for his obedience to Yahweh, so that when Yahweh says "Go," he goes (Gen 12:1-6), a key issue in Abraham's subsequent life is whether he will trust Yahweh. His story thereby announces a key issue in Israel's own relationship with Yahweh. In some subsequent stories it is not clear that Abraham trusts Yahweh (Gen 12; 16; 20), though he does so in others (Gen 13).

The point is explicit when Genesis specifically declares that Abraham put his trust in Yahweh (Gen 15:6). Here Genesis uses the verb *he' ĕmîn* for the first time. Translations often render it "believe," though "the notion of mere 'holding an opinion,' which is one of the senses of the English word 'believe,' is totally absent from the Hebrew."[22] The verb denotes an active self-commitment on the basis of an awareness that there is something here that can be trusted, a self-commitment that had been involved in Abraham's original going when bidden.

Martin Buber sees a difference between "faith" in Israel, where it meant trusting someone, and in the early church, where it meant acknowledging something to be true. Each naturally leads to the other, though in both contexts one is primary.[23] While faith is vital, properly locating faith is also vital; tellingly, in Greek "faith" (*pistis*) can also denote "the faith" (Acts 6:7; Gal 1:23; 1 Tim 3:9; Jude 1:3). Conversely, belief has to become trust, and knowledge has to become acknowledgment. As well as assuming that there is such a thing as truth and thereby questioning the assumptions of a post-modern world, the Scriptures affirm a right kind of knowledge and reject a wrong kind.

Israel's story reflects how it can be hard to believe that something is going to happen and to live on the basis of that belief, and people often live on some other basis. The challenge involved in living in light of unproven claims concerning the future is significant in Ecclesiastes. In the New Testament, the firstfruits and sign or guarantee of things that God will indeed do is the presence and activity of the Spirit: an inner reality (in one's sense of God), a moral reality (in people's walking by the Spirit) and a miraculous reality (in events such as healings). In the Western church, none of these forms of the Spirit's presence and activity may seem evident, so we find ourselves back in Ecclesiastes's position.

---

[22]Walther Zimmerli, *Old Testament Theology in Outline* (Richmond: John Knox; Edinburgh: T&T Clark, 1978), 147.

[23]Martin Buber, *Two Types of Faith* (London: Routledge; New York: Macmillan, 1951), 7-8.

Visionary

The Prophets' visions of the fulfillment of Yahweh's purpose for Israel and for the world take up the content of two longstanding sets of promises of blessing. Yahweh had first laid before Abraham undertakings about land, increase and a covenant relationship, and then in due course had added promises about David and his line and about Zion and the temple. The Prophets' visions really do little more than update and rework these promises. The point is particularly evident in Ezekiel 33–48, where one can trace the link of substance between each chapter and one or another of the promises.

The Prophets speak about how God intends to implement them in the lives of the people whom they address. They also speak about how God will fulfill his ultimate purpose in events that will not take place in the addressees' lifetime but that are nevertheless significant for them; they are realities in light of which they need to live their lives. The same promises are thus the framework for the life of an individual generation and also for the people's long-term destiny. Although Yahweh's Day did not come about in their lifetime, its coming was still important for them, as the final appearing of Jesus did not happen in the lifetime of the congregations whom the New Testament writings address yet was still the vital certainty in light of which they were to live.

Taking up the actual language of "revelation," the book of Isaiah starts by calling what will follow a "vision" concerning Judah and Jerusalem that Isaiah "saw" (Is 1:1). As happens with words such as *vision* and *revelation* in English, this introduction to the book may be using these expressions in a loose sense, but Isaiah does have his visions (notably Is 6). The book of Amos, too, begins by speaking of words that Amos "saw," and Amos later tells people about things he has "seen"—a locust swarm, a fire, a wall, a fruit basket, all of them signaling something to come (Amos 7:1-9; 8:1-3).

Such visions show that Yahweh's revelations can relate something more like nightmares than dreams, something like the canceling of Yahweh's positive purpose, not its achievement. Yet they also show how, surprisingly, the revelation of something in a vision does not mean that the event it portrays is set in stone. The first two of Amos's visions relate how Amos prays and how the event then does not take place. Indeed, Amos's job as a prophet is to be the means of seeing that his visions are not fulfilled. Thus "a 'failed' prophecy" is not the same as a "*'false'* prophecy."[24] A prophecy may fail because it has succeeded.

Further, prophetic visions of events such as the fall of Babylon do not give something like advanced videos of what the events will actually look like. Likewise, while Jesus' coming was a fulfillment of revelations that the Prophets had been given, the relationship between the revelation and the events associated with his coming is not straightforward. A faithful servant like John the Baptizer has a hard time recognizing the relationship between Jesus' activity and the kind of thing the Prophets had spoken of.[25]

Again, many of the detailed links with the First Testament that are made by the Gospels involve striking points of connection between what look like random lines in the Scriptures and aspects of the Jesus story that are not of great inherent significance. At the crucifixion, the soldiers draw lots for Jesus' clothes "so that the scripture might be fulfilled, 'They divided my clothes among them; for my clothing they cast lots.'" The way Jesus died happened "so that the scripture might be fulfilled, 'None of his bones will be broken'; and again another scripture says, 'They will look at the one they have pierced'" (Jn 19:24, 36-37). Only the last of these Scriptures (Zech 12:10) is a prophecy in its context—and it is the one that is not said to be "fulfilled." But in any case, the technical-sounding English word *fulfillment* is misleading. Both the Hebrew verb *mallē'* and the Greek verb *plēroō* are ordinary words that mean "fill," and it is illuminating to take them as suggesting that prophecies are filled full or filled out or filled up as much as fulfilled.

Interpreting

The comment about none of Jesus' bones being broken is the nearest John's Gospel comes to quoting the Torah, insofar as the words recall the Passover regulations (Ex 12:46; Num 9:12), though they also recall Psalm 34:20. Thus even here "it is difficult to give the source of this quotation."[26] In any case, no one reading any of these First Testament passages could be expected to realize that they were speaking about the Messiah. Rather, what happens is that the story of Jesus' death and the Passover regulation and/or the psalm are put together, and they then illumine each other.

---

[24] Andrew Chester, *Future Hope and Present Reality* (Tübingen: Mohr, 2012), 1:134.
[25] See further the paragraphs under "Coming One, Son of God" in section 5.1 below.
[26] C. K. Barrett, *The Gospel According to St John* (London: SPCK, 1962), 464.

It is in this way that the details of the Scriptures commonly go about interpreting Jesus, in taking the First Testament as of key importance to understanding him. The allusiveness of the link between revelation and event confounds our ways of thinking, but it opens up the question whether there is a bigger framework for what is going on than we can perceive, whether both are part of a bigger tapestry that God is weaving whose existence emerges as holes appear in the curtain that surrounds the world. Paradoxically, when it is hard to identify the scripture referred to (as is so with Jn 19:36, and with Mt 2:23), this difficulty intensifies the point. We see only the edges of the tapestry.

Conversely, while it is possible to understand the First Testament Scriptures without knowing about Jesus (at least, people living before Jesus were assumed to be able to do so), knowing Jesus adds to an understanding of their significance. While John implies to Gentiles, "You will fully understand Jesus only if you go via the Scriptures," to Jews he implies, "You will fully understand the Scriptures only if you go via Jesus." In light of the fact that God's purpose reached its climax in Jesus, it is possible to perceive a new significance and purpose (rather than a new meaning) in the Scriptures (Rom 1:2; 4:23-24; 15:4; 1 Cor 9:9-10; 10:11). Sometimes individual pieces of data in isolation may say little, but when a number are brought together, a recognizable total picture may emerge.

The Scriptures provided a revelation about God and implicitly about his purpose in Jesus, though they did not always succeed in being revelatory. A revelation may stay sealed (Dan 8:26; 12:4). It may need an interpreter to explain it (Acts 8:30-31). The author of Isaiah 53 likely understood the *meaning* of that chapter better than we do, and the same may be true of the people to whom he delivered it. But the passage has continued to be a mystery to exegetes, and maybe both author and hearers were unclear about aspects of its meaning. Further, even if the mediator and recipients of the revelation know its *meaning*, they may not know its *reference* and thus may not know its *significance* for them (compare the comments in 1 Pet 1:10-12). The eunuch in Acts 8 did not know that Jesus was the supreme embodiment of the servant vision in Isaiah 53 (in this sense, he did not know its reference), and thus he did not understand its revelatory significance.

Strangely, if a revelation refers to some future event, only the occurrence of the event may make the revelation itself intelligible. There are parallels between dreams and revelations; both can be the subject of *pesher*, revelatory interpretation. One must not be too hard on the disciples who only after the resurrection "believed in the scripture and in the word Jesus spoke" (Jn 2:22), any more than on John the Baptizer.

A broader point can be made. While revelation is a key aspect of Christian faith, a revelation may not immediately answer all questions even for people who yield to it in an act of simple faith. Paul's understanding of Jesus and the gospel issued from an interweaving of the revelatory appearing of Jesus to him on the way to Damascus, the moment of intuition when he saw how to read the Scriptures in connection with that revelation, the Scriptures themselves on which he then pondered, and the report of Jesus that was handed down in congregations. Jesus' appearing and speaking to Paul gave him a key clue to God's revelation concerning God's intentions for the Gentile world, but this experience was succeeded by lengthy thinking and reflection. The process whereby he gained that revelation was not wholly supranatural, and God did not then dictate his letters to him.

The Revelation Unveiled

John the Baptizer "is the one spoken of through the prophet Isaiah when he says 'The voice of one crying out in the wilderness, "Prepare the Lord's way"'" (Mt 3:3). One is tempted to say, "No he isn't: the prophecy referred to something that was happening six centuries before Jesus." In what sense is John's voice that voice? Did the prophecy receive only partial fulfillment in that century and now receive a further fulfillment? But the New Testament uses language of this kind when the original prophecy was completely fulfilled. In his revisionist interpretation of Deuteronomy 30:11-14 (Rom 10:6-8), "Paul gains leverage on the text by claiming immediate revelatory illumination; the rabbis gain leverage on the text by appealing to majority opinion within the interpretive community"[27] (modern scholarly method follows the rabbis).

---

[27]Richard B. Hays, *Echoes of Scripture in the Letters of Paul* (New Haven, CT, and London: Yale University Press, 1989), 4.

One might have thought that the First Testament's message about God's actions was of self-evident meaning, but it is not so. At least, people don't get it. God had a longstanding intention to make Gentiles and Jews together sharers in the promise of God, and that fact was explicit enough in God's promise to Abraham, but people like Jonah didn't get it. With hindsight, at least, Paul can see how the Prophets indicate that someone like Jesus who gets rejected and executed would be the one through whom God's intention would find fulfillment. But he recognizes that the means of fulfilling the intention, and maybe the intention itself, needed to be the subject of a revelation (Eph 3:4-5; cf. Rom 16:25-26). So the revelation unveils how the fact that Jesus is living in or among Gentiles as well as Jews in the congregation is their hope of the glory of the resurrection and the consummation of God's purpose (Col 1:26-27): it unveils this *mystērion.*

> There is no evidence in the letters that Paul—in contrast to other ancient au-
> thors such as Philo—ever sat down with the biblical text and tried to figure
> out what it might mean by applying an exegetical procedure abstractable from
> the particular text that he was reading. Rather, he seems to have leaped—in
> moments of metaphorical insight—to intuitive apprehensions of the meanings
> of texts without the aid or encumbrance of systematic reflection about his
> own hermeneutics. . . . There are constraints on Paul's interpretation of
> Scripture, but the constraints arise primarily from material (i.e. theological)
> concerns rather than from formal methodological considerations. The her-
> meneutical foundation for his reading is the conviction that the Law and the
> Prophets bear witness to the gospel of God's righteousness, now definitively
> disclosed in the death and resurrection of Jesus Messiah.[28]

So Paul does not generally utilize a method of exegesis, though many of the key arguments he makes on the basis of a scriptural passage survive the application of modern exegetical method to them. But method can be cold.

Understanding the Scriptures may require a revelation, and yet the Scriptures themselves do have a "revelatory function. . . . The voice of Scripture, regarded as authoritative in one way or another, continues to speak in and through later texts that both depend on and transform the earlier."[29] God "spoke" in the past through the prophets, someone "testified"; but in addition

---

[28]Ibid., 160-61.
[29]Ibid., 7, 14.

Jesus "says" in the present words that originally come in Psalm 22:22 [MT 23] and Isaiah 8:17-18, and the Holy Spirit also "says" (Heb 1:1; 2:6, 12-13; 3:7). It is such words from the First Testament that God speaks now, which are alive, active and piercing now (Heb 4:12).

2.3 TESTIFIED TO

The Scriptures affirm that the insight written into the world and into human experience is true but incomplete or insufficient. Human beings can easily miss central aspects to it. It is the story that runs through the Scriptures that provides the key to real insight, a clue or a series of clues that human insight otherwise generally misses.

While the insight that comes only from the Scriptures expresses itself in declarations revealing what God has promised, promises are also incomplete without some fulfillment of them. So the insight that comes only from the Scriptures continues in the story of what God has done. The story points to "the difference between a genius and an apostle"; the apostles and the other scriptural narrators tell a story they did not devise. They point away from themselves, like John the Baptizer.[30] They remember and pass on key aspects of the story of Israel, the story of Jesus and the story of the infant church, witnessing to what God had been doing and to what Jesus had done. In the process they interpret it, and they interpret Jesus in light of the First Testament and the First Testament in light of Jesus. Their witness contradicts much regular so-called insight and sometimes gets the witnesses into trouble.

Remembered and Passed on

While the truth about God is written into the way God relates to the world and to all humanity, then, this truth is easy to miss, and Israel's story and Jesus' story give it a vivid expression that makes it clearer. After beginning with the promises about what God intends to do, Israel's story gives testimony to God's keeping of his promises. Jesus' life makes clear that he is the embodiment of God. His death and resurrection give the most vivid possible expression to what God had always shown himself to be, the one who pays the price for human waywardness and refuses to be defeated by it. It is

---

[30]Barth, *CD* I, 1:113. The phrase in quotation marks is the title of an essay by Søren Kierkegaard (see *The Present Age, and Of the Difference Between a Genius and an Apostle* [repr., New York: Harper, 1962], 89-108).

through Jesus that God's ultimate purpose will be fulfilled. He is the guarantee of it, because it already becomes actual in his resurrection. The New Testament brings the process of promise and fulfillment to its climax, though not to its end; it still leaves people living by God's promises.

As the basis of Israel's life is the story of God's involvement with it, the basis of any congregation's life is the gospel story, "the message of the truth of the gospel" or "the true message of the gospel" (Col 1:5). "Christian faith is not whatever a modern Christian may happen to believe . . . but faith related to Jesus and to the God of Israel."[31] It involves belief and action that match what Jesus was and taught. It thus involves remembering. The First Testament is therefore concerned with passing on what God was doing with Israel and how God spoke to Israel, and the New Testament is concerned with passing on what Jesus was and taught. Luke begins his Gospel by referring to his predecessors who applied themselves to compiling an account of the Jesus story, based on what was passed on by the original "eye-witnesses and servants of the message [*logos*]"; he is now producing his version (Lk 1:1-2).

In theological usage, the word *tradition*, the noun that denotes "passing on," can refer to ways of thought and practices that developed after scriptural times, but our concern here is with its use to describe what was passed on and found its place within the scriptural writings. Within the New Testament, the "passing on" covers the general nature of the faith and of the lifestyle that links with this faith; it also covers specific aspects of Jesus' words and actions. The term occurs with reference to Jesus' commissioning the disciples to reenact the last meal they had together, and more generally with reference to his dying for our sins and his rising from the dead, and to the way both relate to the Scriptures (1 Cor 11:2, 23; 15:3; Phil 4:9; Col 2:6; 1 Thess 2:13; 4:1; 2 Thess 2:15; 3:6; 1 Tim 6:20; 2 Tim 1:14; 2 Pet 2:21; Jude 3). The New Testament itself is the formal deposit of that passing on. In form it corresponds to it, especially in being dominated by Gospels that were written to pass on the story and teaching of Jesus, but also in including letters that passed the tradition on to congregations in a form that worked out its implications for issues that concerned them.

---

[31]James Barr, *The Bible in the Modern World* (London: SCM Press; New York: Harper, 1973), 118.

Remembering is the other side of passing on. It is an overstatement to say that no biblical command is as persistent as the command to "remember,"[32] but it is not much of an overstatement. Books such as Deuteronomy and Psalms emphasize remembering and underline how remembering what has been passed on is vital to a religious, spiritual and ethical life lived in light of what God has done.[33] Paul praises the Corinthians for remembering what he passed on to them (1 Cor 11:2). Remembering centers on the Lord's Meal, and the Lord's Meal centers on remembering.

Paul's praise is qualified. The Corinthians' celebration of the Lord's Meal rather too closely follows social convention, with its division between well-to-do and ordinary people, whereas for Paul the bread and the wine are "the primary expressions of the unity of the congregation and . . . the means to that unity."[34] Part of the background of the Lord's Meal is the practice of table fellowship in Jesus' ministry, but the Corinthians have not assimilated what Paul "passed on" concerning the way this table fellowship worked (1 Cor 11:23).

Written and Handed Down

Being a witness can mean testifying to truth that people do not wish to hear, and a *martys* (the Greek word for witness) may end up as a martyr. In the early story of the church, there was a role to be played by Peter, whose name would be well known, who would tend the sheep and would pay the ultimate price of martyrdom for doing so; there was also a role to be played by one whose name was not on everyone's lips in the same way but who was a good friend of Jesus, "the disciple Jesus loved" (Jn 21). The one would be a martyr, the other would be simply a *martys*, who would be in a position to keep giving his testimony to what Jesus had done and might even stay alive to do so until Jesus returned.

The task of tending the sheep can be passed on to the next generation, so that Peter is dispensable. The task of giving firsthand testimony cannot be

---

[32]Elie Wiesel, *From the Kingdom of Memory* (New York: Summit, 1990), 9; cf. Miroslav Volf, *Exclusion and Embrace* (Nashville: Abingdon, 1996), 235.

[33]See John Goldingay, *Do We Need the New Testament?* (Downers Grove, IL: InterVarsity Press, 2015), 119-37.

[34]Cf. James D. G. Dunn, *The Theology of Paul the Apostle* (Grand Rapids and Cambridge, UK: Eerdmans, 1998), 609-20, following Gerd Theissen, *The Social Setting of Pauline Christianity* (Philadelphia: Fortress, 1982); see 165-66; quotation from 616.

passed on in the same sense, but such a friend of Jesus can write down his testimony, and he did. Yet John's Gospel, perhaps the last of the scriptural Gospels to be written, does contain more overt reflection on Jesus' significance than the other three Gospels. There is no necessary link between time and depth of reflection, but staying alive and having time perhaps made it possible for Jesus' friend not only to give his firsthand testimony in person but to write it down in a more reflective fashion. The church is built on Peter; it is also built on John.

Jesus in John, and John himself, speak much of testimony.[35] "We speak of what we know and we witness to what we have seen," Jesus declares. "What he has seen and heard: this is what he witnesses to. . . . The one whom God sent speaks God's words, because God does not give his Spirit by measure." God gave words to Jesus; he passed them on (Jn 3:11, 32, 34; 17:8). Jesus himself speaks in self-referential fashion: he is the messenger, but he is also the message. He speaks of eternal life, and it is through him that eternal life comes to people (Jn 3:15-16). The world is characterized by deceit; he speaks the truth (e.g., Jn 5:33; 8:32, 40, 44-46). His deeds witness to who he is; the Father witnesses to who he is; the Scriptures witness to who he is (Jn 5:36-39).

They are not separate testimonies. "The Father's form is not seen—but it can be discerned in the works of Jesus; his voice is not heard—but it is echoed in the scriptures," and it continues in the work of the Holy Spirit through the disciples, the people who have been with Jesus from the beginning (Jn 15:26-27; cf. Lk 1:2; Acts 1:21-22).[36] The disciples are sanctified by or in the truth, dedicated to the service of the word (the message) that is true (Jn 17:17). Jesus' sharing this truth with them is an indication of how close they are to him. They are his friends, not slaves who don't know what their master is doing (Jn 15:15). They are thus in the same position as Abraham, who was God's friend (Is 41:8; 2 Chron 20:27; Jas 2:23), or Moses, who was called God's servant but to whom God spoke face to face in the way one speaks with a friend (Ex 33:11).

---

[35]On the motif of witness in John, see Andrew T. Lincoln, *Truth on Trial* (Peabody, MA: Hendrickson, 2000); also Richard Bauckham, *The Testimony of the Beloved Disciple* (Grand Rapids: Baker, 2007).

[36]John Ashton, *Understanding the Fourth Gospel* (Oxford and New York: Oxford University Press, 1991), 525-27 (differently expressed in the 2nd ed., 2007, 501-3).

The disciples are witnesses (Acts 1:8), and the Gospels are the deposit of their testimony (cf. Jn 21:24). They saw and heard things that they could hand down. Only such testimony provides access to the facts for people who did not see and hear these things. Witness is thus a vital means of access to truth. Someone who knows tells people who do not know. Luke wrote his Gospel so that a reader might have some certainty about things he had been told aurally (Lk 1:1-4). Jesus' acts are vital to the response of faith in him. Yet "for those who receive the message of Jesus' disciples, as for the readers of the Gospel [of John], *the works have been transformed into words*."[37]

Interpreted

Jesus is the one witnessed to, but with his passing, it is no longer possible for anyone to witness his signs. But seeing for oneself was never either the necessary or the sufficient route toward a proper response to Jesus. Many who saw did not believe. Thomas believed on the basis of seeing, but there is a blessing on people who have not seen and yet have believed. It is for people who have not seen that John wrote his Gospel, so that they might know about the things Jesus did in the presence of his disciples and might believe that he is the Anointed One, the Son of God, and thus have life through him (Jn 20:29-31). Further, while God's revelation was embodied in Jesus (Jn 1:1-18), it was also expressed in his words, which people can still have access to. "My teaching is not my own but his who sent me. If someone is willing to do God's will, this person will know of the teaching, whether it is from God or I speak from myself" (Jn 7:16-17). The Gospel preserves the teaching.

The writing down of the disciples' testimony followed the precedent set by the First Testament Scriptures. At the Reed Sea Moses and Miriam led the Israelites in a proclamation of what Yahweh had done, but that proclamation needed not to be lost on the airwaves. It had to become a story that Israel told and eventually put into writing. The first advantage that attaches to the Jewish people is that they were entrusted with God's *logia* (Rom 3:1-2; cf. Acts 7:38). While *logia* suggests sayings or instructions or oracles, one could broaden the point and note the importance of the Jewish people's being in a position to tell that story.

---

[37]Ibid., 522 (2nd ed., 498).

What is handed on thus centers on an account of some things that happened. Yet the account incorporates interpretation. Mark emphasizes that
God's reign arrived in Jesus. Matthew makes Jesus Act 2 to the First Testament's Act 1 and has Jesus interpreting Torah. Luke makes Jesus Act 1 to an
Act 2 in the church's life.[38] John indicates how the Holy Spirit interprets Jesus
in the life of the church. Samuel–Kings is an interpretation of the story of
the monarchy that points to its significance for Judah in light of the fall of
Jerusalem. Chronicles is another interpretation of that story that points to
its significance for Judah in the Persian period.

Actually, there is no such thing as an uninterpreted story. Only by interpreting events does one generate a story, rather than simply record a collection of facts. As testimony the Gospels offer both facts and interpretation
in their inevitable combination. They offer not the "arbitrary imposition" of
theological meaning on "objective facts" but "the way the witnesses perceived the history, in an inextricable coinherence of observable event and
perceptible meaning."[39]

The disciples' own testimony and interpretation depended on the First
Testament Scriptures. Whether or not Jesus would have been intelligible
without them, actually it was these Scriptures that made him intelligible. The
preaching of Peter on Pentecost (Acts 2) depended on it substantially. The
gospel of God is something God announced ahead of time through the
Prophets in the "holy writings" (Rom 1:2) through which Jesus is understood.
They are prophetic writings that announce beforehand what the Anointed
One will be. The Scriptures saw in advance and announced the news in
advance (Gal 3:8). Thus they themselves gave testimony to him; Moses
"wrote about me" (Jn 5:40, 46; cf. Lk 24:27).

Yet we have noted that there is not a single unequivocal quotation from
the Torah in John. So how does this anticipatory testimony work? John
begins by declaring that the message about Jesus goes back to the beginning
of what Moses wrote (as it were) in Genesis 1. He describes Jesus as the
embodiment of the grace and truthfulness of which Moses speaks. He

---

[38]Though perhaps the relationship of Luke and Acts is less cozy than this description implies: see
Andrew F. Gregory and C. Kavin Rowe, eds., *Rethinking the Unity and Reception of Luke and Acts*
(Columbia: University of South Carolina Press, 2010).
[39]Richard Bauckham, *Jesus and the Eyewitnesses* (Grand Rapids: Eerdmans, 2006), 5.

reports John the Baptizer's description of Jesus as the lamb of God. He compares Moses' lifting up the snake in the wilderness with Jesus' lifting up on the cross. He goes on to report Jesus' miraculous feeding of a crowd in a way that recalls but surpasses the feedings of which Moses was the agent (Jn 6). Paralleling scriptural material outside the Torah, John describes Jesus as the real shepherd and the real vine.

The Scriptures and the Story

The First Testament Scriptures give their testimony to Jesus by forming part of the resource material in light of which people understand Jesus. Matthew begins his Gospel with an account of Jesus' ancestry marked by reference to Abraham, David and the exile, inviting the reflection that the story of Jesus continues the testimony to God's action that appears in the story of Abraham, the story of David and even the story of the deportation to Babylon.

So along with the things that Jesus does and says and the things that happen to him, these Scriptures are key to the way believers come to understand Jesus, the way they argue for his being recognized by other Jews and the way they deal with apparent objections to the idea that he can be the Anointed One. When things that happen do not make sense, looking at them in light of the Scriptures may mean they become intelligible. It is troublesome that all the babies in Bethlehem die as a consequence of Jesus being born there, but setting the tragedy in the context of Jeremiah's words about Rachel weeping for her children makes it a little easier to live with (Mt 2:16-18). Indeed, passages from the Scriptures play a key part in each of the five vignettes that comprise Matthew's story of Jesus' birth, by also helping to make intelligible how he could be born of a virgin and be one who embodied God's presence, how he was born in Bethlehem rather than Jerusalem, how he then went off to Egypt, and how he subsequently went to live in faraway Nazareth (Mt 1:18–2:23).

"Whatever was written ahead of time was written to teach us, so that through endurance and through the Scriptures' encouragement we might have hope" (Rom 15:4). The Scriptures often portray the people of God having experiences they might wish did not come their way, but they put up with them; and Jesus is the climactic illustration. It contributes to the achievement of God's purpose to bring about the world's salvation. The Scriptures thus inspire people to endurance and hope.

The church's vocation is to give testimony, to give faithful witness. It has been described as our first responsibility after keeping sabbath, as our central vocation as believing human beings.[40] The church is a powerless entity, and witnessing is the only thing the powerless can do (cf. Jn 9:25). But what an important task it is. "The ministry and therefore the witness of the community is essentially and in all forms and circumstances (1) the declaration of the Gospel . . . (2) the explanation or explication of the Gospel . . . (3) evangelical address, i.e., proclamation and explication in the form of application."[41] And "in this powerless witness the power of truth to defeat lies comes into its own."[42]

Yet it won't therefore be surprising if being a *martys* leads into being a martyr, for the congregation in general as for individuals. At first hearing, the idea that the lynching of a Jew is of key significance for humanity seems an expression of stupidity and an affront, not an expression of insight (1 Cor 1:23; Gal 1:18). But the preaching of this message is the Spirit's means of piercing through people and opening their eyes to see that what they thought was folly is actually insight (1 Cor 2:6-16). The word of God (that is, the gospel message) is the Spirit's *sword* (Eph 6:17). The gospel is the power of God for salvation (Rom 1:16). It shares in the power that regularly attaches to God's words (e.g., Gen 1:3, 6; Ps 147:15; Is 40:8; 55:10-11; Jer 23:29).[43]

Counterintuitive but Powerful

When God speaks, his message is indeed alive, active and sharp; it penetrates and exposes (Heb 4:12-13). It has this power whether it is a message spoken within the Scriptures that also addresses the contemporary congregation, as may be the case in the context of that statement about the sharpness of God's word (see Heb 3:7–4:10),[44] or whether it is the message of the gospel (Heb 13:7), or the word that creates the world (Heb 11:3 [*rhēma* there rather than *logos*]). Jesus, too, "carries everything [in creation] by his powerful

---

[40]Barth, *CD* III, 4:73; IV, 3:554-614.
[41]Barth, *CD* IV, 3:844, 846, 850.
[42]Bauckham, *Theology of the Book of Revelation*, 163.
[43]Cf. C. E. B. Cranfield, *A Critical and Exegetical Commentary on the Epistle to the Romans* (Edinburgh: T&T Clark, 1975), 88.
[44]See the comments on this passage at the end of the paragraphs headed "Interpreted," above.

word" (Heb 1:3; *rhēma* again). His words are his means of acting. It is by speaking that he rescues and condemns. "The words that I have spoken to you are spirit, and they are life"; Jesus' word (his message) had the power to make the disciples clean (Jn 6:63; 15:3).[45]

A piece of news can have such power. Abraham Lincoln's emancipation proclamation in 1863 had no effect in Texas until it was publicly announced there two years later, but then the news revolutionized the life of slaves; hence the celebration of Juneteenth, the date when the proclamation arrived. News about a Jew being executed would not seem very impressive or transformative, and therefore someone proclaiming its importance would look stupid. Paul knows that actually it is vitally important and transformative, and therefore he is "not ashamed" of it. His statement may be a litotes: he is wildly proud of it.

In Jesus all the treasures of insight and knowledge are located. It is important that people don't fall uncritically for human insight. Our turning away from God means that human insight can be empty and deceitful, based on something "passed on" by human beings that is of this-worldly origin rather than something that reflects the insight embodied in Jesus (Col 2:3, 8). Through this Anointed One in whom God's fullness dwells, we are filled (Col 2:10); we don't need anything else, any other teaching. But the message to which the Scriptures testify goes against what we are naturally inclined to think, as members of a humanity that turned away from God. Being given their testimony to counteract the results of that turning away means being given insight that the world in general doesn't possess; the world is thus characterized by foolishness.

Even the congregation can easily think that insight lies in what is actually worldly foolishness. We have to become fools in order to becomes truly wise (1 Cor 3:18-23; cf. Job 5:13; Ps 94:11). "The whole of man's intellectual wisdom must be submitted to the foolishness of the cross."[46] God has turned the world upside down. "Weakness is strength; foolishness is wisdom; those of no honor or standing topple those of honor, wisdom, and power." The

---

[45]Cf. Rudolf Bultmann, *Theology of the New Testament* (repr., Waco, TX: Baylor University Press, 2007), 2:60-61.

[46]T. F. Torrance, summarizing Calvin's teaching in *Calvin's Doctrine of Man*, new ed. (Grand Rapids: Eerdmans, 1957), 169.

shameful bodily parts receive more honor from the honorable ones. The last, Paul, becomes the first.[47] The way Paul talks about God involves an ongoing exercise in "code-switching."[48]

When people who believe they have the truth are in a position of power, their belief can encourage divisiveness, exclusion, persecution and violence. People who believe that Jesus is the truth must therefore continue to remind themselves that backing the message by the weapons of power makes their stance deconstruct. Their witness tells of how God overcame power by submitting to it not by exercising it. Paul came to Corinth in weakness, yet also with power and effectiveness (1 Cor 2:1-5), partly because God did powerful things when he preached (cf. Rom 15:18-19): "It would never occur to him that the miraculous would *not* accompany the proclamation of the gospel."[49] But it was God's acts of power that made the difference.

2.4 IMPERATIVE

God's insight finds further expression in assertions about how he expects us to live our lives. God's expectations cover the obligations of community and individual; they interweave ethics and worship and spirituality; and they bring together directives that relate to a variety of historical, geographical and social contexts. Fulfilling such expectations is not the way people first enter the realm of God's grace or of covenant. "Ethics can claim no primacy in theology."[50] But fulfilling such expectations is intrinsic to living in that realm.

Welcomed and Contextual but Worrisome

God's first imperatives appear in the creation story and the Eden story. Implicitly they depend simply on God's authority. Human beings are not God's partners or coworkers, but neither are they slaves or robots. They are God's servants, and servants do what the master says.

---

[47]Jerome H. Neyrey, *Render to God* (Minneapolis: Fortress, 2004), 187-88.

[48]Pheme Perkins, "God's Power in Human Weakness," in A. Andrew Das and Frank J. Matera, eds., *The Forgotten God*, Paul J. Achtemeier Festschrift (Louisville and London: Westminster John Knox, 2002), 145-62 (on 147).

[49]Gordon D. Fee, *God's Empowering Presence* (Peabody, MA: Hendrickson, 1994), 849.

[50]Oliver O'Donovan, *Finding and Seeking* (Grand Rapids and Cambridge, UK: Eerdmans, 2014), 6.

Whereas we may be inclined to object to anyone telling us what to do and inclined to question what we are told, the First Testament is enthusiastic about God's commands. It delights in them, loves them and gets comfort from them (e.g., Ps 119:16, 40, 48). We are privileged to have them. Jesus' ready submission to the Father expresses the attitude the First Testament assumes, though in practice Israel was not so keen on obeying God's commands, any more than the church is.

"The grace of God in Jesus Christ is not only the foundation but the content, the decisive form, of the claim addressed to us in the divine command,"[51] and the First Testament presupposes an equivalent conviction. It assumes that God's commands do express insight and offer the secret to a life that implements God's purpose, attains personal fulfillment and finds blessing. People such as Adam and Eve who flout God's commands are just stupid. Basic commands such as worshiping Yahweh alone, not making images, not attaching Yahweh's name to projects to which it does not belong and keeping the sabbath are delightful expressions of insight. A summary of the First Testament's expectations such as the dual command to love God and love neighbor is likewise an expression of insight.

The First Testament's delight in God's *many* commands indicates a recognition that we have and need more than the basic two or the basic ten. We need the insight that spells out their implications. So both Testaments spell them out for us, in ways that recognize the necessity to do so in different contexts. The New Testament does it in recognition of the geographical diversity of the believing communities. What needs be said to the Corinthians differs from what needs to be said to the Thessalonians. The First Testament does it in recognition of the historical diversity of Israel. The imperatives in Exodus 21–23, in Leviticus and in Deuteronomy reflect different historical and social contexts. God's imperatival insight is both eternal and timely, both universal and contextual. It is divine and also human, worked out through the aid of the Holy Spirit by people such as Paul and the anonymous thinkers whose reflection lies behind the imperatives in the Torah.

---

[51]Barth, *CD* II, 2:632.

Genesis does not describe the creation relationship between God and humanity as covenantal, though in a broader sense one can say that the covenant of grace existed from creation; it denotes the fellowship that originally existed between God and humanity, which was then disturbed but fulfilled in Jesus.[52] Still less is the creation relationship between God and humanity based on human deeds rather than on grace, as is implied by the phrase "covenant of works."[53] Covenant in the way the First Testament uses its word *bərît* suggests a gracious commitment by God that comes in only after things have gone wrong.

Thus the first covenant is God's commitment to Noah, which has no imperatives attached. In Genesis 1-11 we do have both imperatives and a covenant, but they are not related. The situation changes little in Genesis 12–50, where God again issues some imperatives and makes covenant commitments but doesn't relate the two very integrally. At Sinai God takes a step in the direction of interrelating his action toward Israel and his expectations of Israel (see Ex 19:3-8; 24:1-12), and in the steppes of Moab Moses works out the implications of their interrelationship (see Deuteronomy). Now that Yahweh has not only promised to rescue Israel from its serfdom but has actually done so, he is in a position to lay down some expectations.

Law and Legalism

If possessing the Torah is a privilege, why can it seem that "all of the New Testament is obsessed with its anxious relationship to the Law and the Prophets"?[54] What is the Torah for?

"As we move through Romans the most obvious function of the law is that of defining and measuring sin and transgression."[55] Neither Jews nor Gentiles can get right with God on the basis of doing the right thing. No one can be put right by means of deeds prescribed by the Torah, because through the Torah there is awareness of shortcoming (Rom 3:20; cf. 4:15). This function of exposing waywardness corresponds to one role of the Torah's instructions within the First Testament; in the story of Josiah's reformation, discovering what the Torah says makes wise people panic.

---

[52]Barth, *CD* III, 1:44; IV, 1:22.
[53]Westminster Confession of Faith 7:2.
[54]Harold Bloom, *Jesus and Yahweh* (New York: Riverhead, 2005), 36.
[55]Dunn, *Theology of Paul the Apostle*, 133-34.

The Torah as a whole is the story of the early stages in the relationship between Yahweh and Israel. It is a story, though it has imperatives embedded. Yet the word *tôrâ* itself commonly also refers to the actual instruction given at Sinai (and subsequently in Numbers and Deuteronomy), instruction dominated by the declaration of divine requirements that must be kept rather than transgressed, with sanctions attached to their transgression.[56] The word *tôrâ* thus gets translated by the Greek word *nomos* and then by the Latin word *lex* and then in English by the word "law." Such translations are systematically misleading. Although Deuteronomy is the book that most systematically expounds the nature of God's expectations, and it is thus dominated by commands, calling Deuteronomy "law" is still misleading. While the equation Torah = obligation is firmly rooted in Deuteronomy, it is not the case that "the equation *Torah* = law is firmly rooted in Deuteronomy itself."[57]

Christians have often assumed that Jewish faith in the Second Temple period was characterized by legalism or nomism, that such legalism was the kind of religion Paul was concerned to oppose, and that such a religion was in continuity with the faith of the First Testament.[58] Discussion of the questions raised by those assumptions is complicated, because "legalism" can be understood in various ways.[59] "Nomism" commonly corresponds to one of its meanings, the idea that people get right with God on the basis of things they do rather than on the basis of God's grace.

No doubt there were Jewish people who held this nomistic view, as there are Christians who hold it, but the standard Jewish view is that God chose the Jewish people by his grace, and they were then to respond to his initiative with the obedience detailed in the Torah. "Covenantal nomism," as this view might be called, "is the view that one's place in God's plan is established on

---

[56]Cf. Stephen Westerholm, *Israel's Law and the Church's Faith* (Grand Rapids: Eerdmans, 1988), 106-9, 136-40.

[57]Against James D. G. Dunn, *The Partings of the Ways* (London: SCM Press; Philadelphia: Trinity Press International, 1991), 24.

[58]See, e.g., Martin Noth, "The Laws in the Pentateuch: Their Assumptions and Meaning," in *The Laws in the Pentateuch and Other Studies* (Edinburgh: Oliver and Boyd, 1966; Philadelphia: Fortress, 1967), 104-5; Rudolf Bultmann, *Primitive Christianity in Its Contemporary Setting* (London and New York: Thames and Hudson, 1956), 59-71.

[59]See Bernard S. Jackson, "Legalism," *Journal of Jewish Studies* 30 (1979): 1-22; Kent Yinger, "Defining Legalism," *Andrews University Seminary Studies* 46 (2008): 91-108.

the basis of the covenant and that the covenant requires as the proper response of man his obedience to its commandments, while providing means of atonement for transgression. . . . *Obedience maintains one's position in the covenant, but it does not earn God's grace.*[60] It is not involved in "getting in," but it is involved in "staying in."[61]

Admittedly, this analysis is more like theory than practice, and in a good sense. If obedience were required for Israel to maintain its position in the covenant, the covenant would have been annulled long before the exile and certainly long before Jesus. Obedience is Israel's proper response, but when obedience is not forthcoming, God cannot bring himself to cast Israel off. Fortunately the same is true of the church.

Torah and Covenant

Further, the distinction between getting in and staying in is harder to maintain than it may seem. If obedience is vital in order to experience life, that fact may not seem very different from the idea that acceptance by God is conditional on obedience.[62] Both ideas are present in Judaism and both fit Paul's "pattern of religion."[63] Paul asserts both that God chooses who will hear and receive the gospel message and that people decide to believe, and commit themselves; he seems not to have felt a need to harmonize these two statements.[64] "On the issue of the relationship between (initial) justification and final judgment, and between faith and obedience, . . . *NT teaching has the same or at least a very similar inter-relationship*" as that in the First Testament or much of Judaism.[65]

Within the First Testament, the question of the Torah's significance arises in another way if one asks about the relationship between Abraham and Moses, or between Sinai (standing for Yahweh's expectations) and

[60]E. P. Sanders, *Paul and Palestinian Judaism* (London: SCM Press; Philadelphia: Fortress, 1977), 75, 420; expanded on 422.

[61]Cf. E. P. Sanders, *Paul, the Law, and the Jewish People* (London: SCM Press; Philadelphia: Fortress, 1983), 6.

[62]Cf. James D. G. Dunn, "In Search of Common Ground," in Dunn, ed., *Paul and the Mosaic Law* (Tübingen: Mohr, 1996), 309-34 (on 312).

[63]James D. G. Dunn, "Epilogue," in Reimund Bieringer and Didier Pollefeyt, eds., *Paul and Judaism* (London and New York: T&T Clark, 2012), 208-20 (on 215).

[64]Cf. Sanders, *Paul and Palestinian Judaism*, 446-47.

[65]James Dunn, *The New Perspective on Paul* (Tübingen: Mohr, 2005), 67.

Zion (standing for Yahweh's gracious commitment).[66] Whether or not it is appropriate to talk about the Sinai-Moab covenant as *conditional* on Israel's obedience, it does *require* Israel's obedience. The commitment between the two parties needs to be mutual if it is to be real. Likewise, "for Jesus, forgiveness cannot be earned, . . . but our repentance is the only adequate response to God's forgiveness."[67] While forgiveness is undeserved and unconditioned, Jesus indicates that forgiveness is conditional: if you don't forgive other people, God doesn't forgive you (Mt 6:14-15). He seems to imply that grace is unmerited but conditional.[68] Perhaps the language of conditionality is misleading, but whether or not it is appropriate, Jesus is reaffirming the structure of Yahweh's relationship with Israel.

It is not the case that in the First Testament "the idea of the divine 'mercy' and 'grace' stands on a legalistic basis" so that "it is Law . . . that says the final and decisive word in the Old Testament view of man's relation to God," compared with which "the New Testament idea of redemption constitutes in fact a veritable revolution; for it declares that sovereign Divine Love has . . . broken through the order of justice and merit."[69] The contrast between the old dispensation and the new is not a contrast between law and gospel.[70] Talk of grace "does not of itself produce a contrast between 'grace' and 'Law,' because for the Jews the Law was a *charis* or a gracious revelation of God."[71] Thus already "the Law is completely enclosed in the Gospel. It is not a second thing alongside and beyond the Gospel. It is not a foreign element which precedes or only follows it. It is the claim which is addressed to us by the Gospel itself and as such, the Gospel in so far as it has the form of a claim addressed to us, the Gospel which we cannot really hear except as we obey

---

[66]Cf. Gerhard von Rad, *Old Testament Theology* (Edinburgh: Oliver and Boyd; New York: Harper, 1962), 1:339.

[67]L. Gregory Jones, *Embodying Forgiveness* (Grand Rapids: Eerdmans, 1995), 121.

[68]Cf. John Piper, *Future Grace* (Sisters, OR: Multnomah, 1995), 11.

[69]Against Gustaf Aulén, *Christus Victor* (London: SPCK, 1931), 95-96. Ironically, Aulén's misperception derives from his reading the First Testament through the eyes of later Christian tradition, the practice he resists in his reading of the New Testament.

[70]See, e.g., Daniel P. Fuller, "Progressive Dispensationalism and the Law/Gospel Contrast," in *Biblical Theology*, ed. Scott J. Hafemann (Downers Grove, IL: InterVarsity Press; Leicester, UK: Inter-Varsity Press, 2002), 237-49.

[71]Edward Schillebeeckx, *Christ* (New York: Crossroad; London: SCM Press, 1980), 122.

it."[72] Hence "only the believers obey, and only the obedient believe."[73] And if there were no law in the sense of commands concerning behavior, grace would not be the same sort of thing.

Grace and Conditions

In this sense, "covenantal theology is characteristic not only of Jewish thinking in this period, but also of Paul's whole worldview." The Torah and Paul hold together as an integral whole what God has done and what we must do. The prophets and Jesus hold together as an integral whole what God is about to do and what we must do. "Jesus' eschatological message and his ethical message constitute a unity"; he is "both the prophet who proclaims the irruption of God's Reign and the rabbi who expounds God's Law."[74]

Like the Sermon on the Mount, then, the Torah was never designed as a means of getting into a relationship with God. It was designed to shape the life of people who have already been granted life. While the contents of the Torah issued from a wide range of historical and social contexts, linking the material in Exodus and Leviticus with Sinai declares that all of it works out the implications of the exodus and the covenant making at Sinai. Conversely, placing Deuteronomy on the other side of the period during which the exodus generation died affirms the legitimacy and necessity of adapting the original revelation to later contexts.[75]

Insofar as the Torah is a true statement of God's expectations of people, not surprisingly it broadly corresponds to insights about attitudes and behavior that are recognized by peoples other than Israel, whether in the Middle East, in Greece or in traditional societies elsewhere. God made all humanity in the divine image and hardwired all humanity with an awareness that we should love our neighbor or administer justice in a fair way or avoid coveting. This is not to say that all people everywhere have accepted such principles, even in theory, only to say that there is little in the Torah that would surprise ethical thinkers in societies other than Israel.

---

[72]Barth, *CD* II, 2:557.
[73]Dietrich Bonhoeffer, *Discipleship* (repr., Minneapolis: Fortress, 2003), 63. Most of the sentence is in italics.
[74]Bultmann, *Theology of the New Testament*, 1:19; he italicizes the first quotation.
[75]Brevard S. Childs, *Old Testament Theology in a Canonical Context* (London: SCM Press, 1985; Philadelphia: Fortress, 1986), 54-56.

The relationship of the Prophets to the Torah implies a similar assumption. Prophets tell forth what God expects of the people they address, though they do so in a less specific way than the Torah does. Indeed, their focus lies more on what people should not have been doing. They do sometimes speak in a way that virtually picks up the language of the Torah or refers directly to it (e.g., Amos 2:4), to remind people of their failure. But it is unusual for them to do so. They, too, think that it's obvious what God expects of people and that people hardly need the Torah to tell them.

The New Testament's assumption is not that God's dealings with his people were previously law-based but now are so no longer, though it was and is easy for people to think that way. It is that Jesus' coming renders that mistake harder to make than it was before, not least because it provides a potentially more effective way in which the Torah's own concerns can be embodied in people's lives.

> Through the Torah I died in relation to the Torah so that I might live in relation to God. I have been crucified, with the Anointed One. I myself no longer live; the Anointed One lives in me now. In that I now live in the flesh, I live by faith in the Son of God who loved me and gave himself up for me. I do not set aside God's grace. Because if righteousness comes through the Torah, then the Anointed One died for nothing. (Gal 2:19-21)

2.5 INSPIRING

There is a further form of God's insight that is the most surprising. The Scriptures incorporate examples of the way people are invited to praise God and pray, especially in the Psalms. For the most part this invitation takes the form not of further imperatives telling us how to praise God or how to pray, but the form of examples of things that God is willing to have said to him in praise and prayer. They comprise teaching that is designed to inspire people to pray and praise.

Teaching

Although this Scriptural material is inspiring, it actually is the subject of imperatives.

> Be filled with the Spirit, speaking to each other in psalms, hymns, songs that are Spirit-inspired, singing and playing with your inner being to the Lord,

giving thanks all the time on behalf of everyone in the name of our Lord Jesus, the Anointed One, to God the Father, submitting to one another in reverence for the Anointed One. . . . Pray on every occasion in the Spirit with every prayerful request, and to this end be alert with every continuing request for all the saints, and for me, so that a message may be given me when I open my mouth, to make known freely the gospel mystery for which I am an ambassador in a chain. (Eph 5:18-21; 6:18-20)

While the expressions of worship urged by this exhortation doubtless include Spirit-inspired songs referring to Jesus, such as ones incorporated into the New Testament (e.g., Lk 1:46-55, 68-79; 2:29-32), the "psalms" to which it refers surely include or comprise the psalms in the Psalter. If the Psalms were the place where Jews and Christians always used to learn to pray,[76] this role fits their aim. Perhaps the individual psalms (or most of them) started off life as expressions of praise and prayer composed to express what people needed or wanted to say to God in a specific context. But their inclusion in the Psalter gives them a new significance. The Psalter's comprising five books, like the Torah, suggests that teaching people to worship and pray is its own intention.

In English translations, the Psalter's five-book structure is explicit in the headings to Psalms 1; 42; 73; 90; 107. While these headings are not part of the Hebrew text, the text does have codas at the end of Psalms 41; 72; 89; 106 that make the same point by means of their distinctive blessings and amens. In dividing into five books of teaching, parallel to the Torah itself, the Psalter is "the five-fold answer of the congregation to the word of God in the five books of Moses."[77] For every word that God speaks to us, there is an answering word from us. Not that (e.g.) Psalm 1 corresponds to Genesis 1; Psalm 2 to Genesis 2; and so on. The conversation between God and his people is not preprogrammed in this way. Rather the Psalter introduces us into a living conversation and shows us how to engage in it.[78]

Further, the Psalter begins with a declaration concerning the good fortune of the person who attends to Yahweh's Torah. Initially one would

---

[76]So Eugene Peterson, *Working the Angles* (Grand Rapids: Eerdmans, 1987; repr., 1993), 50.

[77]Christoph F. Barth, *Introduction to the Psalms* (New York: Scribner's; Oxford: Blackwell, 1966), 4; cf. Peterson, *Working the Angles*, 54.

[78]Peterson, *Working the Angles*, 56.

assume that this declaration refers to the Torah of Moses, but the five-book structure of the Psalter opens up the possibility that it is the Psalter itself that is here designated as Yahweh's Torah. The Psalter is then Yahweh's teaching about praise and prayer, in the form of 150 examples of things you can say to him.

Whichever is the correct understanding of Psalm 1, the implication of the Psalter's structure and of its presence in the Scriptures is that it is designed to teach people how to worship and pray—or rather to show people how to do so, given that it does take the form of examples rather than an exposition of principles or rules. It perhaps implies something about worship and prayer, that they are caught, not taught. It is through seeing and listening to people worship and pray that we learn how to worship and pray.

The Scriptures thus make the assumption that worship and prayer are not activities that come naturally—or rather, that the way we naturally worship and pray may not be the way God appreciates. A comparison with Babylonian and Egyptian prayers and praises suggests one sense in which it is so, if it is fair to contrast the First Testament psalms with Egyptian psalms, which offer praise only in general terms and not in relation to the deity's doing anything, and Babylonian psalms, which offer praise only as a lead-in to prayer and not for its own sake.[79] Certainly worship and prayer in the Psalms resolutely affirm that Yahweh alone is God and that he alone must be worshiped or entreated, which contrasts with the assumption that there are many gods whom one might worship and whose help one might seek.

Invitational

One can thus contrast the praise and prayer of the Psalms with that of other Middle Eastern peoples; one can identify a different contrast with the worship and prayer of Western churches. Modern Western prayer often assumes that the chief significance of prayer is to change the people praying, and many prayers amount to self-resolve ("Lord, help us to be more loving/committed/ accepting of others . . . let us do small things with great love. . . . Help us to be midwives of the kingdom"). The insight of the Psalms in this connection concerns the reality of God and of God's involvement in the world.

---

[79]So Claus Westermann, *The Praise of God in the Psalms* (Richmond: John Knox, 1965; London: Epworth, 1966) = *Praise and Lament in the Psalms* (Atlanta: John Knox; Edinburgh: T&T Clark, 1981), 36-51.

For a book called *təhillîm* ("praises"), the Psalter starts in an odd way, not only in the declaration about paying attention to Yahweh's teaching (Ps 1) but also in the subsequent declaration concerning Yahweh's decree about his anointed (Ps 2). This latter is odd both because it is a declaration rather than an act of praise or prayer and because it is a declaration that found rather little fulfillment throughout First Testament times. It thus leads oddly but appositely into the protests that follow, beginning with Psalm 3. "Ask of me," Yahweh has invited, "and I will make nations your possession" (Ps 2:8). The succeeding psalms take up the invitation.

Protest psalms of this kind dominate the Psalter; it is another reason for wondering at the title *təhillîm*. Through the Psalter, psalms affirming Yahweh's commitment to the king and to Israel recur from time to time, but they are surrounded by or interwoven with protest psalms urging Yahweh to fulfill his commitments. Their presence in Yahweh's book constitutes an invitation to pray in the way they do and an assurance that people may do so with impunity.

The Psalms thus offer inspirational insight into God's commitment to Israel—insight that inspires worship and prayer. Indeed, they link with all four forms of insight we have considered in this chapter. They respond to the world that God created and that is the locus of God's ongoing activity. They take up God's declarations of intent and urge God to fulfill them. They take up the story of God's acts, rejoice in them and urge God to continue so to act. They take up the Torah's exposition of Yahweh's expectations and acknowledge that it is impossible to worship and pray without being people who live by this Torah.

Variety is a feature of the protest psalms that God commends. There are features that recur in them. The most common and prominent is the protest itself, which describes the trouble that assails the people who are praying, but they also incorporate some form of plea for God to listen and act, and commonly some declaration of trust and avowal of commitment. Yet as noticeable as the recurrence of such features is the variety in the way they are expressed and the variety over whether these features appear at all. While God's insight thus offers teaching on prayer and requires that people pray to the one God, within the framework of its insight it invites people to pray as they need to in their situation. The insight and inspiration do not involve a formula or a single model but a collection of illustrations.

The community and the individual have the responsibility and the freedom to work out which psalm needs praying in what circumstance. One can see this freedom being exercised in stories in Chronicles where the community takes up the invitation. The prayers of people such as Hannah, Jeremiah, Ezra, Nehemiah, Daniel, Mary and Zechariah imply the assumption that the psalms in the Psalter comprise examples to guide people in formulating their own prayers as well as prayers that they may straightforwardly follow.

One further surprising feature about the praise and prayer of the Psalms is their lack of focus on the shortcomings of the people who come to pray. In a commentary on the Psalms, sixth-century Roman writer Cassiodorus identified a group of seven "Penitential Psalms" (Pss 6; 32; 38; 51; 102; 130; 143),[80] but only one or two of them are actually penitential. There is more penitence in prayers outside the Psalter such as Ezra 9; Nehemiah 9; and Lamentations. The Psalter puts greater emphasis on the need for people to be able to claim commitment to God and to right living if they are to come to worship or pray. Their emphasis is in keeping with the Prophets' declarations that Yahweh is not interested in the worship or prayer of people who are not so committed. The Scriptures thus encourage people not to be inhibited in worship and prayer by "worm theology," while also taking seriously the question whether they are committed to a life of faithfulness to God and to others.

Doxological

In the introduction to this volume we noted that the First Testament does theology by means of praise and prayer, and the Psalter is the chief repository of that theologizing. The doxology of the Psalms has several foci. It relates to who Yahweh is in himself, as the one who is characterized by grace and mercy. It relates to his acts as creator and as the one who delivered his people when they were helpless. It relates to his acts in the personal life of Israel and of the individual. Protest psalms presuppose that God has acted

---

[80]See his *Explanation of the Psalms*, 3 vols. (repr., New York: Paulist, 1990, 1990, 1991) (it is not clear whether Cassiodorus was the first to designate them in this way).

that way and could do so again, so that their doxology challenges God to be God. Thanksgiving psalms rejoice in the fact that God has acted this way again, and they indulge in doxology for the sake of God's glory, and to encourage other people to join their doxology and thereby have their own trust in God built up against the moment when they need to call on God.

The kind of praise psalms that make no reference to my need are the purest form of doxology. They are the doxology of heaven. They make no link with my need, either a present need or one from which God has just rescued me. They do not mention me. They focus simply on God. They thus have parallel significance to that of much sacrifice in the temple. Christians customarily think that the significance of sacrifice centers on my need to find forgiveness. While this is a main focus of the New Testament's references to sacrifice, the New Testament knows that there are other significances attaching to sacrifice, and in the First Testament the link between sacrifice and sin is a minor motif. The first significance of sacrifice is that it gives concrete and costly expression to praise, and surely the purest sacrifice is the one that involves simply giving something to God for no other reason than that God is God.

While the Psalter begins as teaching and is dominated by protest, it ends in such praise. The principle implied by the attitude taken in the praise of the Psalms becomes explicit in the Mishnah, which begins with a body of teaching on Blessings (that is, Praises), among which is the provision of forms of praise for anyone who sees something remarkable such as a shooting star or an earthquake or a flash of lightning, but also in connection with more everyday things and even in connection with bad things that happen.[81] Everything created by God is to be received with thanksgiving; it is then sanctified by God's word and prayer (1 Tim 4:4-5).

Except for Revelation and some of Paul's letters, the Psalter is the most densely packed theological tractate in the Scriptures. Paul himself noticeably falls into doxology when he has been involved in dense theological exposition (notably, Rom 11:33-36; 16:25-27), and Revelation falls into doxology as a way of doing theology (e.g., Rev 4–5), while Ephesians and 1 Peter start with such doxology. Doxology is a (maybe "the") natural way to do theology.

---

[81]Mishnah Berakoth 9; cf. N. T. Wright, *Paul and the Faithfulness of God* (London: SPCK; Minneapolis: Fortress, 2013), 411.

"Prayerful reflection on God, God's ways, God's work, God's purpose, and ultimately God's faithfulness" is "that task we loosely call 'theology.'"[82] How could one expatiate on the person of the great God in blank and impassive fashion, rather than being involved in and drawn into worship?

Actually biblical and theological study has managed to do so for quite a while. For Augustine, in contrast, autobiography naturally took the form of doxology. *Confession* means relating how God has been involved in my life. Acknowledging my waywardness rather than thinking that I can do something for God discourages pride and encourages doxology. Augustine's framework of spirituality and thinking is rather like that of the Psalms, where talk about my personal needs and talk about God's greatness and love interweave. For Luther and Calvin, thinking and worship, biblical study and commitment to God, belong together in an intuitive rather than a calculated fashion. In the context of the Enlightenment, mind and spirit came to operate as separate realms, and holding them together remains an act of will rather than a natural instinct.

2.6 DIVERSE

One might have thought that the Scriptures would offer straightforward and unequivocal answers to questions, answers that would immediately win the assent of readers. They do not do so, partly because most serious questions are complex, mysterious and unamenable to straight answers. Biblical faith involves not having answers to all questions but having the central clues that enable one to live with questions and to trust God over questions to which we do not have the answers. In addition, the Scriptures are often impolite, coarse and aggressive. They are culturally rooted; but they also speak beyond their context.

Multihued

Jesus urges people to choose between a road leading to destruction and one leading to life, to choose between two masters (Mt 6:24; 7:13-14). He follows the teaching of Proverbs, which urges people to choose between two mutually exclusive ways of life (e.g., Prov 4:14; 15:19). Deuteronomy lays before people life and death, blessing and curse. John's Gospel sees things in black

---

[82]Wright, *Paul and the Faithfulness of God*, 403 (the first quotation is in italics).

and white: light over against darkness, the world below over against the world above, belief over against unbelief. You are either in or out. Revelation closes by emphasizing that its prophecy needs to be taken really seriously, without adding anything or taking anything away (Rev 22:18-19).

Yet elsewhere Jesus and the scriptural writers make clear that things are more complicated than one pithy statement may imply. The Scriptures let their antitheses deconstruct. In Joshua, is a Canaanite like Rahab in or out, is an Israelite like Akan in or out? In John's Gospel, is Nicodemus in or out? Is Peter in or out? Let alone, is Judas in or out? Are Jews good or bad, in or out? Jesus is the only way to God (Jn 14:6); but the mind/message enlightens everyone (Jn 1:9). Jesus does not pray for the world (Jn 17:9); but love for the world was what made God send Jesus (Jn 3:16).[83] Scriptures that see things in terms of black and white, of in and out, voice something important in cultural contexts that are not inclined to perceive things that way, and something important for people who are not inclined to see them that way. Scriptures that see things as less black and white, less in and out, voice something important that complements and is complemented by the other sort of Scriptures, and something important to the opposite sort of context and for the opposite sort of people.

As God's insight expresses itself in the Scriptures in a number of forms, so its content is also multicolored. Jesus is servant, king, priest, prophet, savior, master, martyr, redeemer, teacher, shepherd, "Son of man." The New Testament needs these varied images because his role or position is too complex and rich for one or two images to convey it. Letting himself be killed was a sacrifice that cleansed people, a battle that robbed their enemy of his power, a price he paid that freed them from bondage, an offering that compensated for their wrongdoing. The New Testament points both to the propriety of baptizing people who have made their own confession of Jesus as Lord, and to the propriety of baptizing children on the basis of their being members of a family within the covenant. It declares that we come to count among the faithful simply on the basis of our trusting in Jesus and not on

---

[83]Cf. Miroslav Volf, "Johannine Dualism and Contemporary Pluralism," in Richard Bauckham and Carl Mosser, eds., *The Gospel of John and Christian Theology* (Grand Rapids and Cambridge, UK: Eerdmans, 2008), 19-50 (on 21) = Volf, *Captive to the Word of God* (Grand Rapids and Cambridge, UK: Eerdmans, 2010), 94.

the basis of what we do, and that we come to count among the faithful on the basis of what we do and not simply on the basis of our trusting in Jesus; and it supports both these declarations by adding, "You only have to look at the example of Abraham to see that" (Rom 4; Jas 2).

In the First Testament, there is a difference between Proverbs on one hand and Job and Ecclesiastes on the other.[84] The two halves of the book of Daniel take different stances on a series of key questions: the first half portrays God involved with his people in the dispersion, active in the world now, implementing his reign, engaged in political events and enabling his servants to be active in politics, whereas the second half focuses on Jerusalem and portrays God not active in the world or implementing his reign or engaged in political events, while his servants' role is to help their people understand what is going on and to stay faithful.[85] Some First Testament writings emphasize the offering of costly worship to God and put less emphasis on caring for the needy, while other parts have the reverse emphasis. Sometimes different works take different stances because of the contrasting nature of the situations of the people to whom they write, sometimes because they thereby witness forcefully to their individual point.

Eventually "unity of doctrine was assured by the canon and not by some normative system of dogmatics. But that means this unity is *only a relative one*. . . . The canon reflects a multiplicity of conceptions of Christian faith."[86] It also reflects the complexity of truth itself; and it means that the canon does not imply a simple unity of doctrine. It opens up vistas, though it also sets boundaries. The inclusion of many of the other apocalypses and gospels that we know would change its nature.

Uncouth

The Scriptures can be coarse. While God's message may taste nice (Ezek 3:1-3), it goes sour inside you (Rev 10:9-11). Often it does not even taste nice. The Prophets are nasty about their people, about leaders, about women, about other nations. Jesus calls his people's leaders a bunch of snakes (Mt 23:33), says that one of his disciples is a devil (Jn 6:10) and calls another "Satan" (Mk 8:33). The Gospels speak of Satan entering into Judas (Lk 22:3; Jn 13:27),

---

[84]See the paragraphs headed "Insight Written into How Life Works" in section 2.1 above.
[85]See John Goldingay, *Daniel* (Dallas: Word, 1989), 329-34.
[86]Bultmann, *Theology of the New Testament*, 2:141.

and Peter speaks of Satan having entered the heart of Ananias (Acts 5:3). First John 3:10 says that people who do not do right or do not love their brother are the children of the devil. Paul describes his fellow Jews as always heaping up their sins to the limit (1 Thess 2:16) and tells Elymas he is a son of the devil (Acts 13:10).

Revelation speaks of a group of people "who say they are Jews but are not" and describes them as "a synagogue of Satan" (Rev 2:9; 3:9). John portrays Jesus as calling the Jews the offspring of the devil (Jn 8:31-59).[87] While such language seemed okay to John and to the churches that accepted John (while not accepting many other gospels) and has seemed okay to countless generations of followers of Jesus, it has become a problem in the West over recent decades as anti-Judaic or anti-Semitic.

Calling Jews the devil's offspring has indeed been used to justify Nazi attitudes, but then the Scriptures have been used to justify all sorts of attitudes—slavery and abolition, democracy and autocracy, genocide and pacifism.[88] There are many possible ways of "excusing" New Testament writers from their anti-Judaism. They are themselves Jewish writers, and their works reflect a conflict within Judaism, not one in which Judaism and Christianity are two separate religions. In John's Gospel, Jesus and his disciples are among "the Jews," and they are sometimes described thus. The Jews to whom Jesus and the Gospel show hostility are the Jewish leaders of the day, the people who are trying to kill Jesus, not Jews in general.

The New Testament writers might in this sense be described as anti-Jewish but not anti-Israel,[89] and the polemic in Paul, Acts, Matthew and John is part of a dispute within Judaism about who counts as Israel. It involves sibling rivalry, prophetic critique and un-Western bluntness.[90] One can also compare Hosea's anti-Ephraimite stance or Jeremiah's anti-Judahite stance, especially in their context of a battle about what it really meant to be Israel—

---

[87]On anti-Judaism in John, see, e.g., the essays in Bauckham and Mosser, *Gospel of John and Christian Theology*, 143-208; R. Bieringer et al., eds., *Anti-Judaism and the Fourth Gospel* (Assen: Van Gorcum, 2001); Luke T. Johnson, "The New Testament's Anti-Jewish Slander and the Conventions of Ancient Polemic," *JBL* 108 (1989): 419-41; Adele Reinhartz, "The Gospel of John," in Paula Fredriksen and Adele Reinhartz, eds., *Jesus, Judaism, and Christian Anti-Judaism* (Louisville: Westminster John Knox, 2002), 99-116.
[88]Examples in Bieringer et al., *Anti-Judaism and the Fourth Gospel*, 16.
[89]See Dunn, *Partings of the Ways*, 145.
[90]Ibid., 161.

about whether being Israel involved worshiping only Yahweh. Indeed, from time to time the Scriptures are anti-lots-of-people: Canaanites, Philistines, Assyrians, Babylonians, Edomites, Moabites, Romans . . .

John's "anti-Judaism" may reflect a context after the fall of Jerusalem when much of Judaism was needing to think through its own nature and was doing so by defining itself more sharply. In effect rabbinic Judaism set itself forward as the only valid Judaism, and this mainstream Judaism thereby denied Jews who believed in Jesus the right to see themselves as part of the Jewish community.[91] John's description of Jesus' interaction with his fellow Jews thus reflects interaction between his congregation and the Jews of his day. While in principle this perspective may well be right, as each Gospel tells the story in a way that interacts with its context, it is hazardous to make this idea too privileged a key to the Gospel's interpretation.[92] It opens up possibilities with regard to the identification of the Jews in John, but it is impossible to know which of the many possibilities is right.

Confrontational

The coarseness and uncouthness of God and of the Scriptures draws attention to the culture-relative nature of some of our assumptions concerning the kind of person God must be and the kind of speech God must approve. The Scriptures assume that we should be able to be straight without being violent, as do other writers in their world. The Qumran documents, too, refer to other groups as comprising men of the pit or of sin or of Belial. "The slander of the NT is typical of that found among rival claimants to a philosophical tradition and is found as widely among Jews as among other Hellenists. . . . The way the NT talks about Jews is just about the way all opponents talked about each other back then."[93]

What responsibility does the New Testament carry for the way its language has been open to being used in an anti-Jewish and anti-Semitic way? The question also arises concerning the use of the Scriptures to justify war, slavery and the oppression of women. Why didn't God inspire books that

---

[91]Cf. James D. G. Dunn, "Let John Be John," in Dunn, *The Christ and the Spirit* (Edinburgh: T&T Clark; Grand Rapids: Eerdmans, 1998), 1:345-75 (on 370-72).

[92]Reinhartz, "Gospel of John," 114-15.

[93]Johnson, "New Testament's Anti-Jewish Slander," 429; he goes on to provide the evidence for the statements.

couldn't be used that way? Perhaps their capacity to be misleading is the
price of effectiveness in their original context. Perhaps the question underestimates our human capacity to pervert anything at all that God inspires.
One might ask why God did not include in the Scriptures either a statement
that explicitly said "Do baptize babies" or one that explicitly said "Whatever
you do, don't baptize babies," but if God had done so, I am sure we would
have found ways of reinterpreting the instruction.

Much contemporary discussion simply presupposes that anti-Judaism
would be wrong and in conflict with the central message of the Scriptures,
the message of love, and that it is thus part of the fallibility of the Scriptures.[94]
At such points the Bible is "found wanting with regard to central
ethical values."[95]

There are a number of assumptions here. They include the conviction that
love is the central message of the Scriptures, that someone who is loving
cannot also hate, and that a modern assessment of what is right has priority
over the Scriptures' assessment of what is right, as well as the assumption
that a writer such as John is exclusivist and implies that the church replaces
Judaism as God's people, that this view is wrong, and that John's anti-Judaism
bears part of the responsibility for anti-Semitism.

Suppose we turn such assumptions on their head on the basis of the
possibility that the "central ethical values" of our contemporary world
might be fallible? The question then becomes, in what way does the anti-
Judaism of the New Testament give us something to think about and challenge our values? Modern people are inclined to want Jesus to have been
"the only modern man who lived in the ancient world" and one who thus
didn't share ancient views and assumptions that are often disliked in the
Western world.[96] The Scriptures confront our assumption that our Western
views must be right—including our relativism and our politeness. They declare that God indeed has one way of achieving the world's salvation but
that everyone is invited to walk this way. If we are to relate Christian anti-
Semitism to the Scriptures, perhaps it issues from "Christian theology's

---

[94]E.g., Roger Burggraeve and Marc Vervenne, eds., *Swords into Plowshares* (Louvain: Peeters;
Grand Rapids: Eerdmans, 1991).
[95]Bieringer et al., *Anti-Judaism and the Fourth Gospel*, ix.
[96]E. P. Sanders, "Jesus, Anti-Judaism, and Modern Christianity," in Fredricksen and Reinhartz,
Jesus, Judaism, and Christian Anti-Judaism, 31-55 (on 34).

perverse incomprehension of Paul's vision for eschatological reconciliation, a vision that seeks . . . to embrace Jews and Gentiles alike within the scope of God's unfathomable mercy."[97]

If the attitude toward the Jews in John is one of "pain and . . . anger"[98] arising from the way people who believe in Jesus have been persecuted and eventually expelled by the synagogue authorities, then the Gospel is behaving in a way analogous to the way the Psalms behave toward attackers. John's community is no more a group able or desiring to persecute its enemies than the psalmists are. It is a powerless people crying out, not a powerful people inciting a rampage. While it is an exaggeration to say that the Scriptures lack an "ethic for enemies,"[99] the Psalms and John, at least, do think that both punishment and forgiveness are mainly God's business, not ours.

Time-Transcending

The Scriptures reflect a body and a process of interpretation whereby the significance of God's speech is continually discerned for new contexts. This process happens (for instance) between Exodus, Leviticus and Deuteronomy, between Kings and Chronicles, within Isaiah, between the First Testament and the New Testament, between the Gospels, and between the Epistles. It indicates that God's speech is both time-rooted and time-transcending (the term *timeless* is less illuminating).

The process whereby we understand God's speech is also time-rooted and time-transcending. My understanding reflects who I am in my context, which is both its strength and its limitation. Understanding may also be time-transcending. Through the Scriptures God enables us to see things that we would not otherwise have seen, things that may not correspond to the Scriptures' inherent meaning but that we see only through them. We owe it to ourselves and to God to seek to discern what other people have been able to see in these Scriptures because of the context in which those people lived and what God has enabled other people to see through these Scriptures.

The Scriptures "must be read . . . under the guidance of the Spirit as a witness to the gospel." They thus become "a metaphor, a vast trope that signifies and illuminates the gospel of Jesus Christ." Meaning is "not so much

---

[97] Hays, *Echoes of Scripture in the Letters of Paul*, x.
[98] Ashton, *Understanding the Fourth Gospel*, 293 (2nd ed., 196).
[99] See Donald W. Shriver, *An Ethic for Enemies* (New York: Oxford University Press, 1995).

like a relic excavated from an ancient text as it is like a spark struck by the shovel hitting rock. Consequently, for Paul, original intention is not a primary concern." Yet in reading the Scriptures primarily as narrative and promise rather than as rules, "Paul can hardly be accused of imposing his own conceptions on the earlier tradition." "No longer can we think of meaning as something contained by a text; texts have meaning only as they are read and used by communities of readers."[100] To put it in the terms Paul uses when he reminds Timothy of his relationship to the First Testament Scriptures (2 Tim 3:14-17), these Scriptures that come from before Jesus' day have had an extraordinary capacity to instruct him about the faith in Jesus that brought him salvation, a capacity that issues from the fact that they were and are "God-breathed."

One can overstate the point about the Scriptures' capacity to speak independently of their original context, or underestimate it, or oversimplify it. There is a difference between what Paul does with Exodus 34 in 2 Corinthians 3, what he does with Genesis 12 in Galatians 3 and what he does with Genesis 15 in Romans 4. In each letter his shovel hits the rock and sparks fly. To put it more theologically, each piece of interpretation is Spirit inspired. In each case he moves from the present to the text. But with 2 Corinthians 3 he could hardly hit the rock again and see the same spark fly; the experiment is unrepeatable. His insight is a right-brain one. In Galatians 3 he assumes that God's speaking to Abraham needs to be understood in light of the experience of the Spirit by believers, and it is on this basis that he finds a reference to the Spirit in Genesis 12. Genesis refers to progeny and land; Paul "translates" these into the gift of the Spirit. "The fulfillment precedes the promise, hermeneutically speaking."[101] In Romans 4 his interpretation perhaps had a left-brain origin; his argument is more exegetical, and it can be discussed on left-brain terms. Indeed, it needs to be open to such validation if it is to be convincing.

That fact links with a more general point. The individual Scriptures came into being as a result of an act of communication between God and people in which the words' inherent meaning in the context was important, but they then became Scriptures because they also spoke beyond their original

---

[100]Hays, *Echoes of Scripture in the Letters of Paul*, 149, 155-56, 157.
[101]Ibid., 109.

context. It would be weird, irresponsible and risky if we treated them as merely historical documents, but also weird, irresponsible and risky if we abandoned interest in what they meant as acts of communication between God and people in their original context. For this reason it is wiser to speak of their having an inherent *meaning* that links with their origin in an act of communication, but of their having vast potential for *significance* outside that context as they are read and used.

That reference to Paul's description of the Scriptures as God-breathed draws attention to the fact we noted at the beginning of this chapter. The chapter has been handling the ideas that appear in doctrinal talk of inspiration, authority, canon, inerrancy, revelation and word of God.[102] The inspiration of the Scriptures as the word of God signifies that they have the power to effect God's purpose and have that capacity to speak beyond the context in which they were uttered. It does not indicate whether or not they are factually inerrant, and the nature of the scriptural narratives makes clear that factual inerrancy or consistency is not a priority for them, though broad factuality is important to them. Their canonical authority signifies that they are our key resource and norm for our thinking because they alone can tell us what God was doing in the story of Israel and the story of Jesus. As the written expression of God's revelation to his prophets, they tell us what God intends to do in bringing his purpose to completion.

---

[102]See further John Goldingay, *Models for Scripture* (Grand Rapids: Eerdmans; Carlisle, UK: Paternoster, 1994).

3

GOD'S CREATION

✝

While the Scriptures focus on God's participation in the story of Israel and the story of Jesus, both Testaments set this participation in the context of God's involvement with the cosmos and with humanity as a whole, and they speak about the nature of the cosmos (section 3.1), of the human world and of human life as a whole (sections 3.2-5), and of the way things have gone wrong with humanity and with the world (section 3.6). God's involvement with creation is a presupposition of the link the Scriptures see between the insight expressed in the story of Israel and of Jesus and the insight expressed in the creation of the world itself, and between the message embodied in that story and the message embodied in creation.

In English, *creation* can refer both to the world as it now exists and to the act that brought it into being. The ambiguity has advantages and disadvantages. It is important that *creation* denotes more than something that happened a long time ago. The Hebrew verb translated "create" (*bārā'*) also has a dual reference, though a different one. It denotes a sovereign act of God at the Beginning, though it does not denote creativity, nor does it refer to continuing creation or continuous creation. Its second application is to sovereign acts of God in Israel's life (e.g., Is 41:20; 45:7-8): "Israel's reflections on God's creative power are continually made in a context of suffering and defeat."[1] As the original creation was an act of sovereignty, so in new acts of

---

[1] Brevard S. Childs, *Old Testament Theology in a Canonical Context* (London: SCM Press, 1985; Philadelphia: Fortress, 1986), 33.

sovereignty God continues to act as creator.[2] At the same time, the Scriptures do emphasize that creation indeed happened "in the beginning." It is not just an ongoing activity of God but something that took place once. Creation does need to be related to what followed—the story of Israel, the coming of Jesus and the End; they need to be understood in light of creation as their foundation.[3]

World, too, is a complicated word, as are its Hebrew and Greek equivalents. They can refer to the entire good earth as a whole, human and nonhuman. They can refer to humanity as a whole as the object of God's care and as destined to acknowledge God. They can also refer to the systematized structure of power that resists God and attempts to control humanity.

3.1 THE HEAVENS AND THE EARTH

"In the beginning God created the heavens and the earth" (Gen 1:1). "The heavens are yours, the earth also is yours," because you established them and created them (Ps 89:11-12 [MT 12-13]). It is hardly right to say that really "the doctrine of creation means anthropology—the doctrine of man."[4] The doctrine of creation makes affirmations about God's relationship with the world and reminds us that there is more to God's creation than us.

God is one who gave the world its order, light, life, beauty and goodness. His creative action was an assertion of sovereignty, and he continues to be active in the world in sustaining it. Yet it also has its ambiguities and it seems not to be a completed project. Further, its goodness is compromised by the activity within it of other, created supernatural beings, who may be the agents of God's action in the world but may also work against God's designs. Satan or Leviathan is the great embodiment of such resistance to God.

Order, Goodness, Beauty
The creation as a whole is like a building that God designed and constructed. It is indeed a cosmos, a whole whose parts fit together (see Gen 1). It is securely founded (Job 38; Ps 24). It works ecologically and in a way that shows it is not centered on humanity (Job 38; Ps 104). God built it as a home. It's

---

[2]Cf. Otto Weber, *Foundations of Dogmatics* (Grand Rapids: Eerdmans, 1981), 1:463-507.
[3]Cf. Francis Watson, *Text and Truth* (Edinburgh: T&T Clark; Grand Rapids: Eerdmans, 1997), 225-75.
[4]So Barth, *CD* III, 2:3.

like a tent for living in (Is 40:22). More specifically, God lives in the heavens, from where he can administer things on earth and keep an eye on earthly events (1 Kings 8:30; Pss 2:4; 11:4; 104). Of course the heavens and the earth cannot contain Yahweh (1 Kings 8:27), any more than my home can contain me. But they can be a place where Yahweh is at home.

As its builder, God is in a position to decide how the world works and to ensure its security and stability. The world's order includes the structuring of night and day, of stars and planets and sun and moon. These establishments undergird the seven-day week and lunar month, and also the annual cycle of seasons and festivals. The order includes the grouping of plants and animate life into species that reproduce themselves; pomegranate seeds produce pomegranates, lambs give birth to lambs.

How do they do so? It's been said that the New Testament "offers no ideas about the beginning of creation, about the creation of the world and humankind,"[5] but actually a passage such as the opening of John's Gospel makes some significant statements about these matters. It declares that everything came into being through God's mind/message, and that what came into being through him was life, which was then the light of humanity (Jn 1:2-4). Thus what God created was good (Gen 1). Whereas certain false teachers reject marriage and some kinds of food, in reality everything God created is good, and is to be accepted with thanksgiving (1 Tim 4:3-5). The earth is the Lord's and everything in it (Ps 24:1); therefore in principle anything in it can be eaten, though God may set limits to our freedom in that connection (as he did for Israel) and though we are called to eat and drink for God's glory and for other people's upbuilding rather than for their fall (1 Cor 10:25-26, 31-32).

The goodness of the world includes its beauty. The word for "good" in Genesis 1 (*ṭôb*) is often used to describe someone who is "lovely" (e.g., Gen 24:16; 26:7), and it wouldn't be surprising if that connotation applies in Genesis 1. The more explicit word for "beautiful" (*yāpeh*) comes most frequently in the Song of Songs (e.g., Song 1:8, 15, 16), which systematically mines the potential of the natural world in its beauty in order to convey the beauty of the man and the woman who appear in the

---

[5]Karl Löning and Erich Zenger, *To Begin with, God Created* . . . (Collegeville, MN: Liturgical, 2000), 45.

poems. Elsewhere, the First Testament speaks of the beauty of trees and their fruit, of animals and of jewelry (2 Chron 3:6; Is 4:2; Jer 11:16; 46:20; Ezek 31:3).

In confronting people who opposed the idea that God was really the creator, Irenaeus declared: "While human beings, indeed, cannot make anything out of nothing, but only out of matter already existing, yet God is in this point pre-eminently superior to human beings, in that he himself called into being the substance of his creation, when previously it had no existence."[6] Although the idea of creation out of nothing is not one that would interest the authors of Genesis, in the context of debates in Irenaeus's day it was an appropriate articulation of something implicit in biblical faith. It enunciates an implication of the declarations that "what is seen did not come into being through what was visible" (Heb 11:3) and that God is "the one who stretched out the northern sky over the waste, suspended earth over nothingness" (Job 26:7).[7]

Such affirmations are as near as the Scriptures themselves come to the idea that God created the world out of nothing rather than by shaping it out of already-existent raw materials. If one had asked the authors of Genesis who made the raw materials that God used, they would surely affirm that God did so, but they were more interested in the fact that God made something orderly out of materials that would otherwise have lacked shape or purpose or coherence. "What fascinates the biblical narrators about creation is not that there is something there that was not there earlier, but that something new is underway that was not there—nor could have been—before the creation."[8] It is God's capacity to do something creative when things look out of order that makes creation good news. That fact links with the way Isaiah 40–55 speaks in terms of creation when it promises the coming great act whereby God will restore Israel.

God's Assertion of Sovereignty at Creation

There was a serendipitous aspect to the process of creation whereby God tried things out to see whether they worked and then acted to make up

---

[6] *Against Heresies* II.10.4.
[7] Cf. Barth, *CD* III, 2:152; he notes that the creation of nothing first appears in 2 Maccabees 7:28, "God did not make [the things in heaven and earth] out of things that existed."
[8] Löning and Zenger, *To Begin with*, 10.

for the shortfall when they didn't (Gen 2). This aspect to God's creative activity matches nicely the scientific account whereby species came into existence and mutated into other species in an experimental fashion that involved the survival of the fittest. It also matches the way the Scriptures describe events following one another in history in a way that doesn't look planned. Yet the Scriptures can also describe God undertaking the work of creation in a carefully organized fashion (Gen 1), which suggests planning and forethought. God used his insight in creating the cosmos (Prov 3:19-20; 8:22-31): "Wisdom began as the inventive design in God's imagination that initiated the process of creation."[9] Yet wisdom or insight also work by trying out possibilities, thinking about how they turn out, abandoning some experiments, and making new plans in light of experience and reflection, and the Scriptures suggest that God's insight can work in this way, too.

If there are monsters in the world, they are not invaders from some other galaxy breaking into God's worlds but beings created by God. It is in such a connection that Genesis 1:21 uses the verb *bārā'* for the first time since the opening of the chapter. The usage links with the fact that this verb carries as much the resonances of sovereign power as those of creative activity. There is no prospect of any alien monsters making serious inroads into God's world; God turns Leviathan into a pet dolphin (Ps 104:26). Yahweh's rhetorical questions about who can control Leviathan or Behemot (Job 40–41) require no answer.

So creation was a moment when God asserted sovereignty.

Yahweh began to reign, he put on majesty;
  Yahweh put on, girded on might.
Yes, the world stands firm, it does not collapse;
  your throne is standing firm since long ago—you are from of old.
Rivers lifted up, Yahweh, rivers lifted up their voice,
  rivers lift up their crushing.
Above the voices of many waters, majestic, the sea's breakers,
  Yahweh was majestic, on high. (Ps 93:1-4)

---

[9]Leslie C. Allen, *A Theological Approach to the Old Testament* (Eugene, OR: Wipf and Stock, 2014), 33.

Creation was the beginning of God's reign. Beneath the world's smooth surface are tumultuous forces that could seem to threaten its stability, forces that find expression in earthquakes, volcanoes and tsunamis. God asserted sovereignty over such forces in creating the world. While they may assert themselves again, they will not finally succeed. "Yahweh took his seat over the flood, and Yahweh took his seat as king forever" (Ps 29:10). This assertion of authority happened as Yahweh's voice thundered over the mighty waters, a voice powerful and majestic (Ps 29:3-4).

It is by speaking that one exercises authority. The director says, "Light," and there is light. Parents name their baby, and they determine how the child will be known. Grandparents bequeath part of their estate to their grandchild, and the blessing comes to the child. A president says, "There is to be a project to put a man on the moon," and there is. A centurion tells a soldier to go, and he goes. It was by speaking in these ways that God created the cosmos (Gen 1).

Creation can also be described as the result of a birthing process (Ps 90:2); God is the mother of creation. Its coming into being is mysteriously wonderful, though it involved labor. Yahweh's establishing his authority in the world was easy in one sense; other forces had no hope of successfully resisting Yahweh. Yet it involved effort and the overcoming of the pathetic defiance of resistant forces (Pss 74; 89). But as a result the cosmos is indeed secure.

Providence

Israel knew that the cosmos does not always appear secure. The security of Israel's own world could be imperiled by invaders (e.g., Pss 46; 124). But the world stands firm (Job 26:10-13; 38:8-11). We need not worry about its security, though perhaps we should worry about our vandalizing or despoiling it, not least because the builder himself could claim the right to demolish it. He once nearly exercised that right (see Gen 6–8). He then said he wouldn't ever do so again, but we would be unwise to assume that we can therefore do as we like. Maybe God won't ever destroy the world, but won't necessarily stop us doing so.

The good world that God created has not lost its goodness. It's still alive and alight. Look at the birds in the heavens, which God feeds, or look at the wild flowers with which God clothes the countryside (Mt 6:26-30). In other words, God did not merely set the world going like someone winding up a clock and then leaving it to get on with its work. God makes springs gush, waters the earth from his penthouse suite, makes things grow for animals and human beings, arouses the sun in the morning and retires it in the evening, gives life and terminates life, causes earthquakes and ignites volcanoes (Ps 104).

So the power and goodness shown in the once-for-all creation continue in God's keeping the world in being and exercising sovereignty over it. Creation is "gift and blessing."[10] God rested, but God works (Jn 5:17). The word *providence* usefully covers these two forms of involvement, sustaining and governing.[11] It suggests the provision of what we need and the experience of things working out in our lives in ways we could not have arranged. It denotes

> the almighty and ever present power of God by which God upholds, as with his hand, heaven and earth and all creatures, and so rules them that leaf and blade, rain and drought, fruitful and lean years, food and drink, health and sickness, prosperity and poverty—all things, in fact, come to us not by chance but by his fatherly hand.[12]

The appropriate responses to God's providence, then, are trust, obedience and petition.[13]

We have noted that God exercises his kingly sovereignty in historical events in a variegated fashion.[14] The Scriptures suggest a parallel point about his sovereignty in nature and human experience. They make strong affirmations about this sovereignty that justify the Heidelberg Catechism's statements, just quoted. God not only gives life but terminates life (Ps 104:29-30). The earth literally includes the realm where we end up when we die, whether our resting place is a rock-hewn tomb or a grave dug in the ground. As the underworld, the earth is thus also the abode of the dead, Sheol. Darkness

---

[10]James W. McClendon, *Systematic Theology: Doctrine* (Nashville: Abingdon, 1994), 148.

[11]See, e.g., G. C. Berkouwer, *The Providence of God* (Grand Rapids: Eerdmans, 1952), 57-134.

[12]Answer 27 in the Heidelberg Catechism of 1563, in the English version approved in 2011 by the Synod of the Christian Reformed Church in North America, www.crcna.org/welcome/beliefs /confessions/heidelberg-catechism.

[13]Barth, *CD* III, 3:246.

[14]See the comments on God's sovereignty in section 1.2 above.

and silence are its characteristics. We are safe and secure there, as God keeps an eye on us and no other power rules there. But pending resurrection day, God is not normally active there (e.g., Pss 6:5 [MT 6]; 30:9 [MT 10]; 88:10-12 [MT 11-13]).

We have noted, further, that the Scriptures sometimes say that God caused famine or infertility or sickness, but on other occasions that these things simply happen. They thereby again suggest that the sovereignty of God operates in different ways or to different ends in different contexts.[15] Providence works out in varying ways, in varying relationships with the exercise of human freedom and of creation's freedom.

Ambiguity and Incompleteness

As well as providing the cosmos with order and predictability, God is sovereign in relation to its unpredictable events. On one hand, he can cause them. He didn't make the cosmos such an ordered place that it has no room for his making it do surprising and alarming things or for its doing such things on its own initiative. On the other hand, he is in a position to set limits to its volatility. There is indeed a unity about it that makes it a cosmos. In its order and its volatility it manifests his greatness, his commitment and his sovereignty (e.g., Job 38–41; Pss 19; 29; 36; 104). It expresses his generosity; we can share in the world because God invites us to, though we cannot behave as if we own it.

God's relationship with the world means not only that creation can help us understand God's dealings with us but also that the heavens and the earth can give God their worship (e.g., Ps 148). It means we can pray for material blessing (e.g., Ps 67), though only if we recognize the link between such blessing and a commitment to *ṣǝdāqâ ûmišpāṭ*—to faithfulness in the way we make decisions—because *ṣǝdāqâ ûmišpāṭ* are key characteristics of God himself that are embodied in creation.[16] "By Yahweh's word the heavens were made"; and "Yahweh's word is upright and his every act is done in trustworthiness." So the created world is an embodiment of that uprightness and trustworthiness; and "the earth is full of Yahweh's commitment [*ḥesed*]" (Ps 33:4-6).

---

[15]Again, see the comments on God's sovereignty in section 1.2 above.
[16]See further *OTT* 2:647-709.

Arguably, the result of the process whereby the world came into being looks too extraordinary to be simply the product of time plus chance. In many respects it looks like the result of planning (Is 40:12-14; Job 28). Some scientists can therefore argue that it looks like something designed by someone. Yet paradoxically, the goodness of the world also includes some ambiguity. The world as God created it, rules it and manages it is full of surprises, and not just nice ones. It's not what we would have made it. Thus other scientists can retort that there's as much evidence that works against the idea that the world evidences design. Nature is a means of Yahweh's blessing people but also a means of bringing disaster. Creation issued from Yahweh's action, but from the Beginning there have been elements within the created world that have asserted themselves over against Yahweh. The creation project looks incomplete.

Indeed, the creation is still groaning and suffering labor pains (Rom 8:22). The reason is not that it was once fine but that it has become spoiled; the Scriptures do not speak of creation being fallen. It's more like a pregnant woman who hasn't yet given birth. Human beings were created in order to facilitate the creation's coming to completion as the world that God intended. They were to control it and subdue it (*kābaś*, the word for conquering a country by invasion; Gen 1:28). Paradoxically, in this way they were to serve it and care for it (Gen 2:5, 15). It's not the case that God created the world for humanity's sake;[17] we were created for its sake. But we have failed to serve it, and it has therefore not reached its destiny. In the terms of Genesis 3, instead of ruling over creation, human beings let it rule them, and the result has been ongoing tension with the animal world and laborious toil in getting things to grow. But God is committed to bringing ambiguity to resolution and the world to its destiny.

Supernatural Beings

The fact that there is only one God, Yahweh, does not preclude the existence of other gods of lower status than God, but Yahweh's deity is such that Yahweh alone can properly be described as God; other gods belong to a metaphysically different category of being.[18] In other words, actually there

---

[17]So John Calvin, *Institutes* I.14, 22: cf. T. F. Torrance, *Calvin's Doctrine of Man*, new ed. (Grand Rapids: Eerdmans, 1957), 23.

[18]See the trenchant argument in Christopher J. H. Wright, *The Mission of God* (Downers Grove, IL: InterVarsity Press; Nottingham, UK: Inter-Varsity Press, 2006), 136-88.

aren't any other real deities. In English we can make that point by distinguishing between God and the gods, which corresponds to a real distinction in the thinking of both Testaments though they cannot make the distinction typographically. Hebrew *'ĕlōhîm* and Greek *theos* cover both God and also gods (English commonly falls short of words corresponding to key Hebrew or Greek ones, such as *hesed* and *ṣədāqâ*, or *agapē*, so it's nice that things sometimes work the other way). Thus the two Testaments occasionally use expressions such as *'ĕlōhê hā'ĕlōhîm* and *kyrios tōn kyrieuontōn* ("God of gods," "Lord of lords"; e.g., Deut 1:17; 1 Tim 6:15) to safeguard the point in question.

One might locate discussion of other supernatural beings with discussion of God, but it belongs more appropriately with discussion of creation. What these other supernatural beings have in common with God fades into insignificance alongside what distinguishes them from God. They are created entities; like human beings, they come into existence, they are dependent on God for their existence, and they can die (see Ps 82). "The biblical traditions not only overcome a merely naturalistic understanding of heaven. They also resist the typically religious *divinization* of heaven and its powers. Like earth, heaven is *created*."[19] The declaration that these other beings are only gods and not God is important because there is a lot to be said for polytheism or idolatry. You can, for instance, find a god who suits you. So that assumption needs confronting.

As well as *'ĕlōhîm* and *theos*, the two Testaments have a number of other words to denote supernatural entities other than God, such as aides or angels, sons of gods, leaders and powers. In general, these beings exist in order to be the means of God implementing his will in the world. Among them are some that serve God quite faithfully. Supernatural aides appear as messengers from God in the story of Jesus' birth (Mt 1:18–2:23; Luke 1:5–2:20). The eastern philosophers arrive because they have seen Jesus' star in the east or at its rising (Mt 2:2). Here the old story of the self-assertive morning star (Is 14:4-21; Ezek 28:1-19) is turned on its head. Jesus is the Morning Star who is not eclipsed. The risen Jesus has seven stars in his hand; they are the aides overseeing the seven congregations (Rev 1:16, 20; cf. Is 40:26).

---

[19]Michael Welker, *God the Spirit* (Minneapolis: Fortress, 1994), 139.

Matthew and Luke also refer to "an angel of the Lord" (Mt 1:20-25; 2:13-20; Lk 1:11-20; 2:9-15), who is named Gabriel in Luke (Lk 1:26-38). Gabriel had already appeared in Daniel, as had Michael, who reappears in Revelation (see Dan 8:16; 9:21; 10:13, 21; 12:1; Rev 12:7; also Jude 1:9). In Matthew the angel brings messages designed to ensure in various ways that Jesus' birth happens in accordance with God's intent. In Luke he brings messages that enable Zechariah, Mary and some shepherds to understand what is happening. The angel appears to Joseph in dreams, to Zechariah when he is burning incense in the temple and to Mary in unspecified circumstances. After Jesus' birth, a crowd from the heavenly army joins the angel to praise God.

An angel of the Lord appears again at the other end of Jesus' story to strengthen him in Gethsemane (Lk 22:43)[20] and then to roll away the stone on his tomb so that the women can see he is gone and so that the angel can tell them what to do next (Mt 28:1-7). Such an angel also appears a number of times in Acts (Acts 5:19; 8:26; 10:3; 12:7, 23; 27:23) and many times in Revelation. Plural "angels" appears on many other occasions, often in connection with announcements about the End (e.g., Mk 1:13; 8:38; 13:27).

God implements his purpose in the world by means of such agents.

Rebellious Angels and a Rebellious World

Some supernatural beings avoid accepting their role as means of implementing God's intentions, and maybe others sometimes do what God wants but at other times don't. In fact, they are like human beings. Psalm 82 is a forthright expression of protest at the failure of the gods to exercise authority in a faithful way and thus to protect the poor, the vulnerable, the oppressed and the needy, and a challenge to God to do something about it. The powers that God created are in rebellion against God, though they nevertheless continue to exercise an ordering function, like human authorities.[21]

It was the rulers of this age who crucified the glorious Lord, not realizing what they were doing (1 Cor 3:8). While both Testaments thus assume that there are supernatural entities behind the human religious and political powers that are humanly responsible for such an act, neither Testament talks

---

[20]This verse is missing from some important manuscripts.
[21]Cf. John Howard Yoder, *The Politics of Jesus*, 2nd ed. (Grand Rapids: Eerdmans; Carlisle, UK: Paternoster, 1993), 140-42.

about these entities a great deal; they focus more on the human powers. The astounding story[22] of the enigmatic "great wrath" that "came on Israel" and deprived it of victory over Moab (2 Kings 3:27) suggests an awareness that the Scriptures themselves do not pretend to provide all the answers about the relationship between Yahweh and other gods;[23] Jesus can also speak allusively about wrath (Lk 21:23).

The Scriptures do assume that there is more to earthly religious powers and empires than meets the eye. The assertion that other gods exist is not simply a piece of theological theory. It offers part of the explanation for the way God's will is not implemented in the world. "The world is ruled by many powers and our experience knows no solution to the permanent struggle between them."[24] Indeed, "the visible surface of the godless world and its history . . . is covered by a thin skin, and when it bursts open, terrifying realities creep out of its uncanny depths": dragon, antichrist and antispirit, and a host of evil spirits (Rev 12–13).[25] "These powers are both earthly and heavenly, divine and human, spiritual and political, invisible and structural" (e.g., Col 1:16), though we encounter the supernatural in the earthly: "The powers are simultaneously the outer and inner aspects of one and the same individual concretion of power."[26] The embodiment of rebellious supernatural powers is a rebellious world.[27] The absolute sovereignty of God is not incompatible with God's declining simply to put down all resistance to that sovereignty.

The New Testament also refers often to demons, which hardly feature in the First Testament. This contrast is a symbol of the fact that Jesus' coming brings to a climax the conflict between God and the powers that resist him.[28]

---

[22]Cf. David Penchansky, *Twilight of the Gods* (Louisville: Westminster John Knox, 2005), 11.

[23]See the discussion of this passage in Burke O. Long, "Letting Rival Gods Be Rivals," in Henry T. C. Sun and Keith L. Eades, eds, *Problems in Biblical Theology*, Rolf Knierim Festschrift (Grand Rapids and Cambridge, UK: Eerdmans, 1997), 222-33.

[24]Ulrich Mauser, "One God Alone," *Princeton Seminary Bulletin* 12 (1991): 255-65 (on 261).

[25]Mathias Rissi, *The Future of the World* (London: SCM Press; Naperville, IL: Allenson, 1972), 11. See further Walter Wink, *Unmasking the Powers* (Philadelphia: Fortress, 1986).

[26]Walter Wink, *Naming the Powers* (Philadelphia: Fortress, 1984), 11, 107 (both quotations are in italics in the original). Wink assumes that the mixed nature of such supernatural figures as both good and demonic extends to the angels of the churches in Rev 2–3 (*Unmasking the Powers*, 69-86).

[27]See further the paragraphs under "The World" in section 3.6 below.

[28]Cf. Barth, *CD* III, 3:529-30.

"A prominent element in Paul's thinking about the nature of the old age is the conviction that it is in the grip of evil supernatural powers."[29] The significant place of these powers in Jewish writings of the period likely means Paul himself affirms their reality; he is not merely making an allusion on the basis of formal belief in them on the part of his readers and/or in the culture.[30]

Likewise, while one could ask whether the heavenly cabinet idea in Job 1–2 is "properly theology" or part of a worldview,[31] one also has to consider whether our unease about such an idea is simply part of our worldview and to consider on what basis we go with our unease. "The popular demythologizing of these powers in current theology, whereby they represent the structures of human society which oppress people, may well be a valid reinterpretation of a NT concept but it is a reinterpretation." The writer of Ephesians "himself believes the powers to be spiritual agencies in the heavenly realm standing behind any earthly or human institutions (cf. 6:12)."[32]

Yet it is indeed noteworthy that neither Testament says much about them. Paul "did believe in spiritual powers and treated the subject with immense seriousness. But the spiritual powers he focused his theological and pastoral concern on were not the 'rulers and authorities,' but the power of sin and death."[33]

Rebellious Religion

Other supernatural beings attract human worship and thus arouse God's jealousy (1 Cor 10:20-22). Another scriptural term for them is thus *idols*. They are entities that look as if they are something but are really nonentities. One consideration lying behind the exhortation to avoid being yoked with

---

[29]George Eldon Ladd, *A Theology of the New Testament* (Grand Rapids: Eerdmans, 1974), 400 (rev. ed., 440).

[30]So T. K. Abbott, *A Critical and Exegetical Commentary on the Epistles to the Ephesians and to the Colossians* (Edinburgh: T&T Clark; New York: Scribner, 1897), 32-33.

[31]Cf. Roland E. Murphy, "Reflections on a Critical Biblical Theology," in Sun and Eades, *Problems in Biblical Theology*, 265-74 (on 273).

[32]Andrew T. Lincoln, *Ephesians* (Dallas: Word, 1990), 64. See further "Liberation from the Powers," in M. Daniel Carroll R. et al., eds., *The Bible in Human Society*, John Rogerson Festschrift (Sheffield: Sheffield Academic Press, 1995), 335-54.

[33]James D. G. Dunn, *The Theology of Paul the Apostle* (Grand Rapids and Cambridge, UK: Eerdmans, 1998), 110. See chapter five below.

unbelievers (2 Cor 6:14–7:1) is the importance of avoiding idolatry,[34] which implies being yoked to those nonentities. We are bound to be yoked to something, so it had better not be the wrong thing. It is tempting to think that the supernatural entities are more significant than they are, more important even than Jesus, but God does not address them in the way he does when he is addressing the Son. They themselves are bidden to worship the Son; they are earthly means of God acting, but the Son sits on a divine throne, sits at God's right hand (Heb 1:4-14).

While humanity has an inbuilt awareness of the basic truths about God and about right and wrong, it is inclined to suppress this awareness and to devise a religion of its own. The instinct to recognize a higher power and to recognize right and wrong is too intrinsic to ignore, but humanity thus ends up with a stupid religion and an immoral morality (Rom 1:18-32). The Jewish people don't do quite the same thing, in that they are privileged to have been reminded of the truth about God and about a proper response to God, but their failure to live by that revelation means their eventual state is not so different.[35]

The New Testament is thus inclined to a negative stance in relation to other religions. Their adherents simply need to be converted. For all the multiplicity of their gods, their adherents acknowledge that they do not know what they need to know; Paul therefore tells the Athenians about something of which they are self-confessedly ignorant (Acts 17:22-23). The First Testament takes the same stance in relation to the traditional religion of Canaan because of the way it beguiles Israelites, though the attitude of Israel's ancestors to the religion of the priest-king of Salem, Melkizedeq, is characterized more by something like "ecumenical bonhomie."[36]

Yahweh inspired Israel to take up traditional expressions of worship such as sacrifices, psalmody and festivals in spring and fall, and to transform them by connecting them with the way he had delivered Israel from Egypt.

[34]See, e.g., Margaret E. Thrall, *A Critical and Exegetical Commentary on the Second Epistle to the Corinthians* (Edinburgh: T&T Clark, 1994), 1:475-76.
[35]According to James D. G. Dunn (*Theology of Paul the Apostle*, 115-19), Paul sees the Jewish people as also affected by "misdirected religion," but the critique of Rom 2:1–3:20 surely rather concerns their behavior. Circumcision and other aspects of their religion were "of great value" (Rom 3:1-2).
[36]G. J. Wenham's phrase in "The Religion of the Patriarchs," in A. R. Millard and D. J. Wiseman, eds., *Essays on the Patriarchal Narratives* (Leicester, UK: Inter-Varsity Press, 1980; Winona Lake, IN: Eisenbrauns, 1983), chap. 6.

They could thus turn them into ways of celebrating what Yahweh had done, of keeping its memory alive for them and of responding to what Yahweh had done. The downside to this strategy was that Israel was always inclined to forget the transformation and simply live by the tradition in its original significance, which related more immediately to people's everyday needs and everyday life.

The New Testament includes no parallel commission to take up traditional expressions of worship to commemorate what Jesus had done, but the church later did so in adapting festivals such as Christmas and Easter. This strategy had the same downside, and in Western culture the Christianized version of the traditional forms has disappeared. These festivals once again belong to the gods, though this need not be true of the Christian calendar as a whole.[37]

The Devil

Theologically, in a description of biblical faith there is arguably no place for the devil, or for sin: "We do not believe 'in' the devil. . . . We do believe 'against' the devil; the devil's power is real but invalid."[38] Yet the Scriptures talk about the devil and about sin, and we need a way of thinking about them. One might locate them in an appendix to a biblical theology, which puts them in their place. Yet they are interwoven with the main body of the Scriptures' own thinking.

Before Jesus' last meal with his disciples, "the devil already had in mind that Judas Iscariot, son of Simon, should betray him."[39] Jesus also knew that he had come from God, that it was time for him to leave the world and go back to God, that his dying would show the disciples the full extent of his love and that his Father had put everything into his power (Jn 13:1-3). The sovereign purpose of God is much greater than the power of the devil, and God uses that power not to stop the devil doing what he wants to do but to harness it to the divine purpose. Jesus knows that Judas will betray him before Judas himself knows; and he virtually

---

[37]See the paragraphs under "Words and Acts" in section 7.2 below.
[38]Weber, *Foundations of Dogmatics*, 1:489; cf. Nigel G. Wright, "Charismatic Interpretations of the Demonic," in Anthony N. S. Lane, ed., *The Unseen World* (Carlisle, UK: Paternoster; Grand Rapids: Baker, 1996), 149-63 (on 163).
[39]Probably not that he had already put it in *Judas's* mind (though manuscripts vary); it is later in the chapter that Satan enters Judas (Jn 13:27).

commissions Judas to do it, by giving him his special piece of bread (after which Satan enters him) and telling him to go quickly to do what he is going to do (Jn 13:21-30).

It is when Satan enters Judas and Judas goes out into the night to betray Jesus that the Man is glorified and God is glorified (Jn 13:31). Jesus will be humiliated by his death and then glorified by his resurrection, but he will also be glorified by the death, and so will the Father. Jesus' death is the climactic revelation of the Father as the God who has been paying the price for people's waywardness all through history and especially in Israel's story, and God is making use of Satan in order to bring about a revelation of himself as God. Satan is "a force hostile to God but permitted so to act by God to serve his will."[40]

The First Testament also refers to a *śāṭān*, but he does not have the profile of an entity that focuses rebellion against God. The Hebrew word denotes an ordinary military or legal adversary, and a *śāṭān* acts as a legal adversary in court-like scenes over which God presides (Job 1–2; Zech 3). There are contexts where the New Testament speaks of Satan in terms more reminiscent of these First Testament references to a *śāṭān* (e.g., Lk 22:31). Conversely, the First Testament does assume that there is a supernatural entity that is a concentration of resistance to God, an entity denoted by terms such as Leviathan (e.g., Job 41:1), Rahab (e.g., Ps 89:10 [MT 11])[41] and the serpent (e.g., Job 26:13), but not by the word *śāṭān*. It is the monster or serpent figures rather than the "adversary" that are the First Testament equivalents to Satan in the New Testament. It is suggestive that none of its terms imply a being that is human-like. There is something beastly and monstrous about this entity.

It is possible to live "in accordance with the one who rules the realm of the atmosphere, of the spirit that is at work now among disobedient people" (Eph 2:2). Genesis 3 spoke only of a this-worldly entity getting humanity to disobey God; Ephesians speaks of a supernatural entity doing so. Further, whereas Paul argues that sin rules now because something went wrong at

---

[40]Dunn, *Theology of Paul the Apostle*, 38.
[41]To be distinguished from the Rahab of Josh 2, whose name is spelled differently.

the Beginning (as Genesis implies), John adds that sin rules because "the devil lurks behind every particular sin" (Jn 8:44; 1 Jn 3:8).[42]

We have to stand firm against the devil; we struggle not against flesh and blood but against the rulers, the authorities, the world powers, the evil spiritual entities in the heavenly realm (Eph 6:11-12). There is an individual quasi-personal entity active in the heavens and on earth; his center of operations is above us, not below us, as it is often conceived.[43] Ephesians may imply that negative supernatural influences somehow come upon us from the air around us; they are in the atmosphere, as we say. The devil dominates the atmosphere of the world in which we live.

The description of him as ruling the realm of the atmosphere could avoid the idea that he rules the heavenly realm itself, though he does exercise some power there. His aim or modus operandi is to get people to live the opposite way to the one that God lays down; our struggle is a struggle to live God's way. Temptation comes to us from our own lower nature, and believers, too, have to struggle against that temptation, which is the way to death. Satan tempts us to fulfill the desires of our lower nature—to go shopping or travel or buy a bigger house or have an affair or work 24-7.

3.2 THE HUMAN COMMUNITY

While creation does not revolve around humanity, humanity has a prominent place in creation, at least on planet Earth. Humanity's own nature is corporate or communal. It involves relationality, which means that individual human beings are social beings who live in relationship with other human beings. But relationality has another aspect: individual human existence is complemented by corporate human existence, by communality or *koinōnia*. Paul's notion of the body helps express this reality. It denotes more than the fact that the parts relate to one another. It suggests that they are part of a whole that is itself a reality.

As God created it, human communality takes diverse forms in peoples and cultures. A particularly significant form of it is the village community,

---

[42]Rudolf Bultmann, *Theology of the New Testament* (repr., Waco, TX: Baylor University Press, 2007), 2:25.

[43]Cf. Markus Barth, *Ephesians* (Garden City, NY: Doubleday, 1974), 1:228-29.

which is also a context for caring for the needy and the outsider. More ambiguity attaches to the city.

Communality

A story in Numbers 20:14-21 illustrates the point about the reality of the corporate entity. Each "you" or "your" in this passage is singular. It speaks as if referring to one person.

> Moses sent envoys from Qadesh to the king of Edom: "Your brother Israel has said this. You yourself know all the hardship that has befallen us. . . . Now. We're in Qadesh, a city on the edge of your territory. May we pass through your country? We won't pass through fields or vineyards . . . until we have passed through your territory." But Edom said to him, "You're not to pass through my territory or I'll come against you with the sword to meet you." The Israelites said to him, "We'll go up by the highway. If we drink your water, I and my flocks, I'll pay for it. Come on, it's nothing. We're going to pass through on foot." But he said, "You will not pass through," and Edom went out to meet him with a substantial force, strongly armed. Edom refused to let Israel pass through his territory, and Israel turned away from him.

While part of the background to this exchange is that behind Israel and Edom stand the individuals Jacob and Esau, and representing them are the individuals Moses and the Edomite king, nevertheless the passage also implies a corporate awareness. The Israelites are a collection of individuals, but Israel is also a "he," as is Edom. That awareness compares with the fact that a city such as Los Angeles or London, a state such as California, a country such as England, or a nation such as the United States or the United Kingdom has a corporate personality and character, and also has a corporate responsibility for what it is and what it does. We could even say that the world as a whole has a corporate personality and character.

It's often said that Western people are individualist, but the point needs nuancing. Westerners are individualist and nonrelational in the sense that they may ignore other individuals and seek to be self-contained or to avoid being vulnerable to other individuals. Yet they have a harder time avoiding being part of the corporate personality of their culture. Paradoxically, indeed, precisely by being individualist they are being part of their culture. In a community such as Southern California, many Christians and others don't think community is a reality, but they are deeply shaped by their cultural community.[44]

In the decades before individualism became a pejorative term, it was sometimes customary to portray the Scriptures as evolving from a corporate view to an individual view of humanity. One way of seeing that development involved portraying it as a move from the communal nature of Israel's religion to the faith of the New Testament, which is a matter of individual choice. Another way of seeing it finds the move from corporate to individual in the prophets who promise that people will no longer have to complain that the parents have eaten sour grapes whereas it is the children who have a bad taste in their mouth; people will now pay the penalty for their own sins (Jer 31:29-30; Ezek 18). But these prophets are making a different point; they are responding to people's inclination to blame their parents for their own fate, and they are being challenged not to do so.[45]

Nowadays we might portray a development from corporate to individual as a negative evolution. In reality, throughout both Testaments God deals both with communities and with individuals. "Modernity generated two rival myths-of-origin about the I and the we. . . . According to the one the individual constructed society, according to the other society constructed the individual."[46] By nature human beings are individuals and members of larger wholes, to which they contribute and by which they are affected, whether or not they are aware of it and like it.[47]

A People and a Culture

As individual human beings are diverse in characteristics such as physical attributes and ways of thinking, so are communities. In a twenty-first-century Western context, diversity is important, at least in theory. This

---

[44]Cf. Cyril S. Rodd, *Glimpses of a Strange Land* (Edinburgh: T&T Clark, 2001), 274.

[45]See, e.g., John Barton, *Ethics in Ancient Israel* (Oxford and New York: Oxford University Press, 2014), 53-55.

[46]Oliver O'Donovan, *Finding and Seeking* (Grand Rapids and Cambridge, UK: Eerdmans, 2014), 59.

[47]See, e.g., José Ignacio González Faus, "Anthropology: The Person and the Community," in Jon Sobrino and Ignacio Ellacuría, eds., *Mysterium Liberationis* (Maryknoll, NY: Orbis, 1993), 497-521.

awareness draws our attention to "God's blessing of diversity,"[48] which begins in Genesis 1–11. The opening pages of the Scriptures tell the story of the development of culture, cities, communities and nations. The development constitutes the further unfolding of the creation process. At the same time, it reflects how the "very good" of Genesis 1:31 is compromised by human waywardness.

The Scriptures do not view human culture as inherently evil, and they accept its conventions, even while setting them within the context of the gospel and letting the gospel purge, radicalize, broaden or otherwise modify them. The culture provides the Scriptures' forms of literature, such as proverbs, dialogues and psalms. The epistles greet people in a similar way to epistles outside the Scriptures, though they modify the greeting in light of the gospel.[49] Like other cultures, the Scriptures use narrative, and their narratives use the techniques of narrative in other cultures, but they also use narrative in innovative ways in light of the nature of their message (see Genesis to Kings, the Gospels).

Cain takes up the task of serving the earth that God had given his father, and Abel adds to it the keeping of sheep. The two of them devise ways of making offerings to God. Abel's initiative works better, but with a horrifying aftermath. Condemned to wander even farther from Eden than his parents, Cain sets about building a city. A few generations later his descendants are inventing musical instruments and inventing poetry, but using poetry to boast of a revenge killing.

The other side of the flood, Noah discovers how to ferment grapes but also discovers the downside to that discovery. His sons and their descendants are the means whereby God's commission to fill the earth gets implemented. The development and spread of nations is a further outworking of that creation purpose to fill the earth, but the building of the city with a tower that will enable the builders to make a name for themselves leads to further catastrophe.

The notion of a "people" comes as close as the Scriptures do to the notion of race, but the idea of race as a way of categorizing people on the basis of physical characteristics such as skin color came into usage only in recent

---

[48]Allen, *Theological Approach to the Old Testament*, 114.
[49]Cf. Anthony C. Thiselton, *1 Corinthians* (Grand Rapids: Eerdmans, 2006), 30.

centuries. The Scriptures take for granted a world that is multiethnic and see all humanity as made in God's image. While they oppose intermarriage on religious grounds and show some awareness of ethnic prejudice, they do not oppose intermarriage on ethnic grounds. They open with God's involvement with all ethnic groups and end with a body of worshipers from every tribe, language, people and nation.[50]

The Local Community

In a society without modern communications, government policies do not have much effect at a local level. Most Israelites lived some distance from their capital and lived in their own local worlds. Although the books in the First Testament were no doubt produced in the city, and they reflect city life, the city was not the context for most people's lives. People lived in a village (or on a homestead), and their community was the village where they had their homes as they worked the farmland surrounding it.

Things were not so different in Jesus' day, though Judea and Galilee then saw more urban development. Jesus' teaching thus takes much of its imagery from the life of the farmer and the shepherd, and his concern with matters such as conflict resolution, generosity and making loans to people who have got into difficulties would be especially significant in village communities. Such communities need to be ones where people live in good relationships with one another, support one another when they get into difficulties, resolve conflicts and deal with wrongdoing.

Like the Torah, Jesus' teaching thus takes up the characteristics, potentials, hazards and challenges of community life. Relationships with one's "neighbor" were already a focus of Exodus 20–22; neighbors and friends are a focus in Proverbs (e.g., Prov 27). The Torah often refers to the fellow members of one's community as one's brothers (and sisters) (e.g., Deut 22:1-4): it encourages the community to take family obligations as the model for community obligations.[51] The Scriptures expect the community to see that its vulnerable members are looked after, and they know that the development of wholesome community life is a vital aspect of human flourishing.

---

[50]See J. Daniel Hays, *From Every People and Nation* (Downers Grove, IL: InterVarsity Press; Nottingham, UK: Inter-Varsity Press, 2003).

[51]This is less clear in gender-inclusive translations that use expressions such as "members of your community" to translate words that more literalistically denote "brothers."

In such a community, we weep with the people who weep, and we rejoice with the people who rejoice (Rom 12:15)—though the context suggests that this assumption relates to identifying with people outside the community and not just inside. The protest psalms likewise presuppose that other people join in your prayer when you are in desperate need, and the thanksgiving psalms presuppose that other people join in your rejoicing when you are delivered from that need.

One way a community makes life work is by encouraging people to behave in a way that brings them honor rather than shame because they are people of integrity, faithfulness, courage and generosity. Honor rather than shame is thus an emphasis in Proverbs (e.g., Prov 10:5; 11:16; 12:4; 13:5). One significance of the story of Job, however, is that a community can mistakenly shame people because their lives don't work out in the way one would expect if they were people of integrity. To be abandoned by God is a reason for shame, whether you deserve it or whether you do not. It is thus an element in prayer for oneself and in prayer against other people (e.g., Pss 25:1-3; 31:17 [MT 18]; 69:6-7, 19 [MT 8-9, 20]; 71:1, 13, 24; 119:6, 31, 46, 78, 80, 116).

"Seek first his sovereignty and his way of treating people right, and all these things will be given you as well," Jesus says (Mt 6:33). "All these things" comprise food, drink and clothing. Jesus doesn't want people to save up for tomorrow, but neither does he want them to go without. He doesn't preach a prosperity gospel in the sense of promising an SUV or a holiday home, but he does promise that people will have plenty in order for life to flourish. He declares that quiet, ordinary people are "blessed": they will gain possession of the country, or even the world (Mt 5:5) (but whereas translations do usually assume that the Greek word *gē* means "earth" here, it means "country" on the preceding five occasions when it appears in Matthew, and it has that meaning in the passage from which Jesus takes up these words, in Ps 37:11). One way or the other, gaining possession is an aspect of being a "blessed" community.

Here, too, Jesus' stance corresponds to the one he finds in the First Testament. People who live in awe of Yahweh by walking in his ways are "blessed" in that they enjoy the fruit of their labors, they do well, they have big families (Ps 128). God's blessing of Abraham and his family finds expression in the flourishing of Isaac's crops and herds (Gen 26:12-14), though the flourishing issues in conflict and trouble. It had already happened to Abraham and Lot (cf. Gen 13–14), and it will recur spectacularly when Jacob swindles Esau out of the "blessing" (the privileges of the firstborn that go with his responsibilities) and in his subsequent relationships (Gen 27–34). On the other hand, such blessing does give people scope for hospitality and generosity (Gen 18). Alas, paradoxically, while wisdom should issue in prosperity and influence or power, prosperity and power are then inclined to encourage stupidity (as Solomon's story vividly illustrates). Proverbs and Jesus note that people come to trust in their wealth and forget its vulnerability.

Will ordinary people gain possession of the country or the world in the sense that they will own it or rule it or enjoy it? The Scriptures subvert the notion of owning land and suggest that the human vocation is to serve it rather than rule it. The good news in the First Testament that lies in the background to Jesus' language is that gaining possession does suggest security, provision and independence (though not of God).

The Needy and the Outsider

"Two paradoxical facts intrigue and challenge the theologian": the societies of abundance (which need no hope) and the poor (who have hope).[52] On one occasion, Jesus does encourage a wealthy person to sell everything and give to the needy (Lk 18:18-25), but it is not the Scriptures' usual tack in connection with questions of wealth. Instead, they emphasize the obligation that comes with wealth: use it in a way that glorifies God and ministers to the needs of God's people, especially people who don't have resources of their own. Jesus' bidding to this particular individual reflects the fact that wealth is a trap.

One might even say that the love of money is the root of all evils, or at least of all kinds of evil (1 Tim 6:10). The Torah and the Prophets provide much evidence of this fact. Rules in the Torah try to maneuver people who have resources into using them for the benefit of the needy. Prophets protest at the way wealthy people sidestep this maneuvering. Such sidestepping no

---

[52]João Batista Libâno, "Hope, Utopia, Resurrection," in Sobrino and Ellacuría, *Mysterium Liberationis*, 716-27 (on 716) = *Systematic Theology* (Maryknoll, NY: Orbis, 1996), 279-90 (on 279).

doubt continues on the part of people such as the writer and most readers of this book, who belong to the global socioeconomic elite.[53]

While giving is one aspect of this generosity, lending is another. In Western economies, lending is a way of making more money. The Scriptures do not totally exclude such "business" lending, but they emphasize lending that earns no interest, lending that functions to help people survive when they are in trouble, on the assumption that they will be in a position to pay back the debt in due course.

Such lending can characterize relationships within a mutually supportive society. This year I lend to you, next year you lend to me. Such an approach to lending has the potential to form part of a kind of local economic system, though not one that works with the rules of Western market principles. It is an aspect of the way the Scriptures suggest an ideology that might be called relationism rather than democratic capitalism or market socialism.[54] I lend to someone in this way on the basis that he is my "brother" (e.g., Lev 25:35-37; Deut 15:7-8)—one does not charge interest within the family.

Reminders that even the poor person is "your brother" occur in connection with the way someone in debt to you may end up as your "servant." Since the Second World War, most translations have used the word *slave*, but KJV's *servant* is more appropriate: an ʿ*ebed* is not someone who is the property of a master. He or she is a family servant like the man whom Abraham commissions to find a wife for Isaac, or a temporary bondservant or indentured servant like the Englishmen who paid for their passage to the Americas on this basis. The Torah thus allows for a man who gets into insoluble economic difficulties to pay his debts by undertaking a limited term of such service.

This form of servitude could function as a safety net for people who get into difficulties and could enable them to get a fresh start if they are duly released at the end of their six years' service. The regulations about release of land (the "jubilee"), too, are designed to enable people to make a new start. They have a social angle (a concern to undergird households and families), an economic angle (a concern to undergird the way land is distributed

---

[53]Cf. Craig L. Blomberg, *Neither Poverty nor Riches* (Downers Grove, IL: InterVarsity Press; Leicester, UK: Inter-Varsity Press, 2000), 11.

[54]Michael Schluter and John Ashcroft, eds., *Jubilee Manifesto* (Leicester, UK: Inter-Varsity Press, 2005).

among all Israelite families) and a theological angle (a basis in the fact that both people and land belong to God).[55]

Bond service is thus an inner-Israelite arrangement; it relates to the fact that every family has land. It could not apply to foreigners who come to live in the village for some reason (maybe they are on the run, or maybe they have got into economic difficulties in their home country). Israelites are expected simply to be generous to them, as Boaz is to Ruth. The same expectations apply to widows and orphans (the latter term will not necessarily imply they are children). Boaz's concern for Naomi again illustrates the principle, and the Ruth story perhaps points to the reason why widows and orphans would be vulnerable: Elimelek's land had apparently already become forfeit. The expectation of generosity also applies to Levites, who were allocated no land.

In the village, responsibility for seeing that the Torah's vision gets implemented rests with the body of elders as the people with power and resources in the community. They will also be responsible for justice in the sense of resolving conflicts in the village. Their responsibility will include dealing with issues such as murder, assault and misappropriation of land. The focus of the implementation of justice is restorative and religious, not simply retributive or rehabilitative or deterrent. It restores relationships and makes reparation for harm.[56] Justice means putting things right. A further element in this picture is the conviction that a person who wrongs another has also offended God. So they must put things right both with God and with the other person (see Num 5:6-10).

The City

While the imperatives of the Prophets, Proverbs and the Sermon on the Mount come under pressure in the village, they may be more vulnerable in the city. In Israel, the significant development of the city takes place as a consequence of the development of the state, which needs the city as a means of administration—not least of collecting taxes. City and village then live in codependence. But for various reasons the city seems also to be a context in which some people can accumulate wealth at the expense of others; and if

---

[55]Christopher J. H. Wright, e.g., *The Mission of God* (Downers Grove, IL: InterVarsity Press; Nottingham, UK: Inter-Varsity Press, 2006), 291-93.

[56]See Christopher D. Marshall, *Beyond Retribution* (Grand Rapids and Cambridge, UK: Eerdmans, 2001).

economic difficulties drive people to the city, their difficulties may increase there. Thus while wealth and poverty can be a reality in the country, they may be more endemic in the city.

Such factors make justice more of an issue in the city. The First Testament also implies that the city is a place where honesty and fairness in trading and in the resolving of conflict are imperiled, so that the community needs systems for safeguarding them. In the village, responsibility for such justice lies with the community's elders meeting at the city gate, and it's possible that this arrangement is less susceptible to corruption than the more formalized system that would be needed in the city—though here, too, the administration of justice was hardly professionalized. Justice thus has different connotations from the ones that hold in urbanized and industrial societies.

This difference holds in connection with penalties for wrongdoing. The First Testament has no idea of the imposing of fines, which presupposes that a person has wronged the state, and neither is there any practice of incarceration. One principle of justice is that it requires a wrongdoer to make restitution for wrongdoing. Another principle is that the punishment should not exceed the crime, as Lamek's did (Gen 4:23-24). To put it poetically, an eye for an eye or a tooth for a tooth is appropriate; excessive punishment is not. While the Torah prescribes the death penalty for many offenses, including (for instance) adultery, the First Testament tells of virtually no implementation of the death penalty, and a declaration such as "someone who hits one of their parents should be executed" is more a statement of theological ethics ("assaulting a parent is really wicked") than a law.

Parallel considerations apply to the notion of social justice. The Hebrew equivalent is *mišpāṭ ûṣĕdāqâ*, which is commonly translated "justice and righteousness."[57] The Hebrew expression reframes the idea of social justice. *Mišpāṭ* denotes the exercise of authority or government, which can belong to the head of a household, or to the elders, or to the king, while *ṣĕdāqâ* denotes the faithfulness to community relationships and relationships with God with which one goes about the exercise of *mišpāṭ*. Such social justice is as much local as centralized. It is expressed by people who have power, who

---

[57]Cf. Moshe Weinfeld, *Social Justice in Ancient Israel and in the Ancient Near East* (Philadelphia: Fortress, 1995).

are to exercise that power to see that everyone is treated fairly and that (for instance) the community behaves in a caring rather than an exploitative way.

The origins of the city as Genesis describes it, and the wrongdoing that flourishes there, might make one expect the Scriptures to see it as an inherently questionable and wayward human invention, as might apply to the associated development of music and poetry and the fermenting of grapes. But God affirms them all. David sees the city as a necessity and chooses one as his capital, and retrospectively Yahweh identifies with his choice (Ps 132). It becomes a place where he manifests his faithfulness and power (e.g., Ps 46), Israel's equivalent to Mount Zaphon (Ps 48), the *real* Mount Zaphon. It is the place where Yahweh deigns to have a palace (the temple), in addition to the one in the heavens, where people can come to bring their needs and plead with him to intervene on their behalf. And the Scriptures' vision for the future is not a reversion to village life but a new heavens and earth, a new world, that is embodied in a new Jerusalem— albeit one that recognizes the necessary relationship between city and country (Is 65:15-25; Rev 21:1–22:5). The moral, social and material collapse of Jerusalem does not make God abandon it. In some fulfillment of the vision in Isaiah, there were times when one could see Jerusalem turned into a recreated city; it gave up the worship of other deities, the creation of images, and the contravening of the sabbath that characterized it before the exile. The personal commitment of people such as Ezra and Nehemiah, as well as that of the "wise teachers" to whom Daniel 11 refers, contributed to this renewal.

The city is not especially a place where very many people live,[58] but a center of power and administration as well as a place of refuge, and also a place where inequality, corruption, fraud and oppression flourish. Yet the city becomes key to the spread of the Jesus story and to the development of congregations of people who believe in Jesus. Having become the city of God, the holy city, Jerusalem never loses its significance. For all the vicissitudes of its history, it provides an image for the city that will stand forever, the New Jerusalem. The Scriptures thus start in a garden but end in a city.

---

[58]See J. W. Rogerson and John Vincent, *The City in Biblical Perspective* (London and Oakville, CT: Equinox, 2009).

Jonah pictures a great city as characterized by waywardness and as destined for judgment but as able to repent and find pardon.

3.3 THE NATION

While the city is a human invention that God takes up and works with, the development of different nations in their individuality seems to be a more direct outworking of God's creation of humanity.[59] Although God summons Abraham out of the civilizations of Mesopotamia and the ancient city of Ur, away from his country, his people and his family, he promises to make him into a great *nation*, the ancestor of many nations and a blessing to the nations (e.g., Gen 12:2; 17:4; 18:8). Israel is both an ʿ*am* and a *gôy*, even before its arrival in the land—both a people and a nation (Ex 33:13; Deut 26:5; Josh 3:17). It is an entity that sees itself as ethnically one, a huge family, as well as a body whose members are aware of forming one political unit. The First Testament's focus on Israel as a nation, and on the other nations of the day and Yahweh's expectations of them, complements the New Testament's relatively great focus on the congregation, and the common focus in Christian faith on the individual's coming to believe in Jesus, when "the conception of the 'holy nation' in its strict sense has faded altogether."[60]

God is thus concerned for all the nations. Land is then intrinsic to their nature. Central government perhaps is not; it is a practical necessity while also a mixed blessing. The Scriptures' perspective on the superpower is less ambiguous. There is no doubt that it is a kind of antigod, even if God can make use of it.

Nations

In keeping with God's promises to Abraham, the Prophets include spectacular promises about the nations' destiny (e.g., Is 19:18-25), while Revelation takes up the words of Psalm 86:9 to declare that "all the nations will come and worship" before Yahweh. They will walk by the light of the holy city, the new Jerusalem, and their splendor and honor will be brought into

---

[59]Contrast Barth, *CD* III, 4:305-9. The background of Barth's comments lies in the ideology of peoplehood propagated in Germany between the two world wars. But even in the 1950s a judge in the United States affirmed an interracial couple's guilt of a felony on the basis that God made white people white, black people black, and that they should stay separate.

[60]Martin Buber, *Two Types of Faith* (London: Routledge; New York: Macmillan, 1951), 173.

it (Rev 15:4; 21:24-26). In the meantime, they benefit from Yahweh's deliverance of Israel when this deliverance involves putting down the superpower, because the superpower is also their oppressor. This deliverance establishes the kind of God Yahweh is and establishes the basis on which Yahweh operates in the world, character traits that work for the nations' benefit when they are in need. Yahweh's action in relation to Israel models his positive intention for nations. He is also their deliverer, sovereign and provider.

In both Testaments, God's choosing some people does not imply rejecting others. When Jesus chooses some people out of the world, his action is set in the context of God's loving the world as a whole, and it is apparently an expression of that love (Jn 3:16; 15:19). Likewise, God's choosing Israel does not imply rejecting the rest of the nations.[61] They were created by Yahweh, they live in Yahweh's world, and even now they are summoned to worship Yahweh (e.g., Pss 47; 66; 67; 113; 117) and to do so not least on the basis of what he has done for Israel. Yahweh's reigning means that

> The world indeed stands firm, it will not totter;
>   he decides for the peoples with uprightness.
>
> He will govern the world in faithfulness
>   and the peoples in trustworthiness. (Ps 96:10, 13; cf. Ps 98:9)

English translations commonly have Yahweh "judging" the world, but the verb (*šāpaṭ*) is the word for "judging" the poor—that is, giving judgment with regard to them, exercising authority for their benefit.[62]

One way Yahweh does so involves their being drawn to Zion because it stands high above them metaphorically as the location of Yahweh's house, and they somehow know they need to learn from Yahweh about the ways they themselves should live; Yahweh's teaching will thus issue in the resolution of conflicts between them (Is 2:2-4). Yahweh intends to bring to an end the toll of death and mourning that issues from war, and he is preparing a great banquet on this mountain to celebrate the fact (Is 25:6-8). While it will be an occasion when he removes the disgrace from his people, it will also bring relief and celebration

---

[61]See, e.g., Joel Kaminsky, "Did Election Imply the Mistreatment of Non-Israelites?" *Harvard Theological Review* 96 (2003): 397-425.
[62]See the comments on *mišpāṭ* in the paragraphs under "The City" in section 3.2 above. "Faithfulness" is *ṣedeq*, related to the word *ṣĕdāqâ*, on which those paragraphs also comment.

for all peoples. Indeed, by being Yahweh's servant, Israel was to be the means of Yahweh's "just and gentle government"[63] coming to them (Is 42:1-4).

Blessing and Honor

One way, perhaps *the* way, this intention was to be realized was by virtue of Israel being a covenant for the peoples—that is, being an embodiment of what it means to have Yahweh in covenant relationship with you. It was in this way that Israel would be a light to the nations (Is 42:5-7). The image restates the talk of Abraham's descendants being a blessing to the nations (Gen 12:1-3).[64] To be light or blessing, Israel doesn't actually have to do anything beyond let Yahweh be lord of its own life, though even this commitment is too much (cf. Is 42:18-25). Before the book of Isaiah ends, however, it does picture survivors of the catastrophe that has fallen on Israel reaching out to the nations, and even representatives of the nations themselves being involved in so reaching out (Is 66:18-24).

Israel will thus be honored before other peoples. As honor rather than shame is an appropriate ambition within a community, so it is an appropriate ambition in relationships between communities (Jer 2:26 makes the link). Shame is a grievous reality; Jeremiah 46–51 makes it a prominent motif in describing Yahweh's putting down of Egypt, Moab and Babylon. It is thus also a motif in Israel's prayers. Israel can rejoice in occasions when Yahweh did not leave it to experience shame as a result of his failing to deliver it in response to its pleas (e.g., Ps 22:5 [MT 6]). It can also grieve before Yahweh in times when he is letting it live in shame (e.g., Ezra 9:7; Neh 1:3; Dan 9:7-8).

Paradoxically, however, giving too much attention to honor can issue in losing it. The very possession of honor and majesty can threaten to compromise the honor and majesty of the One to whom alone honor and majesty inherently belong; certainly the possessors of majesty and honor can (indeed, inevitably will) become proud of them in a way that infringes on God's honor and majesty, and they therefore risk forfeiting them; indeed, they inevitably will (see Is 2:5-22).

---

[63] *Mišpāṭ* again. The phrase in quotation marks was applied by people in Britain to their government in the eighteenth century, and later by people in the United States to theirs.
[64] See the paragraphs under "Promising" in section 2.2 above.

The Psalms point out the threatening consequences if nations fail to be faithful and trustworthy. When they are in an uproar, Yahweh silences them (Ps 46). The Prophets also speak of the downfall of individual nations when they get turned into substitute gods or when they are guilty of war crimes (e.g., Is 13–23; Amos 1–2), and Revelation declares terrible fates for the nations. As Yahweh's action against Pharaoh for oppressing an underling people models the way he is willing to relate to any superpower, so his action against the Amaleqites or the Canaanites models the fate threatening other nations that attack the weak or sacrifice their children. The Prophets incorporate parallel warnings about Israel itself as a nation. Like Israel, then, the nations are faced with a choice. God lays two possibilities before them. As is the case with Israel, however, even if they choose destruction, it need not turn out to be the end; there is the possibility of restoration (Is 19:18-25 is again the spectacular expression of the point).

Yahweh is directly involved in the political affairs of the nations as their actions affect his people. "Yahweh has foiled the nations' policy, frustrated the peoples' intentions" (Ps 33:10). Sometimes he works in their affairs by means of members of his people—as when he commissions Elijah to anoint a new king in Syria (1 Kings 19:15). The temptations for Israel are to trust in the nations, or to fear the nations, or to admire the nations and their insight. It's a demanding challenge that Israel should live by trust in Yahweh in its political life. It's demanding when the Israelites are in Egypt and when they are on their journey through the wilderness. It's demanding for Judah when it's a political entity under pressure from Assyria and under related pressures from Syria and Ephraim (see, e.g., Is 7; 30).

Territory

Promising that Abraham will become a great nation is associated with telling him to go to a particular country, and it leads naturally into promising that his people will have this territory as their own (Gen 12:1-7). Abraham responds by building a series of altars in the country, in the north, the center and the south, and he thus declares Yahweh's name over the land, like a modern explorer planting a flag there. Yahweh can later refer to this country as "my country" (e.g., Jer 2:7; Ezek 38:16; Joel 1:6). It's not a practical problem to Yahweh that the country currently belongs to the Canaanites. After all, he has the power and the right to reallocate territory. That fact might be a moral problem, though, and it led to Yahweh waiting quite a while before fulfilling his promise to Abraham, waiting until he could do so without being unfair to its current occupants (Gen 15:16).

The Scriptures will continue to speak of Israel's land as belonging to Yahweh. While he will settle Israel there and in a sense it will belong to them, they live there as tenants rather than owners. They must therefore live in the land in a way that is agreeable to its real owner. The land is a place for them to implement the Torah. Right living in the land is a major focus in the vast tracts of requirements and exhortations in Exodus to Deuteronomy. Failure to live in accordance with the owner's expectations is liable to lead to his suspending or terminating the lease, as he did to the previous occupants— and it does have that result for Israel.

Yahweh's giving Israel its territory is a particular instance of a broader activity. It was Yahweh who gave the Philistines their land and who gave the Syrians theirs (Amos 9:7). Yahweh expects all nations to live in "their" land (that is, his land) in a way that matches his expectations.

Territory and peoplehood or nationhood are tied together. A people or nation's identity lies in part in its land. A nation without a land is an odd idea. The link reflects something about the way God created humanity. It is the corporate equivalent to God's creating individual human beings as people with bodies.[65] As a nation, Israel thus is a territorial entity. It is rather odd that the Jewish people's attachment to their land is now sometimes subject to critique whereas "the attachment of Native Americans or Australians to their particular rocks, trees, and deserts is celebrated as an organic connection to the Earth which 'we' have lost."[66]

More explicitly in Genesis, spelling out the blessing of Abraham in terms of increase and territory fits with the nature of God's activity in creation. There God had already spelled out the nature of the blessing he intended by speaking of humanity increasing and filling the territory. God repeats that threefold motif in speaking of blessing, increase and territory

---

[65]Cf. the comments of Thomas F. Torrance, "The Divine Vocation and Destiny of Israel in World History," in *The Witness of the Jews to God*, ed. David W. Torrance (Edinburgh: Handsel, 1982), 85-104 (on 103).

[66]Daniel Boyarin, *A Radical Jew* (Berkeley and London: University of California Press, 1994), 251.

for Abraham as the one in whom God's creation intention will thus be realized, as a model of God's intention for humanity and the world as a whole ('ereṣ is both the word for "earth" in Gen 1 and the word for "land" in Gen 12).

The New Testament makes little reference to the link between the Jewish people and its land. The Gospels may simply take the link for granted. If land is bound up with peoplehood, the Jewish people's continuing significance will entail the continuing significance of its land.[67] Further, the geographical location of the events of Jesus' life, death and resurrection will mean that the land cannot lose its significance. Paul's omitting reference to the land when he enumerates Israel's privileges (Rom 9:4; Eph 2:12-13) may link with the fact that he is writing to Jewish and Gentile believers in Rome and Turkey for whom the land is not as directly significant as it might be for people in Judea.

That omission also suggests a theological point. Abraham's family was chosen as a bridgehead into all the world's peoples, and now all the world's families are coming to share his blessing, so Abraham's family's filling the 'ereṣ of Canaan linked with God's purpose for the 'ereṣ as a whole. It fits with the fact that God's kingdom is not to be confined to the land of Israel but to occupy the whole of the earth,[68] though this does not imply that nations and therefore land go out of existence.

State

While the New Testament does speak in Romans 13 of the authority of an imperial power such as Rome, the First Testament has more to say about responsibility for proper government. That responsibility rests on nation as well as on city and village. Israel starts off as a people and a nation, then eventually becomes a kingdom—a nation with a central government. The word for "kingdom" is as near as Hebrew gets to a word for "state." It signifies a particular form of central organization that as such has the capacity to

---

[67]But Nicholas C. R. Brown ("For the Nation: Jesus, the Restoration of Israel and Articulating a Christian Ethic of Territorial Governance" [PhD diss., Fuller Theological Seminary, 2015]) notes points where the Gospels imply the link.

[68]Cf. N. T. Wright, *Paul and the Faithfulness of God* (Minneapolis: Fortress; London: SPCK, 2013), 366-67.

protect its people and to guard against social disorder—to limit people's freedom to do what they like in the way they did in Judges (Judg 21:25).

Psalm 72 expounds the responsibility that rests on a national government. It speaks in terms of monarchic rule, but its account of the priorities expected of the king transfers to presidential systems and parliamentary democracies. The prayer's first concern is that government should give itself to *mišpāṭ* and *ṣədāqâ*, to an exercise of authority that recognizes mutual obligations and commitments and encourages people to live in relation to each other in light of such obligations and commitments.[69] Such faithful exercise of authority and the safeguarding of mutual faithfulness within the nation is the first obligation of government. Human self-centeredness then means that government must be concerned to protect the powerless, the needy and the exploited from the people with power and resources, who will take advantage of them. The trouble is that the people in government are themselves likely to be the problem. The psalm's promise is that a government that accepts the priority it emphasizes will also succeed in making the nation flourish, because (it implies) there is a moral link between prosperity and faithfulness within the community.

Israel was a state—soon two states—for only a few centuries in First Testament times; shortly Ephraim, then Judah, became provinces of a foreign empire. As Samuel pointed out, central government is indeed as likely to be a burden as a liberation (see 1 Sam 8:11-17), but it did bring Israel external political stability (that is, it dealt with people such as the Canaanites and Philistines) until the arrival of those imperial powers. Turning Abraham's family into a nation and then into a state made it pretty inevitable that it should operate in the way that a state does, and be involved in war, for instance, because war is what states do in order to protect their people.

In due course God apparently abandoned the idea of working by means of a state. One might infer that being a state had not facilitated Yahweh's aim of attracting all the nations to recognize Israel and thus to recognize Yahweh himself, but the Scriptures do not make explicit any reasons for God's abandoning the idea. Neither Testament is uneasy about the fact

---

[69]See the comments on these words in the paragraphs under "The City" in section 3.2 above.

that Israel once was a nation or a state and as such was involved in war making, or (in particular) about Joshua's action against the Canaanites (see Acts 7 and Heb 11), though both Judaism and Christianity are uneasy about it.[70]

The Scriptures regard war as simply an aspect of human life, an aspect of the fact that conflict is a fact of human life. They do see conflict as resulting from human rebellion back at the Beginning, and they promise a day when people will no longer make war, but in the meantime they accept war as a reality. So Jesus' only comment about war is that it will continue until the End (e.g., Mk 13:7), and he is more accepting of soldiers than of rich people. Faith in God is key to fighting a war, as it is to everything else (Heb 11:34).

The Scriptures thus do not fret over war and other forms of human violence in the way that people do in the Western world. "The problem of war" is not a problem in either Testament.[71] Part of the reason for our fretting issues from the Enlightenment; part of it issues from the fact that modern war takes a much heavier toll on humanity because of our technological advances. So the Scriptures do not help us directly with the problem we feel about war, but they talk much about war and help us precisely by virtue of coming at the subject from a different angle.

With apparent approval, the Scriptures can picture war as a way of putting down oppressive powers and liberating the oppressed (see Gen 14), of war as a way of resisting the attack of another people and punishing the attackers (e.g., Ex 17:8-16) and of war as a way of punishing wrongdoers in general (e.g., Num 31:1-3). They can enthuse over deliverance that involves no war making (Ex 14–15) and over the avoidance of war (Num 20:14-21). Whereas war is a major way nations gain territory, the Scriptures do not imply that it would be all right for Israel simply to invade Canaan and take the land by force because God had promised it to them. We have noted that their occupation of the land can only be justified because its occupants deserve to have it taken from them (e.g., Gen 15:16). If these passages from the Scriptures are providing rationalizations for actions that were really self-serving, it adds

---

[70]See, e.g., Robert Eisen, *The Peace and Violence of Judaism* (Oxford and New York: Oxford University Press, 2011).

[71]Contrast the title of Peter C. Craigie's *The Problem of War in the Old Testament* (Grand Rapids: Eerdmans, 1978).

rather than takes from the force of the assumption that Israel could not simply appropriate another people's territory because it wanted to do so.[72]

The Superpower

Much of the biblical story unfolds against the background of a sequence of Middle Eastern superpowers—Egypt, Assyria, Babylon, Medo-Persia, Greece, Rome.[73] The Scriptures assume that these empires exist only because God allows them to, but he usually does so without directly involving himself with them or intervening in history. Occasionally he asserts himself against them, as happened at the exodus and the Reed Sea. His object there was to demonstrate the fact that he was king and that Pharaoh was not king, and certainly was not God. Paul takes up God's comment in Exodus, "For this purpose I raised you up, so that I might show my power through you, and so that my name might be proclaimed through all the earth," and Paul adds his gloss, "So then, on whomever he wishes, he has mercy, and whomever he wishes, he hardens" (Rom 9:17-18). Subsequently God harnesses the Assyrian and Babylonian superpower to his purpose in bringing trouble to his people. The Assyrian king is Yahweh's agent (e.g., Is 10:5-6). The Babylonian king is Yahweh's servant, and Judah and the other smaller nations must submit to him (Jer 27). Of course the superpower does not see it that way (e.g., Is 10:7-15), or does so only nominally. Further, it is inclined to trust in its vast military and information resources (e.g., Is 47).

Yahweh then uses one superpower to put down another. Its destruction comes as *šōd* from *šadday*, as destruction from the Destroyer; Yahweh's Day will come for it (Is 13:6, 8). Yahweh thus harnesses Persia to bring Judah deliverance, stirring up the Persian king's spirit in this connection (Ezra 1:1). Metaphorically speaking, indeed, Cyrus becomes Yahweh's Anointed, a kind of Gentile King David (Is 44:24–45:7), and one of his successors commissions Ezra to see that life in Jerusalem is structured by Yahweh's Torah (Ezra 7). The law of God is also the law of the king. No doubt the emperor has his reasons; he wants his empire to be kept in an orderly state. But without realizing it, he is Yahweh's agent.

---

[72]See further *OTT* 1:474-505; 3:548-82.
[73]See further *OTT* 2:758-88.

The circumstances of Jesus' birth and early life interact with the policies and acts of the superpower (Mt 2:1-23; Lk 1:5–2:40). It is the edict of Rome that causes him to be born in Bethlehem. The arrival of a possible Anointed One makes Rome's local puppet nervous; he wants to eliminate him, and he is ruthless in seeking to do so (Mt 2:1-18). It is this act that causes Jesus to live in Egypt and in due course to return but then to go to live in Nazareth. He is carried to and fro by superpower politics. Yet at each point events can be linked with passages from the Scriptures, suggesting that there is a bigger picture of which the superpower is unwittingly part and which it does not frustrate. The superpower seeks to serve itself and to frustrate God. In the short term it may do the former, but it will not do the latter.

Indeed, in due course the master will become the servant. The superpower can be unwittingly used by God, and it is challenged to acknowledge Yahweh as God and join in the joyful worship of the nations. Its alternative destiny is that Jesus should brandish an iron scepter over it, or give over this scepter to his people (Rev 2:2:27; 12:5; 19:15). The expression comes from Psalm 2, which promises that the Davidic king will exercise authority over the nations unless they submit themselves to Yahweh. Isaiah 52:13–53:12 offers another take on that acknowledgment, in picturing the nations recognizing Yahweh's servant, the other side of his humiliation and exaltation; he carries their wrongdoing as well as carrying Israel's. Likewise the humiliation of Israel will be reversed (Is 49:22-23). Acknowledging the people of Yahweh and acknowledging Yahweh are tied up together (e.g., Is 45:14-17; 49:7; 55:1-5). But for Egypt and Assyria, too, defeat and humiliation are not the last word (see Is 19:18-25).

Putting down the superpower is logistically necessary if Israel is to be restored. Putting down war-making nations is logistically necessary if peace is to come to Israel and to other nations. Putting down oppressors is theologically necessary if moral order is to be established in the world. Yahweh thus takes redress from the superpower (e.g., Jer 50:15-18). Promising to put it down is pastorally necessary if Israel is to keep going in the midst of its helpless domination by the empire: the good news for Israel is that Yahweh is "a passionate God, one who takes redress" (Nah 1:2).

The Underling

When Jesus tells someone who collected taxes for the Romans to follow him (Mt 9:9), he hardly implies a negative assessment of his work; at least, that judgment is not implicit when he gives the same bidding to fishermen, or to members of the military. It is simply not a factor. He has dinner with Matthew and other tax collectors and sinners, earning the disapproval of people who knew that it was important to stay pure. But associating with them in this way is a demonstration of *ḥesed*, of steadfast love or commitment.

Yet the Scriptures are "a history of faithful resistance to empire."[74] In New Testament times, with some plausibility Rome claimed to rule the world. Revelation presupposes that such a claim "could only be heard as a blasphemous usurpation of God's sole rulership and could only be resisted." God is the *kyrios* and the *pantokratōr* (Rev 1:8; 4:8; 11:17; 15:3; 16:7; 16:14; 19:6; 19:15; 21:22).[75] Revelation is "a political resistance document. . . . It seeks to rally the seven churches to a stance of courageous witness against a culture that dangles seductive defilements before the people of God."[76] It is thus "the most explicitly counter-imperial book in the New Testament."[77] It is "one of the fiercest attacks on Rome and one of the most effective pieces of political resistance literature from the period of the early empire." Further, "its thoroughgoing criticism of the whole system of Roman power includes an important element of economic critique."[78] Revelation 17–18 likely takes up from Isaiah 23:15-18 the image of Tyre as a whore; Rome is a whore "because her associations with the peoples of her empire are for her own economic benefit. To those who associate with her she offers the supposed benefits of the *Pax Romana*," but these are "the favours of a prostitute, purchased at a high price. The *Pax Romana* is really a system of

---

[74]The phrase comes from the subtitle of Richard A. Horsley, ed., *In the Shadow of Empire* (Louisville and London: Westminster John Knox, 2008). Cf. Theodore W. Jennings, "Paul Against Empire," in Alejandro F. Botta and Pablo R. Andiñach, eds., *The Bible and the Hermeneutics of Liberation* (Atlanta: SBL, 2009), 147-67.

[75]M. Eugene Boring, "The Theology of Revelation," *Interpretation* 40 (1986): 257-69 (on 258, 259).

[76]Richard B. Hays, *The Moral Vision of the New Testament* (San Francisco: Harper, 1996), 170.

[77]Greg Carey, "The Book of Revelation as Counter-Imperial Script," in Horsley, *In the Shadow of Empire*, 157-76 (on 157).

[78]Richard Bauckham, *The Climax of Prophecy* (Edinburgh: T&T Clark, 1993), 338.

economic exploitation of the empire."[79] One might also see Rome as the epitome of patriarchal power, and see God's putting down Roman power as restoring the situation at the Beginning in which there are no power structures among human beings. God rules all humanity; no human beings exercise authority over human beings.

Wherever one looks in the Scriptures, they assume that the superpower is an embodiment of rebellion against God that is to be put down, but this putting it down is God's business. In the meantime, the people of God is to submit to its authority insofar as it can give Caesar what is Caesar's without compromising on giving God what is God's (Mt 22:15-22). It was put in power by God, like all governmental power (Rom 13:1-7).

Roman citizens in Rome perhaps had less to fear of the Roman authorities than some other people within Rome's orbit; the Roman believers ought therefore to pay their taxes with a smile on their face. But it seems likely that Paul had noticed that Rome sometimes did wicked things, yet he still declares that people who do good have no need to fear the worldly authorities because their focus lies on putting down wrongdoers. As is the case when he declares that "troubles generate endurance and endurance generates proved character" (Rom 5:3-4), he is defining how things are supposed to be. Exceptions to the rule should not be allowed to make people forget the rule. First and Second Kings as well as the Prophets indicate that God can still work through the superpower.[80] That fact does not make it unfair for God to judge the superpower (cf. Rom 3:1-8).

Daniel offers the Scriptures' widest perspective on the empires, seeing Babylon, Medo-Persia and Greece as a sequence that implicitly tells the entire story of the superpowers, a sequence that is in due course terminated by God's bringing in a different kind of superpower. Second Temple Judaism extended the sequence by adding Rome, and the New Testament follows. While Daniel sometimes speaks of God giving power to an imperial ruler, it sometimes simply describes such powers as arising. God's involvement lies only in their fall.

---

[79]Ibid., 347.
[80]See Jacques Ellul, *The Politics of God and the Politics of Man* (Grand Rapids: Eerdmans, 1972).

3.4 HUMAN BEINGS

Humanity was made in God's image in order to exercise responsibility for the world on God's behalf. We were created to care for one another, to enjoy freedom and to work. We were created male and female, and marriage plays an important role in our fulfilling our vocation. So does the life of the family.

Responsibility

Humanity bears the image of its creator (Col 3:10). God made humanity in his image, after his likeness (Gen 1:26-27); the second noun restates and underlines the first. There is no indication in the Scriptures that this image has been lost or spoiled through sin; they rather indicate that it abides.[81] In Genesis, the implications of being in God's image are spelled out in the words that follow. It implies responsibility to rule the world. In the background is the way a king would sometime erect images of himself in different parts of his realm to symbolize his rule there.[82] One would be expected to show regard for the image, as one is expected to show regard for the portrait of a king or queen (just yesterday as I write, a British man was in court for defacing a portrait of the queen). One is therefore expected to show regard for other human beings and not curse them (Jas 3:9). The basis for saying that human life is sacred is the fact that human beings are made in God's image.

Being human is thus a matter of vocation and responsibility in relation to God and to the world, rather than a matter of rights. Admittedly, such a comment may be proper only to people who do not have to worry about their rights and who are in a position to honor or ignore the rights of people who may get trampled on.[83] People with some power such as the writer and most readers of this book have an obligation to be concerned for the rights of other people rather than their own.

---

[81]See John F. Kilner, "Humanity in God's Image," *Journal of the Evangelical Theological Society* 53 (2010): 601-17; contrast Barth, *CD* I, 1:238-41. The discussion in G. C. Berkouwer, *Man: The Image of God* (Grand Rapids: Eerdmans, 1962), in effect locates the problem of this disagreement in the fact that systematic theology commonly uses words differently from the Scriptures' use of them; it may make a scriptural point, but it does so using words in its own way.

[82]See J. Richard Middleton, *The Liberating Image* (Grand Rapids: Brazos, 2005).

[83]See the illustrations in David Novak, "God and Human Rights," in Isaac Kalimi, ed., *Jewish Bible Theology* (Winona Lake, IN: Eisenbrauns, 2012), 89-99.

As created in God's image, humanity was part of God's good creation. As moral selves, however, human beings were not yet either good or bad, but were at the beginning of the journey that would shape them as moral people. "Adam . . . stood at the beginning of his 'career' not at the end."[84] Being created opened up the possibility of being good or bad; at least, it did so at the Beginning. But humanity failed to exercise sovereignty over the world as God intended and yielded to its authority instead.[85] As a result humanity found its relationship with the world fraught, and creation never reached its goal. God put all things under humanity's feet, but things haven't worked out in the way God intended.

But we do see Jesus crowned with glory and honor because of suffering death (Heb 2:6-8), which constitutes the guarantee that God's purpose will find fulfillment. There is hardly scriptural ground for saying that "we derive wholly from Jesus not merely our potential and actual relation to God, but even our human nature as such. . . . We are partakers of human nature as and because Jesus is first partaker of it."[86] But we can say that Jesus is "the paradigm case of the truly human." He fulfilled our vocation to subdue the earth and take responsibility for it, pioneering the way for us, whom he wishes to see as his brothers and sisters, sharing our human fragility as creatures of flesh and blood, reaching maturity through suffering, living by trust in God, protesting about his experience and learning obedience through suffering (Heb 2:5-14; 5:7-8).[87]

One might have hoped that the renewing of humanity's image in Jesus (Col 3:10) would then mean progress toward the fulfilling of God's purpose that humanity should rule the world well on God's behalf, though there doesn't seem to have been any such progress.

Relationality

It's often said that being in God's image implies having the capacity to be in relationship with God, and/or that the spelling out of this image in terms of male and female implies that human relationality is a key aspect of the image

---

[84]Herman Bavinck, *Reformed Dogmatics* (Grand Rapids: Baker, 2004), 2:564.
[85]See the paragraphs under "Ambiguity and Incompleteness" in section 3.1 above.
[86]Barth, *CD* III, 2:50.
[87]Anthony C. Thiselton, *The Hermeneutics of Doctrine* (Grand Rapids: Eerdmans, 2007), 241, 242.

of God.[88] Neither implication is inherent in the idea of being in God's image, but both are implicit in the broader account of humanity in Genesis 1–2.

The first thing human beings discover about themselves in the Scriptures is that they are addressed by God; God has already addressed the creatures of sea and sky, though not at the same length, and not as the recipients of his gifts. We understand what it means to be human when we start from our being created, addressed, blessed, commissioned to get the world under control, generously (though a-carnivorously) provided for, bidden to serve the ground, given wide permissions but subjected to slight restrictions, liable to lose our lives for ignoring the restrictions and then subjected to temptation. God goes looking for the first man, asks him and his wife questions, expresses anguish at the way they've ignored his prohibition, declares consequences and pronounces punishments, provides them with clothing and, while he banishes them from his orchard, persists in the relationship outside it (Gen 2–4).

So sin does not separate humanity from God, though it does make it hard for humanity to fulfill its vocation. Any understanding of what it means to be human has to focus on the fact that human beings stand before God and live as the objects of God's blessings and lordship. We receive life as a gift (or rather a loan) from God. The appropriate response is "astonishment, humility, awe, modesty, circumspection and carefulness." The fact that God himself became a human being like us makes that response even more appropriate.[89]

Interhuman relationship is also integral to being human. It's no good the man being on his own; he will need a partner if he's to undertake his commission. The animals cannot fulfill the role. The orchard needs more human beings in order for the commission to find fulfillment; the man on his own cannot generate them, and the animals cannot help him. So the woman is created in order that the two of them can have children and can together fulfill that commission.

Their relationship is thus task-oriented. There is nothing in Genesis 1–2 about a joy in the romantic relationship of Adam and Eve or about their being friends. "The myth of romantic love"[90] has to be read into these

---

[88]See the discussion in ibid., 223–40.
[89]Barth, *CD* III, 4:339, 340.
[90]James W. McClendon, *Systematic Theology: Ethics* (Nashville: Abingdon, 1986), 133.

chapters. Fortunately (we may think), later stories in Genesis imply a recognition of these facets of being human. Elsewhere in the Scriptures, the Song of Songs especially has this emphasis. It portrays sexual relationships as ones in which men and women find delight, though even here the Scriptures recognize the frustrations and pains of these relationships. They are ones in which insight and folly wrestle (Prov 7).[91]

It fits with these awarenesses that in Genesis 3 itself it is the man-woman relationship that is immediately the context in which there is failure; the man and the woman fail each other and fail God, blame each other and blame God. While their mutual relationship and their relationship with God are not broken, they are messed up. The story of Cain and Abel then implies that human beings have some responsibility to and for one another as well as to God and the world, or as an aspect of responsibility to God. "In its basic form humanity is fellow-humanity," and I am to love my neighbor as a person like myself. I therefore look at him or her eye to eye, seeing and letting myself be seen, hearing and letting myself be heard, giving and receiving help, and doing so gladly, in a togetherness in which "both are companions, associates, comrades, fellows, and helpmates." As such we are indispensable to one another.[92]

It's possible to define what it means to be human in terms of the person in itself or its parts—for instance, a human being is essentially a soul or a body or the combination of the two.[93] Discussions of embryology and life-support machines may presuppose only a biophysical definition of the human. But "understanding *the human* cannot be adequate unless it arises *in relation to the 'Other.'*"[94] The declaration that "Paul's theology is relational," that "he was not concerned with God in himself or humankind in itself," applies to the Scriptures as a whole. The Scriptures do not speak much about "God in himself or humankind in itself" in the manner of Christian theological debate and formulawtion when these necessarily come to work within the framework of European philosophical thinking. They are con-

---

[91]Cf. Brevard S. Childs, *Biblical Theology in Crisis* (Philadelphia: Westminster, 1970), 184-200; Childs goes on to note that sex is a subject on which the New Testament's perspective is rather narrow and needs to be read in light of the First Testament.
[92]Cf. Barth, *CD* III, 2:285 and 250-71; second quotation from 271.
[93]See section 3.5 below.
[94]Thiselton, *Hermeneutics of Doctrine*, 181.

cerned with God in relation to the world and with humanity in relation to God, with men and women in their relationships with one another, and with Jesus as God's response to humanity's plight.[95]

Freedom for Life

An unexpected feature of the Eden story is the presence of temptation or testing. God tells Adam not to eat of the good-and-bad-knowledge tree despite the evident usefulness (in connection with God's commission to him) of the life skill he could apparently acquire from it, and one of the creatures that God made suggests to Eve that they should ignore God's instruction. When Jesus has been baptized and has had the Spirit descend on him, the first thing that happens is that he goes through a similar experience. The story of Job begins by telling us that his suffering is a test, and one can see various ways in which it functions that way, though Job never knows. Indeed, that unawareness is one aspect of the test.

God's creation intent includes putting pressure on human beings so that they may grow to maturity. It's not a total answer to "the problem of suffering," but it's one of the assumptions with which the Scriptures approach suffering. The question is not where suffering comes from, but what you do with it. One thing you have to do is argue: with God (as Job does), with yourself (e.g., Pss 42–43) and with the immediate source of temptation (as Eve and Adam do not).

I devised the first two headings in this section (responsibility and relationality) without realizing that they parallel Barth's first two headings for his discussion of humanity. He then adds this third heading, "freedom for life."[96] It draws attention to what one might call God's commission to human beings to be themselves, a commission reflected in the Bible's portrayal of humanity. God made us into creatures distinct from him and then wants us to live—to choose life. The appropriate response is again astonishment, humility, awe, modesty, circumspection and carefulness.

In the urban world it may be surprising to find work treated at the beginning of Genesis as an aspect of the freedom for which we were created.

---

[95]Dunn, *Theology of Paul the Apostle*, 53.
[96]Barth, *CD* III, 4:324.

In the Scriptures, work is our vocation.[97] But we were not created for em-
ployment—that is, to work for someone else. Becoming someone else's
"servant" in this way is a life-saving possibility if one gets into a mess, but it
is not the ideal. Still less is it the ideal that "each day men sell little pieces of
themselves in order to try to buy them back each night and week end."[98] In
the Scriptures, work is part of the activity of the family.

At the same time, rest is an aspect of the freedom for which we were
created. The First Testament is particularly interested in "the good life,"[99]
which is epitomized in the enjoyment of being able to sit under your vine
and fig tree and to invite people to join you there (e.g., 1 Kings 4:25; Zech 3:10).
It means enjoying "wine that cheers the human heart, making the face shine
with oil, and bread that sustains the human heart" (Ps 104:15).

God thus created the world as a good place and located the first human
beings in a wonderful orchard, and the Scriptures do not forget it. "There is
hardly a word so characteristic of the Old Testament as the word joy."[100] "It
is astonishing . . . how many references there are in the Old and New Testaments to delight, joy, bliss, exultation, merry-making and rejoicing, and how
emphatically these are demanded from the Book of Psalms to the Epistle to
the Philippians."[101] Not only does the Song of Songs enthuse over the joy of
sex; it is noticeable that Ecclesiastes often talks about joy (e.g., Eccles 5:20;
11:8-9), despite or maybe because of the constraints on human "freedom" of
which it speaks. Our freedom does not mean we can find ultimate freedom
or significance through what we do or experience or through our hard
thinking or through possessing power ("there is no passage in the Bible in
which power as such, whether physical, mental or political, is praised as
good or even desirable, much less as the supreme good").[102]

Yet once we grant the constraints that God has put upon us, we can enjoy
thinking and possessing and experiencing and doing things. That principle
applies most spectacularly to acceptance of our mortality. Without irony,

---

[97]Cf. Jürgen Moltmann, *On Human Dignity* (Philadelphia: Fortress; London: SCM Press,
1984), 45.
[98]C. Wright Mills, *White Collar* (New York: Oxford University Press, 1951), 237.
[99]Cf. R. Norman Whybray, *The Good Life in the Old Testament* (Edinburgh: T&T Clark, 2002).
[100]Ludwig Köhler, *Old Testament Theology* (London: Lutterworth, 1957; Philadelphia: Westminster,
1958), 151.
[101]Barth, *CD* III, 4:375.
[102]Barth, *CD* III, 4:391.

that enthusiasm about wine, makeup and bread appears in a psalm that resolutely acknowledges that God is both the one who gives life and the one who withdraws it (Ps 104:27-30). "To consider that we shall die means, in contrast to all attempts at evasion, to accept oneself; to assent to that to which we can assent only with God; to admit that one day we shall no longer exist but will stand before a final 'too late.'"[103] Such an admission opens up freedom.

"We can see that New Testament ethics [Old Testament ethics, too] is one powerful summons to take frankly and seriously the existence of man in his limited time as such and therefore to grasp it to-day, at once, this very moment, as his opportunity."[104] "To be a man is to be in the sphere where the first and merciful will of God toward his creatures, His will to save and keep them from the power of nothingness, is revealed in action." Then, second, "he is a being which is summoned by the Word of God." And further, it follows that "the being of man is a history," not something static. "Man lives in his time." "That man is in time means . . . that he always is now."[105] That fact makes us vulnerable in relation to the past and to the future, but fortunately, for God "now" includes our past and our future.

Male and Female
The creation of male and female relates to God's purpose for the world, and man and woman share in an egalitarian vocation in connection with subduing the earth and serving the ground, though admittedly, our own concern for an egalitarian society comes from Enlightenment thinking. The Old Testament's concern is "to humanize society from the side of Israel's faith."[106]

Jesus welcomes women among his followers, and on the whole they show themselves better followers than the men, yet he does not include any women among the Twelve, and his women followers are not called "disciples."[107] He leaves a glass ceiling in place. The life of the early Christian congregations likewise sometimes recognizes the creative role

---

[103]Barth, *CD* III, 4:591.
[104]Barth, *CD* III, 4:584.
[105]Barth, *CD* III, 2:145, 150, 157, 437, 527.
[106]Brevard S. Childs, *Old Testament Theology in a Canonical Context* (London: SCM Press, 1985; Philadelphia: Fortress, 1986), 182.
[107]See the discussion in John P. Meier, *A Marginal Jew* (New York: Doubleday, 2001), 3:73-80.

of women in mission and ministry but also places constraints on them. In adapting to the realities of the culture in this way, Jesus and people such as Paul continue the practice of the First Testament, where priests were men but prophets could be women. Both men and women were made in God's image and thus shared in the work for which God created humanity, but a greater monetary value could be put on a man as a worker (e.g., Lev 27).

Thus neither Testament puts into effect the implications of men and women together being made in God's image. The Scriptures can be used to support twenty-first-century Western concerns such as egalitarian relationships (and matters such as leadership and the importance of theologians), but we are indeed using them to support our concerns, not reflecting ones that are intrinsic to them. The two Testaments are adapting to their cultural context, and Western Christians are adapting to theirs.

The stories in the First Testament offer a series of insights on what it means in their context to be a man or a woman. The portraits again relate to expectations and stereotypes from their culture, and they are not necessarily offered in the conviction that these expectations and stereotypes are normative, but they do give people in other contexts some portraits to think against.

In First Testament stories, violence is a feature of masculinity; the motif features in many of the stories of the judges, but supremely in the story of David. Violence often operates within the family, and it is often associated with sex. Politics and sex are likewise interwoven. The David story also illustrates the terrible toll that can be exacted of a family in association with and in the wake of sexual disorder. The accumulation of women is a mark of status for a man such as Gideon or David, and in Samson's life, women feature as mother, wife, whore and lover. The cheapness of a woman's position finds clearest expression in the horrifying story of the Levite's secondary wife in Judges 19.[108] At the same time, the books tell stories of women who stand out, such as Deborah as a leader, Hannah as a person who knows how to pray, Ruth and Naomi as

---

[108]The traditional translation "concubine" is misleading; the term refers in some way to her not having the same status as a "primary wife," perhaps in connection with her children's inheritance rights.

women who stand by each other in a man's world, and Esther, who finds herself pushed into a position of abuse but can use that position to bring about her people's deliverance.

To judge from remarks about the Essenes in Philo, Josephus and Pliny the Elder, a commitment to staying single and celibate was a known phenomenon in Jesus' world; their remarks cohere with features of the Qumran scrolls. This commitment did not imply rejection of marriage as such but rather an acceptance of the vocation to singleness for oneself as a sign of giving oneself wholly to God, as part of being a community that sought to prepare for the moment when God would bring about the restoration of Israel.

Celibacy might thus be a natural and unremarkable adjunct of a prophetic calling for people such as John the Baptizer and Jesus. Their celibacy might be given further impetus by the idea that celibacy relates to a focus on the future, on the coming of God's reign. On the other hand, the declaration that men are not independent of women nor women of men (1 Cor 11:11) doesn't apply just to marriage.[109]

Marriage

Genesis 1–2 pictures marriage as the lifelong union of a man and a woman, and the First Testament gives a less patriarchal portrait of the relationship between husbands and wives than we might have thought.[110] Men and women were interdependent, with women as well as men involved in the management of the family's work and life. A wife was not her husband's property,[111] except in the sense that wife belongs to husband and husband to wife. Indeed, the technical Hebrew words for husband and wife, which etymologically imply master and mastered or owner and owned, hardly appear in the First Testament. Usually "his wife" or "her husband" is more literally "his woman" and "her man."

Yet in all their aspects, manhood and womanhood are compromised by human waywardness, and there are a number of ways of falling short of

---

[109]Barth, *CD* III, 4:163.

[110]Cf. Carol Meyers, "The Family in Early Israel," in *Families in Ancient Israel*, Leo G. Perdue et al. (Louisville: Westminster John Knox, 1997), 34.

[111]See Christopher J. H. Wright, *God's People in God's Land* (Exeter, UK: Paternoster; Grand Rapids: Eerdmans, 1990), 183-221.

God's vision for it. Jesus offers a telling comment on marriage when asked a question about divorce (Mt 19:1-12; Mk 10:1-12). He recognizes the Genesis 1-2 vision of marriage but also acknowledges that Deuteronomy's divorce regulation works with the fact of human stubbornness. That stubbornness means that divorce happens and that women then need papers that establish their status. Genesis itself suggests further insights. While the point about marriage is to further God's purpose in the world, human rebelliousness issued in a spoiling of the relationship as well as in the compromising of the vocation. Henceforth, God says to Eve, "your desire will be for your man but/and he himself will rule over you" (Gen 3:16). There are several ways of interpreting this statement; maybe the woman's desire is a good sexual desire, but the man's sexual relationship with her is oppressive, or maybe her desire is more like lust, and/or maybe his ruling is more general and refers to what we call patriarchy. Whatever the interpretation, the relationship is spoiled.

When Jesus implies that people who are seriously committed to the Torah will live by the creation standard of Genesis 1-2 rather than the allowances of Deuteronomy, his disciples are horrified. The Epistles indicate that not all believers come anywhere near this standard. For instance, "The 'church of the saints' in Corinth was a sociological beargarden."[112] There are men involved in marriages that ignore the rules in Leviticus 18 and men who have recourse to prostitutes (see 1 Cor 5-7), and some people have reacted by renouncing marriage and the household, rather like the Essenes. Paul opposes that reaction (his instruction that slaves should stay slaves is related). Husbands and wives should engage in sexual relations with each other rather than risk immorality as a result of trying to be celibate, and likewise people should marry unless they have the charism of singleness. While married people cannot focus on God in the exclusive way celibates can, as the world awaits the Lord's coming, celibacy is a gift and therefore not everyone's calling.

Paul's instructions about women's dress when they are leading worship (1 Cor 11:2-16) also involve a kind of compromise between creation ideals and practicalities. To put it another way, they imply a recognition that the

---

[112]Peter R. L. Brown, *The Body and Society* (New York: Columbia University Press, 1988; London: Faber, 1989), 36-41, 52.

End has not yet come: "for *as well as* being a new creation the believer still belongs to the natural order," and "the restraints of mere convention" retain some importance.[113] We have noted that one has to turn to the Song of Songs for a less equivocal enthusiasm for and exploration of the relationship between a man and a woman that is not dominated by a concern about order or children or property.

While 1 Corinthians 7 "was to determine all Christian thought on marriage and celibacy for well over a millennium," Ephesians "handsomely corrected the chill tone of Paul's answer to the Corinthians. It presented the relations of husband and wife as a reflection of the primal solidarity brought back by Christ to the universe and to the church" (see Eph 5:21-33).[114] For men in particular, marriage involves taking up your cross and following Jesus, because it involves a "cutting off of self-will"; its mutual love is joyful but also sacrificial.[115] While Colossians 3:18-19 simply urges wives to submit to husbands and husbands to love and not be harsh to wives, Ephesians 5:21-33 turns upside down the obvious implications of such an instruction: the way husbands are to love their wives is by giving themselves up for them; so the way wives are to submit to their husbands is by letting them do so.[116] Thus "marriage is a kind of discipleship program for second-class Christians,"[117]—for instance, for men who need to learn about self giving. But it works (when it does) because the reality of love in the relationship can have a transforming effect.

Family

The New Testament begins with an implicit recognition of the importance of family (though perhaps the word should be avoided, because what family means in different scriptural contexts is different from what it means in different contexts in the Western world). The relationship of father and son is integral to the way God's purpose comes to its climax in Jesus, and the incarnation happens through the birth of Jesus into a family. Indeed, his birth brings a family into being—it turns a marriage into a family, or it adds what Western thinking might term a new nuclear family to the extended family

---

[113]Cf. Anthony C. Thiselton, "Realized Eschatology at Corinth," *NTS* 24 (1978): 510-26 (on 521).
[114]Brown, *Body and Society*, 54, 57.
[115]Kallistos Ware, *The Inner Kingdom* (Crestwood, NY: St Vladimir's Seminary Press, 2001), 123.
[116]Cf. Michael J. Gorman, *Cruciformity* (Grand Rapids and Cambridge, UK: Eerdmans, 2001), 261-66.
[117]Thomas A. Bennett in a personal comment.

or families to which Joseph and Mary belonged. That extended family plays a role in the drama of his birth (Lk 1:5-80). Jesus grows up in the context of a family and joins in family pilgrimages to Jerusalem (Lk 2:41-51). The portrayal fits the picture in the First Testament, where the family is the context in which people gain insight, learn what God has done and learn God's expectations of them.

There a typical situation might be one where a village was home to a hundred or two hundred people divided between two or three or four extended families, each of which would comprise a number of households. In Jerusalem and other big cities things would be different, but for the vast majority of people who lived in villages or homesteads, the latter were the base for the regular life of tending the extended family's land in accordance with the commission in Genesis and the allocations in Joshua. The extended family is thus the people's work unit and the unit in which the faith is taught, and in both respects it is the unit through which God's creation and redemption purpose is put into effect. It provides the structures for life as a whole, including worship, discipline, generosity, hospitality and care for the stranger. If a household gets into economic difficulties, the extended family has responsibility for helping it get through them.

The First Testament assumes that everyone belongs to an extended family. So people who move to a village from another country or another part of Israel are adopted into a family, as are orphans and widows—at least such is the theory, though the rules about gleaning imply that things did not necessarily work out that way. Servants likewise are members of the extended family; it is the society's safety net. In the New Testament, the place of servants within the family is suggested by a story like that of the centurion's concern for his "boy" (Mt 8:5-13). In practice, family life as the First Testament describes it is often dysfunctional, and God works through it in its dysfunctional nature. Rivalry, conflict, deception and trickery are among its consistent characteristics.

The New Testament also shows some concern for the structure of the family and for safeguarding its order and obligations (e.g., Eph 6:1-4; Col 3:20-21; cf. also 1 Tim 5:4, 8). This concern likely underlies the rules in the Torah about who may marry whom, which Paul affirms (1 Cor 7). The community needs ways of safeguarding the stability of the extended family when it becomes a place of conflict and oppression, not least in connection with sex.

The New Testament sees God's being a Father (*patēr*) as lying behind the notion of family (*patria*) (Eph 3:15), rather than the other way around, and it recognizes the family's importance by taking it as an image for the congregation. One's fellow believers are one's brothers and sisters (e.g., Rom 8:29; 1 Cor 8:11-13; Gal 1:2; 1 Pet 2:17). It was closer to being literal reality in Israel; it is metaphorically so for a congregation of believers in Jesus. They are "the household of faith" (Gal 6:10).

Turning family into a metaphor in this way also subverts the family and undermines its importance. Such subversion is explicit elsewhere. On one occasion when his family show up, Jesus declares that his real family are the people who do the Father's will (Mk 3:31-35). Some people have left their families on his account, and he promises them replacements (Mk 10:29-30). Indeed, he has come to divide families, and his followers have to hate their family (Mt 10:34-37; Lk 14:26). The congregation becomes a believer's primary group.

3.5 THE PERSON

The way the Scriptures think about the elements that make up the human person need not have direct theological significance, but it does point toward some insights about the human person. Talk of the flesh can speak simply of bodiliness, but it can also suggest our physical frailty and in other contexts our moral frailty. Our physical frailty links with our vulnerability to suffering, which can link with our moral weakness, though it need not. Body and soul can operate semi-independently, but it is odd for them to do so; they are intrinsically related. The soul is the self, and the self embraces both the outer person and the inner person. The heart in scriptural thinking more often denotes the mind than the emotions; both these are also intrinsic to the true self. The spirit suggests the dynamic of the person; the human spirit is our "natural" point of contact with the divine spirit.

Human Life and Its Frailty
Genesis 2–3 pictures humanity as free to eat from a life tree and thus to begin a life that would last forever. So the human body was not created in a way that

would mean people automatically lived forever, and what we directly know of the human body fits with that implication. Life starts when God shapes you in the womb, gives you breath and pulls you out of the womb (Pss 22:9-10 [MT 10-11]; 139:13-16), and it then follows a natural cycle of birth, growth, maturing, plateauing, declining and dying. Absent the life tree, in due course we give the life breath back to the one who gave it (Lk 23:46; Acts 7:59).

A kind of frailty is built into human existence. Jesus thus shares in human weakness as an aspect of sharing in human nature (Heb 5:2), and Paul makes many references to his personal weakness.[118] Life *in* the flesh is thus different from life *according to* the flesh. Life in the flesh means vulnerability and fragility, yet it is something in which one can glory, as one could not glory in life according to the flesh. It is in the context of this weakness of the flesh that one experiences the power of the Spirit, the power of the age to come.[119] Human life is thus a combination of frailty and strength, as divine breath, spirit, is poured into it in its frailty. "All flesh is like grass, and its splendor is like a flower in the grass. The grass withers and the flower falls. But the Lord's word lasts to the ages" (1 Pet 1:24; cf. Is 40:6-8).

Some experiences of frailty are our own fault. When his friends bring before Jesus a man who is totally handicapped, Jesus tells him that his sins are forgiven (Mk 2:5), and after healing a man who had been handicapped for thirty-eight years, Jesus tells him not to sin any longer (Jn 5:14). In both cases he implies that the man's suffering had something to do with his sin. The background to Yahweh's declaration "I am your healer" (Ex 15:26), "the divine Magna Carta in the matter of health and all related questions,"[120] includes expressions of disillusion and a challenge to obedience (cf. Jer 33:6; Ps 107:17-18). Paul, too, assumes a link between sin and suffering when he speaks about sickness and premature death in the Corinthian congregation: it issues from the way people are eating the Lord's bread and drinking his cup, without discerning Jesus' body—that is, without recognizing that they are one body (1 Cor 11:17-32).

---

[118]Cf. Krister Stendahl, *Paul Among Jews and Gentiles and Other Essays* (Philadelphia: Fortress, 1976), 40-52.

[119]See Gordon D. Fee, *God's Empowering Presence* (Peabody, MA: Hendrickson, 1994), 822-26; also David Alan Black, *Paul, Apostle of Weakness* (New York: Lang, 1984).

[120]Barth, *CD* III, 4:369.

On the other hand, one significance of the story of Job is that people's individual suffering does not always result from their personal wrong-doing, and many other biblical stories illustrate the same awareness. John 9 has as its background the fact that suffering can issue from sin, and the disciples ask whether a man had been born blind because of his own sin or that of his parents. In his case the answer is neither. He was born blind "so that the works of God might be manifested in him," the work of God being the work that God does through Jesus, who heals the man. Similarly, Lazarus's illness is "for God's glory, so that God's Son may be glorified through it" (Jn 11:4). The book of Job comprises the Scriptures' most systematic reflection on human frailty. It says nothing that does not also occur elsewhere, but it brings the Scriptures' insights together. Human suffering can be corrective, can be a context in which God is glorified, can be a test of our relationship with God, can drive us into pressing God with protests, can be an experience through which God reaches out to us and can be an experience that properly shatters our assumptions about who God is and who we are.

Another form of weakness characterizes Israel and characterizes the believing communities. Except for a century or so in the era of David and Solomon, and another century at the very end of the First Testament period, Israel and the Jewish people were never politically powerful; they were regularly subject to the control of bigger powers. Further, within Israel, the Torah and the Prophets often focus on the relationship between the strong and the weak, emphasizing that the powerful people (those who can exercise *mišpāṭ*) have responsibility to do the right thing by the ordinary, weak people (to show *ṣədāqâ* toward them). They emphasize that powerless people such as widows, orphans and the landless have rights. While the followers of Jesus are mostly not poor people, they are powerless people, and in the first congregations of believers such as the one at Corinth there were few powerful people (see 1 Cor 1:26-31). Yet the powerless were embodying an aspect of regular humanity, because frailty is an aspect of humanness that throws into relief the power of God, which is also realized in weakness (1 Cor 1:18–2:5). It has been said that black Christianity has been embodied, life affirming, present (people present to one another and aware of the presence of God) and open to the depth of human suffering.[121] In that respect it has modeled the nature of all humanness.

Flesh/Body and Soul

Flesh (*sarx*) can thus suggest human nature in its frailty, and it can also denote humanity's lower nature. Elsewhere the word has a neutral significance. "The Mind/Message became flesh and dwelt among us" (Jn 1:14); "Jesus the Anointed One has come in the flesh" (1 Jn 4:2, 3). Flesh simply denotes created human nature in its physicality. It is such human nature that Jesus took. In these contexts, flesh is a way of referring to our total humanness (body and soul, if you like). The trouble that comes to Jesus' servants means that their bodies share in the experience of death through which Jesus went, but this experience opens up the possibility of Jesus' life being exhibited in their bodies, in their mortal flesh (2 Cor 4:10-11).

Whereas Jesus came from David's family as regards the flesh, he was declared Son of God in power as to the spirit of holiness through the resurrection from the dead (Rom 1:4). That statement does make a contrast between flesh and spirit that links with the contrast between weakness and power. But Western thinking has also been inclined to draw a different contrast between the material and the spiritual, between body and soul, a dualism in which the two are seen as opposed, or a duality that may simply imply that they are somewhat independent of each other. The suspicion is then that the spirit or soul is the real person and that it's easy to imagine the spirit or soul happily surviving separation from the body or surviving the death of the body.

But the New Testament does not put spirit (*pneuma*) or soul (*psychē*), and body (*sōma*) or flesh in the neutral sense (*sarx*), over against each other, as the First Testament does not put *nepeš* and *bāśār* over against each other. Body and soul can be distinguished, but they belong together. Jesus speaks of the risk of both being destroyed in hell (Mt 10:28). "A man's body is no mere adornment, or external convenience; it belongs to his very nature as a man" (hence the human instinct to give it decent burial).[122]

---

[121]James W. McClendon, *Systematic Theology: Ethics* (Nashville: Abingdon, 1986), 79-84.
[122]Augustine, *City of God* 1.23.

The two can operate semiseparately. A person can be absent in body but present in spirit (1 Cor 5:3-4; Col 2:5). The body can be in one place, but the person can be somewhere else, in some sense (2 Cor 12:1-3). In a committee meeting I may be present physically, but in my spirit I may be elsewhere. The same can be true of my students during a lecture; they are physically in the classroom, but their spirits may be somewhere else. We may speak of spirit and body as the inner and outer person, but this language is misleading. The so-called inner person has some independence of the so-called outer person and can be wandering about elsewhere when the outer person is stuck in one place. Although body and spirit are interdependent, then, they can to some degree function separately or be in tension. In my mind I may want one thing, but with my body I may do something else (Rom 7:22-23). I may be wasting away outwardly but renewed inwardly (2 Cor 4:16)—or the reverse.

Admittedly, when Paul says, "Though I am away from you in the flesh, in the spirit I am with you, rejoicing as I see your order and the firmness of your faith toward the Anointed One" (Col 2:5; cf. 1 Cor 5:3-4), he may not be referring to the natural capacity of the human spirit to be somewhere different from the body. His words may carry the overtones of "in the Spirit I am with you." It is because of the Spirit's involvement with him that this presence with the Colossians or the Corinthians is possible. Yet if the Spirit's involvement with us through Jesus is a heightening or fulfilling or restoring of something that is built into creation, this would fit with the way anyone can be present with someone in spirit though absent in body.

Death means losing our bodies for a while (2 Cor 5:1-10). This experience is not a welcome one. It's like being naked. It would be preferable to be present with people as a whole person, as it is preferable for me and my students to be present in a meeting or a class as whole persons. The body is too integral to being human for the separation of body and spirit to be a satisfactory situation. The body is not something inessential that outwardly clings to the real self, which is the spirit. The body "belongs to its very essence," so that a person does not *have* a body but *is* a body. The body *is* the self; to put it less paradoxically, the body is the embodiment of the person.[123]

---

[123]Cf. Dunn, *Theology of Paul the Apostle*, 56.

If Jesus is magnified in my body, he is magnified in *me* as an essentially embodied person; presenting our bodies to God means presenting *ourselves* to God; and our bodies are "members of the Anointed One" (1 Cor 6:15; cf. Phil 1:20; Rom 6:12-13; 12:1).[124] My body is not something that belongs to the world external to me. It is *my* body. It is through my body that I get my primary experience of myself and also of my dependence on others. While the spirit is also relational and communal, part of the body's importance lies in its being more obviously, outwardly, relational and communal.[125] Mind and body are also not set over against each other: presenting my body to God is associated with being transformed through the renewing of my mind (Rom 12:1-2). It means getting back to the way we were created to think (Rom 1:20-21, 28).

The way body and spirit can be semiseparable links with our human capacity to distinguish ourselves from ourselves in a certain fashion, as we think about what we do and what happens to us. We can be at odds with ourselves or estranged from ourselves. We can control ourselves or lose control of ourselves. While losing control clearly can be negative, it can mean bringing back the estranged self. We can subdue ourselves, give ourselves, yield ourselves, expend ourselves, rule over ourselves (Rom 6:12-13; 12:1; 1 Cor 7:4; 9:27; 13:3; Phil 1:20). We can argue with ourselves (Pss 42:5, 11 [MT 6, 12]; 43:5). The Scriptures thus accept the experience of tension involved in our relationship with ourselves, whereas the tension is evaded in different ways by gnosticism (with its dualism of soul and body), mysticism (if this term implies that developing our relationship with God involves escaping the body) and asceticism (with its reckoning that the body needs to be treated toughly). All three involve seeing the body as not an aspect of the real and essential me.[126]

"The resurrection of the body is important: if my body is not resurrected, I am not resurrected. The resurrection of the body is . . . less a secondary add-on to eternally existing souls or spirits than it is the necessary destiny of creatures defined essentially in part by their embodiment."[127] While Paul

---

[124]Bultmann, *Theology of the New Testament*, 1:194.

[125]Thiselton, *Hermeneutics of Doctrine*, 47, 240-56.

[126]This paragraph incorporates a summary of Bultmann, *Theology of the New Testament*, 1:192-97.

[127]Amos Yong, *Renewing Christian Theology* (Waco, TX: Baylor University Press, 2014), 38. In *Theology of the New Testament*, 1:198-99, Bultmann goes on to suggest that Paul is interested in the

can speak in terms of wishing to be released from the body (2 Cor 5:1-10), this longing relates to its physical vulnerability rather than its moral weakness, and it generates a desire for a new, heavenly "dwelling" to replace this earthly one rather than a desire or assumption that we can escape physicality.

Soul/Self

When God created Adam, he shaped him from dirt and breathed living breath into his nostrils, and the man "became a living soul" (Gen 2:7 KJV). The word *soul* has a range of meanings in English, like *nepeš* in Hebrew and *psychē* in Greek. English can use expressions such as "there wasn't a soul there" as well as expressions such as "soul music" and "soul food" and "things that did my soul good." In speaking of the man becoming "a living soul," Genesis is talking about his becoming a person; the New Testament can likewise use the word *psychē* to denote a person (e.g., Acts 7:14; Rom 13:1; 1 Cor 15:45; 1 Pet 3:20). To judge from Genesis, a person comprises a physical body plus some breath, though paradoxically, even without the breath a body (that is, a corpse) can be called a *nepeš* (e.g., Lev 21:1, 11). *Body* and *soul* and other such terms "do not refer to *parts* of man . . . but rather always mean *man as a whole*, with respect to some specific possibility of his being."[128]

In a modern Western context the assumption that the body embodies the person may be intelligible on a new basis, since we know that the physical workings of the brain are essential to the functioning of the person and to who the person is. Without the brain, there is no person. It doesn't mean human beings are "merely" bodies. It does mean there is no person without a brain. But neither is the brain the entirety of the person; the body is the person's embodiment.[129]

The Scriptures assume that our moral commitments need to cover both thinking and action. The Ten Commandments urge people to avoid murder,

---

body and in resurrection only because it symbolizes the way we have a relationship with ourselves, but here he seems to be imposing an idea on Paul. See further the critique in, e.g., Richard B. Hays, "Humanity Prior to the Revelation of Faith," in Bruce W. Longenecker and Mikael C. Parsons, eds., *Beyond Bultmann* (Waco, TX: Baylor University Press, 2014), 61-77.

[128]Rudolf Bultmann, *Existence and Faith* (New York: Meridian, 1960; London: Hodder, 1961), 130; cf. Thiselton, *Hermeneutics of Doctrine*, 261.

[129]See further Joel B. Green, *Body, Soul and Human Life* (Grand Rapids: Baker; Milton Keynes, UK: Paternoster, 2008).

adultery and perjury. Jesus declares that such avoidance is not enough; disciples must avoid anger, desire, swearing, resistance and bias (Mt 5:21-48). He doesn't give reasons, and his words can place a burden on people who feel some guilt about an occasional angry or lustful thought that doesn't seem within their control, but it fits with the insight in Proverbs that the heart or mind is the wellspring of life. The human person is one whole. If someone is to be whole as a person (*teleios*; Mt 5:48) there needs to be some consistency between the working of the inner person and of the outer person. It is in any case hard to be one thing on the outside and something different on the inside. Actions issue from attitudes and affect attitudes. It may be no good trying to control actions unless you do something about attitudes, and vice versa.

Jesus is not interested in inner attitude rather than outward action, which would let people off the hook in one direction. But it might be easy for believers to focus on outward observance such as tithing or avoiding profanity, as he says Pharisees and theologians do. One should not be too harsh on the Pharisees and theologians; the Torah does stress outward action, as is its nature as a rule book. A concern with attitude surfaces more in a book such as Proverbs and in the Prophets, though the Torah's references to attitudes such as trust and compassion show that it presupposes the point Jesus makes. The Torah expresses it in the command to love with your entire mind or heart, your self or soul and your strength (Deut 6:5) and in the Decalogue's closing command about coveting. Contentment is a hard virtue, whether its object is a house or a spouse or some stuff. Dissatisfaction is a root of much trouble. In looking for both an inner and an outward commitment, then, Jesus is once again filling out or filling up or making explicit the implications of the Torah and the Prophets (and the Writings), as he says (Mt 5:17).

Heart/Mind

Jesus once speaks of heart and soul and mind (Mt 22:37), but he hardly implies a threefold division of the inner person; and Paul once speaks of spirit and soul and body (1 Thess 5:23), but understanding him to imply that human beings are made up of three parts would make him speak inconsistently with the way he and other biblical writers speak elsewhere. Rather it compares with other formulations (Deut 6:5; Mk 12:30; Lk 10:27; as well as Mt 22:37) in conveying rhetorically a complete personal soundness. Such aspects of the way the Scriptures speak draw our attention to the fluid nature of the distinctions we make between aspects of the person.

The two Testaments use the terms *lēb/lēbāb* and *kardia* to refer to the heart in the sense of the whole inner person, including the mind, the emotions and the will. Pharaoh hardens his heart (Ex 8:15). Robe makers need to be wise of heart (Ex 28:3). Moses' ideas don't come from his own heart (Num 16:28). Solomon prays for an understanding heart (1 Kings 3:9). Jeroboam devised something out of his own heart (1 Kings 12:33). God asks whether the adversary has set his heart on Job (Job 1:8). Refusal to acknowledge God in light of what he had revealed led to people's stupid heart being darkened (Rom 1:20-21). The heart feels desire (Rom 1:24). God's Torah needed to be written into people's hearts (Rom 2:15). Circumcision of heart is the kind that counts (Rom 2:29). The love of God is poured out into our hearts (Rom 5:5). Paul has sorrow in his heart (Rom 9:2). With the heart people believe (Rom 10:8-10). We make decisions with our hearts (2 Cor 9:7). The heart signifies the mind as much as the emotions.

While *lēb/lēbāb* is the main Hebrew word for "mind," Greek has *nous* as well as *kardia,* so there is an overlap between the words for heart and the mind in New Testament terminology. God gave people over to a base mind (Rom 1:28). People need to be transformed by the renewing of their mind (Rom 12:2). They need to be fully persuaded in their own mind (Rom 14:5) and not to be shaken in mind (2 Thess 2:2). One could substitute *kardia* in these passages and not significantly change their meaning, though one could not rewrite all the *kardia* passages with *nous*; the link with thinking rather than emotion is essential to *nous*.

In Hebrew "heart" also covers "conscience," the sense that one has done wrong (e.g., Gen 20:5-6; 1 Sam 24:5; 25:31; 2 Sam 24:10; Job 27:6). Greek again has a separate word (*suneidēsis*; Jn 8:9; Acts 24:16; Rom 2:15; 9:1) and another separate word for people's feelings, which it locates in the guts (*splanchna* and the verb *splanchnizomai*). These feelings are a motivation for Jesus' action (e.g., Mk 1:41; 6:34; 8:2; 9:22) and for believers' relationships with one another (Phil 2:1; 3:12; 1 Jn 3:17).

Different cultures are inclined to evaluate different aspects of the inner person in different ways. Scholarly Western thinking has been inclined to view reason as good and emotions as bad,[130] and it can therefore be attracted to Paul's stress on the mind; he urges people to avoid being stupid (Gal 3:1, 3), doesn't want the Thessalonians to be "out of their mind" (*apo tou nous*; 2 Thess 2:2) and emphasizes that worship should involve the mind as well as the spirit (1 Cor 14:14-15). The attitude of ordinary Western people and of people in traditional cultures may be different. They may be attracted to the way people in both Testaments express joy and pain. The mixed nature of the Scriptures' talk of the heart, and the New Testament's use of other expressions, reminds us that the facets of the inner person are interwoven and that emotions give energy to action. Indeed, many moral judgments, at least, are intuitive and are only subsequently rationalized.[131]

Human Spirit/Divine Spirit

Human life is a combination of frailty and strength. Divine breath, divine spirit is poured into a frail body. "My message and my preaching were not in persuasive words of insight but in a demonstration of the Spirit and of power, so that your trust might not be in human insight but in God's power" (1 Cor 3:4-5). "What is born of the flesh is flesh, and what is born of the Spirit is spirit" (Jn 3:6). "God is spirit" (Jn 4:23). Among terms that refer to human nature such as *flesh*, *body*, *heart* and *soul*, *spirit* is the term that is most redolent of God and most suggests God's involvement with human beings.

When Paul says, "If we live by the Spirit, let us also walk by the Spirit" (Gal 5:25), he may not be suggesting "an explosively working power" but rather a guiding by a definite tendency;[132] the Spirit is an ethical norm, as is implicit in references to "walking according to the Spirit" and "setting the mind on the things of the Spirit" (Rom 8:4-5).[133] Yet Paul is also pointing to the need for God to do something miraculous to get us to walk in the right way. The double resonances of *holiness* have the same implication. Holiness

---

[130]See Thomas Kazen, *Emotions in Biblical Law* (Sheffield: Sheffield Phoenix, 2011), 12.
[131]Cf. ibid., 14.
[132]Bultmann, *Theology of the New Testament*, 1:207; and see further 191-227 on the emphases of the different terms such as *flesh*, *body*, *heart* and *soul*.
[133]Bultmann, *Theology of the New Testament*, 1:336-37.

suggests the metaphysically supernatural and extraordinary; it also suggests the morally supernatural and extraordinary.

Spirit suggests a reality that contrasts with the human. The spirit of God is God's distinctive dynamism that transforms the human. The implication of 1 Corinthians 2 is that "talk of 'spirituality' and of 'wisdom' comes to nothing unless God's Holy Spirit activates the message of the cross and brings it home afresh."[134] Athanasius asks, "What kinship could there be . . . between the Spirit and the creatures? . . .The Spirit is from him [God]."[135] Paul's use of *pneumatikos* denotes "what pertains to the Holy Spirit, not human spirituality."[136] Like is known only by like," so "humans do not on their own possess the quality that would make it possible to know God or God's wisdom"; only God can know God, so only God's Spirit can reveal God.[137] *Pneumatikos* does not denote "spiritual" in the sense of inner or noncorporeal over against physical or earthly.[138] "Small case 'spiritual' probably should be eliminated from our vocabulary" given that it tends to suggest religious, nonmaterial, mystical "or, even worse, 'the interior life of the believer.'" Paul never uses the word to refer to the human spirit or to "spiritual life"; it "primarily refers to the Spirit of God, even when the contrasts are to 'earthly' bodies and 'material support.'"[139]

In a Christian context, *spirituality* needs to mean what Paul calls the new life in the Spirit, but in practice *spirituality* easily suggests a move "from the *vitality* of a creative life *out of* God to the *spirituality* of a not-of-this-world life *in* God. . . . A clean line divides spirituality from everyday life," and "spiritual experiences" contrast with "sensory ones." "*Soul-searching* takes the place of practical *conversion*."[140] *Spirituality* denotes a human inclination to attend to aspects of life that are other than merely material. Talk about spirituality then has little to do with the way the Scriptures talk about the spirit of God or the Spirit of God.

---

[134]Thiselton, *1 Corinthians*, 57-58.

[135]Athanasius, *The Letters of Saint Athanasius Concerning the Holy Spirit* (London: Epworth, 1951), 1:22; cf. Thiselton, *1 Corinthians*, 58.

[136]Thiselton, *1 Corinthians*, 192 (the words are italicized).

[137]Gordon D. Fee, *The First Epistle to the Corinthians* (Grand Rapids: Eerdmans, 1987), 110.

[138]Fee, *God's Empowering Presence*, 30.

[139]Ibid., 32.

[140]Jürgen Moltmann, *The Spirit of Life* (London: SCM Press; Minneapolis: Fortress, 1992), 83-84.

Yet the spirit is "that dimension of the human person by means of which the person relates most directly to God."[141] It is the aspect of our person that we have most in common with God. Paul can talk of "my spirit" when "it is clear in the context that the Holy Spirit is very much in view as well" (e.g., 1 Cor 5:3-4; 6:17; 14:14-15). "The believer's spirit is the place where, by means of God's own Spirit, the human and divine interface in the believer's life."[142]

The First Testament does imply that Athanasius has overstated the point. "The possibility of perceiving God in all things, and all things in God, is grounded theologically on an understanding of the Spirit of God as the power of creation and the wellspring of life" (cf. Job 33:4; 34:13-14; 104:29-30). Thus "every true experience of the self becomes also an experience of the divine spirit of life in the human being."[143] There *is* a natural kinship between the Spirit and creatures, but our human turning away from God compromised that kinship. The Scriptures do not make clear whether it simply impaired it (so that a person can still reach out to God or respond when God reaches out) or actually destroyed it (so that whenever a person reaches out to God they are doing so because God has already begun a process of recreating it).

We were created spiritual (*pneumatikos*), but we became fleshly (*sarkinos*) (1 Cor 3:1). It is not an absolute distinction. The Corinthians are "infants in the Anointed One," not outside him. Since humanity turned away from God, it is our default position to form attitudes and make decisions on a basis that leaves God out and leaves other people out. The First Testament story makes it clear; the life of the Corinthians does so. God's winning us back reverses our default position, though the life of Israel and the life of the Corinthians indicate that there is no necessity about the way it works out.

3.6 Waywardness and Its Consequences

In considering heavenly powers, local communities and cities, nations and superpowers, and the makeup and life of the individual, we have seen that nothing is as good as it was when God created it. It is compromised and spoiled by the way human beings have acted. Yet human beings are victims as well as perpetrators.

---

[141]Dunn, *Theology of Paul the Apostle*, 77.
[142]Fee, *God's Empowering Presence*, 25.
[143]Moltmann, *Spirit of Life*, 35.

A Series of Images

The two Testaments have a series of images to convey the nature of human wrongdoing, and it's unwise to fix on one as conveying the essence of it.[144]

The title of this section takes up the image of waywardness, which suggests leaving the road that God sets in front of people as the right way and choosing to go another way (e.g., Jer 3:21).

Wrongdoing can be described as an act of rebellion against God. People were familiar with the use of the verb *rebel* in the nontheological sense (e.g., 2 Kings 3:7; 8:20), and its etymological sense is therefore quite likely to be in people's mind when they use this image for wrongdoing (e.g., Is 1:2; Jer 3:13). It involves rejecting God's authority. He is in a position like that of a king or parent, and we are in the position of rebellious children or defiant subjects.

Wrongdoing can be described as unfaithfulness, like the unfaithfulness of someone who goes back on a commitment and/or commits adultery (e.g., Ex 21:8; Jer 3:20). So it involves going back on one's commitment to Yahweh and consorting with other deities (e.g., Jer 5:11; Lam 1:2). It can be described as a broader faithlessness (*reša*'), which is the most general Hebrew word for wrongdoing (compare *adikia* in Greek). It is the antonym of faithfulness (*ṣədāqâ*), so that the pair of terms set up a contrast between living rightly in relation to God and other people, and ignoring the obligations that inhere in those relationships.

Wrongdoing can be described as trespassing on God's rights or honor. A woman who committed adultery would be doing so in relation to her husband's rights or honor (Num 5:12, 27). In relationships with Yahweh, a classic instance is Akan's taking some of the plunder from Jericho that belonged to Yahweh, not least as the one who brought about the city's destruction (Josh 7:1). Another form of trespass on God's rights or honor is involved in marrying someone from another people, who would be the servant of another deity (Ezra 9–10). The idea of wrongdoing as profanity (*ḥănupâ*; Jer 23:15) is related. It means failing to treat the holy as holy—worst of all, treating the Holy One as if he were not really God. In effect, it is godlessness (*asebeia*; e.g., Rom 1:18).

---

[144]Cf. G. C. Berkouwer, *Sin* (Grand Rapids: Eerdmans, 1971), 255.

Wrongdoing can be described as transgressing the rules that God has laid down, crossing over the boundaries with which he has circumscribed his people's life (e.g., Deut 2:14; 12:10 for the literal usage; Deut 17:2; 26:13 for the theological usage). Humanity's wrongdoing started off as disobedience: alongside a wide range of scope for decision making, Yahweh laid down one prohibition, but as a result of one person's disobedience to the one prohibition, humanity as a whole ended up as sinners. Adam's action can thus be described as boundary crossing of this kind (Rom 5:14, 19). "Sin is lawlessness" (1 Jn 3:4). It issues in there being a record of the occasions when people have broken the law (Col 2:14).

While Genesis does not describe Adam and Eve's disobedience as "sin," that word does come in the Cain and Abel story (Gen 4:7). It commonly renders Hebrew and Greek words that in everyday speech suggest failing or falling short, not because people have tried hard and not succeeded but because they haven't really tried: one could argue that humanity's original sin is sloth.[145] "All have sinned and fallen short of God's splendor" (Rom 3:23). Although the Hebrew and Greek words have these similar etymologies, in the Scriptures they are hardly ever used in an everyday sense—like the English word *sin*, in fact. People would likely therefore not be very aware of the sense of "falling short" suggested by etymology.

A Wayward Community

As a subset of the fact that being human is a corporate as well as an individual reality, waywardness characterizes corporate entities (families, communities, cities, nations, congregations, the world) as well as individuals. Sin is a corporate affair from the beginning. From the beginning it involves a married couple, then a family, then a village (Gen 3–4). Genesis brings its account of sin to a climax with an emphasis on how "bad" things have become (*ra'*) and how the entire earth is filled with violation or violence (*ḥāmās*) (Gen 6:5, 11, 13; 8:21).

The word *ra'* carries the same double connotation as "bad" in English. It's the opposite of pleasant or beautiful and the opposite of honorable or upright or righteous. It suggests a contrast with the goodness of the world as God created it ("good," *ṭōb*, came nine times in Gen 1–2). The equivocal

---

[145]See Barth, *CD* IV, 2:403-83.

nature of the Hebrew words compares with that of the English words *bad* and *good*, the ambiguity exploited in the question "Why do bad things happen to good people?" The double use of the word suggests that it is quite appropriate that bad things happen to bad people and good things to good people.

The word for violence or violation carries another double connotation, the idea of people doing violence to God's rules and doing violence to one another, and it hints at links between these two, that violating God's rules leads to violence between people and/or that violence toward other people involves violation of God's rules for human life; one way or another, things are ruined (Gen 6:11-12).

After the flood, likewise sin involves a family and a nation (Gen 9–11). Yahweh subsequently warned Israel as a nation that the possession of territory could become a distraction. It could lead Israel astray as the fruit tree led Adam and Eve astray. It did so, and Yahweh threw Israel out of his territory for a while, as he had thrown out its previous occupants and had thrown out Adam and Eve from his orchard. Likewise the city to which God made a commitment became the city Yahweh abandoned because of its faithlessness (see esp. Lamentations). In the unfolding of the book of Isaiah, the horizon broadens from a focus on Judah (Is 1–12) to a tour of the nations around (Is 13–23) until the prophecies stand back and talk about the world as a whole (Is 24–27), polluted by humanity's violating of Yahweh's rules for its life and its violence.

So a society can be characterized by greed, waste, laziness, overwork, racism, sexism or inequality. A nation can make war for the sake of revenge or of gaining territory, or it can fail to take action against oppressors. "The Western world has been shaped and defined by a spirit that exhibits another constitution, other interests, other goals, and other power structures than the Spirit of God." This other spirit "cultivates and spreads individual and community self-relations in the sense of self-certainty, self-possession, and the constant increase of this self-relation that serves self-production." It "aims at the cult of the abstract, private person and of the stratified, monocentric institution, as well as the cognitive or cognitively controllable domination of the world."[146] "In the story Americans tell themselves, every great problem

---

[146]Welker, *God the Spirit*, 279, 280, 281.

from independence to slavery to totalitarian threats is finally solved by the *ultima ratio* of war," whereas "the biblical master story pivots upon a slave people who ran away 'in urgent haste' (Deut. 16:3), upon a Savior who enters the capital city riding on a donkey and who is called the Prince of Peace."[147]

In a twenty-first-century context, as in Genesis and in Isaiah, the corporateness of human experience does not stop at one's own society or nation. The world's societies and peoples are interdependent. Culture is global. The economic process, the political process and the cultural process are acted out in economic struggles and the exploitation of nature, in the struggle for power and the control of power, and in the struggle for educational, racial and sexual privileges.[148] The individual members of the society or the nation or the world may then suffer several consequences. They may be the direct victims of the waywardness, and/or they may inevitably share in responsibility for it, and/or they may be so influenced by their group that they personally come under the grip of the attitude in question. Escaping the effect of sin in these connections is even more complex than is escaping the bondage of individual sin. That fact adds to the burden of sin on the individual.

The World

The ultimate expression of this reality is the world as a whole. While the world can stand for creation in its entirety (Jn 1:10; 17:5, 24), it also stands for the human creation as it has turned its back on God, and specifically as it opposes Jesus. Theologically, the world is a possible source of truth for the church, the context in which the church lives and the object of its mission,[149] but it is also an embodiment of resistance to God, a sphere set over against God, "an independent super-self over all individual selves." The creation got turned into the world, and the spirit of the world is then "the atmosphere to whose compelling influence every man contributes but to which he is also always subject." The world is characterized by darkness and opposition to God and to the realm of light. "The essence of the

---

[147]James W. McClendon, *Systematic Theology: Witness* (Nashville: Abingdon, 2000), 361-62.
[148]Cf. Jürgen Moltmann, *The Church in the Power of the Spirit* (London: SCM Press; New York: Harper, 1977), 163-89.
[149]Francis Watson, *Text, Church and World* (Edinburgh: T&T Clark; Grand Rapids: Eerdmans, 1994), 9-11.

kosmos . . . is *darkness*," not as a shadow or affliction imposed on it (as in Is 9:2 [MT 1]) but as its own inherent nature; "the world appropriates to itself its darkness." It is characterized by falsehood (since Jesus comes to bring truth [Jn 18:37]) and by blindness.[150]

It is thus in "desperate" need.[151] "The whole world lies with the evil one" (1 Jn 5:19). The Torah lays down rules designed to make it impossible for people to be short of food, shelter, clothing, work, rest, family, community or freedom. But "the world" is a system or context in which we can methodically deprive people of food, shelter, clothing, work, rest, family, community and freedom, and in which we do so. The world is the antikingdom.[152] Its deeds are evil (Jn 7:7).

The world is very powerful because it is presided over by supernatural powers, though they have power only because humanity lets them have power, not because their power and God's power are inherently similar. Christians may comment ruefully that "it's a fallen world," but it's not a fallen creation. It is the world that is under the control of "the prince of this world" (Jn 12:31). The beast has been allowed to exercise authority over "every tribe, language, nation, and race," so that "the inhabitants of the earth" as a whole have been deluded into worshiping the beast (Rev 13:7-8), even though this does not apply to "the people whose names are written in the lamb's book of life."

This world is also set over against the world to come, characterized chronologically as well as spatially. This age stands over against the age to come (1 Cor 2:6-8; Eph 1:21). Talk in terms of this age as opposed to this world refers to the same entity but draws attention to its temporal limitation, both retrospective and prospective. By nature we walk "in accordance with this world, this age," literally, "this world's age" (Eph 2:2).[153] The contrast between this age and the age to come and the contrast between this world and the world to come are distinct but related. The distinctive phrase "this world's

---

[150]Bultmann, *Theology of the New Testament*, 2:26-27; 1:207; 2:15.

[151]D. Moody Smith, *The Theology of the Gospel of John* (Cambridge and New York: Cambridge University Press, 1995), 80, 81 (he uses that word twice).

[152]Jon Sobrino, *Jesus the Liberator* (Maryknoll, NY: Orbis, 1993; Tunbridge Wells, UK: Burns and Oates, 1994), e.g., 24.

[153]Cf. J. Armitage Robinson, *St. Paul's Epistle to the Ephesians*, 2nd ed. (London: James Clarke, [?1904]), 48 (and 153-54 for other such expressions in Ephesians). English translations have phrases such as "the way of this world" to produce a more natural English expression.

age" makes the point that the problem of this age is its being dominated by this world, but also that the rule of this world is limited to this age. The destiny of this world is to lose its power when this age passes.

God stood over against the world in Israel (Israel is the world); it is what the Prophets are about. God stood over against the world in Israel's history (the empire is the world); it is what the visions of Daniel are about. God stood over against the world in the time of Jesus. God stands over against the world in the life of John's church. The New Testament thus takes a negative stance toward the world,[154] though this stance does not mean a negative attitude toward people. Indeed, the world is the object of God's love and self-sacrifice. The New Testament has a negative stance toward the *kosmos* and toward the leaders who prop it up and work with it the way it is, yet not toward human beings in general. The disciples are the light of the world (Mt 5:14). It was for love of the world that God sent his Son to it to deal with its sin and be its savior, and he then sends his disciples into the world as he was sent into it (Jn 1:29; 3:16-17; 4:42; 12:46; 17:18).[155]

Degrees of Sin and Stupidity

We are all sinners, yet some people are sinners in a special sense. Matthew's account of John's baptizing activity illustrates this double assumption. John urges repentance in general terms but also confronts particular groups who especially need to put their lives right and are not to think that his baptism can bring them purification in isolation from such change.

These great sinners are the people's religious leaders, as is the case for the Prophets. The Pharisees and Sadducees are a brood of vipers (Mt 3:7-10). They kill, especially their parents, according to ancient tradition; John is inverting their own claim to an honored parenthood.[156]

John's urging people in general to repent and be baptized may also seem odd. The Jewish people are to be the beneficiaries of God's reign arriving and

---

[154]Compare H. Richard Niebuhr's exposition of "Christ Against Culture" in *Christ and Culture* (repr., San Francisco: Harper, 2001), 45-82, though Niebuhr is not enthusiastic about this way of seeing the relationship between these two.

[155]Cf. Miroslav Volf, "Johannine Dualism and Contemporary Pluralism," in Richard Bauckham and Carl Mosser, eds., *The Gospel of John and Christian Theology* (Grand Rapids and Cambridge, UK: Eerdmans, 2008), 41 = Volf, *Captive to the Word of God* (Grand Rapids and Cambridge, UK: Eerdmans, 2010), 118.

[156]See Craig S. Keener, "'Brood of Vipers,'" *JSNT* 28 (2005): 3-11.

of their overlords being put down. Yet evidently they too need cleansing. The assumption corresponds to the Torah's assumption in its rules about purification. Yes, "all have sinned and fallen short of God's splendor" (Rom 3:23).

Reactions to Jesus were strangely mixed. On one hand, Jesus summoned individuals who then abandoned their jobs and families and went with him (Mt 4:18-22). Crowds followed him on the basis of his teaching and healing (Mt 4:23-25; cf. Mt 7:28-29; 8:16). People were filled with awe and glorified God (Mt 9:8; cf. Mt 9:33). On the other hand, in Gadara he was asked to leave (Mt 8:34). Some theologians thought he was blaspheming (Mt 9:3). Some Pharisees asked why he ate with tax collectors and sinners and hypothesized that he expelled demons by means of Beelzebub (Mt 9:11, 34; 10:24).

In John, chapter after chapter tells how people fail to get Jesus: Nathanael, Mary, Nicodemus, the Samaritan woman, the people who want to make him king, the disciples, the Judeans in general. Often one has some sympathy with them, as with the Judeans who don't understand his remark about destroying this temple, and with Philip when he asks how they can feed five thousand people. Yet even when Jesus' words are quite clear, they are misunderstood, because people have to change their categories of thought in order to get Jesus. There's a miracle involved. It's only after the resurrection that some people get it (Jn 2:22).

People's dimness is illustrated by the story of Jesus giving sight to a man who had been born blind, and doing so on the sabbath. It leaves the Jerusalem leadership at a loss. One can hardly improve on the man's own words: "Well, this is extraordinary, that you don't know where he comes from, and he opened my eyes. We know that God doesn't listen to sinners, but if someone is godly and does his will, he listens to this person. It has never been heard of that someone opened the eyes of a person born blind. If this man was not from God, he couldn't have done anything" (Jn 9:30-33). All the leaders can do is throw the man out.

People are also not very good at knowing themselves. Peter illustrates the point (e.g., Jn 13:1-11). Abraham, Isaac and Jacob had long ago illustrated it. It's one of the ways in which human beings are slaves of sin (Jn 8:34). The Gentile world's thinking is characterized by emptiness and ignorance; the light has gone out in people's minds and they have lost all sensitivity

(Eph 4:17-19). The loss of moral awareness or insight starts in resistance and ends in all forms of wrongdoing. The life of the Gentile world is characterized by a hardening of people's mental arteries. The hardening issues in their alienation from God, their understanding being darkened and their lives being characterized by sensuality, impurity, greed, deceit and anger. "Sin is properly of the mind."[157] One could say that its essence is stupidity.[158] It involves suppressing the truth through *adikia* and judging others for doing so when we do the same thing (Rom 1:18; 2:1). "Sin is not a matter of weakness, but of lying and blindness." We end up blind, but it's because we have made ourselves blind.[159]

When the apostles preach the gospel, they are responsible for doing so without watering it down, but people are responsible for the way they react. To people on the way to salvation the message about Jesus' death (embodied in the lives of people whose own ministry threatens them with death) will smell lovely and will be life-giving; to people on the way to death it will smell unpleasant and be death-dealing (2 Cor 2:14-17).

Godlessness

Back at the Beginning, it seemed a good idea to take action to safeguard the future, to take control of one's destiny, to exercise responsibility for oneself. It wasn't a good idea (see Gen 3). "The sin of man is the pride of man."[160] That pride lies in refusing to trust and to obey. While it is the process involved in Genesis 3, subsequently the making of the gold calf provides a great illustration.[161] Pride indeed goes before a fall.[162]

This fall meant that people's relationship with one another became skewed. From now on, men ruled over women, and/or husbands ruled over wives. Motherhood meant hurt (watching one son kill the other). Work became toilsome. Relationships with the animate world involved ongoing conflict. The flesh became the lower nature, and yielding to the lower nature henceforth seemed a good idea. In the stories of Cain and Abel, of Lamek, of Noah

---

[157]T. F. Torrance, summarizing Calvin's view (*Calvin's Doctrine of Man*, 116).
[158]See Barth, *CD* IV, 2:410-45.
[159]José Ignacio González Faus, "Sin," in Sobrino and Ellacuría, *Mysterium Liberationis*, 532-42 (on 533) = *Systematic Theology* (Maryknoll, NY: Orbis, 1996), 194-204 (on 195, 196).
[160]Barth, *CD* IV, 1:413.
[161]See Barth, *CD* IV, 1:423-32. Barth goes on to consider a sequence of First Testament stories.
[162]Barth, *CD* IV, 1:478.

and his sons, and of the migrants in Shinar (Gen 4–11), the flesh won the argument, as it did in Eden. Humanity followed the inclinations of the lower nature. This dynamic generated both short-term and long-term trouble. Henceforth blessing and curse work themselves out in conflict in the world, with God on both sides of the battle. God is sovereign all right, chastising and destroying and scattering, but also engaging and urging and protecting and restraining. People resist God and worship him (Gen 4:26; 8:20-23).

Outside the orchard, God continued to provide for people, to act for them and to speak with them. They didn't lose their relationship with God; the realm outside the orchard was not one from which God was absent. But sin pollutes. The clash between moral wrong and the character of God means that moral wrongdoing and unfaithfulness to God are defiling (e.g., Ps 106:39). People need purifying if they are to be in God's presence (e.g., Prov 20:9).

So we are godless (*asebeis*; Rom 5:6). It is a remarkable description, because the world has always been full of gods and full of religion, but Paul dismisses all of it with a word. People are *atheoi* (Eph 2:12): this word can denote both people who forsake God and people God forsakes. Paul's dismissal encompasses both pagan religion and Jewish religion. It would now encompass Christian religion, which can no more save people than any other.

As well as being godless, we were weak and alienated (Rom 5:6-11). We were neither in the right nor good; we were sinners; we were enemies. We were weak or feeble as a consequence of our turning our backs on God's way long ago. God had then turned away from us, abandoned us to our own devices and left us helpless to do anything about our situation. There was consequently a kind of stalemate between God and us that we could do nothing about. Such is the implication of the story that the first part of Genesis tells, and God's gracious and then long-suffering involvement with Israel did little to change the situation for Israel and even less to change it for the rest of the world.

For someone who is in the right and does the right thing in relation to you, you might be prepared to die. A mother may be prepared to stand between a bullet and her grown-up son who had been a loving son to her (and even do so for the son who has let her down). For someone who is good, you

might be prepared to die. Another woman who sees that mother's action and
is impressed by its goodness might herself then be prepared to risk her life
to protect the mother. But in relation to God, we were people who had
turned our backs on our responsibility to God. We were neither in right
relationship nor good. We were sinners: people who had willfully failed God,
offended against his expectations. And we were enemies.

Was God then hostile to us? Did God attack us? Or is it that we are hostile
to God? Do we attack God? There are many forms of enmity and hostility.
Different forms and degrees of enmity and hostility have obtained in recent
years between the United States and (say) Iraq under Saddam Hussein, Iran
under Ahmadinejad, Venezuela under Chavez and North Korea under Kim
Jong-il. Different forms of enmity and hostility can obtain between members
of the Democratic and Republican parties or the British Conservative and
Labour parties; they can rail at each other in public yet then (we are told)
laugh and joke over dinner.

Different forms of enmity and hostility can obtain within the family:
parents and children, wives and husbands can rail at each other, and one
or other can walk out of the house but then come back. The Scriptures
often describe God railing at people, particularly at Israel. They describe
Jesus railing at his disciples. They describe Paul railing at churches. Paul
himself describes God giving humanity up to the consequences of its own
turning its back on God. His reference to God and us being enemies
follows immediately on his reference to wrath that we need rescuing from
(Rom 5:9), which implies hostility on God's part. Apart from the last, these
railings are most like spats within the family, which usually do not end up
in outright war.

Less frequently, the Scriptures describe human beings railing at God. Job
is the spectacular example (Job also accuses God of treating him as an
enemy). But the Scriptures do speak of us as rebels, which is an indication
that we need to see ourselves as at enmity with the one against whom we
rebelled. Again, this dynamic parallels an outbreak of hostilities within the
family. We were like children who ignored their mother's house rules and
made her throw them out of the house. Humanity serves under the lordship
of all sorts of other entities, often without realizing it. By nature human
beings serve sin, the Torah, the lower nature.

By Nature Deserving of Wrath

In Paul's account, sin lay in the fact that people did not praise God or give thanks to God though they could see the basic facts about God from the created world. Instead they suppressed the truth, and as a result lost it. Their foolish mind became darkened. Thinking to be wise, they became foolish. They did not so much give up praise as redirect their praise to created images of created beings such as animals, like the gold calf (the passage alludes to Ps 106:19-20). And God abandoned them, with the result that their action issued in a life of impurity and a dishonoring of their own bodies, and in all manner of wrong such as greed, envy, murder, strife, deceit and malice. In this way God's wrath was revealed against godlessness and wrongdoing (Rom 1:18-32).

So God's hostility issues in wrath. People who decline to turn to God are storing up wrath for themselves on the day of wrath and of the unveiling of God's judgment (Rom 2:5-8; cf. Rom 5:9; 1 Thess 1:10). It will be the day when God gives recompense to everyone in accordance with their deeds (Rom 2:5, taking up Ps 62:12 [MT 13]). The expression "the day of wrath" picks up ones the First Testament uses (e.g., Ezek 7:19; Zeph 1:15, 18), where it is another term for "Yahweh's Day." Whereas the people of God think Yahweh's Day will be a day of blessing for them and a day of judgment on other people, things may work the opposite way (Amos 5:18).

That Day of Yahweh is the climactic one that will bring about the ultimate fulfillment of Yahweh's purpose, yet it is also a day that finds fulfillments in history. The fall of Jerusalem in 587 BC is "the day of his angry fury ... the day of his anger ... the day of your anger ... the day of Yahweh's anger" (Lam 1:12; 2:1, 21, 22). God's wrath is a reality within history as well as a reality that comes into play at the End. Already, "God's wrath is revealed from heaven against all godlessness and wrongdoing on the part of people who suppress the truth by wrongdoing" (Rom 1:18). There is an inbuilt process whereby stupid action generates disaster. There is also an interventionist process whereby God brings punishment on wrong action.[163] Failing to recognize Jesus' body makes one liable to

---

[163]See, e.g., Gene M. Tucker, "Sin and 'Judgment' in the Prophets," in Henry T. C. Sun and Keith L. Eades, eds., *Problems in Biblical Theology*, Rolf Knierim Festschrift (Grand Rapids and Cambridge, UK: Eerdmans, 1997), 373-88.

judgment and leads to illness and early death, though at least we may then experience judgment in this age and not at the End (1 Cor 11:27-34). Thus judgment can be a form of discipline. There is no purgatory after death, but there is purgatory before death.

"We were by nature deserving of wrath" (Eph 2:3 TNIV). "By nature" has the sense of "in ourselves."[164] What happens by God's grace (Eph 2:5) then contrasts with how things are by nature. Through decisions taken at the beginning of human history, something happened that changed things for humanity in a way that ruled out any going back. Henceforth all human beings were born into a context that was morally askew, and they inevitably share that skewedness. The "original sin" of the first human beings changed what all future human beings are "by nature." They would be deserving of God's wrath, and they could be restored to the possibility of walking in the right way only through God's taking some extraordinary, generous action. In other words, it could happen only "by grace." Although the contrast between nature and grace came to be used in a more defined way in theological discussion,[165] that more technical use in theological study is not so far from Ephesians's understanding of humanity and of salvation.

The Scriptures are not trying to prove God's existence by appeal to nature. They are almost doing the opposite; at least, they imply that such an argument cannot work. The world indeed exists only because God's power brought it into being, and anyone ought to be able to see this fact and thus respond to God with the appropriate submission of themselves, but instead they suppress this truth by wrongdoing. There is thus a link between godlessness and wrongdoing. The implication is not necessarily that godlessness issues in wrongdoing toward other people. Many godless people are concerned for right to be done in the world. But wrongdoing can relate to godlessness. It is in our interests (we think) to live for ourselves without caring about other people, but in order to live that way we have to ignore God.

---

[164]Robinson, *Ephesians*, 156.
[165]See, e.g., Augustine, *On Nature and Grace*; John Calvin, *Commentaries on the Epistles of Paul to the Galatians and Ephesians* (repr., Grand Rapids: Eerdmans, 1948), 222-24.

Sin the Power

Did things come to be this way because of a flaw in the way humanity was created? Rather, sin issued from decisions humanity took at the Beginning. Human beings were created to share in the glory of God's sovereignty over creation (cf. Ps 8), but they forfeited it. They were created to enjoy the eternal glory to which the life tree was the gateway, but they surrendered it and were thrown out of God's orchard where they could have access to that tree. They were made in God's image, but they failed to realize the point about being made in God's image (cf. Heb 2:5-9). Though they did not lose the image, it needed renewing. By its inherent created nature, life in the flesh involved a physical and emotional frailty and a need to trust in God and obey God. The trust and obedience were not forthcoming. Instead of exercising authority over the animate world, humanity yielded to the authority of one of its representatives and decided to make its own decisions about how to gain the kind of wisdom it needed to live life. This decision skewed things for everyone who was to follow. Henceforth humanity lives according to the flesh, not just in the flesh.

How could it be that God involved himself so profoundly with the world and with Israel, yet both the world and Israel in overlapping ways behaved as they did toward him? How could it be that our response to him eventually took the form of killing his Son? Looking back to the beginning of the story begins to suggest an answer. There was no flaw in the way Adam and Eve were created, but in the garden a suggestion about suspicion, distrust and disobedience came to them from outside them. Soon afterwards sin was crouching at their son's door like another wild creature. The other side of the killing of Jesus, Paul can see sin as

> a compulsion or constraint which humans generally experience within themselves or in their social context, a compulsion towards attitudes and actions not always of their own willing or approving. . . . Sin is that power which makes human beings forget their creatureliness and dependence on God, that power which prevents humankind from recognizing its true nature, which deceives the *adam* into thinking he is godlike and makes him unable to grasp that he is but *adamah*. It is that power which turns humankind upon itself in preoccupation with satisfying and compensating for its own weakness as flesh.[166]

---

[166]Dunn, *Theology of Paul the Apostle*, 112-14.

While wrongdoing is a complex business that benefits from being described by means of a wide range of images, it is also a single coherent thing. "Sin is among those anti-God powers whose final defeat the resurrection of Jesus Christ inaugurates and guarantees."[167] Sin came into the world to enslave a base of operations, became an enslaving power that got everyone into its power there, unleashed Death, its cosmic partner, even took control of the Torah and turned it into its own agent. One could almost have included it in the discussion of supernatural powers.[168]

Sin and death came, they saw, they conquered. "*The power of sin* . . . forces all men without exception into slavery."[169] There is some mystery about these two forces—in fact, there are several forms of mystery. Where did they come from? How did they exercise their power? Why did everyone give in to them? What was the relationship between their power and human responsibility? The Scriptures do not clarify the answer to these questions, though this omission does not undermine the assertions. We know that sin and death did and do have power, yet that we were and are responsible for our decisions about right and wrong. We do not find ourselves saying, "Sin made me do it, against my will." Yet we are victims of sin as well as perpetrators of sin.[170]

Sin and Death

So death came to all human beings in that all sinned, even if they did not sin in the way Adam did and in the way Israel did, by disobeying explicit instructions from God. In a sense their sin could not have been itemized and kept account of, but the fact that they died is an indication that they were sinning and paying for it (Rom 5:12-14). They were aware of God and of their responsibility to God even if they had no direct revelation from God in the way Adam had or in the form the Torah would eventually take, and they preferred darkness to light (Jn 3:19).

People's frailty meant they needed access to the life tree, but they lost it. The first human beings were warned not to eat of the good-and-bad-

---

[167]Beverly Roberts Gaventa, "The Cosmic Power of Sin in Paul's Letter to the Romans," *Interpretation* 58 (2004): 229-40 (on 231). The next sentence summarizes her subsequent paragraphs.
[168]See section 3.1 above.
[169]Bultmann, *Theology of the New Testament* 1:249.
[170]See Ian A. McFarland, *In Adam's Fall* (Chichester, UK, and Malden, MA: Wiley-Blackwell, 2010).

knowledge tree because they would then die, but they chose to do so anyway. They did not die that day, but they eventually died, and so did everyone who followed (cf. Rom 5:12). Adam lived to be 930, Seth to be 912, Enosh to be 905, Kenan to be 910, Methuselah to be 969 (Gen 5). You hold your breath through the account of each man: maybe someone will reach a millennium. But no one does. Each of their little paragraphs ends with the solemn epitaph "then he died." The exception is Enoch (and later Elijah), who simply disappears (Gen 5:24), which maybe hints at some other possibility, but that exception deepens the refrain's poignancy. The wages of sin is death (Rom 6:23).

Yet the First Testament is strangely accepting of mortality. It does not fret over it, except perhaps in those opening pages. It does rail and protest at people dying before their time. That protest is reflected in Daniel 12, the closing page of the First Testament (on the assumption that Daniel is the latest book), which includes the First Testament's only promise of a form of resurrection. But it accepts people dying and going to be with their ancestors when their time comes. It knows that death is more or less the end; after death there is only a rather boring existence in Sheol. But it is okay about that fact.

The First Testament also portrays death and Sheol reaching into this life when people are overcome by illness and attack (e.g., Pss 18:4-5 [MT 5-6]; 30:3; 86:13). Death does not wait until people die to dominate them. Morally, too, by nature we are "dead in connection with our transgressions and shortcomings" even while we are alive, as we walk in the ways of this age and focus on the fulfillment of our own desires (Eph 2:1-3). It is the cause and/or result of our death rather than the nature of it. The world has nothing to hope in or hope for (Eph 2:12). It is in the same position as the people in Ezekiel's dry bones vision, where the community's deadness consists in its being without hope (Ezek 37:11). Where there's hope, there's life. By hope, both passages refer to an objective reality rather than an inner attitude, though the objective reality (or the lack of it) logically generates the inner attitude. "It is not hope that makes the future into God's future; it is this future that awakes hope."[171] The fact that life was going to end in nothing at best, in wrath at worst, made it a kind of living death. Death had got hold of us now.

---

[171]Moltmann, *Church in the Power of the Spirit*, 197.

So we were dead as Jesus was dead. We had no future. We were dead in the sense of hopeless in connection with our wayward acts. This analysis again parallels the one presupposed in Ezekiel 37 and also suggests a parallel with Genesis 1–3. While human beings were not created inherently immortal, they were intended to eat of the life tree and therefore to be able to live forever, but their disobedience to God's command and their indulging their desire for the discernment tree meant they gave up that possibility.

The Lower Nature

In speaking of sin's power, Paul refers to the "sinful body," the mortal body in which sin can reign (Rom 6:6, 12). More often he refers in this connection to the "flesh" (e.g., Rom 7:18, 25). He doesn't imply that the body is inherently sinful—or rather, it is no more so than the heart and the mind. Still less is it the case that the body as opposed to the mind is the source of sin.[172] When used to refer to our sinful nature, the "flesh" can be said to have "desires" (e.g., Gal 5:16-17), which indicates that "flesh" is seated in the inner person as well as in the outer person, in the mind and soul as well as in the body.

The story of Israel's journey from Egypt to Canaan (1 Cor 10:1-13) sees the people's problem as misdirected desire. It lay in what they wanted. Their wanting found expression in their attitude to parties, images, sex, complaining and seeing how far they could push God. In the Decalogue, the exhortation not to covet comes as the unexpected coup de grâce; it's not hard to avoid worshiping other gods or breaking the sabbath or killing someone, but this final exhortation overcomes a person's sense of doing okay.

When Paul describes the way someone might come to an awareness of sin, he refers to this command, "You shall not covet" (Rom 7:7-8). His awareness links with the account of the first, disastrous act of disobedience (see Gen 3:6).[173] It fits the way he earlier moved on from humanity's declining to treat God as God, to God's giving humanity up to its desires, which found expression in misdirected sexual desire (Rom 1:24-27).

---

[172]Cf. Augustine, City of God 14.3.
[173]See the discussion under "'The Hermeneutics of Misdirected Desire," in Thiselton, Hermeneutics of Doctrine, 257-82.

Conversely, in his lists of the works of the flesh, sexual sin commonly comes first, and coveting follows.[174]

The crucial question is whether we live not merely "in the flesh" but "in accordance with the flesh" in the sense of "in accordance with the lower nature." The New Testament does not make the linguistic distinction in quite this way; both "in the flesh" and "in accordance with the flesh" can have positive, neutral or negative connotations, as is the case with the nouns "body" and "flesh." But as a piece of theological analysis the distinction works, as does that between "human bodiliness, to be affirmed and rejoiced in, and human fleshliness, always to be guarded about and against."[175] Living in the flesh or living in the body is one thing; living in accordance with the lower nature involves "a turning away from the Creator, the giver of life, and a turning towards the creation. . . . It is in this sense, then, that 'fixing the mind on the things of flesh' is to be at war against God (Rom. 8:7)."[176]

The influence of the flesh manifests itself in acts such as sexual immorality, humanly devised religion, hostility to other people, jealousy, ambition, envy and drunkenness (Gal 5:19-21). The New Testament's lists of sins (cf. Rom 1:28-32; 1 Cor 3:3; 5:9-11; 6:9-10) compare with the ones the First Testament sees in Israel. They combine what we might see as the more serious, such as murder, and the more trivial, such as gossip, but these two have in common that they are sins in the context of the community and they point to the fact that even the more trivial can end up having cataclysmically destructive effects on a community.[177]

While the parallel account of the fruit of the Holy Spirit (Gal 5:22-23) seems mostly to take a random order, paradoxically the fruit of the lower nature may be catalogued with more logic. The list begins with sex (immorality, impurity and vice) then goes on to false religion (idolatry and sorcery). The longest sequence covers personal relationships (hostilities, rivalry, envy, fits of rage, ambitions, disputes, splits and jealousies), and the account comes finally to acts of intemperance (drinking bouts and carousing). The wider context of the list illustrates the kind of things the catalog refers to; it speaks

---

[174]Cf. Dietrich Bonhoeffer, *Discipleship* (repr., Minneapolis: Fortress, 2003), 264.

[175]Dunn, *Theology of Paul the Apostle*, 73 (though he seeks to equate the theological distinction with a linguistic distinction between *sōma* and *sarx*).

[176]Bultmann, *Theology of the New Testament*, 1:239.

[177]Dunn, *Theology of Paul the Apostle*, 124.

of believers attacking one another (literally, "biting and devouring one another") and of conceit, provocation and envy. So while the list begins with sexual immorality, the context also makes clear that the "flesh" does not refer especially to sex, any more than to the body rather than the spirit. Our spirits are indeed as fleshly as our bodies.

The introduction and conclusion to the list make clear that it is not intended as an exhaustive inventory, and within each of the broad categories there are overlaps. There are culture-relative features about it; idolatry and sorcery are more characteristic of traditional societies than of the modern West, though Western life in the secular world and the church suggests that sex, personal relationships and intemperance are crosscultural problems.

The context also implies that believers should not worry that they are more troubled by internal conflict in these areas than they once were. The Holy Spirit generates conflict over them instead of acceptance of them and thus encourages resistance to them; one motivation is that people who do indulge in such acts don't come to share in God's reign (Gal 5:17-21). Living in accordance with the lower nature means living in light of the present age, which is passing away. Living in accordance with the Spirit means living in light of the fact that the new age has begun. The former is the natural life of people who do not live with Jesus, the latter the natural life of people who live with him.[178]

---

[178]Cf. Fee, *God's Empowering Presence*, 816-22.

4

GOD'S REIGN

✝

"Sovereignty belongs to Yahweh; he rules over the nations" (Ps 22:28 [MT 29]). The sovereignty of God has a firm place in Christian theology,[1] but it can suggest something so all-inclusive that it loses purchase. Although it is important that everything is under God's ultimate control even when the world acts in rebellion, so that nothing happens without God's permission, the idea of God's reign (*malkût, basileia*) is more dynamic. The Scriptures emphasize the motif of God asserting his sovereignty or implementing his reign. In this sense, the sovereignty of God "has too seldom been a key category in Christian theology."[2] "The kingdom of God" means "God coming in power to rule."[3] Against the background of the existence of an "anti-Kingdom,"[4] God asserts sovereignty from time to time against the background of other powers having been asserting theirs. God's reign denotes a king's successful assertion of authority and power over forces that oppose it.

We will consider God's reign in Israel (section 4.1), God's reign proclaimed by Jesus (section 4.2), the resistance to that proclamation and reign

---

[1]See the discussion in section 1.2 above.

[2]James W. McClendon, *Systematic Theology: Doctrine* (Nashville: Abingdon, 1994), 64. Cf. Jon Sobrino, "Central Position of the Reign of God in Liberation Theology," in Jon Sobrino and Igancio Ellacuría, eds., *Mysterium Liberationis* (Maryknoll, NY: Orbis, 1993), 350-86 = *Systematic Theology* (Maryknoll, NY: Orbis, 1996), 38-74. But contrast the caveats in John P. Meier, *A Marginal Jew* (New York: Doubleday, 2001), 3:243-52, with the summary on 289.

[3]Meier, *Marginal Jew*, 3:148.

[4]Jon Sobrino, *Jesus the Liberator* (Maryknoll, NY: Orbis, 1993; Tunbridge Wells, UK: Burns and Oates, 1994), e.g., 24.

(section 4.3) and God's turning that resistance into a means of achieving his purpose to reign in a worldwide people (section 4.4).

4.1 In Israel

So God is sovereign in the world as a whole, and nothing happens without his willing it or allowing it; he could close the world down tomorrow if he chose. But he doesn't force people to acknowledge his rule, perhaps because forced acknowledgment is not real acknowledgment. Having tried twice to gain willing human acknowledgment so as to effect his sovereign purpose in the world through humanity as a whole (see Gen 1–11), God tried a different tactic in settling on one group that might become his bridgehead into the world.

Yahweh chooses Israel to be this bridgehead. It is an act of grace rather than an act based on Israel's being fit for the task in some way, and belonging to Israel ethnically is neither sufficient nor necessary to being part of this people of God. Yahweh's reigning over this people implicitly rules out its having human rulers, but Yahweh accedes to Israel's desire for a human king. He could be the agent of God's reign—potentially at least, though not so much actually. Subsequently, God's reign is sometimes effected by means of the sovereignties of the superpowers, but that is a rather paradoxical expression of Yahweh's reign, and Yahweh also intervenes in the rule of the superpower to assert his own reign.

God's Promise and Its Fulfillment in Israel
Yahweh is the God of Israel. He is the God of this people more fundamentally than he is the God of a territory, of a city, of a sanctuary or of particular persons—though not more fundamentally than he is the God of the whole creation. In turn, Israel is the people that belongs to Yahweh more fundamentally than it is a nation or state or geographical entity. As a people, it is a community bound by familial ties, but its familial unity is not sufficient to define its identity. It is a people that belongs to Yahweh, and in order to be what it is supposed to be, it needs to be a people that recognizes Yahweh as its God. When it fails to do so, it may not exactly cease to be Israel, but it enters a kind of twilight zone in its identity.

If individuals fail to make their commitment to Yahweh (e.g., if a man refuses circumcision), they cut themselves off from their kin (Gen 17:14). Conversely, lacking the blood tie does not exclude someone from becoming a member of Israel. Israel's boundaries are permeable in this direction, too. Someone from a different background can be adopted into Israel, as an individual can be adopted into a new family. A person who acknowledges Yahweh and recognizes that Israel is his people becomes a de facto Israelite. People may long remember that he or she is ethnically a Moabite or a Hittite, though the vast increase in the Jewish community in the land during the period leading up New Testament times presupposes that peoples such as the Edomites/Idumeans who had come to commit themselves to the God of Israel can then be treated simply as "Jews."

"The special service of Israel within the totality of the elected community consists . . . in the hearing, the reception and the acceptance of the divine promise."[5] In effect, God's promise to Abraham was that he would see God's creation blessing fulfilled in him. God was unwilling to have his creation plan frustrated or to abandon it in favor of (say) a focus on the relationships of individuals with God. Israel comes into being as a people in fulfillment of the creation purpose and the ancestral promise. Israel comes to be a people with its own land on the basis of the same purpose and promise. Yahweh's sovereignty is implemented in his giving Israel the territory he had promised. The point runs through the story of the Israelites' miraculous crossing of the Jordan and of the miraculous collapse of Jericho's walls, and of the subsequent extraordinary victories of Joshua's ragtag army. They did not gain control of their territory because they fought hard but because Yahweh gave it to them.

The book of Joshua emphasizes how complete was Yahweh's fulfillment of his promises in this connection. God's promises to Abraham had found partial fulfillment in Genesis, but through no fault of their own the people had ended up in the wrong land. It might seem that the promises now find complete fulfillment. Yet the book of Joshua also includes another side to the story. There was much territory that Israel still needed to possess. While the account sometimes says that Israel "did not" take all the land, which

---

[5]Barth, *CD* II, 2:233.

might hint that they should have done, it sometimes says that they "could not," which does not suggest that they were at fault. The book of Joshua makes clear that Israel continues to experience a fulfillment that leaves God still with something to do and leaves God's people living with partial fulfillment but living in hope. The pattern of "now but not yet" continues through the First Testament into the New Testament and persists through the history that has since passed.

The Scriptures' talk of God's reign thus relates both to present and to future, and does so in a number of ways—for instance,

1. God's reign will come one day.
2. God's reign will come one day, but we experience anticipations of it today.
3. God's reign will come soon.
4. God's reign will come soon, but we experience anticipations of it today.
5. God's reign is here today, but it will become complete one day.
6. God's reign is here today, but it will become complete soon.

In Daniel, arguably the scriptural book most focused on God's reign, that reign features as a present reality in the first half of the book and a coming reality in the second half.

Privileged and Honored

Israel is the people Yahweh chose; the object of election was a people, not individuals. Only in Deuteronomy does the Torah use the actual word *choose* to make the point about Israel's position: "You are a people holy to Yahweh your God. It was you that Yahweh your God chose to become a special people for him from all the peoples on the face of the ground" (Deut 7:6). As Yahweh's possession, Israel is like the piece of land possessed by a family (*naḥălâ*; e.g., Deut 9:26), something special to Yahweh and treasured (*səgullâ*; e.g., Deut 26:18), a people for which Yahweh was prepared to give up claims on other peoples (Is 43:1-7), an object of love (Deut 7:7-8), like a son Yahweh loved and comforted (Hos 11:1-9). Therefore, when Israel cried out, Yahweh listened, was mindful, looked and acknowledged (Ex 2:23-25).

The Scriptures do not indicate why God decided to work via an entity that is basically ethnic rather than one chosen on the basis of their skin color, their hair color, their gifts, their holiness or their own decision. Deuteronomy does comment that the reason for choosing Israel in particular was not that it was more impressive in numbers or in character. Israel's position as God's people issued entirely from God's sovereignty and grace and not from human deserve or choice—as Romans 9–11 more or less argues.

The idea of election "is as offensive to our human reason as it is central to the Bible."[6] "The 'doctrine of predestination,' the doctrine of the divine election of grace has fallen under something of a shadow during the course of its history." But "the election of grace is the sum of the Gospel," the gospel in a nutshell. It signifies that

> God is God in His being as the One who loves in freedom. . . . All the joy and the benefit of His whole work as Creator, Reconciler and Redeemer, all the blessings which are divine and therefore real blessings, all the promise of the Gospel which has been declared: all these are grounded and determined in the fact that God is the God of the eternal election of His grace.

The trouble is that "in this free decision of God we have to do with the mystery of God, i.e., with the divine resolve and decree whose basis is hidden and inscrutable. We were not admitted to the counsel of God as He made His election, nor can we subsequently call Him to give account or to make answer in respect of it."[7] We just have to accept what he does as an expression of his wisdom and faithfulness.

While there is thus no explanation of the rationale for this act of choice that is based on love, there are expectations that follow from the choosing. Israel must live the way Yahweh expects, otherwise choice and faithfulness can turn to repudiation and redress. And it must live on the basis of a trust in Yahweh that assumes he can take it to its destiny and that no obstacles can prevent his doing so. Yahweh is the only one to whom Israel is to look in crises, and the one from whom it seeks guidance.

As well as saying nothing about the basis for Yahweh's choice of Israel, Deuteronomy says nothing about reasons in the sense of Yahweh's intentions,

---

[6] Lesslie Newbigin, *A Faith for This One World?* (New York: Harper; London: SCM Press, 1961), 77; cf. *The Gospel in a Pluralist Society* (Grand Rapids: Eerdmans; London: SPCK, 1989), 80.
[7] Cf. Barth, *CD* II, 2:13-14, 20.

nothing of what Yahweh aims to do with or through Israel, though the book's setting in the Torah carries implications about that question. Whereas Genesis does not explicitly speak about Yahweh "choosing" Abraham or Israel, oddly it does suggest part of the answer to why Yahweh does so. It is because Abraham and the people descended from him are indeed God's bridgehead into the world as a whole. Yahweh does speak of "recognizing" Abraham and in that connection refers to the way all the nations will find blessing through him (Gen 18:18-19). While choosing Israel goes along with rejecting some other peoples such as the Canaanites, these rejections relate to particularities about those peoples and/or to a particularity about how Yahweh is working out his purpose. Choosing Israel does not imply repudiating the nations as a whole; rather the opposite. Yahweh can relate in quite a positive way to people such as Philistines and Egyptians notwithstanding the problematic relationship they will have with Israel later, and representatives of such nations can be a rebuke to Israel. And individual Canaanites or Moabites who choose to identify with Israel are welcome to do so, as the stories of Rahab and Ruth show.

Israel's Wider Family

Yahweh's choosing Israel meant entering into a covenant relationship with Israel. That second simple statement conceals much complexity. There are various relationships that are described as involving a covenant; the word for covenant (bərît) can be applied to various forms of relationship, such as treaties and contracts as well as covenants; and the First Testament can be speaking of relationships that we might describe as covenantal even where it does not use the word for covenant.

Before entering into a covenant relationship with Abraham or with Israel, Yahweh made a covenant with the whole humanity that would descend from Noah. The covenants with Noah and with Abraham focus on a promissory commitment on God's part, as does Yahweh's covenant with David; a commitment does not have to be reciprocal in order to be called a covenant.

The covenant with Israel is more reciprocal. On the basis of what Yahweh has done for Israel, he looks for a responsive covenant commitment. Beyond Joshua, the First Testament does not explicitly refer very much to the covenant, but it does presuppose a relationship with the same dynamic. To the

Israelites belong the adoption, the splendor, the covenants, the Torah, the worship and the promises; and from Israel the Anointed One came (Rom 9:4).

So "Jacob I loved, but Esau I hated" (Rom 9:13; cf. Mal 1:2-3)? The Greek and Hebrew verbs translated "hate" (*miseō, śānēʾ*) do not denote a feeling so much as an action. Used in a strong sense, they imply rejection or repudiation. But further, "hate" over against "love" can suggest merely making a preferential choice. So the New Living Translation has "I rejected Esau" (the Common English Bible has this translation in Malachi though not in Romans), and the New International Reader's Version has "I chose Jacob instead of Esau."

Paul's argument in Romans 9–11 shows how God's choice of Jacob over Esau again relates to God's intention to make his mercy known to other peoples as well as Israel. Paul has already looked behind the choice of Jacob over Esau to the choice of Isaac over Ishmael, and he could also have noted God's commissioning of Abraham over his brothers and his focusing on Abraham rather than his nephew Lot and Lot's descendants Moab and Ammon. But "the election of Israel is set in the context of God's universality," and it "does not imply the rejection of other nations." It is "founded only on God's inexplicable love." It is "instrumental, not an end in itself," and it is "part of the logic of God's commitment to history." It is "fundamentally missional, not just soteriological":[8] that is, God's election of Israel is centrally concerned with God's intent to make himself known to the whole world, not merely with rescuing Israel itself.

So God's choice of one brother over the other does not rule out God's concern for the nonchosen one, despite all the tension and war making between Israel and the peoples it was related to. Israel does not seek to take over the territory of Edom, Ammon or Moab. Ishmael's story comes nearest to making the point explicit: for all the tough treatment of Hagar and her son, Ishmael receives his own promise of blessing and receives the covenant sign of circumcision. The peoples descended from Ishmael are not the line of which the Anointed One will be born, but they are children who inherit a promise from God.

---

[8]Christopher J. H. Wright, *The Mission of God* (Downers Grove, IL: InterVarsity Press; Nottingham, UK: Inter-Varsity Press, 2006), 263 (all these phrases are italicized in the original).

The context of God's declaration in Malachi is a time of fraught relations between Judah and its neighbor communities, who seem to have regretted Judah's becoming a province in its own right; they would have liked to take it over themselves. Edom in particular came to occupy much of southern Judah. Further, Judahites are inclined to marry people from these other communities. It is one thing if such people acknowledge Yahweh, as Ruth did (it has often been assumed that the story of Ruth was written in this period). It is quite another thing if they maintain their own religious allegiance, as is presupposed in Ezra and Nehemiah. It imperils the existence of Judah and thus that of Israel as Yahweh's people.

A kind of converse of the tense interrelationship between the community in Judah and its neighbors (some of whom were its relatives) is the tension in other parts of the empire between Judahites and the dominant communities there. In the Persian period, Judahites are legally free to move back to the country from where their families had come, but many did not do so—as has been the case for the millennia that have followed. Exile became dispersion. In Daniel and Esther trouble comes to Judahites not directly from the emperor himself but from his underlings, who manage to manipulate him into action that threatens the Judahites' death.

Whereas Daniel focuses on tensions involving Judahite leaders, the crisis in Esther involves the entire people. It threatens the annihilation of the entire community, a final solution to the Jewish problem. The book of Esther testifies to God's ensuring the survival of his people. It does so, and he does so, in a paradoxical way. God's deliverance does not happen in the manner of the exodus and the crossing of the Reed Sea. The story makes no mention of God or of religiously grounded action on the Judahites' part. It no doubt assumes that God brings about the deliverance, but it portrays it brought about not by extraordinary acts of God but through a combination of coincidence and the undertaking of brave human action. Yet it testifies to the working out of God's election of Israel.

Yahweh as King

Yahweh's rescue of Israel at the Reed Sea and his victory over the Pharaoh is the occasion to which the Scriptures trace back a confession of Yahweh's being king in Israel. He acted in majestic power, and his act invited the declaration, "Yahweh will reign forever and ever" (Ex 15:6, 18). Pharaoh had been seeing himself as king, and like your average human king or leader had been exercising power in a way that lacked insight or morality. Yahweh has not previously acted as king, in the sense of being termed "king" or described as reigning. The new situation requires that he starts behaving like a king. Being king also requires that "Yahweh is a warrior" (Ex 15:3). The story so far has implied that he is not a warrior by nature, but as the ancillary side to his nature, he has the capacity to be one, and he is willing to give expression to it when necessary. It is in these ways that "he will be what he will be" (Ex 3:14), will be whatever is required in changing situations.[9]

Subsequently, from time to time tumultuous powers assert themselves against Yahweh's people and attempt to overwhelm the city where Yahweh dwells, but they fail. Yahweh's protecting Jerusalem provokes a challenge to the world to recognize who is really king:

> All you peoples, clap hands,
>> shout to God with resounding voice.
> Because Yahweh, the One on High, is awe-inspiring,
>> the great king over all the earth. . . .
>
> Make music to God, make music;
>> make music to our king, make music.
> Because God is king of all the earth;
>> make music with understanding.
> God has begun to reign over the nations;
>> God has sat on his holy throne.
> The lords of the peoples have gathered,
>> the people of Abraham's God.
> Because the shields of the earth belong to God;
>> he has gone up very high. (Ps 47:1-2, 6-9 [MT 2-3, 7-10])

It is an outrageous challenge because "great king over all the earth" is a title claimed by the king of Assyria, the superpower of the day. Little Israel declares that actually its God is that king who has become king or has begun to reign over the nations (Pss 95–99 offer other formulations of the declaration). As Yahweh had asserted his sovereignty in enabling Israel to occupy

---

[9]See the introductory paragraphs to chapter one above, "God's Person."

the country the Canaanites claimed, so he did in frustrating Assyrian attempts to take Jerusalem. Even more outrageously, the psalm declares that
the so-called lords of the nations are going to acknowledge Yahweh, to
become part of Abraham's people, in keeping with Yahweh's intention that
all the nations should find blessing in Abraham.

Elsewhere in the Psalms, God's reign refers to God's power exercised
within creation, God's inherent majesty as lord among the other powers in
the heavens and God's sovereignty exercised on behalf of Israel and over
Israel.[10] In all three aspects, this reign is present but not complete, so that
declarations about it are always overstatements. When it looks as if Yahweh
is not acting as king, the faithful nevertheless declare that "Yahweh is king
forever and ever; nations have perished from his country" (Ps 10:16). Maybe
the faithful are reminding themselves and reminding God of the way he has
acted as king, or maybe they are speaking by faith about what God will do
or is doing or must be doing, and daring him to do it. God is involved in
forceful action, in aggressive force, to implement his sovereignty in the
world. (Forceful action and aggressive force are less misleading terms than
violence in this connection, since *violence* often seems by definition a form
of action that is ethically questionable. The First Testament has a word for
illegitimate violence [*ḥāmās*], and it never attributes it to Yahweh.)[11]

The exodus and the Reed Sea deliverance established Yahweh's reign over
Israel in particular. Israel is the immediate object of the reigning to which
the song of Moses and Miriam refers. Yahweh is in a special sense Israel's
king (e.g., Is 44:6). Israel is a kingdom (*mamlākâ*) of priests (Ex 19:6). The
Israelites are Yahweh's subjects; they acknowledge Yahweh alone. At least,
that is the theory. In practice, Israel does not live as if Yahweh is king, and
he takes aggressive and forceful action against Israel itself. Indeed, it is a
more prominent feature of the First Testament than the use of aggressive
force against other peoples.[12] Even then, God's action involves an assertion
of sovereignty not just to show that God is sovereign but "in order to

---

[10]Cf. Bruce Chilton, *Pure Kingdom* (London: SPCK; Grand Rapids: Eerdmans, 1995), 32.
[11]Cf. Rob Barrett, *Disloyalty and Destruction* (London and New York: T&T Clark, 2009), 58. On
   God and violence, see the discussion in Heath A. Thomas et al., eds., *Holy War in the Bible*
   (Downers Grove, IL: InterVarsity Press, 2013).
[12]Cf. Barrett, *Disloyalty and Destruction*, 10.

transform a bad and unjust historical-social reality into a different good and just one."[13] Hence the fact that the proclamation of God's reign is good news.

Divine Kingship and Human Kingship

Israel is thus a nation over which a divine king reigns. Moses rules over it on Yahweh's behalf, but he is not king; he is the king's servant. He does give Israel permission to appoint a king if it wishes, with certain safeguards including the requirement that the king keeps a copy of Moses' Torah next to him and studies it assiduously (Deut 17:14-20). In due course some Israelites ask Gideon to rule over them; they do not use the word *reign* or *king*, but they do make explicit that it is to be a permanent and hereditary rule (Judg 8:22-23). In his finest moment, Gideon declines, on the basis that Yahweh is the one who is to rule over them. His son subsequently likes the idea of being his people's ruler, and the people with power in Shechem appoint him king, but the mutual commitment is short-lived, and so is the experiment with kingship (Judg 9). On the other hand, the book of Judges concludes with a retrospective comment suggesting that the lack of central government was part of the reason why people could do what they liked in the horrifying way they do in its stories (Judg 21:25).

The issues arise on a new basis when Israel's elders want Samuel to appoint a king such as other nations have. It is a logical development for a developing nation, but Yahweh's reaction is like Gideon's, only more so. To ask for a king is to repudiate Yahweh as king (1 Sam 8:7), as well as to do themselves a disfavor. In light of the reactions of Samuel and of Yahweh, it is then surprising to read of Yahweh instructing Samuel to anoint Saul, though he does not speak of Saul as king but as *nāgîd*, something more like "chief" (1 Sam 9:16). In due course Yahweh's choice of Saul is made known to the people as a whole, and they declare, "Long live the king" (1 Sam 10:24).

Saul proves himself in rescuing the people of Jabesh-gilead from a vicious attack by the Ammonites, and Samuel invites them to Gilgal to inaugurate the kingship; there they make Saul king. Samuel reminds them, "You said to me, 'No, because a king is to reign over us,' when Yahweh your God was your king. So now, here is the king whom you have chosen."

---

[13]Sobrino, *Jesus the Liberator*, 71.

Yahweh thunders before the people, "and all the people said to Samuel, 'Pray for your servants to Yahweh your God so that we may not die, because we have added to all our offenses the wrong of asking for a king'" (1 Sam 11:14-15; 12:12, 19).

In Saul's reign the results of having a king are mixed, but Yahweh gets Samuel to anoint David as Saul's successor and makes a far-reaching commitment to him. Yahweh declares, "I appointed you as chief" (*nāgîd* again), but then adds that he will establish his son in his kingship (*mamlākâ*) "in perpetuity," so that David's own throne will be established in perpetuity; it amounts to a covenant given to David (2 Sam 7:8, 12-13, 16, 28; 23:5). Shepherd becomes a common image both for God and for the king in Israel, as it is elsewhere in the Middle East.[14]

There is thus a poignant contradictoriness about Yahweh's attitude to kingship in Israel. The idea of human kings implies a rejection of Yahweh as king, yet Yahweh goes along with the idea. He does so not merely grudgingly but energetically; God does not do things by half measures. Indeed, the permanency of the commitment Yahweh makes to the Davidic line of kings implies that the suspending of the human monarchy in 587 cannot be its end. Yet at the same time a prophet such as Zephaniah reminds Jerusalem in the frightening circumstances of the seventh century that it should nevertheless not be afraid, because "the King of Israel, Yahweh, is in your midst." Yahweh is the King of Israel who counts, even during the reign of the great King Josiah. Isaiah 55:3-5 sets another question mark by the human kingship when it declares that the promises attaching to David are being extended to the people as whole, back where they originally belonged before that earlier generation's ill-fated rejection of Yahweh as king.

Yahweh's reign in Israel was thus compromised by Israel's insistence on having a human king. The compromise was not merely theoretical. In practice, Israel's kings as often as not used their power to lead the people away from a practical recognition of Yahweh's kingship rather than to lead them in accepting Yahweh's kingly authority. The sovereignty of leaders such as kings was supposed to be constrained by the Torah, and in effect the vocation of prophets was to call the kings to account for failing to work

---

[14]See Jeffrey J. Niehaus, *Ancient Near Eastern Themes in Biblical Theology* (Grand Rapids: Kregel, 2008), 34-55.

within the life-giving constraints of the Torah. The failure issues in Yahweh's turning his forcefulness on them. Then "the radical contribution of the prophets lay, not in denying God's warlike activity . . . but in projecting Israel as God's new enemy."[15]

When Other Powers Reign

Israel's rebelliousness was not the only force that compromised Yahweh's reign in Israel. Imperial powers did so. Admittedly, when Assyria, then Babylon, then Persia ruled the Middle East and ruled over Ephraim and Judah, they did so within the framework of Yahweh's reigning. They did so not merely because Yahweh's sovereignty underlies all events. Assyria and Babylon were specifically the means of Yahweh's own sovereignty being exercised against Ephraim and Judah (and Persia was the means of its being once again exercised for Judah). Yet there is something not finally satisfying about a situation in which God's reign has negative implications for his people and in which the nation through which God's reign operates is not itself interested in being the means of God's reigning.

The fall of Jerusalem meant that God abandoned his people. It was not merely that they felt abandoned or that God seemed to have abandoned them; God confirms that he had done so (Is 54:7-8; cf. 2 Chron 12:5). Israel had thought that he would never do so; Lamentations expresses the awareness that this conviction has been shown to be false, and that people cannot complain. Their situation is not one in which they can pray the protest psalms that are prominent in the Psalter, which lament the way God has abandoned the people when they didn't deserve it. The prayers in Lamentations express the awareness that they deserved it.

Yet they do not infer that this acknowledgment means they cannot protest to God about the awfulness of what has happened and seek to get God to deliver them or hope that God's faithfulness might still mean he might restore them. And many a prophetic promise assures them that God's abandonment will not be final (Is 54:7-8 itself does so). Psalm 137 expresses the same conviction on behalf of people who had been taken into exile, not left in Jerusalem. From God's side, Jeremiah 29 promises that exile will not last forever. The

---

[15]Brevard S. Childs, *Old Testament Theology in a Canonical Context* (London: SCM Press, 1985; Philadelphia: Fortress, 1986), 185. Further on this "nightmare," see *OTT* 2:254-349.

exiles need to settle down for now, but God's eventual plan for them is šālôm, not disaster, a gathering back in the land, not a permanent exile.

They were indeed permitted to return, and they rebuilt the temple, the city walls and the city itself. But they stayed in a much reduced state, as their continuing prayers suggest (e.g., Ezra 9; Neh 9). Their position is a little like that of a Native American community on a reservation, compared with how things had once been when this land was their land. Israel had been reduced to Judah, and Judah had been reduced to something small and insignificant. Solomon's empire was nearly as big as California. Judah is now the size of a small county. It is a province (one could see it as a colony) of the Persian Empire, which controls it and milks it. It no longer has a son of David on the throne. It is surrounded by those other provinces that have designs on such independence as it has, and the Edomites occupy southern Judah as far as Hebron. People can't grow enough to eat as well as pay their taxes, and they have to go into debt servitude. The promises of the Prophets have seen some fulfillment, but they had promised much more.

It is thus astonishing and significant that the community makes a point of affirming that its God is "the God of our ancestors" and also "the God of heaven" (Ezra 7:27; Neh 1:5). It is also important that he is "the God in Jerusalem" (Ezra 1:3) and that they have the privilege of worshiping him there. They become a community that does pay attention to the Torah (e.g., Neh 8–10), which includes asking what Moses would say if he were here now. Throughout Israel's story it has asked that question and incorporated the answers in the Torah as it developed over the centuries. The process issues in the completion of the Torah in the century or two after the exile. As time goes by, the people show that Yahweh has fulfilled his promise to write the Torah into their minds and hearts, so that they give up worshiping other gods, making images and ignoring the sabbath.

God's Reign Is Here?

When Israel was defeated by Babylon, it was a sign of Yahweh's sovereignty, but an ironic one. Yahweh's sovereign purpose for Israel was hardly being implemented in its life. When Cyrus the Persian was about to bring Babylonian power to an end, it meant Yahweh was starting to reign again (Is 52:7-10). Yahweh was acting as king, asserting authority in the world, in order to free Israel from imperial domination. In this connection, a prophet heard the proclamation of a herald (*məbaśśēr*): the Septuagint renders this word with a form of the verb *euangelizomai*, which Jesus uses to refer to heralding the good news (e.g., Lk 4:18, 43). The herald speaks of *šālôm*, of good things, of deliverance, and indeed proclaims, "Your God has begun to reign!" Translations have "your God reigns," but the verb (*mālak*) is perfect, which suggests something that has happened, not something that simply is happening. There is a sense in which Yahweh always reigns, and it has been Yahweh's reign that has brought about Judah's domination by Babylon, but the prophet is talking about a new assertion of that reign or an assertion that takes a different direction.

The advent of the Persians did bring freedom from Babylon, but it still meant a foreign power dominating Judah and burdening it, which continued with the Seleucids and (after a century of freedom) with the Romans. This experience might seem harder to justify as treatment that the Jewish people simply deserved; hence the longing of people such as Mary and Zechariah for a day when God would bring down the powerful from their thrones and rescue the people from the hand of their enemies (Lk 1:52, 74). The question still pressed itself on Jewish and Gentile believers under the sovereignty of the Romans. The reality of persecution underlined the point. John's Revelation thus promises that God will put Rome down. Yet Zechariah had also referred to the forgiveness of his own people's sins, which implies a similar stance to that of prayers from the Persian period (Ezra 9; Neh 9; Dan 9). Such prayers recognize that their sin continues to have an effect on the people's destiny.

In the 160s BC, the visionary who was inspired by God to adopt the persona of Daniel and who shared his visions of relief and restoration (Dan 7–12) was aware of the fact that the promises about Israel's restoration that were given through Jeremiah had not really been fulfilled; punishment and distress continue. He asks what has happened to them and when things will be put right (Dan 9). The Damascus Rule, known from Qumran and elsewhere, speaks in similar terms (1.5-6; 3.9-17; 5.20–6.5).

It's not exactly that exile continues.[16] The visions in Daniel come from someone in Jerusalem, not someone living in a community in exile.[17] Indeed, while Jesus' declaration about God's reign fits the way Rome's rule was experienced as oppressive in Judea, one significance of Paul's not talking about God's reign may be that Rome's rule was not experienced in this way in the cities around the Mediterranean in his time (cf. Rom 13).[18] It is indeed the case that a gathering of Israel from all over the world is an important element in the promises of some Prophets. But for Judah, God had brought about a new exodus, a new entering into the land, a new building of the temple and a restoring of city and community. Ezra and Nehemiah thus tell a story about a partial realization of God's promises. Yet the people still live in servitude to a foreign power. "The problem of Ezra-Nehemiah is not so much one of continuing exile but of incomplete restoration."[19]

To say "God's reign is here," that "Yahweh has become king" (Is 52:7-10), is inclined to suggest the definitive and final arrival of a regime or realm in which God rules, analogously to a declaration that Rehoboam (for instance) has become king (1 Kings 14:21). Yet the story of the period from the 530s down into the Roman period, and those prayers, make clear that Yahweh is not reigning in a dynamic sense in the life of his people. It is the pattern that runs through the story of the people of God. Declarations made at the Reed Sea, at the end of the period of Babylonian rule in the Middle East, and on the eve of the collapse of Seleucid authority in Jerusalem in the 160s BC turn out not to be final statements.

---

[16]Against N. T. Wright, *The New Testament and the People of God* (Minneapolis: Fortress; London: SPCK, 1992), 268-72; Wright, *The Climax of the Covenant* (Edinburgh: T&T Clark, 1991; Minneapolis: Fortress, 1992), 141. Cf. J. Ross Wagner, *Heralds of the Good News: Isaiah and Paul "in Concert" in the Letter to the Romans* (Leiden and Boston: Brill, 2002), 30; Brant Pitre, *Jesus, the Tribulation, and the End of the Exile* (Tübingen: Mohr; Grand Rapids: Baker, 2005), esp. 31-40. See Maurice Casey's critique, "Where Wright Is Wrong," *JSNT* 69 (1998): 95-103 (on 99-100). In his reply Wright does describe exile as "a shorthand to mean 'the time of desolation begun by the Babylonian destruction,'" as "a *period of history* with certain characteristic features, not a mere geographical reference" (Wright, "Theology, History and Jesus," *JSNT* 69 [1998]: 105-12 [on 111]).

[17]N. T. Wright (*Paul and the Faithfulness of God* [Minneapolis: Fortress; London: SPCK, 2013], 139-63) describes Dan 9 as the proper starting point for arguing that we understand Israel's need as a return from exile, but Dan 9 speaks only of Jerusalem's restoration and not at all of exile.

[18]Cf. Gerd Theissen, *The Social Setting of Pauline Christianity* (Philadelphia: Fortress, 1982), 36; and the paragraphs under "The Underling" in section 3.3 above.

[19]Steven M. Bryan, *Jesus and Israel's Traditions of Judgement and Restoration* (Cambridge and New York: Cambridge University Press, 2002), 16; see further 12-20.

4.2 THROUGH JESUS

In Jesus' day, the situation is thus the one the Jewish people had been experiencing on and off for centuries. They are the unenthusiastic underlings of an empire, gaining some benefits from that position but exploited by the superpower. In Jesus God again asserts himself as king. But the termination of the superpower's rule needs to be accompanied by a transformation of his own people's relationship with him. It requires a response of repentance on their part. Jesus comes to bring renewal to Israel in its own relationship with God, a renewal that comes about through the pouring out of God's spirit on his people.

God's Reign Has Arrived

The time has come for a change of government, a revolution.[20] While love is integral to Jesus' proclamation, the proclamation of love is a commonplace, and "the programmatic centre of Jesus' ministry was not the concept of love, but that of God's rule."[21] And in the New Testament, God's reign is not a motif, an idea or a new belief. "Jesus was announcing the kingship of YHWH as something which was in the process of *happening*."[22] God's rule is "a present reign of blessing" and "the gift of life bestowed upon his people."[23] Eight months or so before Jesus' birth, his mother expresses her joy in the fact that his birth will mean that God

> has brought down powerful people from their thrones
> and exalted lowly people,
> has filled hungry people with good things
> and sent the rich away empty,
> has come to the help of his boy Israel,
> being mindful of mercy,
> as he said to our ancestors,
> toward Abraham and his offspring forever. (Lk 1:52-55)

---

[20]Cf. David Wenham, *Paul: Follower of Jesus or Founder of Christianity?* (Grand Rapids and Cambridge, UK: Eerdmans, 1995), 40-41.

[21]Bruce Chilton and J. I. H. McDonald, *Jesus and the Ethics of the Kingdom* (London: SPCK, 1987; Grand Rapids: Eerdmans, 1988), 3.

[22]N. T. Wright, *Jesus and the Victory of God* (Minneapolis: Fortress; London: SPCK, 1996), 563.

[23]George Eldon Ladd, *A Theology of the New Testament* (Grand Rapids: Eerdmans, 1974), 70, 72 (rev. ed., 68, 70).

A supernatural visitor appears later to Jesus' adoptive father to tell him that his son "will rescue his people from their sins" (Mt 1:21). Inspired by the Holy Spirit and prophesying, Jesus' great-uncle rejoices that in these events God has stirred up

> salvation from our enemies,
> > yes, from the hand of all the people who repudiate us . . .
> to grant us, without fear
> > (being rescued from the hand of our enemies)
> to serve him in holiness and doing right
> > before him all our days . . .
> to grant his people knowledge of salvation
> > through the remitting of their sins. (Lk 1:71, 74-75, 77)

They thus see Jesus as coming to bring about a restoration of Israel with two aspects.[24] The one that may have concerned most people was their longing for deliverance from Roman rule. Like the Prophets, Mary, Joseph and Zechariah say nothing of the Anointed One leading Israel itself in putting down its overlord and taking it into political power over the nations; Mary does imply that God is the one who will take action along those lines. Joseph and Zechariah also talk about the other aspect; they recognize that this restoration involves the people being rescued from their sins, because the reason for God's letting Israel be dominated by a series of superpowers has been its unfaithfulness to God over the centuries.

"The reign of heaven has arrived (ēngiken)," John the Baptizer thus declares; Jesus later says the same thing (Mt 3:2; 4:17). In John's use of the expression, the verb is anticipatory, like Mary's verbs. By "arrived," he means it is at the gates; it is not yet inside the city. His way of speaking parallels that of other prophets who had spoken of God having begun to reign when they meant God was about to assert sovereignty (notably, Is 52:7). Jesus' use of the same words presumably has the same implication.

The people's situation in the time of Mary, Joseph, Zechariah, John and Jesus is similar to the one that had obtained in earlier centuries. Only the empire's name is different. "In the calamitous and pain-ridden history within which Jesus stood it was impossible to find any grounds or indeed any

---

[24]Cf. Wright, *Jesus and the Victory of God*, 264-74.

reason at all which would serve to explain and make sense of the unqualified assurance of salvation that characterized his message."[25] But his actions begin to provide grounds for believing his proclamation. When he goes about "heralding the good news about sovereignty," he is also involved in "healing every illness and sickness among the people" and expelling demons from them, and he commissions the Twelve to heal, resuscitate, cleanse and exorcise as they also proclaim that God's reign has arrived (Mt 10:1-8).

In due course Jesus brings about the renewal of his disciples by breathing the Holy Spirit onto them in an act that represents a renewing of the way they were created (Jn 20:22): "he breathed into them" is the same verb in the same form as appears in the Septuagint in Genesis 2:7, and the same verb as in Ezekiel 37:9.[26] Ezekiel promised a renewal of creation, and the situation of the Jewish people and of the rest of the world indicates that this renewal had not yet happened. Jesus brings that renewal, though the Spirit can be poured out only after Jesus has died and risen (Jn 7:39).

Dethroning the Opposing Power

The prominence of exorcism in Jesus' ministry links with the declaration that God's reign has arrived: "If it is by God's spirit that I throw demons out, then God's reign has come upon you" (Mt 12:28; Lk 11:20). "The reality of the Evil One" is "the ultimate dimension of the anti-Kingdom."[27] The exorcisms are symbolic victories in Jesus' conquest of the powers that assert themselves against God. They indicate that "God's reign is among you" (Lk 17:21). God's reign means God putting down everything that conflicts with it, including Satanic power and the pain and sorrow that issue from it (demons were also commonly associated with ghosts, so that victory over demons could imply victory over death).[28]

Being demonized could be a manifestation, too, of the overwhelming domination of familial or social or political pressures and stresses. People have come under the control of powerful, hostile alien forces. They are no longer themselves. The social and political pressures of Roman rule in Judea

---

[25]Edward Schillebeeckx, *Jesus* (New York: Crossroad; London: Collins, 1979), 267.

[26]It also comes in 1 Kings 17:21 (cf. John R. Levison, *Filled with the Spirit* [Grand Rapids and Cambridge, UK: Eerdmans, 2009], 368-72).

[27]Sobrino, *Jesus the Liberator*, 93.

[28]Cf. Peter G. Bolt, "Jesus, the Daimons and the Dead," in Anthony N. S. Lane, ed., *The Unseen World* (Carlisle, UK: Paternoster; Grand Rapids: Baker, 1996), 75-102.

might thus manifest themselves in illnesses.[29] Jesus' healings would then be another sign that the liberating rule of God was replacing the repressive rule of Rome. They were both acts of restoration for individuals and part of God's great act of restoration for Israel as a whole.[30] Thus Jesus' deliverance of the afflicted Gerasene not only deals with his individual needs but reaches toward the restoration of his place in his community—indeed the transformation of it, as it sends him to tell them about Jesus (rather than letting him follow Jesus) (Mk 5:1-20).[31]

God's reign is thus to benefit the people of Judea by putting the reign of God in the place of the reign of Rome and of other supernatural beings. The proclamation of God's reign is complemented by the denunciation of the antireign.[32]

Nevertheless Jesus' activity rather fazes John the Baptizer. It's not what he expected God's reign to involve. Jesus' coming did not issue in the fulfilling of the main promises about a coming king expressed in the Prophets (e.g Is 9; 11) and in the declarations made by his parents and by John's. The Prophets did not speak of casting out demons, such a prominent feature of Jesus' activity. While for some people in his context exorcism and healing may have had messianic connotations,[33] there is no one-to-one correspondence between Jesus' acts and the promises in the Prophets. Yet this facet of the relationship between prophecy and fulfillment is typical;[34] there was enough correspondence to bear witness to the declaration that he was fulfilling promises that Israel in its weakness and humiliation at the hand of the superpower would hear good news about healing and resurrection from death and would experience those realities in its midst (e.g., Is 35; 61; Ezek 37). Prophets such as Elijah and Elisha had been involved in healing, and the Gospels' implication is that such activities are indeed an indication that God has begun to reign. The king has entered the city and made his presence felt among the needy people just inside the gate, even though he

---

[29]Cf. Richard A. Horsley, *Jesus and the Spiral of Violence* (repr., Philadelphia: Fortress, 1993), 183-84.
[30]Cf. also Michael Welker's comments on demon possession in *God the Spirit* (Minneapolis: Fortress, 1994), 198-200.
[31]Amos Yong, *Renewing Christian Theology* (Waco, TX: Baylor University Press, 2014), 193-97.
[32]Cf. Jon Sobrino, "Central Position of the Reign of God in Liberation Theology," in Sobrino and Ellacuría, *Mysterium Liberationis*, 350-88 (on 364-65) = *Systematic Theology*, 38-74 (on 51-52).
[33]See, e.g., Ben Witherington III, *The Christology of Jesus* (Minneapolis: Fortress, 1990), 156.
[34]See sections 2.2 and 2.3 above.

has not yet advanced on the rebels occupying the palace. It is still necessary to pray that God's reign may come (Mt 6:10; Lk 11:2).

Jesus did not talk much about his own reign; he rather talked about God's (but see Jn 18:36; Eph 5:5; Col 1:13). In the Synoptics Jesus' own kingship does not belong to this age but to the age to come. "He did not bring the kingdom; it was rather the kingdom that swept him along in its wake."[35] In announcing God's reign, "Jesus' concern was to announce: God in strength. At every point Jesus' announcement directs our attention to God."[36]

"Are you the king of the Judeans?" Pilate asks him (Jn 18:33). Jesus is not very enthusiastic about this way of framing the question. He cannot deny being a king, but his reign is not "from this world," as is evidenced by his not having his servants fight to stop him being arrested. There is neither any need to attempt to stop him trying to be king nor any point in doing so. But rather than speak in terms of being a king, he here prefers to speak in terms of being a witness. His job is to tell the truth (Jn 18:37).[37] Pilate's famous "What is truth?" finds its answer in the fact that Jesus' whole life and teaching is an embodiment of grace and truthfulness; he came to witness to the true light (Jn 1:8, 14, 17).

Israel Renewed, Reconstituted and Repentant

"Jesus had a mission to the nation of Israel."[38] He came to restore Israel to the kind of position one would expect it to have as God's people.[39] "Jesus did not intend to found a church *because there already was one.*" He did intend the reformation of the community that already existed.[40] He summoned them to turn to God in light of what God was doing in implementing his reign and thus sanctifying his name, in line with intentions declared by

---

[35]Chilton, *Pure Kingdom*, 8, summarizing Rudolf Otto, *The Kingdom of God and the Son of Man* (repr., London: Lutterworth, 1951), 97-107.

[36]Bruce D. Chilton, *God in Strength* (Freistadt: Plöchl, 1979), 287.

[37]Given that he goes on to say that he was born to testify to the truth, the NIV 1984's paraphrase "You are right in saying I am a king" makes his statement incoherent; contrast TNIV's more literal "You say that I am a king."

[38]Scot McKnight, *A New Vision for Israel* (Grand Rapids and Cambridge, UK: Eerdmans, 1999), viii.

[39]James M. Scott sees "Jesus' vision for the restoration of Israel as the basis for a biblical theology of the New Testament" (the title of his essay in *Biblical Theology*, ed. Scott J. Hafemann [Downers Grove, IL: InterVarsity Press; Leicester, UK: Inter-Varsity Press, 2002], 129-43).

[40]Wright, *Jesus and the Victory of God*, 275, following Gerhard Lohfink, *Jesus and Community* (Philadelphia: Fortress, 1984); what follows is indebted to Lohfink, *Jesus and Community*, 7-29.

the Prophets (e.g., Is 52:7-10; Ezek 36). He did form a group of disciples, who were his real family and his "little flock," the people who do God's will (e.g., Lk 8:19-21; 12:32). His forming a group of *twelve* links with his concern with a renewed *Israel*; they are "prophetic symbols of the regathering of the twelve tribes of Israel."[41] They compare with the Qumran council of twelve. They are going to judge the twelve Israelite clans (Mt 19:28). "Judging" (*krinein*) looks like a Hebraism; it implies ruling (*šāpaṭ*). He thus commissions one representative for each of the twelve clans to take part in implementing the project of rescuing Israel, the lost flock (cf. Ezek 34). Doing right by Israel is then Paul's way of talking about restoring Israel and thus about God's reign.[42]

In association with his proclamation of God's reign, John the Baptizer declares "a baptism of repentance with a view to remission of sins," and when John has been arrested, his cousin takes up his proclamation and declares that people are to repent and believe the good news (Mk 1:4, 15). Repentance is the business of individuals (e.g., Lk 13:1-5), of families (Lk 16:27-30), of local communities (e.g., Lk 10:10-15) and of the nation as a whole (e.g., Acts 5:31). When God is about to assert his sovereignty, repentance is a good idea on everyone's part, though especially on the part of leaders. Jesus underscores the point when he asserts that people who are to get into the heavens' reign need a righteousness exceeding that of the people who made a point of obeying the Torah and teaching it (Mt 5:20). The exposition that follows (Mt 5:21–7:27) indicates the nature of that more demanding righteousness.

As in Isaiah 40–55, then, when a prophet proclaims that God's reign has come and makes a promise to Israel, he also issues a demand. He's not exactly issuing conditions; he's more indicating the kind of response that God's coming requires. God's reign is arriving, so people had better repent. While "without repentance there can be no new life, no salvation, no entry into the Kingdom," it can be the shining of the light that generates repentance rather than the other way around. It is the fact that God forgives that transforms people's thinking.[43] Yet the shining of the light must have that effect.

---

[41]Meier, *Marginal Jew*, 3:148.
[42]Cf. Wenham, *Paul: Follower of Jesus or Founder of Christianity?*, 80.
[43]Kallistos Ware, *The Inner Kingdom* (Crestwood, NY: St Vladimir's Seminary Press, 2001), 43, 46-47.

Preaching forgiveness without repentance implies that grace is cheap, whereas actually grace cost God the life of his Son, and it costs his followers their lives.[44]

Of what are people to repent? Prophets often speak of people worshiping other deities, they speak of people with resources ignoring the needy, and they speak of Israel thinking it has to look after its own destiny and seeking to do so by political or military means. In the Gospels, the call to repentance by John and Jesus perhaps refers to the general sinfulness of ordinary people who are involved in what Paul will later call the sins of the lower nature, which include sexual sin and also hatred, jealousy, rage and ambition. God's reign challenges them to a new way of life, as John points out, and as is suggested by the First Testament's common verb for repent (*šûb*, "turn"). While the Sermon on the Mount does not directly expound the nature of the sin that Jesus has in mind, it may thus indirectly do so. The general nature of the sinfulness presupposed by this call may also parallel the assumptions about the people's sinfulness that underlie prayers such as the one in Daniel 9, the sense that Israel is under chastisement for its waywardness.

Etymologically, the New Testament word for repentance (*metanoia*) suggests a new way of thinking. Even people whose life is in reasonable order and who don't need to turn may need such a revolution. This assumption corresponds to one underlying the prophetic proclamation of God's reign. The people of God are inclined to think that they can work out the way God will act by looking at his acts in the past, and that they can use this knowledge to evaluate what people such as prophets say, but that assumption binds them to the idea that God is only likely to do again what he has done previously, and he is inclined to have other ideas (Is 55:8-11). Prophets also speak of people becoming disillusioned about whether Israel can ever experience restoration, and that sin might be more of a problem. People need to "turn" from that assumption and trust in Jesus and in his capacity to bring about their restoration.

In response to John and Jesus, people came to confess their sins and receive a ceremonial washing away of them. They were used to regular

---

[44]Dietrich Bonhoeffer, *Discipleship* (repr., Minneapolis: Fortress, 2003), 44-45.

bathing to deal with the way their lives stood in contrast with God's life, metaphysically or morally. This new washing is a one-time version that corresponds to a more general contrast between their life and what God expects.

Living in the Realm Where God Reigns

Like God's original choice of Israel, the announcement of God's reign with its associated promises of blessing does not come to people on the basis of their deserving it or of their being impressive in other ways. The blessings are proclaimed for people who have nothing to be proud of, who grieve over their insignificance, who long for God's righteous purpose to be fulfilled, who are persecuted and slandered for that concern and for their association with Jesus. It is by these negative qualifications that they will show themselves to be a prophetic community. They will have their longing fulfilled, they will possess the land in freedom, they will experience God's comfort, they will find themselves at home in God's reign, they will receive God's reward (Mt 5:3-12). One can see this profile embodied in the kind of people Matthew and Luke describe at the beginning of their Gospels, Zechariah and Elizabeth, Mary and Joseph, Simeon and Anna. Elizabeth has been described as the "prototype of the Spirit-filled life," before Jesus has been born as well as before Pentecost.[45]

In the midst of his description of such a personality profile, Jesus interweaves another set of personal qualities that need to go along with ordinariness, grief and longing. To participate in the realm of blessing, the community needs to be merciful, pure and peacemaking; it is this sort of community that will receive mercy from God, will see God, will be treated as God's family. It will then be salt throughout the land and light throughout the house (Mt 5:13-16). Jesus refers here to being a light to the world, but in the first instance, the "world" will denote the people of God corporately and/ or in its worldly nature. Jesus issues "a challenge to Israel to be Israel."[46] When the people of God becomes the people of God by manifesting this personality profile, attracting the world will look after itself. If the community

---

[45]Yong, *Renewing Christian Theology*, 59.
[46]Wright, *Jesus and the Victory of God*, 288.

fails in being merciful, pure and peacemaking and thus drawing Israel to glorifying God, it might as well be trashed.

The reign of God that Jesus announces thus implies obligations that the people ought to accept. The revolution brought by the arrival of God's reign involves a "transformation of social relations."[47] Will people take part in that revolution? God's reign is not imposed on the people who are designed to be its beneficiaries. They are urged to share in the festive rejoicing at its arrival. "Being sad in Jesus' presence" is "an existential impossibility: his disciples 'do not fast.'"[48] But people are not compelled to take part in the revolution. There's a sense in which "the coming of God's Reign is a miraculous event, which will be brought about by God alone without the help of men." All that human beings can or have to do in face of it is "keep ready or get ready for it."[49] Whereas the social gospel emphasized the ethical demand of the kingdom, "Jesus appears to proclaim the imminence of God's kingdom," and "even today, talk of 'building' or 'spreading' the kingdom . . . is current, and stems from the belief that Jesus preached an ethical cause" when actually he preached "a divine reality."[50] David wanted to build God a temple, but "God's temple can only be built by God's own self."[51]

Jesus' parables do make clear that there is a link between God's promise and human activity,[52] and other references to God's reigning also show how it involves an interaction between the divine will and the human will. While the First Testament regularly assumes that God wins the victory in war, there are wars in which he does so without human participation, but others in which he works via human participation. In the 540s BC God brought in his reign through Persia putting Babylonia down. God utilizes human agencies that don't realize that they are his agents. In Revelation, too, it is

---

[47]Horsley, *Jesus and the Spiral of Violence*, 324.

[48]Schillebeeckx, *Jesus*, 201.

[49]Rudolf Bultmann, *Theology of the New Testament* (repr., Waco, TX: Baylor University Press, 2007), 1:4, 9.

[50]Bruce Chilton, "Introduction," in Chilton, ed., *The Kingdom of God in the Teaching of Jesus* (London: SPCK; Philadelphia: Fortress, 1984), 1, 6.

[51]Bonhoeffer, *Discipleship*, 223.

[52]Cf. Chilton and McDonald, *Jesus and the Ethics of the Kingdom*, 24-47.

expected that God will use human participation, but it is the participation of martyrdom.[53]

The Shepherd and the Under-Shepherds

Israel was supposed to be the place where God reigned. It was supposed to be God's priestly kingdom. In practice the Israelites are like shepherd-less sheep (Mt 9:36). They were first in that position after Joshua's death, when they got lost socially, morally and politically. Subsequently they had shepherds, but these shepherds usually failed their flock. So do the shepherds of Jesus' day, with the result that the people are again harassed and helpless. God had promised them proper shepherding and had also promised that they would be gathered in. So Jesus was sent to the lost sheep of the household of Israel (Mt 15:24). He "saw himself as their divinely-sent and divinely-endowed shepherd." He is God's apostle, and they are his apostles.[54]

To change the metaphor, part of their task is to pray God to bring the moment of the great harvest by sending out the harvesters. The harvesters are the supernatural aides who will gather numerous but scattered Israel when the Man comes, in keeping with the Prophets' promises (Mt 13:39; 24:31). That work by these aides will be an aspect of God's reign arriving, and such praying is one way by which the disciples will seek God's reign. The action needed if God's reign is to begin is teaching, healing and praying (Mt 9:35-38). In sending out the Twelve, then, Jesus does not imply that they are the harvesters any more than that they bring in God's reign. Indeed, it would be odd for Jesus to tell them to pray for God to act and then to send them as if they were the answer to their own prayers.

Jesus does send them to the lost sheep of the household of Israel. Their work relates to the gathering in of these sheep. They undertake the work of shepherding that has been neglected, like twelve leaders of the twelve clans that make up Israel. The idea is that God's reign will arrive, and that the Man will come in glory in the way described in Daniel 7, as they complete this commission (Mt 10:23). The nations will then be swept into recognizing what God has been doing and into acknowledging God.

---

[53]Richard Bauckham, *The Climax of Prophecy* (Edinburgh: T&T Clark, 1993), 210-37.
[54]Witherington, *Christology of Jesus*, 143.

After Jesus' execution, resurrection and departure, the apostles and the rest of the believers (Acts 2:44) assume that their vocation, too, is to bring good news of Israel's restoration. In their midst, too, people get healed and raised from death, and in their midst people can also see the implementing of another promise (see Joel 2:28-29). There is again no one-to-one correspondence between events in Acts and prophetic promises; the Prophets said nothing about tongues of fire or speaking in tongues (a key feature of Pentecost), neither about hospitality and sharing (key features of community life in Acts). But once more there is enough overlap for it to be plausible to claim that prophetic promises are finding fulfillment. And in a broader sense, one can see Pentecost and the gift of tongues as the reversal of Babel and as symbolizing the broader solution to the problem of the human tongue (recognized also in Jas 3).[55]

The apostles, too, baptize people, the sign of people's turning to God, finding cleansing and joining the reconstituted community. The apostles have to add a new reason for repentance, the killing of Jesus. They also make explicit that there is to be a delay before God brings about the consummation of his purpose (Acts 3:19-21). As they await that moment, they see themselves as the embodiment of a renewed Israel, which the rest of Israel is urged to join.

The task Jesus gives them is to be his witnesses all over the world (Acts 1:8). In the context, it would be natural for them to see this witness as meant for the worldwide Jewish community that was destined to experience God's restoration, not to the Gentile world, which would then be drawn through seeing what God was doing for Israel. And initially, it was to the Jewish community that they gave their witness, though Matthew's version of Jesus' closing commission (Mt 28:16-20) does make explicit that they are to disciple all the nations.

Now and Then

A generation or two after Jesus, it remains hard to see that God is reigning. After his death and resurrection, John has a vision of God reigning, with Jesus alongside him (Rev 4–5). The fact that God reigns and that Jesus reigns underlines the necessity and the possibility of the putting down of evil on

---

[55]Cf. Yong, *Renewing Christian Theology*, 97-98.

which the rest of Revelation focuses. John's vision recapitulates the vision in
Ezekiel 1–3, and behind it the vision in Isaiah 6, and behind that vision the
confession in Exodus 15.

But Revelation is testifying to a reality that contrasts with the experience
of John's audience, who could not see God reigning in their life. Ezekiel's
vision likewise affirms the reality that his audience would be tempted to
question, the idea that Yahweh was sovereign in Babylon. Isaiah's vision was
set over against the fact that the earthly sovereign had just died (Is 6:1), and
over against the fact that it was hard to believe in Yahweh's sovereignty when
Assyria and Ephraim were asserting theirs. In contrast, however, the confession in Exodus 15 issues from the fact that Yahweh has indeed asserted
his sovereignty over the sovereign of the day.

Revelation goes on to relate "the song of Moses, God's slave, and the song
of the lamb":

> Great and wonderful are your deeds,
>> Lord God Almighty,
> Just and true are your ways,
>> King of the ages,
> Who will not revere, Lord,
>> and glorify your name?
> Because you alone are holy,
>> because all the nations will come,
> And they will bow down before you,
>> because your judgments have been revealed. (Rev 15:3-4)

Like most of Revelation, the song reworks phrases from the First Testament,
in this case that earlier Song of Moses in Exodus 15. The link is apposite in
light of the way the context in Revelation reworks motifs from the story of
the plagues that Yahweh had brought on Egypt, which came earlier in
Exodus. Prostration before God in worship as the one enthroned links with
submission to God in action as the one enthroned—in both cases, over
against prostration before Rome and submission to Rome.

Many Jews hoped for the coming of an Anointed One, for the restoration
of Israel's freedom and for the resurrection of the dead. Some Qumran
writers argue that the coming of the End would bring a great change and
that their people have a vocation to live in the present in preparation for that

event. For Jesus, too, God's reign is "the final reality,"[56] yet his declaration about God's reign follows the pattern of the earlier declarations of it: it does not lead into its final implementing.

On the basis of Jesus' resurrection and the pouring out of the Spirit, Jews who believed in Jesus knew that the End had arrived. "There had been a decisive shift in the possibilities confronting humankind. An epoch characterized by the power of sin and death had been overtaken by a new epoch, one marked by grace and faith."[57] Yet they still awaited the consummation of these events. "The whole of Christian existence—and theology—has this eschatological 'tension' as its basic framework."[58] "The ends of the ages have come"; yet "the end, when he surrenders the sovereignty to God the Father" is still to come (1 Cor 10:11; 15:24). In Galatians Paul places the stress more on the first fact and on the change of attitude it warrants, in 1 and 2 Thessalonians more on the second.[59]

The pattern of events and responses thus follows that instanced at the exodus, in Joshua, in the restoration from the exile and in the Maccabean deliverance.[60]

The Spirit

The activity of God's Spirit in the church is the sign that God's reign has begun in a new sense, and it is the guarantee of its consummation. The bestowal of God's Spirit is a down payment that enters on a contractual obligation and guarantees the fulfillment of that obligation (2 Cor 1:21-22; 5:5; Eph 1:14). It is the seal by which God marks people as his own (2 Cor 1:22-23; Eph 1:13; 4:30). It is the firstfruits, the pledge that God will bring in the final harvest (Rom 8:23). (Paul can also speak in 1 Cor 15:20, 23 of Jesus' resurrection as the firstfruits of ours.)[61]

On the basis of his disciples' love for and submission to Jesus, he promises that he will ask God to give them another *paraklētos* (Jn 14:16). We don't

---

[56]Sobrino, *Jesus the Liberator*, e.g., 67.

[57]James D. G. Dunn, *The Theology of Paul the Apostle* (Grand Rapids and Cambridge, UK: Eerdmans, 1998), 318.

[58]Gordon D. Fee, *God's Empowering Presence* (Peabody, MA: Hendrickson, 1994), 803.

[59]Cf. Wayne A. Meeks, *The First Urban Christians*, 2nd ed. (New Haven, CT, and London: Yale University Press, 2003), 171-80.

[60]See further chapter eight below.

[61]Fee, *God's Empowering Presence*, 806-8.

know why John uses this word for the Holy Spirit. A *paraklētos* can be an advocate (1 Jn 2:1), but John's Gospel doesn't mention this role. Another conventional translation is "comforter," and the *paraklētos* does act as comforter, though perhaps not in the sense that word often has. One could say that Jesus himself came as a comforter, in light of the First Testament's use of this expression. After the fall of Jerusalem in 587 BC Jerusalem "had no comforter" (Lam 1:2, 9, 16, 17, 21). While in the immediate context, "comfort" suggests consoling, in the broader context it suggests action to put things right that will bring another level of comfort (e.g., Is 49:13; 51:3). Such comfort is a result of God reigning (Is 52:7-10). Jesus came as the comforter who would restore Israel to what it was supposed to be and who would see to the fulfilling of God's promises to it. He is now leaving. Paradoxically, his departure is the means to completing the fulfillment of that intent, but the intent still needs implementing. So God will replace Jesus on earth by "another comforter" to get on with that work. It will never be necessary for this other comforter to leave them; he will be with them permanently.

Jesus does also say that after his resurrection he himself will come to them (Jn 14:18), and further that "we" (Jesus and the Father) will come to them and make "our" home with them individually (Jn 14:23). The Holy Spirit will be "with them" (*meta*), and the Father and Son will make their home "with" people individually (*para*). The Holy Spirit will live with them (*para*) and will be/is among them (*en*; manuscripts vary over the verb's tense) (Jn 14:17). "I am in my Father, you are in me, and I am among you" (Jn 14:20). The *paraklētos* will be "the spirit of truth," the true spirit, the faithful spirit. As Jesus is the truth, the embodiment of faithfulness, this spirit will be the truth, not an embodiment but an ongoing expression and manifestation of God's faithfulness. He will be the truthful spirit in the sense that he will declare the truth, which the world (which includes the Jewish people) cannot receive.

A further conventional translation of *paraklētos* is "counselor," which also corresponds to the role of Jesus and of the Holy Spirit as making up for Jesus' departure. The Holy Spirit is an adviser or teacher (Jn 14–16), reminding them of what Jesus said and bringing home its significance. He will guide the disciples into truth and tell them about the things that are coming, through being able to speak what the Father and the Son say (Jn 16:12-15).

The things that are coming are in the first instance Jesus' death, but then also the outworking of the significance of that event in the exposure and condemnation of the world. This exposure and condemnation belong to the final judgment, but through the Spirit as through the Son this judgment happens now. "The Spirit already proclaims the truth that will one day be manifest, and the judgement that will then be executed."[62] "On that day you will no longer ask me anything" (Jn 16:23).

Further, the Spirit will convict or expose the world with regard to its guilt by convicting or exposing it for not recognizing Jesus and for killing him instead, which brings out its guilt. This result will come about because Jesus' death means his going to the Father and means the condemnation of this world with its prince (Jn 16:8-10). How does the Spirit convict the world? It happens through the church,[63] through its life, its acts and its words.

4.3 THE RESISTANCE

It's both surprising and not surprising that the Jewish people reject Jesus. It's surprising because he is announcing God's reign and their restoration. Yet it's in keeping with Israel's resistance to God's prophets over the centuries.

> "Ye would not" (Mt. 23[37]). It can all be summed up in these words directed to the inhabitants of Jerusalem. This is the riddle of the existence of Israel in its relationship to Jesus. . . . Jerusalem had opposed to the gathering of Jesus the oldest and thickest and most impregnable of all its walls—its own unwillingness: "Jerusalem, thou that killest the prophets, and stonest them which are sent unto thee."[64]

It's a mystery, but it's not a mystery, because Jesus is a threat to the existent political and religious powers. The First Testament pattern recurs: Jesus confronts people, they don't want to have anything to do with it, and they end up cut down though not cast off. The people of God is always secure in God's commitment to it, but it is always vulnerable to his chastisement.

---

[62]C. K. Barrett, *The Gospel According to St John* (London: SPCK, 1962), 76.
[63]Ibid., 405-6.
[64]Barth, *CD* IV, 2:261.

The Puzzle

The Israelites affirmed at the Reed Sea that Yahweh reigns, but they were soon objecting to the manner in which Yahweh reigned in their lives. In the time of Samuel, they rebelled against Yahweh's reign by asking for a human king to reign over them. In the sixth century, Yahweh declared that his reign had arrived, and he terminated Babylonian rule over them, but most of the exiles did not return to Jerusalem with the reigning Yahweh. The ultimate assertion of God's reign by Jesus followed this pattern; neither did it win people's allegiance. The message/messenger that had been the means of making the world was in the world, but the world didn't accept him; the world is full of misapprehension about God, mysteriously preferring its misapprehension to the truth. And even his own people did not accept him. The First Testament illustrates the point; the story of Jesus illustrates it again (Jn 1:1-11).

Why should it be so? Unbelief is a bewildering mystery. Paul wrestles with it in Romans 9 and concludes that Israel was predestined to reject the message, which at one level is simply a reformulation of the question of why it happens. Jesus analyzes some of the reasons in Mark 4. Sometimes Satan takes the message away as soon as people hear it, which also simply reformulates the question. Some people accept it for a while but abandon it when persecution comes, which once more reformulates: Why do people persecute those who accept this message? Some people abandon it because trouble comes to them; they thought it was going to solve their problems, but it doesn't. Some initially accept it, but the worries of this life get in the way of their assimilating it.

The stories of Israel in the wilderness (Ex 14–17; Num 11–20) illustrate this dynamic in Israel, and Israel's subsequent inclination to turn to Ba'al, the Master, implies something similar. They need the crops to grow and they need children to be born; can Yahweh look after such things, or do they need to turn to another expert? Lacking crops and children is a problem; having them can also be a problem. Moses warns about the ease with which Israel could put Yahweh out of mind when they are comfortably off in the land, and Jesus adds reference to "stuff," to the deceitfulness of wealth, the desire for more things, that also gets in the way of assimilating the message (Mk 4:19).

When Jesus sends out the Twelve to announce God's reign and to back it up with its signs, he warns them that they, too, are not to assume that people will welcome them or listen to them (Mt 10:9-39). They are like sheep among wolves. They are to allow for the possibility of being handed over to councils and flogged in synagogues, arrested and brought before governors and kings, betrayed by family members, hated and persecuted, and called Beelzebul, as Jesus was. Persecution is "the climate in which Jesus lived,"[65] and the one in which they will live. He knows that he comes to bring a sword, not peace. They have to be prepared to be killed because of their proclamation and the signs they give.

Jesus later reiterates that the mystery of opposition that he has faced will also face his followers (see Mt 24; Mk 13; Lk 21), though their predicament will at least be the means of the good news being proclaimed to all the nations. It will then be the case that "you are not the ones who are speaking, but the holy spirit" (Mk 13:11). Such pressures will mean families and communities being riven by conflict and hatred. The disciples will be hated by all nations (Mt 24:9).

Jesus as a Threat

Evidently it is not "any more immediately obvious to the world that Jesus alone is Lord, God and Savior, than it was to the nations around Israel that YHWH alone is the God of heaven and earth, Creator of the world and Ruler of all its nations."[66] Many people will turn away from the faith and will betray and hate each other, and the love of most will grow cold. But the disciples are to stand firm until the end, and they will be delivered—even if (paradoxically) they lose their lives (Mt 24:9-14). They are encouraged never to lose hope. Many people will take no notice of the message; but in other people it will produce stupendous fruit.

Jesus' story does point to some factors in people's mysterious resistance. He imperils people in power. "The 'cross' of Jesus Christ was a political punishment" related to "the threat which the Suffering Servant poses to the powers of the world"; taking up the cross does not denote an acceptance of one's illness or loss, or "an inward experience of the self," or a "subjective

---

[65]Cf. Sobrino, *Jesus the Liberator*, 196.
[66]Wright, *Mission of God*, 130.

brokenness, the renunciation of pride and self-will."[67] It means accepting persecution and martyrdom. "I die every day" (1 Cor 15:31), Paul declares, in the sense that he faces death every day in the course of his witnessing (cf. TNIV). Indeed, "whenever Christ calls us, his call leads us to death."[68] But his disciples can take up their cross and lose their life yet save it, in the sense that the Man will acknowledge them rather than be ashamed of them when he comes (Mk 8:34-38).

Jesus also imperils people in religious power. Like the Christian church, Judaism does not have one view on questions of theology and spirituality— for instance, on whether to look for God speedily (or eventually) to put down the Romans, and on the role of the Anointed One in doing so. But people with an investment in the status quo—usually the people who hold power now—cannot be expected to enthuse about change. The issue in the controversy between Jesus or Paul and other Jews is "*the hope of Israel*: Jesus' announcement that the hope was being realized, Paul's belief that in Jesus' cross and resurrection it had indeed been realized."[69]

So Jesus gets into trouble for proclaiming that God's reign is arriving, and specifically for proclaiming that it is arriving in his person, and for his associated declaration that some aspects of the Torah (or of their interpretation of it) are now less important than people think, that the temple is now less important than people think, and that his time is no time for fasting but that they will feel like fasting when he is gone (Mt 9:14-15). After he defends his disciples for picking some heads of grain on the sabbath and after he himself heals a disabled man on the sabbath, religious leaders determine to destroy him. Is it because he breaks sabbath, or claims to be greater than the sabbath, or speaks of the arrival of something (or someone) greater than the temple, or constitutes a threat to their views or to their authority (Mt 12:1-14)? None of these possibilities constitutes a very rational explanation. The difficulty in providing an answer again suggests that his rejection is something of a mystery. Eventually Jesus speaks of how he will be betrayed by one of the

---

[67]John Howard Yoder, *The Politics of Jesus*, 2nd ed. (Grand Rapids: Eerdmans; Carlisle, UK: Paternoster, 1993), 125, 127.
[68]Bonhoeffer, *Discipleship*, 87.
[69]Wright, *Jesus and the Victory of God*, 380.

Twelve and abandoned by the rest of them (Mt 26:20-25). Why does Judas do it? For money? That explanation, too, seems insufficient.

One way or another, the implementing of God's reign and the termination of other reigns does meet with opposition. It is thus both surprising and not surprising to read of Jesus' declaration of terrible judgment on the big towns in Galilee where he had performed his signs. They have not repented, as he urged people to do in light of the coming of God's reign (Mt 11:20-24). By implication, the crowds that followed him were not representative of their cities; already the pattern is that only a minority responds to him. His generation stands in contrast with the people of Nineveh who repented at Jonah's preaching (Mt 12:41). His hometown is worst of all (Mt 13:53-58).

Confronted and Decimated

While crowds follow Jesus, then, it does not mean that the people as a whole do so. And it is not given even to the crowds to understand what God's reign means (Mt 13:11). The towns where he does most of his miracles do not repent, nor do the religious leaders; indeed the entire generation fails to do so (Mt 11:20; 12:38-41). When a Gentile manifests extraordinary trust in his power, Jesus comments that many Gentiles will join in the party "in the kingdom of heaven" while members of Israel, people who belong to that kingdom, will be thrown out (Mt 8:5-13).

In John the "Jews" feature prominently in similar connections. The context of some of John's references to Jewish hostility suggests the people's leadership (e.g., Jn 1:19; 5:10, 15, 16, where TNIV has "the Jewish leaders"); the New Testament elsewhere suggests that most of the Jerusalem leadership indeed opposed Jesus. Other expressions of Jewish hostility may also apply to the Jewish leaders or may refer to ordinary members of the Jewish community (e.g., Jn 2:18, 20; 6:41, 52; 7:11, 13). Other references to the Jews are neutral (e.g., Jn 2:6, 13; 5:1). Yet others denote Jews who believe in Jesus (Jn 8:31; 12:9, 11). "Salvation is from the Jews" (Jn 4:22). Whereas the Synoptic Gospels refer rarely to "the Jews," Acts frequently does so, and this link supports the idea that in his references to the Jews John is making a connection with the experience of the church. In Acts, too, Jews who believed in Jesus and Jews who did not believe can take a confrontational stance to each other and can use language that offends Western people (e.g., Acts 13:6-11, 44-51; 28:17-28).[70] To complicate matters further, Paul's letters are "in dialogue and dispute not with non-Christian Jews, but with fellow Christian Jews," and it is in this context that Paul's principal treatment of the Torah was formulated.[71]

The situation in the time of Jesus and Paul recapitulates the one that obtained through the ministry of the Prophets, and the result is the same as the one that came about in 722 BC and in 587 BC. The Prophets threatened that Yahweh would cast Israel off, and Yahweh did cast off the people as a whole, while also allowing some leftovers to remain. The diminution of the people sometimes involved the outward people being reduced to mere leftovers, as happened between the time of Elijah and the time of Ezekiel. Sometimes the outward people stay numerous and the reduction takes place in the proportion that sees and hears, as happened in Elijah's day and in Paul's. Either way, paradoxically this process is God's way of reaching the whole world, just as much as making the whole people flourish was a way of reaching it.

Once more the pattern within the First Testament repeats itself when the people as a whole do not recognize Jesus, but God ensures that there continues in existence "leftovers in accordance with election by grace—but if by grace, no longer on the basis of deeds, since grace would no longer then be grace" (Rom 11:5-6). Israel had come into being as God's people in the first place on the basis of grace. As there was nothing distinctive about Israel to commend it to God (cf. Deut 7:7-8; 9:5-6), the preserving of a remnant in its history likewise happened on the basis of grace. The people who escaped the gradual diminution of the nation over the centuries from Solomon to the exile escaped on that basis. It is not the case that the faithful people survive and the faithless are eliminated. The remnant always exists on the basis of grace.

So the manner of God's operating continues as it had been in the past, when God had felt free to cast off a whole generation or a whole segment of Israel, even to decimate it, without finally abandoning the people as a whole. The majority had the same experience as Pharaoh or the Canaanites. They

---

[70]See further the paragraphs on the "Uncouth" aspect to the Scriptures in section 2.6 above.

[71]James D.G. Dunn, "In Search of Common Ground," in Dunn, ed., *Paul and the Mosaic Law* (Tübingen: Mohr, 1996), 309-34 (on 310).

were inclined to resist God, and God was inclined to encourage their resistance as an act of punishment. So God made them even less able to see and hear. God sees that the terrible prayer in Psalm 69 is fulfilled in them (Rom 11:7-10). But if Israel comes to trust, it can be grafted back in (Rom 11:24). Everything depends on trust.

The Necessity

The sort of people who respond to Jesus are children, not the wise and learned, and even they respond only because God opens their eyes (Mt 11:25-27). Yet in the same breath Jesus invites everyone who is tired to come. Perhaps what makes them tired is the obligations that the wise and learned put on the "children," the ordinary people, who have a harder time than the wise in fulfilling them (cf. Mt 23:4). These obligations form a contrast with the easy yoke Jesus puts on people (Mt 11:28-30). There is a sense in which he is utterly demanding, but a sense in which his demands are easier; they relieve them from other concerns (Mt 6:25-34).[72] Rather than being overanxious about obeying the Torah, they can follow its own encouragement to be relaxed about other people's rigorous interpretation of its implications (Mt 12:1-14).[73] They can go back to its relative simplicities.

But they do have to take up their cross in the sense of being prepared to join Jesus in accepting martyrdom if it should be required, as happens to some people in both Testaments. Innocent suffering alone does not make someone a martyr; it is the acceptance of it as the cost of giving your witness, and the self-dedication to it, that makes suffering creative and makes death sacrificial (2 Tim 4:6), and turns someone into a person who bears witness.[74]

Jesus' warnings are fulfilled in the lives of his representatives in Acts. While sometimes his representatives get released from prison, on occasion miraculously (Acts 5:17-20; 12:1-11), sometimes they do get martyred. The first fact reflects the fact that God has the power to bring about such events, the second reflects the fact that such intervention is not his general way of acting. The Scriptures offer no way of determining why deliverance happens in particular cases and not in others. They imply that we should

---

[72]Cf. Margaret Davies, *Matthew* (Sheffield: Sheffield Academic Press, 1993), 91-92.
[73]Cf. R. T. France, *The Gospel of Matthew* (Grand Rapids and Cambridge, UK: Eerdmans, 2007), 451.
[74]Ware, *Inner Kingdom*, 113, 115.

not infer that the reasons lie in the deserving of the people involved. Maybe it's random.

The prospect of his own rejection and martyrdom hangs over Jesus' story from the beginning. At his baptism (Mt 3:17), God declares that Jesus is his son, taking up words from Psalm 2. That psalm describes God's kingly son as God's Anointed but also as such someone whom the world's rulers attack. In those words at his baptism God goes on to speak of Jesus as the son he loves, which would recall the story of Abraham's offering of Isaac in Genesis 22, a story familiar and influential on Jewish thinking. God further speaks of Jesus as the one in whom he takes delight, taking up words from the description of Yahweh's servant in Isaiah 42:1-4, where he is someone who has to put up with opposition in order to fulfill his task of announcing Yahweh's rule among the nations. None of the phrases that lie behind the words at Jesus' baptism are without a solemn aspect.

It is in keeping with these declarations that Jesus speaks of having a baptism to undergo, a drowning; he has to drink God's wrath (Mk 10:38). He goes on to speak of the Man having come to give his life as a ransom or redemption price for many (Mk 10:45). It wouldn't be surprising if that language made people think of Israel's redemption from Egypt and/or of the picture of Yahweh's servant suffering "for many" (Is 53:10-11). When Peter made his declaration that Jesus is the Anointed One, Jesus began to tell the disciples that the Man has to suffer, be rejected and be killed, though then to rise from death (Mt 16:21).

His suffering repeats a pattern that runs through the scriptural story. Prophets often become martyrs. But its necessity is based on something beyond such inevitability. Somehow there is a relationship between talk of God's reign and the likelihood of Jesus' martyrdom. There was a sense among some Jewish people that their restoration is never going to come until they have paid for their wrongdoing and faithlessness. The two aspects of Israel's restoration interrelate. Indeed, there may need to be greater tribulation before there can be restoration, before God's reign can arrive. Jesus knows that he is destined to pay the price on his people's behalf, in effect to undergo this tribulation.[75]

---

[75]See Pitre, *Jesus, Tribulation, and the End of the Exile*; and see further chapter five below.

A Vine with Its Fruit

As a Jewish leader, Nicodemus is the kind of person one might have expected to understand Jesus, but he doesn't realize the gulf that separates him from understanding (Jn 3)—though his role later in the Gospel indicates that he is not to be written off. There is a contrast between Jesus' interactions with him and with the Samaritan woman (Jn 4). Her nationality and gender make her the kind of person one might not expect to understand, but she comes to do so. This contrast between Jew and Samaritan corresponds to the way the spread of the gospel turned out.

"You [Samaritans] worship what you do not know, we [Jews] worship what we know, because salvation is from the Jews. But the time is coming (and it's now here) when the true worshipers will worship the Father in/by spirit and truth" (Jn 4:22-23). The fact that Jews worship what they know implies that there must be some sense in which they worship God in/by spirit and truth now. But Jesus brings a new outpouring of God's spirit for them and a new manifestation of God's truth. For people such as Samaritans (who here stand for outsiders generally), he makes true worship possible, worship that corresponds to who God is and that reflects God's dynamic. "The Father seeks such people as his worshipers" (Jn 4:23). The implication is not that the Father is looking around for people who will commit themselves to that kind of worship, so that the responsibility lies with them. It is that God is the shepherd out looking for the sheep, or the father out looking for the returning wayward son, looking for people like the Samaritan woman who can be turned into true worshipers through Jesus' coming. "God is spirit, and the people who worship must worship in/by spirit and truth" (Jn 4:24).

Nicodemus needed to realize that Jesus is the real vine and his Father is the gardener (Jn 15:1). Israel had been the vine that God planted in the land of Canaan, the vine that turned it into the land of Israel (Ps 80:8-16 [MT 9-17]; Is 5:1-7; Jer 2:21; 12:10; Ezek 15; 19:10-14; Hos 10:1).The image of the vine suggests fruitfulness, which would imply *mišpāṭ* and *ṣədāqâ* (Is 5:1-7), and fruitfulness is the idea Jesus takes up. He implies the same fruitfulness: in New Testament terms, *agapē*. By claiming to be the real vine, he also implies that he is the real Israel. The Prophets have protested that Israel has failed to produce fruit, and Jesus reaffirms their protest and their declaration of

judgment (Mk 12:1-9). His Father's activity as gardener corresponds to that
in Isaiah 5:1-7, though it is less radical in John than in Mark. In Isaiah, God
destroys the vineyard, and in Mark the vineyard owner kills his tenants who
tend it. Indeed, the axe is already at the root of the trees, and trees that do
not produce good fruit will be thrown into the fire (Mt 3:10). In John 15, God
simply cuts out fruitless branches.

So a congregation that failed to grow would die. And a congregation that
did grow would be pruned (for instance, it might be persecuted, or perhaps
be confronted by a message that pruned it). The reason why fruitfulness is
important is that it glorifies God (Jn 15:8). The vital thing is to stay part of
the vine. Congregations have to stay in association with Jesus and to keep
living by his words. The way people stay with Jesus and Jesus with them is
by Jesus' words staying with them (Jn 15:6-7). The way one stays in the vine
is by loving.

The corporate vine needs to produce the fruit of the Spirit (Gal 5:22-23).
It is a working out of serving one another in love as opposed to biting and
devouring each other. "The flesh/Spirit contrast in this passage, therefore,
has . . . to do with 'love, joy, peace, forbearance, kindness, goodness, and
gentleness' within the believing community." The passage expounds "primarily the ethics not of the individual, but of the community of faith."[76] The
fruits of the Spirit "are defined by *free self-withdrawal and self-giving for the
benefit of other creatures*, whether given in a liberating manner or received
in a liberating manner." Free self-withdrawal gives other people space for
free self-development.[77]

It is in this connection (among others) that the Torah serves love. The
fruit of the Spirit is the kind of thing the First Testament expects to see in
the life of Israel, and the kind of thing Jewish tradition and much pagan
thinking affirm. It expects this fruit in the sense of urging that it should
appear, though not in the sense that it anticipates it will appear. Believers in
Jesus likewise do not produce the Spirit's fruit unmixed with the fruit of the
lower nature. But sometimes one does see that fruit. In the First Testament,
Jonathan is an embodiment of love, the Psalms of celebration, Joseph of

[76]Fee, *God's Empowering Presence*, 883.
[77]Welker, *God the Spirit*, 248-49.

peacemaking, Job of long-suffering. They indicate that the Spirit is bearing fruit, whether or not they use that language.

Chosen and Not Cast Off

It's unwise to rely on descent from Abraham. God can use stones to generate new descendants of Abraham (Mt 3:9). Yet in light of the position Israel had been given by God, once more one asks how they could have failed to recognize their Anointed One. The answer is not that God's promises have failed (Rom 9:6-13). To begin with, God's promises never applied to everyone within the people to whom they were given. The promise to Abraham applied only to Isaac's line, not to Ishmael's, and only to Jacob's line, not to Esau's. "Jacob I loved, but Esau I hated": Paul is referring to choosing and rejecting in connection with a particular purpose,[78] and the basis for choosing and rejecting was not what people deserved but the requirements of that purpose.

God's purpose operates on the basis of God summoning a people, not of a people volunteering, and on the basis of God's selecting a people, not of a people electing to serve God. Thus Augustine notes that "it was because [the disciples] had been chosen, that they chose [Jesus]; not because they chose Him that they were chosen."[79]

Yet Paul is not talking about predestination or election in the sense in which this idea has often been discussed in theology. He is talking about a people, not about individuals, and talking about a role in God's purpose, not about whether people go to heaven. Neither is he interested in the question of divine sovereignty in relation to human freewill (he would laugh at our concern to safeguard human freewill, partly because he is concerned to affirm God's freewill, compared with which our freewill is a triviality). In both connections his experience of Jesus bowling him over on the Damascus road reframes the presuppositions of our concern. He "went to Damascus without any preparation" and "as one who was to quite a special degree proof against the Gospel";[80] his experience there came out of the blue. His

---

[78]See further the comments on Rom 9:13 in the paragraphs headed "Israel's Wider Family" in section 4.1 above.

[79]*On Grace and Free Will* 38 [xviii] (*NPNF* 1, 5:460).

[80]Johannes Munck, *Paul and the Salvation of Mankind* (London: SCM Press; Richmond: John Knox, 1959), 15; cf. Anthony C. Thiselton, *The Hermeneutics of Doctrine* (Grand Rapids: Eerdmans, 2007), 475.

experience is the great illustration of how "the exaltation of man, which in defiance of his reluctance has been achieved in the death and declared in the resurrection of Jesus Christ, is as such the creation of his new form of existence as the faithful covenant-partner of God."[81]

So is God rejecting most of the Jewish people, and therefore being unfaithful to them? No, says Paul, because one has to see God's action in relation to the Jews as part of a bigger picture, of that bigger purpose (Rom 9:14-21). God is concerned to be merciful and compassionate on the widest front, and his choice and nonchoice are a paradoxical means to that end. It was for this reason that Pharaoh also got what might look like a bad deal. It was to make him the means of proclaiming God's name in all the earth, which has certainly happened. Encouraging him to be stubborn (when he was already so inclined) was a means to that end. Paul's argument "bears witness to the *freedom* of God's mercy, but the freedom to which it bears witness is the freedom of His *mercy*."[82]

If Paul shared our modern concern to safeguard human freedom, he could point out that Pharaoh is no more *forced* to give in to this encouragement than anyone is *forced* to give in to the encouragement to believe in Jesus. Indeed, he could have pointed out that Exodus itself speaks of Pharaoh stiffening his own resolve as well as of God stiffening his resolve.[83] But Paul is not so concerned. And if he were in a position to take into account the possibility that some readers would understand the theme of God's choice in the framework of the eternal destiny of individuals, he could point out that the dynamics of God's dealing with Pharaoh say nothing about whether you will meet Pharaoh in the new Jerusalem.

What was true of Ishmael, Esau and Pharaoh is true of that majority of Jewish people in Paul's day who have declined to believe in Jesus. They contribute to God's plan to fulfill a merciful purpose for the whole world (Rom 9:22-29). It is through their unbelief that God is going to be "true to the promises to Abraham, promises which declared *both* that he would give him a worldwide family *and* that his own seed would share in the blessing."[84]

---

[81]Barth, *CD* IV, 2:499.
[82]C. E. B. Cranfield, *A Critical and Exegetical Commentary on the Epistle to the Romans* (Edinburgh: T&T Clark, 1975), 472.
[83]Cf. James D. G. Dunn, *Romans* (Dallas: Word, 1988), 2:564.
[84]Wright, *Climax of the Covenant*, 236.

Secure and Vulnerable

There is a *mystērion* about Israel (Rom 11:25). A *mystērion* is not a mystery, something that we can't understand. It's something that we wouldn't have guessed that has been revealed. The *mystērion* about Israel is God's decision to make Israel's unfaith the way of opening up the gospel to Gentiles, and then to make Gentile faith the way of winning Israel back to faith. The gospel's reaching the whole world is to bring about the restoration of Israel to flourishing, by making Israel jealous of what it sees its own God doing in the world. God thus cleverly reverses the original intention to attract the world by blessing Israel.

If Israel's rejection means such blessing for the world, imagine what blessing Israel's restoration will mean for Israel itself! It will transpire that Israel as a whole can be rescued from God's wrath and can join in the coming resurrection of the dead, along with the leftovers who have believed in Jesus along the way (Rom 11:11-26). Unfortunately, in the short term this clever plan of God's was just as frustrated as God's earlier plans. The church's treatment of the Jewish people did not encourage the Jewish people to want to have anything to do with the one whom the church claims to be the Anointed One.

So in the twentieth century maybe God formulated yet another clever plan in bringing about by other means over recent decades the exponential growth in Jewish recognition of Jesus. Secularization and the secularization of the Jewish people in particular lies at the background of this development—that is, many Jews who have come to believe in Jesus were people for whom their Jewish faith was no longer real. So perhaps God has used the evil of secularization as the means of Jewish people coming to see the need to break out of its parameters in order to discover the truth.

Calvin concluded that in Romans 11:26 "Israel" means an expanded Israel, a renewed people of God embracing both Jews and Gentiles,[85] and this understanding would fit the development of Paul's argument in Romans 11.[86] But everywhere else in Romans 11 "Israel" means "the Jewish people," and there is no clear instance anywhere in the New Testament of it meaning

---

[85]John Calvin, *Commentaries on the Epistle of Paul the Apostle to the Romans* (repr., Grand Rapids: Eerdmans, 1947), 437.
[86]Cf. Wright, *Climax of the Covenant*, 249-51.

anything else. Admittedly it's hard to read the reference to Israel in Galatians 6:16 as alluding to the Jewish people; it would be a novel point to introduce in the coda to the epistle.[87] But it's also hard to read it as referring to the church, which would also be a novel point to introduce in the coda. This unclarity perhaps epitomizes the sense in which Paul hasn't reached an unambiguous view of the relationship between the Jewish people, the communities that trust in Jesus, and the Israel of the Scriptures.[88]

While it's more likely that Romans 11:26 refers to the Jewish people, little hangs on the point, because Paul does affirm both that the whole Jewish-Gentile church will be saved and that the whole Jewish people will be saved. The gifts and summons of God are irrevocable (Rom 11:29).

Does he mean every individual Jew will be saved? That question again involves imagining him thinking in terms of individual believers, which he is not doing. He is speaking of a mass turning of the Jewish people that will be the reverse of the mass turning away from Jesus that he has witnessed. Writing in the 60s AD, he knows that a whole generation has passed since Jesus' death and resurrection and that a whole generation of Israel has forfeited its place in Israel and can never get it back, so that the story of Israel between Sinai and Canaan has repeated itself. But that earlier event did not derail God's purpose to take Israel as whole to its destiny, and neither will this repetition of that event have that effect. The End will come, the deliverer will arrive, the new covenant will be implemented: when Jesus comes, he will turn ungodliness from Jacob and take away their sin (Rom 11:26-27). Thus Israel as a whole will be saved from God's wrath along with Gentiles. God's wrath has come on Israel, as Roman 1–3 argues, and has done so in a way that will continue to operate until the end (1 Thess 2:16). But at the end God's mercy will be revealed to Israel in a new way (Rom 11:31-32).[89]

Jesus speaks like a prophet in declaring that the end has come on Israel. He also speaks like a prophet in recognizing that this end would be a kind

---

[87]Cf. Gerd Lüdemann, *Paulus und das Judentum* (Munich: Kaiser, 1983), 27-30; E. P. Sanders, *Paul, the Law, and the Jewish People* (London: SCM Press; Philadelphia: Fortress, 1983), 174.

[88]Cf. Sanders, *Paul, the Law, and the Jewish People*, 171-79.

[89]Karl P. Donfried, "The Theology of 1 Thessalonians," in Donfried and I. Howard Marshall, *The Theology of the Shorter Pauline Letters* (Cambridge and New York: Cambridge University Press, 1993), 1-79 (on 69-70).

of interim end, not a complete one.[90] The crowd before Pilate chillingly declared, "His blood be on us and on our children" (Mt 27:25), but the God of Israel cannot grant this prayer. The story of Israel at Sinai already establishes Israel's security and vulnerability, and Romans 9–11 expounds it further. It expounds a "particularist universalism,"[91] a universalism that excludes as well as a particularism that includes.

4.4 GOD'S SECRET PLAN: ISRAEL EXPANDED

So God lay behind Israel's short-term rejection of Jesus, because it facilitated the sharing of the message with the world. Although Jesus focused on the Jewish people itself, God always intended to make the existence and the restoration of Israel the means of reaching the world. The Torah is now annulled to that end. How, then, are we to think of the relationship between the community of Israel and the community of people who do recognize Jesus? It's not that Israel is cast off, nor that the Gentiles are subordinate to Israel, but there comes into being one new entity that embraces Jews and Gentiles who believe in Jesus, that shares both the long-term security and the short-term vulnerability of Israel.

Greater Things Than Me

While Jesus came to announce God's reign and to restore the Jewish people, it transpired that God also had this other secret plan and that Jesus' own intention, too, was to create one new humanity out of Jews and Gentiles and to reconcile both to God through the cross (Eph 2:15-16). The way the Scriptures speak in this connection recalls the way Joseph says that it wasn't his brothers who sent him to Egypt but God (Gen 45:8) or the way John says that Caiaphas didn't speak of his own accord when he commented that it was advantageous for one man to die for the entire nation (Jn 11:51). Sometimes breathtaking consequences must be more than accidents.

The excitement of Mary and Zechariah (Lk 1) relates to the fact that Jesus' birth means the restoration of Israel, and in his lifetime Jesus did not concern himself with the Gentile world; implicitly he worked within the framework of Isaiah 60–62, that God's fulfilling his promises to Israel would draw the

---

[90]Against Bryan, *Jesus and Israel's Traditions of Judgement and Restoration*, 87, who contrasts Jesus and the prophets.

[91]Daniel Boyarin, *A Radical Jew* (Berkeley and London: University of California Press, 1994), 201.

world to acknowledge Israel's God, so that the temple would then fulfill its destiny to be a prayer house for all nations. When a Canaanite woman sought help from him, he resisted her, though he eventually granted her request (Mt 15:21-28). She was like people such as Jethro and Rahab in the First Testament, individuals who seize the chance to acknowledge what the God of Israel is doing and whom one can see as harbingers of something much bigger. The apostles likewise initially focused on testifying to the Jewish community that was destined to experience God's restoration, not on the Gentile world; it would be drawn through seeing what God was doing for Israel. If God brings about the restoration of Israel, the acknowledgment of the nations will look after itself.

In the event, this scenario failed to work out. God visited his people to redeem them, but they did not recognize the time of their visitation (Lk 1:68; 19:44). Jesus thus speaks of turning directly to the nations (Mt 21:33-44; 24:14). In the years that follow, opposition from Jesus' own people continues be more evident than welcome, and the Man will still not come. The turn to deliberate witness to Gentiles comes with Jesus' appearance to Ananias in Damascus and then with God's appearance to Peter in Jaffa (Acts 9–10). One might nevertheless see this development as a natural one, given that the Gentile world was indeed to be drawn to acknowledge Israel's God (cf. Mt 28:16-20). And with hindsight, one might not be so surprised that the Jewish people itself continued to be at best equivocal in its response to the apostles, though one would have no reason to expect that the Gentile world would be more responsive.

Jesus did say that his disciples would do greater things than him (Jn 14:12). In terms of wonders, while they do heal, exorcise and resuscitate, they don't do anything like feeding five thousand people out of virtually nothing. But when Jesus gave that promise, he had just spoken of the world coming to recognize that they are his disciples if they love one another (Jn 13:35). More likely his promise is fulfilled as they spread the news of God's reign around the eastern Mediterranean, as far as Rome, and as they do so in the Gentile world, not just working within Judea and Samaria and among Jews. It is his going to the Father that makes it possible (Jn 14:12).

Paul's commission thus includes bringing the offering of the Gentiles to God (Rom 15:16), in fulfillment of those expectations expressed in the

Prophets (e.g., Is 60). The significance of his "conversion experience" is that it was a "commission to proclaim the gospel, that is, to serve Christ among the Gentiles."[92] Throughout the eastern Mediterranean, "from Jerusalem and in a circle as far as Illyricum I have filled out the gospel of the Anointed One" (Rom 15:19): while he himself did not preach in Jerusalem or Judea, he still sees the gospel as going out from Jerusalem to the world as a whole.[93]

"The apostle, to whom the world seemed rather small, who in his excited hope of the approaching end of the world could not hurry fast enough from one country to another, so as at least to have made an opportunity for Christ to be known," and who thinks in terms of nations and peoples rather than of individuals, "was not a man made for working out small details—no one can be so made who believes himself called to accomplish gigantic tasks in so short a time."[94]

The Torah Reaches Its Goal

The gospel is for all. "'All' is one of the really key words in Romans."[95] This fact does not clash with God's having entered into a special relationship with Israel, and Paul is tethered to a "devout ethnocentrism" in the early chapters of Romans. "Scripture is the tether, because Scripture tells the story of God's election of Israel. If Paul's gospel nullifies this election, it means that God's past dealing with his people was false dealing, that he made promises on which he is now reneging. At issue is 'the moral integrity of God.'"[96] Indeed, "the driving question in Romans is not 'How can I find a gracious God?' but 'How can we trust in this allegedly gracious God if he abandons his promises to Israel?'" Hence Paul's claim that

> his gospel does not annihilate the law but establishes it. . . . Paul's procla-
> mation presents the righteousness of God not as some unheard-of soterio-
> logical novelty but as the manifestation of a truth attested by Scripture from
> the first. When he says that his message confirms the Law, he refers not to the

---

[92]J. Christiaan Beker, *Paul the Apostle* (Philadelphia: Fortress, 1980), 3-6.

[93]Günther Bornkamm, *Paul* (New York: Harper; London: Hodder, 1971), 53.

[94]Quoted without reference as from the work of Adolf Jülicher by Munck, *Paul and the Salvation of Mankind*, 53 (though Munck calls it an "unjust judgment").

[95]Dunn, *Theology of Paul the Apostle*, 372.

[96]Richard B. Hays, *Echoes of Scripture in the Letters of Paul* (New Haven, CT, and London: Yale University Press, 1989), 47. The internal quotation comes from the chapter heading to Leander E. Keck, *Paul and His Letters* (Philadelphia: Fortress, 1979), 117-30 (rev. ed., 1988, 110-22).

specific commandments of the Pentateuch but to the witness of Scripture, read as a *narrative* about God's gracious election of a people.[97]

(Likewise, while Hebrews sees some aspects of the Torah as deficient, "there is not a trace of anti-Judaism" in Hebrews "or any sense that God has rejected Israel in favor of Gentile believers in Jesus. . . . Hebrews is no more supersessionist than Jeremiah.")[98]

The Torah's rules about worship and purity reflect both God's choice of Israel and his intention to reach the world through Israel. The rules themselves rarely give reasons for their injunctions other than obedience to Yahweh as the holy one and the need to embody separateness for the holy one.[99] Thus one reason God gave Israel the Torah was to provide it with boundary markers, to keep Israel distinct. But ironically, the reason for keeping Israel distinct was to make it possible for it to be God's means of bringing blessing to the rest of the world, and the First Testament does not treat the boundary as impermeable. The stories of Rahab and Akan confuse the boundary between Israelite and Canaanite,[100] as does the story of Ruth and of the welcome given her by the people of Bethlehem, and the story of David and Uriah the Hittite. The commitment that the Moabite Ruth showed to Naomi anticipates the way a Samaritan models care for someone who belongs to another group (Lk 10:25-37).

If one lived in a mixed community, caring for one's neighbor could involve compromising that boundary. The story about the Samaritan and the Jew thus confuses the boundary between Jew and Samaritan. In the First Testament,

> figures are constantly turning up, who, quite away from the given place, outside the nation Israel, seem nevertheless to have become genuine recipients of God's revelation. But this last possibility appears more and more to have the significance of a corrective. Those who perhaps boast of their membership instead of boasting in God must be checked and shamed. Those who

---

[97]Hays, *Echoes of Scripture in the Letters of Paul*, 53.

[98]Richard B. Hays, "Here We Have No Lasting City," in Richard Bauckham et al., eds., *The Epistle to the Hebrews and Christian Theology* (Grand Rapids and Cambridge, UK: Eerdmans, 2009), 151-73 (on 165).

[99]Childs, *Old Testament Theology in a Canonical Context*, 87.

[100]Cf. Dan Hawk, *Every Promise Fulfilled: Contesting Plots in Joshua* (Louisville: Westminster John Knox, 1991).

within this membership do not become recipients of revelation must be given a sign of judgment. The freedom of grace which is so easily forgotten and so lightly treasured must be made manifest.[101]

In another sense Paul's view of Judaism, too, is not ethnocentric, because his argument in Romans 4 is that from the beginning God's relationship with Israel is not merely ethnically based; God's promise of blessing had always had in mind Gentiles as well as Jews.[102] God thus terminates the Torah's role as boundary marker (see Acts 10–11) not because he previously took an ethnically exclusive position but because his concern for "all" is now to be achieved in a different way.[103] In light of God's changed missional strategy, outward markers of identity that require separation become "irksome,"[104] though trusting in Jesus does not mean the end of distinctive ritual markers of identity; baptism is an outward rite that constitutes a distinctive identity marker for the reconstituted people of God.[105]

Which Chosen People?

At a meeting of apostles and elders in Jerusalem, James speaks of how God has acted "to take *from the nations* a people for his name" (Acts 15:14). This Jewish-Gentile body is "a chosen race, a royal priesthood, a holy nation, a people that is a personal possession" (1 Pet 2:9), which God can call "my people" (e.g., 2 Cor 6:16). It is his "special people" (Tit 2:14). Such passages call this Jewish-Gentile body by means of terms that originally applied to Israel as God's people, (though they had been applied to other nations in Is 19:25). So is there one people of God or two? Has this Jewish-Gentile body replaced the Israel to which those terms earlier applied? What is now the significance of Israel as God's people? If the two basic heads of Jewish theology are "monotheism and election, God and Israel,"[106] how are we to think

---

[101]Barth, *CD* I, 2:210.

[102]Hays, *Echoes of Scripture in the Letters of Paul*, 55-57.

[103]N. T. Wright argues that this is the significance of Paul's opposition to circumcision: e.g., *Jesus and the Victory of God*, 381. But it is not the argument Paul uses, and it would be illogical, because it would have been quite possible to extend circumcision to Gentiles (and one can imagine the scriptural argument to support this, which would involve appeal to the way Ishmael as well as Isaac was circumcised).

[104]Dunn, *Romans*, 1:436-37.

[105]In critique of Dunn, see especially Douglas A. Campbell, *The Deliverance of God* (Grand Rapids: Eerdmans, 2009), 444-55.

[106]Wright, *Climax of the Covenant*, 1.

about Israel in light of the existence of a church that became largely Gentile? And how are we to think of the church in light of the existence of Israel?

Paul invites the Corinthian believers to see the Israelites of the exodus and wilderness period as "our ancestors," even though most of the Corinthians are Gentiles (1 Cor 10:1; 12:2). God's *ekklēsia* at Corinth comprises people "made holy through the Anointed One, Jesus, called holy ones" (1 Cor 1:2). In itself *ekklēsia* need not imply that they are Israel-like, but the addition of "made holy" and "holy ones" pushes the implication in that direction (cf. Ex 19:5-6). They have been grafted into the olive tree of Israel.[107] The church is a reworked, enlarged version of Israel. "Israel is the people of the Jews which resists its election; the Church is the gathering of Jews and Gentiles called on the ground of its election."[108] The church is "the messianic pilgrim people of God typologically shaped by Israel's story." The implication is not that the church is a separate entity from Israel that uses Israel's story to enable it to understand itself. It is that "the Church is simply Israel in the time between the times."[109] Gentile believers in Jesus become "honorary Jews."[110]

Or one could say that the church is a subset of the people of God. "The name the church gives itself" is "the church of Jesus Christ,"[111] a description that draws attention to the fact that the church "is not created, formed and introduced by individual men on their own initiative, authority and insight. It is not the outcome of a free undertaking to analyse and come to terms with the self-revealing God by gathering together a community which confesses Him." It derives from the Word made flesh, and its life is lived for Jesus' sake.[112]

Yet phrases such as "church of Christ" never occur in the New Testament. The New Testament's expression is "church of God" (e.g., Acts 20:28; 1 Cor 1:2; Gal 1:13). That title is also more frequent than the phrase "the body of the

---

[107]Cf. Hays, *Echoes of Scripture in the Letters of Paul*, 95-96.
[108]Barth, *CD* II, 2:199.
[109]George Lindbeck, *The Church in a Postliberal Age*, ed. James J. Buckley (Grand Rapids: Eerdmans, 2004), 146, 150; cf. Joseph L. Mangina, "God, Israel, and Ecclesia in the Apocalypse," in Richard B. Hays and Stefan Alkier, eds., *Revelation and the Politics of Apocalyptic Interpretation* (Waco, TX: Baylor University Press, 2012), 85-103 (on 86).
[110]Krister Stendahl, *Paul Among Jews and Gentiles and Other Essays* (Philadelphia: Fortress, 1976), 37; cf. Lindbeck, *Church in a Postliberal Age*, 151.
[111]Jürgen Moltmann, *The Church in the Power of the Spirit* (London: SCM Press; New York: Harper, 1977), 66.
[112]Barth, *CD* I, 2:213-17 (quotation from 213).

Anointed One" (only 1 Cor 12:27; Eph 4:12). Whereas calling itself "the church of Christ" usefully implies that the church has to "make Christ its starting point in its own self-understanding,"[113] calling itself "the church of God" even more usefully implies that it will have to make God its starting point.[114] While "Christ is his church's foundation, its power and its hope," and for the church of Christ "christology will become the dominant theme of ecclesiology," the church belongs within "the trinitarian history of God's dealing with the world."[115]

One Flock, One Tree

It is as he undertakes his mission of preaching, healing and baptizing, and finds the Gentile world responding, that Paul seeks to make sense of what happens in light of the Scriptures and finds in it a shrewd divine plan. The renewed Israel was always destined to be an Israel that embraced the nations. As Paul focuses his ministry on Gentiles, an element in the prophetic promises is finding fulfillment. It fits the Torah, too. The Torah's priorities are faithfulness, mercy and worship, and these concerns reappear in the vision of the person on whom God's spirit comes (Is 11; 42), but that vision also extends them beyond Israel to the nations.[116] Salvation is from the Jews, but it is just as much for Samaritans (Jn 4). There is a harvest to be reaped there.

Thus "church is not defined by differentiation *from* Israel, but rather by inclusion *in* Israel and identification with Israel's blessings."[117] Jesus died not only for the Jewish nation but for the scattered children of God, to bring them together and make them one (Jn 11:51-52). In their original First Testament context, the expressions "children of God" and "scattered" suggest the Jews of the dispersion, but here it comes to refer to Gentiles who are to become children of God. Israel was God's flock; God was Israel's shepherd. But as there are sheep in the present flock who do not really belong to it and thus do not respond to Jesus' voice, he has sheep in other pens who will

---

[113]Moltmann, *Church in the Power of the Spirit*, 68.

[114]Edmund Schlink suggests that—in keeping with the order of the creed—the church should be considered in connection with the Holy Spirit (*The Coming Christ and the Coming Church* [Edinburgh: Oliver and Boyd, 1967; Philadelphia: Fortress, 1968], 96).

[115]Moltmann, *Church in the Power of the Spirit*, 5-6.

[116]Welker, *God the Spirit*, 109-24.

[117]Dunn, *Theology of Paul the Apostle*, 507.

respond and thus show that they are his sheep; he must fetch them and combine them with the present flock so that there is one flock under one shepherd (Jn 10:16).

"The task of mission . . . is founded, in fact and in time, on the church's relationship to Israel. . . . Israel is Christianity's original, enduring and final partner in history."[118] It is not the case that the church has replaced Israel, that Israel has been superseded and rendered obsolete. The church is "reassigned to Israel's drama."[119] The Scriptures hardly justify the further declaration that Israel retains its own "vocation for salvation," side by side with the church.[120] There was to be one flock, one tree. But the church is "limited, non-universal and non-Catholic as long as Israel exists parallel to it."[121]

In developing the image of the one olive tree, Paul infers that it is the unfruitfulness of some branches that makes possible the grafting in of new ones (Rom 11:17-24). John 12 hints at a stronger version of Paul's point when it juxtaposes some Gentiles' request to see Jesus and the Jewish crowd's refusal to believe in him: this disbelief issued from God's blinding their eyes so that they couldn't see and find healing. "They *couldn't* believe" (Jn 12:39). Yet in pointing to this tough-minded understanding of God's own tough-mindedness, Jesus refers to passages in the Scriptures that qualify it. While Isaiah 6:10 threatens blindness, it is not the last exposition of this theme in Isaiah; God is also committed to opening these eyes. And while Isaiah 53 begins by wondering at people's past disbelief, it goes on to testify to the way they then came to believe.

Thus the gates in the new Jerusalem's walls are inscribed with the names of Israel's twelve clans. "They are in an especial sense *their* gates and, in the fact that they are continually open, an *invitation to the people Israel to enter into salvation.*" It is a reflection of the fact that Jesus *is* first and above all the fulfillment of all the promises to Israel.[122] God seals 144,000 from the twelve Israelite clans (Rev 7:1-8), who would correspond to "all Israel" being saved (Rom 11). They have on their foreheads the lamb's name and his father's

---

[118]Moltmann, *Church in the Power of the Spirit*, 135.

[119]J. R. Daniel Kirk, *Jesus Have I Loved, but Paul?* (Grand Rapids: Baker, 2011), 61.

[120]Moltmann, *Church in the Power of the Spirit*, 137.

[121]Ibid., 350.

[122]Mathias Rissi, *The Future of the World* (London: SCM Press; Naperville, IL: Allenson, 1972), 74.

name (Rev 14:1). They have not defiled themselves sexually but have kept themselves pure; they follow the lamb wherever he goes; they were purchased to be firstfruits from humanity to be offered to God and to the lamb. Alongside them, however, is a huge multitude from all the nations who are acknowledging God and the lamb, who will also be protected and comforted (Rev 7:9-17). They come out of the great ordeal. They go through hunger and thirst, heat and mourning, but they come out the other side. The eternal gospel is then proclaimed to them (Rev 14:6).

One Humanity, One Building

To use further images, there is one new humanity, one new person and one new temple. As there is no suggestion that one flock or tree is *replaced* by another, so it is with the new humanity. Whereas Gentiles were far away from Israel and thus far away from Jesus and from God, they have been brought near, by Jesus' blood (Eph 2:11-23). Before Jesus, in Roman times proselytes who had been far away had been brought near, like Jethro and Ruth earlier, but the Gentile nations as a whole were separate from Israel. They may not have lacked all knowledge of and relationship with God, but they were far away from the kind of knowledge and relationship that Israel had in possessing the covenants, with the hope that they proclaimed. They didn't know about the Anointed One or have anticipatory experience of the benefits of Jesus' coming, as Israel did.

Now there is the possibility of a mass conversion of Gentile nations. Gentiles are no longer foreigners, and not even merely sojourners, but fellow citizens and members of the household, or bricks in the building that is actually God's temple, God's dwelling. Further, before Jesus, there could be tension between Jews and Gentiles. Jews could see the Torah as obliging them to keep some distance from Gentiles lest they contracted taboo, and Gentiles could be suspicious of Jews for their exclusiveness.

When Jesus died, he abrogated the Torah and thereby removed the barrier between Jews and Gentiles. He brought about peace between them and made it possible for there to be one new person. The two can be in harmony because both the people who were near God before and the people who were far away have access to God on the same basis. Gentiles are now fellow citizens with the holy ones, the people of God as a whole. They are members of God's household. Both groups have access to the Father, whereas previously only Jews did, and even the position of Jews has changed because Jesus has abolished those regulations in the Torah.

Jesus was always "the secret goal of Torah" (Rom 10:4), "the climax of the covenant."[123] When the Torah reaches its goal and loses its significance as a marker of Israel's distinctiveness, in a sense it comes to an end. "Why would the confession of Jesus as the Messiah necessarily upset the basic fabric of Judaism and the Torah?" The reason links with the fact that "the rupture between the Torah and Christ establishes the equality of Jew and Gentile, because in Jesus the 'dividing wall' of the Torah (Eph. 2:14) is broken down;" both are right with God on the basis of trust.[124]

To put it yet another way, the situation of Israel's ancestors (before God gave Israel the Torah) made clearer the real basis for a relationship with God (Rom 4). God's gift of the Torah risked obscuring it. Now that Jesus has annulled the Torah, even Jews enjoy peace with God on a different basis, or on a basis they were not as clearly aware of before. Jesus preached peace to the people who were near as well as those who were distant (Eph 2:17-18). Jews are reconciled to God through Jesus as Gentiles are. We are one through Jesus, because he annulled the Torah, and we are one by means of the one Spirit, through whom the one God lives among us. We are one edifice built on one foundation with one cornerstone or keystone, so that wondrously, "together with one voice [we] may glorify the God and Father of our Lord Jesus, the Anointed One" (Rom 15:6).[125] God has destined us for adoption to sonship through Jesus (Eph 1:5). There is only a single sonship (cf. Rom 8:15, 23; Gal 4:5), the position occupied by Israel as a people that is now extended to Gentiles.

The Surprising Disclosure

God has thus given Paul insight into the *mystērion* of the Anointed One (Eph 3:4). As in Romans 11, a *mystērion* is not the same as a mystery. It is something vitally important, impressively smart, humanly unguessable, previously unknown and now revealed. This surprise disclosure concerns that

---

[123]Wright, *Climax of the Covenant*, 241.
[124]Beker, *Paul the Apostle*, 184, 250.
[125]Fee, *God's Empowering Presence*, 873, 811.

fact that "the Gentiles are joint heirs, a joint body, joint sharers in the promise that lies in the Anointed One, Jesus, through the gospel" (Eph 3:6).

Wherein lies the novelty? The Gentiles coming to know God alongside and with Israel is not itself a new disclosure. One key aspect of the novelty may be hinted by the recurrent word "joint" (the Greek prefix *syn*) in that sentence. The First Testament does envisage the Gentile nations flocking to Jerusalem (Is 2:2-4), and it pictures Gentiles individually grabbing the coat-tails of Jews and asking whether they can tag along with them because they recognize that God is with them (Zech 8:23). Such Gentiles might be adopted into the family in a full sense so that everyone forgets that they had Canaanite or Moabite or Edomite origin, though the stories about people such as Rahab, Ruth and Doeg suggest that often (at least) an awareness of their different background persisted.[126] It happens when Brits become US citizens; the awareness does not imply inferior status. Further, the Torah emphasizes the obligation to care for resident aliens in a way that assumes that they continue to be resident aliens, not people born of Israelite parents. They are a little like a child who everyone always knows was adopted. Yet such a child is a full member of the family, and foreigners and whole foreign families can become full members of the covenant community and take part in Passover if they make that commitment (Ex 12:43-49).

The new revelation is that God always intended to bring into being a people in which Jews and Gentiles had the same status. There is none of the subservience of which the First Testament sometimes speaks when describing the great reversal whereby Israel's own subservience is abolished (e.g., Is 45:14).[127] The idea is not simply that Gentiles are admitted to Israel as the people of God. It's that the notion of "people of God" is revised. The people of God now comprises the people who trust in Jesus as the Anointed One, Jews and Gentiles. Gentiles and Jews are part of the people of God on the same basis and on equal terms. The distinction is not abolished, but it does not imply superiority or inferiority.

Beyond this point, "the disclosure concerning [God's] intention" related to "bringing unity to all things through the Anointed One, things in the heavenly realm and things on earth" (Eph 1:9-10). "From the ages" the secret

---

[126]Cf. the paragraphs under "God's Promise and Its Fulfillment in Israel" in section 4.1 above.
[127]Cf. Sanders, *Paul, the Law, and the Jewish People*, 172-73.

purpose of "the one who created all things" was "that God's manifold insight should be made known to the powerful rulers in the heavenly realm through the church" (Eph 3:9-10). That purpose has now been made known, and the shared access of Jews and Gentiles to God displays it. That shared access puts the rulers in their place. Jesus has put them in their place, and the life of the church is the evidence of that fact.

Thus bringing Jews and Gentiles together had more far-reaching implications than one would have guessed from the Scriptures, because the significance of Jesus was much greater than one could have guessed from the Scriptures. The surprising disclosure is *to mystērion tou Christou*, the surprising disclosure about the Anointed One (Eph 3:4). Such is "the *mystērion* hidden for ages and generations but now disclosed to the saints, to whom God wanted to make known the glorious riches of this *mystērion* among the nations, which is the Anointed One among you, the glorious hope" (Col 1:26-27). People are to know "the *mystērion* of God, the Anointed One, in whom all the treasures of insight and knowledge are hidden" (Col 2:2-3). Here, too, it is the revelation of God's reaching out to the nations.

A Renewed Jerusalem

Judaism had a number of ways of envisaging the new Jerusalem: as a transformed earthly city, as an existent heavenly city, as a heavenly city that will come down to earth at the End, as a preexistent heavenly city that Adam had seen.[128] In Revelation, the new Jerusalem, the holy city, is the new world in its concrete form. Unlike the original Jerusalem, it is of heavenly origin (Rev 21:1-10).[129] Whereas the holy city has been trampled underfoot and has become the scene of the Lord's execution (Rev 11:1-8), now a renewed and transformed version of it comes into being.

It hardly follows that "there is thus a radical break in the history of Israel, which throws its continuity utterly into question."[130] Revelation speaks of a new *Jerusalem* and uses the phrase "holy city" of the old and the new. It suggests continuity as well as discontinuity, in the manner of a prophetic book such as Isaiah. Jerusalem is trampled underfoot only for a limited period

---

[128]Rissi, *Future of the World*, 46-51.
[129]Ibid., 55.
[130]So ibid., 56.

and "the new Jerusalem points . . . to a particular hope: the final fulfilment
of the Old Testament's promises for Israel."[131]

Revelation takes up the image of a new Jerusalem from the Prophets (Is
65; Ezek 40–48). The background is the destruction of the old Jerusalem,
and Revelation may also presuppose the destruction of Jerusalem in AD 70.
But at least as significant for Revelation is its concern to encourage congregations to dissociate themselves from their own cities that were themselves
associated with "the great city, Babylon the mighty city" (Rev 18:10). Because
they were part of the Roman Empire, other cities had to work with the values,
assumptions and methods of this "Babylon," and the congregations there
need to distance themselves from them.

Where does that leave the congregations? John wants them to see themselves as outposts or colonies of "the holy city, the new Jerusalem" that John
can see "coming down from heaven from God" (Rev 21:2). In contracting
out of their cities they do not become homeless or city-less. They become
part of this other home and city. Their position parallels that of Jews in the
Dispersion, for whom their loyalty to the earthly Jerusalem ultimately had
priority over their loyalty to the ordinary city in which they lived.

Like the new heavens and the new earth, it is a new Jerusalem in the sense
of being a renewed Jerusalem. It is thus a new Jerusalem in the same way as
the church is a new Israel: Jewish Jerusalem becomes international Jerusalem, in fulfillment of Isaiah 2:2-4. God had promised his presence with
Israel after its exile (Lev 26:11-12) and had promised that the nations would
recognize that God had granted that presence (Ezek 37:26-28). Mount Zion
would see a banquet to which all peoples are invited, where God would bring
death and mourning to an end and wipe away the tears from everyone's faces
(Is 25:6-8). Revelation 21:1-4 combines these promises so that the covenantal
relationship whereby God is Israel's God and Israel is God's people applies
to a body drawn from all the nations.[132]

The city is monumental in size (Rev 21:10-21). The nations walk by its
light and bring their splendor and glory there instead of giving them to
Rome (you gotta serve somebody). There is no curse there, and there is

[131]So Rissi himself, ibid., 65.
[132]Cf. J. Ramsey Michaels, *Revelation* (Downers Grove, IL: InterVarsity Press; Leicester, UK: Inter-
Varsity Press, 1997), 236.

healing for the nations. There is no temple, or sun or moon, because God and the lamb are its temple and its light (Rev 21:22-25). While there being no sun or moon fits with Isaiah 60, there being no temple sets Revelation apart from all other Jewish expectation.[133] Jews and Samaritans will no longer have to dispute which is the true temple because worship will not involve the right mountain. Because God is spirit, it will be worship in spirit and truthfulness (Jn 4:19-24).

Secure and Vulnerable

God is committed to the restored, renewed, expanded Israel, the Jewish-Gentile community that believes in Jesus, as God was committed to the original Israel. But its Gentile members can't afford to feel superior just because branches were broken off so that they could be grafted in. They have to remember that the roots support them; they don't support the roots. And they have to remember that they could go the same way. As was the case for the original Israel, if you don't continue in God's kindness, "you too will be cut off" (Rom 11:16-23). "The church lives . . . in particular vexations and in jeopardy of her relationship to Christ through the temptations offered by the religious world which tried to undermine the life and teaching of the church from within" (Rev 2–3) and through "oppression and bloody persecution" from without (Rev 6:9-11).[134]

The experience of Israel on the way to Canaan provides the church with a telling warning. The journey that Israel had to undertake was in theory a straightforward one. It's a couple of weeks' walk. It's a tough walk, and they will need Yahweh's provision, but Yahweh has proved himself capable of ensuring that they will get to the destiny he intends. Yet they themselves have already had a hard time trusting him to do so, and on their journey they continue to have a hard time trusting. It is a time of recurrent crisis and protest, protest that they address to Moses rather than to Yahweh. Moses and their other leaders also get overwhelmed by the pressures of the journey, and neither Moses nor Miriam nor Aaron gets to the land. Yahweh does provide for the community and take them

---

[133]Rissi, *Future of the World*, 61.
[134]Ibid., 15.

through the crises, but he gets pretty irritated with them. Indeed, there is a "profound originality" about

> a divine-human pact in which both parties complain endlessly about each other. . . . Israel complains about Moses, Moses complains about Israel, God complains about Israel, Israel complains about God, God complains about Moses, and Moses complains about God. That such a narrative should have been preserved and elevated to the status of sacred scripture and national classic was an act of the most profound literary and moral originality.[135]

It is a time of testing and of rebellion and chastisement, though also a time of mercy. A chilling aspect is that it makes the Israelites wish they had never left Egypt. Putting on rose-tinted spectacles, they see life back there as preferable to undertaking this journey. The assertion of this conviction comes to a climax when they are on the verge of entering the land itself but are convinced that they can't do so. As a result Yahweh declares that they will not enter. Their generation will be stuck in the wilderness until they die, and only the next generation will enter the land (Num 13–14). Yet God is still committed to fulfilling his promise of blessing (Num 22–24).

So the wilderness generation was stubborn and rebellious and incurred God's anger, anger issuing in an oath that they would not be allowed to enter Canaan (Ps 95:7-11). The psalm picks up that motif with the implication that the same thing could happen again. Israel's reactions to events set a pattern for their life in the land; it is for this reason that the stories are there in the Torah.

The threat of this dynamic does not cease to hold for the expanded Israel. We are the household to which Jesus will be faithful only if we hold onto our confidence and the hope in which we glory (Heb 3:6–4:11, taking up Ps 95:7-11). The stories about how the entire community that went through the Reed Sea and enjoyed God's provision died in the wilderness because of idolatry, sexual immorality and dissent are in the Scriptures to act as a warning to the church (1 Cor 10:1-13). And the New Testament's account of the congregations at Corinth and elsewhere means that "one cannot (on

---

[135]Jack Miles, *God: A Biography* (New York and London: Simon and Schuster, 1995), 133; cf. *OTT* 1:454 (that chapter expands on the comments here).

New Testament grounds) contrast the shame of Israel with the splendor of the church, for the church shares in Israel's imperfections."[136]

The axiom that the gifts and calling of God are irrevocable (Rom 11:29) "contains the consolation which the Church and the Synagogue have in common, but which also they can hear and receive only in common."[137]

---

[136]Mangina, "God, Israel, and Ecclesia in the Apocalypse," 87.
[137]Barth, CD II, 2:303.

5

GOD'S ANOINTED

The reign of God was declared, and the expanded Israel came into being through God's sending his Anointed One, Jesus. In this chapter we will look at Jesus' person and life (section 5.1), at what he achieved by his death (sections 5.2-5) and at the significance of his resurrection (section 5.6).

5.1 JESUS' LIFE

There is "one God, the Father (from whom all things exist, and we exist toward him), and one Lord, Jesus the Anointed One (through whom all things exist, and we exist through him)" (1 Cor 8:6). "In the beginning was the *logos*," the mind/message;[1] "the *logos* was with God, and the *logos* was divine" (Jn 1:1). He became "the mediator between God and human beings, a human being, the Anointed One, Jesus" (1 Tim 2:5). He was extraordinarily born, Spirit-endowed, a prophet, an unexpected kind of Anointed One, the "Man," one who aroused conflict, but one who brought the presence of God.

The Human Person

Jesus was one "born of the seed of David in terms of the flesh" (Rom 1:3). In Matthew, he appears as "the Anointed One, descendant of David, descendant of Abraham" (Mt 1:1). In Mark, he arrives abruptly and unannounced from his home village in the north (Mk 1:9). In Luke, he is set in the political context of Augustus Caesar and Herod the Great (Lk 1:5; 2:1). Each Gospel goes on to portray him as a human being of extraordinary good sense, sound

---

[1]See sections 1.2 and 1.4 above.

reason and creative imagination. He says things that surprise people, but not merely for effect, and he does so whatever the cost. He paints the world as it is: no better, no worse. He manifests all the true human traits of anger and joy, goodness and toughness, friendship, sorrow and temptation.[2]

John's Gospel also incorporates those features, but here his background lies first in that position going back to the Beginning, and his foreground then lies in the fact that the mind/message became flesh (Jn 1:14). Starting from his divine status adds emphasis to this subsequent declaration.

John nuances his point by speaking in terms not of his becoming a human being but of his becoming flesh, in "its weakness and its mortality."[3] The word *sarx* has the connotations of *bāśār* in Hebrew rather than those of *sarx* in Paul, though Paul does declare that God sent his Son in the image of sinful *sarx* (Rom 8:3). Jesus is one with us in our sinful humanity, though in Jesus' case, being flesh does not imply sinfulness. It does imply frailty and limitation; flesh is set over against Spirit (Jn 3:6; 6:63; cf. Is 31:1-3; 40:6-8). Jesus gets tired and thirsty (Jn 4:6-7). He doesn't know everything (Jn 5:6).

John thus combines strong assertions of Jesus' origin as the supernatural, divine, glorious agent of God and strong assertions of his humanness. Denying that Jesus really came in the flesh is a marker of not really acknowledging Jesus at all (1 Jn 4:2; 2 Jn 7). He didn't just *seem* like a human being. He *was* a human being. He got tempted—in every way like us (!) (Heb 4:15). He prayed, and did so with urgent cries and tears, submitting to God and learning obedience, and through such experience attaining maturity (Heb 5:7-9; cf. Heb 2:9). Prayer, adversity, learning, experience and maturing are of the essence of being human. As well as being one with us in our sinful humanity, he is one with us in our suffering humanity.

More specifically, he is a man born under the Torah (Gal 4:4); "the Word did not simply become any 'flesh,' any man humbled and suffering. It became Jewish flesh."[4]

Looking at Jesus in his humanness, with his capacity to be sad, needy and fearful, people could be tempted to infer that claiming he is God must be a

---

[2]Leonardo Boff, *Jesus Christ Liberator* (Maryknoll, NY: Orbis, 1978), 80-99.
[3]Martin Luther, *Sermons on the Gospel of St. John Chapters 1–4* (St. Louis: Concordia, 1957), 111; cf. Tord Larsson, *God in the Fourth Gospel* (Stockholm: Almqvist, 2001), 36.
[4]Barth, *CD* IV, 1:166.

mistake. God is the consuming fire, the all-powerful one. The idea that "God reveals himself in a specific human being and, moreover, in the suffering of this human being must seem strange, even absurd, viewed against this background. . . . What kind of God shows himself as being weak, thirsty, deserted, sad, fearful, persecuted and dying?" The idea that God took the same body and soul as every one of us seems contrary to reason, even absurd.[5]

While the Western scholarly difficulty is to know how to talk about Jesus being divine because we know he was human, for other sorts of people the correlative difficulty is to know how to take seriously the idea that Jesus really was human because we know he was divine. The difficulty is sometimes encouraged by a doubt about whether creation itself is really good and thus is really compatible with deity. If one sees deity and body as antithetical, it's hard to think in terms of God becoming human, of the embodiment of deity as opposed to indwelling or inspiration. In post–New Testament times this raised further difficulties when Christian thinking came to conceive of God as one who couldn't feel or suffer or change.[6]

The Death and the Birth

Contrary to common assumptions, Jews might not think that the idea of God becoming human was inherently impossible. Humanity was made in God's image (Gen 1:26-27), and God had sometimes appeared in human form (e.g., Gen 18). Yahweh interacts with Israel in a human-like way and in a servant-like way. The idea that God should be embodied in a human being fits with the fact that "the God of the Hebrew Bible has a body," so that the controversial question would be not whether *someone* can be God's embodiment but whether *Jesus* can be God's embodiment; it would carry the implication that God is a dying and rising God.[7]

---

[5]Larsson, *God in the Fourth Gospel*, 36-38 (quotation from 38), summarizing comments by Luther: see (e.g.) *Sermons on the Gospel of St. John Chapters 6–8* (St. Louis: Concordia, 1959), 80; *Sermons on the Gospel of St. John Chapters 1–4*, 102-14; cf. Rudolf Bultmann's comments on Jn 1:14 (*The Gospel of John* [Oxford: Blackwell; Philadelphia: Westminster, 1971], 62-63, and elsewhere).

[6]Cf. James D. G. Dunn, *The Christ and the Spirit* (Edinburgh: T&T Clark; Grand Rapids: Eerdmans, 1998), 1:32.

[7]The first sentence of Benjamin D. Sommer's *The Bodies of God and the World of Ancient Israel* (Cambridge and New York: Cambridge University Press, 2009), 1, followed by a comment from 135-36 that refers to Harold Bloom, *Jesus and Yahweh* (New York: Riverhead, 2005), 6-7. Cf. the comments on whether Jews could think in terms of Trinity in the paragraphs under "Fluidity" in section 1.2 above.

In the Scriptures, however, "the glory of Jesus is also the glory of God," so that God's glory, too, is "the glory of suffering and death. . . . The moment of Jesus' death is also the moment of the Father's glory." The combination of John's stress on Jesus' oneness with the Father and his depiction of the humiliation of the Son does carry scandalous implications for an understanding of God.[8] "The cross seems an impossible *locus* for God," but "the key to revelation is found in Christ hanging on the cross." The way God has revealed himself "is as a weak, humble, persecuted, and dying human being."[9]

So the execution of Jesus and his being raised from death meant a "structural shift" in the pattern of Jewish beliefs for his followers. An understanding of God cannot now be separated from God's having been caught up in this execution and resurrection.[10] "The person who believes in me does not believe in me but in the one who sent me, and the person who sees me sees the one who sent me" (Jn 12:44).

Yet when one goes back to the story of God's involvement with the world and with Israel over the centuries, this understanding of God does not seem so novel. God has been sacrificing himself and denying himself and paying the price for the world's sin and for Israel's sin over the centuries. But it does mean a paradigm shift to see things that way and to realize that Jesus embodies God in his dying as well as in his power.

The manner of Jesus' conception meant that he was linked to humanity through his mother, and specifically to David through his adoptive father, but that he represented a wholly new start, a new Adam, through the special involvement of the Holy Spirit in his conception. God's work in pursuing his purpose for the world involved a number of miraculous conceptions, such as those of Isaac and Samuel. Jesus' conception topped them all by virtue of its not involving physical human fatherhood at all; Jesus was born of Mary through the agency of the Holy Spirit (Mt 1:18-25).

Being born without the involvement of a man would not imperil his true humanity, any more than Adam and Eve's being created by God imperiled

---

[8]Larsson, *God in the Fourth Gospel*, 287, 188, summarizing Bultmann, *Gospel of John* (e.g., 429-30).

[9]Larsson, *God in the Fourth Gospel*, 36, commenting on Luther's exposition of Jn 8:28 (see *Sermons on the Gospel of St. John Chapters 6-8*, 382-83).

[10]Wayne A. Meeks, *The First Urban Christians*, 2nd ed. (New Haven, CT, and London: Yale University Press, 2003), 180.

their true humanity. But neither was such a birth either necessary or sufficient in order to establish his deity. The incarnation is "the great mystery"[11] independent of the manner of the birth. "The mystery does not rest upon the miracle. The miracle rests upon the mystery. The miracle bears witness to the mystery, and the mystery is attested by the miracle."[12]

The Gospels' emphasis lies on Jesus being born through that agency of the Holy Spirit more than on the mere fact that his mother was a virgin. His being virgin-born is not something the New Testament puts great emphasis on, as if it were important enough to put in a creed,[13] though it does point to the idea that regular human nature in itself "possesses no capacity for becoming the human nature of Jesus Christ, the place of divine revelation."[14]

Spirit-Endowed, Prophet

At the beginning of his ministry, John the Baptizer declares, "I saw the Spirit coming down like a dove from heaven, and it stayed on him" (Jn 1:32). A comparison with the other Gospels draws attention to the second clause, "and it stayed on him." There was nothing very novel about God's Spirit coming upon someone; it could come and go, as happens in the stories in Judges and in the story of Saul (cf. also Ps 51:11 [MT 13]).[15] On Jesus, it stays. John links two other statements with this observation. The staying designates Jesus as the one who baptizes people in Holy Spirit, not just in water like John himself (Jn 1:33). People will be immersed and overwhelmed by God's Spirit. It is a similar experience to the one that came to the figures in Judges and to Saul, and the experience that Joel envisaged (Joel 2:28-29 [MT 3:1-2]). It is this coming and staying of God's Spirit that designates Jesus as God's Son (Jn 1:34).

The story of Jesus' ministry rarely makes explicit that the Spirit is at work, which is perceived retrospectively in light of his resurrection. "The Spirit was not [around] yet, because Jesus had not yet been glorified" (Jn 7:39). The subsequent emphasis on the Spirit is an aspect of the way "Spirit" becomes

---

[11]G. C. Berkouwer, *The Work of Christ* (Grand Rapids: Eerdmans, 1965), 88.
[12]Barth, *CD* I, 2:202.
[13]Andrew T. Lincoln, *Born of a Virgin?* (London: SPCK; Grand Rapids: Eerdmans, 2013), reflects further on the subject.
[14]Barth, *CD* I, 2:188.
[15]Cf. the comments on "resting" and "alighting" in the paragraphs under "Person as Well as Force" in section 1.3 above.

the way of referring to God's activity in the world.[16] But the talk of the Spirit's "staying" implies that in Jesus' entire story God's Spirit was indeed operating through him or that he was operating through God's Spirit. When the Spirit has come on him, he leaves the Jordan full of the Spirit, and he is led by the Spirit into the wilderness to be tempted by the devil. He then returns in the Spirit's power to Galilee, where he declares that the Lord's spirit is indeed on him as one anointed to proclaim good news to Israel in its oppressed state (Lk 3:22; 4:1, 14, 18).

As one so anointed, he speaks as a prophet. The First Testament occasionally talks about the literal or metaphorical anointing of prophets (1 Kings 19:16; Is 61:1). Preaching, teaching (with authority: Mt 7:28-29), healing, cleansing and bringing people back to life were the acts of a prophet like Elijah. Jesus has the supernatural knowledge of a prophet (Jn 2:24-25; 4:18-19; 6:64, 70; 11:4, 11, 14; 13:1; 16:30, 32; 18:4), though the extent of this supernatural knowledge makes him a superprophet. It is as a superprophet that Jesus is "sent"[17] with God's message (Jn 8:16, 28, 42). His origin does not lie in this world; he does not arise out of this world, like a great human leader. He comes here as if from another planet and returns as if to that other planet. This world is not his home. "I came from the Father and came into the world. I am leaving the world again and going to the Father" (Jn 16:28). He has one task to fulfill for the Father, and he fulfills it (Jn 4:34; 17:4). He comes to execute his Father's will in the world (Mk 12:1-11).

The language of sending also suggests the idea of his being God's envoy, aide or "agent,"[18] and when you deal with the agent of someone (a king, or president, or pope, or mafia boss), you deal with the actual person. In the First Testament, this phenomenon is represented by the figure of Yahweh's aide. There is no indication that people in New Testament times found their way into declaring that Jesus was divine by upgrading him from being

---

[16]According to Michael Welker (*God the Spirit* [Minneapolis: Fortress, 1994], 191), E. Jüngel sees the resurrection as making it possible to perceive this fact (Welker gives no reference).

[17]Cf. John Ashton, *Understanding the Fourth Gospel* (Oxford and New York: Oxford University Press, 1991), 308-9 (2nd ed., 2007, 211-12).

[18]See Peder Borgen, "God's Agent in the Fourth Gospel," in John Ashton, ed., *The Interpretation of John*, 2nd ed. (Edinburgh: T&T Clark, 1997), 83-95.

someone like Gabriel.[19] But Jesus does represent God yet remain distinguishable from God in the manner of God's aide.[20]

When he enters Jerusalem from Bethphage, the crowd calls him the prophet from Nazareth. His attack on people buying and selling in the temple is the action of a prophet. His cursing the fig tree is the work of a prophet. The religious leaders are afraid to act against him because people see him as a prophet (Mt 21). In Jerusalem he continues to teach like a prophet, though his stories imply that he has much more significance.

Coming One, Son of God

He himself goes on to ask his enigmatic question about whether the Anointed One is (merely) the descendant of David (Mt 22:41-45). He points to Psalm 110:1, "The Lord said to my lord, 'Sit at my right hand until I put your enemies under your feet,'" which is "the Old Testament text which appears most often in direct quotations or in indirect references in the New Testament" (e.g., Acts 2:34-35; 1 Cor 15:25; Heb 1:13).[21] As Jesus notes, it is a psalm about the human king and God, and Jesus now "waits for his enemies to be made into his footstool" (Heb 10:12-13).

John the Baptizer, who had talked about Jesus "coming," asks whether he is "the coming one," the expression Malachi had used of one who would be "coming" and would be acting to bring purifying judgment on Israel (see Mt 11:2-6; cf. Mt 3:11). People would not have expected the Anointed One to focus on healing, exorcising, teaching and proclaiming that God's reign was imminent, and such proclamation was what John himself did. Perhaps Jesus was another herald of the Anointed One, like John himself? Perhaps people were to look for someone else as the Anointed One? It was not an unreasonable hypothesis.

Jesus sidesteps John's question and points to the indications that his activities suggest a different way of thinking about him. His acts do correspond to ways in which the Book of Isaiah speaks, specifically in chapters around the declaration that God has begun to reign (see Is 35:5-6; 61:1). So Jesus' reply doesn't make any concessions. He grants John's premise but denies his conclusions. Look again at the fact that the blind see, the disabled walk, the

---

[19] Again, see the paragraphs under "Fluidity" in section 1.2 above
[20] Cf. Ashton, *Understanding the Fourth Gospel*, 2nd ed., 284-91.
[21] Martin Hengel, *Studies in Early Christology* (Edinburgh: T&T Clark, 1995), 133.

people with a skin condition are cleansed, the deaf hear, the dead come back to life, and the poor hear good news. It may not be what the Anointed One was expected to do, but it's pretty impressive, isn't it? John has to reframe his way of thinking about what the Anointed One might do.

When Jesus heals a demonized man who was blind and mute, Matthew does report people wondering whether he might be "the son of David" (Mt 12:22-23), and Matthew's account of Jesus' arrival in Jerusalem (Mt 21:1-11) has Jesus arriving on a donkey, in the way Zechariah 9:9 describes Israel's king. While people spoke of him as a prophet, they could also see his arrival as messianic. They implicitly did so in taking up the words of Psalm 118:25-26. Yet Matthew also notes Zechariah's observation that a donkey is an everyday, ordinary, lowly creature. Jesus is not on a horse. His arrival has the ambiguity that attaches to his response to Peter's confession (Mt 16:13-21).

With hindsight, a different form of ambiguity attaches to the declaration from the heavens at his baptism that he is the Son of God, taking up Psalm 2 (Mk 1:11). The phrase describes God's adoptive relationship with the Davidic king (see further 2 Sam 7), and being God's son does not therefore suggest being divine. It does mean that God is uniquely committed to Jesus as the one through whom God's purpose is to be effected in the world, and it means that Jesus is committed to serving his Father to this end and is destined to share his Father's authority and recognition by the world. "No one recognizes the Son except the Father, nor does anyone recognize the Father except the Son and anyone to whom the Son wishes to reveal him" (Mt 11:27). Jesus is not speaking of intimacy or identity of nature but of mutual recognition and commitment.

In the psalm itself, the descriptions "anointed" and "son of God" thus describe the current king. The First Testament itself does not talk about the coming of a future anointed one. While it affirms that God will stand by his promises to David's household, the word *māšîaḥ* never applies to someone God will send in the future, only to a king or priest who already exists. A parable of its nonpreoccupation with the matter is that it has no regular term for this person, parallel to its term "the Day of Yahweh."

Another parable of its nonpreoccupation with the coming of an Anointed One is that most of the passages that the New Testament applies to Jesus in this connection do not themselves have anything to do with this figure. They are not promises that are implemented in Jesus in any straightforward sense. Their words are given a new significance that can be unrelated to their original meaning. The sequence of references in Matthew 1:18–2:23 illustrates how the prophecies are more "filled out" than "fulfilled."[22] Matthew does allude to one passage that we might see as inherently "messianic" in meaning; God promises that someone from Bethlehem will come to rule over Israel (Mic 5:2; Mt 2:6), because Bethlehem is David's city. Yet even that passage does not use the word *māšîaḥ*, and even here further questions arise: Jesus did not rule Israel and still does not do so. Many First Testament promises tell readers more about what Jesus still needs to do and will do than about what Jesus has already done.

What Kind of Anointed One?

"Jewish messianology exploded into the history of ideas in the early first century B.C.E., and not earlier, because of the degeneration in the Hasmonean dynasty and the claim of the final ruling Hasmoneans, especially Alexander Jannaeus, to be 'the king,' and because of the loss of the land promised as Israel's inheritance to the gentile and idolatrous nation Rome." Yet "one can no longer claim that most Jews were looking for the coming of the Messiah."[23]

Matthew does describe Jewish theologians as expecting someone who would be a ruler to shepherd Israel, and Herod realized that the arrival of such a person implied a threat to his position (Mt 2:1-17). Mary knew that Jesus was destined to reign over Israel on the throne of David (Lk 1:32-33). Zechariah knew that his birth heralded God's rescuing the people from the hand of their enemies (Lk 1:74). Thus for many people

> the Messiah was supposed to win the decisive victory over the pagans, to rebuild or cleanse the Temple, and in some way or other to bring true, god-given justice and peace to the whole world. What nobody expected the Messiah to do was to die at the hands of the pagans instead of defeating them; to mount a symbolic attack on the Temple, warning it of imminent judgment,

---

[22]See the comments on this verb in the paragraphs headed "Visionary" in section 2.2 above.
[23]James H. Charlesworth, "From Messianology to Christology," in Charlesworth, ed., *The Messiah* (Minneapolis: Fortress, 1992), 3-35 (on 35).

instead of rebuilding or cleansing it; and to suffer unjust violence at the hands of the pagans instead of bringing them justice and peace.[24]

The kind of hopes of the Anointed One that many people held makes it not surprising that Jesus was unenthusiastic about being called by this term.

In Mark, we have noted, Jesus appears like a hurtling comet, announced by John the Baptizer but without father, without mother, without genealogy, having neither beginning of days nor end of life, and he then consistently looks at things in a quite different way from his disciples and from other people. He has his own agenda to fulfill, with a timing he intends for it; or rather, he has God's agenda to fulfill, with a timing God intends for it. "What has that got to do with you and me?" he says to Mary when the wine runs out. "My hour has not yet come" (Jn 2:4). That hour is the hour for his glorifying by his death and his going to his Father (Jn 12:23; 17:1; cf. Jn 7:30; 8:20; 12:30; 13:1).

When he asks the disciples who they think he is (Mk 8:27-38) and Peter says, "You're the Anointed One," his unexpected, bald response is, "Don't say it to anyone." It matches his useless attempts to get people not to talk about his extraordinary acts (e.g., Mt 8:4; 9:30-31). He goes on to tell his disciples that he is going to be attacked, rejected and killed, but that he will then rise again. In light of his bold confession of Jesus as the Anointed One, Peter cannot make sense of what Jesus says. The sequence of events is both made more puzzling and more intelligible in Matthew's version, where Jesus initially responds to Peter's confession with the comment "Flesh and blood did not reveal it to you, but my Father in the heavens," and adds that this recognition by Peter will be the beginning of the history of the church (Mt 16:17-18).

It's not that Jesus avoided speaking of himself as the Anointed One and that the church retrojected this idea into his story and attributed to him a desire to keep his vocation secret.[25] Paradoxically, recognizing that Jesus is the Anointed One is both a great insight and a quite misleading one. While Jesus was a fulfillment of God's commitment to David, having a king like David hadn't been God's own idea but had involved going along with Israel's ideas, and anyway Jesus wasn't immediately going to do the kind of thing

---

[24]N. T. Wright, *The Resurrection of the Son of God* (London: SPCK; Minneapolis: Fortress, 2003), 557.

[25]So William Wrede, *The Messianic Secret* (first published 1901; Eng. trans., London: Clarke; Greenwood, SC: Attic, 1971).

that God had promised in connection with that fulfilment. When Pilate asks, "Are you the king of the Jews?" Jesus stays equivocal: "You said it" (Mt 27:11). It would be misleading to say "Yes" or to say "No." He was executed as someone who was alleged to claim to be king of the Jews (Mt 27:37), a claim he did not dispute even though he did not make it nor enthuse over it.[26] Calling him the Anointed One was misleading, but denying being the Anointed One would be even more misleading.[27]

Through John's Gospel, whether people will recognize Jesus as the Anointed One is a key question, and when Jesus is put on trial, the key question is whether he claims to be a king. The Gospel's aim is to get people to recognize that Jesus is the Anointed One and Son of God. Whereas "Jesus Christ" has become a kind of proper name in much of the New Testament, when John describes his aim in these terms (Jn 20:21), "the Anointed One" is still a designation. Yet the terms "Anointed One" and "Son of God" have gained more transcendent implications than the ones they have in the other Gospels; they "connote the belief that Jesus is . . . divine and of heavenly origin."[28] "I am he" (Jn 4:26).

But in John 18–19 Jesus declines to assert or defend himself like a king. His kingship is not of this world, not in the sense that it is inoperative in this world but in the sense that it is not derived from this world. It's an eternal kingship, though not in the sense that it is merely a future one. It is a presently effective one. Jesus does not share kingship with earthly powers; his kingship is the only kingship.[29] But "it is only as Christ crucified that the Messiah claim can be incorporated into Christology."[30] It fits with that fact that in Paul *christos* is particularly used in references to Jesus' death and resurrection. "The Anointed One died for the ungodly" (Rom 5:6). "The Anointed One died for our sins" (1 Cor 15:3).[31]

---

[26]On the historical plausibility of this explanation of his execution, see, e.g., Nils A. Dahl, *The Crucified Messiah and Other Essays* (Minneapolis: Augsburg, 1974), 10-36; cf. Larry W. Hurtado's discussion in *Lord Jesus Christ: Devotion to Jesus in Earliest Christianity* (Grand Rapids and Cambridge, UK: Eerdmans, 2003), 56-60.

[27]Cf. W. Bousset, *Jesus* (New York: Putnam; London: Williams and Norgate, 1906), 178-79.

[28]Hurtado, *Lord Jesus Christ*, 362.

[29]See Hengel, *Studies in Early Christology*, 333-57.

[30]Dunn, *Christ and the Spirit* 1:28.

[31]See Werner Kramer, *Christ, Lord, Son of God* (London: SCM Press; Naperville, IL: Allenson, 1966), 26-28; cf. Hurtado, *Lord Jesus Christ*, 100.

The "Man"

One might have thought that the execution of someone who claimed to be king would put an end to such claims. For John, it rather meant reformulating them. The elevation involved in crucifixion is a symbol of an elevation to kingly honor or glory.

John the Evangelist and the other John who speaks for him, John the Baptizer, both begin by establishing who Jesus "really" is. He is the one whose being goes back to the Beginning and the one who takes the world's sin. The first disciples of John and of Jesus then start from where an ordinary Jew would start. Jesus is a rabbi whom they follow and accompany in order to learn from him (Jn 1:38-40). But he is also "the Anointed One," the one of whom Moses and the Prophets spoke, "the Son of God" and "the King of Israel" (Jn 1:41, 45, 49). All three expressions come from Psalm 2.

In response to Nathanael, Jesus wants to go back to something like the two Johns' perspective (Jn 1:51). He wants to be seen as the Man, the one who bridges heaven and earth and who is the means of God's aides acting on earth and going back to heaven to report on their activity and to get fresh orders (Jn 3:13-14). The imagery corresponds to the way the First Testament speaks of Yahweh's aides.

"Man" is more literalistically "son of man," an odd phrase in English and Greek but less odd in Hebrew and Aramaic. It parallels expressions such as "son of righteousness," which means "righteous man"; so "son of man" is a term for "human being." God regularly used this expression in addressing Ezekiel. It denotes a human figure in Daniel 7, where it designated a figure set over against a more senior person on a throne. The vision's explanation indicates that the more senior figure stands for God, while the ordinary figure stands for God's holy ones—perhaps for Israel itself, perhaps for a supernatural person like Michael or Gabriel who then represents the body of God's supernatural aides. In later Jewish works from the same general period as the New Testament, "the Man" comes to denote a figure of heavenly origin who will implement judgment on the world's wickedness: see e.g., 1 Enoch 46–48; 62.

When the crowd ask their question about the lifting up of the Anointed One, they ask, "How can you say that the Man must be lifted up? Who is this Man?" (Jn 12:34). They prefer to speak in terms of the Anointed One, and they do not understand the "Man" talk. But "Anointed One" was a misleading title because it could suggest heading an insurrection against Rome, while "Man" was less likely to raise this problem. It was not as common as "Anointed One" or "Prophet" as a way of describing someone through whom God would bring about the fulfillment of his purpose.[32] It did not have an established significance; Jesus could fill it with the content that was appropriate for him.

To Peter, Jesus says not that "the Anointed One" but that "the Man" will be handed over to be crucified, and when the high priest asks whether he is the Anointed One, Jesus answers in terms of the Man (Mt 26:2, 64). It does designate him as more than an ordinary human being and as existing before his showing up on earth, though it does not in itself designate him as divine. It also does suggest a claim to be the final judge. While the picture of Jesus appearing on the clouds at the End links with Daniel 7, his coming from heaven at the beginning does not have such a link. But as the Man he indeed connects earth and heaven.

In 4 Ezra 13 the Man is described as God's Son, and in 4 Ezra 7:28-29 the same description is applied to the Anointed One, which invites the inference that the Man and the Anointed One are the same person there, as they are in the New Testament. Further, 4 Ezra speaks of the Anointed One dying. The Psalms' references to the attacks to which Israel's king is subject, the description in Isaiah 52:13–53:12 of the affliction, anointing and exaltation of Yahweh's servant, and the allusion in 4 Ezra to the death of the Anointed One would open up the possibility that Jesus' talk in terms of the suffering and death of the Man might be intelligible to some people, even if the likes of Peter didn't welcome it. In his lifetime people were unable to see the lifting up of the Man in crucifixion as itself his exaltation (Jn 12:23).

The One Who Arouses Conflict

Cross and resurrection signify Jesus' passage from this world to the world above. Why does the passage take that form? "For John the sentence passed on Jesus is above all the final act in the long, sad story of Jesus' rejection by his own people."[33] Jesus arouses conflict and opposition. When he defends

---

[32]See, e.g., Ragnar Leivestad, "Exit the Apocalyptic Son of Man," *NTS* 18 (1971–1972): 243-67.
[33]Ashton, *Understanding the Fourth Gospel*, 547 (2nd ed., 523).

the disciples for picking some heads of grain on the sabbath, heals a disabled man on the sabbath and speaks of the arrival of something (or someone) greater than the temple, the religious leaders start plotting to kill him (Mt 12:1-14).

Martha, Mary and Lazarus give a dinner in his honor (Jn 12): Martha serves (in this story, she seems not to mind), Lazarus sits there just watching and relaxed (!), Mary pours perfume over Jesus' feet, Judas protests this waste. A crowd of Jews come to see the resuscitated Lazarus, and many are coming to faith in him. The chief priests therefore plan to kill Lazarus as well as Jesus. The Passover crowd celebrates Jesus in a way that suggests recognizing him as the Anointed One, though the disciples do not realize the significance of what they are doing. The Pharisees are bewildered about what to do as the whole world has gone after him. To underline that point, some Greeks (that is, Gentiles) come and ask to see him, which is for him a sign that the moment of his glorifying (by death) is imminent.

The Gospels talk about three groups of people opposed to Jesus, the Pharisees, the Sadducees and the theologians (the "scribes"). The Pharisees were people concerned for the application of the Torah to everyday life in such a way that they and other people could live in accordance with Moses' teaching. But they resented Roman authority and looked for a day when God would bring the people's subordination to an end and restore Israel.

The Sadducees had distinctive theological views over against the Pharisees, notably a rejection of the idea of resurrection, but their further distinctiveness lay in being the group with authority over the community, under the Romans. They cooperated with the Roman authorities. This political arrangement meant that they could be reasonably well-off. In anticipation of the day when God would free and restore Israel, a further group, the Essenes, who are unmentioned by the Gospels, withdrew from Jerusalem on the basis that it was perverted by the Sadducees' leadership.

The theologians could belong to any of the three groups, while most ordinary people likely focused on trying to make ordinary life work in tough times. But the ordinary people were involved in the "spiral of violence," as victims of the violent rule of Rome who were drawn toward protest, resistance and eventually revolt.[34] The Gospels do not refer to the Zealots as people who advocated violent rebellion against Rome; as far as we can tell, the Zealots did not exist until the revolt that led to the fall of Jerusalem in AD 70.[35]

The people's leaders were broadly agreed that Jesus was a false prophet and an agent of Satan who must therefore be put down. If he withdrew, as he sometimes did (e.g., Mt 15:21), he could avoid being provocative, but he could not fulfill his vocation that way. Eventually he had to go to Jerusalem, which goaded them into taking action against him. But when he said he "must" thus suffer (e.g., Mt 16:21), he referred to more than its political inevitability. Lynching prophets was part of the pattern of Israel's relationship with God. It was a religious inevitability. It also links with broader human patterns of sacrifice and violence.[36]

The Son and the Creator

When you met Jesus, you encountered God in person. "Only a God could be so human."[37] While God in person encounters people in Jesus, it does not mean there is a kind of aura about Jesus. You know you are meeting an ordinary man. Yet what he does (the power and the grace) and what he says (the insight and the authority) indicate that he is not just an ordinary man. God has granted him to have life in himself in the same way as God does (Jn 5:26). He does the kind of thing God does. God continues acting even though it is the sabbath; so does Jesus. Jesus does what he sees the Father doing. The Father raises the dead and gives them life; Jesus gives life to people. The Father has entrusted judgment to Jesus.

He is the "shining radiance of God's glory" (Heb 1:3); paradoxically, in looking at Jesus we look at the brilliance of the sun and do so without going blind. It was through Jesus that God made the worlds, and as one who shares God's nature, he is still "carrying everything by his powerful word" (Heb 1:3; cf. Jn 1:1-3). Thus the revelation of God's glory in Jesus, the revelation of Jesus' glory, involves the exercise of the creator's power. "The first of the signs that

---

[34]See the analysis in Richard A. Horsley, *Jesus and the Spiral of Violence* (repr., Philadelphia: Fortress, 1993).

[35]See, e.g., John P. Meier, *A Marginal Jew* (New York: Doubleday, 2001), 3:565-67.

[36]See René Girard, *Violence and the Sacred* (Baltimore and London: Johns Hopkins University Press, 1977).

[37]Boff, *Jesus Christ Liberator*, 178.

Jesus did" involved an act of creative power, the turning of water into wine with some extravagance, by which Jesus "manifested his glory" (Jn 2:11). He manifests his splendor in bringing about the feast of joy associated with the fulfillment of God's purpose.[38]

So Jesus reveals God's power as well as his love, in his life and in his death and resurrection. In the Synoptic Gospels he begins by casting out an impure spirit and healing people (Mk 1:21–2:12). The sequence of stories involves the exercise of authority. No doubt the occasions also involve compassion, to which the Gospels occasionally refer (e.g., Mt 14:14; 15:32; 20:34). Yet the people who had impure spirits or were sick will have had other people in their families and communities who showed them compassion. What they needed was not compassion but power, and it is this power that has the prominence in the stories. Jesus heals people with terrible afflictions and with trivial ones (Mt 8:5-14). As his exorcisms are manifestations of supernatural power, so are his resuscitations. His marvels provide evidence that his message is true. He is like Moses or Elisha, only more so; he walks on water, like Elijah, but also calms a storm there in the manner of Yahweh putting down the powers of disorder embodied in the tumultuous waters of the sea. It provokes the disciples to ask, "So who is this, that even the wind and the sea obey him?" (Mk 4:41). While his actions leave the disciples bemused, they subsequently realize that the actions are ones that require people to bow in homage and declare "you are the Son of God" (Mk 6:45-52; Mt 14:22-33).

While none of the actions need make Jesus more than a prophet like Elijah, the Judeans have already worked out that the way he talks about God as "my Father" means he is making himself equal with God (Jn 5:18). He calls God *Patera idion*, his own Father, his Father in a sense that does not apply to everyone else, though like any son, he does not make himself equal with God in authority. He does nothing of himself but does only what he sees the Father doing. He happily accepts his subordination to his Father. He just wants to please his Father. And like any father, God "loves the Son and shows him all the things he himself does" (Jn 5:20). Indeed, the Father has not merely delegated to the Son the prophetic capacity and authority to judge and to give life but has granted the Son to "have life in himself" (Jn 5:26).

---

[38]Cf. Hengel, *Studies in Early Christology*, 293-331.

Further, like any son Jesus is equal to his Father in the sense that he is made of the same stuff, and he is equal in authority in relation to humanity precisely because of that giving on the Father's part and that submission on the Son's part. His talk in terms of being subordinate to the Father and obedient to the Father, of doing and speaking only what the Father bids him do and speak, is simultaneously a denial of authority and an assertion of authority.[39] And like any son, he deserves to be honored as the Father is honored.

The Image and the Presence

God's Son is God's image (Col 1:15). God made humanity as his image in the world so that humanity could represent God there and exercise God's authority there, like God's firstborn. Later, God adopted Israel as his firstborn son and then adopted the Israelite king as his son who would represent God and exercise God's authority in the world. Now Jesus acts as God's Son, with the authority that attaches to being the firstborn.

Again, in itself language of this kind would not establish that Jesus is one in nature with his Father. But further (Col 1:16-19), by means of this Son everything in the heavens and on the earth was created; specifically, everything that exercises any authority. It came into existence through him and for him. He existed before it did, and it all holds together through him, as the president's authority holds the nation together. As well as still having that authority over creation that derives from involvement in its origin, he is in particular head over the church. As well as being the beginning, he is the firstborn from the dead, so that he might now have the preeminence in the midst of it all. His having that authority was possible because the fullness resided in him—that is, the fullness of God's own person dwells in him bodily (cf. Col 2:9).[40] That word, *bodily*, emphasizes "the encounterable reality of the divine indwelling in Christ."[41]

"If you knew the gift of God, and who it is who says to you 'Give me something to drink,' you would have asked him and he would have given

---

[39]Rudolf Bultmann, *Theology of the New Testament* (repr., Waco, TX: Baylor University Press, 2007), 2:51.

[40]See T. K. Abbott, *A Critical and Exegetical Commentary on the Epistles to the Ephesians and to the Colossians* (Edinburgh: T&T Clark; New York: Scribner, 1897), 219-20.

[41]James D. G. Dunn, *The Theology of Paul the Apostle* (Grand Rapids and Cambridge, UK: Eerdmans, 1998), 205.

you living water" (Jn 4:10). For a Middle Eastern person, thirst and water is a telling image. The Samaritan woman may have had to make laborious daily journeys to bring water home. People out in the wilderness or on a journey have to husband water carefully; miscalculation can become a matter of life and death.

So coming into the presence of God is like finding water (for people in other climates, it is like waking up and finding the sun shining). And being unable to come into that presence is like being parched with thirst (or like suffering from sun deprivation). Someone who cannot get to the temple, the place of the guaranteed presence of God, has this kind of experience of being parched: "My whole being thirsts for God, for the living God; when shall I come and see the face of God [Targum]/appear before God [MT]?" (Ps 42:2 [MT 3]).

Israelites knew that God was not confined to the temple, otherwise most Jews would have lived nearly all their lives out of God's presence. Psalm 42 assumes that the suppliant can talk to God and be heard even when unable to get to the temple. But there is something special about going there. David had asked Yahweh make a home in such a place, and Yahweh had reluctantly agreed. It meant you could have a special assurance about meeting with God there, which logically somewhat downgraded other places and could give people away from Israel even less assurance about meeting God.

The presence of Jesus means the presence of God, a presence analogous to that presence in the temple. Being in contact with him is like having an internal spring of water welling up to eternal life (Jn 4:14). There is no longer any need to feel that thirst when one cannot get to the temple. One has an internal source of water. One can be aware of being in God's presence with the same certainty that one could have in connection with the temple. So perhaps the Samaritan woman is not changing the subject when she asks about the right mountain on which to worship God.[42] Likewise, Jesus' reply reexpresses his point about water. Worshiping God is a matter of spirit and truth, not place (Jn 4:23).

Jews who believe in Jesus will still worship in the temple, as Acts shows. But the temple's eventual destruction by the Romans will not raise tricky

---

[42]See the paragraphs under "Spirit and Truth" in section 1.3 above.

questions of theology or spirituality. A river of living water flows from the throne of God and of the Lamb (Rev 22:1-2), and a person who is thirsty can come to Jesus and drink. Streams of living water will flow from the person who believes in him. John glosses this promise by telling us that Jesus is speaking of what will come about through the Spirit being given (Jn 7:37-39).

5.2 Jesus' Death: Embodying and Modeling

To what end does Jesus let himself be killed, and to what end does God let it happen? Why does Jesus have to drink the cup of poison that his Father gives him (Jn 18:11)? Why was he "handed over by God's fixed plan and foreknowledge" to lawless people to be crucified (Acts 2:23)? The preaching in Acts doesn't seek to answer that question. It confines itself to declaring that the execution and the resurrection happened and that therefore people should repent of their involvement in his death, and also that the possibility of finding forgiveness and restoration is still open. It doesn't make a link between the execution and the possibility of forgiveness.[43]

To some readers, the chapters in the Gospels describing the crucifixion "are not likely to be more than the record of a shocking miscarriage of justice, carried out with violence." But "to disciples they are the record of events to which they owe their life."[44] How is that so? The New Testament interweaves a series of images for understanding what Jesus achieved through accepting execution. They do not form part of a scheme, and it seems unprofitable to argue for the priority of one of them.[45] It's more profitable to ask how they individually illumine what Jesus achieved, to let the many metaphors stand. They are "fragments" of the cross.[46]

This consideration extends to the way the New Testament speaks of Jesus' death in terms of sacrifice. Sacrifice has many significances, and the New

---

[43]Cf. Frances M. Young, *Sacrifice and the Death of Christ* (London: SPCK, 1975), 64.

[44]R. H. Lightfoot, *St. John's Gospel* (Oxford and New York: Oxford University Press, 1956), 259.

[45]Cf., e.g., Stephen R. Holmes, "Death in the Afternoon," in Richard Bauckham et al., eds., *The Epistle to the Hebrews and Christian Theology* (Grand Rapids and Cambridge, UK: Eerdmans, 2009), 229-52; Charles B. Cousar, *A Theology of the Cross* (Minneapolis: Fortress, 1990), 86-87.

[46]Cf. Kevin J. Vanhoozer, "The Atonement in Postmodernity," in Charles E. Hill and Frank A. James III, eds., *The Glory of the Atonement*, Roger Nicole Festschrift (Downers Grove, IL: InterVarsity Press, 2004), 367-404 (on 371, 401); cf. David Tracy, "Fragments: The Spiritual Situation of Our Times," in John D. Caputo and Michael J. Scanlon, eds., *God, the Gift, and Postmodernism* (Bloomington: Indiana University Press, 1999), 170-80.

Testament appeals to a number of them, not just to expiation. Further, while he "uses sacrificial ideas, Paul does not develop these but leaves them inchoate."[47]

The analogy with sacrifice points to a further insight. The same sacrifice can do several things. A fellowship sacrifice expresses joy on the part of the offerer, embodies gratitude to God and enhances communion among family and friends. Similarly, when my wife lays on a dinner party, it does a number of things: it is act of love toward me, a demonstration of love toward me (which is a different point), an act of creativity that gives her pleasure, a means of ensuring that we ourselves get fed and an act of fellowship with the people who come. These are not alternative interpretations of a dinner party. They are all things that the dinner party achieves.

By letting himself be executed, Jesus achieves a number of things. He embodies what it means to be God and what it means to be a human being (section 5.2). He carries humanity's wrongdoing and makes reconciliation with humanity possible (section 5.3). He cleans humanity from its defilement and makes restitution for its wrongdoing (section 5.4). He frees humanity for a new service (section 5.5). "The meaningless has a secret meaning,"[48] or a series of meanings.

Why Have You Abandoned Me?
Toward the end of his life, Jesus is betrayed and abandoned, and God does not respond to him (Mt 26:36-46). But he stands firm. There is a sense in which he is in control of what happens. John's Gospel describes his last hours in a way that especially makes this point. "We often speak of the passion of Christ but ... his passion was also his action."[49] It was "his last prophetic sign,"[50] but a sign that had been signaled often enough.[51] God had signaled it in his words at Jesus' baptism with their allusion to Genesis 22 and

---

[47]W. D. Davies, *Paul and Rabbinic Judaism*, 2nd ed. (repr., New York: Harper; London: SPCK, 1962), 242.

[48]Boff, *Jesus Christ Liberator*, 117.

[49]Tom Smail, *Once and for All* (London: DLT, 1998; Eugene, OR: Wipf and Stock, 2006), 58. Cf. Jürgen Moltmann, *The Trinity and the Kingdom of God* (London: SCM Press; New York: Harper, 1981), 75.

[50]Edward Schillebeeckx, *Jesus* (New York: Crossroad; London: Collins, 1979), 318.

[51]See Scot McKnight, *Jesus and His Death* (Waco, TX: Baylor University Press, 2005).

Isaiah 42. Jesus himself had signaled it and suggested its significance, even if the disciples didn't get it.

Jesus cries out, "My God, my God, why have you abandoned me?" (Mt 27:46). It's a reasonable question, though it's a rhetorical one. In the context of Psalm 22, which Jesus is taking up, it's not a question about theodicy but a way of saying, "You've abandoned me, and there's no basis for your doing so, so come back and rescue me!" In due course God does, but for the moment God sits in the heavens resolutely watching his Son suffer and resolutely declining to terminate his suffering when he could do so. The "terrible irony" of the name Yahweh, which implies "I will be present whenever and wherever I will be present," is that "the opposite also is implied: 'and I will be absent whenever and wherever I will be absent,' including at the destructions of his Temple, at the German death camps, at Golgotha."[52]

Accepting persecution and even martyrdom is an aspect of the way prophets fulfill their ministry, as appears in the story of Jeremiah and in the account of serving God in Isaiah 40–55. At Jesus' baptism, God begins from Psalm 2 but moves on to Genesis 22 and ends in Isaiah 42; Matthew later sees Jesus as embodying the portrait of God's servant in that passage (Mt 3:17; 12:15-21). He embodies it in his healing ministry. He may also embody it in withdrawing from a situation of conflict and in telling people not to talk about him, because the religious leaders seeking to kill him are bent reeds and flickering wicks, and withdrawal from the context in which he is being provocative reduces the risk of making them break and die out or postpones the moment when they have to make their final choice.

When he speaks of the necessity that he should be lifted up and thus die, the crowd comments, "We have heard from the Torah that the Anointed One remains forever" (Jn 12:32-34). How can Jesus talk about such a necessity? He does not immediately answer this question, but John soon afterwards quotes Isaiah 53:1: "Lord, who has believed our message, and to whom has the Lord's arm been revealed?" (Jn 12:38). The necessity links with the portrait of God's servant in Isaiah 52:13–53:12. "Servant of Yahweh" is commonly a title for the king, and this portrayal pictures that servant as

---

[52]Bloom, *Jesus and Yahweh*, 27-28.

someone lifted up on high and anointed like a king,[53] after being the subject
of attack and humiliation. It might form a kind of answer to questions
raised by passages such as Psalm 51 (because it promises exaltation, the
other side of humiliation) and even more Psalm 89 (because it presupposes
undeserved humiliation).

Yahweh's Arm

As well as combining motifs from such psalms, Isaiah 52:13–53:12 adds an
extra possibility. Like the king in Psalm 51, but unlike the king in Psalm 89,
this servant's humiliation is peculiar to him, and it is not shared by the
people; it is his problem. Like the king in Psalm 89, but unlike the king in
Psalm 51, this servant's humiliation is undeserved. Taken together, these
features come close to suggesting the distinctive feature of Isaiah 52:13–
53:12: the servant suffers undeservedly over against his people and for his
people. His willingness to do so makes God glad to take him from humiliation to exaltation.

Rejection and death are not the end of the story in Isaiah 52:13–53:12;
abuse is followed by restoration. Jesus knows that rejection and execution
cannot be the end of his story. The vision involving the Man in Daniel 7 will
also be an encouragement to face martyrdom knowing that it will not be the
end. Jesus must endure it, but he will be raised from the dead, not at an End
that may happen only in centuries' time but after two or three days. As the
Man he will "come in his Father's splendor with his aides" to be the agent of
God's judgment and to inaugurate his reign as king; some of the people who
are listening will see it (Mt 16:27-28).

In the event, it did not happen in quite that way, as is often true of the
relationship between prophets' talk about the future and the way things
work out. God's statements of intent always contain implicit if not explicit
conditional clauses (cf. Jer 18; Ezek 33): "Things will turn out in this way
unless I find reason to change my mind" because of the reaction of human
beings or because of reconsideration on my part. Commonly, it is because
God prefers to avoid acting in judgment.[54] Thus commonly, while something

---

[53]I take *mišḥat* as a form from the verb *māšaḥ*, "anoint," not one from *šāḥat*, "spoil": see, e.g., John
  Goldingay, *The Message of Isaiah 40–55* (London and New York: T&T Clark, 2005), 491-92.
[54]See the paragraphs under "Unwilling Judgment" in section 1.1 above.

happens by way of fulfillment, the declaration is not as final as one would have expected.

Further, while Isaiah 52:13–53:12 explicitly speaks of humiliation followed by exaltation, it also points to the insight that the humiliation is itself a strange form of exaltation. In the vision, humiliation is past and exaltation is future. Yet "we" (the servant's own people) have already come to believe in what they had been told about the servant and have perceived that God's arm was revealed in him. In their thinking and attitude and lives, he is exalted already, even though his visible exaltation and his recognition by nations and kings has not yet happened. It is on this dynamic that Jesus riffs. His lifting up (onto the cross) will be an exaltation that draws all people to him. As is the case in Isaiah 52:13–53:12, while there is a linear sequence of cross then resurrection, humiliation then exaltation, there is also a more subtle simultaneity of a humiliation that is also an exaltation.

A third significance of Isaiah 53:1 lies in its declaration that in the humiliation of the servant, the Lord's arm is revealed. The prophet has already spoken of a revelation of Yahweh's arm in the sight of all the nations that brings about deliverance; Yahweh's arm will be raised against Babylon, in bringing in his reign (Is 52:10). Yahweh fulfilled that promise as Cyrus brought to an end the rule of Babylon in the Middle Eastern world. While Cyrus did so only to replace it with his own rule, this transition nevertheless brought some freedom to communities such as the Judahites who had been under the domination of Babylon.

Isaiah 52:13–53:12 then speaks of a radically different revelation of Yahweh's arm. It, too, is a revelation that has already taken place; the passage is not referring to a coming revelation in the servant's exaltation, which will be easy to see. The revelation that has already happened was one that people could easily miss, and for some time people did miss it. But they have now perceived it, through the process they go on to describe in their testimony. They have come to see that their first estimate of the servant as a sinner had to be wrong, that rather he was afflicted with them and because of them, undeservedly, and that he was making his acceptance of this affliction into an offering to Yahweh.

Speaking of Yahweh's arm having been revealed implies that Yahweh was involved in the process of his servant's affliction, which the servant could

then turn into an offering. It was Yahweh who "determined the crushing of
the one he weakened" and who "let the wrongdoing of all of us fall on him"
(Is 53:6, 10). In a paradoxical way, Yahweh's arm was revealed in the servant's
affliction. This affliction was an act though which Yahweh achieved something at least as significant as what was achieved through putting Babylon
down. Yahweh was manifested in the affliction. He was the suffering God.

The Revelation and the Embodiment

Jesus' self-giving thus constituted an incarnation or representation of what
God's love means and thereby of what love means.

"The Torah was given through Moses" (Jn 1:17). Moses was the mouth-
piece for a revelation of God's will; he was given the revelation of God's
nature as grace and truthfulness (Ex 34:6-7). But he was not a personal
embodiment of grace and truthfulness in the sense that Jesus was. While
Jesus did not bring a novel revelation concerning God's nature as grace
and truthfulness, he did bring a newly vivid and concrete embodiment of
that nature. "God spoke to our ancestors of old in many different ways
through the prophets, but in these last days spoke to us through a son"
(Heb 1:1-2). In this one person all those individual truths about God (some
of which were easy to miss) were embodied. Jesus was not "the peripeteia
of a drama of salvation"—that is, a sudden turn of events or an unexpected
reversal. "Rather, in him the One becomes involved who has long been
involved—God himself."[55] In him the invisible one became visible. He was
"God going about on the earth."[56] "The person who has seen me has seen
the Father" (Jn 14:9).

While nothing new found expression in the speaking that came about
through Jesus, then, there was the difference of a vivid, concrete incarnation
in a person, someone who could be seen. It is in this sense that "in Jesus God
has superseded all the prior revelation to previous generations that are attested in the Old Testament Scriptures."[57] Previously, no one saw God
(Jn 1:18). In this sense there had been no revelation. Moses wanted to see
God's glory and was not allowed to; the shining splendor of God's face
would be too devastating, like looking directly at the sun (Ex 33:18-23).

---

[55]Otto Weber, *Foundations of Dogmatics* (Grand Rapids: Eerdmans, 1981), 2:7.
[56]Ernst Käsemann, *The Testament of Jesus* (London: SCM Press; Philadelphia: Fortress, 1968), 9.
[57]Hurtado, *Lord Jesus Christ*, 499.

There were people (including Moses) who did see God in some sense, and who saw God's face, and John knew those stories. He also knew that the embodiment of God in Jesus provided a different kind of seeing.

While Jesus comes from God and therefore brings a special revelation such as can derive only from someone who comes from God, the revelation oddly has none of the content one would expect. It tells us little about "the things above and below, the things in front and behind" in the manner of revelations such as those in Enoch. "There are no heavenly mysteries revealed to Jesus by God except those disclosed in his own life and death."[58] The revelation concerns only himself and his significance for them.

It is focused in the "I am" sayings: I am the bread of life, I am the light of the world, I am the good shepherd. They are less statements about him than statements about the predicate. You want to know about the bread of life—it's me. You want to know where the world can see light—it's me. You wonder who will ever be the flock's good shepherd—it's me. Put simply, I am the one. In this sense he reveals nothing except that he is the revealer, the one the world has been looking for.[59] He didn't need to reveal anything about God because his people knew from their Scriptures who God was; what John and other New Testament writers needed to handle was the explication of the relationship of the God of Israel to Jesus.[60]

So "no one has ever seen God, but a one and only offspring, God, who is close to the father's heart, he has given an account of him" (Jn 1:18). The second occurrence of the word *God* in this statement may be a later addition to the text, but if so, it makes explicit something implicit. Being one who embodies grace and truthfulness, and being God's only son, and being one who can give an account of God, Jesus *is* himself divine. Instead of "give an account," English translations have "make known," but this waters down the statement. The regular meaning of *exēgeomai* is "relate" or "narrate," to tell a story or to give a full account of something (e.g., Acts 21:19). An *exēgēsis* is such a full account. Jesus relates God or narrates God. When we read Jesus' story, we read God's story.

[58]Ashton, *Understanding the Fourth Gospel*, 551 (2nd ed., 527).
[59]Bultmann, *Theology of the New Testament*, 2:65-66.
[60]Marianne Meye Thompson, *The God of the Gospel of John* (Grand Rapids and Cambridge, UK: Eerdmans, 2001), 141.

It is this grace and truthfulness that constitutes the glory of God that people saw (Jn 1:14). "When I touch Him, see Him, and physically crucify Him, . . . I am touching God, I am seeing God with my physical eyes, and with my physical hands I am crucifying the Son of God, for in Him you will assuredly encounter God." After all, "they crucified the Lord of glory" (1 Cor 2:8).[61]

There is a sense in which the Son lays aside the divine glory in becoming a human being, and even more in letting himself be killed (Phil 2:1-11). There is another sense in which he manifests that glory in doing so. "For John the incarnation is not a self-emptying but a manifestation of divine glory, and the cross itself an instrument of exaltation."[62] And the cross "is no longer the pillory, the tree of shame." Jesus' death "is rather the manifestation of divine self-giving love and his victorious return from the alien realm below to the Father who had sent him."[63] Jesus does not simply cry out there in abandonment; his last words on the cross are a shout of triumph.[64] And while it was also a reality in his earthly ministry, Paul speaks of it in the present tense as well as the past (Col 2:9). Jesus remains an actual embodiment of God.

The incarnation is one aspect of what saves us in the sense that it meets our need to see who God is, as well as making it possible for God to forgive us for wrong we have done.[65]

An Embodiment of Suffering

Thomas Cranmer gave the Church of England for its regular worship a confession that declares, "We acknowledge and bewail our manifold sins and wickedness, which we from time to time most grievously have committed, by thought, word, and deed, against thy divine Majesty, provoking most justly thy wrath and indignation against us."[66] Half a millennium later, the idea that our sin is our basic problem is not as prominent in Western Christian thinking. As an expression of a similar theology to

---

[61]Luther, *Sermons on the Gospel of St. John Chapters 6–8*, 104, 105.

[62]Ashton, *Understanding the Fourth Gospel*, 486 (2nd ed., 461).

[63]Käsemann, *Testament of Jesus*, 10.

[64]Ashton, *Understanding the Fourth Gospel*, 489 (2nd ed., 464).

[65]See Anastasia Scrutton, "'The Truth Will Set You Free,'" in Richard Bauckham and Carl Mosser, eds., *The Gospel of John and Christian Theology* (Grand Rapids and Cambridge, UK: Eerdmans, 2008), 359-68.

[66]From the confession at Holy Communion in *The Book of Common Prayer* of 1549 and repeated in subsequent prayer books.

Cranmer's, the cathedral dedicated to St. Lazarus in Autun, Burgundy, had a Romanesque tympanon (an ornamental panel above a window or door) with an extraordinary portrayal of the last judgment. In 1770 the enlightened cathedral clergy had it plastered over. It no longer suited the times. This procedure at the apex of the French Enlightenment reflected a paradigm shift in modernity that "reversed the forensic relationship between God and humans. No longer must human beings, as sinners, give account before the throne of their God, but God must justify himself—in view of the suffering of the world, for example—before the forum of human reason."[67]

In the twenty-first century, too, we may be more inclined to see ourselves as victims than as villains. For us, the significance of the cross is then that it identifies God as one who shares our suffering. For us, theodicy is more important than atonement—the justification of God rather than our justification.[68] And while the development of theological thinking in the centuries immediately after the New Testament solidified the idea that Jesus belonged "within the unique identity of the one God of Israel," theological thinking was less successful in appropriating the corollary of "the revelation of the divine identity in Jesus' human life and passion."[69]

Whereas many people don't understand how the atonement worked, they may recognize that Jesus' dying for them was somehow an embodiment of love.

> In this we are justified in the blood of the Anointed One and reconciled to God, that it was through this matchless grace shown to us that his Son received our nature, and in that nature, teaching us both by word and by example, persevered to the death and bound us to himself even more through love, so that when we have been kindled by so great a benefit of divine grace, true charity might fear to endure nothing for his sake. . . . Each one is also made more righteous after the Passion of Christ than before; that is, he loves

---

[67]Reinhard Feldmeier and Hermann Spieckermann, *God of the Living* (Waco, TX: Baylor University Press, 2011), 469 (they note that this tympanon has now been restored); cf. the comments in the paragraphs under "An Embodiment of Love" in section 5.2 above.
[68]See, e.g., Smail, *Once and for All*, 40-57.
[69]Richard Bauckham, *God Crucified* (Grand Rapids: Eerdmans, 1998), vii, ix (2nd ed., *Jesus and the God of Israel* [Carlisle, UK: Paternoster, 2008; Grand Rapids: Eerdmans, 2009], x, 59).

God more, because the completed benefit kindles him in love more than a hoped-for benefit.[70]

By his death, as the Apostle says, God's charity toward us is commended. . . . Since token of such great love toward us has been shown, we are moved to, and kindled with, love of God, who has done so much for us; in this way, we are justified, that is, we are released from our sins, and so we are made just. Indeed Christ's death justifies us, as by it charity is kindled in our hearts.[71]

"Man can revolt against a God aloof from all suffering, enthroned in undisturbed bliss or apathetic transcendence. But is it possible to revolt against the God who revealed all his com-passion in Jesus' Passion?"[72] Actually, yes, it is possible, but this revelation might overcome that rebellion.

A Model of Love

Humanity's original problem lay in wanting to be like God and in being afraid of the fact that God alone was God.

Jesus is God's incarnate overture to alienated humans grasping for divinity as the only security against the contingency of creaturehood. In Jesus, God demonstrates that divinity, equality with God, is not something to be coveted, because divinity is not something God exploits at our expense. In Jesus, God takes on the very form that humanity, instructed by the tempter, regards as slavery, namely, creaturehood, to demonstrate that creaturehood is not a condition of existential peril rooted in ontological deficiency. Even when drunk to the dregs to which humanity can be reduced by evil itself, namely, violent death on a cross, creature-hood remains the locus of glorification, exaltation, inextinguishable union with God. To be fully human, including experiencing annihilation's "look-alike"—death—is not a deprivation of divinity but a privileged way to participate in divinity. God conquers death not by avoiding it, as Adam and Eve hoped to do by seizing divinity, but by embracing it. In the outstretched arms of God's love on the cross, death is finally slain.[73]

---

[70]Peter Abelard, *Commentary on the Epistle to the Romans* (Washington, DC: Catholic University of America Press, 2011), 167-68.

[71]Peter Lombard, *The Sentences Book 3*, distinction xix.1 (Toronto: Pontifical Institute of Mediaeval Studies, 2008), 78 (cf. Hastings Rashdall, *The Idea of Atonement* [London: Macmillan, 1919], 370-71).

[72]Hans Küng, *On Being a Christian* (Garden City, NY: Doubleday, 1976; London: Collins, 1977), 435.

[73]Sandra M. Schneiders, "The Lamb of God and the Forgiveness of Sin(s) in the Fourth Gospel," *Catholic Biblical Quarterly* 73 (2011): 1-29 (on 7-8).

Adam (and then Noah, Abraham and Israel) was unwilling and then incapable of living by the pattern of grace and commitment; the patriarchs' lives indicated that God had to do something more than God had done at creation. Humanity in its bodiliness (its createdness) turned out to have been morally too weak from the Beginning, and Adam and Eve's action had changed the dynamic of relationships with God. Henceforth humanity was not merely body but "flesh." What God eventually did in Jesus was take on that fleshly human nature yet live the life of commitment and obedience that humanity had so far failed to live. People opposed this one who was embodying God and God's ultimate purpose, and set about killing him. They were taking to its logical conclusion the rebellion against God that went back to the Beginning.

God wanted Jesus to take whatever came from them, and Jesus continued to offer that commitment and obedience that embodied what it meant to be God and also what it meant to be truly human. The very opposition to God that was expressed in killing Jesus became the means whereby God overturned the order of things that humanity worked with. There is now a more realistic possibility of resisting the temptation to eat of that tree, because the vision of Jesus hanging on another tree stands before us. The power in the story of Jesus' execution lies in its capacity to win commitment. Paul knows from his own experience that God is quite capable of using the kind of power that overwhelms people against their will, though the story of his conversion shows that this overwhelming is but a stage to winning submission, not merely a requiring of submission, so that even his story proves the rule.

There is a glory belonging to Jesus that is revealed in his turning water into wine (Jn 2:1-11), and then there is a glory revealed in his submitting to martyrdom. The revelation at Cana anticipates the martyrdom revelation, though the martyrdom revelation is then incomplete without the resurrection and ascension. Is Jesus' death a means to his glorification, or is it the glorification itself?[74] Is Jesus glorified despite the cross or through the cross? Jesus' death is a revelation of who God is. Jesus embodies that revelation in becoming incarnate (Phil 2:5-11), then in washing his disciples' feet, then in

---

[74]See Tord Larsson, "Glory or Persecution," in Richard Bauckham and Carl Mosser, eds., *The Gospel of John and Christian Theology* (Grand Rapids and Cambridge, UK: Eerdmans, 2008), 82-88.

being willing to die for them. Because it reveals who God is, his humiliation is his glorification. Jesus' death is his glorification. He is glorified through the cross.

The Wisdom of the Cross

Whereas before Jesus the nations lacked the understanding of God that Israel had, and lived with an understanding that was at best partial and often twisted, after Jesus the gospel is to be preached to them so that they no longer live in such obliviousness or falsehood. Yet the Scriptures' understanding of God's ways with the world looks really stupid.

> The crucifixion of Jesus, in which the old æon said its last word, was by no means a specially shameful act when seen in this context, but an act of very primitive self-preservation and self-defence. Far from being an act that can be laid to the charge of the people of Israel particularly, it was an act in which they behaved and proved themselves as the representatives and accredited agents of all nations as never before or since.[75]

The Scriptures' understanding makes both sense and nonsense to God's people (1 Cor 1:18–2:15; cf. Is 29:14; 40:13; 64:4; 65:17). It makes sense in that God's people comprises ordinary human beings; it is not dominated by intellectuals. God chose such a people to put the world in its place and to get it to enthuse about God rather than about ourselves and our insight, our power, our prestige or our position, which ordinary people cannot do (cf. Jer 9:24). So even an intellectual like Paul enthuses and preaches about something simple and consequently feels fearful and feeble in doing so.

People's extraordinary response to this simple message is a demonstration of the story's power. It is also a demonstration of the Spirit's power and an indication that it takes the Spirit to open someone's eyes to the truth of the story's implausible interpretation of Jesus' execution. God indeed overwhelms and compels but does so by winning adherence and submission through the credible and persuasive nature of the message. At first sight it doesn't make sense; it's counterintuitive. On reflection, it's clearly right. That process of recognition is how real change comes about in people, which is

---

[75]Barth, *CD* I, 2:62.

why the execution story, which looks like something stupid, is actually the epitome of insight.[76]

The particular form of its counterintuitive nature might make it immediately more credible to ordinary people than to powerful people. It's tempting to refuse to acknowledge weakness. Yet there can be a powerful effect when someone does acknowledge weakness, especially someone who one thought was strong—indeed who is known to be strong. It does place before these ordinary people the temptation to think that they have found instant access to intellectual prestige. They have to keep reminding themselves that the heart of the revelation of God's insight is a man being executed, something that is simple and thus remains stupid looking.

They have to keep reminding themselves. Perhaps the very counterintuitive nature of the point underlies that fact. The execution story is God's power to people who are "being rescued" (1 Cor 1:18); it enables them to keep taking the stance that rescues them from God's wrath. In contrast, it looks stupid to people who are perishing.

The illogic of the way God acted to rescue the world in Jesus was in keeping with the illogic of his relationship with Israel. God chose a people that had neither power nor insight, nor greater integrity than other people, and God persisted with this people even though it persisted in its resistance to giving God its allegiance and to relying on God. God thus demonstrated an insight formulated by God before the ages, yet not obvious, and missed by the rulers of this age (peoples like Babylon and Rome) who thus crucified the glorious Lord (1 Cor 2:6-8). It is indeed the pattern of Israel's own story: "What eye did not see and ear did not hear and did not come into the human heart, such things God prepared for those who love him" (Paul quotes Is 64:4).

In dying, Jesus was embodying what it really meant to be God, and also embodying what it really meant to be a human being. The mystery of the Immortal One's dying relates not only to solving problems that lie in our past but to reshaping us for the future.

---

[76]See further Richard B. Hays, "Wisdom According to Paul," in Stephen C. Barton, ed., *Where Shall Wisdom Be Found?* (Edinburgh: T&T Clark, 1999), 111-23.

5.3 JESUS' DEATH: CARRYING WRONGDOING

So Jesus' death expresses God's love for us and thus arouses love for God in us. But the idea that this arousing of love in itself resolves things between us and God is too simple. We needed more than a manifestation of love, and "a theology of the atonement seeks to bring together the depth of moral evil as men know it in themselves, and the work of Jesus."[77] It is because Jesus' execution involves dying *for* us that it is a revelation of who God is; his dying for us was a means of reconciling, cleansing, making restitution, liberating and conquering evil. It was not only something other than a pointless suicide; it was more than a heroic martyrdom.

When God had Jesus die, he was doing something that affected his relationship with us. That's what made it an act of love. First, he was carrying our wrongdoing and thus effecting our reconciliation.

Offering Reconciliation

God's action in Jesus was designed to offer us reconciliation. Reconciliation, a central theme in the New Testament,[78] primarily has to do not with our attitude toward God but with God's attitude toward us and our wrongdoing.[79] Talk of reconciliation in the Scriptures presupposes that humanity (Jewish and Gentile) had got out of harmonious relationship with God. We were like a husband who has betrayed his wife, or a son his father, or a man who has stolen his best friend's girl. It is appropriate for the father/wife/friend to be angry. The background of scriptural talk of reconciliation is the fact that God is angry with us, even though he also loves us.

The New Testament emphasizes the fact that God is angry with the world, has expressed his anger in the past, does so in the present and will do so in the future. "God's anger is revealed from heaven against all impiety and faithlessness on the part of people who suppress the truth in faithlessness" (Rom 1:18). "You are storing up anger for yourself on the day of anger and of the revealing of God's right judgment" (Rom 2:5). "God's anger comes on

---

[77]D. M. MacKinnon, "Subjective and Objective Conceptions of Atonement," in F. G. Healey, ed., *Prospect for Theology*, H. H. Farmer Festschrift (Welwyn, UK: Nisbet, 1966), 169-82 (on 181).

[78]See Ralph P. Martin, *Reconciliation* (London: Marshall; Atlanta: John Knox, 1981; rev. ed., Eugene, OR: Wipf and Stock, 1989).

[79]George Eldon Ladd, *A Theology of the New Testament*, rev. ed., ed. Donald A. Hagner (Grand Rapids: Eerdmans, 1993), 495 (cf. 453 in the first edition).

disobedient people" (Eph 5:6). People can be imagined pleading with the mountains, "Hide us from the face of the one sitting on the throne and from the lamb's anger" (Rev 6:16).

At the same time, the Scriptures also recognize that God is not in the habit of acting out this anger.[80] God's giving Jesus to die for us expressed his commitment to being reconciled to us. "While we were enemies, we were reconciled to God through his Son's death," and "having been reconciled, we will be rescued by his life," so that "we exult in God through our Lord Jesus, the Anointed One, through whom we have now received the reconciliation" (Rom 5:8-11). It means we can indeed have peace with God and that we will not be the victims of God's anger in the future (Rom 5:1, 9). But the act whereby God goes about effecting reconciliation with us is past. It is over before it reaches us.

> The work of reconciliation, in the sense of the New Testament, is a work which is *finished*, and which we must conceive to be finished, *before the gospel is preached*. It is the good tidings of the Gospel, with which the evangelists go forth, that God has wrought in Christ a work of reconciliation which avails for no less than the world, and of which the whole world may have the benefit. The summons of the evangelist is—"*Receive* the reconciliation; consent that it become effective in your case." The work of reconciliation is not a work wrought upon the souls of men, though it is a work wrought in their interests, and bearing so directly upon them that we can say God has reconciled the world to Himself; it is a work—as Cromwell said of the covenant—*outside of us*, in which God so deals in Christ with the sin of the world, that it shall no longer be a barrier between Himself and men. . . .
>
> Reconciliation is not something which is doing; it is something which is done. No doubt there is a work of Christ which is in process, but it has as its basis a finished work of Christ; it is in virtue of something already consummated on His cross that Christ is able to make the appeal to us which He does, and to win the response in which we *receive* the reconciliation.[81]

---

[80]See further the paragraphs under "Unwilling Judgment" in section 1.1 above.

[81]James Denney, *The Death of Christ* (London: Hodder and Stoughton, 1902), 144-46. Denney is referring to a letter from Oliver Cromwell to his son-in-law Charles Fleetwood, Lord Deputy of Ireland, of June 22, 1655, in which he declares, "The Covenant is without *us*; a Transaction between God and Christ" (Thomas Carlyle, ed., *Oliver Cromwell's Letters and Speeches* [New York: Scribner, 1871], 4:125).

"The atonement is history. . . . To try to grasp it as supra-historical or non-historical truth is not to grasp it at all."[82] When Jesus died, the temple curtain was torn in two (Mt 27:51). It was a sign of judgment, an indication that the temple was finished and an anticipation of its destruction, and also a sign of grace, because it suggested opening up the presence of God to people (cf. Heb 9–10).

God's Patience

There is a further significance in John's appeal to Isaiah 53:1.[83] The vision in Isaiah 52:13–53:12 has its setting in the exile, and it relates to the waywardness of Israel that had brought about the exile. That waywardness had not begun in the decades just preceding the fall of Jerusalem. As people lamented, the parents had eaten sour grapes, but it was the children who had a bad taste in their mouth (Jer 31:29; Ezek 18:1-2). That is, the generation that saw Jerusalem fall experienced something that their parents and earlier ancestors had deserved but did not experience. This later generation deserved it just as much, and in this sense they couldn't complain, but they were right that they were unlucky to be the generation that was alive when Yahweh's patience finally ran out.

Their reflection raises a further question. How is it that Yahweh has been so patient over the centuries? After all, that patience was regularly useless, in the sense that it met with no response.

One way of formulating an answer is to note the implication that Yahweh's patience is not contingent on humanity's response. It issues from who Yahweh himself is.[84] A further implication is that Yahweh has been continually paying the price for his people's waywardness. For centuries they have been behaving in ways that suggest contempt for Yahweh, and Yahweh has just taken it. From time to time he has acted in chastisement, but never in the way that the covenant warned. The punishment has never corresponded to the crime. Yahweh has carried the consequences of their waywardness instead of making them carry them. He is like a parent who would have reason to throw a son or daughter out of the house but never does so. In other words, there has been a revelation of Yahweh embodied in the story

---

[82]Barth, *CD* IV, 1:157.
[83]Cf. section 5.2 above.
[84]Cf. Barth, *CD* II, 1:414-22.

of Israel from its very beginning, in the way Yahweh has rolled with Israel's disdain. In effect, Yahweh has been letting Israel crucify him.

We have noted the objection to Christian faith that "Yahweh, aside from all questions of power, diverges from the gods of Canaan primarily by transcending both sexuality and death. More bluntly, Yahweh cannot be regarded as dying. . . . I find nothing in theological Christianity to be more difficult for me to apprehend than the conception of Jesus Christ as a dying and reviving God." On this understanding, it shatters the Tanakh.[85] Actually, Yahweh has always been a dying and rising God, though not in the manner of a Canaanite god. That truth is expressed in Israel's history, and it is embodied in the action Yahweh takes in the ministry of his servant (Is 53:1). It is further embodied in Jesus when he takes up the servant role and embodies its vision.

In heaven God has long been absorbing his anger, but he had also embodied that stance and action in the world and in the life of Israel. Letting Jesus be executed was the ultimate expression of his willingness to absorb his justified resentment and anger in himself rather than express it on the people who had earned it, because he wanted to be reconciled to them.

Carrying Human Wrongdoing

The classic term to describe what Jesus achieved by his death is the word *atonement*. The word's etymology is a guide to its meaning. Without Jesus' dying, there would have been no at-one-ment between us and God. Through his dying, we can be at one. God lets humanity kill his Son and thus lets us do the worst thing imaginable, yet refuses to withdraw from us, and rather absorbs our hostility in himself. Indeed, "Jesus' sinlessness consists in his ability to suffer human evil, particularly the human tendency toward destructive judgment, and to absorb it without passing it on."[86] The notion of absorbing anger corresponds to the more technical idea that God lets himself be propitiated—it's as if he propitiates himself.[87] While the Scriptures

---

[85]Bloom, *Jesus and Yahweh*, 6. See the paragraphs under "The Death and the Birth" earlier in this section.

[86]L. Gregory Jones, *Embodying Forgiveness* (Grand Rapids: Eerdmans, 1995), 122.

[87]It is thus odd that writers who wish to emphasize propitiation describe "absorb" as a "curious notion" (Steve Jeffery and Andrew Sach, *Pierced for Our Transgressions* [Nottingham, UK: Inter-Varsity Press; Wheaton, IL: Crossway, 2007], 215).

do not speak of God absorbing human evil, they frequently speak of God carrying it, which makes a similar point.

The New Testament has two main words for "forgive": *aphiēmi* suggests letting go of the wrongs that people have done to us, while *charizomai* suggests being gracious toward people who have wronged us. The First Testament also has two words. The less frequent one, *ṣālaḥ*, suggests pardoning people; it denotes the forgiveness that someone in authority gives to a subordinate. The more common word, *nāsā'*, is the ordinary word for "carry," so it is this word that suggests carrying someone's wrongdoing. It denotes the forgiveness that anyone might give to a person who has wronged them.

In principle, people who do wrong have to "carry their waywardness"— that is, accept responsibility and either undergo punishment or make restitution (*'āšām*; Ex 28:43; Lev 5:17-18). But one person can "carry" the wrongdoing of another person, one way or another. In the wilderness, people "carried" their parents' unfaithfulness and waywardness (Num 14:33-34)— that is, they involuntarily bore the consequences of it when they didn't deserve to do so. Yahweh's servant voluntarily "carried" people's offenses (Is 53:12)—that is, he bore the consequences of these offenses when he didn't deserve to do so and didn't have to do so.

This formulation is taken up in the declaration that Jesus "carried" our offenses when he did not deserve to (1 Pet 2:24). He was doing so when he died: "His death, and His bearing of our sins, are not two things, but one."[88] In letting himself be killed, he was behaving as one who took the initiative in accepting responsibility for us and who thus accepted the consequence of our action.

Nothing outside God could have this effect. The world was continuing in its waywardness, turning its back on God. If God were to wait until the world came to its senses, he would wait forever. Instead, God carries the world's wrongdoing, accepts responsibility for it—not in the sense that it is his fault but in the sense that he will not behave on the basis of the fact that the world has done wrong and should get what it deserves.

He does so after almost destroying the world, and does so again in restoring the Israelites after the exile, but he does so most spectacularly in

---

[88]James Denney, *The Death of Christ* (London: Hodder and Stoughton, 1902), 98.

sending Jesus into the world, letting the world execute him, then bringing him back from the dead and reaching out to the people who killed him. "God demonstrates his own love for us in that while we were still sinners, the Anointed One died for us" (Rom 5:8).

There used to be enmity between us and God. God's giving Jesus for us expressed God's desire to end the enmity, and our trust in Jesus expresses our response. So now there is at-one-ment, a good relationship, the kind Adam and Eve were designed for.

Doing the Right Thing

What God did in Israel and what God did in Jesus are thus an expression of God's *dikaiosynē*. The traditional English translation is "righteousness," and this translation fits the term's background in secular Greek, where it denotes integrity. But *dikaiosynē* and related expressions are also equivalents in the Septuagint to words such as *ṣədāqâ* that denote doing the right and faithful thing by people with whom one is in a committed relationship. They are "basic Old Testament terms connected with God's covenant with his chosen people. Predicated of God, they designate his faithfulness to the covenant and the fact that of his goodness and grace he constantly reaffirms it"; predicated of Israel, they denote its living within the covenant in obedience.[89]

"God's 'righteousness' and 'faithfulness' are almost identical attributes and correlative actions" (see Rom 3:3, 5); both are "formed fundamentally by God's covenant with Israel. God's saving act in Christ is therefore to be understood primarily as an act of covenant faithfulness and restoration."[90] God's letting Jesus be executed was the ultimate expression of God's commitment to doing the right thing by us, being faithful to us. The cross is the "paradigm of faithfulness."[91]

The word *primarily* is important; in both Testaments God's doing the right thing and acting in integrity includes his acting in judgment.[92] But God did right by us not in the sense that he acted in keeping with our deserts (we

---

[89]Günther Bornkamm, *Paul* (New York: Harper; London: Hodder, 1971), 139.

[90]Douglas A. Campbell, *The Deliverance of God* (Grand Rapids: Eerdmans, 2009), 441, summarizing the views of James D. G. Dunn (see, e.g., *Romans* [Dallas: Word, 1988]) and N. T. Wright (see, e.g., "The Letter to the Romans," in Leander E. Keck et al., eds., *The New Interpreter's Bible* [Nashville: Abingdon, 2002], 10:393-770).

[91]Richard B. Hays, *The Moral Vision of the New Testament* (San Francisco: Harper, 1996), 27.

[92]See Charles Lee Irons, *The Righteousness of God* (Tübingen: Mohr, 2015).

had none) but in the sense that he acted in keeping with his own integrity and commitment to us. God "set forth" Jesus as the one who died for us, "so that he might show he had acted aright in passing over the sins of the past in God's forbearance, so that he might show he had acted aright in the present time, so that he might be both the one who acts aright and the one who treats someone as in the right, through faith in the Anointed One, Jesus" (Rom 3:25-26).

This formulation might hint that there was a "problem" about God having left the sins of the past unpunished. There would then be some tension between the way God acted in relation to Israel and the rest of the world and the way God acted in Jesus. But more profoundly the formulation points to a continuity between God's past forbearance and God's act in Jesus. God's act in Jesus enables us to see the significance of the way God had always related to Israel and to the world. All through Israel's history and the world's history, God had been acting with integrity, acting in the right way, in the sense that his actions expressed his commitment to being in a good relationship with Israel and with the world, and not letting human sin frustrate that intention. Jesus' execution brings this insistence to its fullest expression. There is no tension between passing over sin in the past and treating people as in the right now that they are in a position to trust in Jesus. Both manifest the same instinct to do the right thing by people, the same commitment to faithfulness to Israel and to humanity.

One might even say that righteousness is "Paul's code word for the attribute of mercy."[93] It is for this reason that I can be *simul justus et peccator*, "righteous and a sinner at the same time, holy and profane, an enemy of God and a child of God."[94] Through my life I fail in my commitment to God (I am a sinner), but God does not give up on a commitment to me (I am *justus*, a saint, in that God views and treats me as among the people to whom he is committed to being faithful).[95]

Further, that commitment means that in another sense God does not simply accept me as I am but works out a commitment to taking me to mature holiness. We are *peccatores in re, justi autem in spe*—sinners, but

---

[93]Jerome H. Neyrey, *Render to God* (Minneapolis: Fortress, 2004), 123.
[94]Martin Luther, *Lectures on Galatians 1535 Chapters 1–4*, LW 26 (St. Louis: Concordia, 1963), 232.
[95]Much of these paragraphs follows Dunn, *Theology of Paul the Apostle*, 334-89.

destined to be saints.[96] Perhaps better, we *are* saints, but we are destined to become what we are.[97]

Putting Us Right

Alongside the use of the noun *dikaiosynē*, the Scriptures also use the verb *dikaioō* and the noun *dikaiōsis* in connection with that carrying of human wrongdoing. For these words, English translations often use the words *justify* and *justification* to denote God's putting things right between him and us, but these English words, too, are misleading.[98] They suggest the idea of God as judge, which is indeed an understanding that is accepted in both Testaments. But in this connection they also suggest the idea of God acquitting people who are guilty, of God declaring that ungodly people are innocent (see Rom 4:5). Both Testaments would question this idea. A judge's job is to find the ungodly guilty. One could say that the judge metaphor breaks down at this point, as metaphors always do at some point. Yet the metaphor would be breaking down rather early on. There is nothing more central to the idea of judging than that one justifies the innocent and condemns the guilty.

Behind the difficulty is the consideration we have already presupposed, that Greek words of the *dikaio-* family do not have their context in law, either in secular Greek or in the New Testament, and certainly not a context in Western law. *Dikaiōsis* is closer to the act of treating someone rightly in light of your right relationship with them than to the act of declaring their innocence. In the context of their wrongdoing, it involves saying, "Yes, you did the wrong thing, but I am not going to allow it to break our relationship. I am still committed to you."

Dikaiōsis does not involve a legal fiction. It does not mean treating someone as in the right when they were not. It means treating them as within the covenant people.[99] "The Judge who acts at Calvary is not the

---

[96]From Martin Luther's comments on Rom 4, *Lectures on Romans* (St. Louis: Concordia, 1972), 258. More literally we are "righteous in hope"; but Luther is referring not to my hopeful attitude but to God's intent and thus to my destiny.

[97]Cf. N. T. Wright, *Paul and the Faithfulness of God* (Minneapolis: Fortress; London: SPCK, 2013), 1027.

[98]On the modern debate over justification, see James K. Beilby and Paul Rhodes Eddy, eds., *Justification: Five Views* (Downers Grove, IL: InterVarsity Press, 2011).

[99]So N. T. Wright, e.g., *Justification* (London: SPCK; Downers Grove, IL: InterVarsity Press, 2009), 55-108.

Roman judge who acts according to Roman law, *lex*, balancing crime with punishment, injury with recompense." He is "the Judge of the Old Testament law, the *Torah*, whose concern is to maintain and restore his covenant relationship with his people."[100] Jesus' death is the "quintessential covenantal act."[101]

On our part, in order for the relationship to continue we simply have to trust that God means that he is not going to let our wrongdoing break the relationship. Jesus' death is the evidence of that fact. "As those who are judged by God, and directed to His grace, we are, in fact and objectively, called to faith."[102] It is for this reason that when we are thus "put right through faith, we have[103] peace in relation to God through our Lord Jesus, the Anointed One, through whom we have also gotten access by faith[104] to this grace in which we have come to stand" (Rom 5:1-2). The reality of a peaceful relationship follows from the stance that God takes in continuing to relate to us, and from our trust in God's doing so.

The stance and the trust also mean we can always approach God in the manner of a subject approaching a king or of a worshiper coming to offer a sacrifice. Further, we can boast in hope of God's glory (Rom 5:2)—that is, we can confidently look forward to seeing God's glory at the End. Our sin meant we would have lost any hope of that prospect (Rom 3:23), but God determined that our sin would not have the effect of cutting us off from the tree of life. Our *dikaiōsis* means our being rescued from wrath (Rom 5:9-11).

Grace

So God was like a person who has been wronged but who determines that the act of betrayal will not terminate the relationship, and who wants to put the wrongdoer right with him or her just as a gift, instead of taking redress. All that the offender has to do is believe that it is so and trust the other person. So it is with God (Rom 3:21-24). His letting his Son be executed by

---

[100]Smail, *Once and for All*, 101.

[101]Michael J. Gorman, *Inhabiting the Cruciform God* (Grand Rapids and Cambridge, UK: Eerdmans, 2009), 57.

[102]Barth, *CD* II, 2:766.

[103]Or "let us have"; some manuscripts have *echomen*, some *echōmen*, but the difference does not affect the point under consideration here.

[104]Again, there is manuscript variance over whether Paul included the phrase "by faith," but he certainly assumed it.

us and not insisting on redress for this act puts us right with him. God lets go of that right anger at our wrongdoing, so that there is a peaceful relationship between us, and we stand in a relationship of grace with God (Rom 5:1-2). In a sense, originally (at creation) there did not need to be a relationship of grace between us. The relationship between parent and child or husband and wife or friend and friend is not one of grace in this sense. But the act of determining to stay in relationship despite a betrayal generates something that is in a new sense a relationship of grace, of pure gift.

Given that Yahweh is a God characterized by grace, when humanity went wrong he could hardly let death have the last word. As Moses might have put it, he would look really stupid. Thus "God so loved the world that he gave his only Son, so that each person who trusts in him may not perish but have eternal life, because God did not send his Son into the world to condemn the world but so that the world might be rescued through him" (Jn 3:16-17).

The words neatly combine God's concern for the world and God's involvement with the individual. It is because God loves the world, the *kosmos*, that Jesus came. He intends to reign there. But the way individuals come to be part of the realm where Jesus reigns is by trusting him. They then escape the condemnation and death that are coming on the world; they are rescued from them, and they enjoy the eternal life that God intended for humanity from the Beginning. They start experiencing that life now. It is as if they are restored to the garden and eat of the life tree. So the person who believes in the Son has eternal life. On the other hand, "the person who disbelieves the Son will not see life, but God's wrath stays on them" (Jn 3:36). Life and condemnation are set over against each other (cf. Jn 5:19-27).

God's original act of creation itself was indeed an act of grace in the sense that it arose from God's giving instinct, and keeping creation in being was an act of grace. Then, "grace upon (*anti*) grace," out of the fullness of God's grace and truthfulness that are embodied in Jesus, we have all received (Jn 1:16): "Christian life is based at all points upon grace; as it proceeds, one grace is exchanged only for another."[105] Thus it's possible to base an entire gargantuan volume called *Christ* on the theme of grace.[106]

---

[105]C. K. Barrett, *The Gospel According to St John* (London: SPCK, 1962), 140.
[106]I refer to Edward Schillebeeckx, *Christ* (New York: Crossroad; London: SCM Press, 1980).

In Jesus, "God's grace is not His hitherto unknown or misconceived graciousness, but is His now occurring act of grace." It is not a new "mode of dealing" but "*a single deed*," God's giving Jesus to die. To accept God's grace in vain (2 Cor 6:1) is to reject that gift of God. Grace is the giving of a gift, so it can be spoken of as a *dōrea* or *dōrēma* or *charisma* as well as *charis* (Rom 5:15-17). The same is true of love: *agapē* is a deed. Separation from Jesus' love would be separation from what God did for us in Jesus (Rom 8:34-35). But then because this deed is the decisive event in which the time of salvation has come, "grace may be spoken of as a personified power" that now reigns in sin's place (Rom 5:20-21). Grace is the situation or territory in which we stand (Rom 5:2), and we must make sure we don't fall out of it (Gal 5:4).[107]

A Two-Way Reconciliation

God's willingness to forgo anger and to sacrifice himself indicated that reconciliation was possible from God's side. That fact means it is also possible from our side. The etymology of the word *at-one-ment* indicates that reconciliation has to be a two-way event. "The purpose of forgiveness is the restoration of communion."[108] Both forgiveness and reconciliation presuppose that wrongdoing has come between two parties, and the restoring of the relationship involves both sides.

God did need reconciling to the world, which had turned its back on God and had incurred his anger. God had to reconcile himself to the world's wrongdoing. When we speak of people reconciling themselves to something we commonly mean they have to accept its reality, but not necessarily that they stop being angry about it. God's reconciling himself to the world meant giving up being angry about it. It meant abandoning justified resentment and not counting people's transgressions against them. "Reconciliation includes . . . a change on the part of God as well as on the part of man."[109]

The necessity for the act that expressed God's reconciliation to the world showed how the world also needed to be reconciled to God: "In the Anointed One God was reconciling the world to himself, not counting their

---

[107]Bultmann, *Theology of the New Testament*, 1:289-91.
[108]Jones, *Embodying Forgiveness*, 5.
[109]Leon Morris, *The Apostolic Preaching of the Cross* (London: Tyndale; Grand Rapids: Eerdmans, 1955; 3rd ed., 1965), 249.

transgressions against them. . . . We beg you on behalf of the Anointed One, be reconciled to God" (2 Cor 5:18-20). The acts that objectively embodied God's reconciliation to the world also appealed to the world's subjectivity. They sought to get the world to recognize the extraordinary way in which God had surrendered his justified resentment and anger and had reconciled himself to the world.

The first great biblical example of this dynamic comes in the conclusion of the flood story (Gen 8:15–9:17). God bids Noah and his family come out from the ark and reaffirms his original creation commission to humanity; Noah sacrifices burnt offerings. God promises never again to curse the ground, because humanity is incorrigibly perverse; God has reconciled himself to that fact. But in addition, he makes the Scriptures' first covenant and draws Noah's attention to the sign that he has hung up his bow.[110] He is reconciled to humanity in that other sense. Today is bright sunshine after a day of rain yesterday; each such day comes because God reconciled himself to the world, and thus also seeks to reconcile the world to himself. The Judahites' return from exile came about because God was reconciling himself to them, and it thus appealed to them to be reconciled to God. Jesus' coming, execution, resurrection and proclamation happened because God was thus reconciling himself to the world, and they thus appeal to the world and the church to be reconciled to God.

The declaration that the Corinthians need to be reconciled to God is surprising, because a once-for-all reconciliation between God and humanity was the object of Jesus' coming. The exhortation "be reconciled to God" is "the language of evangelism."[111] It transpires that there is a sense in which God's act of reconciliation need not be once-for-all. The relationship between God and Israel was subject to periodic breakdown. Israel would offend God, God would get angry with Israel, in due course God would set aside anger and reach out to Israel, and Israel would come back to God. The anger did not mean the relationship was ever terminally imperiled. God was never going to give into the temptation to walk out

---

[110]See the paragraphs under "But Wrathful and Not Acquitting" in section 1.1 above.

[111]I. Howard Marshall, "The Meaning of 'Reconciliation,'" in Robert A. Guelich, ed., *Unity and Diversity in New Testament Theology*, G. E. Ladd Festschrift (Grand Rapids: Eerdmans, 1978), 117-32 (on 129); cf. Ralph P. Martin, *2 Corinthians* (Waco, TX: Word, 1996), 138.

on Israel finally. But the relationship could go through rocky periods. This dynamic continues in God's relationship with churches such as that in Corinth.

God's commitment to the world after the flood meant that the world could always come back to God and be sure of finding the relationship restored, though it has not done so. God's grace to Israel at Sinai meant that Israel could always come back to God and be sure of finding the relationship restored, as Israel periodically did. God's grace to Judah in its restoration after the exile meant that Judah could always come back to God and be sure of finding the relationship restored, as Judah did. God's grace in Jesus meant that churches could always come back to God and find the relationship restored.

When a nation is powerful, it is inclined to assert authority by force over other peoples, but it may get further by resisting that temptation, because a willing acknowledgment of authority is better than an enforced one. God's way of acting in Jesus recognized this fact (Col 1:20). Having the fullness of God's person residing in Jesus meant that through Jesus God could reconcile the world to himself by making peace through the blood-shedding associated with his execution. The reconciliation resembled that of a rebellious subordinate power to a superior power, but it was achieved by the superior power's self-sacrifice.

Not with Empty Results

The Corinthians are urged to be reconciled to God and thus not to have received God's grace with empty results (2 Cor 6:1). Receiving God's grace with empty results need not mean they will lose their place among God's people. Rather it means that their accepting God's grace will not have had the intended results in their life. They will be a little like the Jewish people itself in Paul's day. And the present nature of their life together could indeed suggest that they have received God's grace to no effect. They are still stuck in their old ways. They need to respond to Paul's exhortation in order that this situation should not solidify. Rather neatly, in this connection Paul appeals back to one of those earlier occasions when God showed grace. Toward the end of the exile, God declared his intention to restore Judah: "In a time of favor I have listened to you, in a day of salvation I have helped you"

(Is 49:8). Paul adds, "Now is 'a time of favor,' now is 'a day of salvation'" (2 Cor 6:2).

Sometimes the reason reconciliation has to be two-way is that both sides are hostile and a third party needs to bring them together, as is the case when the United States seeks to mediate between Israel and Palestine. The question who initiated the hostility may not be important; the question is whether they are prepared to end it. Sometimes one party is hostile and the hostility is not reciprocated, as was the case between the prodigal son and his father; the father had not responded to his son's departure by turning against his son, and what is required is for the son to swallow his pride and come home. The reconciliation was two-way because the father swallowed his pride before it could assert itself. Sometimes one party is hostile and the other has reciprocated it, but the originally offended party can swallow its justified pride and take the initiative to win back the hostile party.

In connection with reconciliation between God and the world, the first circumstance may be a misleading model if it suggests that God and the world are at odds and Jesus brings them together. Exegetically and theologically this understanding is astray; "it takes the Trinity to make sense of the atonement."[112] Jesus' parable of the prodigal son shows the appropriateness of the second model, though it leaves the father purely reactive to the son's return. The argument of Colossians and Romans points to the third model. God had responded to human rebellion by the exercise of punitive authority, but reconciliation came about because God was also willing to swallow justified pride and forgo the right to enforce submission. Letting Jesus be executed expresses that willingness. The same act seeks to win the human response to get people now to offer ready submission to divine authority. The two parties can then be reconciled, not so much as friends but as master and servant.

Human beings were indeed like children who ignored their mother's house rules and made her throw them out of the house. Yet a mother has a hard time stopping being a mother, and the development of such enmity does not make a mother bar the door; more likely it makes her go out and try to get the children back in for dinner. Jesus' dying for us was and is an

---

[112]Thomas A. Smail, *The Forgotten Father* (London: Hodder, 1980; Grand Rapids: Eerdmans, 1981), 113.

expression and demonstration of *God's* love (Rom 5:8). While we were sinners and enemies, Jesus died for us (Rom 5:6-11). His dying both expresses the way God's enmity does not have the last word and demonstrates such insistence in its not doing so, in order to let our human enmity not have the last word.

It turned people with whom God did not wish to meet into people with whom God was willing to associate again, and it turned people who had gone astray into people who saw that they had done so and wanted to come back. It effected an objective atonement and a subjective atonement; it reconciled God, on God's initiative, and it also reconciled us. Giving his Son to die for us was an extraordinary expression of God's righteousness or covenant faithfulness that was designed to win us to reconciliation so that we become an embodiment or evidence of that righteousness or covenant faithfulness—not that we have to try to be it, but that God's action has made us into it.

5.4 JESUS' DEATH: CLEANSING AND MAKING RESTITUTION

With the best will in the world, even the God who is willing to absorb anger and who desires reconciliation may be inhibited from relating to humanity by the defilement or taboo attaching to human beings in their waywardness. Human beings themselves may become aware of that stain or uncleanness. Lady Macbeth tried and tried in vain to wash the blood of King Duncan off her hands. A man who commits adultery and then accepts that he has done wrong may realize that he remains consequently unclean, and he certainly may be unclean to his wife. People may similarly be aware that things they have done stain them in a way that makes it inappropriate for them to come into God's presence.

Sometimes a cleansing rite may enable people to know that the taint has been cleaned, the taboo removed. A person who is aware of being unclean and needing purification may bathe in the ocean to that end, for a sense of washing off the impurity. Baptism may have that effect, especially if administered in a river or in the ocean.

One significance of sacrifices in the First Testament was that they were God-given means of cleansing people from stain. The New Testament takes up that reality. In dying, Jesus was acting on God's behalf by providing a means of cleansing in the form of a metaphorical sacrifice whereby we could be cleansed and thus able to come into God's presence.

The First Testament sacrificial system also suggests another approach to seeing the significance of Jesus' dying. Wrongdoing puts us in debt to the person we have wronged. The careless driver may wish there were a way of making restitution to the parents of the child he killed. The unfaithful husband may come to his senses and wish there were a way to make amends to his wife. As sinners we may come to recognize how we have not given God the allegiance he deserves. Jesus was also acting on God's behalf and on ours, in providing us with a gift of obedience that we can offer to God to make up for our failure of allegiance, as we identify with his self-giving.

The Stain of Sin

In the First Testament, there were things that could make it impossible for people to come into the temple because they would compromise its sanctity; for instance, they could not enter if they had just had sex or if they had just been in contact with a dead body. Translations regularly use the word *impurity* in this connection, but the translation is misleading as a rendering of the Hebrew word *ṭāmēʾ*. That word does not indicate the lack or compromising of some quality, as is suggested by the word *im-purity*. It rather suggests the presence of a quality, the presence of something rather strange or worrying or mysterious, which issues in the attaching of a taboo to the object that carries it. A number of key taboos seem to relate in some way to the difference between human beings and God—not the moral differences but the differences in nature. They mean you cannot go into the presence of God in the sanctuary when you carry a taboo. It needs to be dealt with first. Those two classic instances of taboo, relating to sex and death, concern aspects of human experience that sharply distinguish human beings from God. It's not that sex (with the appropriate person) or burying a family member is wrong. Sex and death are alien to Yahweh's own being, as they were not alien to the being of other gods (who could have sex and could die).[113]

Moral impropriety and unfaithfulness to Yahweh did have the same effect of staining a person and making it impossible to come into God's presence.

---

[113]Cf. the quotation from Harold Bloom in the paragraphs under "Yahweh's Arm" in section 5.1 above.

These acts, too, were alien to Yahweh's own being. People stained by them would defile the place where Yahweh lived and make it impossible for Yahweh to be present there without compromising who he was.

With mild forms of taboo, you were obliged at least to wait for a few days for the defilement to wear off. When you were affected by one of the more serious taboos, you would need some form of cleansing rite such as a ceremonial washing or the offering of a sacrifice. Moral impropriety would also require repentance and some act of restitution.

Leviticus 4–5 lays out two forms of offering that deal with human shortcomings or failures. Neither is designed to deal with what one might call "proper" sin. If you have worshiped another god or made an image of God or traded on the sabbath or committed adultery, offering a sacrifice will not deal with this wrongdoing. The two forms of offering in Leviticus 4–5 have lesser concerns, as we might see them.

The term for the first of these two forms of offering is the word *ḥaṭṭā't*, which in other contexts is commonly translated "sin." This sacrifice is thus traditionally referred to as the "sin offering," but the translation is misleading. This offering does not deal with the moral and relational consequences of deliberate moral wrongdoing. It deals with the pollution that issues from such wrongdoing, or from those other factors such as contact with death or sex that are not wrong but do make a person taboo, or from doing something wrong by accident. Even if there was nothing morally wrong with your action, it contrasts with some aspect of God's nature and makes you taboo and unable to go into God's presence. First you make an offering that deals with the pollution or taboo, then you can go into God's presence. It is a "purification offering."

Mary makes such an offering after Jesus is born; childbirth makes a woman taboo because of its deathly danger and its involvement with blood, and thus its link with death. Menstruation likewise makes a woman taboo because of its involvement with blood. The Day of Atonement (Lev 16) dealt with the purification of the people as a whole and the associated purification of the sanctuary (which the people's taboos would compromise). It ensured that they were cleansed from the year's accumulated taboos so that these taboos did not make it impossible for God to associate with the people or to be present in the sanctuary.

The Scriptures don't make clear why purification offerings "work"; they just do. God says so. They are God's provision to solve the problem that taboo raises. There is a sense in which God raises the problem (by saying "Don't come into my presence when you are marked by death or sex"), but God also provides the solution. That gracious fact is made more remarkable by the way the First Testament can speak of God himself "making expiation" for human wrongdoing (e.g., Ezek 16:63; Ps 79:9).

The New Testament then takes the purification offering as suggesting a metaphor for understanding Jesus' death. It's as if it were a kind of sacrifice, whereby Jesus makes an offering of himself that effects purification for sin more generally, and on a once-for-all basis.

Jesus' Death as a Purification Offering

Thus God gave his Son *peri hamartias* (Rom 8:3). While *hamartia* is the regular Greek word for "sin," *peri hamartias* is also the standard Greek equivalent to the phrase "as a purification offering" (e.g., Lev 5:6-7); the Greek word thus has a parallel double meaning to Hebrew *ḥaṭṭā't*. The same significance of purification offering likely attaches to *hamartia* when Paul says, "the one who did not know *hamartia*, for us God made into *hamartia* so that we might become God's righteousness through him" (2 Cor 5:21). God gave his Son as a purification offering; God made Jesus a purification offering.

In Romans 7, and thus just before speaking of God giving his Son *peri hamartias*, Paul talks about sin as something we commit even though we don't really intend to.[114] God provides Jesus' death as an offering that deals with our pollution, as God provided the purification offering to deal with the Israelites' pollution. While Jesus had contact with corpses and with carriers of taboo and with sinners, evidently nothing of a moral kind that could make him taboo and unable to be in God's presence ever stuck to his person. He could therefore be an embodiment of the kind of offering that could deal with taboo.

So he "made purification for offenses" (Heb 1:3), and "the blood of Jesus, his Son, cleanses us from every offense. . . . If someone does offend, we have an advocate with the Father, Jesus, the Anointed One, the righteous one, and

---

[114]Dunn notes the link between Rom 7 and Rom 8:3 in *Christ and the Spirit*, 1:198-99.

he is the expiation [*hilasmos*] for our offenses" (1 Jn 1:7; 2:1-2). He is "the lamb of God who takes the world's sin" (Jn 1:29). Gentiles, too, have been brought near to God "through the blood of the Anointed One" (Eph 2:13). The reference to blood suggests that the passage works with the understanding of Jesus' death as a sacrifice that purifies. Like the First Testament idea of God making expiation for people, it is an extraordinary testimony to God's love and God's desire for us to be able to be in his presence.

In connection with Jesus' death, the New Testament focuses on the taint issuing from moral waywardness. The Corinthian church included people who had been sexually immoral, idolaters, greedy or swindlers, but they had been "washed, sanctified, made right, by the name of the Lord Jesus, the Anointed One, and by the Spirit of God" (1 Cor 6:9-11). God had set forth Jesus as "an expiation [*hilastērion*] through faith in his blood," and this action made redemption and reconciliation possible (Rom 3:25). It provided such people with cleansing. While God's nature made God forbearing, and this forbearance was an expression of God's righteousness or faithfulness, God's nature remained in tension with the thing that caused stain, and presenting Jesus as a means of expiation dealt with that issue.

In passages such as ones we have noted, KJV uses the word *propitiation* rather than *expiation*. A key difference is that one propitiates a person, but one expiates an offense. The idea of propitiation presupposes that God is angry with human beings and that they appease God's anger by means of sacrifice. We have noted how wrongdoing indeed makes God angry, but it is not sacrifice that deals with God's anger. Sacrifice does not relate to anger; hence Leviticus never refers to God's anger. God deals with anger in himself. Sacrifice relates to uncleanness.

Nor is it the case that a sacrificial animal carries the punishment that is due to its offerer; this idea "confuses Temple with Law-court, Altar with Gallows."[115] God carries wrongdoing himself. Sacrifice relates to cleansing; it removes the uncleanness that mars the good creation.[116] But the removal of the uncleanness does indeed make possible the relationship with God that

---

[115]J. S. Whale, *Victor and Victim* (Cambridge and New York: Cambridge University Press, 1960), 53. Cf. Thomas A. Bennett, "The Cross as the Labor of God" (PhD diss., Fuller Theological Seminary, 2015), 123-24.

[116]Colin E. Gunton, *The Actuality of Atonement* (Edinburgh: T&T Clark; Grand Rapids: Eerdmans, 1989), 119.

would otherwise be impossible, and in this sense there is not so much difference in effect between talking in terms of expiation or of propitiation.[117]

Sacrifice is thus not designed to bring about forgiveness of sins. It would perhaps be obvious to thinking Israelites (and to adherents of other religions) that such an idea would not make sense. How could sacrifice bring about forgiveness? Rather, by God's declaration a sacrifice could bring about purification from taboos. And the reality of finding release from constraint over coming into God's presence through the termination of the taboo by means of a sacrifice provides another way of understanding Jesus' death.

The rending of the temple veil at the moment of Jesus' death also symbolizes this release. Jesus' death is the sacrifice that generates our cleansing and means we can come into God's presence without compromising it. In the New Testament's revisionist interpretation of Leviticus, the errors that a sacrifice could deal with become our willful waywardness in relation to God and other people, the remission becomes release from the consequences of the waywardness, and the release comes about because Jesus' execution is reframed as a kind of sacrifice that can eliminate it.

Jesus Our Priest

Hebrews systematically expounds this way of seeing the significance of Jesus' death, nuancing it with the image of Jesus as the priest who offers the sacrifice as well as being the sacrifice itself. He could not be a regular priest, because the clan identity that qualified him to be a king ruled out his being a priest. He is a priest along the lines of Melkizedeq rather than of Aaron (Heb 7). While the First Testament does not speak of a coming, future priest, there were some hopes along those lines in Jesus' day, especially on the part of people such as the Qumran community, who saw the Jerusalem priesthood as apostate. It would then be possible to hold a dual expectation of Jesus along the lines of the picture of Moses and Aaron or Zerubbabel and Joshua (see Zech 4).

There is no indication that Jesus was understood in these terms during his ministry, though when he tells a disabled man, "Your sins are forgiven" (Mk 2:5), it is a priestly act. On that occasion, some of his listeners think he

---

[117]As Morris notes while arguing at length for the idea of propitiation (*Apostolic Preaching of the Cross*, 211).

is "blaspheming." He actually says, "The Man has authority on earth to forgive sins"; the evidence is his capacity to heal, to say to a disabled man, "Get up and go home," so that he can walk instead of being carried. It might also be a paradoxical pointer to his priestly authority that he assumes the power to make a declaration about who does not get forgiven (Mt 6:14; 12:31-32).

As a priest, he is able to rescue us completely or forever, because he always lives to intercede for us (Heb 7:25). Hebrews expounds the significance of Jesus as priest and as an offering in connection with seeking to deal with the pastoral issue of people not being sure they were forgiven (Heb 9:9, 14; 10:2, 22). Its point then is that the temple sacrifices could not take care of this matter (as people perhaps thought), whereas Jesus' death had done so.

The problem of not being sure you are forgiven is not a problem to which the First Testament refers, and the First Testament therefore has no provision for handling it. Or if it is a problem, its resolution lies in letting oneself be grasped by the facts about Yahweh's mercy and grace, which the story of Yahweh's relationship with Israel demonstrates and the story of Jesus confirms. But the First Testament does indicate that people could not go into the holiest place, and that the high priest went there only once each year, because the way in there had not yet been disclosed (Heb 9:7-8). The blood of bulls and goats couldn't take away sin, but Jesus' sacrifice did so; by one sacrifice he has forever brought to completion the people who are being made holy (Heb 9:14; 10:3, 14). So now we can have confidence and full assurance of faith about entering the holiest place, because our hearts are sprinkled so that we do not have a guilty conscience (Heb 10:19-22).

Hebrews thus addresses the needs of people who have a distressing problem about consciousness of sin. "They need to *feel* that they are forgiven." They know that Jesus died for them and that their coming to trust in Jesus brought them cleansing from their past sins. But what about the sins they continue to commit? Perhaps they thought they could solve their problem by combining their trust in Jesus with purification rites and the offering of sacrifices, or at least by associating with the Jewish community that lived in the context of the offering of these sacrifices and especially in the context of the Day of Atonement (which was effective for the whole community, wherever people lived). Actually, Hebrews says, the sacrificial system can't solve it. "They must be persuaded that, though the sacrifice of Jesus is unrepeatable, it continues to be effective to cope with their present consciousness of sin, and that there is a practical way of maintaining the sense of unhindered relationship with God."[118] For people aware that they fall to temptation, the good news is that Jesus knows about temptation. The fact that he did not fall to it does not stop him being sympathetic to people who do fall, and his death was like a sacrifice that could cleanse the consciences of such people. So we can approach God's gracious throne, at whose right hand Jesus sits, to find mercy and grace (Heb 4:14-16; cf. Heb 1:3, 13; 8:1; 10:12; 12:2).

Making Restitution

While an adulterer, or a drunk driver who had killed someone, might appropriately be aware of being unclean as a result of their action, and Jesus' dying for such a person could then provide cleansing, their action also places them under obligation to make some restitution in connection with their wrongdoing. A driver who has killed a family's breadwinner would be under obligation to help the family subsist. Twelve-step programs require people to meet with people they have wronged as a result of their addiction and to ask what they can do to make amends. An adulterer would have to look for ways of restoring his wife's self-respect and honor. In 1963 British politician John Profumo had to resign from his government post after an affair that might have imperiled national security. He spent the second half of his life as a volunteer with a charity in east London, initially with the job of cleaning toilets. By the end of his life, he had been restored to public honor. He had made restitution.

The offenses we commit not only place us in debt to the people we wrong; they also put us in debt to God. A wrong against another human being is also a wrong against God, in whose image that person is made. Treating things such as work or shopping or sex or career as god slights God more directly. Jesus' death offers restitution to God on our behalf in a way that can compensate for humanity's faithlessness.

---

[118]Barnabas Lindars, *The Theology of the Letter to the Hebrews* (Cambridge and New York: Cambridge University Press, 1991), 14, 59-60.

As well as the *ḥaṭṭā't*, which relates to people's need of purification in order to come into God's presence, Leviticus 4–5 describes a second kind of sacrifice, the *'āšām*. The term is often rendered in English as "guilt offering," but its distinctive significance is to make restitution for something that a person has done. Like the purification offering, its concern is not so much with deliberate moral wrongdoing as with an offense such as accidentally failing to tithe properly or failing to give testimony in court when you had something relevant to say. If you realize you have made a mistake in this connection, you have to put the matter right, and you also bring an offering to make up for the mistake.

The idea of a metaphorical restitution offering features in the vision of Yahweh's servant in Isaiah 52:13–53:12, which speaks of the servant making his life an *'āšām* (Is 53:10). Jesus' death, too, can then be seen as such an offering, which substitutes for the offering the people cannot make. Many modern translations have the servant carrying the "punishment" for our sin (Is 53:7), which suggests the idea that Jesus' death involved the "penal substitution" of his suffering for ours,[119] but this translation introduces an alien set of ideas into the chapter. KJV, for instance, has "chastisement" rather than "punishment." The chapter's point is not that God is punishing his servant instead of punishing his people. Its point is rather that the servant has been faithful to Yahweh and has not deserved affliction, as other people did, but has shared in their affliction. Indeed, they have treated him as distinctively unfaithful. He has been attacked and persecuted as the price of his ministry to them, at the hand of imperial powers and/or at the hand of Israel's own leaders. He has suffered beyond them because of them.

But in a strange way, the undeserved nature of his affliction opens up a new form or a new level of serving Yahweh for this servant. It gives him something he can offer to God. Both the imperial powers and the people they represent, and the leaders of Israel and the people they represent, need something to offer to God to compensate for their faithlessness. But their very faithlessness means that they have nothing to offer, and anyway they don't see the need to make such an offering because they have not come to see themselves as doing anything wrong and needing to try to make up for

---

[119]Cf. Martin, *2 Corinthians*, 131; Jeffery et al., *Pierced for Our Transgressions*, 52-67.

their waywardness. Yahweh's servant can offer God his faithfulness to God in fulfilling his costly ministry, with the possibility of its compensating for their faithlessness. Rather than being as sinful as or more sinful than they are, he is less so. He can make his undeserved affliction something he accepts as God's will, and he can make it into an offering of obedience to God, which might counteract the effect of the people's own rebelliousness on their relationship with God and compensate for it. Yahweh's servant can make his life an offering on their behalf that might counterbalance their wrongdoing, if God is willing for it to do so.

Jesus, then, knows that such an offering to God is required in connection with the restoration of Israel and with the implementing of God's reign and with Israel finding freedom to serve God. His lynching therefore need not imperil the arrival of God's reign. It will make it possible. He can offer God his whole faithful but persecuted life, culminating in his faithful and undeserved death, and that offering could compensate for the faithless life of as many people as cared subsequently to identify with his offering and let it count for them.[120]

Jesus makes this offering as one who did not acknowledge sin (2 Cor 5:21), in the sense of commit himself to it. He also makes it as God's own Son, so that his self-offering would have a qualitative value that could counterbalance all human wrongdoing. But the New Testament does not make this point, and we should likely not try to be mathematical about the way offerings work. In Leviticus, there is no suggestion that the bigger the offense, the bigger the offering. The Expiation Day observance makes the point clear; the offering of a goat deals with the people's shortcomings over an entire year. Likewise, the presupposition of Isaiah 53 is that one faithful person's willingness to pay the cost of their ministry might compensate for the faithlessness of their entire people.

Trespass

In its account of the *ʾāšām*, Leviticus also uses the word for sin and for the purification offering (*ḥaṭṭāʾt*), which links with how the different ideas about sacrifice and about the significance of Jesus' death bleed into each

---

[120]See Brant Pitre, *Jesus, Tribulation, and the End of the Exile* (Tübingen: Mohr; Grand Rapids: Baker, 2005).

other. The Septuagint likewise uses the expression *peri hamartias* ("as a purification offering") to refer to the restitution offering in Isaiah 53:10. Given
the significance of Isaiah 53 in helping the early church understand the
meaning of Jesus' death, it would not be surprising if the reference to *hamartia* in 2 Corinthians 5:21 specifically designated Jesus' execution as a
restitution offering as well as or instead of a purification offering.

KJV calls the *'āšām* a "trespass offering," which suggests a further insight.
The *'āšām* relates to wrongdoing that constitutes trespassing on God's rights
or honor. Jesus' self-offering on our behalf restored God's honor.[121] Human
wrongdoing involves failing to take God's rights seriously, and humanity
needs to make up for that failure. In that connection, God further expresses
his graciousness in authorizing the Levitical offerings to enable humanity to
offer compensation for trespassing on God's rights.

Jesus' life and death then constitute an offering that does so on a once-
for-all, worldwide scale, and God's providing for this offering witnesses
again to God's desire that humanity should be at one with him. In no way
did Jesus ever fail to treat God as God. Yet God let him be treated as an
embodiment of the opposite characteristic, an embodiment of trespass, and
provided him as an embodiment of the kind of offering that could deal with
trespass (2 Cor 5:21).

Our waywardness does dishonor God, and God's honor needs to be vindicated or satisfied. Anselm asks whether it is fitting for God to remit sin out
of mercy alone.[122] "For him the world is literally 'turned upside down' by sin,"
so that simple forgiveness does not solve the problem.[123] The underlying
concern of retributive justice is to restore order in the universe, "to restore
balance."[124] And even if God were happy to remit sin out of mercy alone, "as
long as a man does not restore what he owes God, he cannot be happy."[125] If
God simply forgives, he leaves us without a way of making restitution.[126]

---

[121]Cf. Joel B. Green and Mark D. Baker, *Recovering the Scandal of the Cross* (Downers Grove, IL:
InterVarsity Press, 2000), 20-22; Anthony C. Thiselton, *The Hermeneutics of Doctrine* (Grand
Rapids: Eerdmans, 2007), 362.
[122]Anselm, *Why God Became Man* 1.12.
[123]Weber, *Foundations of Dogmatics*, 2:212.
[124]See Augustine, *On Free Will* 3.9 (3.26); the phrase quoted comes from Vernon White, *Atonement
and Incarnation* (Cambridge and New York: Cambridge University Press, 1991), 94.
[125]Anselm, *Why God Became Man* 1.24.
[126]S. Mark Heim, *Saved from Sacrifice* (Grand Rapids and Cambridge, UK: Eerdmans, 2006), 315.

What God does in Jesus is reaffirm God's honor, by accepting the penalty for dishonoring it. In this respect "it was Anselm's great contribution to have understood sin as ultimately personal."[127]

To speak of Jesus making restitution to God is not to put God and Jesus on different sides.

> God and Jesus together submit themselves to human violence. Both suffer its results. Both reveal and overcome it. God does not require the death of the Son anymore than Jesus requires the helpless bereavement of the Father. Jesus' suffering is not required as an offering to satisfy God anymore than one member of a team undertaking a very dangerous rescue mission "requires" another dearly loved member to be in a place of peril or pain. They are constantly and consistently on the same side.[128]

"To destroy sin cost God His life in His Son."[129] Once more, "it takes the Trinity to make sense of the atonement."[130]

Seeing Jesus' submission to a martyr's death as a restitution offering helps us further in understanding how "justification" can work. God "set forth" Jesus as the one who died for us, "so that he might be both the one who acts aright and the one who puts a person right through faith in the Anointed One, Jesus" (Rom 3:25-26). While the explanation of atonement as at-one-ment corresponds to that word's etymology, one cannot say the same about the explanation that being justified makes the situation "just as if I'd never sinned." Yet that explanation does convey the significance of justification. Jesus' offering of himself to God as a restitution offering on our behalf transforms a situation in which we were guilty and were under an obligation that we could never fulfill. It makes adequate compensation for the offense. It is just as if we had never sinned. As our representative and substitute Jesus offers his perfect obedience as an offering that can compensate for our defiance and counteract its effects.[131] Thus "as by the

---

[127]Weber, *Foundations of Dogmatics*, 2:211.

[128]Heim, *Saved from Sacrifice*, 309.

[129]P. T. Forsyth, *The Justification of God* (London: Duckworth, 1916; New York: Scribner's, 1917), 183.

[130]Smail, *Forgotten Father*, 113.

[131]On the question whether the act of obedience was simply the submission to martyrdom or the obedience of the whole life, see, e.g., J. R. Daniel Kirk, "The Sufficiency of the Cross," *Scottish Bulletin of Evangelical Theology* 24 (2006): 36-64, 133-54.

disobedience of the one human being the many were made sinners, so through the obedience of the one the many were made *dikaioi*" (Rom 5:19). Another person cannot be punished for you; that doesn't work. But another person can make compensation for you, if you then identify with the offering they have made.

5.5 JESUS' DEATH: FREEING PEOPLE FOR A NEW SERVICE

Jesus' execution covers a further facet to the human predicament. As well as the question whether we have any understanding of what it means to live in love and the question whether God in his justified anger could ever relate to us and the question whether the stain and debt of our waywardness could ever be resolved, there is the question whether we could ever be free to serve God. "Sin is a slavery, and slavery is not abolished by appeals to follow a good example. What is required is a setting free, an act of recreation, or redemption." Humanity's problem is "a disrupted relationship with the creator" and consequently "an *objective* bondage, pollution and disorder in personal and social life."[132] But "God invades creation in the death of Jesus Christ, releases human beings from the grasp of Sin, and transforms those believers into God's own children who await their ultimate final redemption as slaves of righteousness."[133] Acting on God's behalf, Jesus submits to the powers that enslave us, pays the penalty that they demand, and thereby ends their hold on us. We are now free to live for God rather than for sin, the Torah, ourselves and death. Our challenge is to live in light of the facts concerning what God did through Jesus.

Servitude

Humanity was in servitude. People were in bondage to sin; they could not fulfill the expectations in relation to God and their neighbor that they recognized. The Jewish people were in bondage to the Torah insofar as they assumed that doing what the Torah said was the foundation of their life. Gentiles could make a parallel assumption by seeing the performance of right acts as the foundation of their life, so that they were in an equivalent servitude. Jews and Gentiles were in bondage to themselves; they did what

---

[132]Gunton, *Actuality of Atonement*, 160.
[133]Beverly Roberts Gaventa, "The Cosmic Power of Sin in Paul's Letter to the Romans," *Interpretation* 58 (2004): 229-40 (on 239).

their lower nature suggested rather than fulfilling those expectations. And they were in bondage to death, because death follows from failing to live by God's expectations. "The wages of sin is death" (Rom 6:23). God created humanity to enjoy eternal life through eating from the life tree, but the first human beings forfeited that possibility through preferring a different fruit, and that act had irreversible implications.

It is in particular through the command "You are not to covet" that the Torah takes people into bondage (Rom 7:7).[134] Telling Adam not to eat from the tree was designed for humanity's good, for people's protection and maturity, but it enabled the snake to draw attention to the desirability of its fruit. If God had not forbidden it, the snake could not have encouraged an illicit coveting and taking. Sin would have been dead, incapable of doing anything (Rom 7:8). God's command enabled it to spring to life.

Jesus' execution released people from their fourfold bondage to sin, to the Torah, to themselves and to death. In his life as a whole, he was the one person who totally submitted to God's expectations. The commitment of religious people to the Torah made them oppose Jesus because they perceived that he threatened the Torah's position as they understood it. He was going to terminate the operation of the entire edifice of their faith built on the Torah, and they liked that edifice.

In this sense the Torah stirred up their passions to kill Jesus. He was the one human being who could have partaken of the life tree, but instead he submitted to a death tree. He submitted to sin in accepting its penalty even though he was not liable to pay it. His once-for-all, undeserved submission meant the termination of these various authorities over him. And people who identify with him share in that freeing. It was once the case that the expectations laid down by God could say to us, "By your own submission, you belong to me." Sin could say to us, "You belong to me; you can't resist me." Our lower nature could say to us, "You belong to me; I control you." Death could say to us, "You belong to me; your life is forfeit." It is no longer so; God was willing to let Jesus' submission count for other people.

Believers are free from the Torah because they "have been put to death in relation to the Torah through the person of the Anointed One" (Rom 7:3-4).

---

[134]See further the paragraphs under "The Lower Nature" in section 3.6 above.

It used to be the case that the Torah aroused sinful passions in us. "Challenged by the law," which claims us for God and for our neighbor, our self-centeredness "recognizes that it is being called into question and attacked, and so seeks all the more forcefully to defend itself."[135] Paul can see this dynamic in the way he used to relate to the Torah and the way his fellow Jews do—both Jews who believe in Jesus and Jews who don't.[136] In practice, the Torah leads people astray.

When we are no longer under obligation to it, it cannot do so. And because we have paid its penalty (that is, because Jesus paid it for us) we are under no obligation to the Torah. Of course, much of the Torah expresses obligations that applied to Gentiles as well as Jews and that still apply to both, but they do so because of their content not because they are part of the Torah in its capacity as integral to the relationship between God and Israel.

In the terms of A. G. Greimas's actantial model for understanding how narratives work, God (the sender) was concerned to give life (the object) to the people of God (the receiver), and he commissioned the Torah (the subject) as the means of giving this gift, but humanity's lower nature and sin itself (the opponent) rendered the Torah incapable of doing so. God therefore gave the Son as an alternative means of achieving the aim through defeating these two, which in turn made it possible for the Torah to function. God, that is, made possible the fulfilling of the Torah's proper requirement for the people of God (now defined as those who belong to Jesus), with the Torah and the Spirit as the means of doing so (Rom 8:1-4).[137]

Paying a Penalty

So we had come short of God's splendor, but we have been "put in the right [dikaioō] freely, by his grace, through the redemption [apolytrōsis] that comes through the Anointed One, Jesus" (Rom 3:24). Redeeming and putting right (apolytrōsis and dikaiōsis) are both "fundamentally liberative"

---

[135]C. E. B. Cranfield, *A Critical and Exegetical Commentary on the Epistle to the Romans* (Edinburgh: T&T Clark, 1975), 338.

[136]Cf. Dunn's comments, *Romans*, 1:364-65.

[137]See N. T. Wright, *The Climax of the Covenant* (Edinburgh: T&T Clark, 1991; Minneapolis: Fortress, 1992), 204-8. For Greimas's own exposition of his model, see his *Structural Semantics* (Lincoln: University of Nebraska Press, 1983).

notions.[138] When God "justifies" us, it means he makes things right for us and frees us from our servitude to those powers that held us.[139]

It is then because people have been put in the right in this way, made *dikaioi*, that they need no longer to be barred from the life tree. They can share in Jesus' resurrection. "When you were dead people in connection with your transgressions and the uncircumcision of your lower nature, God brought you to life with him. He graced all your transgressions for you. He erased the record concerning us with its decrees, which stood against us. He removed it. He nailed it to the cross" (Col 2:13-14). Jesus' death was the means whereby the penalty for our offenses was paid. It is as if a notice listing them was fixed to the cross.

While speaking of Jesus being punished instead of us gives the wrong impression, he did pay the penalty for our freedom. "He, the innocent One, bears in his own body and being those penal consequences of man's ill-doing and guilt which are his own judgment upon sin. Judgment and penalty are one and the same fact in Christ crucified."[140] We were dead because of our transgressions, so the key to our resurrection was their pardon. God erased the record of our offenses through the process whereby Jesus submitted to death. He thereby also terminated the authority of the supernatural powers through which (tradition said) the Torah was given (Gal 3:19). In paying the penalty for our wrongdoing, Jesus became a curse for us (Gal 3:13). That expression involves a metonymy,[141] as when the Scriptures say that Abraham would be a blessing or that God's servant would be a covenant (Gen 12:2; Is 42:6). Jesus became someone cursed in that he experienced the curse that comes on covenant breakers.

Thus when Jesus died, he died to sin (Rom 6:10), on behalf of people who would identify with him. He personally owed no obligation to sin, but through choosing to identify with us he was in a position to pay the penalty that sin had a right to demand of humanity. The penalty was death, the inability to eat from the life tree and thereby enter into a transformed life that would last forever. Jesus underwent death and thus died

---

[138]Campbell, *Deliverance of God*, 657, 668.
[139]On "Justification," see section 5.2 above.
[140]Whale, *Victor and Victim*, 67.
[141]Ronald Y. K. Fung, *The Epistle to the Galatians* (Grand Rapids: Eerdmans, 1988), 148.

to sin. People who identify with him by being baptized share in the effects of that death and no longer need to die to sin. They have already done so, through their association with Jesus, because his dying to sin counts for them (Rom 6:2). "One man died for all; therefore all died" (2 Cor 5:14). He was our proxy,[142] acting on our behalf and in our place; the preposition "for" (*hyper*) suggests both representation and substitution. The point is underlined by the reminder that Jesus' execution has been portrayed before our very eyes, as if we were witnesses of the event itself (Gal 3:1). This portrayal made us realize that Jesus really had died for us, so that in effect we also died.

So when we are baptized we are baptized into Jesus' death. It is a kind of drowning, a kind of dying, and a kind of burying. It implies a radical break.[143] It means we affirm that his death to sin counted for us as our death to sin. It also means that his resurrection (not just resuscitation) to a new kind of life counts for us. We, too, come out of baptism with a new life, a new freedom, a new citizenship. The old person, the person we once were, has died (Rom 6:6). The "old self" is the whole person we once were, not just a part of us, and the "body of sin" likewise denotes the individual sinful person in their embodiedness. We then start a new walk. While we will still "die" in due course, our death will be more like the ones that Adam and Eve might have died if they had not acted as they did—their death would simply have meant a transition to a new life. The resurrection life we start will be consummated at the coming resurrection, but it begins now.

The penalty for rebellion was death; it would be logically impossible for God and humanity to live together when humanity was living in rebellion. So in Jesus, God personally paid that penalty. The one who was supremely committed and obedient let himself be treated as one who was supremely rebellious and thus be killed. But the fact that there was no basis for treating him that way meant there was no basis for death holding onto him, as it could reasonably hold onto everyone else. And people who associate themselves with him then share in the surplus value of his commitment and death.

---

[142]Martin's term, *2 Corinthians*, 131.

[143]Cf. Dietrich Bonhoeffer, *Discipleship* (repr., Minneapolis: Fortress, 2003), 207.

Living in Light of the Facts

In the year I was born, during the Second World War, my uncle died in combat in order that I might grow up free from Nazi oppression. He died on my behalf and in my place, though it would be years before I could be aware of his paying this price on my behalf and thus come to affirm that he indeed acted as my proxy. His death meant that in effect I died; it was as if I had taken part in that campaign and paid the price for my freedom. Jesus' death had analogous significance for all who would in due course become aware of his having acted in that way as their representative and in their place.

Yet believers can fail to identify with what Jesus did, and think and behave as if they are not free, but then they are not living in accordance with the facts. Their task is to look at themselves in light of the facts and live in light of them by enjoying their freedom.

On June 19 my mostly African American congregation celebrates the emancipation of slaves. While there are people in the congregation whose great-grandparents personally gained their freedom through the proclamation read on June 19, 1865, everyone celebrates the event. The freedom of all African Americans issues from Lincoln's proclamation, which reached Galveston on that day (two and a half years after it was issued). If anyone were now to try to treat an African American as a slave, they can be referred to that event, even though it did not apply directly to this present would-be slave owner or present potential slave. The African American community continues to celebrate the event in order to build up its own awareness and the awareness of the white community that those days really are over and that African Americans cannot be treated as a subordinate or inferior group. An event that happened in the nineteenth century has decisive importance for the present lives of people who identify with it.

Analogously, on July 4 my neighbors celebrate the moment when "they" gained "their" independence from Pharaoh Britain. As a British person I can join in the barbecue but not in the words that implicitly go with it. But even for my neighbors there is something paradoxical about saying that "we" gained "our" independence. They are speaking as if they were involved in something that happened in the eighteenth century; furthermore, many of them trace their ancestry to ethnic groups that were not even represented in that victorious triumph. Yet they still say "we," as if they were involved. They can do so because they have identified with the event and do enjoy the fruits of it. They are like foreigners who join Israel and henceforth join the celebration of Passover (Ex 12:43-49). Whereas I can be deported from the United States, if someone working for the immigration service were to attempt to deport someone who is a citizen, they can show their citizenship papers, establish their status and elude deportation.

In some ways US culture still thinks and behaves as if it is has not quite escaped Pharaoh Britain; its relationship with Europe is that of a young adult who is still not quite at ease about relating to its parents in adult-adult terms. But while the United States is still a postcolonial culture, it is actually its own nation. An event that happened more than two centuries ago has a decisive affect on the present lives of people who identify with it. As African Americans died to slavery that day in 1863, US citizens more generally had died to the British Empire that day in 1776. As African Americans identify with the proclamation of 1863 and participate in its freedom, people in the United States who become citizens identify with the victory of 1776 and participate in its freedom.

It is possible to fail so to identify with what Jesus did and to think and behave as if you are not free, but then you are not living in accordance with the facts. The people who belong to the Anointed One, Jesus, have executed the lower nature with its passions and desires; through Jesus' execution the world has been executed as far as they are concerned, and they have been executed as far as the world is concerned (Gal 6:14). "The world" here signifies a set of attitudes that seeks to impress other people by one's religious practice, to avoid being persecuted because of the message about Jesus' execution, and to exult in a form of religion that is not liable to that persecution. Jesus' execution and resurrection exposed those attitudes as stupid and thus robbed them of their power. It established that the only reality that was worth affirming was the reality of new creation. That rule is the one worth walking by, and people who walk by that rule are the real Israel (Gal 6:12-16). Thus within a few verses the New Testament can affirm that believers "have shed the old self with its actions and put on new" but can then go on to urge them to "put on" attitudes such as compassion (Col 3:10-12), as it can declare that believers have died with the Anointed One but also that they must take up their cross.

Overcoming the Powers That Hold People

Jesus brought about our liberation from sin, the Torah, death and our own lower nature, by the paradoxical tactic of submitting to them and thereby defeating them. He won a victory over these powers and more. When God freed the ungodly from their servitude to those powers that held them, he destroyed these powers, emptied them of their authority. When he nailed the record of our wrongdoing to the cross, he "disarmed the rules and authorities. He showed them up boldly. He triumphed over them through it" (Col 2:15). Jesus came to overcome sin, the Torah, death, evil, Satan, and the principalities and powers that operate in the heavens. He came to do so as God's agent, in his life, his death and his resurrection. Evil is "an appalling and irrational corruption of the good creation. . . . The cross of Jesus does not serve to explain such evil, but to act: to break its power by undergoing its concentrated opposition."[144]

The passage that "is perhaps more often quoted by the Fathers than any other New Testament text"[145] is that Jesus became a human being "so that by means of death he might break the power of the one who holds the power of death, that is the devil, and free those who through all their life were held in slavery by the fear of death" (Heb 2:14-15). What is this fear of death, and how did Jesus win such a victory?

In the First Testament there is little fear of death, only a resentment at it when it comes before a person's time, but maybe in New Testament times (as in the modern West) "through fear of death many men will consent to do things that nothing else could compel them to do."[146] For the readers of Hebrews "fear of death could also and very naturally be accompanied by fear of imperial edicts."[147] Turning death into something that people need no longer fear would deprive the devil of this aspect of his power. The martyrs "won over him through the blood of the lamb and through the

---

[144]Gunton, *Actuality of Atonement*, 84.
[145]Gustaf Aulén, *Christus Victor* (London: SPCK, 1931), 90.
[146]F. F. Bruce, *The Epistle to the Hebrews* (Grand Rapids: Eerdmans, 1964; London: Marshall, 1965), 51.
[147]Robert P. Gordon, *Hebrews* (Sheffield: Sheffield Academic Press, 2000), 19.

message of their testimony [*martyria*]; they did not love their life to the death" (Rev 12:11).

It was when Jesus was lifted up from the earth in being crucified and thus glorified that the prince of this world was thrown out (Jn 12:31-32). Thus he achieved that for which the Son of God appeared, the destruction of the devil's work (1 Jn 3:8). He overcame the devil in a comprehensive legal victory. The devil is bound to lose every case from now on.

The image recalls Zechariah's vision of a court case in which the Adversary accuses the high priest Joshua of being too tainted to fulfill his office (Zech 3). He has a point. There are several bases on which the Adversary might appeal for a guilty verdict, and Yahweh does not dispute them but simply declares the intention to pardon and cleanse.

Jesus' submission to execution spells out the rationale for that declaration. He accepts the guilty verdict on humanity's behalf and submits to the consequences of it, so that they no longer need to do so. There is no way the Adversary can win a case against believers. They too are guilty, but their record has already been nailed to the cross. Michael has defeated the dragon, and he has been thrown down from heaven to earth (Rev 12:7-12). The battle and defeat mean that the accuser can no longer lay charges against believers. They can now give testimony to the fact that Jesus has died for them and satisfied any claim the devil had. It may not mean they save their earthly lives; the power of the dragon on earth may lead to their losing them. But they can be untroubled by that possibility because they know that death is not the end.

The victory of Jesus brings with it the declaration that God reigns; the idea of God's reign and the idea of winning the victory over evil and resistance are closely related.[148] It was when his disciples went about proclaiming that God's reign had arrived and exorcising demons that Jesus declared that he had seen Satan fall like lightning from heaven (Lk 10:18). His achievement is thus in continuity with God's action in the First Testament, as creation and exodus involved a divine victory over evil and resistance. It is also in keeping with promises in the First Testament that God's future action will

---

[148]Cf. Gunton, *Actuality of Atonement*, 59.

involve such a victory (Is 27:1; Daniel).[149] So Jesus initiated a thousand-year binding of Satan (Rev 20:1-3).[150]

Victory Over the World and Its Scapegoating Instinct

Jesus refused to acknowledge the supernatural powers that exercise significant authority over human lives, so they killed him. But in letting them do so, he exposed them as less than what they claimed, and he thus triumphed over them and disarmed them. The church's job is to proclaim that it is so and to avoid getting seduced by them.[151]

> The irreducible fact about Jesus is that he was executed. Yet he did not represent an armed threat to the existing order. He broke no civil or criminal laws. He violated religious laws and customs regarding the Sabbath, hand-washing, and holiness, but in every case the issue hung on interpretation, and no doubt some rabbis would have supported him; at least they would not have condemned him to death. He mainly taught, healed and exorcised. Why then was he such a threat that he had to be killed? . . . They had to kill him, for Jesus represented the most intolerable threat ever placed against the spirituality, values, and arrangements of the Domination System.[152]

The "domination system" is the hierarchical structure of communal life whereby some authorities and people hold sway over others and use violence to do so. The expression is a way of speaking about the "world" with its elemental forces and rules (Col 2:20).[153] "The city of this world . . . holds nations in enslavement, but is itself dominated by that very lust of domination."[154] Jesus' death made it possible for people to be in control of the world's forces instead of being dominated by forces such as technology, fashion, sport, racism and sexism.[155] Jesus declares that the moment when God will reign has arrived. The characteristics of God's reign are a present reality now that

---

[149]Cf. ibid., 60-61.
[150]See further section 8.3 below.
[151]Cf. John Howard Yoder, *The Politics of Jesus*, 2nd ed. (Grand Rapids: Eerdmans; Carlisle, UK: Paternoster, 1993), 144-47, 150, following H. Berkhof, *Christ and the Powers* (Scottdale, PA: Herald, 1962).
[152]Walter Wink, *Engaging the Powers* (Philadelphia: Fortress, 1986), 109, 110.
[153]Ibid., 157. See further the paragraphs under "The World" in section 3.6 above.
[154]Augustine, *City of God* 1, preface.
[155]See Karl Barth, *The Christian Life: Church Dogmatics IV, 4: Lecture Fragments* (Grand Rapids: Eerdmans, 1981), 227-30; cf. Gunton, *Actuality of Atonement*, 182-83.

Jesus has come. So believers are not to live as people subject to the world's rules, because they are no longer "living in the world" (Col 2:20).

The devil thought he could defeat God by sidetracking Jesus (e.g., Mt 4:1-11) or getting him killed; he made use of one of the disciples to that end (Lk 22:3; Jn 13:2, 27). But God turned his action into his own defeat rather than a victory. The devil used people's instinct for scapegoating; Jesus was scapegoated by his own people.[156] But "God made that occasion of scapegoating sacrifice (what those who killed Jesus were doing) an occasion of overcoming scapegoating violence (what God was doing)."

The effect of the event was parallel to the one involving Joseph, who was scapegoated by his brothers but who could see that God was using their scapegoating instinct as the means of keeping his people alive (Gen 50:20). Or it was again like the event involving Yahweh's servant (Isa 52:13–53:12), who was being scapegoated by his fellow exiles but was willing to turn their scapegoating into an offering he could make to God. "The sacrificing of Jesus was the work of sin, but the overcoming of that scapegoating death is the work of God."[157]

Then, "by resurrection Jesus is cleared of the scapegoat charges against him. But the resurrection also acquits those who scapegoated him" because they have failed and because he declines to press charges. "How can God be justified unless God sides with the unanimous victim, unless God vindicates and restores the scapegoat." But then, "if God vindicates the sacrificed, . . . how can God be justified in saving the guilty, i.e., the victimizers? . . . If God is to do justice for victims, how can God fail to do justice against their persecutors?"[158] "He was delivered up for our transgressions and raised for our being treated as in the right" (Rom 4:24).

Bringing Them Back So They Can Serve Another Master

Because Jesus died to sin, self, death and the Torah, and therefore they as a matter of fact have also so died, believers are free and can decline to let sin, self, death and the Torah exercise authority over them. They are free

---

[156]Schneiders, "Lamb of God and the Forgiveness of Sin(s) in the Fourth Gospel," 2. On the framework of thinking, see René Girard, *Violence and the Sacred* (Baltimore and London: Johns Hopkins University Press, 1977).

[157]Heim, *Saved from Sacrifice*, xii, 123, 310.

[158]Ibid., 146, 311.

positively to look for what right living implies of them—to praise, to love, to serve. Indeed, they must do so. Sin must not reign in their mortal bodies; they can and must let God reign in them (Rom 6:12-13). They are not under the Torah, in the sense of being subject to its demands and condemnation, but under grace. They are in a loved and gracious relationship with God because Jesus has died for them. Sin will not have the power to rule over them; they are "free to fight against sin's usurped power, and to demonstrate their true allegiance."[159]

In their freedom they can now do what they could not do before, surrender their lives to God. They are in a position to respond to Jesus' self-giving by determining to live in the same generous way (2 Cor 5:15). Because they have paid its penalty (that is, because Jesus paid it for them) they are under no obligation to the Torah and are in a position to be committed to another. Having expounded the nature of salvation by grace and by faith, the Heidelberg Catechism asks, "But doth not this doctrine make wild and careless folk?" It answers, "No, for it is impossible that those who are implanted into Christ by true faith should not bring forth the fruit of thanksgiving."[160]

Paul does not refer very often to forgiveness; his interest does not focus on release from the guilt contracted by former sins. "The important thing for Paul is release from *sinning*, release from the power of sin."[161] Sin is now "the impossible possibility."[162] "There is no *legitimate room* in the New Testament for the continuation of our sin.[163] In this sense, a person is not *simul justus et peccator.*[164] The formula should be *tunc peccator—nunc justus*: once a sinner, now made right. The believer does not remain a sinner, even though sin does continue.[165] Augustine is closer to Paul. "That every Christian

---

[159]Cranfield, *Romans*, 319.

[160]Cf. Barth, *CD* IV, 1:642.

[161]Bultmann, *Theology of the New Testament*, 1:287.

[162]J. Christiaan Beker, *Paul the Apostle* (Philadelphia: Fortress, 1980), 215.

[163]Cf. G. C. Berkouwer, *Sin* (Grand Rapids: Eerdmans, 1971), 591.

[164]See the comments in section 5.2 above under "Carrying Human Wrongdoing"; and the discussion in James F. McCue, "*Simul iustus et peccator* in Augustine, Aquinas, and Luther," *Journal of the American Academy of Religion* 48 (1980): 81-96.

[165]Cf. the argument between Hans Windisch and Rudolf Bultmann in Windisch, *Taufe und Sünde im ältesten Christentum* (Tübingen: Mohr, 1908); Bultmann, "Das Problem der Ethik bei Paulus," *Zeitschrift für die neutestamentliche Wissenschaft und die Kunde der älteren Kirche* 23 (1924): 123-40; Windisch, "Das Problem des paulinischen Imperativs," *Zeitschrift für die neutestamentliche*

remains a sinner is clear (though for Augustine that is always a secondary affirmation)," but the sins Augustine speaks of are "imperfections, trivialities, something very different from Luther's conception of the ineradicable egoism of all human beings, even Christians."[166]

Jesus' execution thus gains freedom for people, but it does not simply set them free to do as they like. It redeems them, which means transferring them from one service to another. Jesus paid a price for them, which means they come to belong to him as the one who paid the price. He becomes their Master, and they serve him instead of serving those various other masters.[167] They experience what one might call negative liberty; they are no longer under those oppressive authorities. They do not experience positive liberty, a freedom to do what they like, to take control of their own lives with a view to their self-realization,[168] though paradoxically their new service is itself a kind of liberation.[169] Jesus is like a lamb that paid for people by its death and that thus made it possible for them to be "a kingdom and priests on the earth for our God," like Israel (Rev 5:6, 9-10).

Redemption and Ransom

Jesus came to give his life as a ransom or redemption price for many (Mk 10:45). God had originally redeemed Israel from servitude in Egypt; in effect Israel needed redeeming again. The songs of Mary and Zechariah presuppose that all is not well for Israel in their day and that they need to be redeemed, to be delivered, to be rescued—so that they can serve God without fear (Lk 1:68-74). Jesus' language recalls the description of God's servant as one who "gives his life" in a way that will benefit "many" (Is 53:10, 11), but he speaks in terms of a ransom or redemption price (*lytron*; in Hebrew, a *kōper* or a *pədût*) rather than a purification offering or restitution

---

Wissenschaft und die Kunde der älteren Kirche 23 (1924): 265-81; cf. Beker, *Paul the Apostle*, 216; and cf. Bonhoeffer, *Discipleship*, 263.

[166]McCue, "*Simul iustus et peccator* in Augustine, Aquinas, and Luther," 83-84. He refers to Augustine, *On Nature and Grace* 45 [xxxviii] (*NPNF* 1, 5:136).

[167]Cf. E. P. Sanders, *Paul and Palestinian Judaism* (London: SCM Press; Philadelphia: Fortress, 1977), e.g., 497-99.

[168]For the distinction between negative and positive liberty, see Isaiah Berlin, "Two Concepts of Liberty," repr. in his *The Proper Study of Mankind* (New York: Farrar, Straus, Giroux; London: Chatto, 1997), 191-242; cf. Campbell, *Deliverance of God*, 65.

[169]See further the paragraphs under "Fulfilling the Torah" in section 7.1 below.

offering.[170] Jesus' way of speaking provides another instance of the way the New Testament's language takes up metaphors in an informal, intuitive and artless way, rather than a disciplined, strict and fastidious one. One cannot infer too much from an isolated phrase. The New Testament is quite happy to mix metaphors.[171]

Paul speaks similarly in declaring that we are "put right [*dikaioō*] with God freely, by his grace, through the redemption [*apolytrōsis*] that comes through the Anointed One, Jesus, whom God set forth as a means of expiation [*hilastērion*] through faith, by means of his blood" (Rom 3:24-25). Fourth Maccabees 17:21-22 sees the death of the people who gave their lives in Judah's rebellion against Antiochus IV as martyrdom and as such sees it as a substitute life (*antipsychon*; compare *antilytron* in 1 Tim 2:6) and a means of expiation (2 Maccabees 6:12-16; cf. 2 Maccabees 7:37-38, without the sacrificial terminology).[172] Paul speaks in such terms in describing Jesus' death.[173]

The Scriptures do use the notion of redemption with more precise connotations than it has come to have in ordinary Western speech or in theology.[174] In Western culture, redemption often means recovering from loss or from the consequences of bad choices, getting one's life back on track, and it often denotes someone finding their own redemption. In the Scriptures, redemption has to be brought about by someone else. It denotes releasing people from someone or something that has bound or controlled them; and a ransom or redemption price is the payment a person might make to buy someone's freedom or life when their life is forfeit for some reason (e.g., Ex 21:30; 30:12; 35:31-32; Ps 49:8-9 [MT 9-10]; Prov 6:35; 13:8). A ransom can also denote an action that acknowledges God's right to take possession of the firstborn in a family; it implies giving something to God in their place.

The First Testament does not identify anyone to whom Yahweh paid the price when he redeemed or ransomed Israel, and the New Testament does

---

[170]See the comments in section 5.4 above.
[171]James W. McClendon, *Systematic Theology: Doctrine* (Nashville: Abingdon, 1994), 226.
[172]But David Seeley (*The Noble Death* [Sheffield, UK: JSOT, 1989]) argues that the vicarious and expiatory elements in the Maccabees account are subordinate to the idea that the Maccabees set an example for later Jews.
[173]Campbell suggests a common resonance with Gen 22 (*Deliverance of God*, 647-56).
[174]For the latter, cf. Morris, *Apostolic Preaching of the Cross*, 11.

not identify anyone to whom Jesus paid the ransom or redemption price for people. Church fathers occasionally assumed that it was the devil,[175] which is a less outrageous idea than it might at first seem. People are in bondage to the devil until Jesus frees them. Yet the New Testament is reticent with such statements, and the point about the metaphor lies in the commitment expressed in bringing about the people's release and the success in doing so.

Yahweh had given Egypt as a ransom price to get the Israelites out of Egypt (Is 43:3)—that is, he had given up any claim on Egypt in this connection. He had redeemed the Israelites from there (*pādâ*, Deut 9:26) and would redeem them from other experiences of bondage (Ps 44:26 [MT 27]). He has redeemed them in the sense of restored them (*gā'al*; e.g., Ex 15:13; Is 43:1). This verb has a further connotation: it suggests someone taking action on behalf of a person in their extended family. Such a redeemer or restorer might pay a debt and thereby free a person who was in servitude as a result of economic difficulties. The verb draws attention to the relationship that is expressed in the paying of a price as well as in the action. So Jesus acts as our guardian or next of kin (or brother: Heb 2:11-17) in treating us as members of his family and making it possible for us to be free people again.

Redemption and Covenant

The predicament from which people are redeemed need not be their fault. It may not have issued from their sin; it may have issued from other people's oppressiveness. But the redemption can involve delivering people from sin (Ps 130:8), as was the case when God redeemed people from Babylon (Is 50:2). It then meant forgiving them and getting them out of the mess they had got into through their wrongdoing. So it is with Jesus' act of redemption: "Through the Anointed One we have redemption, by means of his blood, the remission of errors" (Eph 1:7). God qualified us to share in what belonged to the saints in the realm of light, by rescuing us from the realm where darkness rules and transferring us to the realm where Jesus reigns. Through him we thus have redemption; and redemption can be equated with the

---

[175]See, e.g., Origen's comment on Ex 15:16 (*Homilies on Genesis and Exodus* [Washington, DC: Catholic University of America Press, 1982], 295-96); but this idea is more an incidental or homiletic comment (subordinate to the idea that Christ defeated the devil) than a systematic theory (cf. Rashdall, *Idea of Atonement*, 259-61).

forgiveness of sins (Col 1:13-14). Our being forgiven is the means of our redemption.

Redemption, rescue and forgiveness then all link with covenant. Yahweh redeemed Israel from Egypt because of a covenant commitment to his people, and his act of rescue issued in a new covenant at Sinai. Jesus came to restore Israel, which involved granting it forgiveness and freedom, and his act of rescue issued in a new covenant. Yahweh's action in redeeming Israel from Egypt came to draw people outside Israel to acknowledge Yahweh, and Israel's restoration would naturally include the recognition of Yahweh by the rest of the world. Genesis, the Psalms and Isaiah emphasize the point. Israel didn't want this restoration on Jesus' terms, and the world didn't want to be so drawn, so they killed him. Jesus is there entirely for humanity, yet for that very reason he collides fatally with humanity.[176] But God raised him from death because God could not tolerate this killing.

A covenant is sealed by a sacrifice. Two sacrifices are especially significant in connection with the achievement of redemption, though the New Testament again allows their significance to mingle and allows the idea of expiation to interweave with them. In Exodus, the first sacrifice is that at Passover. Once more, the significance of the sacrifice is hard for Western thinking to articulate, because it presupposes ideas with which a traditional culture was at home and which the Scriptures could take for granted and do not articulate.

The Passover sacrifice draws attention to the fact that blood is about to be spilt, and it safeguards against the offerers being the victims of the blood-shedding (Ex 12). Yahweh intends to act in judgment against people who have been resisting his purpose and holding onto his son and to do so by taking their sons. But where a family kills a lamb and daubs its blood on their door, this blood will be a sign that a death has already occurred, and it will protect them from any further blood-shedding. Jesus' death has an effect like that of the Passover offering. The breaking of his body and the spilling of his blood achieve something analogous to (but more spectacular than) what the original Passover sacrifice achieved (Mk 14:12-26). Jesus is our Passover sacrifice—and therefore we must live as people whom he has redeemed (1 Cor 5:7-8).

---

[176]Weber, *Foundations of Dogmatics*, 2:192.

Jesus' death is also like the subsequent sacrifice at Sinai that sealed the Sinai covenant (Heb 8–9). As an aspect of covenant making, killing the animal involves a self-curse. It is an acted prayer that one may experience what the animal experiences if one fails to keep one's covenant commitment; hence the spattering of the altar and the people with blood (Ex 24). Both Yahweh and the people are implicated in this prayer. By offering bulls as a sacrifice, Moses was the mediator of the Sinai covenant.

By offering himself as a sacrifice, Jesus is the mediator of a more spectacular new covenant. It is established on better promises, of a resurrection to come. Jesus was able to go into the most holy place (in heaven), on the basis of his sacrifice of himself, thus "obtaining eternal redemption [*lytrōsis*]." His dying brought about "redemption [*apolytrōsis*] from the transgressions under the first covenant," so that "the people who are called could receive the promise of the eternal inheritance" (Heb 9:12, 15). As well as commemorating the Passover sacrifice, then, the Lord's Meal commemorates Jesus' death as the means by which the new covenant is sealed (1 Cor 11:23-25). "The shed blood is a sign that God has proved this covenantal faithfulness precisely by undergoing the sanctions, legal and relational, for covenantal disobedience."[177]

"God transforms the murder of his emissary into a deed of his *faithfulness* to Israel (in biblical terms, covenant); he turns the death of his emissary, planned and brought about by men, into the establishment of *definitive and irrevocable faithfulness* to Israel (in biblical terms, new covenant) and thus preserves his claim on the chosen people of God."[178] He has freed it so that it can serve him.

5.6 JESUS' RESURRECTION

Jesus, who was "born of the seed of David in terms of the flesh," was "designated son of God with power in terms of the holy spirit through his raising from the dead people" (Rom 1:3-4). The statement about his birth refers to a necessary but not a sufficient qualification for someone to be designated God's Anointed One: he was born of the right line. That fact is a fleshly thing, an indispensable physical reality, but only a physical reality. Ironically, Jesus

---

[177]Vanhoozer, "Atonement in Postmodernity," 398.
[178]Gerhard Lohfink, *Jesus and Community* (Philadelphia: Fortress, 1984), 25.

seems not to have been physically born of David's line; it is his relationship with his adoptive father that makes him a descendant of David. But adoptive parenthood is as valid as physical parenthood. Jesus really was part of Joseph's fleshly family and was one flesh and blood with him.

Jesus' resurrection is a sign that his submission to the powers that enslave us has been successful. It signifies his vindication, his exaltation, his victory, his being put in a position of authority in the heavens. When he ascends there, he takes with him the people who identify with him. In spirit they live in the presence of God, citizens of this world and of that other world, of this age and of the age to come.

Raising

"In the biblical traditions every experience of salvation begins with a cry *from the depths*" like that of the Israelites in Egypt (Ex 3:7). "Analogously, the raising from the dead to eternal life begins with Christ's tortured and terrified cry on the cross."[179] When he died, Jesus presumably went to Sheol like anyone else, as the Apostles' Creed says (Acts 2:31 implies as much). But there was extra reason for him to do so. It linked with his mission. Isaiah 13:12-21 imagines the Babylonian king reaching Sheol and being derided for ending up in the same state as everyone else—or worse, because he has not been buried properly. In contrast, when Jesus reaches Sheol, he is in a position "to announce to the Old Testament saints the benefits of his victorious redemptive work," to tell them that they "are part of the company of those redeemed through Jesus" (cf. 1 Pet 4:6).[180] So there is good reason for him to go to Sheol.

But he does not stay there. The grass did not grow on the sepulcher of Jesus.[181] Jesus was put to death, at the hands of lawless people, and it looked like a final defeat. "But God raised him, loosening the pains of death, because it was not possible for him to be held by it" (Acts 2:23-24). His resurrection was a definitely physical event. His body was gone from the tomb. Thomas was free to feel the wounds in his hands and side (Jn 20:27).

---

[179]Jürgen Moltmann, *The Way of Jesus Christ* (San Francisco: HarperCollins; London: SCM Press, 1990), 211.

[180]Hurtado, *Lord Jesus Christ*, 632-33; cf. Matthew Levering, *Jesus and the Demise of Death* (Waco, TX: Baylor University Press, 2012), 23.

[181]Boff, *Jesus Christ Liberator*, 122.

Jesus was not merely resuscitated, like the dead people whom Elijah, Elisha and Jesus himself brought back to life.[182] When Elisha or Jesus resuscitated people, they eventually died again. When God resurrects Jesus, and when he resurrects us, matters are different. Jesus was raised to a new, supernatural kind of life. In his resurrection, God established "a new reality of life," a new life that comes "out of himself." It was an event analogous only to the original creation.[183] Jesus' resurrection is more like that envisaged in Daniel 12:3. While resuscitation required power, this kind of resurrection requires much greater power. The holy spirit was involved: his holy spirit and God's Holy Spirit.[184] In Daniel the idea that God would bring about people's resurrection had an implicit theological basis, that surely God cannot simply abandon the martyrs to death, and Jesus had added a theological argument of broader import, that once God becomes people's God, how could he be content for them to stay dead? (Mk 12:27). Resurrection now also has a historical basis: Jesus' resurrection is the beginning of the resurrection of other dead people.

"In the resurrection of Jesus Christ there has taken place God's solemn declaration of His faithfulness to the world and man."[185] While it might have been necessary for the first believers to know that Jesus did not stay dead, there might have been no necessity for them to think in terms of his rising from death in a physical or visible sense, or of their own being raised from death in this way. It was not required in the context of Judaism, and in the context of paganism it was a crazy idea. There are other ways of understanding the experience of a continuing life after death.[186]

But as John relates the story, the disciples are not unreasonably confused and distraught when Jesus tells them he is leaving them, because he is like a father to them and his death means they are orphaned. He tells them he will

---

[182]Cf. Wolfhart Pannenberg, *Jesus—God and Man* (Philadelphia: Westminster; London: SCM Press, 1968), 77. Pannenberg goes on to note that New Testament understanding of resurrection has a background in Jewish expectations in its day. See further N. T. Wright, *The Resurrection of the Son of God* (London: SPCK; Minneapolis: Fortress, 2003).

[183]Walter Künneth, *The Theology of the Resurrection* (London: SCM Press; St. Louis: Concordia, 1965), 73-74.

[184]Paul uses the Hebraic expression "spirit of holiness" as in Ps 51:11 [MT 13] with the same allusiveness about whether this is God's spirit or the psalmist's spirit.

[185]Barth, *CD* IV, 3:299.

[186]Cf. Wright, *Resurrection of the Son of God*, 209-10.

not leave them in that position but come back, and they will see him, though he will not continue to interact with the world. Because he lives, they will live; and at last they will recognize that "I am in my Father, and you are in me, and I am in you" (Jn 14:18-20). In speaking of "coming," he is hardly referring to the coming of the spirit of truth, to which he has just alluded, because he distinguishes this spirit from himself. Nor is he referring to his own "second coming," since the consequences of the coming that he describes are not ones that will have to wait until then; his resurrection will bring them about.

Vindication and Exaltation

Jesus' resurrection implies his vindication. Someone who had been executed could hardly be the expected Anointed One. Only his resurrection made it possible to believe that he was. The unexpected but decisive fact that distinguished Jesus from the many other people who were born of the seed of David was that he did not stay dead.

While his dying would raise a question about whether he was the Anointed One, it opened the way to a confirming of that fact through his resurrection. It leads to his designation as son of God, in keeping with God's declaration in Psalm 2:6. "Paul's references to Jesus' divine sonship all involve primarily connotations of God's direct involvement with Jesus, Jesus' special status with God, and Jesus' consequent honor and authority."[187] The accusations on whose basis he was executed were not true. Yet the resurrection was not an event that the world saw, as the execution was. Only people who were in some sense committed to the executed Jesus saw it—or rather, saw its aftermath. What it did was vindicate their commitment, for them.

> This was an act of God in time, reversing history's judgment as represented by the authorities, by the opponents, even by the hapless friends of Jesus. All these read history's judgment to be: death to this one. The resurrection opposed that judgment by entering God's own judgment: life, Life to this same one. God reversed all human judgment by identifying the life of Jesus of Nazareth afresh with God's own life, so that from that time, and in accordance with an eternal purpose of God, the history of this man, Jesus of Nazareth,

---

[187]Hurtado, *Lord Jesus Christ*, 22; see further 101-8.

was to be counted identical with God's inner history, in such a way that in the knowing of Jesus Christ God could be truly known.[188]

It is his triumph, but only because it is also God's triumph. Perhaps the impossibility of his being held by death implies that there was an energy in Jesus that made his coming back to life inevitable. Perhaps he could have raised himself from death (cf. Jn 10:17-18). But the New Testament speaks more often in terms of God raising Jesus than of Jesus rising in the manner of someone getting up in the morning by their own will and decision (see, e.g., 1 Cor 15). "Jesus' lordship is a status granted by God, a sharing in his authority. It is not that God has stepped aside and Jesus has taken over. It is rather that God has shared his lordship with Christ, without its ceasing to be God's alone."[189]

Jesus' resurrection is to be distinguished from his exaltation,[190] but it is an aspect of his journey from death to the presence of God; "in the resurrection and ascension of Jesus Christ we have to do with an inwardly coherent event."[191] Mary must not try to hold onto him as he makes that journey, though once it is done, he can come back and appear to the disciples as the risen, ascended and glorified Lord who is also manifestly one with the incarnate and crucified Lord. His resurrection means his exaltation to God's right hand, of which his pouring out the Holy Spirit is evidence (Acts 2:33), and it has to be God who grants this exaltation.

The resurrection provides the evidence that Jesus is the Anointed One, not merely because he is brought back from death but because it means his exaltation. It means Jesus sat down at the right hand of the majesty on high, and in this respect he is in a much more exalted position than any angel (Heb 1:3-14). Although the lion-lamb is not on a throne in John's vision of heaven, angels, human figures and exotic supernatural figures join in declaring, "To the one who sits on the throne and to the lamb be praise and honor and glory and power to age-long ages" (Rev 5:13).

Raising Jesus from death thus involved the exertion of sovereign power because it was also a stage in putting him in that exalted position at God's

[188]McClendon, *Systematic Theology: Doctrine*, 247 (the whole quotation is italicized).
[189]Dunn, *Theology of Paul the Apostle*, 254.
[190]Cf. Wright, *Resurrection of the Son of God*, 227.
[191]Barth, *CD* IV, 2:142.

right hand above all powerful entities, and thus in authority over the church (Eph 1:19-22). Previously it had been quite reasonable for humanity to serve these powerful entities; indeed, God had authorized this submission (Deut 32:8). Now the situation has changed, and people should acknowledge the authority of Jesus.

Victory

Whereas "heaven to us has come to mean a future state of perfect bliss," to Paul it is another present realm where the same struggle goes on as happens on earth.[192] The Scriptures work with a duality between the earthly world and the heavenly world, though not with a dualism; there is neither an absolute distinction nor an antithesis between the two worlds. The heavenly realm is above the earthly realm. There are of course limits to the spatial metaphor. Nikita Khrushchev is said to have commented that the first cosmonaut had not seen any God when he flew into outer space; it is not self-evident that biblical writers would expect that one would do so. The heavens are a metaphor for Heaven, for a realm outside the physical realm.

In that realm, as in ours, there is a conflict involving wicked spiritual entities (*pneumatika*; Eph 6:12). It is not surprising that our involvement in the heavenly realm and its involvement with us became troublesome (Gen 6:1-4). The realm of the spirit is affected by waywardness, in heaven as on earth. Christians thus sometimes refer to "spiritual warfare." Both the world below and the realm above are affected by rebellion against God, but Jesus' death and resurrection brought about a significant victory over the rebellious powers in the realm above. Paradoxically, this victory introduces or magnifies tension in relationships between believers and rebellious supernatural realities. In this world believers have a partial experience of the heavenly world. They are aware of living in God's presence, and they can perceive God involved in that world. God talks to them and they respond; they talk to God and God responds. God rescues or heals, and they respond with thanks; they appeal to God, and God rescues or heals. Divine aides visit them, and they give these aides hospitality, perhaps without realizing who they are (Heb 13:2). Faith means being sure of what they cannot see (Heb 11:1).

---

[192]J. Armitage Robinson, *St. Paul's Epistle to the Ephesians*, 2nd ed. (London: James Clarke, [?1904]), 12.

"The God of our ancestors raised Jesus . . . ; God exalted this man at his right hand as leader and savior, to give Israel repentance and remission of sins" (Acts 5:30-31). "The means of salvation for Luke is the exaltation of Jesus."[193] Salvation signifies forgiveness, the forgiveness of Israel and its salvation or restoration as God's people. Jesus' exaltation means he is God's means of bringing about that salvation, forgiveness and restoration. His disciples will be able to storm the gates of Hades with his message and open the gates to God's realm for people to run from one to the other, so that their binding and loosing will have consequences in heaven, not just on earth (Mt 16:18-19).

Jesus' execution was not an experience imposed on him against his will but an event over which he was Lord. Further, its physical nature as crucifixion pointed to the fact that it was actually his exaltation, a manifestation of his majesty and of his Father's majesty. There is another sense, then, in which there might be no need for him to be raised, or at least for this raising to be a publicly witnessed event.

Yet as well as it being impossible for him to stay dead, it was pretty useful that his having been raised should be an event that people could know about. It offered a more conventional demonstration of his majesty. While his submission to death was a paradoxical kind of glorious triumph, it was his rising from death that showed it to be so. "Cross and resurrection stand in the relation of riddle and interpretation"; yet at the same time, there is an "inner harmony" between them, in that "the preaching of the cross is dependent on the resurrection message" as well as vice versa.[194] Consideration of "Jesus Christ, the Lord as Servant" leads into consideration of "Jesus Christ, the Servant as Lord."[195]

Authority

So Paul preaches Jesus as Lord (2 Cor 4:5). While there was a lordship that he exercised in the story told earlier in the Gospels, the New Testament speaks of him as Lord in a new sense after his resurrection. His own announcement that God's reign had come thus yielded in the preaching of the apostles to the announcement that Jesus had risen from death and himself

---

[193]Green and Baker, *Recovering the Scandal of the Cross*, 73.
[194]Künneth, *Theology of the Resurrection*, 151 (the first part of the quotation is in italics).
[195]Barth, *CD* IV, 1:135.

reigned as Lord. While his resurrection was an assertion of God's sovereignty and power that evidenced the fact that God indeed reigned, it also means that Jesus is not only "the firstborn of/from the dead" but "the ruler of earth's kings" (Rev 1:5). He can say not only "I was dead, and now—I am alive forever and ever" but also that as a consequence "I hold the keys of death and Hades" (Rev 1:18). "To him glory and power" (Rev 1:6—the sentence has no verb).

Jesus' incarnation and death meant he did not care about power in the manner of a human ruler or emperor. His elevation means that he, not Caesar, is the real Lord. The triple description of him as savior, lord and anointed (Phil 3:20) is "counter-imperial." The last two nouns might seem obviously so, but "savior," too, which is an unusual word for Paul, is the emperor's self-description.[196] The portrayal rephrases Jesus' message, "not in some newly invented and peculiarly Christian language but *in* and thereby *against* the public discourse of Roman imperial theology." It takes up the familiar titles of Caesar (Son of God and Redeemer are other examples) and scandalously reapplies them.[197] The idea that Jesus is Lord links with the assumptions of empire,[198] as the description of Yahweh as Lord belongs commonly in the context of Israel's subordination to an imperial lord—it appears little in the narrative books but it flourishes in the Psalms and the Prophets.

The New Testament writers were not fixated with taking a stand against the empire, and there were scriptural reasons for using such titles.[199] Yet "every step Paul took, he walked on land ruled by Caesar. Every letter he wrote was sent to people who lived within Caesar's domain"; and "the narrative Paul believed himself and his communities to be inhabiting produced

---

[196]Cf. Wright, *Resurrection of the Son of God*, 228, 232, following Peter Oakes, *Philippians* (Cambridge and New York: Cambridge University Press, 2001); see esp. 138-40.

[197]John Dominic Crossan, *God and Empire* (San Francisco: Harper, 2007), 141; cf. Crossan, "Roman Imperial Theology," in Richard A. Horsley, ed., *In the Shadow of Empire* (Louisville: Westminster John Knox, 2008), 59-73 (on 73); Joerg Rieger, *Christ and Empire* (Minneapolis: Fortress, 2007), 23-67.

[198]See Elizabeth Schüssler Fiorenza, *The Power of the Word* (Minneapolis: Fortress, 2007), and her critique of the "reinscription" of imperial language for God and Jesus, *The Book of Revelation*, 2nd ed. (Philadelphia: Fortress, 1998), 219. Neil Elliott applies the same critique to Romans: see *The Arrogance of Nations* (Minneapolis: Fortress, 2008), 15.

[199]See Seyoon Kim, *Christ and Caesar* (Grand Rapids: Eerdmans, 2009); Scot McKnight and Joseph B. Modica, eds., *Jesus Is Lord, Caesar Is Not* (Downers Grove, IL: InterVarsity Press, 2013).

a clash with Rome and its empire." It is by way of affirmation that Jesus is the real Lord that Paul focuses his own ministry on the Roman empire as a whole, aiming for Rome itself and even for its most western border, and growing Jesus communities enacting that lordship of Jesus throughout the empire that pretended Caesar to be lord.[200] Arguably, "Paul's principal conviction was not that Jesus *as the Messiah* had come, but that God had appointed Jesus Christ *as Lord*."[201] When he began proclaiming that Jesus was the Son of God, immediately after Jesus appeared to him (Acts 9:20), he may have simply meant that Jesus was the Anointed One. But it would not be surprising if Acts takes these words as a declaration that Jesus is Lord and Son of God (cf. Rom 1:4)—and that the emperor is not.[202]

There is another, different significance to the use of titles such as "Lord." In the proclamation in Acts 2, Peter declares that on the coming day of bloodshed and darkness "anyone who calls on the Lord's name will be rescued" (Acts 2:21; cf. Rom 10:9-13). Here, "the Lord" is the exalted Jesus, but in the prophecy Peter is quoting (Joel 2:28-32 [MT 3:1-5]) the Lord is Yahweh. Paul speaks of every knee bowing to Jesus as Lord (Phil 2:5-11), and he is again recycling a declaration about Yahweh (see Is 45:22-25).

Such examples of the ease with which the New Testament applies to Jesus' scriptural passages in which the Lord is Yahweh "connote and presuppose the conviction that in some profound way he is directly and uniquely associated with God."[203] His being raised from the dead did not in itself mean that he was God incarnate or Lord of all creation.[204] But his appearing to Paul as the exalted Lord, which leads immediately to Paul's recognizing that he is the Son of God in the sense of the Anointed One, almost as immediately leads to his recognizing that Jesus is Lord and Son of God in the sense that he himself is divine.[205] It is expressed by Thomas in his recognition of the risen Jesus as "My Lord and my God" (Jn 20:28).[206]

---

[200]Wright, *Paul and the Faithfulness of God*, 1271, 1281, 1484-1504.
[201]Sanders, *Paul and Palestinian Judaism*, 514.
[202]Cf. Wright, *Resurrection of the Son of God*, 728-31.
[203]Hurtado, *Lord Jesus Christ*, 114.
[204]Cf. Wright, *Resurrection of the Son of God*, 23-25.
[205]Ibid., 397-98.
[206]See further section 1.4 above.

In the Heavenly Realm

Having seated Jesus in the heavenly realm after raising him from death, God has also seated believers there with Jesus in order to demonstrate the reality of the divine grace (Eph 1:20; 2:6-7). They live in and enjoy God's blessing "in the heavenly realm" (*en tois epouraniois*; Eph 1:3; the phrase recurs in Eph 3:10; 6:12). While this blessing is *pneumatikos* (Eph 1:3), it would be best not to call it "spiritual" blessing or to refer to a "spiritual" realm; in English that word is inclined to suggest something inward. The heavenly, spiritual realm is not inward or smaller than the physical realm but bigger. Blessings in the heavenly realm do have to do with the Spirit, but they are not inward as opposed to outward and material. The New Testament sets the Spirit over against humanity's lower nature, not over against its outer nature, and its inner nature is part of the lower nature, while the First Testament sets God's spirit over against humanity's feeble nature.

Jesus' sitting denotes being in a position of authority over other authorities; our sitting likewise implies that we are no longer bound to accept the authority of other powers. We can fight against them (Eph 6:12). In sitting us in a position of authority with Jesus in the heavens, God demonstrates his insight to the other authorities in the heavenly realm (Eph 3:10). This insight has devised a way of bringing into being a new Jewish-Gentile humanity and making it possible for all peoples to approach God in the heavenly realm with freedom and confidence (Eph 3:2-12).

So Jesus' resurrection means believers continue to enjoy physical life but also relate to that other realm. They, too, have not merely been resuscitated or even merely resurrected to a new form of earthly life but raised to a life in heaven. Their spirits are in heaven though their bodies are on the earth. They are therefore to seek the things above, to set their minds on the things above (Col 3:1-2). Their treasure, after all, lies there (Matt 6:20-21).[207] Being raised into the heavenly realm now in their spirits, and living now in their spirits in the presence of God, they are to focus on that reality. It is currently invisible to other people, but one day it will be made manifest.

The focus on heaven does not mean that people's present, earthly lives don't matter. The body on earth and the spirit in the heavenly realm still

---

[207]Cf. Abbott, *Critical and Exegetical Commentary on the Epistles to the Ephesians and to the Colossians*, 278.

comprise one person. Jesus himself promises them things in the realm of the material and outward such as inheriting the earth or land, food and clothing, though he tells them not to worry about them (Mt 5:5; 6:25-34). The focus on heaven revolutionizes people's lives on earth rather than depriving them of significance.

It is in light of their having been raised with Jesus that believers are to kill (*nekroō*) earthly practices such as sexual immorality, greed (which is idolatry), anger, malice, deceit and the instinct to divide (Jew and Gentile, us and them, slave and free), making distinctions whose significance has been abolished for people who have put off the old self and put on the new one (Col 3:5-11). In their place they are to cultivate other practices that reflect heavenly realities, such as compassion, humility, gentleness, patience, forgiveness and peaceableness—everything that expresses a care for other people as the overarching principle. They are to clothe themselves in the characteristics of their heavenly nature (Col 3:12-15).

Life and Presence

We were "dead," but God "made us alive with the Anointed One—by grace you have been rescued—and with him raised us up and enabled us to sit in the heavenly realm, through the Anointed One, Jesus" (Eph 2:5-6). "Life" means living in the heavenly realm, enjoying easy access to the presence of God, living for the glorious praise of God, having hope and therefore living in hope, with insight into the nature of God's project in the world. Death is to be in the opposite position, to exist without easy access, to exist for ourselves, to exist without hope and without understanding.

With Jesus we have been raised from such death to such life. This understanding of life and death corresponds to one that appears in the Gospels. It also appears in the Psalms, more paradoxically: evidently these realities did not have to wait until Jesus came for them to be real for the people of God. In the Psalms, too, death can be a reality that gets hold of people in this "life." Oppression and attack in effect put people into Sheol, and God's rescue delivers them from Sheol. It makes it possible to enjoy "life forevermore" (Ps 133:3)—that is, life until the end of one's life.

Thus the "normal" life into which the Psalms invite people is one where I can "live in Yahweh's house[hold] all the days of my life" (Ps 27:4). Jesus raises believers to new life so as to enjoy that access to God's heavenly presence. They are able to take part in meetings where God's agents sort out what will happen on earth (Jer 23:18). They enter the presence of God, discover what God is doing and as a result are then able to serve God more effectively in this world.

To put it another way, believers died with Jesus "from the elements of the world," which imposes rules regarding what people can handle, taste or touch, which can impose some sort of discipline but not achieve anything very effective in dealing with the lower nature (Col 2:20-23). Such rules resemble highway speed limits, which restrain some driving excesses but do not turn people into safe drivers. But believers have been "raised with the Anointed One," though their new life is "hidden with the Anointed One in [the presence of] God" (Col 3:1-4).

The fact that Jesus is alive and that he lives in God's presence is hidden from most people, and so is the fact that believers are alive and live in God's presence. Though they live in the heavenly realm, having access to the heavenly court, no one can see this reality, even if its results are perceptible in their lives. They are as susceptible to death as other people are. Jesus' final manifestation will change these things for him and for them, because they will be manifested with him "in splendor." But at the moment they are like royalty walking through the streets in ordinary clothes. They will then be wearing the royal robes that reflect who they actually are. The sons and daughters of God will be revealed (Rom 8:19).

Thus, not only does our identifying with Jesus' death and making it our own mean that in effect we paid the death penalty.[208] Jesus' resurrection meant he then started a new kind of life, and our identifying with his act and making it our own also means we started a new kind of life, one "lived by faith in the Son of God," by faith in him as the one who died and rose for us in his representative and substitutionary way (Gal 2:19-20). Indeed, "if Jesus has been raised, then the end of the world has begun. . . . God himself has confirmed the pre-Easter activity of Jesus." It makes clear that "the Son of Man is none other than the man Jesus who will come again." The resurrection "constituted only the beginning of the universal resurrection of the

---

[208]See section 5.5 above.

dead and the end of the world." Because of the passage of two millennia it's hard now to hold onto the essential relationship between Jesus' resurrection and the end of the world. But we need to do so if we are to see the significance of Jesus' resurrection.[209]

Jesus' resurrection thus "marks the start of the reality of eternal life. . . . The reality of the resurrection is the assault of life upon the spatio-temporal reality of death."[210] Neither his vindication nor his exaltation is widely acknowledged now, but they will be so acknowledged. The actuality of his resurrection in the present (rather than its being an event to come in the future) makes it possible for his followers also in some measure to share now in his resurrection, vindication and exaltation. His resurrection appearances make it possible for them to know about his vindication and his exaltation, and thus about the coming consummation of his resurrection and exaltation, and about theirs.[211]

---

[209]Pannenberg, *Jesus—God and Man*, 67-68, 106, 107.
[210]Künneth, *Theology of the Resurrection*, 75-76 (part of the quotation is in italics).
[211]See further chapter eight below.

6

God's Children

┼

Death and resurrection led into Pentecost. At Pentecost, the Holy Spirit overwhelmed the entire community of people who believed in Jesus, and this overwhelming issued in something spectacular that required explanation and thereby opened up the possibility of telling other people about Jesus (Acts 2). Another version of the sequence occurred when the believers were all filled with the Holy Spirit and spoke the message about Jesus boldly (Acts 4:31). On subsequent occasions there is no overt link between filling and proclamation; the filling or coming is simply an indication that the pouring out is being extended to people in Samaria, to proselytes and to people who had missed out earlier (Acts 8:15-17; 9:17; 10:44-46; 19:1-7). It is a crucial aspect of the story of the people that acknowledges Jesus and of their experience as individuals.

6.1 The Congregation

The community that believes in Jesus is a new manifestation of the people of God that God brought into being with Abraham. But it is a new manifestation, whose nature as a Jewish-Gentile community, embodied in congregations around the Eastern Mediterranean, makes for a new portrait within the New Testament. So there is both continuity and diversity in the way the two Testaments envisage the life of God's people. The community of believers in Jesus is a household (for which eating together is a key activity), a temple, a kingdom, a school, a priesthood. It is worldwide and local, one but diverse, selected but outreaching, inclusive but holy.

Community and Individual

Given that being human is both a corporate affair and an individual affair, it is not surprising that relationships with God are both a corporate affair and an individual affair. The congregation relates to God; God's aim was to form a people, a new humanity. Individuals also relate to God. Whereas Western Christianity can make God's involvement with individuals an excuse for not taking the community seriously, there could be occasions when Israelites made the corporate nature of the community an excuse for evading individual responsibility. In themselves, however, both Testaments maintain a balance. They speak of God's activity in, with and through the community; they also recognize that the individual enjoys God's provision and must respond to God's expectations.

At the end of the world's story, when the work of restoring all things is complete and God finally says "It's all over," there will be a body of people who "will be his peoples, and God himself will be with them." But in addition, God will give living water to the individual person who is thirsty, and God promises to the victor, "I will be his [or her] God and he will be my son [or daughter]," whereas the people who are cowardly, unbelieving, disgusting, murderous, immoral, sorcerous, idolatrous and deceitful will fall to the second death (Rev 21:1-8). Jesus describes the lifestyle of a group of disciples or a congregation and mostly uses the plural (Mt 5–7), but his description would also require individual commitment to reconciliation, chastity, honesty, forbearance, love, modesty, charity, prayer, fasting, generosity, trust, self-criticism, discernment and obedience, and he makes that expectation explicit in many singular verbs—"anyone who gets angry with his brother . . . , when you [singular] pray . . . , anyone who listens to my words . . ."

In the Torah, the interweaving of singular and plural is one way the instructions signal the reality of the community, its experience and its responsibility, and also the reality of individuals, their experience and their responsibility. While some singular verbs issue from Israel's being an "it" as well as a "they," many of the Torah's rules explicitly concern the obligations of an individual. The Psalms manifest a parallel dynamic: while they may assume that praise is inherently corporate, both protest and testimony belong equally to the individual and to the community, and it can be difficult to tell whether a given psalm speaks for the one or the other. Much of Proverbs describes the ordinary life of individuals, but its concern is the shaping of the community.

God's aim in sending Jesus was to restore his people, but his people as a whole did not accept him, which put the pressure on the individual. Individuals could not hide behind the people as a whole and abdicate responsibility to decide for themselves whether to welcome Jesus. "Whoever accepted him, to them he gave the freedom to become God's children, those who put their trust in his name, who were brought to birth not through blood nor through human will nor through a man's will but through God" (Jn 1:12).

John especially stresses the individual and focuses on the relationship of the individual believer to Jesus and to God.[1] The vine, a classic image for the people of God, becomes an image for Jesus, and the individual's relationship with the vine is a relationship with him, not directly with the community. It matters that the individual believes in Jesus. Yet John also speaks in the plural of people who accept Jesus and reports on a household coming to believe (Jn 4:53). Acts, too, describes how a household comes to believe (Acts 10; 16:15, 31; cf. 1 Cor 1:16). Perhaps in some way each member of the household made his or her response, but they did so as part of a whole.

The New Creation

So Israel as an entity is Yahweh's son or daughter, and Yahweh is its father or mother, though it does not behave in the way appropriate to a son or daughter. It is an unresponsive child whom Yahweh is tempted to disown, though in the end he cannot make himself do the deed (Hos 11). Individually, too, Israelites are God's children, and Yahweh is their father or mother, though individually, too, they do not behave in the way appropriate to the relationship. They are rebellious children whom Yahweh may chastise, but he stays committed to his sons and daughters (Is 1:2; 43:6-7).

That belonging to God is both a community and an individual matter reflects the way God created humanity. But "if someone is in the Anointed One—a new creation; the old things have passed away: there, new things have come into being" (2 Cor 5:17; cf. Gal 6:15). The idea of new creation,

---

[1] Cf. C. F. D. Moule, "The Individualism of the Fourth Gospel," *Novum Testamentum* 5 (1962): 171-90; cf. George Eldon Ladd, *A Theology of the New Testament* (Grand Rapids: Eerdmans, 1974), 281 (rev. ed., 317).

too, is both a corporate one and an individual one. On one hand, God promised a new heavens and a new earth, embodied in a new city (Is 65:17-25). On the other, the creation of a new person can be the object of prayer: "Create for me a clean heart [a clean inner being, mind, spirit], God, and make new a firm spirit within me" (Ps 51:10 [MT 12]).

The heading to that psalm connects it with Nathan's confrontation of David after David's adultery and murder, but 2 Samuel makes clear that God did not bring about such a new creation for David, though there are other people in the First Testament for whom one can see God did bring it about (people such as Ruth or Hannah). Likewise, in some ways Jerusalem after the exile was a renewed city, but its renewal left much to be desired.

Paul's talk of "new creation," then, could refer to the creation of a new individual person, which suggests an answer to the psalm's prayer. It could suggest the creation of a new Jerusalem, a community in the form of a congregation that believes in Jesus. Either way, it would presuppose that the new age has arrived through Jesus' coming.[2] Yet corporately, and in many cases individually, the Corinthian congregation was evidently more like the city of Jerusalem before the exile and more like David than like his great-grandmother—the new creation has not happened for the Corinthians. Paul is describing the way new creation is supposed to work; his declaration that "if someone is in the Anointed One—a new creation" is a statement like "anyone who stays in him does not sin" (1 Jn 3:6).

Paul's words about new creation follow on from some preceding declarations, that Jesus' love controls us, that we no longer live for ourselves but for Jesus and that we no longer regard people from a worldly perspective (2 Cor 5:14-16). The arrival of a new age and a new creation as a result of Jesus' coming provides a new basis for this transformation. It gives a new motivation and a new foundation for the prayer "create for me a clean heart and make new a firm spirit within me," and for the belief that this prayer will be answered. God has brought into being the new Jerusalem, and thus I ask to be transformed so as to be a citizen worthy of it. It also gives a new challenge to seek such renewal. Calvin's paraphrase is not so far off the mark as

---

[2]See the discussion in Mark Owens, *As It Was in the Beginning: An Intertextual Analysis of New Creation in Galatians, 2 Corinthians, and Ephesians* (Eugene, OR: Wipf and Stock, 2016).

a summary of Paul's implications: "if any man desires to obtain a place in Christ . . . let him be a new creature."[3]

To put it in only slightly different a way, the coming of Jesus makes it both possible and necessary for a person to be born again, born from above (Jn 3:3-7). It is necessary, because one cannot see things straight unless one starts over. And it is possible, because Jesus makes it possible to see straight and start over. To put it in another slightly different way, the coming of Jesus makes it possible to be adopted into a new family, a family one joins through becoming Jesus' brother. To welcome someone into one's family is a creative and new-birthing act that brings new creation and new birth to the person.[4]

A Household

The congregation of believers thus forms a kind of family or household. To become God's children means to become part of a family. It is "a key image" for the community of people who believe in Jesus.[5] In 1934 a synod of the German Evangelical Church, a federation of confessional churches, met at Barmen and over against the stance of the "German Christians" agreed a "theological declaration" in which it defined the church as "the congregation of the brethren."[6] The definition fits the fact that believers are members of God's household (Eph 2:19; 1 Tim 3:15) and are therefore each other's brothers and sisters (e.g., Rom 14:10-21; 1 Thess 4:10). Jesus can speak in terms of the family of disciples replacing the natural family (Mt 12:46-50), and the household is "the basic context within which most if not all the local Pauline groups established themselves."

They differ from a voluntary association or synagogue or school.[7] Brothers and sisters cannot choose each other, and their relationship is not subject to termination.[8] The way I behave must take into account the

---

[3]John Calvin, *The Second Epistle of Paul the Apostle to the Corinthians and the Epistles to Timothy, Titus and Philemon* (Edinburgh: Oliver and Boyd, 1964), 75.

[4]Thomas A. Bennett develops the idea that Jesus' death constituted his laboring to bring a new people to birth ("The Cross as the Labor of God" [PhD diss., Fuller Theological Seminary, 2015]).

[5]Robert Banks, *Paul's Idea of Community* (Grand Rapids: Eerdmans, 1980), 54 (rev. ed. [Peabody, MA: Hendrickson, 1994], 49).

[6]Cf. Arthur C. Cochrane, *The Church's Confession Under Hitler* (repr., Pittsburgh: Pickwick, 1976), 237-42.

[7]Wayne A. Meeks, *The First Urban Christians*, 2nd ed. (New Haven, CT, and London: Yale University Press, 2003), 84.

[8]Cf. Jürgen Moltmann, *The Church in the Power of the Spirit* (London: SCM Press; New York: Harper, 1977), 316 (though he prefers the image of friends to that of brothers and sisters).

spiritual health of other believers as brothers and sisters for whom Jesus died (1 Cor 8:11-13). This motivation corresponds to the one the Torah laid before Israel: members of Israel are to see each other as brothers and sisters and to behave accordingly (e.g., Deut 1:16; 3:20; 15:1-11). Acts pictures the post-Pentecost community as "the fulfillment of two ancient ideals: the Greek ideal of true friendship and the Deuteronomic ideal of the covenant community."[9]

The household is thus an important model for that fellowship, that *koinōnia*, of which individual believers in Jesus are members. Some Christian groups prefer this word *fellowship* to the word *church* with its institutional/ hierarchical associations.[10] As the Scriptures portray it, "religion is a life to be lived in fellowship."[11] One of Paul's favorite expressions is "one another." We are members of one another (Rom 12:5; Eph 4:25); we are to build up one another (1 Thess 5:11; Rom 14:19), to care for one another (1 Cor 12:25), to love one another (1 Thess 3:12; 4:9; 2 Thess 1:3; Rom 13:8), to pursue one another's good (1 Thess 5:15), to bear with one another (Eph 4:2), to bear one another's burdens (Gal 6:2), to be compassionate and forgiving to one another (Eph 4:32; Col 3:13), to submit to one another (Eph 5:21), to have high regard for one another (Phil 2:3), to be devoted to one another (Rom 12:10), to live in harmony with one another (Rom 12:16).[12]

Indeed, of the exhortations in Romans 12:9-21, "not a single one relates to the private life of individual Christians. Formally, the whole series is connected with the passage about gifts of grace. . . . Materially, it contains directions about the life of Christians in relationship with others: first . . . their fellowship among themselves, and then . . . their contacts with the surrounding non-Christian world."[13]

"What is God doing in the world in the interval between resurrection and parousia? According to Paul, God is at work through the Spirit to create communities that prefigure and embody the reconciliation and healing of

---

[9]Richard B. Hays, *The Moral Vision of the New Testament* (San Francisco: Harper, 1996), 123.

[10]Cf. Veli-Matti Kärkkäinen, *Toward a Pneumatological Theology* (Lanham, MD: University Press of America, 2002), 116. Cf. further the footnote comments under "Worldwide and Local" later in this section.

[11]D. N. Buntain, *The Holy Ghost and Fire* (Springfield, MO: Gospel Publishing House, 1956), 62; cf. Frederick Dale Bruner, *A Theology of the Holy Spirit* (Grand Rapids: Eerdmans, 1970), 149.

[12]Gordon D. Fee, *God's Empowering Presence* (Peabody, MA: Hendrickson, 1994), 871-72.

[13]Barth, *CD* II, 2:719.

the world" (see, e.g., Rom 15:7-13). "The church is a countercultural community of discipleship" that "embodies the power of resurrection in the midst of a not-yet-redeemed world."[14]

Eating Together

As a household, a congregation naturally eats together (1 Cor 11:17-34). Eating together is a feature of family life, and eating with people was a feature of Jesus' life. His practice was similar to that of Jewish groups such as the Pharisees and the Qumran community. The last meal he had with his disciples was at one level simply the last such event of many that he shared with his followers and with other people.

"Except in superficial ways," a theologian laments, preachers have "often kept silent on the topic that should have demanded all their eloquence— Jesus Christ crucified for the ungodly"; but fortunately, the celebration of the Lord's Meal makes it impossible to escape that topic, because by its very nature it brings this reality home.[15] The life of believers is lived between what Jesus has done and what Jesus will do, and the Lord's Meal brings home both past and future. We bring home the memory of Jesus dying, until he comes.

The motif of bringing home the memory links the Lord's Meal and the celebration of Passover, which was the context of the meal that the ongoing Lord's Meal continues. "The narrative of the Passover (Exod. 12:1-51) takes the form of a dramatic action in which those who take part become participants in the narrative world of, and in effect 'relive,' the drama of divine deliverance from bondage in Egypt. . . . 'In every generation,' the Mishnah declares, 'a man must so regard himself as if he came forth himself out of Egypt.'"[16] In continuation of that dynamic, the congregation's celebration of the Lord's Meal involves people reliving the dying of Jesus as if they were there. Its effect is to bring home the reality of that event and involve people in it once again, so that its effect on their lives is reinforced. What baptism does on a one-time basis at the beginning of a believer's life, the Lord's Meal does on an ongoing basis.

---

[14]Hays, *Moral Vision of the New Testament*, 32, 196, 198; the second and third quotations are italicized in the original.

[15]Miroslav Volf, *Against the Tide* (Grand Rapids: Eerdmans, 2010), 89.

[16]Anthony C. Thiselton, *The Hermeneutics of Doctrine* (Grand Rapids: Eerdmans, 2007), 527, quoting from Mishnah Pesahim 10:5 (a number of the words are italicized).

The Lord's Meal is a key occasion when its members "come together" in a way that expresses their comprising "one body" (1 Cor 10:17; 11:18). It is both a social and a religious event. It is "an expression not only of the death of Christ for our sins but also of the sharing of bread between those who have and those who have not,"[17] a "practice" that gives "social shape to Christian life."[18] Meal and sacrament came to be separate, so that a meal is not a sacramental event and Holy Communion is not a meal. In the New Testament, sacrament and meal go together, in continuation with the Jewish way. The First Testament practice of sharing a meal with God, as people did at God's invitation at a "well-being sacrifice" or "fellowship sacrifice" (*zebaḥ šəlāmîm*), brings home the reality of the presence of God with his people. It happened at a meal.

Giving thanks for and sharing the same loaf and the same cup of wine is a sign of unity among people who belong to God and who share a relationship with God. Ironically, however, such meals became occasions of controversy, because proper conduct at meals and the proper limiting of participation to people who counted as the faithful rather than as sinners was of great importance. Yet on one hand, the New Testament mentions baptism rather less frequently than we might have expected (it is "indispensable but secondary"),[19] while on the other, at Corinth reference to the meal comes only in connection with the need to address self-centeredness and conflict within a congregation split by wealth as well as by beliefs ("I am Paul's . . .").[20]

Jesus likewise got into trouble for eating with "sinners." Essenes and Pharisees would be inclined to divide Jews into the faithful and the faithless. They knew what faithfulness looked like, and they were committed to living in accordance with that vision and to dissociating themselves from people who dissociate themselves from such faithfulness. In the Christian church that instinct expresses itself in the stance that different doctrinal traditions take to one another (Orthodox, Catholic, evangelical, liberal, Pentecostal, Baptist), and also in the importance attached to certain commitments such

---

[17]John Howard Yoder, *The Priestly Kingdom* (Notre Dame, IN: University of Notre Dame Press, 1984), 93.

[18]James W. McClendon, *Systematic Theology: Ethics* (Nashville: Abingdon, 1986), 218.

[19]Barth, *CD* IV, 4:48.

[20]Meeks, *First Urban Christians*, 159.

as acceptance of or opposition to divorce and remarriage, same-sex relationships, abortion or pacifism. Believers are often inclined to "single-issue" politics and theology.

The proper celebration of and participation in Holy Communion became a particular topic of controversy in the church, and the meal has been "the occasion for the misery of schism and denominational conflict" through history.[21] The development parallels the church practice that has taken us a long way from the notion of "one baptism" (Eph 4:5).

A Temple, a Kingdom

As well as being a household, the congregation is a building, with Jesus as its foundation. Specifically, it is a temple (1 Cor 3:9-17). As the promise to Abraham of blessing for the world has been fulfilled in the coming of God's spirit on God's people, so the promise of Yahweh's dwelling in the temple (especially if people think that God isn't in the Second Temple as he was in the First Temple) is filled out through the coming of God's spirit into the midst of God's people.[22] "We are the temple of the living God," the place where God is present and where he walks with his people (2 Cor 6:16). The temple is built on the foundation of the apostles and prophets with Jesus as the cornerstone or headstone, a structure that is being built together as a holy temple, and a dwelling where God lives by his Spirit (Eph 2:19-22).

The nature of the congregation as a temple is one reason why it can have nothing to do with idols, which are one source of impurity (2 Cor 6:14–7:1). It is another marker of being in continuation with Israel, for whom it is a common theme. The new Jerusalem has no temple, but it is still a "holy city" (Rev 21:2, 10; 22:19).

Further, if anyone within the congregation takes the kind of action that destroys God's temple, God will destroy that person. Rather, the structure needs to be built up (1 Cor 14:12, 26), and believers need to contribute to this upbuilding. It is a criterion for their exercise of charisms and it is one reason why prophecy is more important than tongues unless tongues are interpreted (1 Cor 14:4-5). Even praise and prayer are meant to be shared, for the building up of the body, as the Psalms imply. Praise is a method of testifying

---

[21]Moltmann, *Church in the Power of the Spirit*, 244.
[22]Cf. N. T. Wright, *Paul and the Faithfulness of God* (Minneapolis: Fortress; London: SPCK, 2013), 1074-78.

and teaching; there is a close link between praise and prophecy, as the stories of Miriam and Hannah show (see Ex 15:1-18; 1 Sam 2:1-10). If someone else can't understand my thanksgiving, they can't say amen to it (1 Cor 14:16-17): that is, they can't affirm it for themselves and indicate that they have made a commitment to its perspective. They can't be built up.

Jesus has also made the congregation into a kingdom (Rev 1:6). Its people are therefore free of other overlords and free of any overlords within their own midst. Authority in the church rests with the congregation as a whole, not with "leaders" within it. They are all taught by God and participants in the Spirit.[23] But they are not free to make their own decisions. They are the kingdom of God; he rules them. In the new Jerusalem, God's servants serve him and reign instead of being reigned over by others (Rev 22:3-5).

Jesus has been exalted to a position of authority over all other authorities. The congregation is the body that recognizes this fact and lives in accordance with this reality, so that it is a kind of extension or filling out (*plērōma*) of him, in the sense that it is filled out by him,[24] pending the time when all reality comes to be thus filled out by him (Eph 1:22-23). Over against the Hellenistic Jewish idea that the cosmos was a body permeated by the divine Word, Ephesians here uses the word *ekklēsia* and the image of a body to refer to the entire people that believes in Jesus, which makes it possible to declare that the church is a body permeated by the rule of Jesus.[25] The people of God is a kingdom that acknowledges a different king. The fact that Jesus is Lord also needs to be allowed to subvert rather than reinforce the idea that there is hierarchy within the congregation.

A School, a Priesthood, a Servant
The congregation is a school. Its task is to make disciples (Mt 28:16-20). Given the Ephesians' trust in Jesus and their concern for the holy people, which mean they are part of the people through which God intends to be acknowledged and exalted in the world, Paul wants God to give them a wise

---

[23]Cf. James D. G. Dunn, *The Theology of Paul the Apostle* (Grand Rapids and Cambridge, UK: Eerdmans, 1998), 593-94.

[24]In isolation the language about *plērōma* could imply that the congregation fills out Christ, but the language is allusive, and the idea is not clearly present elsewhere: cf. Markus Barth, *Ephesians* (Garden City, NY: Doubleday, 1974), 1:200-210.

[25]Cf. Andrew T. Lincoln, *Ephesians* (Dallas: Word, 1990), 71-72. See further the paragraphs under "Authority" in section 5.5 above.

and revelatory spirit (which will result from the activity of the wise and revelatory Spirit) in connection with knowledge about God (Eph 1:17). Possession of or by this wise and revelatory spirit is not limited to the individual
shoot from Jesse's stump (as in the promise in Is 11:2) or to the apostles and
prophets (as in Eph 3:5) but given to the whole congregation (cf. Is 55:3-5).[26]

In English "knowing God" suggests a relational, experiential knowledge,
and the Scriptures believe in such a personal or experiential relationship
with God. "Knowledge of God" also means knowledge about God. Thus Paul
can spell out its implications not in relational terms by speaking about love
or intimacy but in terms of the content of the knowledge. He wants people
to know about the hope to which God has called them, the rich, splendid
possession they are to God, and the dynamic power and authority that God
has in relation to people who trust, the power and authority manifested in
raising Jesus (Eph 1:18-19; cf. Col 2:2).

Knowledge also overlaps with acknowledgment or recognition, something that involves the will and is closely related to obedience (e.g., Jn 17:3;
1 Cor 15:34; 2 Cor 10:5; Col 1:9-11; 2 Thess 1:8; 1 Jn 3:1). "When acknowledgment takes place, there is a yielding of the man who acknowledges before
the thing or person he acknowledges. He submits to the authority of the
other."[27] It is the submission of which the First Testament speaks when it
refers to awe for God, the expression traditionally rendered "fear of God," as
well as in its frequent references to "knowing Yahweh" in the sense of acknowledging Yahweh.

The congregation is a priesthood in relation to Jesus' God and Father
(Rev 1:6). It has a special privilege over against the rest of the world in its
service of God and its worship. Further, as a kingdom and a priesthood, the
congregation is a servant. To be a priesthood and a kingdom is a great honor,
and so is being a servant. It implies the master's commitment and protection
(Is 41:1-10). To be a priesthood and a kingdom also points to an expectation
on God's part, and the same point applies to being a servant. It implies a
commitment to fulfilling the task the master wants done. While it is true
that the church exists for others, its position as servant first describes its
relationship with God. "The modern notion of the servant Church . . . seems

---

[26]Cf. Barth, *Ephesians*, 1:162-64.
[27]Barth, *CD* I, 1:207.

to lack any direct foundation in the Bible."[28] The Bible does not speak of the people of God as designed to be a servant of the world, but it does see it as designed to be the servant of God.[29]

The service God wants undertaken does involve a role in relation to the world. The people of God are to serve God by showing the world that God's faithful purpose for it is being fulfilled and by thus becoming a light to the world (Is 42:1-12). As a servant, the people of God is a witness (Is 43:8-13). It is in a position to testify to what God has done and thus to draw the world to acknowledge God. It does so by its existence, because it is the very embodiment of a covenant (Is 42:6), and by its words. Whereas the world is characterized by fear and anxiety, the people of God serve God by showing and telling that we can live by trust not in fear. The church is a counterpolity, living in between the times, and its holiness and communal love offer a radical witness to the world.

Worldwide and Local

The New Testament commonly describes the community that believes in Jesus as the *ekklēsia*.[30] It is the Septuagint's regular equivalent for *qāhāl* in the First Testament, but in ordinary Greek it was not a religious expression but one that denoted an assembly of citizens.[31] The First Testament uses both *ʿēdâ* and *qāhāl* to refer to Israel gathered together; the former is closer to assembly (the Septuagint renders *ʿēdâ* by *synagōgē*), the latter to congregation gathered for worship.

A congregation such as that in Corinth is thus an *ekklēsia* of God that comprises "people who have been made holy through the Anointed One, Jesus," who are "called holy people" and are set in the context of "all the people who call on the name of our Lord, Jesus, the Anointed One, in every

---

[28] Avery Dulles, *Models of the Church*, 2nd ed. (Dublin: Gill and Macmillan, 1988), 100.

[29] See further the paragraphs under "Service" in section 7.2 below.

[30] Elizabeth Schüssler Fiorenza nicely notes that whereas *church* comes from the word *kyrios* and implies an inherently hierarchical entity, *ekklēsia* is more amenable to suggesting "radical democracy" (*The Power of the Word* [Minneapolis: Fortress, 2007], 78). There is dispute over whether *church* is etymologically linked rather to the word *circle* (cf. Barth, *CD* IV, 1:651), which could connect nicely with her theology. Martin Luther was uneasy about the word *church* because it looks suspiciously like the word *curia* (see his exposition of the third article of the creed in his Large Catechism [*Luther's Large Catechism* (repr., St. Louis: Concordia, 1988), 74]; cf. Hans Küng, *On Being a Christian* [Garden City, NY: Doubleday, 1976; London: Collins, 1977], 478).

[31] Cf. Larry Hurtado, *At the Origins of Christian Worship* (Carlisle, UK: Paternoster, 1999), 54-55.

place, their [Lord] and ours" (1 Cor 1:2). While the New Testament most often uses the word *ekklēsia* to refer to a local congregation, an assembly in a particular place, the word can also refer to the people all over the world who are committed to Jesus (e.g., Eph 1:22; Col 1:18; cf. Mt 16:18).

Ultimately the congregation is catholic, *kath' holon*, spread through the entire earth, because its God is the God of the entire earth.[32] Likewise, the people of God is one because God is one. "The unity of the Church is not primarily the unity of her members, but the unity of Christ who acts upon them all, in all places and at all times."[33] "The *ekklēsia* and especially its unity stand at the centre of Paul's newly framed symbolic universe."[34] It is a peculiar use of the word *ekklēsia* "that must have been puzzling to any ordinary Greek."[35] But in this connection, "The plural for 'church' is an inner contradiction."[36]

While the opening of 1 Corinthians does not use the word *ekklēsia* to refer to the worldwide fellowship, it does note that the Corinthian congregation is part of a body of believers that is worldwide as well as local. Any individual congregation needs to think and live with an awareness of belonging to this worldwide fellowship. The mutual obligations of support, charity and hospitality that obtain within a local congregation apply to the extended family worldwide. One congregation cannot behave as if the rest of the church in its country or in the world does not exist (cf. 1 Cor 7:17; 11:16).

When writing to the believers in a particular place, Paul often refers to other congregations and individuals (see, e.g., the greetings in Col 4:7-17). Indeed, "a community which does not see the suffering and testimony of other communities as its own suffering and its own testimony is dividing the one Christ who suffers and acts in all places and at all times" (cf. 1 Cor 12:26).[37] The Christian movement combined tight local communities with a supralocal network of relationships, and it may have been this

---

[32]Edmund Schlink, *The Coming Christ and the Coming Church* (Edinburgh: Oliver and Boyd, 1967; Philadelphia: Fortress, 1968), 108; cf. Moltmann, *Church in the Power of the Spirit*, 338.

[33]Schlink, *Coming Christ and the Coming Church*, 105; cf. Moltmann, *Church in the Power of the Spirit*, 338.

[34]Wright, *Paul and the Faithfulness of God*, 387.

[35]Meeks, *First Urban Christians*, 108.

[36]G. C. Berkouwer, *The Church* (Grand Rapids: Eerdmans, 1976), 77.

[37]Moltmann, *Church in the Power of the Spirit*, 343.

combination, "and not any evangelist, which proved to be the most effective missionary."[38]

In some situations one congregation will give to another, in other situations the direction of giving will be reversed (2 Cor 8:13-15). The principle is equality (*isotēs*). Admittedly this principle is not the only one Paul is working with, otherwise he would have been making the poor Macedonians recipients rather than givers.[39] He has particular reasons to be concerned for the Jerusalem congregation. And he goes on to include a scriptural quotation that refers to sufficiency rather than equality (Ex 16:18).

Oneness with Differentiation

As well as seeing itself as part of a worldwide entity, a congregation needs to preserve its own unity in the way its members think and live. We are all one in the Anointed One, Jesus (Gal 3:28). Our unity is a unity of the Spirit; there is one body, one Spirit, one hope, one Lord, one faith, one baptism, one God and Father of all (Eph 4:3-4). It's therefore a strange thing to take each other to court; such action is not an expression of oneness (1 Cor 6:1-7). The argument again recalls Deuteronomy's recurrent reminders that the community is a body of brothers and sisters. It's a terrible thing to tear the church apart, to split the church, because God is not split and the Anointed One is not split (1 Cor 1:10-17).

So the congregation must not divide into groups attaching themselves to one leader or another according to these leaders' apparent insight. That inclination suggests childishness and fleshliness rather than maturity and spirituality, the qualities that make it possible to be open to insight (1 Cor 3:1-9). Paul, Apollos and Cephas all belong to the Corinthians (1 Cor 3:22), so the Corinthians are foolish to confine themselves to one teacher. God's truth is comprehensive and multifaceted. In emphasizing one aspect we inevitably downplay others. So we need to listen to people who emphasize other aspects.

---

[38] Adolf von Harnack, *The Mission and Expansion of Christianity in the First Three Centuries* (London: Williams and Norgate; New York: Putnam, 1908), 1:434; cf. Meeks, *First Urban Christians*, 108.

[39] Cf. Margaret E. Thrall, *A Critical and Exegetical Commentary on the Second Epistle to the Corinthians* (Edinburgh: T&T Clark, 2000), 2:540.

In what sense is everyone to say the same thing and have the same mind? It relates to a focus on Jesus. Paul talks about different gifts (1 Cor 12) and different vocations (Gal 2:1-10) but not about different insights. There is nothing postmodern about Paul. The scriptural recognition that we do not all say the same thing and think the same way comes from setting Paul in the context of other parts of the Scriptures. Paul does not think the same way as James. Yet this fact would (perhaps) not stop him recognizing the need in another sense to say the same thing and have the same mind by not splitting the church over differences of views among people who acknowledge the same God and the same Jesus. Acts 15 would evidence the point.

The mixed nature of the congregation extends to their position in society. The Corinthian congregation is "diverse, stratified, and divided"; its members come from "different social and economic worlds." They include slave and free as well as Jew and Gentile (1 Cor 12:13; cf. Eph 6:5-9; Col 3:22–4:1; 1 Tim 6:1-2; Tit 2:9-10; Philemon). They include men and women, single, married and widowed (1 Cor 7).

Paul's goal is then not to reform the existing social order. With regard to slavery, "Paul has no word of criticism for the institution as such. In this sense, he was unconcerned about 'social ethics.'"[40] One reason will be that the resurrection and coming return of Jesus changes everything and discourages the development of any impetus for social change. Pending the End, Paul thinks that it is generally better to stay as you are, though you can accept freedom or marry if you wish. Everyone has their charisma (1 Cor 7:7). "Everything can become for me charisma," not excluding "the realms of the natural, the sexual, the private, the social."[41] They are the "*everyday charismata of the lived life.*" The "special" charismata are then no less natural and no more supernatural, but charisms that relate especially to the building up of the congregation.[42]

In due course it will become clear that the church has to settle down for a longer haul, and we may then think of Paul as offering a vision of transcending slavery, the prospect of transposing social and economic diversity

---

[40]Ladd, *Theology of the New Testament*, 529 (rev. ed., 574).
[41]Ernst Käsemann, *Essays on New Testament Themes* (London: SCM Press, 1964), 63-94 (on 75).
[42]Jürgen Moltmann, *The Spirit of Life* (London: SCM Press; Minneapolis: Fortress, 1992), 183.

to a new and more fundamental plane" by means of "an ethic of love-patriarchalism."[43] The basic idea then is "the willing acceptance of given inequalities" and "making them fruitful for the ethical values of personal relationships" with the possibility that one might "alter given conditions from within outwards, without touching the external aspect at all."[44] The approach of the Torah will then become newly important.

Selected but Outreaching

Israel is God's chosen people.[45] The community of people who belong to Jesus come to share in that election; they are God's chosen ones (e.g., Mt 24:22, 24, 31; Rom 8:33; 1 Pet 1:1). In this connection the word *chosen* is regularly plural. It can be used in the singular to refer to God's choice of someone for a particular task (e.g., Acts 1:24), and specifically to Jesus as God's chosen one (1 Pet 2:4), maybe with the same implication. The word's application to believers likewise suggests God using them for a task. They are chosen to be God's servants, as is more obviously the case when the word is applied to the disciples (Lk 6:13; Jn 6:70). If the people who are chosen do individually belong to Jesus forever, that promise is not the point about the reference to their being "chosen" for a task. What is explicit is that the choice is retrospectively eternal. "God selected us through the Anointed One before the world's foundation" (Eph 1:4). In one sense God's selection of the Jewish-Gentile church, and behind that of Abraham's family and of Israel, took place in history. In another sense it took place much earlier. God had anticipated the need for this action and had in some sense taken it.

God then selected us to be holy and blameless in his sight (Eph 1:4). While this statement may imply a challenge, its direct point concerns God's intention. God determined to make us holy and blameless. Whereas there is a sense in which God made us holy simply by appropriating us, changing our status and declaring us to be people who belong to him, making us blameless implies God achieving something in our lives, which likely means

---

[43]John H. Schütz in his introduction to Gerd Theissen, *The Social Setting of Pauline Christianity* (Philadelphia: Fortress, 1982), 14.
[44]Ernst Troeltsch, *The Social Teaching of the Christian Churches* (London: George Allen; New York: Macmillan, 1931), 1:78; cf. Schütz, "Introduction," 15.
[45]See the paragraphs under "Privileged and Honored" in section 4.1 above.

that making us holy has the same implication. We become like an animal that is whole (rather than lame or otherwise defective) and is thus fitting to be offered to God. While *amōmos* (blameless) is one of the Septuagint's equivalents to "whole" (*tāmîm*) in this connection (e.g., Lev 1:3), *whole* is also a term for moral and relational integrity (e.g., Ps 18:23, 30 [MT 24, 31]). God made a commitment to forming a people of integrity. The point will be taken further if Paul also believes that God selected us to be "holy and blameless in love," though it is unclear whether "in love" belongs with and qualifies "holy and blameless" or belongs with and qualifies "having predestined," which follows.

The people of God was designed to be an investment bank, to venture its bag of gold so as to see it grow (Mt 25:14-30). It was designed to be a light: seven gold lamps stand for the seven congregations John writes to (Rev 1:12). They parallel the candelabra in the temple, but they shine out into the world. "You did not choose me, but I chose you, and appointed you so that you would go and bear fruit, and your fruit would last, so that whatever you ask the Father in my name, he would give you" (Jn 15:16). God planted the vine so that it would bear fruit. Its fruitfulness is not the cause of the choice but it is the aim of it. And when the disciples are fruitful, their prayers can be answered. This experience, too, is not the aim of the fruitfulness but the result of it. When Isaiah uses the image of the vine, fruitfulness lies in doing right, which fits the New Testament idea of the fruit of the Spirit, though a natural result of producing that fruit will also be that the disciples are fruitful in their witness. "As the Father sent me, so I am sending you" (Jn 20:21). This sending involved breathing the Holy Spirit into them and their being sent out to forgive people.

From the beginning, God's people was designed to be a magnet, to attract people from outside. The principle is illustrated in the stories of Jethro, Rahab, Ruth and the Eastern philosophers in Matthew 2. God's people is designed to exert a pull on the world, but to do so by being different from the world. Its calling is "to present itself both in the forum of God and in the forum of the world. For it stands for God to the world, and it stands for the world before God," embodying liberty and crying for liberty. In addition, being itself on the way and living in hope, it understands and presents itself "in the forum of the future of God and the world."[46] The congregation is thus a prophetic entity; it was the vocation of prophets to represent God to their people in proclamation and challenge, and to represent their people to God in prayer through their membership of God's cabinet.

Inclusive but Holy
The image of a household marks the believers' close relationship with one another and the commitments it entails, and it links with their possessing family commitments, rituals, language and history—all of which also come to belong to people adopted into a family. It also sets them off over against outsiders.

In 1 Peter the congregation sets up a distance between itself and the world through having a living hope and through being a distinctive people. It is a body of sojourners and aliens. Its members "walk" in a different way. It does not seek to impose its walk on the world or directly to critique the world, but it scandalizes the world by walking differently, not least in its submissiveness to suffering—while being willing to accommodate to the world in other ways (see the household code).[47] It is in the world but not of the world. "Don't be conformed to this age but be transformed by the renewing of your mind so that you may recognize what the will of God is, that which is good, pleasing, and perfect"; indeed, we are to give our bodies to God as a kind of sacrifice (Rom 12:1-2). It goes against our human inclination. It means we have to take a different stance to life from people in the world around, who live as if this age is the real and only one and as if God is not intent on transforming us in the new age into the kind of people he intended us to be from the Beginning. So we will come to offer our *bodies* as a sacrifice only if our *minds* get renewed. Both body and mind are affected by sin, and both body and mind need renewing.

The community of believers lacks the rules about circumcision, food and the sabbath that mark off an observant Jewish community, but it has other rules that mark it off, rules about avoiding idolatry and certain notorious sexual relationships (e.g., 1 Cor 6:12-20), and the practices of baptism and the Lord's Meal. Food sacrificed to idols and sexual immorality were two big

---

[46]Moltmann, *Church in the Power of the Spirit*, 1-2.
[47]Cf. Miroslav Volf, *Captive to the Word of God* (Grand Rapids and Cambridge, UK: Eerdmans, 2010), 65-90.

temptations (Rev 2:14). The argument against both is christological. You can't unite sexually with someone because you are one with Jesus; you can't have anything to do with idols because you are a participant in the body of Jesus. Thus the old purity rules go, but new purity rules take their place. When you're baptized, you surrender yourself to holiness (Rom 6:19-22); the language echoes Ezra 9.[48] The language of purity evokes the idea of priestly set-apartness (cf. Ex 19:6); its force would not be much lessened by the fact that the New Testament mostly uses talk of impurity and holiness out of their context in sacramental observance and uses it to provide metaphors with moral force independent of that connotation.[49]

Holiness is concerned with boundary maintenance; it means a purity that will "safeguard the conditions under which God's people could experience God's (dangerous) holy presence."[50] So "to become a member of the Christian *ekklēsia* meant strong social change." It meant joining a new family that replaced other relationships and sources of identity, it meant hostility from outside society, and it meant avoiding involvement in other worship.[51] While there is thus a place for forbearance and mutual acceptance, there is also a place for the congregation to dissociate itself from people who cause divisions and could trip the congregation up (Rom 16:17-18). Dissociation need not imply refusing to speak to them; its point is the need to repudiate their stance. The congregation needs the discernment to see whether a division in its midst is one to be handled by forbearance or by dissociation. Or rather, it needs to take a different stance toward people bringing trouble from outside the congregation over against the one it takes toward tensions inside the congregation.

Gentiles are characterized by a hardening of the mental arteries that issues in alienation from God and a life characterized by sensuality and impurity. When people learn about Jesus, they come to look at things in a new way and they therefore throw off this old person and put on a new one (Eph 4:17-24). This declaration both describes what happens at that moment

---

[48]Cf. James D. G. Dunn, *Romans* (Dallas: Word, 1988), 1:348.

[49]Cf. ibid., 1:346.

[50]Kent E. Brower and Andy Johnson, "Introduction," in Brower and Johnson, eds., *Holiness and Ecclesiology in the New Testament* (Grand Rapids and Cambridge, UK: Eerdmans, 2007), xvi-xxiv (on xviii).

[51]Cf. Meeks, *First Urban Christians*, 97-107, 183-84.

and defines what people need to make sure they live in light of. It means ceasing to live by desire and starting to live like God, righteous and holy. It means walking in love and thus being imitators of God in the way that children are like their parents (Eph 5:1, in line with Mt 5:48): a "bold saying."[52]

The Corinthians *were* sexually immoral, idolatrous, greedy, drunkards, slanderers and swindlers: and they still behave that way! At Corinth "ethical issues arose precisely because believers shared many of the moral values of the surrounding society," especially in connection with sex.[53] But they were washed, sanctified, put right, because Jesus is our insight, righteousness, sanctification and redemption (1 Cor 1:30; 6:7-11). He makes us part of the people to whom God is committed to doing the right thing, separates us off from others as part of that people, and gets us out of our former servitude into his service, which is our security and our obligation.

In the New Testament, sanctification is thus usually an expression for what happened to people when they came to believe in Jesus. The Corinthian believers were "made holy in the Anointed One, Jesus, called holy people" (1 Cor 1:2; cf. 1 Cor 6:11; 2 Thess 2:13). The translation "called to be his holy people" (TNIV; cf. NRSV) could give the impression that holiness is essentially an aim set before the readers, but the way the adjective or noun *hagios* follows on the verb *hagiazō* suggests that they *are* holy, not that they are merely *summoned* to holiness. But Paul can also say that God's will is your sanctification; it needs to become a reality in people's lives (1 Thess 4:3-7).[54]

The people of God is God's bride, all lovely (e.g., Is 62:5). It is Jesus' bride (Rev 21:9), beautifully dressed for her coming wedding. A persecuted congregation would not feel beautiful, and a sinful congregation (see Rev 2–3) would not feel or be beautiful. So such descriptions can embody a reassurance or a challenge.

6.2 RELATIONSHIPS WITH GOD

The Scriptures have things to say about how people get into a relationship with God, and about this relationship's ongoing dynamic. It comes to us as

---

[52]Barth, *CD* II, 2:576.
[53]Dunn, *Theology of Paul the Apostle*, 690.
[54]Cf. Fee, *God's Empowering Presence*, 880-81.

something transformative that issues from a divine initiative, though it requires our response of accepting, believing, acknowledging and acting. It is expressed in the sacramental signs of circumcision and baptism. It means we are now "in Christ" and "in the Spirit."

A Transformative Happening

As a spiritual leader, Nicodemus is insightful enough to recognize that Jesus is someone sent by God, but Jesus is not impressed, and he throws him back on his heels: "Unless someone is born from above, they cannot see God's realm"; to put it another way, "unless someone is born of water and Spirit, they cannot go into God's realm" (Jn 3:3, 5). Great spiritual leaders like Nicodemus, people committed to teaching and obeying God's word, may have no clue about the radical nature of God's intentions and about the gap between how things are and how God intends them to be. They think they see, but they don't. God's realm or reign is utterly different from what they assume. There is a great regeneration coming, part of the transformation of things that will issue in the disciples sitting on thrones in authority over the twelve Israelite clans (Mt 19:28). But that reign of God begins with Jesus' coming, and thus the great regeneration, the new birth from above, also begins with his coming. The life of the new age, eternal life, begins now. "Eternal life in Judaism, as in Daniel 12:2, is primarily the life of the Age to Come, the life of the resurrection"; through Jesus "the life of the Age to Come is already imparted to the believer."[55] It is open to Nicodemus, but he has to recognize it and enter it.

Living eternal life is thus another way of expressing the idea of entering God's realm. Both are by nature future realities, as one can see from visionary passages in both Testaments (e.g., Is 24; Rev 21). Jesus made it possible to enter God's realm now, to begin to live the life of the new age now, to begin to enjoy eternal life now, through the activity of the Holy Spirit. It involves an intervention on God's part that miraculously wipes away tears and nourishes. The intervention reinforces the assurance that this future world is a real world.

So we worship in/by spirit and truth (Jn 4:23): that is, we worship as a result of a dynamic supernatural intervention on God's part that is embodied

---

[55]Ladd, *Theology of the New Testament*, 256, 257 (rev. ed., 292, 293).

in Jesus as the true manifestation of God. Jesus' own presence evidenced the coming of God's reign by his healings and his proclaiming to poor Israel that God's reign is coming. It becomes experiential for the individual through trusting in Jesus, which makes it possible to enter the realm where God reigns and to gain an anticipatory experience of the age to come, of eternal life. Thus "regeneration means emerging from this mortal and transient life into life that is immortal and eternal"; being born again means more than a new start to the same life, as resurrection means more than resuscitation.[56]

The New Testament has many images to describe this transformative happening:[57]

- It's like being resuscitated from the dead.
- It's like turning from one allegiance to another.
- It's like being admitted to citizenship.
- It's like being cleansed from defilement.
- It's like being rescued from a pit or a shipwreck.
- It's like being born anew, to the life of the age to come.
- It's like being re-created and beginning a new life.
- It's like being adopted into a new family by a new father.
- It's like being acquitted even though the judge recognizes you were guilty.
- It's like being pardoned and having your record expunged.
- It's like being bought out of slavery so that you serve a new and kinder master.
- It's like being reconciled to someone when you've wronged them.
- It's like being accepted by someone as you are, with all your faults.
- It's like being made holy and dedicated to service in the temple.
- It's like being healed.
- It's like being freed from chains.
- It's like being ordained.
- It's like being bathed.

---

[56]Moltmann, *Spirit of Life*, 147.
[57]For what follows, cf. Dunn, *Theology of Paul the Apostle*, 328-31.

- It's like getting engaged.
- It's like getting married.
- It's like being made new.

The Divine Initiative

The multiplicity and the nature of these images shows how life-changing is the event whereby God takes hold of people and they respond to God. It may happen suddenly, as it did to Paul. Or it may involve a process of gradual enlightenment, as it did for the Samaritan woman, the handicapped man and the man born blind (Jn 4; 5; 9). Or it may be a longer process, as it was for Nicodemus (Jn 3:1-15; 7:50-52; 19:38-42) and for the disciples Jesus summoned at the beginning of his ministry, such as the two pairs of brothers he bade to go with him (Mt 4:18-22).

While one might assume that these men must have been listening to him when he issued his proclamation about God's reign (Mt 4:17), the Gospels' explicit point is that their following Jesus starts with his summons. "Being a disciple of Jesus springs from a call on his part. . . . The disciples later on confess to having experienced the compelling force of that call."[58] It is "an imperious command to follow."[59] "Disobedience to the command of Jesus: 'Follow me,' . . . is a phenomenon which is absolutely terrifying in its impossibility."[60] Jesus' summons to Saul who becomes Paul is even more abrupt. While the spectacular way Jesus takes an initiative with those disciples and with Paul is not a paradigm for the way people come to recognize Jesus, it is a telling account of one way it happens.

Although Jesus' first disciples themselves decide to follow him, then, their following is a response to his initiative. In emphasizing God's favor or grace or summons, the account of Jesus and the disciples and of Jesus and Paul corresponds to the story of Abraham, and before Abraham to the stories of Abel, Enoch and Noah.[61] The disciples or Paul are a little like resident aliens or orphans or widows in an Israelite village who find a place in one of its families and discover that the head of the household had decided it should invite some new members. It is as if he had spotted them around the village

---

[58]Edward Schillebeeckx, *Jesus* (New York: Crossroad; London: Collins, 1979), 220.

[59]John P. Meier, *A Marginal Jew* (New York: Doubleday, 2001), 3:51.

[60]Barth, *CD* IV, 2:535.

[61]Cf. Barth, *CD* II, 2:341.

or out in the fields and had set his eye on them and worked out that they could be useful members of the family work force. Their joining the family was not just their decision, or even simply the result of their asking and of the head of the household responding positively to them. People who come to believe in Jesus are responding to an invitation, even if they don't realize it.

"In the New Testament . . . the possibility of faith is not automatically given with the fact that Jesus is present as the revelation of the Father or as the One He is, as the Son or Word of God. . . . 'Flesh and blood hath not revealed it unto thee,' is His reply to Peter's confession" (Mt 16:17). "In face of the incarnate Word at the heart of revelation there seems to be a kind of delaying or questioning or limiting of revelation. Will revelation, this revelation, real revelation, reach its goal after all?" Only to some is it given to recognize God's reign (Mk 4:11-12). "Becoming manifest has to be something specific, a special act of the Father or the Son or both, that is added to the givenness of the revelation of the Father in the Son." The Father has to draw the person, give it to them, give them to the Son (Jn 6:44, 65; 10:29). It is the Holy Spirit who makes it happen (cf. 1 Cor 12:3).[62] We are asleep; we have to be woken up.[63] One cannot decide to be born. Jesus' coming and his conversation with Nicodemus initiate his rebirth.

Our human instinct may be to try to turn the basis of our relationship with God (and with other people) from someone else's initiative to our actions. Paul perhaps implies that it had been his instinct, but he came to recognize that according to the Torah, God's relationship with his people indeed started with God's initiative, with God's promise to Abraham (Rom 4). Only after beginning to fulfill that promise did God start laying down much by way of concrete expectations.

Paul had had a basis for "confidence in the flesh," in his membership of Israel and his own commitment to God; he had the best kind of relationship a person could have on that basis (Phil 3:4-6). Was it only through being grasped by Jesus that he was shaken into the realization that there was another kind of relationship with God, the kind that Abraham had and that Israel's position was based on? Perhaps he hadn't seen it clearly and had read

---

[62]Barth, *CD* I, 1:449.
[63]Barth, *CD* IV, 3:511-14.

the Torah in light of that human instinct to base our relationships on things we do, where possible, so that we can control that relationship.

Certainly he has to deal with believers who try to treat things that way. But the relationship comes about through faith in Jesus, not in oneself— indeed, only with a lack of faith in oneself. Faith abandons our basic human pride; it "is wholly and utterly humility." Faith "is an acknowledgment, a recognition and a confession."[64]

Human Responsibility

Yet Nicodemus takes an initiative in coming to see Jesus, and while Jesus' summons of his prospective disciples initiates his dealings with them, their response must follow. Jesus opens the gate for people, but they have to walk through it. Indeed, it's narrow and few go through it; most go through the wide gate that leads to destruction (Mt 7:13-14). Actually, Jesus apparently tries to make it hard for people, or certainly to make clear the cost people have to pay (Mt 8:18-22).

In Abraham's story, too, God's initiative came first, but Abraham had to respond. God said "Go"; Abraham "went" (Gen 12:1, 4). When the Israelites arrived at Jericho, Rahab had to decide to react in a different way from the rest of her people. Nicodemus had to do something similar in relation to his fellows. Rahab and Akan muddy the distinction between Canaan and Israel (she behaves like an Israelite, he like a Canaanite, and they effectively change places).[65] Nicodemus and the Samaritan woman muddy the distinction between Jews and Samaritans (he responds to Jesus like a Samaritan, she like a Jew). While Nicodemus is more of a "seeker," both Rahab and Nicodemus act surreptitiously; a person can get into trouble for taking a different stance from their community.

In effect it was Rahab's whole household that welcomed the Israelites, and in John one of the first people who decided to follow Jesus quickly brought his brother along (Jn 1:41-42). Rahab and her family become part of the Israelite community, and Jesus' followers become a community around him, the nucleus of the reconstituted Israel. Adoption into a family, at least as an adult, involves a decision by both parties. People who follow Jesus become

---

[64]Barth, *CD* IV, 1:97, 618, 758.
[65]Cf. Dan Hawk, *Every Promise Fulfilled: Contesting Plots in Joshua* (Louisville: Westminster John Knox, 1991).

like brothers to someone who takes them home and presents them to his family. They trust him to be able to do so. He has the right name; he is the eldest son, and he has the power to introduce them into the family. In that context they start a whole new life, as if they are born again, born from above.

The accounts of Paul's confrontation by Jesus in Acts emphasize Jesus' initiative and indeed do not suggest that Paul had much option about becoming a servant of Jesus, and his own talk about being grasped by Jesus (Phil 3:12) has the same implication. Yet Acts also gives the impression that he willingly surrendered to Jesus' sovereignty. In the way he speaks of his relationship with God, which is based on trust, he indicates that he also willingly surrenders now; he is happy to have lost everything because of the surpassing worth of knowing Jesus (Phil 3:7-9).

So belonging to God issues from a two-way act of acceptance. It involves the divine will and a human decision, but there is no formula for determining the relationship between the two aspects. The nondefinable nature of the relationship between divine action and human responsibility surfaces again when Jesus talks about being the bread of life. The people who come to him are the people who are drawn by the Father, the people to whom it is given by the Father, which could seem to limit who may do so. But Jesus emphasizes that "all that the Father gives me will come to me, and I will certainly not throw out the person who comes to me. . . . All that he has given me, I shall not lose any of it" (Jn 6:37, 39).

"Faith in Jesus is impossible without God's initiating will for the world, but human beings retain responsibility for the decision they make in response to God's initiative."[66] The people who come to him are the ones the Father draws. They are taught by God. They are the ones who listen to and learn from the Father. No one can come to Jesus unless the Father has enabled that person to do so (see further Jn 6:35-65). Jesus heals a disabled man and bids him not to sin any longer (Jn 5:14); while evidently there was no great righteousness in him that led to Jesus' choosing him and healing him, God's grace cannot then be presumed on. It demands a response.

---

[66]Gail R. O'Day, "The Gospel of John," in Leander E. Keck et al., eds., *The New Interpreter's Bible* (Nashville: Abingdon, 1995), 9:491-871, on the passage.

Coming to Jesus, believing in him and finding eternal life involve a relationship like that of student and professor. Suppose there is a seminary student who cares nothing for studying the Old Testament, who believes that there is nothing to be learned from the story of Israel three thousand years ago. Such students will learn nothing unless a professor draws them; the professor's task, skill and gift is to open students' eyes to what can be learned. Yet they learn nothing unless they are willing to look in the direction the professor points. If they spend the classes surfing the Internet and write their papers by cutting and pasting from various sources without letting the material go through their brain and spirit, they learn nothing. The professor has to draw; the student has to follow. At some point a magical moment may happen when a student's eyes open. It may never happen to the person in the next seat.

Accepting, Believing, Knowing

In his lifetime the appropriate response to Jesus was to "accept" him (Jn 1:12; 5:43-44) or come to him (Jn 6:35-39; 7:37-39) or look at him (Jn 6:40; 12:44-45) or listen to him (Jn 5:24; 8:45-47) or follow him (Jn 1:37-38). As the word *accepting* suggests, the coming, following, listening and looking are not mere outward actions, but neither do they simply comprise an inner listening and contemplation. They are an interrelated outward hearing/sight and inward hearing/insight.

All those responses implied "believing" in Jesus. People who physically heard and saw did not necessarily listen to him or see into him. Believing is unequivocal. It marks the difference between outward and inward. Becoming God's child involves believing that Jesus is the Anointed One, God's Son (Jn 20:31); such belief is the sign or means of being born of God (1 Jn 5:1). It involves believing his words (Jn 5:47). For people who cannot believe him, it involves believing the things he has done (Jn 10:38). It involves believing in him or believing in his name; there are several ways of expressing the point, with the dative (e.g., Jn 4:21), with *en* (e.g., Jn 3:15) or with *eis* (Jn 3:16). Fortuitously, the possibility of this key response of believing is open to people who have not physically heard and seen; they can believe on the basis of the testimony of people who did listen to him and see into him. Metaphorically, they too may thus listen to and look at him, come to him, accept him and follow him.

"We have come to believe and know that you are God's Holy One" (Jn 6:69).
People "believe" and they "know." Are these two stages? Are they two aspects
of the same activity or experience? Jesus doesn't believe; he only knows. Yet
faith is not set over against knowledge. It is based on knowledge and it issues
in knowledge. "Even if you do not believe in me, believe in the deeds, so that
you may know, really know, that the Father is in me and I am in the Father"
(Jn 10:38). "Now we know that you know all things and have no need that
someone ask you. By this we believe that you came from God" (Jn 16:30).
The world thinks it knows (Jn 7:27-29), but its so-called knowledge is not
real knowledge. Its knowledge is based on what it sees, but real knowledge
issues from believing.

What decides (humanly speaking) whether someone believes and knows?
"If someone is willing to do his will, that person will know of the teaching
whether it is from God or I speak from myself" (Jn 7:17). There is a price to
be paid for recognizing Jesus. It involves submission and self-denial. John
the Baptizer had paid the price in being willing to draw attention away from
himself to Jesus. Nicodemus would have to pay a price, as would other
Jewish leaders. The much-married Samaritan woman would have to do so
in owning up to her past.

Paul gave up his old way of evaluating everything that he possessed,
because of the surpassing worth of knowing Jesus, his Lord (Phil 3:8). Like
faith, this knowing might once again have a cognitive, a conative and an
affective content. The cognitive is suggested by Paul's repeated stress on
"counting." He had come to think differently about Jesus. The conative (the
exercise of the will) is suggested by his reference to Jesus being his Lord. We
have noted the First Testament assumption that "knowing God" implies
"acknowledging God."[67] It means making Yahweh Lord, in an exercise of the
will that would otherwise have been impossible. The affective might be suggested by his contemporary cultural context, where knowledge of God could
imply a mystical awareness, a personal communion with God; it is also suggested by his subsequent spelling out of the knowledge of Jesus as knowing
his resurrection power and knowing participation in his sufferings. Paul can
speak negatively about knowledge, but here he speaks positively about it.

---

[67]See the paragraphs under "A School, a Priesthood" in section 6.1 above.

Believing and Acting

One gets right by God *dia pisteōs christou* (Rom 3:21-22). It would make theological sense to understand this phrase to mean "through the faithfulness of the Anointed One,"[68] the one who is the embodiment of God's faithfulness to us in being willing to pay the price for the way we ruined our relationship with God by betraying it. But *pistis christou* usually refers to our trust in Jesus rather than Jesus' faithfulness (e.g., Rom 3:26), and more likely the phrase makes the point that Jesus makes in John: we are put right by God "through our trust in the Anointed One." What God has done to restore the relationship between him and us becomes effective through our trust in Jesus as the embodiment of that commitment to restoring the relationship. Our act of trust in Jesus responds to God's act in sending him to put things right between us.

There is a sense in which faith is set over against actions. Actions such as getting circumcised or baptized or seeking peace and justice can't put someone into a harmonious relationship with God. Some people thought that Gentiles who came to believe in Jesus needed to accept observances such as circumcision, but that view compromises the principle that being right with God issues from God's grace and from a response of trust in Jesus (Rom 3:21-31). The archetypal story of Abraham makes the point (Rom 4:1-25). Abraham was right with God on the basis of trusting in God's promises. Circumcision subsequently set a seal on his position; it did not contribute to it. His faith did express itself in obedience and faithfulness; he made the move from Babylonia to Canaan and was even willing to turn Isaac into an offering when God said so (as Jas 2:14-26 points out). But these acts of obedience and faithfulness were expressions of faith or trust on the part of someone who was right with God, not ways of becoming right with God.

There is a sense in which faith and action are one. Jesus talks to people about taking action to acquire the food that endures to eternal life, and their ears prick up; everyone wants to know what to do in such a connection. What action is required? Jesus' answer is predictably unpredictable and unacceptable. "The work of God is this: to believe in the one he has sent" (Jn 6:29). "Doing God's will" implies believing in Jesus. The ridiculous

---

[68] See, e.g., Wright, *Paul and the Faithfulness of God*, 836-45.

nature of Jesus' answer is reflected in the ridiculous nature of their response, which is in effect to ask him to do what he has just done, to feed them miraculously. When the Philippi jailer similarly asks what he must *do* to be rescued, Paul and Silas tell him to *believe* in the Lord Jesus, then he will be rescued, he and his household (Acts 16:30-31).[69] Acts uses the aorist tense, whereas John uses the present: there is both an initial act of faith and trust and an ongoing life of faith and trust.

Faith is closely associated with and expressed in submission or obedience (Rom 1:5). Acknowledging Jesus is the first act of obedience (2 Cor 9:13). To put it in some other First Testament terms, there is a close relationship between faith and faithfulness.[70] The faith and obedience are directed toward Jesus, and also toward God. Faith issues from hearing the Lord's message, and it issues in turning to the living God from idols (1 Thess 1:8-9; Rom 10:17). It is active, through love (1 Thess 1:3; Gal 5:6). Faith is not a work, a human achievement, because it involves "the radical renunciation of accomplishment, the obedient submission to the God-determined way of salvation."[71] But faith as a response to God's grace is not merely a passive trust.

Faith is closely associated with hope as well as with action (1 Thess 3:6; 5:8; 1 Cor 13:13). It is integrally related to the way believers relate to other people and to the future. In Western Christian culture, "faith seems not so much an integral way of life as an energizing and consoling aura added to the business of a life shaped by factors other than faith." Thus we talk more about "spirituality," with its emphasis on "the empowerment and healing of autonomous individuals."[72] Further, Western culture is inclined to stress "*my* faith." The New Testament rather points to a stress on "my *faith*," my identification with the faith of the church, in both its subjective and its objective nature—in the church's believing and in the belief the church holds.

[69]Cf. Raymond F. Brown, *The Gospel According to John* (Garden City, NY: Doubleday, 1966; London: Chapman, 1971), 265.

[70]Karl P. Donfried, "The Theology of 1 Thessalonians," in Donfried and I. Howard Marshall, *The Theology of the Shorter Pauline Letters* (Cambridge and New York: Cambridge University Press, 1993), 1-79, on 54.

[71]Bultmann, *Theology of the New Testament*, 1:316.

[72]Volf, *Against the Tide*, 82. In an earlier formulation of this comment (in a foreword to Christian Scharen, *Faith as a Way of Life* [Grand Rapids and Cambridge, UK: Eerdmans, 2008], ix), Volf begins the sentence "the faith seems not," which is also suggestive.

The Sacramental Signs

When God made a covenant with Abraham, he did attach a sign to it; the males in Abraham's family were to be circumcised (Gen 17). The sign did not imply that the covenant promise applied only to the males; God had already established that it applied to all Abraham's descendants. It might seem an odd sign, though it might draw attention to the way the covenant involved God working through procreation. The sign is applied to the organ whereby procreation happens, and to the organ with which men commonly go wrong; it suggests the disciplining of that organ.

After Jesus, "through him you were circumcised with a circumcision not performed by human hands, through the putting off of the lower nature through the circumcision of the Anointed One. You were buried with him through baptism, through which you were also raised with him by means of trust in the working of the God who raised him from the dead people" (Col 2:11-12). Jesus' willingness to die was accompanied by a trust in God's power to raise him from among the dead. Our baptism is an expression of our identification with his dying that thus presupposes a trust in the same power that God employed in raising him.

Further, while there is a sense in which our resurrection still lies in the future, in another sense it has already happened; the image of resurrection overlaps with the image of being born again or entering the realm where God reigns. Identifying with Jesus means that in effect we died and rose when he died and rose; and both our dying and our being raised from death link with our trusting in God's capacity to raise us from death. When people are baptized, they are affirming the significance of Jesus' death as the key event it was, identifying with it and participating in it, like slaves in Texas in 1865 (or African Americans today) affirming the significance of the emancipation proclamation, identifying with it and participating in it.[73]

If baptism involves identifying with Jesus, it involves accepting a commission to take up the cross. New Testament writers "used baptism exactly to summon converts to a socially accountable newness of life" (e.g., Col 3:1–4:6).[74] "To be baptised is to undergo judgement, by accepting the work of Christ in our stead . . . , to accept a sentence of death . . . , to have died with Christ." It

---

[73]See the paragraphs under "Counterintuitive but Powerful" in section 2.3 above.
[74]McClendon, *Systematic Theology: Ethics*, 258.

is thus the means whereby we become part of a new community that lives in light of that fact.[75] Thus in Acts people are commonly baptized in public and in groups. Becoming a believer does not happen to individuals in the privacy of their homes, nor is baptism a rite that happens in a sanctuary. In fulfillment of John the Baptizer's prophecy, people get overwhelmed by the Spirit after hearing the news about Jesus in some public place where people gather, and their baptism follows as the sign of their publicly identifying themselves with Jesus' death and with the community that follows him.[76]

So people were baptized because they and their households came to repentance and faith. On the basis of the New Testament, it is possible to mount an argument for the baptizing of children born within a believing family or for the baptizing of such children when they grow up or for their being treated as part of God's people without requiring baptism. Each of these practices would make a significant partial statement about the significance of baptism; none makes the full statement that New Testament practice implies.[77]

Further, we don't know whether people were immersed in water or had it poured over them,[78] and likewise both practices would make a theological point. Immersion suggests going under, drowning, dying with Jesus. "Believers re-enact that death by participating in the ritual of baptism";[79] this reenactment is not merely an imaginary one.[80] Pouring water on people would fit with the idea that baptism was a cleansing rite.[81] This idea is only implicit in the New Testament (notably in Eph 5:26), but cleansing was one way to think of what Jesus did for people. The idea that the people of God need to be cleansed and renewed goes back to Ezekiel, and Jewish thinking extended that idea to converts. To bring them within the covenant people,

---

[75]Colin E. Gunton, *The Actuality of Atonement* (Edinburgh: T&T Clark; Grand Rapids: Eerdmans, 1989), 184, 188.

[76]Cf. Dunn, *Theology of Paul the Apostle*, 450-54; further, James D. G. Dunn, *Baptism in the Holy Spirit* (London: SCM Press; Naperville, IL: Allenson, 1970).

[77]Cf. Thiselton's discussion in *Hermeneutics of Doctrine*, 512-14, 536-40, and Moltmann's in *Church in the Power of the Spirit*, 226-42.

[78]See, e.g., Meeks, *First Urban Christians*, 150-57.

[79]David Seeley, *The Noble Death* (Sheffield: JSOT, 1989), 102.

[80]Cf. Michael J. Gorman, *Cruciformity* (Grand Rapids and Cambridge, UK: Eerdmans, 2001), 127, though I am not sure he portrays the objective nature of the event sharply enough.

[81]Rudolf Schnackenburg begins his study of baptism here (*Baptism in the Thought of St. Paul* [Oxford: Blackwell; New York: Herder, 1964], 3-9).

converts were bathed to remove their heathen defilement, as well as being circumcised if they were men, so that they become children reborn into a new family.[82]

Likewise, given that circumcision was the sign and seal of Abraham's being right with God by faith, it wouldn't be surprising if baptism was seen as a sign and seal of the fact that people who believe in Jesus are right with God,[83] but this point, too, is not explicit in the New Testament. There, it is the gift of the Holy Spirit itself that is the seal (Eph 1:13; 4:30).

In Christ

Congregations and individual believers are *en Christō*, which is usually translated "in Christ"; phrases such as "in the Lord" are comparable. Paul refers to the redemption that is in Christ Jesus, to being alive to God in Christ Jesus, to our having eternal life in Christ Jesus, to the love of God that is ours in Christ Jesus and to believers being one body in Christ (Rom 3:23; 6:11, 23; 8:39; 12:5).[84] He speaks of his colleagues "in Christ Jesus" or "in Christ," of people who were "in Christ" before he was and of having something to boast about "in Christ Jesus" (Rom 15:17; 16:3, 7, 9).

The phrase *en Christō* is terse and laconic. In English "in" suggests a location, and "in Christ" sounds parallel to "in Rome" or "in their minds" or "in the world" (Rom 1:7, 2:15; 5:13). But in other contexts the preposition *en* can be translated "by/through/with/of," partly because *en* derives its meaning from that of Hebrew *b*. Sometimes *en Christō* suggests "belonging to Christ," so that "in Christ" has the same meaning as "of Christ" (these expressions alternate in Gal 3:26-29). Sometimes it suggests "through Christ" (so some translation in, e.g., Gal 3:14; 5:10). Sometimes it suggests "in connection with Christ" rather more generally: "in connection with Christ Jesus neither circumcision nor circumcision has any value" (Gal 5:6:). So *en Christō* need not always mean "in Christ."

The instrumental "in Christ" is an adverbial expression; the connectional "in Christ" is an adjectival expression. As an adverbial expression, "in Christ" can parallel "in Abraham" and "in Adam." God promised that the world

---

[82]Cf. ibid., 15.

[83]Cf. John Calvin, *Institutes of the Christian Religion* IV.14.1.

[84]Ernest Best (*One Body in Christ* [London: SPCK, 1955]) takes the corporate connotations as the key to understanding the phrase "in Christ."

would find blessing in or with or through Abraham, and that intention comes about in or with or through Christ (Gal 3:8-9, 14). "Abraham and Christ are viewed as representative figures through whom God acts towards the human race: he acts towards them 'in' those figures and they are caught up 'with' them in that divine initiative of grace."[85] Likewise we die in or with or through Adam, and we will be made alive in or with or through Christ (1 Cor 15:22). Adam and Christ represented us; what they did counts for us. Their deed has a decisive effect on us; it is as if we were there, doing what they did.

To put it more strongly, we die because there is an ontological link between us and Adam, a little like the link between children and their parents. This link does not depend on the children's birth. It applies to adopted children as well as birth children; they really become the children of their new parents, and they share in their fate, their troubles and their blessings.

Or the link is a little like citizenship. When people become citizens of a country, they become ontologically Australian or Canadian or whatever, just as Australian or Canadian as people born there. The link need not entail an awareness of a connection (Christians do have a sense of personal connection with Christ, but this awareness is not the implication of the idea of being "in Christ"). If I ever become a US citizen, I might not *feel* an American; I was British for too long. But the fact that I did not *feel* one would not alter the fact that I *was* now one.

Mystical writers use expressions such as "in Christ" as a way of indicating the intimacy and fellowship that we can have with Christ. The Scriptures do presuppose that we have such intimacy and close personal relationship, but they do not use "in Christ" language to refer to it. Being in Christ does not denote an inner or mystical relationship. The phrase has an "objective reference"; it points to the "objective grounds" that make our relationship with Christ possible.[86] *En Christō* does not indicate that we are located in Christ in a spiritual sense. When the Scriptures describe our close personal relationship with God, they speak of this intimacy in terms of close human relationships such as that of children to a father, not in terms of location.

---

[85]See A. J. M. Wedderburn, "Some Observations on Paul's Use of the Phrases 'in Christ' and 'with Christ,'" *JSNT* 25 (1985): 83-97 (on 91).

[86]J. K. S. Reid, *Our Life in Christ* (London: SCM Press, 1963), 24-25.

Indeed, the meaning of *en Christō* is not so different from that of the phrase "with Christ." That actual phrase is rare, but the New Testament makes noteworthy use of verbs that are "with" compounds such as die with, be crucified with, be buried with, live with, suffer with, be glorified with and reign with (e.g., Rom 6:4-8; 8:16-29; Eph 2:5-6; Col 2:12-13; 2 Tim 2:11-12).[87]

The Coming of God's Spirit

So "the law/Torah of the spirit/Spirit of life in Christ Jesus" has freed us from the law/Torah of sin and death (Rom 8:1-2). The unfolding argument in Romans 8 will suggest that the sentence refers to the divine Spirit and not just the human spirit. It parallels the declaration that nobody enters God's realm unless they are "born of water and Spirit" (Jn 3:5). Talk in terms of the Spirit is another way of indicating that something extraordinary happens when people come to believe in Jesus. The transcendent divine spirit makes contact with the human spirit; believers receive "the spirit that is from God" (1 Cor 2:12). The Spirit came on Jesus at his baptism, then drove him to be tempted by the devil (!). He began his work in Galilee by the power of the Spirit, declared that the Spirit was upon him there and expelled demons by the Spirit (Mt 4:1; 12:28; Lk 4:14, 18). He promised his disciples that the Spirit would come to them, and it happened after his resurrection (Jn 20:22; Acts 2; Eph 4:7-10). The filling of the Spirit issued in the proclamation of the gospel in other languages, a form of fulfillment of the promise about prophesying in Joel 2:28-32 in behavior that looks out of control and is rather like drunkenness, and in inspired interpretation of the Scriptures.[88]

Thus spirituality, too, does not emerge from us. "Was it through actions prescribed by the Torah that you received the Spirit, or through listening with trust?" (Gal 3:2). Stories in Acts show how people's experience of the Spirit commonly started. They were praying or listening to someone tell them the Jesus story, and God knocked them over. No observances such as baptism or fasting or going on silent retreats or practicing centering prayer brought about this experience of the Spirit. People just heard and trusted what they heard. If experience of the Spirit starts in that way (Paul argues), surely that is how it continues.

---

[87]See Dunn, *Theology of Paul the Apostle*, 401-4.
[88]See further John R. Levison, *Filled with the Spirit* (Grand Rapids and Cambridge, UK: Eerdmans, 2009), 317-65.

The coming of God's spirit on people can be taken for granted as an aspect of their becoming believers, as they thereby come to share Abraham's blessing (Gal 3:2-5, 14). They receive the gospel "with the Holy Spirit's joy" (1 Thess 1:6). God "gives his Holy Spirit" to them in fulfillment of the vision in Ezekiel 37:14, whose language Paul reflects (1 Thess 4:8). They have the truth about Jesus' execution revealed by the Spirit (1 Cor 2:6-10). They say "Jesus is Lord" by the Spirit (1 Cor 12:3). They are anointed by the Spirit, and the Spirit's dwelling in their hearts is the pledge or guarantee or down payment or first installment of what is still to come (2 Cor 1:21-22). They are sealed by the Spirit (Eph 1:13; 4:30), renewed and immersed in the Spirit (Tit 3:5-6), sanctified by the Spirit (2 Thess 2:13). Through the Holy Spirit God's love floods their hearts (Rom 5:5). They are baptized by the Spirit (1 Cor 12:13), and their worship reflects that fact (see 1 Cor 12–14). They are washed, sanctified and put right "in the name of the Lord Jesus the Anointed One and in the Spirit of our God" (1 Cor 6:11).

In the twentieth century, many Pentecostal congregations experienced realities such as speaking in tongues and healing, but many other Christian congregations who declared in their creeds that they believed in the Holy Spirit would have had a hard time identifying in their life phenomena that suggested the Spirit's activity. Western Christians do not assume that becoming a believer is closely associated with a felt or observable experience of the Spirit coming on and into the person. "The new church member is in effect given the assurance: 'You have believed all the right things and/or received the sacrament of baptism and/or laying on of hands; therefore you have received the Spirit, whether you know it or not.'"[89] The situation in Judaism in Roman times was similar.[90]

In the New Testament the order or logic is the reverse. The discernible reality was the arrival of the Spirit, which generated evidences such as prophesying, miracles, awareness of God's love and relating to God as Father, intellectual illumination and moral transformation.[91] The pouring out of God's spirit on Jews was a sign that the new age had dawned, and the pouring out of God's spirit on Gentiles was a confirmation of the fact.

---

[89]Dunn, *Theology of Paul the Apostle*, 430.
[90]See Levison, *Filled with the Spirit*.
[91]Dunn, *Theology of Paul the Apostle*, 430-39.

In the Spirit

So the coming of the Spirit is integral to people becoming believers and integral to their ongoing life as believers. The Spirit is sent into their inner being so that they begin personally to relate to God as Father (Gal 4:4-6). They are now (if things work out in the natural way) people who hope by the Spirit, walk by the Spirit, are led by the Spirit in a moral way, live by the Spirit, sow to the Spirit, reap eternal life from the Spirit (Gal 5:5, 16, 18, 22, 25; 6:8; cf. Rom 8:11-16). God's working in them means being strengthened with power through God's Spirit in their inner being (Eph 3:16-17). Given that the presence of the Spirit means a sense of sonship, moral renewal, compulsion to witness and the potential to reveal things that God is saying, it corresponds to talk of God's spirit in Isaiah 11; 42; 61, Ezekiel 36; and Joel 2.

Whereas it is questionable whether "in Christ" implies something mystical, "in the Spirit" might more plausibly be seen to suggest a mystical relationship with or experience of God,[92] though talking about it as an "inner" experience would be misleading, because the Scriptures more often see an experience "in the Spirit" as happening "out of the body"—it is an experience of being taken out of ourselves (e.g., Rev 1:10; 4:2; 17:3; 21:10). Spirit enters Ezekiel to lift him up, then takes him off elsewhere (Ezek 2:2; 3:12, 14, 24; 8:3; 11:1, 24). Yahweh's hand comes on him and takes him out into the valley in/by Yahweh's spirit (Ezek 37:1).

In turn, "in the Spirit" can have the same implication as the more frequent expression "according to the Spirit." In Romans 8 Paul reformulates his exposition of the nature of discipleship (see Rom 6) within the framework of reference to the Holy Spirit, as the one who brings about an anticipation of what belongs to the End, to resurrection day (Rom 8:11; cf. Rom 2:5-10). All the realities that belong to the End can become realities now, through the activity of the Holy Spirit. On the basis of what Jesus has done, we walk about now in accordance with the Spirit, not in accordance with the lower nature (Rom 8:4). We think differently, following the promptings of the Spirit; we formulate attitudes different from the attitudes involved in walking about in accordance with the lower

---

[92]Thus Jürgen Moltmann treats with mystical experience in a book about *The Spirit of Life*, 198-213.

nature and following its promptings (Rom 8:5). That change means life, peace, a positive stance toward God and thus a positive attitude of God to us (Rom 8:6-8).

Our walk can thus be described as "in/by the Spirit" as opposed to "in/by the lower nature," if God's Spirit lives in us—and "if someone doesn't have Christ's spirit, this person doesn't belong to him" (Rom 8:9). "If you live in accordance with the lower nature, you are going to die, but if by the Spirit[93] you put to death the body's deeds, you will live; because the people who are led by God's Spirit, these are God's children" (Rom 8:13-14). "Life in the Spirit is nothing less than a condition of moral *maturity*."[94]

So (1) believers are not in the lower nature but in the Spirit; (2) the Spirit of God is in them; (3) they have the Spirit of Christ; and (4) they are led by God's Spirit (Rom 8:9, 14).

First, then, speaking in terms of being "in the Spirit," like speaking of being "in Christ," implies a more intrinsic connection between believers and Jesus than speaking in terms such as "following Jesus"; it indicates that there has come to exist an ontological connection between them and Jesus like that between a child and its adoptive parents or between two people who get married. It suggests being indissolubly connected to Jesus. The natural ontological connection between human beings and the lower nature that exists because they belong to Adam's "family" has been succeeded or replaced by an ontological connection between them and the Spirit.

Such is the theory. It does not always work out that way (otherwise Paul would not have to argue many of the points he does have to argue). Sometimes a man who has left his parents to stick to his wife has not actually cut the apron strings to his mother and is thus torn because he doesn't live in light of his real new position, and he gets into a mess because of that failure. Likewise believers can continue to live as if their ontological connection with Adam were still determinative for their lives, when in reality the connection with the Spirit has replaced the connection with the lower nature, and they have to start living that way.

---

[93]Paul uses a simple dative without a proposition.
[94]Oliver O'Donovan, *Finding and Seeking* (Grand Rapids and Cambridge, UK: Eerdmans, 2014), 8.

The Spirit of Jesus

To put it the second way, the Spirit of God is in believers. As Jeremiah expressed it, God has written the Torah into them. God has made a light go on in their minds in such a way that it stays alight and continues to illumine their way of thinking and thus their way of living. It makes them look at everything differently. Instead of encouraging their minds to be inflexible because they like the way of looking at things that belongs to the lower nature, God encourages their minds to be enthusiastic about conforming to the divine way of looking at things.

God's Spirit is the way God achieves this end, because a person's spirit is the aspect of them that is free to roam. Jesus is a physical person, located in a physical place; he could walk through doors, but he could not be physically present in Jerusalem and Galilee at the same time. Jesus' Spirit is not so limited. It can be prompting them and reminding people of what Jesus has done and what he expects of them and thus be encouraging them to walk about in accordance with the Spirit, in accordance with Jesus.

Thus—to put it the third way—they have the Spirit of Jesus. "'In the Spirit' is chained to Christology"; something can be a "movement of the Spirit" only if it is in keeping with the nature of the Son.[95] Given that the Spirit is the Spirit of Jesus, it is as natural to speak of "Christ in us" as of "the Spirit in us" (Rom 8:9-10; cf. 2 Cor 13:5) and to declare that "Christ in you" is "the hope of glory" (Col 1:27)—or that "Christ among you" is the hope of glory.[96] Ephesians 3:17 prays that "Christ may live in your minds through faith," and the means to this end is "that you may be strengthened through [the Father's] spirit in the inner person" (Eph 3:16).

It has been said of the declaration "Christ lives in me" (Gal 2:20) that the "mystical character" of this text is denied by no one, in the sense that it expresses "that form of spirituality which strives after (or experiences) an immediate contact (or union) of the soul with God."[97] But Paul says nothing here about striving, and the context indicates that he is referring not to a

---

[95]I owe this point to Thomas A. Bennett.

[96]So Christopher J. H. Wright, *The Mission of God* (Downers Grove, IL: InterVarsity Press; Nottingham, UK: Inter-Varsity Press, 2006), 340.

[97]Alfred Wikenhauser, *Pauline Mysticism* (New York: Herder, 1959), 46, 14. Daniel Marguerat includes an extensive bibliography in his nuanced study "Paul the Mystic," in Jan Krans et al., eds.,

mystical experience but to the same reality he emphasizes elsewhere. Objectively and historically, Jesus died for me, and my associating myself with him means that I died. Objectively and historically, he rose from the dead, and my associating myself with him means I, too, began a new life. The objective thereby becomes also subjective.

Yet it is not merely because of our action that it becomes subjective. It becomes subjective because Jesus himself is not just a figure of the past but is "the living Jesus Christ" who himself "overcomes the barrier of His own time and therefore historical distance. Because and as He is present and future in His then act. Because and as He is among us to-day, and will be among us to-morrow, in His then act."[98] "Because we are sons, God sent his Son's spirit into our hearts, crying 'Abba, Father'" (Gal 4:7).

There are two complementary ways we might understand this action or influence of Jesus' spirit. Believers find themselves saying and doing things that they would not naturally do and say. It's as if they have been invaded by something from outside themselves, like people who less beneficently have had demons enter them, so that they act in a way that is not natural to them. They might then be inclined to ask "Where did that come from?" or "I don't know what made me say that." Their freedom in talking to God as Father is an example, as is their further freedom and enthusiasm in prayer (Eph 5:18-20; 6:18-20).

On a more regular basis they will be aware that they think and speak differently from the way they once did. They understand things they did not previously understand (Col 1:9). They may think in terms of this change reflecting the influence of someone else. Married people are often affected by their husband or wife's personality or insights or skills.

The Life of Jesus

This experience may help us understand how we can think about one person living in another person. My parents and my wife live in me in the sense that their character affects me. Although people may not realize it (and even I may not realize it), in certain respects when people meet me they meet my

---

Paul, John, and Apocalyptic Eschatology, Martinus C. de Boer Festschrift (Leiden and Boston: Brill, 2013), 76-93.
[98]Barth, *CD* IV, 2:112.

parents and my wife. Further, I think about my parents and about my wife; they are alive in my mind.

Admittedly, talk of someone living in another person is dangerous. My wife does not merely live in me. She is a person in her own right who exists objectively, independent of me. Talk of her living in me must not issue in my domesticating her or thinking that I have grasped all of her. There is too much of her to be contained in me or apprehended by me.

The language of Jesus living in us is useful because it suggests the closeness and reality of his influence on us, but its danger is to suggest the opposite. The closeness and reality of the relationship lie in the fact that Jesus is in the room with me and is much bigger than me, not that he is inside my spirit and thus limited to its dimensions and to my perceptions. Jesus lives in us in the sense that we embody certain things about Jesus, and insofar as we do so.

Because Jesus, the one endowed by the Spirit and raised in the Spirit, then endows the Spirit, the Spirit can be the link between Jesus and the ultimate fulfillment of God's purpose whose coming his execution and resurrection initiated.[99] The church is waiting for God's Son from heaven; meanwhile the Spirit's activity is a reality in its midst, manifested in phenomena such as prophecy, tongues and healing, and in the graces of the Spirit such as love, faith and hope. The activity of the Spirit is thus an encouragement to hope (Rom 15:13; Gal 5:5).

To put it the fourth way, believers follow the prompting of God's Spirit rather than the prompting of the lower nature. They put to death the deeds of the body. This new prompting characteristically requires outrageous acts of love or faith. Abraham, for instance, was impelled to leave his extended family to depart and live in a foreign country, to go off in pursuit of a victorious army to rescue his nephew, to surrender the chance to gain any financial profit from his success, to live in the conviction that God was going to give him this new country and give him offspring and, when he has offspring, to set off to sacrifice him. His acts are signs that God's Spirit was at work in him.

---

[99]"It is pneumatology that brings christology and eschatology together" (Moltmann, *Spirit of Life*, 69).

Confronted by such demands, there are at least two senses in which one might cry "Abba," in other words, "Father" (Rom 8:15). The cry might be a declaration of commitment so to follow. More likely it is a plea for the help one needs in order to follow the Spirit's prompting. Paul knows the sense of wretchedness aroused by the tension between one's natural inclinations and the commitment God expects of him (Rom 7:24). With regard to the particularities of God's expectations of him as an individual (his equivalent to those challenges to Abraham), he asks elsewhere, "Who is sufficient for these things?" (2 Cor 2:16). But the pouring out of God's Spirit means one can cry out "Father, help us!" and know God's help in time of need (Heb 4:16). Believers can live as obedient children.

6.3 Ambiguities

One might have thought that the wonder of what God did in bringing Israel out of Egypt would simply introduce the people of God into a life of peace and holiness, but it didn't do so. Likewise one might have thought that the wonder of what God did in Jesus and of what God does in the Spirit would simply introduce the people of God into a life of peace and holiness, but it didn't do so. The life of the original Israel and that of the expanded Israel combines fulfillment with suffering and combines obedience with rebellion. "The apocalypse puzzles me. . . . There is something else that puzzles me, however, and that is the church," whose flaws are "all too clearly manifest," and yet "the church is itself a part of the gospel."[100] The apocalypse puzzles us in part because God puzzles us. God has his ambiguities, changes of mind, relentings, conflictedness and capacity to suffer.[101] It is hardly surprising if we do, too. We are involved in a battle, and we have to take up our cross in following Jesus. The experience tests what we are. Being committed to God makes our lives more complicated and conflicted. They have to be lives of ongoing repentance. We are becoming what we are. We are on the way.

---

[100]Joseph L. Mangina, "God, Israel, and Ecclesia in the Apocalypse," in Richard B. Hays and Stefan Alkier, eds., *Revelation and the Politics of Apocalyptic Interpretation* (Waco, TX: Baylor University Press, 2012), 85-103 (on 85).
[101]See chapter one above.

Living with Danger

"I have told you these things so that through me you may have peace. In the world you have trouble, but rejoice, I have overcome the world" (Jn 16:33). Jesus expects the world to hate his disciples as it hated him (Jn 15:18-21). After all, like him they do not belong to it. They have turned their back on it and thus incidentally exposed its own sinfulness. Like him and like the Comforter, they will testify to an alternative, but the world will continue to turn its back on this alternative. Organized religion is part of the world, and Jesus expects organized religion, in particular, to take the same attitude to them as it did to him (Jn 16:1-3). They need to be prepared for this experience so that it has less chance to knock them off balance when it comes to them. The trouble will come because neither the state nor the people of God know (acknowledge) Jesus or his Father. While this pattern is a characteristic of the crisis that belongs to the End (Mt 10:17-39), the End is not confined to the (final) End (Mk 13:9-13), though the period of trouble is kept short for the sake of the elect (Mt 24:22; Mk 13:20). It is one reason why the church is "the waiting community."[102]

So the experience of God's people is one of tribulation (Rom 8). "The new order which had come with Christ was quite different from the Messianic age to which Paul might have looked forward. The Messianic congregation, the saints, the chosen ones, by no means enjoyed a prominent position in the world." They experienced the ordinary problems of humanity, and they were persecuted like Jesus himself, though like him, they will experience glory in the future.[103] A congregation such as that at Rome is "living within a hostile world . . . surrounded and threatened by the night and 'the works of darkness'" so that in its relationship with the surrounding world "a primary consideration has to be successful survival" (see Rom 12:9–13:14). Persecution and acts of malice are to be expected.[104] The emphasis on love in this context is therefore noteworthy, and love is to express itself to outsiders as well as to one another.

Noteworthy also is the emphasis on submission to the authorities, in the conviction that they are under God's authority whether or not they

---

[102]Otto Weber, *Foundations of Dogmatics* (Grand Rapids: Eerdmans, 1983), 2:518.

[103]Nils A. Dahl, *Studies in Paul* (Minneapolis: Augsburg, 1977), 11.

[104]Dunn, *Theology of Paul the Apostle*, 674.

recognize it, and that they are constrained by God's authority and sovereignty like the Babylonian and Persian authorities described in the stories in Daniel. In such First Testament contexts, people were attacked because they were faithful to Yahweh, and they were delivered because they were faithful to Yahweh. In New Testament contexts, that double dynamic continues. While all ordinary people may be vulnerable to harsh treatment by the authorities, noncompliance is likely to increase the possibility of such treatment, and it is thus less wise than submission. As in the visions in Daniel, most believers in Jesus do not have the option of being involved in political affairs, but neither are they encouraged to seek the option of withdrawing from city life.[105]

People do sometimes pay for their faithfulness with their lives (cf. Dan 11:33). The beast is given power to attack the saints and conquer them, which calls for their endurance and faithfulness (Rev 13:7, 10). "The Church itself (in which somewhere the crucifixion of Christ is always being repeated) is to-day faithful and to-morrow unfaithful, to-day strong and to-morrow weak."[106] They have to live by the fact that henceforth the dead who die in the Lord are blessed; they rest from their labor and their deeds follow them (Rev 14:13). They share in Jesus' sufferings, and they share in the comfort that comes through Jesus (2 Cor 1:5). Sharing the persecution and martyrdom reveals that the power belongs to God not to them and leads to glory for God (2 Cor 4:7-15). Both death and life are at work in them, which counts for them for eternity, but there is more. Death is at work in them, but life is at work in other people.

Involved in a Battle

Jesus prays for his disciples as he does not pray for the world (Jn 17:9). He hardly means he refrains from praying for the world at all (in effect he is praying for it in Jn 17:20-23). Yet in a sense "to pray for the *kosmos* would be almost an absurdity, since the only hope for the *kosmos* is precisely that it should cease to be the *kosmos*."[107] But he needs to pray for his disciples over against the world because they need to be protected so that they may be one. Their protection relates to the ease with which they could fall away; they are

---

[105]Cf. ibid., 679-80.
[106]Barth, *CD* I, 2:680-81.
[107]C. K. Barrett, *The Gospel According to St John* (London: SPCK, 1962), 427.

different from the world, and they need to keep their identity (Jn 17:11-12). Quite logically, the world will hate them because they do not belong to it. They therefore need to be sanctified, made holy and kept holy, kept separate and distinctive. The means of that sanctification is the truth, which is God's word (Jn 17:14, 17). It is significant in this connection that Jesus is praying to his holy Father (Jn 17:11).

So believers are involved in a fight—indeed, in several fights. One fight is a battle against the rulers, the authorities, the world powers, the evil spiritual entities in the heavenly realm (Eph 6:11-12).[108] Western believers live in a context where the world tries to get them to operate in a way that denies commitment to God and to one another; for instance, advertisements continually urge them to indulge themselves, and they have to fight against this pressure. Paul's point is that believers have opponents in another dimension.

The Gospels suggest two ways in which such attacks may work: Satan attacks Jesus directly and frontally and also indirectly via another person (e.g., Mt 4:1-11; 16:23). Ephesians implies that believers should not underestimate this second dimension to the pressure that comes to them. The devil is still active "now" (Eph 2:2), in the age in which salvation has come; "whenever the adverb 'now' is used elsewhere in Ephesians, it is to proclaim the present time as the day of salvation."[109] In the fight against Satan and other supernatural powers, our armor (Eph 6:10-17) consists in truthfulness that implies integrity, steadfastness, reliability and consistency; righteousness that implies a commitment to doing the right thing by people; peace in the sense of a unity and harmony that enables believers to stand together as they fight; faith in the sense of a trust that knows we do not fight alone; deliverance in the sense of an awareness that we are destined to be victorious; and the word of God in the sense of the gospel message.

The people whom the New Testament describes as "of the devil" seem to be not nonbelievers in general but people who had believed in Jesus but do so no longer and want to kill him (Jn 8:31-47; cf. 1 Jn 3:8-10).[110] "Why do you

---

[108]See the paragraphs under "The Devil" in section 3.1 above.

[109]Barth, *Ephesians*, 1:229.

[110]So Terry Griffith, "'The Jews Who Had Believed in Him' (Jn 8:31) and the Motif of Apostasy in the Gospel of John," in Richard Bauckham and Carl Mosser, eds., *The Gospel of John and Christian Theology* (Grand Rapids and Cambridge, UK: Eerdmans, 2008), 183-92.

not understand my speech? Because you cannot listen to my message. You are from your father the devil and you want to do what your father desires. . . . The person who is from God listens to God's words. It is because of this that you do not listen, that you are not from God" (Jn 8:43-44, 47). "Did not I myself choose you twelve? And one of you is a devil" (Jn 6:70; cf. Jn 13:2, 27). "If you know these things, you are blessed if you do them. I am not talking about all of you. I know the ones I chose" (Jn 13:17-18). There is a mystery about the relationship between God's choice or the Anointed One's choice, and the devil's activity, and the action of human beings. In a sense the fact that these Jews are of the devil explains the stance they take, but it does not stop the stance being one that *they* take, nor does it make it impossible to urge them to take a different one. And Judas can be both chosen and not chosen.

So believers have reversals. The disciples run away, Peter denies Jesus, Thomas refuses to believe he is risen. Yet they are the people God has given Jesus, and they are people who have responded to God's message.[111] The examples of Judas and of other people who walked out on Jesus during his ministry indicate that it is possible finally to give up on him. But that giving up is different from being people who sometimes get defeated but then reengage the enemy.

Taking Up a Cross

The life of believers is characterized by vulnerability. The pattern of vulnerability begins with Abel, who is unwise enough to have God accept his sacrifice and not his brother's, and with Joseph, who is unwise enough to share his dreams about his brothers bowing down to him. It continues in the experience of the Israelites, who are unwise enough to flourish so spectacularly as to seem a threat to the Egyptians. They then also get attacked by the Amaleqites for no reason other than being there, and by the Philistines for being rivals for the same territory.

Subsequently Israel has smaller basis for complaint about its oppressive treatment by imperial powers, since this treatment is redress for its own unfaithfulness to God. Something more like persecution becomes its experience at the hand of rogue Persians who are Amaleq's spiritual descendants

---

[111]Cf. R. H. Lightfoot, *St. John's Gospel* (Oxford and New York: Oxford University Press, 1956), 261.

(see Esther), of the Seleucids (see Daniel) and of Rome (see the New Testament). While the Scriptures recognize that Israel's continuing waywardness is a factor in the pattern, this waywardness hardly explains the entire experience, particularly on the part of faithful groups and individuals within Israel who suffer as much as or more than the people as a whole.

The pattern reaches its peak in Jesus, who knows he is on the way to an execution by Rome that is engineered by the leaders of his own people. It will not affect him alone. People who want to follow him will need to accept crucifixion as their own destiny (Mk 8:34-38). While some believers will end up as martyrs, many more will be the victims of abuse that falls short of death. Paul gives some account of his experience in this connection (notably in 2 Cor 6:4-10) and also offers a theological insight on it when he speaks of filling up the shortfall in Jesus' affliction on behalf of his body (Col 1:24). He is indeed taking up his cross in connection with completing the work of bringing the gospel message to people such as the Colossians.

Persecution is the price believers pay for spreading the gospel, yet it is also the stimulus to spreading the gospel (see Acts 8). Initially Paul was on the persecuting end of this dynamic; once Jesus takes hold of him he is on the persecuted end of it. Elsewhere he says, "I have been crucified with the Anointed One" and not merely "I was crucified with the Anointed One" (Gal 2:20). "Paul did not think of crucifixion with Christ as a once-for-all event of the past. . . . *I am still hanging with Christ on that cross.*"[112]

His work means he is hard-pressed, perplexed, persecuted and struck down, but not crushed, demoralized, abandoned or destroyed. He is embodying in his own life Jesus' death, but in that way he can also embody Jesus' life and thus be the means of life coming to the people he ministers to (2 Cor 4:7-10). The experience of trouble, hardship, persecution, famine, nakedness, danger and sword is like facing death all day for God's sake, seeming like sheep on their way to slaughter (Rom 8:35-36). Paul thus takes up words from Psalm 44, as Jesus takes up Psalm 22 when he is being crucified (Mt 27:46).

These allusions draw our attention to a key aspect of the significance of the many protest psalms in the Psalter, which issue from the experience

---

[112]Dunn, *Theology of Paul the Apostle*, 485.

of being abandoned by God to undeserved attack by fellow members of
one's own community or by other peoples. Many such protest psalms
issue in an awareness that God has heard the prayer and is committed to
answering it; Psalm 22 is an example, though Psalm 44 is not. Paul shows
the Psalm 22 confidence that God does not finally abandon his people to
such suffering, a confidence that now has a further basis in Jesus' death
and resurrection (Rom 8:31-39). When you follow Jesus you may find
yourself in the middle of a storm, but Jesus will eventually still it
(Mt 8:23-26).

"Peace to you," Jesus says twice on resurrection day and again a week later
(Jn 20:19, 21, 26). It's a regular greeting, but Jesus is speaking of a peace that
counteracts fear (Jn 20:19, 26). In the context of the Scriptures, he is also
speaking of a peace that counteracts apprehension at being in the presence
of someone who mediates the presence and action of God (cf. Lk 5:8-11). In
this latter context, his words would also imply their experiencing *šālôm,* that
things will go well in their lives. The pronouncement gains further significance when it leads into his sending them as the Father sent him. He also
goes on to commission them to forgive people (Jn 20:21-23), which might
suggest a link with the idea of peace with God.

Passing a Test

So being a servant of Jesus can mean arrest, beating, stoning and other forms
of pressure, danger and humiliation (2 Cor 6; 11). Yet believers will not
merely tolerate the troubles that come to them. As well as exulting in their
expectation of God's glory, they will exult in these troubles (Rom 5:2-3).
How could it be? Not only do they contribute to the spreading of the gospel;
such trouble or suffering or affliction (*thlipsis*) can generate endurance, and
endurance can generate proved character (Rom 5:3-4).

The troubles of which Romans 5 speaks are not suffering such as
illness, which like war is something the Scriptures do not agonize or
theologize about as much as Western Christianity does. Suffering and
war are just facts of life. Coping with illness and other "natural" human
suffering may, however, involve something of the same dynamic as is
involved in coping with persecution. These experiences, too, can contribute to taking us to glory.

Troubles are built into how things will be on the way to the End, the final fulfillment of God's purpose (see Mk 13:24, which also speaks of *thlipsis*). As believers move toward that moment, endurance is key. The person who endures to the end is the one who will be rescued (Mk 13:13, where the "endure" compares with "endurance" in Rom 5:3). Jesus' talk of being rescued (from being swept away by God's wrath when the end comes) has an equivalent in Paul's talk of endurance generating proved character, which he links with being rescued from wrath. God will be able to look at us with approval, and we will not be swept away by that wrath.[113]

Persecution and other suffering test people. The dynamics to which the New Testament refers go back to creation; the Eden garden was a place where people experienced temptation and testing.[114] Subsequently, Israel experienced it. Believers may be glad when they go through trials, because the testing of their faith produces endurance (that word again); they know it is the way to maturity (Jas 1:2-4).

There is nothing controversial about the point, though Paul and James had presumably noticed that troubles do not always produce endurance. But they *can* do so, and God wants them to have that effect. It is only living with troubles that can generate endurance. When Paul says that endurance produces a tested and proved character (*dokimē*), he uses a word he may have invented that it is difficult to express in one English expression. It turns believers into people who have been proved—proved to others, no doubt, but in the context also proved to themselves, as they are amazed at what they have gone through and amazed that they have come out the other side still standing.

So proved character produces hope or confidence for that Day, a hope that will not be shamed (Rom 5:4-5). On that day, many people who think they will be okay will find that their assumption was wrong, and they will be shamed. They will not merely be ashamed that they made some assumptions that turn out to be wrong. Their shame will be something more frightening. They thought that on that day they would be able to hold their head high because they belonged to the right people or believed the right things or kept the right observances. They will not be able to hold their head high.

---

[113]On testing, see Barth, *CD* II, 2:636-41.
[114]See the closing paragraph under "Relationality" in section 3.4 above.

They will be rejected and thrown out instead. That is what being shamed will mean for them.

There will be a contrast with people who have had God's love poured into their hearts through the fact that the Holy Spirit has been given them (Rom 5:5). The expression is an odd one; it involves a metalepsis. On Pentecost the Spirit was poured onto people, as if it were a liquid or a fire. But the Spirit was not merely an outward anointing. People needed to be affected by God's teaching in their inner workings, not just addressed externally by God's teaching (cf. Jer 31:31-34). They needed to be grasped by God's love in their inner being. God achieves that effect by a process analogous to the pouring out at Pentecost, a kind of flooding of the wellsprings of the person. "Baptism in the Holy Spirit" is "also baptism in the love of God (Rom 5:5)."[115]

There are a number of senses in which "the love of God" may flood people through the coming of the Holy Spirit. They can be overwhelmed by love for God. They can be overwhelmed by a God-like love for other people. Both would contribute decisively to the process whereby the troubles that come generate endurance, and thus proved character, and thus proper confidence that they will not be shamed at the End. But the passage goes on, with a "because," to talk about Jesus dying for us (Rom 5:6-11), which suggests that it is specifically an awareness of God's love for us that overwhelms us through the Holy Spirit, in keeping with the role Jesus gives to the Spirit in John.

Troubles thus play a role in bringing about the fulfillment of God's purpose for believers, even if they don't live on the eve of the actual End. It is fortunate, because the actual End did not happen in Paul's time, or in the time of believers who have lived over the two thousand years since his day. The dynamic followed the one that had obtained in the experience of the people of God before his day, such as the community in Jerusalem in the time of Antiochus's persecution, which went through the affliction described in Daniel 12:1. Going through such pressure still contributes to the achievement of God's purpose to bring them to glory in the sense of enabling them to play their part in implementing God's purpose in the world and to move toward the enjoyment of resurrection life.

---

[115]Amos Yong, *Renewing Christian Theology* (Waco, TX: Baylor University Press, 2014), 101.

Conflicted

For the Scriptures, the problem of suffering is not as troubling as the problem of obedience. While believers' struggle is not only against flesh and blood, it is against flesh and blood—not only other flesh-and-blood people who tempt them but also their own lower nature.[116] God's people lives with danger from outside, as its convictions constitute a rebuke to the world's, and the world directly attacks it or pressures it to water things down. It also lives with dangers from inside, as it is tempted to assimilate to ways of thinking that do not issue from the gospel and from the Scriptures, or to come to too high an opinion of itself.[117]

Believers are called to live by the Holy Spirit rather than by the lower nature. The Holy Spirit and the lower nature have conflicting desires (Gal 5:17). The tension is between the Holy Spirit and the lower nature, not between their spirit and their lower nature. It is not that soul and body are in tension. In Adam, people's natural state is to have spirit, soul, mind, emotions and body dominated by their lower nature. Even if God's teaching is written into their mind, it's not the only thing written into their mind.

In their natural state, all their aspirations, emotions and actions are affected by sin. It does not mean they are abandoned by God, or it need not mean it. God may still be involved with them, and they do many right things. But Jesus' sending the Holy Spirit on them introduces them into a life of sharper conflict than they knew before. They become the battlefield for a fiercer war between different desires. They have to become disciplined people who are prepared to impose tough requirements on themselves (1 Cor 9:24-27). They have to make sure that they are not people with a sinful, unbelieving heart (Heb 3:12). Fortunately, the Holy Spirit joins in the pressure on them not to give in to wrongdoing.

Paul thus perhaps lived a simpler life before he was overpowered by Jesus than afterwards. Being removed from the realm of darkness where he did not recognize Jesus into the realm of light where he does recognize him introduces conflict into his life, or enables him to recognize conflict in a way he may not have done before. He describes such a struggle in Romans 7:14-25.

---

[116]See the paragraphs under "The Lower Nature" in section 3.6 above.
[117]Cf. Barth, *CD* IV, 2:660-70.

One does not get the impression from the rest of his writings that he lives experientially or continuously with the tortuous tension that the passage describes, nor do the rest of the Scriptures describe human experience in this way. More likely he is speaking about an objective reality whether or not it is felt by people, a general reality that may be felt more sharply by believers.

Believers, at least, want to love God and love their neighbor, and sometimes do so. But from inside them there come other instincts that express a commitment to serving themselves, and their worship and relationships are then concerned to fulfill their needs not to honor God and be a blessing to others. The best part of them wants to serve God and serve their neighbor, but that other part of them fights against that inclination and sometimes wins. In this sense they are still people living by the lower nature; they still live as people sold to sin. The very fact that believers are challenged to offer themselves to God (Rom 6:11-13) presupposes that they may not do so or may not do so consistently. Indeed, an "intensified note of existential anguish and frustration" does dominate Paul's words in the latter part of Roman 7.[118]

The argument of Romans implies a recognition that being told to do the right thing may actually increase people's inclination to do the wrong thing. God therefore starts with us somewhere else, not by telling us to do the right thing but by affirming to us that we are accepted as we are and do not need to do the right thing to achieve that acceptance. Then God tells us to do the right thing on that basis, in response to that fact and on the basis of the presence and activity of God's spirit in our lives. He thus sets up the possibility of our starting again, as if we are facing anew the challenge to eat from any of the trees except the one in the middle of the garden. Jesus' death and resurrection have made crystal clear the principle that is also presupposed in the First Testament, that the starting point of people's relationship with God is God's grace and not their commitment.

Overwhelmed by the embodiment of God's grace in Jesus, the "natural" response of believers will be to give God their commitment and obedience, by serving God and serving the garden as they were created to do. Being loved "naturally" issues in loving. They are still involved in conflict, perhaps

---

[118]Dunn, *Romans*, 1:405.

a sharper conflict than before, and their occasional defeat in the battle is now all the more grievous because they live the other side of God's climactic action designed to affirm and undergird the pattern. So the account in Romans 7 of the human experience of Jesus' followers is sobering, but not finally depressing. It's comforting because it makes clear that there is nothing odd about believers going through this experience of conflict. And further, in the conflict between the Spirit and the lower nature, Jesus' death and resurrection mean the Spirit is destined to win.[119]

Turning

Humanity can be divided into good and bad people. The Scriptures can imply a moral and religious dualism. You are either for Jesus or against Jesus (e.g., Lk 11:23). At the End, the sheep and goats will have different destinies (Mt 25:31-46). But the Scriptures can also imply another sense in which the good is a very small category (indeed, there is just one person in it) and the bad is quite a small category. Most people come between.

Both perspectives feature in the Psalms. The Psalter starts by declaring a blessing on the faithful and affirming that trouble comes on the faithless, and it thus urges people to make sure they belong to the first category. It goes on to plead many times with God to do something about the faithless people (e.g., the people who use violence unjustly) and to take into account the way the people praying have maintained their faithfulness to God and to other people.

But from time to time psalms also make clear a recognition that the people who are broadly faithful do not claim to be sinless. They know that Israel as a whole and individual Israelites have lapses in faithfulness and are at best on their way to actual commitment. They are the righteous, but they are not wholly righteous. Thus the Scriptures' dualism is qualified. Righteousness and wickedness are not coterminous with my group and the rest, my community and the rest, the church and the world. Both the really wicked and the averagely faithful need to be people who are prepared to repent, to "turn."

In Israel, priests and prophets stand for two forms of problem that had two forms of consequences and required two forms of putting right.

---

[119]Cf. Dunn, *Romans*, 1:435.

Unintentional offenses such as ones that bring taboo can be dealt with by offerings. When Israelites had become taboo, they needed a priest to make expiation for them so that their offense could be pardoned (e.g., Lev 4:20, 26, 31, 35).[120] But offerings cannot avail for deliberate wrongdoing; it imperils a person's place in God's people (see Num 15:22-31; Heb 10:26-31). A deliberate wrongdoer "has no refuge to flee to except God Himself,"[121] and prophets thus urge people to repent and cast themselves on God. The word most commonly translated "repent" is šûb, the ordinary verb for "turn." Repentance is not the starting point from which people get into a relationship with God, but it is an aspect of the way they stay in a relationship with God.[122]

Priest and prophet are not rivals in Israel, and a priestly prophet such as Ezekiel or prophetic worship texts like those of the Psalter can combine the two perspectives: "There never was a tension in the Old Testament formulation of the will of God between the so-called ritual and ethical aspects of the divine imperative."[123] On one hand, deliberate waywardness also conveys taboo, while ignoring taboo counts as deliberate waywardness. It is just as well that "the blood of Jesus . . . cleanses us from every offense," so that "if someone does offend, we have an advocate with the Father, Jesus, the Anointed One, the righteous one, and he is the expiation [*hilasmos*] for our offenses" (1 Jn 1:7; 2:1-2).

Both Testaments thus recognize that there are several connections in which one needs to reflect on the moral and religious ambiguity of the people of God. The community as a whole and its individual members always live with the tension between this age and the age to come, between their oneness with Adam and their oneness with Jesus. In addition, there are times of marked rebellion and failure in the lives of communities and of individuals, when issues especially need to be faced and people are in special need of casting themselves on God's mercy—times when "turning" is a pressing image.

---

[120]See section 5.4 above.

[121]A. B. Davidson, *The Theology of the Old Testament* (Edinburgh: T&T Clark; New York: Scribner's, 1904), 318.

[122]Cf. E. P. Sanders, *Paul and Palestinian Judaism* (London: SCM Press; Philadelphia: Fortress, 1977), e.g., 513.

[123]Brevard S. Childs, *Old Testament Theology in a Canonical Context* (London: SCM Press, 1985; Philadelphia: Fortress, 1986), 171, 86.

The Scriptures talk more in these terms than they do in terms of gradual moral or spiritual development.[124] People need to turn right around *now* (Ezek 18). Yet further, John and Jesus speak of repenting because God's reign is here. There are times when the community needs to recognize a special moment that requires a new turning. The arrival of God's reign will be good news rather than bad news only if it meets with that response. This dynamic applies when we see ourselves in light of the arrival of salvation or of death. Making this critical decision may not be something we do once and for all, though neither is it something we do every day.

Recognition

Cleansing and repentance are therefore ongoing features of the life of believers. "Repentance is not just a preliminary stage but lifelong."[125] One reason is that repentance is not merely a feeling of horror and regret at one's failure but a *metanoia*.[126] The word etymologically suggests a change of mind, "a fundamental transformation of our outlook," a conversion. Whereas conversion is an infrequent image for the event whereby people come to belong to God, it is a frequent image for the event whereby people return to God. Such conversion, as "the transformation of the human self in all its spheres or strands," has to stand "*squarely in the center* of the Christian Way."[127] Indeed, through our life the change of mind needs to become more radical.[128] But a time of repentance is thus something positive, not negative, a time of gladness, not of despondency, "a joy-creating sorrow." It is the means of our opening ourselves to God's forgiveness and healing; and even in this self-opening it is God's action that is decisive, not ours.[129]

"There is a reflective moment in the repentance of sin, going far beyond the bare admission, 'We did wrong!' It searches out what wrong we did."[130] The change that the Scriptures look for is thus a change in thinking as well as a turning, or as an aspect of turning. In this connection they presuppose

---

[124]Stanley Hauerwas, *A Community of Character* (Notre Dame, IN, and London: University of Notre Dame Press, 1981), 130.

[125]Kallistos Ware, *The Inner Kingdom* (Crestwood, NY: St Vladimir's Seminary Press, 2001), 43.

[126]See the paragraphs under "Repentance" in section 4.2 above.

[127]McClendon, *Systematic Theology: Ethics*, 254.

[128]Ware, *Inner Kingdom*, 45-46.

[129]Ibid., 48-51; the quotation is from St John Climacus, *The Ladder of Divine Ascent*, step 7.

[130]Oliver O'Donovan, *Finding and Seeking* (Grand Rapids and Cambridge, UK: Eerdmans, 2014), 140.

a tension between our human responsibility for living holy lives and our need for God to transform us. While sometimes we are not sure what is right and we need God to guide us, more often we may know what is right but we are not inclined to do it. When we ask to be directed in Yahweh's ways (Ps 119:35-37), we do not mean that we don't know what these ways are. We mean we need our inclinations to be directed so that we walk in them.

Yet Psalm 119 also makes clear that we need to direct our own inclinations in this connection. God's turning to us has to be met with our turning to God. God's promise to give us a new attitude has to be met by our getting ourselves a new attitude (Ezek 11:19; 18:31). There is a turning that God has to do and a turning that we have to do, and one cannot reduce the relationship between these two turnings to a formula. It is the same mystery as affects an attempt to understand the dynamics of how people first come to faith in Jesus. We must turn to God because God has turned to us (Zech 1:3, 16); or we must turn to God so that God may turn to us (e.g., Joel 2:13-14; Mal 3:7). "You disciplined me, and I let myself be disciplined, like an untrained bullock; let me return; I want to return," Ephraim says (Jer 31:18). There is no reason to take this plea more seriously than other such purported turnings (e.g., Hos 6:4-6), but sometimes God takes the risk of doing so (Jer 31:20).

Isaiah 53 describes the process of coming to enlightenment with particular vividness. It reports the imaginary testimony of people who have witnessed the abuse of a servant of God.[131] He had been disparaged and repudiated by them as one who deserved the trouble that came to him. They saw God as behind his illtreatment. But they came to understand that he was illtreated not because he deserved it but because he was willing to identify with them in their tough experiences and willing to endure even more abuse than they did as the price of exercising a ministry among them. God was indeed behind his illtreatment, but in a different sense from the one they had assumed.

It seems that the phenomenon that forced them to change their assessment of his abuse was the way he responded to it. They couldn't get away

---

[131]I take this servant to be the prophet himself (see John Goldingay, *The Message of Isaiah 40–55* [London and New York: T&T Clark, 2005], on the passage), but his identity does not affect the point being considered here.

from the fact that he simply accepted it uncomplainingly. "He didn't open his mouth," they twice comment, incredulously. As the spiritual puts it, "He never said a mumblin' word." His response to his abuse compelled them to recognize him as God's servant.

Penitence

God may take his people through humiliating chastisement, but humiliation can be fruitful (e.g., Ezek 36:31-32). Shame can be "a gift from God."[132] Being shamed by the contrast between us and Jesus can be crucial to a relationship with God.[133] Shame and trust can then be allies, insofar as both issue from facing reality—the reality about oneself and the reality about God. Yes, God is the chastiser, the destroyer, but at least the disaster people go through has some meaning as opposed to being random; and they will also come to recognize that God himself is distraught at the sight of what they have gone through (e.g., Ezek 5:13; 6:9; 14:23). Further, God's discipline is modeled on that of parents, for whom it is designed to make their children shape up. God wants his children to enter into fullness of life (e.g., Ezek 36–37).

Repentance thus involves feelings as well as action and thought. Whereas the New Testament Greek word for repentance suggests a change of mind, and one of the Hebrew verbs for repentance is the ordinary word for "turn" (e.g., Jer 8:5), the other Hebrew verb for repentance, *nhm* (niphal), denotes regretting and feeling sorry (e.g., Jer 8:6). "The sorrow that fits God's way of thinking effects a change of attitude that leads to salvation, leaving no regret, but the sorrow the world shows effects death" (2 Cor 7:10).

When David manifested some sorrow about his action in connection with Bathsheba and Uriah, his sorrow issued in no change of attitude, and henceforth his life unraveled. Psalm 51 offers him the possibility of expressing the sorrow that leads to life, but the David whose story 2 Samuel tells does not take up the offer. Nevertheless Psalm 51 is the classic scriptural expression of penitence. It shows how penitence does mean casting oneself on God, ashamed and naked.

Like the rest of the First Testament, it recognizes that offering a sacrifice is no use in order to make up for wrongdoing. Sacrifice belongs in the context

---

[132]Jacqueline E. Lapsley, "Shame and Self-Knowledge," in *The Book of Ezekiel*, ed. Margaret S. Odell and John T. Strong (Atlanta: Scholars Press, 2000), 143-73 (see 159).
[133]Cf. Barth, *CD* IV, 2:384-403.

of a healthy relationship with God, and if God restores the suppliant, it will be possible to resume sacrifice. But after being involved in rebellion against God, sacrifice is useless. All one can offer God is oneself in one's crushed, shamed and humiliated state, and appeal to God's grace, compassion and commitment for cleansing, pardon and renewal, for the canceling of a record or the covering of the stain it brings, for God to turn a blind eye to it and put it out of mind, for God to carry the sin rather than require us to carry responsibility for it.

Most other biblical expressions of penitence come outside the Psalms. Isaiah 6 "provides a model for Christian sin-talk" in incorporating a recognition of our lostness before God and of our solidarity in sin with other people, a recognition that comes through being "in the presence of the God who immediately and without being asked" declares our forgiveness.[134] Other expressions of penitence explicitly relate to the waywardness and consequent suffering of the community rather than those of the individual, especially in the imperial domination of Jerusalem and Judah that characterizes much of its story.

The classic articulation of this penitence comes in Lamentations. Like Psalm 51, these prayers recognize that the community's devastated state issues from its rebellion against God. Like other psalms, they focus on a simple articulation of suffering in the conviction that this articulation may move God to act in compassion despite the deserved nature of the suffering. Like Psalm 51, they include an astonishing expression of hope that God may so act, a hope based simply on the very nature of God. They thus combine protest and hope. The articulation of hope on the basis of the affirmation of God's nature comes at the very center of the five prayers and thus at their high point (Lam 3:22-33), yet it does not suggest that the "problem" is thereby solved. Indeed, the prayers close with uncertainty (Lam 5:20-22), which is appropriate to the fact that God has not yet responded to the community's pleas.

Later penitential prayers (Ezra 9; Neh 9; Dan 9) take up this note. Even when exiled Judahites have been allowed to return, and Jerusalem's temple and walls have been rebuilt, imperial overlordship continues and eventually

---

[134]Ian A. McFarland, *In Adam's Fall* (Chichester, UK, and Malden, MA: Wiley-Blackwell, 2010), 158.

becomes more rather than less oppressive. The only thing to do is keep acknowledging the faithlessness that led to it and keep appealing to God's compassion and commitment.

These penitential prayers are articulated by people such as Daniel, Ezra and Nehemiah who are themselves bywords for faithfulness, yet they recognize a challenge to identify with their people in their rebelliousness. They express penitence for what "we" have done, not for what "they" have done. Indeed, they live in contexts where the community is itself in better religious shape than it was in earlier centuries, and the prayers also accept on the community's behalf a challenge to identify with earlier generations rather than to claim that it is more holy. Once more, hope lies only in God, not in the community's having any other claim on God.

In Jesus God takes up this example of identifying with a people that is rebellious and in need of penitence. And "even though the church is holy, it still has to pray (Matt. 6:12): 'Forgive us our debts.'" It is not just individuals who pray that prayer. Indeed, "there is no such great sinner as the Christian church."[135]

Becoming Who You Are

Something new has happened to believers, and they need to live in light of it. The old has passed away, the new has come (2 Cor 5:17; 6:2). The fullness of time has come (Gal 4:4). In everyday life it may be hard to believe that something has happened, to believe that God *has* broken the power of the Torah, of sin, of the lower nature and of the devil. So people often live on some other basis; commonly, they assimilate to their culture. But in reality, they died with Jesus and they have been raised with Jesus; they are therefore to set their minds on things above and to kill what belongs to their lower nature (Col 2:20–3:5). They are to work at their salvation on the basis of the way God is at work in them and/or among them (Phil 2:12-13).

Christian use of the word *salvation* in connection with the individual's eternal destiny makes it easy to misread this exhortation. It is not speaking about individuals working out their individual salvation, but neither is it using *sōtēria* to mean (say) health. The subsequent reference to boasting on

---

[135]Martin Luther, *Lectures on Galatians 1535 Chapters 1–4*, LW 26 (St. Louis: Concordia, 1963), 66 (on Gal 1:11-12); Luther, "Predigt am Ostersonntag," on Mt 28:1, in *Werke*, Weimarer Ausgabe 34/1 (Weimar: Hermann Böhlaus Nachfolger, 1908), 271-77 (on 276). Cf. Barth, *CD* IV, 1:658.

the day of the Anointed One (Phil 2:16) confirms that it is speaking of deliverance from God's wrath on the last day. This deliverance depends on action people take now, on the giving and yielding of themselves to one another described in the context on either side (Phil 2:1-11, 14-16).

That expectation could be depressing were their working toward this deliverance (*katergazomai*) not backed up by God's being at work in them (*energeō*) to bring about the effecting of his will that they should have this kind of life. Their life involves a synergism. A man's relationship with his wife enables him to do things he could not have done before. He is released from needing to try to earn someone's love, and he now acts in love, in connection with knowing he is loved. He looks at life in new ways because he looks at things through her eyes. He has to work at the relationship and at new ways of relating to life, but he does so on the basis of the fact that she is at work in him.

What happens to the body affects the mind; what happens to the mind affects the body. We let our minds be renewed so that we look at things in a transformed way, which makes it possible for our lives to be transformed (Rom 12:1-2). We are then able to recognize the good, pleasing and perfect will of God. The adjectives are ones that apply to a sacrifice; the exhortation refers to a will of God that looks good, pleasing and perfect to God. Under natural circumstances, the expectations that are good, pleasing and perfect to God look unacceptable or frightening to us. We have to let our attitudes be turned inside out so that we recognize them, both in the sense of seeing what they are and in the sense of accepting them.

We live our life in a "now" that comes in between "no longer" and "not yet" and has aspects of both of these. We belong to the new age, and therefore it's natural to live the new life; the person who is born of God does not commit sin (1 Jn 3:9). But we still live in this age, so faithfulness is the subject of an imperative. Freedom is freedom to live in obedience; obedience is a gift of grace—not an accomplishment or a condition for salvation. "A dialectic of salvation/judgment, already/not yet, grace/works is present in the Jewish Scriptures."[136] It was hard for the Jewish people to maintain this subtle position, and it has been hard for believers in Jesus to do so. It's easy

---

[136]Kent L. Yinger, *Paul, Judaism and Judgment According to Deeds* (Cambridge and New York: Cambridge University Press, 1999), 63.

to assume that Jesus indeed died to win us forgiveness and wipe our slate clean but that he then left us to rely on our own strength to become worthy of the coming salvation by our obedience. This assumption abandons the idea that God's grace or God's love makes us radically new and continues to do so.[137]

On the Way

One could sometimes get the impression that Paul believes he has arrived. Indeed, he could give the impression that he had thought so more than once. He thought he had arrived as a Jew, and he could seem to have thought so again when Jesus took hold of him (Phil 3:1-9). Yet he then makes clear that he thinks otherwise: "Not that I have already acquired or already been made complete, but I press on so I may take hold of that for which the Anointed One took hold of me. . . . Forgetting what is behind and straining for what is ahead, I press on toward the mark for the prize of the upward summons of God in the Anointed One, Jesus" (Phil 3:12-14). When he speaks about knowing Jesus and the power of his resurrection, and about sharing in his suffering and in a death like his, it becomes unclear how much of this experience is still future—as attaining the resurrection from among the dead certainly is (Phil 3:10-11).

Before Jesus met him, as a Pharisee he would have combined his certainty that he had arrived with a forward orientation that looked toward resurrection day. He reframed that understanding in light of the link between his Jewish resurrection hope and the actual resurrection of Jesus, and in light of the link between resurrection and suffering. He now realizes that he has arrived in the sense that something of the reality attaching to resurrection day is already a reality because Jesus has already suffered and resurrected, and it has become a reality for him. Yet he still has to go through suffering and resurrection on his way to that final day when he will be found in Jesus and given the prize for completing the course (Phil 3:9, 14). It's a marathon, not a sprint, and not a gradual ascent, and not a competition; he just has to keep going to the end, when all will have won and all will have prizes. "The process of sanctification does not consist in an initial dying with Christ followed in the course of that process by an experience of Christ's resurrection

---

[137]Cf. Bultmann, *Theology of the New Testament*, 2:203-4.

power.... The resurrection power of Christ manifests itself... as also a sharing in Christ's sufferings."[138]

Believers thus live with two related antitheses that underlie the ambiguity of their experience. There is a temporal antithesis between now and then, present and future, this age and the coming age, and also a spatial antithesis between here and there, earth and heaven, the world below and the world above. The two antitheses are related insofar as the life of the new age is already a reality in the world above. They are also parallel in a more negative way; in the present age there is resistance to God's will in the world above as there is in the world below, so that the world above also waits for the new age. But in the meantime, there is a positive relationship between life in this world insofar as the new age is a reality here in the present, and the life of the world above insofar as the new age is a reality there in the present.

It is open to people to have their minds set on earthly things and to ignore the fact that their citizenship is in heaven (Phil 3:19): Paul's words could cover a preoccupation with outward religious observances and forms of discipline or with physical indulgence, in food and sex. Either way, they treat this world as more significant than it is. They also treat this age as more significant than it is; they have forgotten that we are looking forward to the arrival of a Savior from heaven who will transform our lowly bodies to be like his glorious body, which is why Paul is forgetting what lies behind and pressing on toward the mark (Phil 3:12-13).

It's logically possible to drop out of the race and not finish, to "fall out of grace" and get cut off from Jesus. It's the risk taken by believers who get circumcised and thus take on the obligation to live by the Torah on the basis that this commitment is required of them—which is bound to mean they fail (Gal 5:1-4; cf. Rom 11:22). It's thus possible to believe "in vain" (1 Cor 15:2). And if people turn back, it's impossible to restore them; if they have turned their back on the gospel and on what they have experienced of the Holy Spirit, there's nothing to draw them back by (Heb 6:4-12; 10:26-31). But we have God's promise, and we need to persevere so that we receive what is promised (Heb 6:13-20; 10:32-39).

---

[138]Dunn, *Theology of Paul the Apostle*, 487.

6.4 The Congregation's Servants

If we put the point in Western terms, leadership is an important theme in the Scriptures, though the Scriptures more often use the word *servants* to describe leaders of the people of God such as Moses, David and Paul. Moreover, they are usually called God's servants, not the people's servants.[139] The Scriptures do not talk in terms of "servant leadership" to guard against the toxic aspect to the practice of leadership, though they are well aware that leadership is often toxic.

One may distinguish four forms of servanthood in the Scriptures, though the distinctions are not tight and the forms slide into each other. I shall call them charism or gift, practice or role, office or position, and commission or vocation. Such servants may be both male and female. They are fallible.

Charism or Gift

The New Testament sets the idea of charisms or gifts in the context of seeing the congregation as a body. Greco-Roman writers took the human body as an analogy for human society in order to illustrate how it can manifest both diversity and unity and can also need order and hierarchy. Roman historian Livy reports the exhortation by a Roman senator, Menenius Agrippa, urging some striking workers (the body's limbs) to return to work and not to "starve" the governing class (the stomach), as if the latter did nothing; without the stomach, the limbs would die.[140] The body is a whole that functions through the working together of its members, which serve one another and thus serve the whole.

The New Testament takes over this image and declares that we were all baptized by/in one Spirit so as to form one body, and we were all enabled to drink one Spirit (1 Cor 12:13); but it refers to "the body of the Anointed One" and to "members of the Anointed One," not to "the body of the Holy Spirit" or "members of the Holy Spirit."[141] We are to see ourselves as one body (1 Cor 12) and to live as one body (Eph 4:1–5:2). The New Testament then qualifies the image in a number of ways.

---

[139]See further *OTT* 3:708-831.

[140]See Livy, *Ab urbe condita libri* 2.32 (quoted by Dunn, *Theology of Paul the Apostle*, 550-51).

[141]Cf. Veli-Matti Kärkkäinen, *Toward a Pneumatological Theology* (Lanham, MD: University Press of America, 2002), 83.

First, "only in the context of the effects and gifts of grace does the apostle utilize the ancient world's figure of the one body and the variety of its members."[142] The assembly of believers is like the secular assembly, but it's identified by its being the body of the Anointed One rather than (for instance) the body of Corinth. Perhaps the implication is that membership of this society is more fundamental to the identity of believers, as membership of this assembly (*ekklēsia*) is more fundamental than membership of the city assembly.[143]

Second, Paul reverses Menenius's argument. On the basis of their belonging to the one "body" of the Anointed One, the strong and the people with impressive gifts must value the weak and the people with less impressive gifts.[144] These gifts are *charismata*: they exist because of God's grace (*charis*) and not because of human ability. They would not exist were it not for God's gracious giving.

They are also *pneumatika*, "spiritual things" (1 Cor 12:1); it may be the Corinthians' word, but Paul is happy to use it. On its own, *charisma* "has little or nothing to do with the Spirit; it picks up Spirit overtones only by context or by explicit qualifiers."[145] While the word can suggest concrete ways in which the Spirit acts, in itself it is a much broader term. The charisms do bring "the manifestation of the Spirit for the common good," and Paul encourages the Corinthians to be enthusiastic about *ta pneumatika* (1 Cor 12:7; 14:1). That expression again underscores the fact that they are not expressions of human ability but manifestations of divine power.

There are charisms such as a wise message, an informed message, faith, healing, powerful wonders, prophecy, distinguishing between spirits, languages and interpretation of languages (1 Cor 12:7-10). We don't know what many of these expressions denote, but it doesn't matter too much since it is the Holy Spirit who distributes them as he determines (1 Cor 12:11). The first thing at Corinth for which Paul gives God thanks is the grace that has been given to the Corinthians and that is embodied in graces of speech and knowledge that enrich them (1 Cor 1:4-7). The problem is that they have

---

[142]Günther Bornkamm, *Paul* (New York: Harper; London: Hodder, 1971), 195.
[143]Cf. Gorman, *Cruciformity*, 356-60.
[144]See Dale B. Martin, *The Corinthian Body* (New Haven, CT: Yale University Press, 1995), 92-95.
[145]Fee, *God's Empowering Presence*, 33.

become illogically proud of these graces, as if they had achieved them rather than received them as gifts (1 Cor 4:7-8).

After safeguarding the unity of the Ephesus congregation's mutual submissiveness, Paul can rejoice in its diversity of charisms (Eph 4:7-13). "To each one of us grace has been given in accordance with the apportionment of the gift of the Anointed One." The graces there are itemized as apostles, prophets, evangelists, shepherds and teachers (or shepherd-teachers), so "each one of us" does not denote each limb of the body but each limb that exercises one of these functions. The graces are exercised by different people. There is no priest or senior pastor (except God). All the body's limbs are involved in the body's activity; the function of the charisms is to equip the believers as a group to do ministerial work and thus to build up the body of the Anointed One. The people as a whole are engaged in ministry to one another and are thus engaged in this building up. The goal of the building up is again the oneness of the faith and of the knowledge of the Son of God so as to become a mature person, attaining the fullness of the Anointed One.

The congregation as a whole is the embodiment of grace. The point is more explicit in a comment about the Macedonian churches. Despite their poverty they have shown great generosity toward believers in Jerusalem, and this generosity reflects the divine grace that they have been given (2 Cor 8:1-7). When a congregation does something extraordinarily godly, it suggests that God's grace is at work. That involvement does not eliminate the involvement of the human will. In this connection as in others, it's possible to receive God's grace but for it to not have its effect (2 Cor 6:1). Paul urges the Corinthians to excel in the grace of giving.

Practice or Role
The first time someone prophesies, you might not know that he or she is a prophet, but if someone develops an ongoing exercise of such a charism, then that exercise becomes something more like a role. Perhaps a prophet might receive a revelation during the week and deliver it when the congregation meets, or might receive it in the context of worship. As First Testament prophets often reflect the words of their predecessors, so John the author of Revelation couches his prophecy in words from First Testament prophecies, and from elsewhere in those Scriptures.

Messages from prophets were a common feature of church life, and so therefore was the need to distinguish true from false prophecy. Beware prophets who consume people, Jesus says; it's by their fruit that you recognize them (Mt 7:15-20). Three tests for the exercise of charisms are: does it fit with the gospel (does it affirm that Jesus is Lord), does it express love, and does it benefit and upbuild the community (see 1 Cor 12–14).[146] The tests overlap with ones that feature in Jeremiah's critique of prophets who generate their own messages (Jer 23:9-40). The hopefulness of those prophets clashes with what must need to be said in light of people's inclination to serve other deities and to live the kind of lives that must displease Yahweh.

It's a feature of church life that there are different "apostles" who do not recognize each other (e.g., 2 Cor 10–12), as it is a feature of Israel's life that there are different prophets who do not recognize each other (e.g., Jeremiah and Hananiah). Both Testaments issue from contexts in which the community has subsequently made up its mind who are the true and who the false. It's said that history is written by the winners and that the same is true about deciding who should be in the Scriptures. Jeremiah and Paul are the winners, but it was other people who decided that they were the winners, and it was not particularly obvious at the time that Jeremiah was a winner.

Their own words, or stories written about them, do suggest some criteria for recognizing them. They were people who were generally timid in person, though they were more impressive in their writing. They were outsiders, people who did not really belong to the community. They did not get paid or supported. Their *curriculum vitae* is characterized chiefly by a list of experiences of persecution or pressure, or of being in danger of losing their life in other ways. In these contexts they nevertheless also experience God's power, in that they come through the other side of persecution or pressure with it being undeniable that God has achieved things through taking them through the experiences.

The position of the "wise," the experts or advisers, might reflect parallel dynamics. People cannot be simply appointed to the circle of the wise any more than they can be appointed to the circle of prophets. No doubt they can be trained (cf. Dan 1), and one function of the "wisdom literature" is to

---

[146]Cf. Dunn, *Theology of Paul the Apostle*, 594-98.

be textbooks for training people for involvement in the administration. But training will need to build on basic aptitude. Wisdom is both a gift and an achievement. Similar assumptions will underlie the position of the elders in a local community, and then their position in a congregation. The elders were the senior figures in the community. It would be assumed that they had learned a few things by virtue of their years, though the capacity of some senior people to be stupid would need to be countered by or absorbed within the corporate wisdom of the body of elders as a whole.

Office or Position

A group will commonly find that it needs to develop "some patterns of leadership, some differentiation of roles among its members, some means of managing conflict, some ways of articulating shared values and norms, and some sanctions to assure acceptable levels of conformity to those norms."[147] Israel does so in developing a priesthood and a monarchy. Yahweh had declared that Israel was to be "a kingdom of priests" (Ex 19:6). Having human kings stands in tension with that idea and compromises the nation's recognition of Yahweh as King.[148] Yet the stories in the book of Judges illustrate the observation about the need to manage conflict and encourage conformity to some norms.

The last sentence in Judges sums up its narrative as the story of a people doing what was right in their own eyes when there was no king in Israel. Simply having Yahweh as King didn't work. The point is underlined by the fact that the "judges" ("leaders" would be a less misleading translation of the word *šōpəṭîm*) were not the kind of people you would expect to find in leadership positions. They mostly were people of little social standing, little courage and little spiritual or moral insight. As with New Testament charisms, God's using such people shows that it is God who is acting, but it further underlines Israel's problem. Likewise the twelve disciples frequently showed little insight or faith, and among them were a denier and a betrayer.

In Israel, having priests likewise stands in some tension with God's declaration that Israel was to be a body of priests. Whereas Genesis and Exodus

---

[147]Meeks, *First Urban Christians*, 111.
[148]See the paragraphs under "Divine Kingship and Human Kingship" in section 4.1 above.

mention a priest of Salem, priests in Egypt and a Midianite priest, they mention no priests among Israel's ancestors. Cain, Abel, Noah, Abraham and Jacob all offer sacrifices; the latter three apparently do so as head of their families. The first reference to priests in connection with Israel comes in that description of the people as a whole. We are then surprised to find just afterwards references to priests within Israel (Ex 19:22, 24) and subsequently to read of God commissioning the ordination and consecration of Aaron and his sons at Sinai (Lev 8–9).

It is usually assumed that historically the development of the Aaronic priesthood came later, though the history is shrouded in mystery. In terms of the way the Torah tells the story, the theological significance of the priesthood parallels that of sacrifice, of the building of the temple and of kingship. All four seem to enter the story as human initiatives that Yahweh in due course affirms. Kingship and temple are both institutions about which Yahweh explicitly expresses misgivings, yet about which Yahweh then determines to sin boldly:[149] that is, once Yahweh decides to take on these questionable institutions, he does so in a committed, not a half-hearted, manner.

Seeing priesthood (and sacrifice) in the same way does not involve too much connecting of dots. A priesthood can safeguard purity, teach people about Yahweh's expectations and lead worship in a way appropriate to who Yahweh is. As with the monarchy, it is an institution that is equally capable of working against Yahweh's purpose and often does so, as prophetic polemic about Israel's worship indicates.

Christians may assume that the priests' chief task was to offer sacrifice, but when Moses describes the role of the clan of Levi (Deut 33:8-11), it is teaching that comes first. Levi's task was to help people know Yahweh's expectations of them, not least in order to avoid or to deal with the impurity that would make it inappropriate for people to come into Yahweh's presence. Indeed, that first mention of Israelite priests (Ex 19:21-24) has a related concern. More broadly, the Levites act as wardens, gatekeepers, sacristans, caretakers, deacons and music leaders, and they look after the

---

[149]I adapt a phrase from a letter by Martin Luther to Philip Melanchthon (*Letters I* [Philadelphia: Fortress, 1963], 282); in the context I take Luther to mean that we should not be paralyzed by the fact that we sin, given the fact that Jesus died for us.

sacred vessels, supplies, storerooms, temple tax, treasury and tithes (e.g., 1 Chron 23; 26). They thus do many of the jobs for which churches appoint and pay people.

Being Realistic

It would be distinctive of Israel to serve as a priest-people, to be "not a nation with, but a nation of, priests"; in the church what is similarly required is not the abolition of the priesthood but the "radical abolition of the laity."[150] Jesus did tell his disciples not to call anyone teacher, master or father, and not to let anyone treat them that way (Mt 23:8-12). But the Jerusalem believers soon found it necessary to appoint some people to sort out the distribution of food in the congregation (Acts 6:3), and the New Testament speaks of the appointment of groups of elders in congregations (e.g., Acts 11:30; 14:23; 20:17; 1 Tim 4:14; Jas 5:14; 1 Pet 5:5); perhaps it would seem natural for "households" to have "elders." There is talk also of overseers (Acts 20:28; Phil 1:1) and servants (e.g., Phil 1:1; 1 Tim 3:8). When the words come in the singular (e.g., 1 Tim 3:2; 5:1; Tit 1:7), the implication is not that there is only one of them in a congregation. It wouldn't be surprising if the people appointed to such positions were people who had manifested charisms and had developed a role, but there is no indication that it was so. The qualifications related to character and maturity (1 Tim 3:1-12; Tit 1:5-9).

Paul's response to disorder in Corinth did not include telling its priest or its pastor to get a grip of the situation or telling the Corinthian believers to do what their priest or pastor said. Insofar as the congregation had leaders, they were not people who resided in Corinth but people like Paul himself, and their existence issued in more division, not less (1 Cor 1–3). Paul urges the Corinthians to submit to people such as Stephanas, but even they were not permanently resident there (1 Cor 16:15-18). Ministry and responsibility belong to the congregation as a whole (Eph 4:12). Each congregation has a star or aide or spirit, put in charge by God and an embodiment of its spirituality, but these are supernatural rather than earthly figures (Rev 1–3). Only in the second century do some congregations have what we might call a senior pastor.

---

[150]James W. McClendon, *Systematic Theology: Doctrine* (Nashville: Abingdon, 1994), 368-69.

The development of ministry in the church thus followed a similar trajectory to the one in Israel. The development of its ministry involved not so much a shift "from charisma to institution but a shift from the charisma of many to a specialized charisma of just a few."[151] Simply having Jesus as Lord didn't work. Israel and the church start off as egalitarian but disorderly. The trouble is that, as having human kings also didn't work, neither did introducing the "monarchical episcopate," the practice of having one man in authority over a church. Both arrangements had the potential to encourage holiness and restrain error, and they sometimes did so. They also had the potential to encourage error and the misuse of power, and they sometimes did so. The Church of England has argued whether bishops are of the essence of the church (no bishops, no real church) or whether they are simply a great benefit to the church. Are bishops of its *esse* or only of its *bene esse*? A wag has noted that bishops have often led the church astray, so if we have to choose between these two views, the answer is that they are not of its *bene esse*; they must be of its *esse*.

In Israel, Moses, the judges and the kings were the "agents of God's rule,"[152] and the appointment of the Twelve represents another incursion into the structures of Israel. They are to be the people who exercise authority over the twelve Israelite clans, and they will do so because Jesus says so. But Moses is unique in the role he fulfills, and so are the judges. Further, there is a little ambiguity about Moses, more ambiguity about the judges and an intrinsic ambiguity about the kings that is then made concrete in the particularities of their reigns. In Judges "the real, active and determining subject is always Yahweh's *ruach*."[153]

Things change with the monarchy, when the activity of Yahweh's spirit on the king becomes a permanent endowment. The people's request for a monarchy not only compromises their recognition of Yahweh as king. As Samuel points out, it will also have devastating effects on the people's own lives (1 Sam 8:10-18). In those lives as well as in connection with the nation's relationship with Yahweh, it will issue in "the paganization of Israel."[154]

---

[151]Edward Schillebeeckx, *The Church with a Human Face* (New York: Crossroad; London: SCM Press, 1985), 121.

[152]Childs, *Old Testament Theology in a Canonical Context*, 108.

[153]Moltmann, *Spirit of Life*, 43.

[154]G. E. Mendenhall, "The Monarchy," *Interpretation* 29 (1975): 155-70 (see 155).

Whereas the book of Joshua records the allocation of the land to different clans and families on an egalitarian basis, the institution of the monarchy initiates a process whereby powerful, shrewd and successful people can increase the size of their farms at the expense of people who are less sharp and/ or less lucky and/or less hard-working, and can become more and more wealthy and turn the latter into landless peasants or urban poor.

Commission or Vocation

The monarchy and the paganization of Israel are significant elements in the background of the rise of prophecy in Israel, though it's hard to define prophets. The characteristics of prophets may include that they share God's nightmares and dreams, they speak like poets and behave like actors, they are unafraid to be offensive, they confront the confident with rebuke and the downcast with hope, they can be independent of the institutional pressures of church and state, they are scary people mediating the activity of a scary God, and they intercede with boldness and praise with freedom.[155] They embody a reassertion of the principle that Yahweh's spirit breaks into the institution and takes initiatives.

They are usually troublemakers, and leaders are thus inclined to kill prophets (Mt 14:3-12). They are people with mysterious power, sent by God, taking powerful initiatives, and thus embodying God's own person. They are people whom God enables to see things that others can't see, so that they can announce things that are coming when there may be no earthly reason to expect such things. Yet they can also be the agents of forces that work against Yahweh's truth, as kings and priests can be the agents of truthful forces. There can be true prophets who bring a false message, or false prophets who bring a true message. Like priests, they call people to be mindful of the faith that has been handed down.

In the New Testament, "the grounding of apostolic ministry derives from a distinctive apostolic status as *'founders'* of the communities and *as translocal overseers*."[156] Key to their status as founders is their being in a position to give testimony to Jesus' death and resurrection. Without their

---

[155]See further John Goldingay, "Is There Prophecy Today?," in *Key Questions About Biblical Interpretation* (Grand Rapids: Baker, 2011), 311-27.

[156]Thiselton, *Hermeneutics of Doctrine*, 501.

"primary founding witness,"[157] it would be inevitable that "soon the remembered Christ becomes an imagined Christ."[158]

As an apostle or emissary of Jesus, Paul had particular authority in churches he founded (see especially 1 Cor 9), but his authority was more like that of a mother or a pastor than that of an employer or a professor. He expects people to do as he says with the implication that otherwise people imperil their membership of the congregation, but he does so on the basis of a coherence between what he says and the gospel itself (e.g., Gal 2:14). "Apostolic authority was conditional upon the gospel and subject to the norm of the gospel."[159] Of course oppressive leaders often claim that they are serving something outside themselves; but Paul's argument lays him open to people checking out what he says by the gospel. He uses argument, and he appeals to logic; he does not simply lay the law down.

An aspect of being an apostle and theologian is having a role to play in the period between Jesus' death and resurrection and his coming in glory. Paul's being the church's first and greatest theologian is an aspect of his significance. As an apostle, his theology is a "christocentric theology of mission"; Romans is an exposition of his "missionary theology."[160] Over subsequent centuries, the church has commonly kept theology and mission separate. Missiology has only recently become a focus of theology, and the practice of mission has been conducted with more enthusiasm than theological reflection. It was not so at the beginning. Not only was Paul the great theologian and the great missionary; these two were interwoven. He does not stand outside the implementing of God's purpose in the world but inside it, reflecting on it.

Slave and Emissary

Paul is "a slave of the Anointed One Jesus, summoned as an emissary, set apart for God's good news" (Rom 1:1). These designations have overlapping meanings, all of them combining subordination and authority.

---

[157]Ibid., 502.

[158]James D. Smart, *The Strange Silence of the Bible in the Church* (Philadelphia: Westminster; London: SCM Press, 1970), 25; cf. Thiselton, *Hermeneutics of Doctrine*, 502.

[159]Dunn, *Theology of Paul the Apostle*, 572; he refers to John Howard Schütz, *Paul and the Anatomy of Apostolic Authority* (London and New York: Cambridge University Press, 1975).

[160]Dahl, *Studies in Paul*, 71, in an article titled "The Missionary Theology in the Epistle to the Romans."

Paul "saw himself as the slave of Jesus Christ, not the founder of Christianity."[161] Whereas he had been a person of some significance who could take initiatives and act on the basis of them, being confronted by Jesus meant becoming someone who simply took orders. He was summoned like a slave in order to be sent off to do what his master said. He was set apart from other slaves and other tasks to focus on delivering a particular message that his master wanted delivered. He has to do his master's bidding. There were people who especially emphasized Paul's importance over against (say) Peter, and if he had been concerned about his own position he would surely have affirmed them, but instead he critiques them (1 Cor 1:10-17). It was Jesus who was crucified for them, not Paul. He behaves like John the Baptizer in pointing away from himself to Jesus.

To put it another way, he is Jesus' prisoner (Eph 3:1). He is in a Roman prison "because of the Anointed One" (Eph 4:1), but he is also imprisoned *by* the Anointed One, taken captive by him and not free to leave and go and live an ordinary life without constraint. It is so "for the sake of you Gentiles." Everything is for their sake and for his master's name's sake. It is part of his living as Jesus lived; "though I am free in relation to everyone, I have enslaved myself to everyone" (1 Cor 9:19).[162]

The designations *slave* and *emissary* imply that Paul is personally unimportant; the regular translation "apostle" does not convey the hint in the word *apostolos* that it denotes simply someone sent off to deliver his master's messages. It is his master and his message that count. Admittedly, to be a slave is not necessarily unpleasant; everything depends on the master.[163] Being an important person's slave carries an authority of its own and is capable of being used to buttress one's own authority.[164] The same applies to an emissary. Paul gains significance from his association with the master and the message. You don't mess with the slave, because the slave represents the master. You don't turn away an important person's emissary, because the

---

[161]David Wenham, *Paul: Follower of Jesus or Founder of Christianity?* (Grand Rapids and Cambridge, UK: Eerdmans, 1995), 410; cf. Murray J. Harris, *Slave of Christ* (Downers Grove, IL: InterVarsity Press; Leicester, UK: Inter-Varsity Press, 2001), 19; also Richard A. Burridge, *Imitating Jesus* (Grand Rapids and Cambridge, UK: Eerdmans, 2007), 81-154.

[162]See the discussion in Gorman, *Cruciformity*, 181-88.

[163]Cf. Thiselton, *Hermeneutics of Doctrine*, 322-23.

[164]See Dale B. Martin, *Slavery as Salvation* (New Haven, CT, and London: Yale University Press, 1990).

emissary represents that important person. Being an emissary is a gift that issues from God's favor (Rom 1:5). You don't ignore information from someone set apart to bring news from a high authority.

Paul is an emissary by God's will (1 Cor 1:1). The story of God's capturing him and making him a slave (Acts 9) illustrates how this process worked. He had passionately persecuted the church of God. But then God "who set me apart from my mother's womb and summoned me through his grace wanted to reveal his son in me so that I might report good news about him among the nations" (Gal 1:15-16). While he does not describe his experience as a conversion, the word *call* is also misleading; it underestimates the peremptory nature of such a summons. He describes it in terms that come from Jeremiah's account of God's capture of him, and Jeremiah's life illustrates the dynamics of the interrelationship between authority and feebleness. Paul's "decision for Christ" was "not strictly Paul's own, but one made for him"; nor was its way prepared by a gradual realization on his part that his faith was built on a shaky foundation.[165]

Fallible Shepherds

It's tempting to want to be in a position of authority. Paradoxically, in order to get into that position, you need to focus on the opposite ambition, that of being a servant or slave (Mt 20:20-28). The entire body of Israel and the entire body of people who believe in Jesus are servants or slaves of God. Within Israel as a whole there are then individuals who are servants of God, people such as Moses or David. Within the body of believers there are people such as Paul who are slaves of God or of Jesus or of nonbelievers (*doulos*; e.g., Rom 1:1; 1 Cor 9:19; Col 4:12), who are underlings of Jesus or of the gospel (*hypēretēs*; Lk 1:2; 1 Cor 4:1) or who are servants of God or of Jesus or of the gospel or of the church (*diakonos*; e.g., 2 Cor 6:4; Col 1:7, 23, 25) or who are God's day laborers (*synergos*; 1 Cor 3:5-9).

Suppose a person who claims to be someone's slave or emissary is lying? Perhaps he is just serving himself, and his claim to his position is a way to assert his own authority? The claim to some gift of God's favor can always work that way. Paul's letters do suggest two considerations to apply in asking whether someone such as him who claims to be a servant is actually a

---

[165]Bornkamm, *Paul*, 16, 23.

manipulator. One is his acceptance of persecution and other forms of trouble that come to him through his work as servant (see, e.g., 2 Cor 4:7-12; 6:3-10). Related to this criterion is the way his entire message focuses on the centrality of Jesus' execution. It seems implausible that a person mainly interested in exercising power would have thought through so systematically the implications of accepting other people's exercise of power and would have lived by that understanding. But biblical theology can survive without being sure what was in Paul's heart.

"Jesus knew that his followers would be muddled and ambiguous, just as he knew that the nation as a whole would not repent. Both of these beliefs belonged with his awareness that what he had to do for Israel had ultimately to be done by himself alone."[166] One expression of that realism is the way he talks about shepherding. The people of God is a flock, so it has shepherds. The strength and the danger of this mage, too, is the way it combines power and commitment.[167] A shepherd directs the flock about where to go and in doing so makes sure of providing for its needs.

The trouble is that the shepherds of the people of God easily focus on the enjoyment of their power and get more interested in feeding on the sheep than in feeding them. This reality makes God determine to intervene to act as shepherd himself, while also promising a human shepherd who will undertake shepherding in the proper fashion (Ezek 34). Jesus implies that the pattern whereby shepherds behave like thieves is repeated in his day and declares that he is the good shepherd, the kind Ezekiel envisages (Jn 10:1-18).

Rather astonishingly, Jesus then challenges a monumentally fallible servant like Peter to shepherd his flock (Jn 21:16) and appoints shepherds in congregations as part of equipping his people for service (Eph 4:11). The actual word translated "shepherd" or "pastor" comes only once in the New Testament, but the image recurs in the exhortation to a congregation's elders or overseers to keep watch over the flock, to shepherd the congregation and to be wary of wolves who will attack the flock—of teachers who will lead disciples astray (Acts 20:28-31). In shepherding, they need to be wary of aiming to build up their status or wealth (1 Pet 5:1-4). Paul safeguards against

---

[166]N. T. Wright, *Jesus and the Victory of God* (Minneapolis: Fortress; London: SPCK, 1996), 318.
[167]Cf. Timothy S. Laniak, *Shepherds After My Own Heart* (Downers Grove, IL: InterVarsity Press; Leicester, UK: Inter-Varsity Press, 2006), 247-48.

the latter temptation by declining to ask congregations for financial support even though he believes in principle that he could properly do so (1 Cor 9).

Servanthood or slavery might seem unlikely to be related to wealth, but power or leadership is likely to be so related. Leaders become wealthier than the people they lead; wealthy people become more powerful than ordinary people. It's no coincidence that a leader who asks Jesus about eternal life is also identified as rich (Lk 18:18-25) or that Nicodemus was a member of the Sanhedrin and was also wealthy (Jn 3:1; 19:39). Church history has shown that the two Testaments' explicit and implicit judgment on shepherds (Ezek 34; Jn 10) continues to apply.

Having teachers is also hazardous, because it involves using the tongue, that very dangerous part of the body (Jas 3:1-10).

Men and Women

Both men and women are involved in the service of God and in leadership in the people of God. While men alone can be priests in Israel, women can be prophets and can fulfill other leadership roles. While the twelve disciples are all men, women fulfill other leadership roles in mission and in congregational life. First Corinthians 11 presupposes that women have authority to lead in worship by praying and prophesying. Paul does also stress they shouldn't let their hair run wild; it could give the impression of being sexually loose or provoking the desire of the kind of angels that appear in Genesis 6[168] or of being ecstatic prophets like the participants in other religions. Later in the letter he declares that they should keep quiet in church (1 Cor 14:34-35), which seems to conflict with what he said earlier; perhaps he means wives shouldn't argue with their husbands in church, because it would imperil the order of the family.

The same principle may underlie the declaration that "a woman [or possibly a wife] should learn in silence, in complete submission. I do not permit a woman [or wife] to teach or have authority over a man [or a husband]" (1 Tim 2:11-12). Part of the implicit background to such requirements is a concern to fit into the culture of the society rather than stand out from it in an assertion of freedom gained through the gospel. A number of the New Testament's instructions correspond to ones we know from non-Christian

---

[168]See Martin, *Corinthian Body*, 242-49.

exhortations in the historical context. The culture expects people to dress and behave with reserve, grace and discretion. To draw a modern analogy: in much of southern Europe, women of all ages go topless on the beach. It's an expression of their human freedom. In the United States they do not. One can imagine Christian women believing that their freedom entitles them to do the same thing in the United States, even though it would lead to scandal (not to say arrest), and one can imagine Christian teachers bidding them not do so and using arguments about modesty in this connection.

Another aspect of the background to the exhortation to keep quiet and not engage in debate is the activity of men who are teaching a perverted version of the faith (see 1 Tim 1:3-11; cf. 2 Tim 2:14-26; Tit 1:10-16). One result of their activity is conflict and argument in the congregation, and Paul wants its worship not to be characterized by anger and argument.[169]

The false teachers are leading women astray with their teaching, which includes a rejection of marriage (1 Tim 4:3; 2 Tim 3:6). God's original intention had put having children at the center of God's purpose for womanhood; it was why Eve was created. These teachers imply that this vocation is over. Paul knows it is not. He wants the women to listen to proper teaching in order that they may be won back to the truth.[170]

His comment on women being saved through childbirth (1 Tim 2:15) sounds contradictory to the teaching elsewhere in this same group of letters (e.g., Tit 3:4-7). As is commonly the case, "salvation" refers to escaping from God's wrath and entering into life at the end. While salvation is by grace and by faith, the Scriptures affirm that being grasped by grace issues in a certain style of life. For Timothy himself, fulfilling his ministry properly is the way he will rescue himself and his hearers (1 Tim 4:16). For anyone, rescuing oneself will mean continuing "in faith, love, and holiness, with propriety" (1 Tim 2:15). A life of this nature leads to salvation. It means fulfilling our vocation, the reason for God's creating us.

For women, having children is part of that life. This is not to say that every woman has to have children otherwise she will be damned. In the world of

---

[169]In line with the way the letters speak, I refer to their author as Paul; the question whether he wrote them doesn't affect whether they form part of the material for articulating a "biblical theology."

[170]Cf. Jouette M. Bassler, *1 Timothy, 2 Timothy, Titus* (Nashville: Abingdon, 1996), 59-63.

the Scriptures, many women could not have children. The epistle is talking about womanhood in general and urging the community of women not to reject their vocation to bear children.

Paul uses some points from Genesis to underline his point. While his allusion has little to do with the text's own meaning, as is often the case with the New Testament's use of the First Testament, one might say on the basis of Genesis 2 that men will be rescued through tilling the ground, women through bearing children.

"There is neither Jew nor Greek, neither slave nor free, neither male nor female, because you are all one person through the Anointed One, Jesus" (Gal 3:28). Here "Paul makes most explicitly and passionately clear his stake in Christ, namely the erasure of human difference, primarily the difference between Jew and gentile but also that between man and woman, freeman and slave."[171] But the implication is not that Jews cease to be Jews, slaves cease to be slaves, or wives cease to be wives. While racial, social and gender differences do not indicate relative worth or privileged status before God, "social realities conditioned the practice of the principle."[172] In any case, the declaration occurs in the context of a discussion of justification. "Paul does not claim that there are no differences among individuals in sex, nationality, or social position. . . . It would be a mistake to attribute to the Apostle a modern humanistic ideal of equality." He does imply that the common basis of the congregation's relationship with God will transform the way people relate to one another as men and women, Jews and Gentiles, masters and slaves.[173]

---

[171]Daniel Boyarin, *A Radical Jew* (Berkeley and London: University of California Press, 1994), 22.
[172]Dunn, *Theology of Paul the Apostle*, 593.
[173]Dahl, *Studies in Paul*, 109.

7

GOD'S EXPECTATIONS

✝

Halfway through the Torah, we discover that God expects his people to "be holy, as I am holy" (Lev 19:2). It makes us look back over the way we have come and ask what Yahweh has been like so that we can examine ourselves by this criterion. We discover that being like Yahweh means being creative, being life-giving and bringing order (Gen 1–2). It means being easily hurt, being realistic, but not giving up (Gen 3–11). It means giving people hope, giving them land and giving them space and scope (Gen 12–50). It means hearing people's pain, being open and self-revealing, fighting against oppression and giving people freedom (Ex 1–18). It means being categorical, being concrete and practical, being present, being flexible and being more merciful than judgmental (Ex 19–40). It means being available and being frightening (Lev 1–18).

Something of this kind is the piecemeal revelation of God that the First Testament Scriptures offer and that Jesus then embodies (Heb 1:1-2). So henceforth being like God involves being like Jesus. The heart of being like God or being like Jesus then involves being cruciform,[1] though both Testaments indicate that there is more to it. If our love is to resemble God's love, furthermore, it will be electing love (in the sense of deliberate and free), purifying love and creative love.[2] To put it yet another way, theological ethics is concerned with faith, love and hope—our sense of self, of others

---

[1]Michael J. Gorman, *Inhabiting the Cruciform God* (Grand Rapids and Cambridge, UK: Eerdmans, 2009), 105.
[2]Barth, *CD* IV, 2:766-83.

and of time.[3] It's not just love, and it's not just faith and love, but faith, love and hope.

7.1 WALKING

"We are his making, created by means of the Anointed One, Jesus, for good actions that God prepared in advance so that we might walk by means of them." Humanity's story started with God sending human beings into the world with tasks to undertake, but we got sidetracked into fulfilling our own desires, and we turned ourselves into the victims of God's wrath. Fortunately, God's own grace could rescue us from that wrath. We could lay hold on this grace by trusting in God—not by doing anything, which ensures that we don't have reason to be proud of ourselves. But the idea is that we do then undertake the things that God originally intended and planned (Eph 2:8-10). The Torah lays out some aspects of them; the New Testament lays out some more.

The End of the Torah (1)

The Torah is the Scriptures' great resource for a knowledge of God's expectations, a knowledge of what it means to walk in the right way. But Jesus is "the end of the Torah as a way of being in the right, for everyone who trusts" (Rom 10:4). Paul has already pointed out that the Torah was never designed to be the means of being in the right. People who were not in the right with God could not acquire such a status through obeying the Torah. Further (as Paul has also pointed out and will soon note again), the Israel of the First Testament is not one that was zealous for God and that was trying to establish its right status. If only!

So we might see this argument as ad hominem. There were believers who argued as if the Torah were supposed to be integral to a relationship with God, and the Torah can be read that way: "The person who does [what the Torah says] will live by it" (Rom 10:5, quoting Lev 18:5). Yet that statement in the Torah was itself speaking of a people that was already in a living relationship with God by God's grace (cf. Rom 4). Maybe part of the problem is that believers, like other human beings, are inclined to want to base their

---

[3]See Oliver O'Donovan, *Self, World, and Time* (Grand Rapids and Cambridge, UK: Eerdmans, 2013), 97-133.

relationship with God on what they do.[4] Jesus rescued us from that project. He put an end to it.

Thus "with freedom the Anointed One set us free" (Gal 5:1).[5] In Galatians freedom is "the central theological concept which sums up the Christian's situation before God as well as in this world" and also "the basis and the content of Christian 'ethics.'"[6] Paul is not speaking about a freedom to do what we like as long as we don't harm anyone else or a freedom to make our own decisions without external constraint but about a freedom from the obligation to do what the Torah says simply because of its nature as something that binds us, as if this commitment were key to a right relationship with God. Such acceptance of the "yoke" of the Torah is a submission to a form of slavery that means you've given up on what Jesus achieved for you. It means falling away from grace (Gal 5:1-4).

The yoke to which Galatians refers may be especially an obligation to the Torah as laying down means of worship and identity formation. This understanding fits Acts' references to observing the Torah (e.g., Acts 13:39; 15:5; 18:13; 21:17-28) and Paul's own words about our having died with regard to rules about food and festivals, which can only safeguard against the worst excesses of the lower nature (Col 2:16-23). The Spirit's taking possession of believers means "freeing them from the compulsion of sin and the power of death."[7]

Paradoxically, "the Lord is the Spirit; but where the Spirit of the Lord is, there is freedom" (2 Cor 3:17). You might have thought that having a lord and master would mean servitude, but the Scriptures assume that God is one "whose service is perfect freedom."[8] That the freedom Paul describes has a distinctive and paradoxical profile emerges when he also urges the Galatians as free people to serve one another as slaves (*douleuete*; Gal 5:13).

---

[4]Cf. the paragraphs under "The Divine Initiative" in section 6.2 above.

[5]The simple dative *eleutheria* deserves a different translation from *ep' eleutheria*, "for freedom" (Gal 5:13), though it may imply no significant difference in meaning; cf. Ronald Y. K. Fung, *The Epistle to the Galatians* (Grand Rapids: Eerdmans, 1988), 216.

[6]Hans Dieter Betz, *Galatians* (Philadelphia: Fortress, 1979), 255, 257.

[7]Jürgen Moltmann, *The Spirit of Life* (London: SCM Press; Minneapolis: Fortress, 1992), 270.

[8]From the Collect for Peace in the Church of England *Book of Common Prayer* (cf. Murray J. Harris, *Slave of Christ* [Downers Grove, IL: InterVarsity Press; Leicester, UK: Inter-Varsity Press, 2001], 153). The idea goes back to Augustine (see, e.g., *The Size of the Soul* 34: "to serve whom is most useful for all, and delight in whose service is perfect and only freedom").

Further, Galatians goes on to speak of "fulfilling" the Torah (Gal 5:14). Obedient submission to God implies such fulfillment.[9] Does it mean *keeping* the Torah? But Paul doesn't speak of believers "keeping" or "obeying" or "doing" the Torah (the term he picks up in Gal 3:10, 12 and in Rom 10:5, in quoting Lev 18:5; cf. also Gal 5:3). He doesn't give the impression that "walking according to the Torah" corresponds to his understanding of the dynamic of the congregation's life.[10]

On Living Life in Accordance with the Torah

Keeping Torah had been the way Israel was to go about living as God's people, though it was not the way they got into a relationship with God. This understanding might then be a viable Christian stance, but it looks rather like the position of Paul's opponents in Galatians. Understandably, some believers did assume that once you had come to acknowledge Jesus, you would continue (or start) to live life in accordance with the Torah. Men would be circumcised, women would observe the purity rules, everyone would celebrate the festivals, people would offer fellowship sacrifices to express their gratefulness when God answered their prayers and would keep kosher, and so on.

There could be no objection to such things in themselves; they were not wrong, but it would be a different matter when someone insisted that it was obligatory to do so and that this obligation rested on Gentiles as well as Jews. Such an insistence was incompatible with recognition of and trust in Jesus. Further, if people see keeping Torah as key to living for God, they will find it doesn't work. If anything, it is counterproductive, because sin can still use the Torah as a means to entice them and draw them into sin rather than out of it.

Believers received the Spirit through accepting the gospel message, not through observing a rule of life (Gal 3:2). To start insisting on a rule of life is to seek to complete by human activity something that was initiated by divine activity. And the trouble with basing your relationship with God on what you do is that you can never do enough. You can never do everything (Gal 3:10). After all, the Torah is not based on trust (Gal 3:12).

---

[9]Cf. Betz, *Galatians*, 275.

[10]Cf. Brian S. Rosner, *Paul and the Law* (Nottingham, UK: Inter-Varsity Press; Downers Grove, IL: InterVarsity Press, 2013).

In its proper context the Torah is indeed based on trust; God's giving the Torah follows on and builds on the response of trust by Abraham and his descendants. The Torah was given to believers. But looked at in isolation, in Exodus through Deuteronomy the Torah itself speaks almost exclusively in terms of obedience to rules, and it often offers no rationale for these rules. If followers of Jesus make keeping this rule of life a condition of discipleship, they are basing their relationship with God on keeping rules. While circumcision counts for something under the Sinai covenant, in the Jesus covenant it doesn't, even though both the Sinai covenant and the Jesus covenant concern trust working through love.

Paul sees deliberate submission to one aspect of the Torah (such as circumcision) as implying submission to the Torah in its entirety (Gal 5:3). Admittedly, he is happy to observe particular requirements in particular circumstances, including circumcision, and to expect other people to observe particular requirements of the Torah, such as not muzzling the ox when it is treading out the grain (1 Cor 9:9). His point concerns the Torah as a system and as something intrinsic to our relationship with God. If people maintain that a requirement such as circumcision or sabbath is binding simply because it's part of the Torah, such an argument implies that the whole Torah has binding authority and is a requirement for a relationship with God. As a default approach to our lives as believers, that way of thinking compromises a proper understanding of the nature of our relationship with God.

The End of the Torah (2)

The statement that Jesus brought the Torah to its end could also suggest a different idea, though a related one. The Greek word for "end" (*telos*) more often suggests goal or object than termination, and this understanding fits the argument of Romans 10.[11] The end of something can be its aim or purpose.

The Torah's purpose was to tell people who trust in Yahweh what was involved in being faithful to Yahweh in response to what Yahweh had promised them and had done for them. But that aim didn't work. People weren't very interested in being faithful to Yahweh. Jesus came to win them to that desire. He thereby brings about the achieving of the Torah's own aim.

---

[11]See Robert Badenas, *Christ the End of the Law* (Sheffield: JSOT, 1985).

The two understandings of Jesus being the end of the Torah then fit together. Jesus put an end to it, making it no longer binding, because he was
the means of achieving its goal. People are to obey Jesus' Torah, and they will
thus fulfill *the* Torah (Gal 6:2; Rom 13:8-10).[12]

In contrast, some of the people who are theoretically committed to
keeping the Torah end up frustrating it. Jesus has been asked why his disciples transgress the elders' tradition in not observing the recognized hand-
purification ceremonies before eating. Such ceremonies were designed to
make sure one had not had contact with anything that was taboo and thus
that one had kept the Torah. Jesus retorts by ridiculing his interlocutors'
presuppositions. As if ingesting a microscopic amount of something taboo
could defile a person! If people want to be concerned about defilement, they
should think about the serious things that come from inside them, not the
trivial results of not purifying their hands. Otherwise they are frustrating
the Torah's aims, not aiding their achievement.

Jesus thereby made all foods clean, Mark adds (Mk 7:19). In other words,
with hindsight he laid the foundation for the later abolition of the food rules.
But his own immediate point was one about the tradition, which some
people were inclined to prioritize over the Scriptures (if he were questioning
the scriptural purity rules themselves, his argument would deconstruct).
They transgressed God's command about honoring parents in the name of
their humanly devised tradition in order to maneuver their way around that
command. They thus honor God with their words, but their real attitude is
far away from God. Jesus' critique overlaps with the idea of keeping the spirit
of the Torah rather than the letter of it. As commonly understood, that idea
is not a biblical one. Keeping the spirit of the Torah implies a more thorough
outward observance, not an inward observance (cf. Rom 2:25-29). Jesus'
critics don't fulfill the spirit or the letter of the Torah; they frustrate it.

On another occasion, Jesus says to someone who has committed
adultery, "Nor do I condemn you. Go, and from now on don't sin any more"
(Jn 8:11). He's not making a legal judgment, of the kind the theologians
were seeking, and he's illustrating his usual stance as one who hasn't come
to condemn and who leaves it to people to condemn themselves (cf. Jn 8:15).

---

[12]Cf. Morna D. Hooker, "Paul and Covenantal Nomism," in M. D. Hooker and S. G. Wilson, eds.,
Paul and Paulinism, C. K. Barrett Festschrift (London: SPCK, 1982), 47-56 (on 48).

But he's bidding the person not to commit adultery again and also laying on her the more general expectations of someone whose life he has restored (cf. Jn 5:14).

Two dangers threaten Christian freedom, the acceptance of the Torah and the corruption of people's life by the lower nature.[13] Both dangers involve forgetting that Jesus died for us, so that remembering that he did safeguards against both or is the means of deliverance from both. One aim of God's action in Jesus was "that the right requirement of the Torah might be fulfilled in us who walk not in accordance with the lower nature but in accordance with the Spirit" (Rom 8:4). Thus if you love your neighbor, you will fulfill the entire Torah (Gal 5:14). "'The law of the Spirit' is simply a summary way of speaking of the requirement of the law fulfilled by those who walk by the Spirit." It is "the law understood as guidelines for Spirit-directed conduct."[14]

Fulfilling the Torah

Jesus says that he came to fulfill the Torah and the Prophets, not to subvert them (Mt 5:17-20). His declaration leads into an exhortation to his disciples to live lives of a high moral standard and then into some profiling of what that life looks like. They are to manifest a higher righteousness than their spiritual leaders; to forswear anger, lust, prevarication, resistance to attackers and resentment; to be discrete in their exercise of spiritual disciplines; to forsake saving, worrying about the future and judging; and to look to God for the meeting of their needs (Mt 5–7).

This Sermon on the Mount is not a system of rules but something like a vision of character.[15] But taking it seriously will mean people "fulfill" (*plēroō*) the Torah and the Prophets—that is, implement them, in a way that gets at their implications and not just their surface expectations. Jesus wants the Torah to be practiced and taught, not set aside. Fulfilling in the sense of filling out is what Jesus does in spelling out the greater righteousness he speaks of,[16] though *fulfill* can also denote "a process of legal interpretation

---

[13]Cf. Betz, *Galatians*, 258.

[14]James D. G. Dunn, *The Theology of Paul the Apostle* (Grand Rapids and Cambridge, UK: Eerdmans, 1998), 646-47.

[15]Richard B. Hays, *The Moral Vision of the New Testament* (San Francisco: Harper, 1996), 97-98.

[16]Cf. the comments on fulfilling and filling out in the paragraphs headed "Visionary" in section 2.2 above.

in which individual laws are interpreted in such a way that they are made to fit given situations or cases and to facilitate justice."[17]

Paul, too,

> believed that the communities he established represented the fulfillment of the prophetic promises that God would reestablish his temple and place his presence among his people in the period of Israel's restoration. With language reminiscent of Leviticus, Paul says that God's people must be pure in order to constitute an appropriate dwelling place for God's presence.... Paul assumes the shape of the Corinthians' faith should roughly duplicate the shape of Israelite religion as it is described in the Mosaic law.[18]

In his instructions to congregations he does cover aspects of life that are not covered by the Torah (e.g., 1 Cor 7; his attitude to prostitution; or some of the fruit of the Spirit), but precisely by going beyond its explicit formulations, believers may be fulfilling the Torah.

When applied to the Torah, then, as when applied to prophecy, fulfilling suggests something both more and less than simple correspondence. It involves filling it out in a way that matches its inner dynamics, though not directly or necessarily obedience to its specifics—people do not have to be circumcised or keep the sabbath. If you're led by the Holy Spirit you're not under the Torah, but you do more than fulfill its aims, not less (Gal 5:18). In this sense "the 'mind of the Spirit' submits to Torah,"[19] and there is no "law" against the characteristic lifestyle of people who live by the Holy Spirit (Gal 5:23) (while in some connections the Greek word for law has a narrower meaning than the word *tôrâ*, in other connections it can have a broader meaning and denote law or instruction or obligation in a more general sense).

In light of the Scriptures as a whole, what might the "fulfillment" of the Decalogue look like? Perhaps it might imply

---

[17]Hans Dieter Betz, *The Sermon on the Mount* (Minneapolis: Fortress, 1995), 179.

[18]Frank Thielman, *Paul and the Law* (Downers Grove, IL: InterVarsity Press, 1994), 98, 99 (the remarks relate specifically to the Corinthian church, but Thielman sees them as more broadly applicable). See further Thielman, *From Plight to Solution* (Leiden and New York: Brill, 1989).

[19]N. T. Wright, *Paul and the Faithfulness of God* (Minneapolis: Fortress; London: SPCK, 2013), 1109 (the words are italicized).

1. Acknowledge as God only the God and Father of our Lord Jesus Christ.

2. Worship, serve, understand and speak of God in accordance with the Scriptures.

3. Attach God's name only to that to which God's name belongs.

4. Balance work and rest in your life.

5. Honor your parents and your children.

6. Seek peace with your neighbors even when they are your enemies.

7. Give yourself sexually only to your wife or husband.

8. Be generous with your possessions.

9. Use your words to build people up.

10. Be content with what you have.[20]

The Torah in Heart and Mind

God had promised to renew the Sinai covenant by writing the Torah into people's minds (Jer 31:31-34). He did not speak of giving a new Torah; there was nothing wrong with the Torah itself. Jeremiah, for instance, was concerned about people's laxity in basic matters such as commitment to Yahweh alone, refraining from image-making and observing the sabbath. The promise was that people would now be self-disciplined in these matters, and this promise had been kept in the Second Temple period.

The fulfillment the New Testament is concerned about relates to the temptation to focus on less important or less demanding features of the Torah or on traditional expectations that are extraneous to the Torah. The coming of Jesus and the outpouring of the Spirit mean that this other form of "fulfillment" of the Torah becomes possible and expected: a more serious facing of the Torah's own most demanding aims.

An opposite question raised by Jeremiah 31 is the implication that people will no longer need to be taught about walking in God's way but will naturally both know and do it. The New Testament does not assume that God has fulfilled such a promise. Paul teaches people, expects there to be a teaching ministry exercised in congregations and knows that Christian congregations and individuals do not walk in God's way. Subsequent history

---

[20]See also the contemporary Western Decalogue in *OTT* 3:839.

supports his assumption. It is not obvious that Christian congregations walk in God's way more faithfully than Israel did. It is not the case that "in OT times the Israelites knew God's law as an external code, but in the NT dispensation the law of God is set in his people's understanding and written in their hearts."[21]

Notwithstanding the definitional statement that the person who is born of God doesn't commit sin (1 Jn 3:9) and the declaration that our old self was crucified with Jesus, believers still have to put some effort into living in obedience to God, and they don't always do so. They have been baptized into a relationship with Jesus and thus into his death (Rom 6:1-11); they have thereby left the realm where sin or Torah have authority and entered a realm where Jesus has authority. They no longer have either the obligation or the right to do what sin suggests. They are like people who come for refuge to the United States who can and must no longer behave like citizens of the enemy of the United States that formerly bound them (cf. the argument of Col 2:9-23).

What ongoing significance does the Torah have in practice? Paul does not make his answer to this question quite clear, but one might join the dots as follows.[22] Broadly, the Torah, though formulated for Israel, is a true statement of God's expectations of humanity as a whole. The qualification "broadly" does not imply that there are any statements in it that are untrue but rather that there are elements in it that relate to the particularities of Israel's relationship with Yahweh and that also incidentally, but crucially, form a hindrance in connection with reaching Gentiles.

These elements do not directly correspond to expectations of humanity in general, and in this respect they are different from the requirement to love one's neighbor or to administer justice in a fair way or to avoid coveting. They do not directly so correspond, though even the Israel-particular rules are expression of principles that have implications for humanity as a whole. While this distinction between the universal and the Israelite-particular overlaps with the idea of distinguishing between the ethical and the ceremonial, it is not identical with it. On one hand, the sabbath is not mainly a

---

[21]So Fung, *Galatians*, 248.
[22]Cf. E. P. Sanders, *Paul, the Law, and the Jewish People* (London: SCM Press; Philadelphia: Fortress, 1983), e.g., p. 100. Some points in the following paragraphs follow Sanders's discussion.

ceremonial observance, but Paul does not see it as binding on Gentiles (Col 2:16). On the other, Paul abjures the use of images in worship, which is a ceremonial observance.

Broadly speaking, Paul assumes that it's obvious what walking in God's way involves, yet this assumption doesn't mean people have no need of his pointing out what it looks like. What Jesus does is not so much reveal what this way is but make it possible to walk in it. In exhorting people to walk in God's way, Paul can appeal to the Torah, but he doesn't need to do so.

Servants and Ministers

It's misleading to speak simply of God bringing about Israel's freedom from Egypt—period. When Moses "delivered" or "rescued" some girls from some shepherds (Ex 2:17-19), they were then simply free (well, one of them did end up as Moses' wife). When God "rescues" or "redeems" Israel from serfdom, "brings Israel out" from Egypt, "restores" Israel and "delivers" Israel at the Reed Sea, Israel does not simply become free. Yahweh is acting to enable Israel to function as his son or servant. Pharaoh is to "release my son so that he can serve me" (Ex 4:23). The Hebrew verb for "serve" (*'ābad*) covers both work and worship, and Exodus uses it with both senses. Both are aspects of submitting oneself. Exodus underlines the point by its use of the verb "know" or "acknowledge" (*yāda'*): Israel is moving from a forced recognition of Pharaoh to a willing recognition of Yahweh in life and in worship.

Likewise, "Christian freedom" does not imply "permission to do everything and anything."[23] Jesus dies to free us from a negative service into a positive one.[24] The Spirit brings freedom in the sense of "freedom to have a Lord, this Lord, God, as Lord."[25] Our experience is one of "liberation and reenslavement."[26] Being a slave means having no final control over your body, your destiny or your life. In this sense you are powerless. It can nevertheless be a position of honor and satisfaction. Everything depends on the master. The astonishing thing about being a believer is that it releases a person from slavery to a rotten and oppressive master, an enslavement that

---

[23]Daniel Boyarin, *A Radical Jew* (Berkeley and London: University of California Press, 1994), 133.
[24]See section 5.5 above.
[25]Barth, *CD* I, 1:457.
[26]Michael J. Gorman, *Cruciformity* (Grand Rapids and Cambridge, UK: Eerdmans, 2001), 126.

means doing things that you don't want to do and that no sane person would want to do, into a slavery to an upright and honorable master, an enslavement that means doing things that on a good day you don't at all mind doing, things that any sane person would be glad to do.

The Holy Spirit inspires believers to declare that Jesus is Lord (1 Cor 12:3), the basic Christian confession. It is both an objective and a subjective statement. Declaring that Caesar is lord acknowledges his authority in the world and also acknowledges his authority over me. Declaring that Jesus is Lord has the same implication; hence it takes the Holy Spirit's agency to get me to make the confession. Making it presupposes that Jesus is a beneficent but authoritative master and that I am an obedient but trusting servant, finding both liberation from anxiety and constraint in submission.[27]

We are not God's partners but his servants. Jesus is not our buddy but our Lord. Jesus does say that his disciples aren't slaves but friends, but the sense in which it is so is that he has shared with them all that he knows from his Father (Jn 15:15); a master doesn't share everything with his slaves. Further, in that very context he also says that they are his friends if they do what he commands (yet what he commands is that they love each other) (Jn 15:12, 17).

Whereas believers used to be slaves of sin, Jesus freed them, and they then did not receive a spirit of slavery but a spirit of sonship (Rom 8:15). Yet this sonship also involves slavery: they are slaves to doing the right thing (Rom 6:18). They are to live as God's slaves (1 Pet 2:16). "Man, upon whose whole self God's demand is made, has no freedom toward God; he is accountable for his life as a whole. . . . He is like the slave who only has his duty to do and can do now more" (Lk 17:7-10).[28] We are like sons working in the family business, whose father pays them for the things that no one needs to see them doing, such as giving, praying and fasting (Mt 6:1-18). "The covenant is a sanctification, a claiming, a commandeering, an arrest of man for God, not of God for man."[29]

As well as being people who make Jesus Lord, we are like deacons working in the sanctuary, making offerings—of themselves. "I urge you brothers and

---

[27]Cf. Anthony C. Thiselton, *1 Corinthians* (Grand Rapids: Eerdmans, 2006), 191-96.
[28]Rudolf Bultmann, *Theology of the New Testament* (repr., Waco, TX: Baylor University Press, 2007), 1:14.
[29]Barth, *CD* I, 2:81.

sisters through the mercies of God to present your bodies a live sacrifice, holy, to God, pleasing, as your rational religious service" (Rom 12:1). While "your bodies" implies "your whole selves,"[30] talk in terms of sacrifice brings to mind the outward, the body. Whereas Christians sometimes suggest that Jesus wants our hearts, the New Testament assumes he also wants our bodies. If he doesn't have the body, he doesn't have the heart. Offering our bodies is an act of religious service (*latreia*, which suggests outward forms of observance) that is rational or spiritual (*logikos*). Romans 12 will go on to note that we need to be transformed through the renewing of our mind.

Further, Jesus' disciples are people who minister to him (*diakoneō*: Jn 12:26). Ministers are people who have some status but who use their capacities or energy or resources for the benefit of others, like the angels ministering to Jesus and Jesus ministering to people (Mt 4:11; 20:28; Lk 22:26-27). The woman present at his execution ministered to him (Mt 27:55). Other people do so unconsciously (Mt 25:44).

Commitment to God

The Torah's inner dynamics concern commitment to God and commitment to one's neighbor; everything else is an outworking of these commitments (cf. Mt 22:37-40). Even though the statement "God is love" (1 Jn 4:8, 16) is irreversible, love is thus indeed a paramount obligation, and love for God was the first obligation. But the preface "Listen, Israel" is vital to this love command because it reminds the people that they are Israel and thus that God is for them, that they are loved by God, that he is "our God." It might seem that commanding people to love imposes a hard and heavy requirement. Yet "it is not an alien demand which comes to us from without, but it is the demand to be what we are." What would be "impossible and absurd" would be the nonfulfillment of this expectation, which would be a denial of our very being.[31]

How is a command to be holy (Lev 19) or to circumcise your sons or to keep the sabbath (let alone to kill the Canaanites) an expression of love? By "love" Jesus evidently means something different from what it would mean in a Western context, as would also be true of what Deuteronomy means. In

---

[30]Cf. C. E. B. Cranfield, *A Critical and Exegetical Commentary on the Epistle to the Romans* (Edinburgh: T&T Clark, 1975), 598-99.
[31]Barth, *CD* I, 2:374, 382, 386.

our sense of the word, love is hardly the unifying theme in the Scriptures' account of God's expectations, as it is not the one word that defines God.[32] A number of strands in both Testaments make no reference to love, and in the West the word has become empty of meaning.[33]

When 1 Corinthians 13 expounds the nature of love, it uses the word *agapē*, and while one should not draw too sharp a contrast between *agapē* and other words for love, in the New Testament *agapē* does suggest a self-giving commitment that goes beyond liking or emotional attachment. Neatly, the Septuagint uses the related verb *agapaō* in translating the common Hebrew verb '*āhēb* in Deuteronomy, so that this verb is the one the Gospels put on Jesus' lips. Believers who read Jesus' words could thus be reminded of *agapē* as the New Testament describes it. It would not be an inappropriate association. In Deuteronomy, the verb '*āhēb* has the overtones of loyalty and commitment; it has political connotations.

The more distinctive Hebrew word for commitment is *ḥesed*, commonly translated "steadfast love" or the like. In substance it denotes what Moses and Jesus look for when they speak of love.[34] Such commitment will express itself (among other things) in holiness and in acknowledging Yahweh alone, in circumcising your sons and in observing sabbath. It will express itself in an imitation of God's character (Ex 34:6-7). It will express itself in a fulfilling of the threefold basic expectation expressed in Micah:

> implementing judgment
> giving yourself to commitment,
> being diffident in how you walk with your God. (Mic 6:8)

It will express itself in a life of integrity or wholeness—that is, a wholeness in giving oneself to God that contains no dissimulation or qualification.

If people live this way, they will indeed fulfill the aim of the Torah, do the kind of thing the Torah encourages, fulfill the "just requirement of the Torah" (Rom 8:4), not by directly trying to do so but by living their lives in light of the fact that God has freed them from making obedience to the Torah the key to a relationship with God. "Through Christ's death the law is also

---

[32]See section 1.1 above.
[33]Hays, *Moral Vision of the New Testament*, 200.
[34]See the paragraphs under "Loving, Compassionate and Gracious" in section 1.1 above.

liberated, namely from the power of sin and death." It is freed to resume its function of being a revelation and a measure of what God expects of us.[35] Believers live by love and live by the Spirit, and thereby also live by the Torah (Rom 8:4).[36]

Walking by the Holy Spirit

Relating to God thus implies obedience and deference. The vocation of God's people involves a walk. It means walking in God's way—both the way he lays out and the way he himself walks. In the New Testament, an initial acknowledging of Jesus as the Lord has to be continued as a walk, a walk "in accordance with the Spirit" (Rom 8:4), which will also be a walk "in [the company of] the Anointed One" (Col 2:6); that is, a walk "in accordance with the Anointed One," in keeping with his teaching (Col 2:8).

Walking begins in the Scriptures as walking about with God and then as walking about in front of God (halak hitpael; Gen 5:22, 24; 6:9; 17:1; 24:40; 48:15). The first expression suggests companionship and friendship; the second suggests openness and integrity but also safety. The Torah and the Psalms talk later about walking in Yahweh's ways (the more common qal or piel of halak; e.g., Deut 28:9; Pss 119:3; 128:1) or walking by Yahweh's teaching or rules (e.g., Ps 119:1; Jer 32:23; Ezek 5:6). Further, "walking" suggests a commitment that runs through life as a whole. There is a consistency about a walk; the walk is an expression of character, and it effects a shaping of character. In the lives of Noah and Abraham it goes with being "whole" (tāmîm; Gen 6:9; 17:1) in the sense of being wholly committed to walking that way; translations traditionally have "blameless," but the word is a positive one, suggesting integrity and uprightness.

It is a response in covenant. It involves love and delight (in God's commands and in the stories of what he has done). It involves heeding the Torah, the Prophets and the Writings. Paul had been committed to "walking" by the "way" of the Torah and being "led" in its ways (e.g., Ps 119:1, 35), and he was prepared to continue "walking" in that way and being "in line with the Torah" as a believer (Acts 21:21-26). But the pouring out of the Spirit in fulfillment of God's promise to Abraham meant that this way of thinking about

---

[35]James D. G. Dunn, Romans (Dallas: Word, 1988), 1:437.
[36]Cf. Sanders, Paul, the Law, and the Jewish People, 103-4.

living the right kind of life was no longer his default way. He rather thought in terms of walking by the Spirit or being led by the Spirit or being in line with the Spirit (Gal 5:16, 18, 25), and he urged on other people that way of conceptualizing the believer's walk.

Expressions such as "being led by the Spirit" are nicely ambiguous in that they suggest both something that the Spirit brings about and something that involves our activity. Living a life with the characteristics Paul describes is a natural result of being overwhelmed by the Spirit; it is a fruit of the Spirit. Yet it is also something willed by us; we are to walk by the Spirit, to keep in line with the Spirit. Paul has in mind a similar dynamic to that in Psalm 119. We need knowledge of God's will through the insight the Spirit gives so that we can live a life worthy of the Lord (Col 1:9-10).

People sometimes speak of having been led by the Spirit to (say) have lunch in one restaurant rather than another, which results in their meeting someone and God doing something. While the Scriptures support the idea that God acts this way, it is not what they mean by "being led by the Spirit." People also speak in terms of being led by the Spirit when they are following an impulse that comes from within their own spirit, and such an impulse may also issue in opening oneself to God's will, but neither is it what the Scriptures mean. The leading of the Spirit concerns our moral life and the way we relate to others (see Gal 5:13-15; also Rom 8:12-14). It is leading that reflects the moral priorities of God's Spirit. The phrase reflects the essential link between "the Holy Spirit and the sanctification of the community—ethics."[37]

Living by the Holy Spirit issues in caring, celebration, peacemaking, forbearance, thoughtfulness, integrity, fidelity, tenderness and restraint (Gal 5:22-23). It means gentleness to win back someone who does wrong, realistic modesty about the possibility of going wrong oneself, sharing the weight of such burdens with the people who carry them, not taking yourself too seriously, testing your own actions rather than comparing yourself with other people, and carrying the burden you have to carry (Gal 6:1-5). It means walking in the light or by the light (1 Jn 1:5-7).

---

[37]Reinhard Feldmeier and Hermann Spieckermann, *God of the Living* (Waco, TX: Baylor University Press, 2011), 229.

Awed

Believers are called to walk after God, to follow God. Admittedly, Jesus does not bid everyone to follow him, as he bids everyone to repent; he bids only some to follow him, in order to become people who share in his activity (Mt 4:17-22). Such following "is not merely a metaphor for absorbing and practicing his teachings."[38] Following means giving up their work, their security and their family obligations, and it tends to lead to trouble, though he is with them in that trouble and brings them out the other side. It means following him to martyrdom (Mt 16:24-25). Jesus "does not say that the disciples will occasionally fall into the midst of the wolves. It says they are *sent* there. No, it does not say their suffering is a rare anomaly; it is the rule. The pattern was established before they came along. They were called to suffering because they were called to follow the one who suffered" (Mt 10).[39]

There are thus two different vocations. All are servants, ministers, slaves, people who follow God; in another sense not all are followers.

It does not mean there are two levels of expectation or devotion. The Sermon on the Mount applies to everyone. Paul's preaching of the gospel is designed to produce "faithful obedience among the nations" (Rom 1:5). "If you love me, you will keep my commands," Jesus himself says (Jn 14:15).

All are expected to be in awe of God. Translations often speak of "fear" of God, but the word *fear* is misleading. In Greek and in Hebrew, the same words refer negatively to being afraid or scared and also positively to awe or submission. In connection with attitudes to God, they occasionally imply the first meaning; there are sometimes reasons to be afraid of God. More characteristically they presuppose the second, with the associated implication of obedience. It is this awe in relation to God that is the foundation of insight (e.g., Prov 1:7). Modesty and discretion in giving, praying and fasting are appropriate as part of an awed life in relation to God (Mt 6:1-18). We know what it is to be in awe of the Lord (2 Cor 5:11). Paul's words recall the First Testament expression, but the Lord here is Jesus, whose judgment he has just referred to.

---

[38]John P. Meier, *A Marginal Jew* (New York: Doubleday, 2001), 3:54.
[39]Miroslav Volf, *Against the Tide* (Grand Rapids: Eerdmans, 2010), 118.

Awe issues in obedient submission, but it has affective implications. The Philippians are to work out their salvation with awe and trembling (Phil 2:12), the same attitudes that slaves show to their earthly masters (Eph 6:4). "'Hope' and 'fear' equally belong to the structure of 'faith' . . . as correlatives: Just because faith is 'hope,' it is also 'fear' and vice versa."[40] In his exposition of the Ten Commandments in his Small Catechism, Martin Luther begins by paraphrasing the first commandment as implying that "We should fear, love, and trust in God above all things," but in expounding the other commandments, he mentions only fear and love.[41] Barth prefers to reverse these two and speak in terms of love and fear.[42]

So love expresses itself in fear (1 Pet 2:17, notwithstanding 1 Jn 4:18), in the sense of awe, and in wonder (e.g., Ex 15). Awe expresses itself in recognition of our openness to God (Ps 139). It expresses itself in respecting and in honoring God. "True and right knowledge of God" means "he is so known that due honor is paid to him." So "what is the method, of honoring him duly?" "To place our whole confidence in him; to study to serve him during our whole life by obeying his will; to call upon him in all our necessities, seeking salvation and every good thing that can be desired in him; lastly, to acknowledge him both with heart and lips, as the sole Author of all blessings."[43] It expresses itself in joy, relaxedness and diffidence, in submission to Yahweh's plans and wisdom.

There is a difference between the position of people who believe in Jesus and the position of the Israelites at Sinai (Heb 12:18-29). But it is thus not the difference that one might expect. Believers are not confronted by frightening audiovisual phenomena but by the heavenly Jerusalem: that difference makes the stakes higher and makes the experience more worthy of awe. If the Israelites did not escape when they failed to respond to God at Sinai, "How much less will we, if we turn away from the one who warns from the heavens?" Thus we need to "serve God pleasingly, with reverence and awe, because our God is a consuming fire," like Israel's (Deut 4:24). So people are

---

[40]Bultmann, *Theology of the New Testament*, 1:322.
[41]*A Short Explanation of Dr. Martin Luther's Small Catechism*, rev. ed. (St. Louis: Concordia, 1965), 5.
[42]Barth, *CD* II, 1:35-37.
[43]John Calvin, *The Catechism of the Church of Geneva* (Hartford, CT: Sheldon and Goodwin, 1815), 10. Cf. Barth, *CD* III, 2:182-86.

to make every effort to enter the sabbath rest that God is offering and thus cease from their own work, so they don't perish as many Israelites did (Heb 4:11).

Trusting

"It is by the Spirit through trust that we are looking forward to what we hope for, for being made right"—or more likely, "it is by the Spirit through trust that we are looking forward to what we hope for, which issues from being made right" (Gal 5:5).[44] Either understanding sums up Paul's insight into the way life works for believers. First, it works by the Spirit, on the basis of God's manifest, powerful irruption into their lives, which makes them do things they would not otherwise do (such as pray to God as Father). Second, correlatively, it works through trust. They do not come into a relationship or grow in a relationship with God on the basis of things that they do, such as get circumcised or get baptized or keep the sabbath or have regular times of prayer or read the Scriptures or undertake religious practices. It works through their trusting in the promise of the God who has burst into their lives. Third, its essence lies in looking forward. It is not about what God is doing in the present but about what God will do at the End. It centers on hope: not on taking a hopeful attitude without having concrete reason, but on an expectation grounded in what God has already done. In line with the first translation above, we could say that the center of that hope is God's final declaration that we indeed belong to the people to whom God has been doing the right thing over the millennia. In line with the second translation, we could say that the basis of that hope is the declaration God has already made that we indeed belong to that people.

"Don't be afraid" is a key biblical imperative. "Trust God" is the positive equivalent. Confidence replaces fear. One aspect of humanity's original failure was a refusal to trust God's word and God's goodness.

Trust is the key issue in Abraham's life, sometimes positively, sometimes negatively. It is a key issue in Israel's life on the way from Egypt to Canaan. It is then a key issue in Israel's life in Canaan. Will Israel trust Yahweh for its material needs, or turn to the "Masters," the Ba'als, as experts in making

---

[44]The former is the more usual understanding, represented by NRSV and TNIV; for the latter, see Fung, *Galatians*, 226-27.

crops grow? Will Israel trust Yahweh for its numerical future, for the flourishing as a people that was a key element in Yahweh's promise to Abraham,
or turn to the Masters in this connection, too, as entities that could look after
the fertility of its womenfolk? Will Israel trust Yahweh for its political future,
when it faces the pressure of the superpower, or will it turn to human allies
or rely on its military resources or turn to mediums and diviners? Will Israel
trust in the invisible Yahweh or bolster its faith by making itself images of
Yahweh? Will it trust in Yahweh, or either trust in itself or become despairing
of its future (self-confidence and despair being the two false alternatives
to trust)?[45]

A fundamental reason for resting on the sabbath is not exhaustion.
Resting is an expression of trust in God to meet one's needs.[46] "The Sabbath
commandment demands the faith in God which brings about the renunciation of man, his renunciation of himself, of all that he thinks and wills and
effects and achieves. It demands this renouncing faith not only as a general
attitude, but also as a particular and temporal activity and inactivity on the
Sabbath as distinguished from other days."[47] A willingness to observe the
sabbath requires a trust that one will nevertheless be able to grow enough
food for the family to survive. It also links with the command not to covet,
which implies being satisfied with having less than we could have if we
worked harder.

In turn, both these observances link with tithing. Giving up a tenth of
your animals and of what you grow again suggests risk, and contentment
with less than one might have. It recognizes that everything belongs to God
as its giver. Psalm 37 expounds that trust so radically that it offends readers
who have plenty to eat with its assertions about the way God has never failed
to ensure that the faithful and their families get enough to eat. It neatly pictures trust as "rolling" your way onto Yahweh (Ps 37:5).

The Torah shows that God's promises and people's trust in them come
before God's laying down rules; trust therefore trumps circumcision (Gal 3).
While the after-the-fact argument in Galatians is that God then gave the

---

[45]Cf. Jürgen Moltmann, *Theology of Hope* (London: SCM Press; New York: Harper, 1967), 22-26.
[46]Cf. Scott J. Hafemann, *The God of Promise and the Life of Faith* (Wheaton, IL: Crossway, 2001),
44-50.
[47]Barth, *CD* III, 4:59. Barth thus makes the sabbath the first command in his description of humanity's responsibility to God.

Torah to keep Israel under control, the logic of the Torah's own argument is that the Torah expounds how living by trust in God works out. "In relation to the Anointed One, Jesus, neither circumcision nor uncircumcision counts for anything, but trust working through love," and the entirety of this Torah is summed up by the command to love one's neighbor (Gal 5:6, 14).

The Sacred

While one reason for keeping the sabbath is that it is an expression of trust in God, there are other reasons. The sabbath is a day for refreshment and renewal, and modern executives are wise to take a day off. They then follow God's example (Gen 2:1-3). Actually, God had been having a relaxed and enjoyable time while engaged in the work of creation (Prov 8:22-31), like a lucky executive, but he nevertheless stopped work on the seventh day (in Hebrew, *stop* and *seven* are similar words) because the week's work was over. Work and joy can go together; stopping work and joy can go together. The job was done, and it was good to stop and look back at it.

So God blesses the sabbath, which implies making it a blessing, making it bountiful; inactivity is fruitful. Israel will prove the sabbath to be "a weekly celebration of the creation of the world, the uncontestable enthronement of its creator, and the portentous commission of humanity to be the obedient stewards of creation."[48] More paradoxically, stopping work and continuing work can also go together; in his sovereignty God continues active, providing for animals on the seventh day, as a human farmer does (Ps 104:10-18; cf. Jn 5:17).

God made the sabbath sacred. It's a human instinct to mark off some time, space, acts and/or people as sacred. The First Testament worked with that instinct. Israel's festivals took over the idea of sacred time and turned familiar festivals into a commemoration of Yahweh's act of deliverance. Israel's sanctuaries in the wilderness and in Jerusalem took over the idea of sacred space and harnessed them to faith in Yahweh. The first believers in Jesus continued to worship in the temple, to observe the festivals and to offer sacrifices. There is little controversy over these matters within the New Testament.

---

[48]John D. Levenson, *Creation and the Persistence of Evil* (Princeton, NJ, and Chichester, UK: Princeton University Press, 1994), 120.

Theologically the gospel may point toward the abolition of the category of the sacred, but the gospel did not bring about this abolition. Whereas the New Testament has no vision for sacred space, later generations established sanctuaries, to which they even applied the word *church*.[49] In the New Testament, baptism and the Lord's Meal are not sacred acts in the manner of sacrifices, but later generations brought them in from ordinary life into ritual and liturgical contexts in sanctuaries, so that they lost something of their significance.

In the New Testament, the only priesthood is that of Jesus and that of the congregation as a whole, but later generations assimilated the congregation's ministry to Israel's. The New Testament has no festivals such as Christmas and Easter, but later generations devised such festivals by a process analogous to Israel's.[50] Maybe we have to accept the First Testament's implication that the human instinct to mark off the sacred is part of the way God created humanity.

In the New Testament, the first day of the week is resurrection day, but it is not a sabbath, as it later became, and the sabbath is the most prominent topic of controversy in connection with the sacred. In Israel, the sabbath had taken up the idea of sacred time and harnessed it, and guarding the sabbath came to epitomize the keeping of the covenant. Nehemiah indicates how much of the reason for this development was contextual: when Judah is a little community surrounded by and involved with other communities that do not observe the sabbath, sabbath observance indeed marks Judah out, as it marks out a Jewish community today.

In Jesus' day, guarding the sabbath was still a marker of such commitment, though the contextual logic of this emphasis has disappeared. In his context, Jesus affirms varying degrees of freedom about the sabbath. He doesn't feel bound by contemporary interpretations of sabbath observance, and he doesn't regard sabbath observance as the one principle that cannot be overridden by another principle (Mt 12:1-14). He notes that the Torah indicates as much in implying that it is fine to circumcise on the sabbath (Jn 7:22-24). But further, with him, someone bigger than the temple is here (Mt 12:6), and with him, in effect, someone bigger than the sabbath is here. The Man is

---

[49]Cf. the comments under "Spirit and Truth" in section 1.3 above.
[50]Cf. the comments under "Rebellious Religion" in section 3.1 above.

Lord of the sabbath (Mt 12:8). God can carry on working on the sabbath, on the basis of being God; Jesus can do the same (Jn 5:16-17).

After him, no one is to judge anyone else in connection with sabbath observance (Col 2:16). The potential judges will be people who hold to some theological views and devotional practices that combine elements of traditional Jewish faith with other traditions from contemporary culture. The practices they commend include matters relating to drink as well as food, but the account of them makes no mention of circumcision; their stance overlaps with the Torah's concerns, but it is not identical with them. They want believers to follow their way of thinking and practice, and they warn them that they will not reach maturity or a full experience of God if they fail to do so. These teachers are thus compromising the ultimate significance of Jesus. Such practices can constitute attempts to reach out to God and find him (Acts 17:27), and as such they can be God-inspired. Yet holding onto them and trying to get other people to hold onto them after Jesus has come is to hold onto the shadow when the reality has arrived.

This consideration need not mean that faith in Jesus has no place for disciplines relating to food and drink and for rites and observances. Jesus assumes people will fast, and he talks about baptizing people and about "doing this in remembrance of me." Yet his words about baptism and about this Passover-style celebration show how these observances relate to his having come. Likewise any observance of discipline regarding food and drink and any observance of festivals, months and sabbaths will now relate to his having come. They do not have independent or supplementary significance, as if he were not enough. People who behave as if the observances have such significance as means of spiritual development in their own right, and not insofar as they are an expression of creaturely trust, have abandoned their connection with the head from which the body does grow (Col 2:19).

Purity

Israel's forms of sacrifice and its purity rules also took over customs that the Israelites shared with their neighbors and channeled them to the worship of Yahweh and to Israel's vocation. Israel's priests were equivalent to the priests of other peoples, but they, too, were harnessed to the overseeing of worship proper to Yahweh and to keeping Israel pure so that it could fulfill its vocation.

Purity means being unadulterated by whatever compromises the quality or nature of a thing. Both Testaments use the image of purity as a category for thinking about moral and religious propriety (and one of Jesus' aims was to deal with our moral and religious impurity). It suggests being uncompromised by anything inappropriate to a relationship with God.

We have noted that the First Testament uses the image of purity in a further connection—possibly the one that lies behind its application to moral and religious questions.[51] Many sacrifices and other rites were concerned with expiating or dissolving impurity that was nothing directly to do with wrongdoing. Two classic forms of impurity relate to death and to sex. The clash between death or sex and the nature of God meant that a person could not go straight into the sanctuary from having sex or tending a dead body.

If, then, you've just had to bury a member of your family, something of the touch of death attaches to you, and you cannot go straight into the sanctuary, otherwise you're compromising the sanctuary's nature as the place where God lives. You first need to undertake a cleansing rite to remove that touch, and to do so not merely for your sake but for the sake of the community as a whole that would risk God needing to abandon the sanctuary because it was compromised. This awareness of the gulf between God and death also found expression in the taboo that attached to menstruation and childbirth, both of which involve blood and interweave life and death in a mysterious way (e.g., Lk 2:22-40). Menstruation is a sign of life, yet it involves losing blood, a sign of death. Childbirth brings life but also threatens the life of a mother.

Likewise, if you've just had sex, you need to undertake a cleansing rite before going into the sanctuary. There is nothing wrong with sex, which God created, as there is nothing wrong with burying a family member. The taboo arises from the fact that sex is foreign to God himself.

It may be no coincidence that other religions believed in gods that did engage in sex and could die. Israel's observances affirmed aspects of the true

---

[51]See section 5.4 above.

nature of God. The taboo relating to death also links with the hesitation about eating meat. At creation God gave humanity plants to eat; eating meat came after the presence of sin in the world. God does not henceforth ban the eating of meat but requires the draining of an animal's blood as a sign of respect for life.

Western churches mostly abandoned these taboos, though there was no theological reason for doing so, and the Church of England Book of Common Prayer of 1662 includes a form for the service "commonly called churching of women" after childbirth. The idea of a taboo attaching to death and sex is a suggestive one in the West in the twenty-first century. We are inclined to treat sex as God and to avoid thinking about death. Likewise the qualifications on the eating of meat are suggestive in a context where we treat meat simply as a commodity.

In English we can conveniently distinguish between the holy and the sacred, whereas both words correspond to aspects of the equivalent single words in Hebrew and Greek, *qādôš* and *hagios*; hence I use the word *sacred* throughout this book. We do let the usage of the words *holy* and *sacred* overlap, which matches the fact that Hebrew and Greek have only one word and points toward the likelihood that there is a substantial link between the two ideas.

7.2 WORSHIP

The essence of fulfilling the Torah or walking in freedom or walking by the Holy Spirit lies in being committed to Yahweh with one's entire being (Deut 6:5; Mk 12:29-30). Everything else is a spelling out of that commitment. It's a commitment that we work out in serving God in our lives out in the world but also one that we work out in serving God in worship. This worship involves words and acts and a fullness of the Spirit that expresses itself in praise, protest, intercession and thanksgiving.

Service

Western Christians like to emphasize that God is relational and that God's intention from creation was to have a relationship with humanity, but God says nothing about such questions in Genesis 1–2. It's thus not explicit whether or in what sense worship would have had a place in the Eden garden, though some expression of recognition and appreciation would be appropriate toward God as humanity's master and provider. The first worship we hear of takes place outside the garden, as a human idea. Adam and Eve's first son takes an initiative, and their second son declines to be outdone. For reasons that are unstated, Yahweh likes Abel's offering more than Cain's, Cain is hurt, and worship becomes the occasion of the first murder (Gen 4).

On the other hand, when Yahweh brings the Israelites out of Egypt, it is explicit that he does so in order that they may serve him instead of serving Pharaoh (e.g., Ex 3:12; 10:3, 7, 8, 11, 24, 26). Israel is Yahweh's son and therefore Yahweh's servant (Ex 4:23). Israel's service of Pharaoh involved undertaking tasks such as laboring on construction sites. Their service of Yahweh was to involve holding a festival for him in the wilderness. In connection with such service of Yahweh, modern versions translate the verb ʿābad "worship," whereas it is the verb that regularly means "serve." The translation introduces a division between two aspects of service and obscures the significance of worship. There is a service of God that we offer by undertaking tasks in everyday life, and a service we offer by means of symbolic actions and words.

How does worship serve God? For some people, the idea that sacrifice generates "a nice smell for Yahweh" (e.g., Lev 1:9, 13, 17) could imply that sacrifice is a way of feeding the deity. But the Torah does not make this assumption, any more than Paul does when he uses this imagery (Eph 5:2; cf. 2 Cor 2:14-16). The vividness of the metaphor compares with the Christian assumption that God likes the sound of our hymn singing. Perhaps in this connection our relationship with God compares with our relationships with other human beings. Husbands and wives do practical things for each other and also give each other flowers and birthday cards, and say "I love you." So "serving" includes worship but covers the whole of life.

While the church's task is to serve God, its members are to serve one another (e.g., Rom 15:25; 2 Cor 9:1; Heb 6:10).[52] In Corinth, worship was characterized by disorder and self-indulgence, whereas it is to be concerned with the congregation's edification and thus by "self-surrender and service

---

[52]On the sense in which the people of God serve the world, see the paragraphs under "A School, a Priesthood, a Servant" in section 6.1 above.

in renunciation of one's rights. . . . Paul's directions for worship are simply a practical application of the 'theology of the cross.'"[53]

Churches have "services" on Sunday, and the language corresponds to a way the Scriptures speak about worship as a service people offer to God. "Let us serve God pleasingly, with reverence and awe" (Heb 12:28): the verb and the related noun (*latreuō*, *latreia*) are the ones that have been used earlier to describe temple worship (Heb 9:1, 6, 9, 14; 10:2). Paul sees this service of God as one of Israel's privileges (Rom 9:4). Admittedly, church "services" easily become primarily a means of fulfillment for the worshipers, so that the notion of service disappears; it would be one way of interpreting what was going on in the worship at Corinth. In Israel, people could be enthusiastic in their worship yet not match this "service" with a life outside worship that corresponds to who God is. With further paradox, whereas Christian worship does not cost worshipers anything, Israelite worship was costly, yet it could still be unacceptable to God because of this mismatch (e.g., Is 1:10-20).

As well as speaking of worship as service, Paul can say, "I serve God in my spirit," and say that he does so "in the gospel of his Son" (Rom 1:9)—that is, by preaching this gospel—and he will go on to urge his readers to a "service" that involves presenting themselves (literally their bodies) to God as a sacrifice (Rom 12:1-2). It will be an outward, physical act of worship or service of a different kind from sacrifice, but one that is *logikos*—it follows logically from what has preceded, and it is worship that is "worthy of thinking beings."[54] It is service that will be "holy" and "pleasing to God."

In holding together worship of God and dedication to God, the New Testament follows the Torah, which spells out the injunction to "be holy as I am holy" as involving respect for parents, sabbath observance, not making idols, reverence in connection with offerings, leaving part of the harvest for the needy, and forswearing theft, lying, deception, false oaths, fraud and holding back people's wages (Lev 19:1-13). In Romans, too, "the *dedication* expressed in the sanctity of the cult" extends "into everyday relationships,"

---

[53]Günther Bornkamm, *Paul* (New York: Harper; London: Hodder, 1971), 187.
[54]The Jerusalem Bible translation; cf. N. T. Wright, "The Letter to the Romans," in Leander E. Keck et al., eds., *The New Interpreter's Bible* (Nashville: Abingdon, 2002), 10:393-770, on the passage.

so that "holiness" applies not simply to specially set-off acts, persons and places but to everyday acts by ordinary people in their everyday lives.[55] Like the Torah, then, Romans holds together aspects of a relationship with God that easily come apart.

Words and Acts

Serving God involves words and acts, both as it happens in temple or church and as it happens in the rest of life. Another Hebrew word commonly translated worship (*hištaḥăwâ*) more literally means "bow down." In Psalm 95:7, all the words for worship are body words, "bow down, bow low, kneel"; and the kneeling is not the dignified version practiced by Episcopalians like me with the aid of a nice kneeler and with something to lean on, but the kind of prostration practiced by Muslims.

What then matters is what you are bowing down to. The first key consideration about worship is the identity of its object. Israel is to worship only Yahweh, the one God, the God whose being is now expressed through the coming of Jesus and the pouring out of the Holy Spirit. The second key consideration is that worship cannot involve images of God, even if people think they are helpful. The reason is that by their nature they encourage people to confuse the real God with gods who can be imaged, and specifically they are bound to misrepresent the real God, who is one who acts and speaks, unlike these other gods.

Sacrifice formed a natural part of the life of Israel, and the New Testament hints that the first believers in Jerusalem took part in the daily worship of the temple (Acts 2:46; 3:1). Jewish faith assumed a regular pattern of daily prayer, partly associated with the morning and evening sacrifices. While references in the Scriptures and in Jewish writings suggest that the pattern changed over the centuries, the principle was that people in Jerusalem could come to the temple to pray at set hours and that people who could not do so could join in from a distance (see Dan 6).

An understanding of Jesus' death as a once-for-all sacrifice implies that temple sacrifices are redundant insofar as their main point is atonement and cleansing. Yet atonement is not the main point about sacrifice in the Torah.

---

[55]Dunn, *Theology of Paul the Apostle*, 545. Dunn sees Paul as introducing a new idea, but the idea runs through the Torah.

Sacrifice is more centrally an expression of commitment, praise, thanksgiving and fellowship.[56] Most sacrifices could thus continue after Jesus had made his once-for-all sacrifice. Even atonement sacrifices could continue as memorials. While Western thinking understands "sacrifice" to suggest loss suffered for the sake of someone, in a traditional society it connotes giving something to God, and it has "a positive, even joyous meaning"; sacrifices were occasions of feasting and celebration.[57] Their joy is expressed in shouting, movement, music and prostration (e.g., Pss 105; 145).

The two Testaments suggest complementary assumptions about the rhythm of worship, in connection with annual, weekly and daily patterns. The Torah emphasizes the annual festive occasions of Flat Bread/Passover, Pentecost and Shelters, which draw together the cycle of the farming year and the commemoration of God's acts in bringing Israel out of Egypt. These family occasions of pilgrimage and a week's holiday have a paramount importance for worship, which makes the dynamic of Israel's worship different from the one that has developed in the West, where worship occupies an hour or so each week. The Psalms suggest further the spiritual significance of the pilgrimage festivals for people who could go to the temple only once or twice a year or for people who could not get there at all from some reason (see, e.g., Pss 42–43; 63; 84; 122).[58]

The New Testament hints that the early believers also continued to observe the festivals (e.g., Acts 20:16), no doubt with a Jesus-oriented recalibration. The festivals have no equivalent in the New Testament, but the church in due course developed an equivalent calendar that commemorates the events related in the New Testament, comprising Advent, Christmas, Epiphany, Ash Wednesday, Lent, Easter and Pentecost. While the weekly sabbath is of key importance to Israelite faith, it is not explicitly a worship occasion in the First Testament, though it has become so by New Testament times (e.g., Acts 16:13). Yet it wouldn't be surprising if it were the occasion for the teaching of Torah that is emphasized especially in Deuteronomy. The

---

[56]Compare Barth's comments on sacrifice as an expression of thanksgiving for God's revelation, and thus of joy and amazement (*CD* II, 1:215-21).

[57]Larry Hurtado, *At the Origins of Christian Worship* (Carlisle, UK: Paternoster, 1999), 24.

[58]See the paragraphs headed "Splendor, Name" in section 1.3 above.

New Testament hints that the believers met on the first day of each week, resurrection day (Acts 20:7; 1 Cor 16:2).

Be Filled with the Spirit

Only a tiny number of believers in Jesus lived near the temple, and the worship practices in which most believers were involved, including the meal that commemorated the Lord's death pending his return, focused on the home. The community's ethos was thus not so different from Israel's, given that most people lived too far from the temple to go there regularly (earlier Israelites did go to the "high places," but the First Testament is equivocal about that worship).

Deuteronomy assumes that the home is the proper place for remembering what God has done for his people and for discussing God's expectations of them. Gatherings in the home would involve women and men, children and adults, landowners and servants, natives and foreigners. The congregations of believers in Jesus worshiping in homes were similarly mixed. Israelite worship would be backward looking and forward looking, and the believing congregation's worship would be similar: believers were to proclaim the Lord's death (backward) until he comes (forward). Yet "whether a community without cult was practical and sustainable . . . is another question."[59] It certainly was not sustained. As well as developing a festal calendar, Christian faith did reestablish sanctuaries and a priesthood, and turned the Lord's Day into a sabbath and the Lord's Meal into something a little like a sacrifice.

The link between worship and the rest of life is implicit in the New Testament's talk about the Holy Spirit. Parallel to the natural link in the Torah between respectful treatment of the offerings and ensuring that needy people could take something from the harvest is the New Testament's link between worship and mutual submission, which are the fruit of the Spirit: "Be filled with the Spirit, speaking to each other in psalms, hymns, songs that are Spirit-inspired, singing and playing with your inner being to the Lord, giving thanks all the time on behalf of everyone in the name of our Lord Jesus, the Anointed One, to God the Father, submitting to one another in reverence for the Anointed One" (Eph 5:18-21).

---

[59]Dunn, *Theology of Paul the Apostle*, 548.

This exhortation assumes that worship addresses other people as well as God (cf. Col 3:16-17); it is designed to glorify God and to edify other people. Though it comes from the inner person, the need to address other people requires it to be outwardly expressed; both outward and inward are necessary. There is no reference to worship being offered for one's own sake or as edifying for oneself.

In a congregation such as that at Corinth, worship unfolds in accordance with the promptings of many different people. There is no set order, and this flexibility opens up the way to disorder, but that problem does not lead Paul to suggest that someone should have the responsibility to function as the worship leader. The worship involves much speech and song to God and much speech and song to other members of the congregation. Both men and women could lead in praying and prophesying, in keeping with the fact that women and men relate to God on the same basis (Gal 3:28).[60]

When people "come together as a congregation" (*en ekklēsia*; 1 Cor 11:18) in this way they share messages in tongues and prophecy (1 Cor 14:22-28). As well as chanting First Testament psalms, they share "songs that are Spirit-inspired": the expression suggests psalm-like compositions analogous to ones known from Qumran and to ones included in the New Testament such as the songs of Mary and of Zechariah. Paul's letters were read at such gatherings (Col 4:16). While the congregation was involved in teaching one another by means of their prophecies, tongues and songs, this sharing did not exclude there being leaders who "admonished" the congregation (1 Thess 5:12). One can imagine this gathering taking place each Sunday, after the manner of a sabbath meal, with the prayers following Jewish patterns (*bārûk ʾattâ ʾădōnāy ʾĕlōhênû* . . . , "Blessed are you, Lord our God . . .") and with the Scriptures being read, but we have no direct evidence that these things were so.

Praise

Paul's exhortations in Ephesians match the way he begins the letter with praise, thanksgiving and prayer, which parallel the three dominant ways of addressing God in the Psalms. He begins, "Praised be the God and Father of our Lord, Jesus, the Anointed One" (Eph 1:3), and he goes on to explicate

---

[60]Cf. Gordon D. Fee, *God's Empowering Presence* (Peabody, MA: Hendrickson, 1994), 885.

the reason for this praise in terms of all that God has done for people in Jesus. This praise matches that which begins 1 Peter (1 Pet 1:3-12). The message of the gospel is a word of grace, and thus the being of humanity is "a being in gratitude": *eucharistia* responds to *charis*.[61]

The Psalms of praise worship God for the wonder of creation and for the wonders of what God had done in Israel's history (e.g., Pss 33; 104; 147). New Testament praise parallels that pattern in worshiping God for what he has done in Jesus. Such praise thus relates not to what God has done for this generation of Israelites or for this particular congregation but for what God has done for the world as a whole and for his people as a whole. While it can thus put an emphasis on the rational nature of the worship, it can become praise that is wordless. In the Psalms two of the common words for praise are *hālal* (as in hallelujah) and *rānan,* which seem to be onomatopoeic words for praise that involve simply a *lalala* sound or a *nanana* sound. And the Psalter closes with a psalm that simply urges people to *hālal* and gives no reasons (no doubt the previous 149 psalms have given the reasons).

Given that "sacrifice" has come to suggest loss suffered for the sake of someone but that in a traditional society it connotes giving something to God and has "a positive, even joyous meaning," sacrifices were occasions of feasting and celebration.[62] Praise is expressed in joy (e.g., Ps 100), and the joy associated with offering sacrifice is expressed in shouting, movement, music and prostration (e.g., Pss 105; 145). In a New Testament context, praise in tongues would have an equivalent place as a form of praise that doesn't edify the congregation but does communicate with God (1 Cor 14:2).

The praise of a congregation will focus on what God did for it in Jesus, and this focus will characterize its meeting for the Lord's Meal. Worship is an event when we remind ourselves of our setting in the context of the history of God's involvement with the world and with his people, in remembrance and hope, and when we set into that context our daily pains, joys, failures, hopes and awarenesses about the world (which therefore find expression there).[63] The congregation breaks bread and drinks wine from the

---

[61]Barth, *CD* III, 2:166-67.
[62]Hurtado, *At the Origins of Christian Worship,* 24.
[63]Cf. Jürgen Moltmann, *The Church in the Power of the Spirit* (London: SCM Press; New York: Harper, 1977), 261-62.

chalice "in remembrance of me" (1 Cor 11:23-25). It "proclaims the Lord's death" and does so "until he comes" (1 Cor 11:26). Paul's comments on either side of this reminder make the link between worship and the rest of life, the link the Corinthians seem unaware of (1 Cor 11:17-22, 27-34). Psalm 95 makes the same link: praise needs to lead into attentiveness to what God has to say, which may well confront our praise.

In John's vision, the 144,000 in heaven make music and sing a new song (Rev 14:1-3). The newness of the song might lie in its focus on Jesus compared with the First Testament songs, which their praise takes up and extends. They (and the people from all nations who join them) are protected, purchased, offered, resting, with their deeds following. Their security issues from their keeping themselves pure, following the lamb everywhere, being truthful, blameless, enduring, obedient and faithful to Jesus. The song of Moses and of the lamb (Rev 15:1-4) then responds to God's acts of wrath that mean God's right acts have been revealed. The praise of Revelation, like the praise of the Psalms, would often involve making affirmations that belie the way things look outside the context of worship. One significance of praise is then that it is "world-making" in the sense that it denies that the way things look (where Assyria or Rome is Lord) is the real world and declares that the real world is one where Yahweh reigns.[64]

> The Christian life, the life of the children of God, consists in these two concepts of love and praise. . . . Christian love cannot be understood except as the thankfulness which the believer owes to God in His revealing and reconciling work. The totality in which God wills to be loved by us according to His commandment excludes all self-glorying, all claims which he who loves might make to the loved One on account of his love. . . . Therefore the love of God—and it is at this point that it merges into the praise of God—means that in our own existence we become a sign of what God as the one Lord has done and is for us.[65]

Prayer

Christians often understand prayer as something meditative; a good time of prayer is one after which we feel better. But the significance of prayer lies

---

[64]Cf. Walter Brueggemann, *Israel's Praise* (Philadelphia: Fortress, 1988).
[65]Barth, *CD* I, 2:371, 400, 401.

rather in the fact that God listens to it. "Here is a statement which is still quite uninfected by Cartesianism. It is not as if our prayer were the certain thing and His hearing the uncertain, but precisely the opposite."[66]

Prayer has its background in our position as servants in relation to our master or of citizens in relation to our king or as children in relation to our father. This relationship involves humble and heartfelt submission, but it is a mutual relationship that also implies God's commitment to us. The servants of God, the citizens of God's kingdom, can thus call on him as "my God" and "my Lord" and look to him in the way that servants look to their master or mistress (e.g., Pss 16; 123). They can have that expectation because they are God's servants or slaves—or children: "Abba is vocative; it is prayer before it is theology." Prayer is the context in which the word occurs in the New Testament; indeed, "to pray *to* Jesus rather than *through* him, *to* the Spirit rather than *in* him, as the established habit of our prayer, is to betray a doubt about our relationship to the Father."[67]

The basis for prayer in the relationship of servants to masters makes it natural to stand for prayer and makes it odd if a servant praying is concerned to be visible and fancy rather than discrete and straightforward (Mt 6:5-15). Kneeling, which again implies prostration so that one's head touches the ground and so that one thus "licks the dust" (e.g., Eph 3:14), is a mark of a strong awareness of the need to lower oneself (e.g., Mt 26:39). Yet we need never think that our prayer will be considered shameless and unacceptable (Lk 11:5-8).[68]

Jesus encourages his disciples to pray "in his name" and to expect to get answers (Jn 15:16). They may do so by closing their prayers with the phrase "in his name," but there is more to it. It implies praying in accordance with who Jesus is. The content of Paul's prayers further illustrates the nature of prayer in Jesus' name, as does "The Lord's Prayer." First, it is not "my" prayer but prayer that speaks in terms of "our" and "we." It implies praying the kind of prayer Jesus would pray; the Gospels illustrate what that is. It implies being prepared to submit to the Father and to take "No" for an answer, like

---

[66]Barth, *CD* III, 4:107.
[67]Thomas A. Smail, *The Forgotten Father* (London: Hodder, 1980; Grand Rapids: Eerdmans, 1981), 160, 169.
[68]See David Crump, *Knocking on Heaven's Door* (Grand Rapids: Baker, 2006), 71-72.

Jesus. Paradoxically, God grants the prayer that says "Not my will but yours." In effect, Abraham presupposes the point when he agrees to offer his beloved son to God.

Such prayer (Jesus says), like giving and fasting, brings a reward (other than having the prayer answered) because it is a form of service we offer to our master. The content of the Lord's Prayer points to why this is so. It is a prayer for God's name to be hallowed, God's reign to become a reality, and God's will to be done. Although this prayer is also "the beginning and end of moral thinking,"[69] our task is not to bring about the earthly hallowing, reigning and obedience that it speaks of, but to urge God to do so. It is a prayer that may stimulate the heavenly cabinet to take action along those lines. The things for which we pray for ourselves are bread, forgiveness, protection and deliverance. The fact that God knows we need these things is a reason for praying simply, but not a reason for failing to pray (Mt 6:7-13).

The assumptions about prayer in the Scriptures contrast with common Western assumptions. The point about prayer is to change God, not me; it is not to get me to assimilate to what God already intends. Prayer is designed to persuade God to take action in the world. The point about prayer is not therapeutic; it is not to make me feel better. It is not a veiled form of personal commitment ("Lord, make us more concerned for justice"). It is not a means of personal formation. The point about prayer is to get God to act. One of the powerful arguments in this connection in both Testaments is that one's prayer arises out of a concern for Yahweh's name, as well as for one's own suffering.

Protest

Prayer is a major way the Scriptures assume we handle "the problem of suffering." They focus on it more as a matter of spirituality than as an academic issue. Their question concerns how we live with suffering rather than how we understand it. In the Scriptures, "the experience of suffering belongs before God."[70] They know that the cry of people who are wronged and the cry of their blood shout out to God (Gen 4:10; 18:20-21; Ex 2:23-24; 5:19-23).

---

[69]Oliver O'Donovan, *Finding and Seeking* (Grand Rapids and Cambridge, UK: Eerdmans, 2014), 147.
[70]Feldmeier and Spieckermann, *God of the Living*, 361.

Even people whose suffering is deserved can cry out in this way and expect to be heard (Lam 1:4, 8, 11, 21, 22).

Such prayers of protest can issue both from individuals and from the community as a whole: there are "I" protests and "we" protests, though the distinction between individual and community prayers may be hard to draw. The prayers that comprise Lamentations are communal, but one of them takes "I" form; one can compare the prayers of a kings such as Jehoshaphat, leading his people (2 Chron 20), and of a king such as Hezekiah, praying on his people's behalf but praying alone (2 Kings 19). The believing congregation is a body of people who call on the Lord's name (1 Cor 1:2), and those who call on the Lord's name get rescued (Rom 10:13).

The Psalms illustrate the nature of such prayer, and Jesus' prayers (e.g., Mk 14:32-39; 15:34) reflect the same understanding of prayer. Paul also takes up the Psalms' way of praying (e.g., Rom 8:36), as do people who have been martyred for their testimony to Jesus (Rev 6:9-11). In light of Jesus' death and resurrection, they appeal for the Man to hasten the time when he comes to bring justice (Lk 18:1-8). These prayers are confrontational, urgent, pressing, questioning, pleading, disjointed and challenging. They characteristically give most space simply to describing the raw need out of which the prayer issues. Whereas Western prayer gives little space to describing the situation and considerable space to suggesting action God might take, biblical prayer reverses these proportions. It gives considerable space to lamenting the situation (hence the common modern term *laments* for these prayers of protest) in the conviction that it may thereby get God's attention. It assumes that it can then leave it to God to work out precisely how to go about delivering the people in need and putting down their attackers.

And it receives answers—at least, it often does so. The Psalms imply that the answers commonly come in two stages. Hannah (1 Sam 1) pours out her pain to God, and eventually the priest Eli realizes what is going on and brings God's answer. God has heard her prayer, and Hannah goes home transformed. But so far she has received only stage one of an answer—she knows God has listened to her prayer and made a commitment to dealing with her need, but he has not acted yet. Then God does act, and Hannah has seen both stages in the answering of her prayer. Prayers of protest such as Psalm 22 close with a declaration that God has answered the prayer, and it is referring to stage one; stage two will need to follow. Other prayers of protest incorporate no sense that God has answered in even the stage-one sense (e.g., Ps 88). Presumably you then come back tomorrow and tomorrow and tomorrow until you get a response, like Job, even if eventually you have to submit, like Jesus.

The risk of prayer is not only that God may not answer. It is that the answer may be confrontational, like God's response to Job. Or it may be negative, like God's response to Jeremiah. In partial possible protection against a snorting response from God, the Psalms assume that in uttering my protests I need to be able to claim that I am basically a person committed to God's ways, like Job or Paul or Jesus, or I need to make my confession in order to get things straight between me and God.[71]

Intercession

Intercession regularly features in the opening sentences of Paul's letters, in the expression of a desire that the readers may receive (characteristically) grace and peace. Ephesians follows this wish by an act of praise and then by its first main intercession, which has its starting point in thanksgiving (Eph 1:2-22). Intercession features again (Eph 3:14-19) at a climax of the letter; arguably, indeed this report of Paul's intercession is resuming the earlier one, so that intercession dominates the first half of the letter. In both contexts it is closely associated with theological exposition, so that the subject of intercession is the Ephesians' theological understanding, and the theological exposition is incomplete without the intercession. Praise again follows (Eph 3:20-21), so that in turn both the exposition and the intercession are set in the context of praise; praise provides the outer framework for the theological exposition. Intercession is incomplete without theology. Theology is incomplete without intercession and praise. Praise is incomplete without theology.

In the similar opening of Colossians (Col 1:2-23) it is also hard to tell where the report of Paul's intercession and thanksgiving ends, as his prayer becomes an exposition of the truth about Jesus. Paul's prayer is that God may fill the congregation with a knowledge of his will through all the insight that the Spirit gives, so that they may live a life worthy of the Lord, grow in

---

[71]See the paragraphs under "Penitence" in section 6.3 above.

knowledge of God, endure with steadfastness and give thanks for what God has done for us in Jesus.

So Paul prays for different congregations and wants them to pray for him in light of the pressures on him, so that he will be able to fulfill his ministry (Eph 6:18-20; cf. Col 4:2-4; 2 Thess 2:16–3:5). He wants believers in Rome to share in the struggle involved in that ministry by their prayers, a struggle that involves being able to neutralize the opposition of communities that oppose Paul's work though they believe in Jesus (Rom 15:30-32). They will be involved in this struggle as they take an active part in the arguments in the heavenly cabinet. The same applies to Epaphras as someone who is wrestling or contending or standing up for the Colossians in prayer (Col 4:12). What has happened to Paul (notably, his imprisonment) will turn out for his salvation "through your prayer and the provision of the Spirit of the Anointed One Jesus" (Phil 1:19). The Philippians' praying plays a role in bringing it about.

The example of a Canaanite woman (Mt 15:21-28) suggests that intercessory prayer may involve struggling *with* God and refusing to take "No" for an answer. Abraham's prayer for Sodom (Gen 18) contrasts with his submission when God requires him to offer his son; praying for other people is different from praying for oneself. It involves asking, seeking, knocking (Mt 7:7-11) for other people. "If you stay in me and my words stay in you, ask whatever you want, and it will happen for you" (Jn 15:7). In the past the disciples have not asked in Jesus' name; now they will do so. They will receive and will have full joy (Jn 16:24). What is new here is not that they have not asked God for things before and received them, because Israelites have always done so. What is new is that they now do it in Jesus' name, in light of the embodied revelation of who God is and their new insight into God's purpose, and thus in firmer conviction.

The intercessory prayers of prophets such as Amos and Jeremiah and of leaders such as Ezra and Nehemiah parallel the prayers in the Psalms and suggest that the prayers of protest in the Psalter could be used as intercessory prayers; one protests and pleads on behalf of other people in their suffering. These prayers of leaders and prophets then illustrate how in using the Psalms one prays not for "them" but for "us."

It could seem that "Jesus, by his silent complicity in his own victimization, which God required as the price of our redemption, appears to condone by example the passive acceptance of violence by the oppressed."[72] Christian unease with psalms of protest could have the same implication. The use of the protest psalms as intercession safeguards against the danger of this dynamic. Perhaps it is fine for the oppressed to accept people's violence as long as their brothers and sisters are not doing so, in their action or in their prayers. The point about the vindicatory psalms is then that they are prayers for God to put down the people oppressing those for whom I am praying.

Once again, it is clear that the point about prayer is not to change us but to change God. Yet our boldness in seeking to do so may be encouraged by an awareness of the possibility that we are responding to God's invitation. When Abraham went about seeking to be a blessing to Sodom by interceding for this center of faithlessness and oppression, he did so because God appeared to him, told him of his intention regarding Sodom and Gomorrah, and apparently stood there waiting to see whether Abraham wanted to say anything to him. Whatever the right way of understanding the text at this point,[73] there is no doubt that the close of the conversation between Abraham and God, in which Abraham urges God to have a change of mind about Sodom, comes when "Yahweh finished speaking with Abraham" (Gen 18:33).

Intercession is the vocation of a prophet, and it is explicitly as a prophet that Abraham later intercedes for Abimelek when he has brought Abimelek trouble rather than blessing (Gen 20). Prophets are people who are allowed to attend meetings of the heavenly cabinet, partly to overhear its deliberations and decisions so that they can then pass them on down below, but also so that they can join in the deliberations by pleading for someone. The prophetic community then shares in that freedom.

Thanksgiving

Thanksgiving and praise overlap in our use of the words, and they do so in the Scriptures, but in substance there is a difference worth preserving. Whereas praise denotes worshiping God in light of the big truths about God and of what God has done, thanksgiving responds to what God has done

---

[72]Sandra M. Schneiders, "The Lamb of God and the Forgiveness of Sin(s) in the Fourth Gospel," *Catholic Biblical Quarterly* 73 (2011): 1-29 (on 3).
[73]See the alternative versions of Gen 18:22 in different translations.

just now. Meetings for worship are occasions when things happen. God speaks, God heals people, and God acts in judgment (see e.g., 1 Cor 5; 11–14).[74] They are thus occasions for thanksgiving.

So Ephesians 1 moves from praise for what God has done for the entire believing community to praise for what God has done for the Ephesians in particular. Other letters begin with thanksgiving (cf. Phil 1:3-6) that relates not directly to what God has done for the writer but to what God has done for the people he writes to. The frequent references to prayers for these churches suggest that God's actions have been responses to these prayers. Thanksgiving may include a response of gratitude to God for who they are and what they have done (cf. 2 Cor 9:11-15), a gratitude to God for what God has done for them (in part because of what it signifies for other people) or a gratitude to God expressed on their behalf.

In Colossians 1:3-8, we've noted that it's difficult to know when the thanksgiving stops; one could argue that it continues through Colossians 1:3-23.[75] Something similar is true in 1 Thessalonians 1 and 2 Thessalonians 1. In 2 Corinthians 1:3-11 the thanksgiving relates to what God has done for Paul; perhaps it is partly for this reason that it takes the form of an act of praise (*eulogētos* . . .) rather than thanksgiving.[76] Experiencing God's comfort (sustaining him through persecution and delivering him from it) makes it possible to comfort other people by telling them of this sustaining and deliverance, in which they can also share. In Turkey Paul and his companions

> despaired of life itself. But we ourselves received the death sentence within ourselves so that we might not be relying on ourselves but on the God who raises the dead. From such a death he rescued us and will rescue us, and we have set our hope in him that he will yet rescue us, as you also join in helping by your prayer for us, so that from many faces [turned up to God in prayer][77]

---

[74]Hurtado, *At the Origins of Christian Worship*, 56-61.

[75]See R. McL. Wilson, *A Critical and Exegetical Commentary on Colossians and Philemon* (London and New York: T&T Clark, 2005), 78.

[76]See the discussion in Peter Thomas O'Brien, *Introductory Thanksgivings in the Letters of Paul* (Leiden: Brill, 1977), 233-58.

[77]Cf. C. K. Barrett, *A Commentary on the Second Epistle to the Corinthians* (London: Black; New York: Harper, 1973), 67-68.

the grace extended to us may be given thanks for by many people on our behalf. (2 Cor 1:8-11)

Eucharistia responds to *charisma*. Their praying contributes to his comfort; his consequent thanksgiving and testimony contributes to their comfort.

The logic of thanksgiving in these letters once more makes for a correspondence with the Psalms. Psalms of thanksgiving mix address to God with address to other people. They are both thanksgiving and testimony. In their nature as thanksgiving they give glory to God (cf. 2 Cor 4:15), but one reason they have this effect is that they are expressed outwardly so that other people hear and have their hope and trust in God built up. Paul's exhortation about tongues (1 Cor 14:14-17) presupposes that thanksgiving addressed to God is also testimony addressed to other people, which therefore needs to be intelligible.

Whereas thanksgiving psalms express themselves in terms of what God has done for "me" or "us," it would not be surprising if (like prayer psalms) they were used not only by the people who have experienced God's action but by others who give thanks on their behalf and with them. It would commonly be the case that a thanksgiving psalm would accompany a thank offering (the word *tôdâ* covers both), and the thank offering would be a communal occasion when the worshiper's family and friends joined in the celebratory sacrificial meal and joined in giving glory to God.

We have considered the scriptural ways of worshiping and praying in the order praise, prayer, thanksgiving, and this sequence suggests the nature of the pattern of spirituality that emerges from the Scriptures. It compares and contrasts with the sequence suggested by the acronym ACTS: adoration, confession, thanksgiving, supplication. But the sequence praise, prayer, thanksgiving is not a simply linear one. Thanksgiving leads into further praise for who God is, and the sequence of elements in the pattern forms an ongoing spiral rather than a linear sequence or a circular one.

The Ambiguity of Worship
In Luke's Gospel, Jesus appears in the context of worship (Lk 1:5–2:52). The background of his story is Zechariah's making the sacrificial offerings there. His mother's response to the prospect of his birth takes the form of a psalm of the kind that people sang there, as does Zechariah's response to his son's

birth. When Jesus is born, angels worship God, and the shepherds join in. In accordance with the Torah, Jesus is circumcised, and Mary offers the appropriate purification sacrifice in the temple. In the temple courts a man and a woman offer prophetic greetings to Joseph, Mary and Jesus. The only other story we are told about Jesus' first thirty years concerns a Passover visit to the temple when he is twelve years old.

Through his ministry he is a frequent participant in the worship of the temple and of the synagogue. The synagogue is often the context for his teaching and healing, while one of his signature acts is to clean up his Father's house, the place that was supposed to be a prayer house (Mk 11:15-17; Jn 2:11-17). He is passionate about the temple, though his reply to a question about his authority for his action in the temple implies that it is not so important, as it becomes a metaphor for Jesus himself: "Destroy this temple, and in three days I will raise it up" (Jn 2:20-21).

After his resurrection the believers continue the pattern of engagement in worship, gathering for prayer and praise in someone's room in Jerusalem and going up to the temple at the regular times for prayer there. A feature of their praise and prayer is the tumultuous involvement of the Holy Spirit (Acts 2:1-4; 4:31). Then a strange feature appears in Stephen's address to the Sanhedrin, where he notes the comment in Amos that the Israelites didn't offer sacrifices in the wilderness and the comment in Isaiah that the idea of building a house for God doesn't really make sense, and he implies that the willfullness people showed in killing Jesus is a continuation of the willfullness of which the First Testament speaks (Acts 7).

Acts thus picks up the First Testament's ambivalence about the temple and its worship.[78] The first acts of worship in Genesis are humanly devised responses to God, though responses that in principle God welcomes (e.g., Gen 4:3-4; 8:20-21; 12:7). The reason God gives Moses for the Israelites needing to leave Egypt is to offer sacrifice to him in the wilderness (Ex 3:18). As Stephen notes, God commissions the building of the wilderness sanctuary, but the Jerusalem temple is a place that David dreams up (see 2 Sam 7). Yet Yahweh agrees to its building and comes to live there, so that it becomes a prayer house (see 1 Kings 8). Several other prophets as well as the ones

---

[78]See further section 1.3 above.

Stephen quotes are scathing about worship because the service of God that people offer in the temple is not matched by a service of God out in everyday life. Subsequently, although one would have thought the temple was vital to Judaism, Judaism managed without it.[79]

There are many reasons for the ambiguity in the Scriptures' attitude to worship. It can take over as the all-important aspect of people's relationship with God. It can be taken over. People come to think that worship has a greater importance than it does. But they can also think it has a lesser importance than it does. People who emphasize worship need to think about action out in the world and do it. People who emphasize action out in the world need to think about worship and do it.

7.3 MUTUAL COMMITMENT

If you're allowed only one answer to the question about the ultimate command in the Torah, then that command is the one that concerns commitment to Yahweh (Deut 6:5). But if you're allowed two, then alongside it you might well put the command about being committed to your neighbor (Lev 19:18). The Testament of Issachar (a Jewish writing from a century or two before Jesus) urges, "Love the Lord and your neighbor" (5:2),[80] and Jesus also combines these two commands in responding to someone who asks him about the most important command in the Torah (Mt 22:37-39). We could call them the two sides to walking in freedom and to walking by the Holy Spirit. The Torah covers many aspects of relationships with other people: marriage, divorce, sex, family, children, war, violence, power, the state, money, possessions, poverty. . . . Jesus sees all its teaching as issuing from this basic command. Love thus fulfills the Torah. But the Torah will help us see how love needs spelling out—what love means in practice. Love thus working itself out is a feature of congregational life that will speak to outsiders, even if the congregation itself is only on the way to unity. It suggests how members of a family (ideally) relate to each other. It has implications in the area of speech, stuff and hospitality. It implies mutual submissiveness, and it involves living with the tension between absolute principles

---

[79]See Daniel R. Schwartz and Zeev Weiss, eds., *Was 70 CE a Watershed in Jewish History?* (Leiden and Boston: Brill, 2012).
[80]Cf. Eduard Lohse, *Theological Ethics of the New Testament* (Minneapolis: Fortress, 1991), 15.

and ways in which we can be flexible with one another. It commits the church to self-discipline.

The Other Love

Believers in Jesus thus "fulfill the Torah" by caring for one another, because the Torah is fulfilled in that one sentence, "Care for your neighbor as you care for yourself" or "as a person like yourself" (Gal 5:14, quoting from Lev 19:18; cf. Rom 13:8-10). Of course Paul oversimplifies; he would hardly disagree with the Jewish view affirmed by Jesus, that the Torah as a whole is summed up by the twofold love command (Mt 22:40). A suggestive aspect of the formulation in Leviticus is that it doesn't merely speak in terms of caring for everyone. It urges me to care for the person near me.[81] The Torah and the Prophets (and the Writings) then help people to see what caring for one another or serving one another looks like.

One function of the Torah in connection with people's moral lives is that it exposes human waywardness: "The first result of man's confrontation with God's command is that he is proved relentlessly and irrefutably to be its transgressor."[82] A second function is that it can deter people from wrongdoing; law in society especially has this function. But

> the third and principal use, which pertains more closely to the proper purpose of the law, finds its place among believers in whose hearts the Spirit of God already lives and reigns. . . . Here is the best instrument for them to learn more thoroughly each day the nature of the Lord's will to which they aspire, and to confirm them in the understanding of it. . . . For no man has heretofore attained to such wisdom as to be unable, from the daily instruction of the law, to make fresh progress toward a purer knowledge of the divine will. . . . The servant of God will also avail himself of this benefit of the law: by frequent meditation upon it to be aroused to obedience, be strengthened in it, and be drawn back from the slippery path of transgression. In this way the saints must press on.[83]

"The one who loves God, the second commandment tells us, will love his neighbour as himself. This is no less the Gospel than the first

---

[81]See Linda Woodhead, "Love and Justice," *Studies in Christian Ethics* 5 (1992): 44-61 (on 49-50).
[82]Barth, *CD* II, 2:742.
[83]John Calvin, *Institutes of the Christian Religion* II.7, 12.

commandment. . . . It is a real fact, and it can be stated and understood, that the children of God will love their neighbour as themselves."[84] It's not the case that "love to God has no sphere of activity outside of love to one's brother."[85] But it is the case that it's implausible to claim to love the invisible God if you don't show love to your visible neighbor (1 Jn 4:19–5:3). The fact that the theologian who quizzes Jesus over the identity of his neighbor is concerned about putting himself in the right (Lk 10:29) shows that he "does not know that only by mercy can he live and inherit eternal life. He does not want to live by mercy." While he acknowledges that he doesn't understand the second command, he also reveals that he doesn't understand the first.[86]

Another approach to the question what it is to love one's neighbor starts from the conviction that the center lies "in the fact that I praise God, i.e., bear witness to my neighbour of the love with which God in Jesus Christ has loved me and him. To love the neighbour, therefore, is plainly and simply to be to him a witness of Jesus Christ," by speaking of the way God has helped me, by being a sign of the offered help of God by my word and action, and by the attitude I show to him in doing so.[87]

The Nature of Love

Paul prays that the Ephesians may be rooted and founded in love (Eph 3:17). The context suggests that this expression implies being rooted and founded in Jesus; it is another way of saying that Jesus is living among them. As human persons we are not bounded and unaffected by other people, like something inanimate such as a table that is clearly distinguishable from its physical surroundings. A strong relationship with someone means he or she becomes part of us and we become part of them. They affect the way we think, not only because we consciously take account of them but because we assimilate them. They become part of the fiber of our being. Who they are is part of us, and we are part of their life. Being rooted and founded in Jesus' love opens up the possibility of grasping the infinite dimensions of that love,

---

[84]Barth, *CD* I, 2:412.

[85]Albrecht Ritschl, "Instruction in the Christian Religion," in Albert Temple Swing, *The Theology of Albrecht Ritschl* (New York and London: Longmans, Green, 1901), 169-286, section 6 (175); cf. Barth, *CD* I, 2:434.

[86]Barth, *CD* I, 2:417-18.

[87]Barth, *CD* I, 2:440, and the pages that follow.

even though that very statement involves a contradiction (Eph 3:17-19). Believers can become filled with regard to the fullness of God.

Elsewhere, Paul prays that people's love may abound in insight so that they can discern what is best and be pure and blameless for the day of the Lord, filled with righteous fruit (Phil 1:9-11). "The idea is that Paul's readers may have the ability to discern, and then to practice in their corporate life as believers, the really important matters of community living."[88] In faith, hope and love and through the charisms "the force field of the Spirit concretizes itself in such a way that human memories and expectations, human contacts and human understanding, human attentiveness and human self-withdrawal become possible *in the Spirit*" so that human beings "become members and bearers of this force field."[89] Indeed, "the criterion of the Spirit's activity is cruciformity, understood as Christ-like love in the edification of others rather than oneself."[90]

When Jesus is leaving his disciples, he wants them to love one another (Jn 13:34). Is it the thing he has most grounds for being anxious about in leaving them? He will know it is a demanding expectation. Peter evades it, as he responds by asking where Jesus is going. The Gospel's readers will know it is a demanding expectation, from their experience of congregational life. And/or is the logic like that in Isaiah 49:1-6, where the prophet doubts whether his vocation will ever find fulfillment, and God's response is to add to its demand? Jesus, then, says, "I'm leaving you" (which is demanding), "so here's another expectation: love one another. And to add to it, people's recognizing me depends on you now, and your love for one another is key to that process." Perhaps it worked. About AD 200, Tertullian relates that outsiders comment on "How they love one another (for they themselves hate one another) and how they are ready to die for one other (for they themselves will sooner kill each other)."[91]

"Love is genuine" (Rom 12:9). Translations render the phrase "Love is to be genuine," but Paul includes no verb; the phrase is more like a thesis

---

[88]Ralph P. Martin, *Philippians* (repr., London: Marshall; Grand Rapids: Eerdmans, 1980), 69.

[89]Michael Welker, *God the Spirit* (Minneapolis: Fortress, 1994), 240.

[90]Michael J. Gorman, *Cruciformity* (Grand Rapids and Cambridge, UK: Eerdmans, 2001), 60 (the words are in italics).

[91]*Apology* xxxix.7.

statement,[92] a definition of love. It's easy for love to be deceptive, as the Psalms stress, and it can be deceptive in various ways. Unconditional love can fail to hate the evil and cling to the good. Positively, we are to show to one another the kind of affection that is appropriate within a family. That love within the believers' new family also expresses itself in honoring one another; it is tempting to reckon that my charism is important, but in love I honor other people's (Rom 12:10).

It is possible to see the implications of God's grace worked out in three ways for humanity—in justification, in sanctification and in vocation.[93] In loving my neighbor, I fulfill my vocation.

A New Command?

Jesus calls loving one another a new command, though he knows that the Torah long ago articulated it. The context hints that its novelty lies in its being a love that reflects the love he has showed them in being willing to die for them and/or in being willing to offer menial service to them even though he is their teacher; compare his later repetition of the command (Jn 15:12-17). It's a fresh command rather than a novel one (*kainē* rather than *nea*). It subverts distinctions between masters and servants. It makes everyone friends. It also makes everyone stewards or servants (1 Pet 4:10). It's a command that belongs to the new age that has dawned (1 Jn 2:7-11). At the same time, it's a reassertion of what creation implied, when all were designed to be friends and servants or brothers and sisters. So its novelty lies in reasserting the creation vision by subverting the hierarchy of master and servant, and even more in requiring that we are willing to die for one another. It implies a following of the example of a servant such as Jeremiah and the one who speaks and appears in Isaiah 50 and 53, whose sacrifice the New Testament sees as expressing what mutual service means and as issuing a summons to the church (e.g., 1 Pet 2:21-25).

The congregation is the place where *agapē* is embodied. First Corinthians 13 suggests that "it is love alone that counts, love alone that triumphs, and love alone that endures."[94] Its exposition indicates that "the key to the nature of love is concern and respect for 'the other.'" This love

---

[92]Cf. Dunn, *Romans*, 2:739.
[93]Barth, *CD* IV, 1:145-46 (but Barth expresses the point christologically).
[94]Barth, *CD* IV, 2:825.

"*creates* value rather than responding to value." It *sets* value on people, whereas *erōs* wants the other person, focusing on the lover's desires.[95] We can thus equate love in a general way with self-giving; it involves a movement away from oneself and a turning to the other. "Christian love turns to the other purely for the sake of the other. It does not desire it for itself. It loves it simply because it is there as this other, with all its value or lack of value." It is willing "to give itself away; to give up itself to the one to whom it turns for the sake of this object. To do this the loving man has given up control of himself to place himself under the control of the other, the object of his love."[96]

There is a kind of love that is essentially "an appetite, a yearning desire, which is aroused by the attractive qualities of its object" and which seeks the other in order to possess and enjoy him or her. A second kind of love expresses itself in doing what the other person wants in order to gain or keep his or her approval. A third kind of love implies "a whole-hearted surrender" whereby we become the willing servant of the other, content to be at his or her disposal, a love that instinctively consists "not in getting, but in giving" and is "neither kindled by the attractiveness nor quenched by the unattractiveness of its object."[97]

All these forms of love come into our relationships with other people and with God, but the last is the distinctive expression of God's stance in relation to humanity and of the stance God looks for in our relationships with others. Its implication is not necessarily that people have warm feelings for one another but that they sacrifice themselves for one another (cf. 1 Jn 3:16).

Jesus desires that his joy may be in his disciples and that their joy may be filled up or fulfilled or filled out (*plēroō*). It depends on doing what he says and thereby staying in his love for them. By implication, that dynamic is already embodied in him; he has joy through his love-obedience relationship with his Father. And what he says is, love one another as he has loved them,

[95]Thiselton, *1 Corinthians*, 217, 219, 223 (his emphasis); he refers to Anders Nygren, *Agape and Eros* (London: SPCK, 1957).
[96]Barth, *CD* IV, 2:733.
[97]I adapt these descriptions from Philip S. Watson's "Translator's Preface" to Nygren, *Agape and Eros*, viii-ix. Much of Nygren's associated thinking and further ways of expressing the distinctions may be questioned, but the distinctions are useful.

which is embodied in dying for one another (Jn 15:10-13). It will be a source of joy.

Insiders and Outsiders

"When Christians nowadays speak of love . . . , the word almost always has *universal* overtones," but in the New Testament "interpersonal love almost without exception means *love for one's brother in the faith*." John refers only to loving one another, not to loving one's enemy, though this omission won't mean he restricts the imperative.[98] In connection with relationships with outsiders, the New Testament is more inclined to speak of honoring, being peaceable, blessing, abstaining from redress and doing good. These are all expressions of love, but the New Testament generally keeps the word *love* for the relations of believers to one another.[99] They are to do good to everyone, especially people within the trusting household (Gal 6:10). It is an implication of the congregation's being a new kind of family, or a replacement for the family in the lives of people who have given up their loyalty to their birth families. The congregation is a gathering of brothers and sisters in a home. The idea of a "house church" is not merely that a house provided a convenient meeting place.

On one occasion Jesus tells people to love their enemies, in accordance with the way the Torah expects people to love their neighbors even when they wrong them. Israelites are not exempt from the obligation to resist telling an untruth or coveting or stealing just because the person has behaved like an enemy to them. If Jesus is offering an innovative interpretation of Leviticus 19:18, it's an interpretation of that command, not a replacement of it.[100] Most enemies will be other people within the people of God. He will not have his disciples cutting down the implications of the Torah, as if they only had to love their good neighbors (Mt 5:43-48).

People who thought they could confine their love to the congregation would be vulnerable to Jesus' story about Jews whose evasion of a commitment to help their fellows contrasted with the action of a Samaritan, whom they would also treat as not a member of the family. Loving a neighbor

---

[98]See, e.g., Verhey, *Great Reversal*, 144.
[99]Gerhard Lohfink, *Jesus and Community* (Philadelphia: Fortress, 1984), 106-15 (quotation from 109-10).
[100]Cf. Hans Dieter Betz, *The Sermon on the Mount* (Minneapolis: Fortress, 1995), 309.

or an enemy can be more radical than one might have thought. Although the Septuagint uses *agapē* as a general-purpose word for love, in the New Testament the word also becomes equivalent to *ḥesed* in the First Testament. There, Ruth the Moabite in her remarkable embodiment of *ḥesed* toward Israelites parallels that of the Samaritan (Ruth 1:8; 3:10), while Joseph in his forgiveness of his brothers exemplifies the way love within the family may need to be more radical than one might have thought.

Paul does bid the Thessalonians to love outsiders (1 Thess 3:12), but this stance does not stop him relishing the idea of judgment coming on his opponents (1 Thess 2:14-16; 2 Thess 1:5-10). There is likewise apparently no inconsistency between telling people to bless their persecutors rather than cursing them and looking forward to God's punishing them (Rom 12:14-21). At first sight Paul's series of exhortations alternates between a concern with attitudes to other members of the congregation (e.g., "contribute to the needs of the holy people") and attitudes to outsiders ("bless the people who persecute you"), but this would be a bit odd. The New Testament makes clear that believers were sometimes attacking one another, as has been so through church history, so it wouldn't be surprising if Paul were again urging the believers to live as one, so that there is some consistency of focus, and he is concerned throughout with relationships within the congregation.

While the move from charisms to love in Romans 12 parallels the one in 1 Corinthians 12–13, Paul doesn't seem here to be making a polemical point, as if he knew they were attacking each other. Any congregation is subject to temptation with regard to charisms and relationships (not least in their interconnection) and needs to watch its attitude to both. Some congregations, like the Corinthians, will be good at charisms and will need to focus on love; other congregations, like many in the modern West, will be good at love and will need to be encouraged to manifest charisms.

On the Way to Unity

Jesus prays that his disciples and the people who will come to believe through them may be one, like him and his Father (Jn 17:20-23). The Gospels, Acts and the Epistles make clear that it's quite a prayer. Talk of unity might make people think of the oneness of Jewish and Gentile believers and the oneness of congregations, which are designed to be one in purpose and vision. Jesus has given them the glory that God gave him to the end that they may be one. One implication is that the glory he has given them involves his execution, which is then the key to oneness and to the world's recognition of him.

The conflict and the unity of which the New Testament speaks relate to the worldwide community of believers as well as the local congregation. "What happened among Christians at Antioch mattered to those in Jerusalem, and vice versa."[101] Meeting and talking, and writing letters, were the obvious ways to try to resolve conflicts.

The goal of oneness is significant in connection with the exercise of charisms. Their aim is to bring the saints to completion (*katartizō, katartismos*), which implies a completion in unity. Sometimes "completion" presupposes a broken unity that needs restoring (1 Cor 1:10), but the word can simply presuppose that the congregation is on the way to completion and oneness, like a married couple growing in oneness. The congregation is to strive for this completion (2 Cor 13:11). Its apostles' task is to bring its faith to completion (1 Thess 3:10).

In the meantime there is some inevitability about people being thrown about by differences among believers, even though these differences obscure the oneness of the faith, and the point about exercising charisms is to enable the saints to attain the unity that issues from the faith (which is one) and the knowledge of the Son of God (which is one) (Eph 4:12-16). The exercise of charisms is involved in the building up of the body of the Lord so that it becomes a mature person, and in attaining the Lord's fullness. "The law of growth for the individual" is "more and more to live as part of a great whole,"[102] rather than more and more to find oneself.

The congregation's oneness embraces truth and love. On one side, at present the Ephesian congregation can be convulsed by disagreement about Christian teaching, like a group of children who can be knocked over by a wave. It's as if some people are deliberately scheming to deceive other people

---

[101]Wayne A. Meeks, *The First Urban Christians*, 2nd ed. (New Haven, CT, and London: Yale University Press, 2003), 113.
[102]J. Armitage Robinson, *St. Paul's Epistle to the Ephesians*, 2nd ed. (London: James Clarke, [?1904]), 102.

about what the truth is. God's intent is that through the charisms that are exercised, the congregation should reach the unity that issues from the fact that the faith is actually one and that Jesus is actually one. They will thus proclaim the one truth about Jesus to one another and to the world. On the other side, at present, the congregation can be affected by bitterness and malice (cf. Eph 4:26-32). God's intent is that through the charisms that are exercised, the congregation should reach a unity in kindness, compassion and forgiveness.

"Christian ethics is first of all a call to participate in a distinctive community, the Church," and it is as the church fulfills this call that it will "provide the responsible witness to the surrounding society" that God seeks.[103] Recognizing the truth together and learning to live in this kind of love together are both the means and the goal of growing as a body into a coherent relationship with the head of the body. This vision for the church again restates the Torah's vision for Israel that the work of God within his people should speak out to the world.

Jesus' prayer for his disciples has similar implications. One could see the unity of Father and Son as a unity of truth and love: Jesus has been delivering the true message that his Father gave him, and the Father and the Son live in a relationship of mutual self-giving. For the disciples to be one like Father and Son might initially seem to refer to an existent unity he wants them to maintain, but he goes on to speak of their being "brought to completion into one" (*teteleiōmenoi eis hen*). It is this unity that will then lead to the world's recognizing Jesus and recognizing them. Then God's purpose for the world will have been achieved.

"It is striking to what a high degree, in the whole of the New Testament, the Church is related to the discovery of the gospel by the world" (e.g., Mt 5:13-16; Jn 13:35; 1 Pet 2:9); indeed, "the essence of the Church cannot be thought of apart from that peculiar movement towards the outside, the world."[104] John H. Yoder lists a series of practices that embody the essence of Christian existence and could make sense to the world outside, so that they are "practices of *witness*."[105] They are that the community is formed

[103] Andrew T. Lincoln, *Ephesians* (Dallas: Word, 1990), 269.
[104] G. C. Berkouwer, *The Church* (Grand Rapids: Eerdmans, 1976), 47, 391.
[105] James W. McClendon, *Systematic Theology: Doctrine* (Nashville: Abingdon, 1994), 379.

through reconciling dialogue, people share possessions, people of different races come together, all people have roles in the community, and everyone is free to speak in the meetings of the fellowship.[106] "For Paul the *reconciliation* and *mutual welcome* of all those 'in the Messiah' took precedence over everything else."[107]

A Family Lifestyle

Matthew 5–7 lays out Jesus' priorities for the disciples in their life together and in relation to other people. For the readers of the Gospel, it is a description of the life of believers in their mutual relationships as a congregation and in relation to outsiders. Those priorities are reconciliation, chastity, honesty, forbearance, love, charity, prayer, fasting, modesty, generosity, trust, self-criticism, discernment and obedience. Paul likewise urges people to bless those who persecute them rather than cursing them and to let redress be God's business, as the First Testament says (Rom 12:14-21; Deut 32:35; Prov 25:21-22). His reference to overcoming evil with good rather than being overcome by evil may indicate that he has in mind winning the person to repentance (which is more clearly the point in Prov 25:21-22 itself). Either way, if I react to someone's wronging me by wronging them, they've won. The vocation of disciples is to "embody forgiveness," an embodying that does not stop when it meets with no response and thus has to take the form of loving the enemy.[108]

Negatively, Jesus denies the importance of possessions and also of family. In the social context, family had an extra level of importance compared with its importance in the Western world, partly because of the significance of Israel as a people that comprised a huge family and that shared out possession of the land on a family basis.[109] Instructions such as those in Matthew 5–7 lay out sample rules for the family life of the new company of brothers and sisters that is formed by a congregation (Mt 5:23-24, 47; 7:3-5; cf. Mt 12:46-50). They are expected to be

---

[106]See John Howard Yoder, *For the Nations* (Grand Rapids and Cambridge, UK: Eerdmans, 1997), 43-46.
[107]Wright, *Paul and the Faithfulness of God*, 12.
[108]See L. Gregory Jones, *Embodying Forgiveness* (Grand Rapids: Eerdmans, 1995), esp. 241-78.
[109]Cf. N. T. Wright, *Jesus and the Victory of God* (Minneapolis: Fortress; London: SPCK, 1996), 398-405.

communities that embody this family lifestyle, in their relationships with one another and with people outside the family. It is the way their light will shine (Mt 5:14-16).

Acts and the Epistles speak more explicitly about believers as a family of brothers and sisters and appeal to that bond as the basis for their relationships, following the example of the Torah. First Thessalonians speaks nineteen times about "brothers" (in general, at least, it will be referring to siblings of both sexes within the family of believers), and it lays out a number of priorities for them in light of the fact that Jesus is coming back and that this life is short (1 Thess 4:1–5:21):

- sexual purity
- not wronging or taking advantage of a brother or sister
- love for one another
- living a quiet life
- working for yourself, not depending on others
- sobriety and watchfulness, as an expression of faith, hope and love
- honoring people who work hard among you and admonish you
- openness and discernment in connection with prophecy

Without referring to the congregation as a family, Ephesians 4:25–5:20 focuses its priorities on the desired difference between nonbelieving Gentiles and believers:

- truthfulness to one another; don't lie (because we are members of one body)
- working with your hands; don't steal (so as to have something to share with the needy)
- kindness, compassion and forgiveness; don't be angry for more than a day, or be bitter, brawling, slanderous or malicious
- being filled with the Spirit; don't get drunk
- speaking to one another with hymns, prayers and thanksgiving; don't speak in an unwholesome way (be concerned to build people up)
- being like God and like Jesus; don't give the devil a foothold or grieve the Holy Spirit (with whom you were sealed for redemption day)

Speech, Stuff and Home

Speech is of broader significance to this family lifestyle.[110] Words can be life-giving, "sweet to the taste and healing for the body" (Prov 16:24). They can be performative; they do things. They can speak truth, wisdom and awe for God and can bring love. They can also speak deception, stupidity and god-lessness and bring hate, and thus be destructive of other people, the community and oneself (Prov 10:18-21). "How long will you torment my spirit, crush me with words?" Job asks (Job 19:1). "The mouth of the faithful is a fountain of life," while "the mouth of a fool is imminent ruin" (Prov 10:11, 14). There is thus something to be said for silence (e.g., Prov 17:27). But the New Testament also shows that we sometimes need the courage to speak words of reproof, as the context of the neighbor-love command implies (Lev 19:17-18). Even such words can be life-giving. True words belong in the context of true relationships; the First Testament turns a blind eye to lies told by powerless people to their powerful oppressors (e.g., Ex 1:15-21).

In Hebrews 13, the equivalent priorities to the ones in 1 Thessalonians or Ephesians are:

- caring for other believers
- caring for believers in prison
- contentment rather than love of money
- rejection of strange teaching
- praise
- intercession
- hospitality
- sexual purity
- emulation of and submission to leaders
- acceptance of persecution as discipline
- sharing what you have

Love expresses itself in "sharing in the needs of the holy people" and "pursuing hospitality" (Rom 12:13). There are links between the two sets of expectations. Abandoning anxiety because you trust in God makes it more

---

[110]See further *OTT* 3:668-81.

feasible to give generously to people who are needy.[111] "Paul never says: 'There is neither rich nor poor,'" even to the Corinthians among whom there are problems about the relationship of rich and poor, and he does not imply an ideal whereby the congregation pools its resources in the way described in Acts. "It is not that the rich man sells all that he has and contributes to the poor or to the congregation's common fund; rather, he opens his home to the congregation and, perhaps, provides for it at his own expense." This assumption will link with the references to congregations meeting in people's houses (Rom 16:1-5; 1 Cor 16:19; Col 4:15; Philem 2).[112]

Generosity and hospitality thus combine, and demonstrating them enables a person to evade the warning about how hard it is for the rich to get into God's realm (Mt 12:16-30). The New Testament picture again corresponds to that in the Torah, which also emphasizes lending and not merely giving—as does Jesus (Lk 6:34-35).

Ordinary people will need to be guided more by Jesus' exhortation not to save treasure on earth but to save it up in heaven, which indicates where your heart is, and not to try to serve God and money (Mt 6:19-24). In this connection they are not to worry about food or clothing but to seek God's reigning and God's putting things right; they will have those things as well (Mt 6:25-34). As Paul put it, if you sow generously, you will reap generously (2 Cor 9:6). He is wisely allusive about the nature of the reaping, but like Jesus he would be sure both that they will have a reward stored up in heaven and that they will have enough in this life, though he would not want to be held to the idea of limousines and private jets.

In being generous toward fellow believers, we are involved in a "ministry toward the holy ones"; Paul is not afraid to manipulate the Corinthians into doing the right thing in this connection (2 Cor 9:1-5; and 2 Cor 8–9 as a whole).

Mutually Submissive

"A life worthy of our summons," our summons to be God's holy people, has four characteristic virtues (Eph 4:1-2), though they may comprise related pairs. First, it means being lowly and meek. Even if we are intelligent and

---

[111]Verhey, *Great Reversal*, 17-19; cf. O'Donovan, *Finding and Seeking*, 174-75.
[112]Nils A. Dahl, *Studies in Paul* (Minneapolis: Augsburg, 1977), 28.

important, we abandon self-respect, adopt a low opinion of our own importance and ideas, don't take ourselves very seriously and don't dismiss believers who do take themselves too seriously. Further, we accept our powerlessness without being frustrated by it because we know God is the only one who can achieve things, we know God is involved with our concerns if they are God's concerns, and we don't get too troubled about believers who are attached to power.

The third and fourth characteristics are that we are patient and accommodating. We are long-tempered and tolerant in accepting people who are different from us rather than assuming we are right, and we are broadminded in relation to people who are sure they are right and who dismiss us. Further, we carry one another as we care for one another, we are happy to bear other believers even though they are a burden, or rather because they are a burden, because love needs a burden to bear. We know we can't fulfill our vocation without the help of people who are a burden to us. Love thus expresses itself in bearing other people's burdens, which (to judge from Gal 6:2) includes their moral failures.

Love means thus keeping the unity of the Spirit through the bond of peace, living in light of there being one body (to which we all belong), one Spirit (who indwells this one body), one hope (that God's manifold wisdom is going to be revealed to the rulers and authorities through the church), one Lord (whom we all serve), one faith (which we all profess), one baptism (into the one body), one God and Father of all (who is over all, through all and in all) (Eph 4:3-6). "It was a startling experiment in human life which the Apostle was striving to realize."[113] The first pair of virtues, in particular, would have seemed more like vices in the ancient European world (though in the context of the First Testament they would seem like virtues), and only in theory are they virtues in the church.

The congregation is to be one in thinking, in caring and in spirit (Phil 2:1-16). That oneness will express itself in refusing to act out of ambition or concern with one's status and rather having ambitions for the status of others; people will do everything without grumbling at one another or quarreling with one another. That stance will naturally emerge from a

---

[113]Robinson, *Ephesians*, 94.

relationship with Jesus and with the Spirit, and from the inspiration of Jesus' own attitude in his willingness to ignore questions about his own status in order to become a human being, and then in letting himself be executed as if he were a criminal. In being one in this way, the congregation will work at its salvation and be blameless and pure, and be a shining light among its contemporaries as it thus holds on to and/or holds forth[114] the living word of the gospel.

When Paul elsewhere urges people not to have too high an opinion of themselves (Rom 12:3), the exhortation begins with a "because." This attitude will be an example of being transformed and not living in the fashion of this age. The earlier background to the expectation lies in the temptation for Jews to look down on Gentiles and for Gentile believers to look down on Jews (Rom 2–4; 11).[115] Diffidence about oneself and caring for other people are the central challenges for a congregation, not least because they go against our natural instincts. Believers are to express their charisms with energy but without assuming that their particular charism alone matters. They are to "think the same things as one another"—come to a common attitude (Rom 12:16). This way of thinking implies more than living in harmony in the sense of being willing to live together while preserving one's own views. It implies living in unison, subordinating one's own views, instincts and convictions to those of the community as a whole.

Jesus' love "controls" us (*synechō*; 2 Cor 5:14). The word can denote a positive compulsion or a negative constraint. Both meanings would be applicable, though in the context the latter may more likely be the point.[116] Indeed, "the transforming work of the Spirit relates Paul (and every believer) to others as their 'slave.' To live otherwise is to return to 'the flesh'" (Gal 5:13).[117]

The Absolute . . .

Paul's comments on attitudes to food rules and sabbath take a different tack; they imply the possibility of being united while conflicted. The Roman

---

[114]If we must choose one of these implications of *epechō* then the context suggests the latter (against Gerald F. Hawthorne, *Philippians* [Waco, TX: Word, 1983], 103).

[115]Cf. Dunn, *Romans*, 2:732.

[116]See Margaret E. Thrall, *A Critical and Exegetical Commentary on the Second Epistle to the Corinthians* (Edinburgh: T&T Clark, 1994), 1:408-9.

[117]Gorman, *Cruciformity*, 55.

church was divided in its convictions about the status of the biblical rules concerning food, sabbath, fasts and festivals, which raised fundamental issues concerning the nature of the gospel. Paul has a firm view about which side is theologically right, but he wants the church to stick together, committed to "living with fundamental disagreements" (Rom 14:1–15:6).[118]

In a Western context we are used to being different from other people; indeed, we rejoice in standing out from the crowd. In a first-century context the pressure might be the other way, and Paul urges people not to apply this pressure but to let people be different. Although he attributes weak faith to people who insist on rules about food and about days that one observes, he wants those of strong faith to cherish these people and hold them in the congregation. They are God's servants, not the servants of other believers, and the stance they take is between them and God. They are responsible to God for it.

Further, it's a matter of love. If you attempt to impose your freedom on people to whom that freedom looks like apostasy, you risk driving them to act in a way that they can't see is right before God and/or to abandon their adherence to Jesus, instead of contributing to their edification. You thus imperil their relationship with God, perhaps fatally.

It's therefore also a matter of faith. If the "strong" are pressuring the "weak" to act in a way that doesn't reflect their own relationship with God, they are pressuring them not to live out of their faith relationship with God, than which nothing worse could be said.

And third, it's a matter of witness. If the congregation is torn apart by conflict over such an issue, it brings discredit on the faith it allegedly stands for and obscures the greater importance of doing right by one another, living in peace and rejoicing enthusiastically together in the Holy Spirit.

Love will accept rather than exclude. Whereas each group will be tempted to dismiss the other, either as too liberal or as too narrow, each must recognize the other as accepted by Jesus. The weak in faith need to see the importance of faith alone; the strong in faith need to see the importance of love, even to value "love rather than integrity."[119] The peace of Jesus is to rule

---

[118]Dunn's title for a study of the passage, *Theology of Paul the Apostle*, 680.
[119]Krister Stendahl, *Paul Among Jews and Gentiles and Other Essays* (Philadelphia: Fortress, 1976), 52.

in the congregation's hearts, and they are to be gracious to one another.[120] As members of one body they are called to peace—the body is in a mess when its different parts are fighting one another (Col 3:15).

Furthermore (Rom 15:1-8), it's a matter of the strong serving the weak, which is the regular pattern of Christian discipleship in following Jesus; the argument in Philippians 2 would also fit here. We follow Jesus by not pleasing ourselves in following our own convictions despite the fact that other people insult us ("they aren't really living in obedience to the Scriptures"). In a sense, talk of "mutual acceptance" is misleading. Paul's vision is not of two groups coming to accept each other. It's that one group (the majority?) should accept the other despite the fact that it's not accepted by it.

To revert to two of his earlier concerns in discussing this issue, such acceptance is necessary so that the congregation may worship with *one* mind and voice and may commend God to the Gentile world. After all, Jesus became a servant of the Jews so that "the Gentiles might glorify God for his mercy." The "strong" in Rome must do the same. People must accept each other as Jesus accepted them, with an acceptance that does not first require that they see everything correctly. And further, both groups are going to stand before God's judgment seat, so it would be wise to leave judgment to God (Rom 14:10-11).

... and the Flexible

Jesus managed to combine "strenuous commands," teaching that is rigorous and all-demanding, with an embrace of people that could accept the "ethically dubious," in imitation of a Father who was both perfect and merciful; the same is true of Paul.[121]

First Corinthians 7:1–11:1 deals further with issues that require believers to be flexible. The confident and the cautious need to live together, and having rights doesn't mean you have to insist on them. The issue is not my

---

[120]English versions translate *eucharistoi* "thankful," and Col 3:16, 17; 4:2 go on to talk about being grateful to God; but the context in Col 3:15 suggests human relationships, and "gracious" is the word's meaning in its only other occurrence in the Greek Bible (Prov 11:16) as well as on many other occasions elsewhere: cf. T. K. Abbott, *A Critical and Exegetical Commentary on the Epistles to the Ephesians and to the Colossians* (Edinburgh: T&T Clark; New York: Scribner, 1897), 290. Similar issues are raised by the use of *charis* in Col 3:16; 4:6.

[121]See Richard A. Burridge, *Imitating Jesus* (Grand Rapids and Cambridge, UK: Eerdmans, 2007), 78-79, 154. The phrase "strenuous commands" comes from Anthony E. Harvey, *Strenuous Commands* (London: SCM Press; Philadelphia: Trinity Press International, 1990).

freedom but what is beneficial and constructive for other people, their encouragement to keep walking rather than stumble, and therefore the glorifying of God.[122] That stance is the one Paul claims to take (1 Cor 11:1).

To put it another way, the freedom of believers is a freedom to care for other people instead of being in bondage to themselves. "The Gospels portray Jesus as a free person," in regard to what he eats or who he associates with and how he speaks. It's not a freedom to exercise his rights but a "freedom for the sake of the good of others," which reaches its "apogee . . . in the free laying down of his own life." This "freedom in the service of goodness" has its basis in God's goodness; "the goodness of God is what frees for goodness."[123] Indeed, "Godhead in the Bible means freedom. . . . It is thus, as One who is free, as the only One who is free, that God has lordship in the Bible."[124]

Sometimes it is pastoral concerns that make flexibility possible and/or necessary. There are grey areas.[125] In working, rather than relying on the support of the people to whom he brings the gospel, Paul is not following Jesus' instructions.[126] But then, when the disciples act in a way that seems to contravene the sabbath, Jesus' response is not to say "It's not really contravening the sabbath." Rather he points to situations in the Scriptures when people ignore the Torah. There are situations in which it's okay to do so. Human need and divine service can override the sabbath (Mt 12:1-14).

This stance fits with the flexibility of the Torah itself. Some Israelites at Sinai couldn't celebrate the Passover because they had had contact with a dead body. "No problem," says Yahweh: "celebrate it next month" (Num 9). The people as a whole decide it's okay to act similarly in a later context (2 Chron 30). Zelophehad's daughters appeal against the idea that in the absence of brothers, they should not be able to inherit the family land. Once more Yahweh says, "Okay" (Num 27), and the rule is modified again later (see Num 36). Such changes are but the tip of an enormous iceberg. A

---

[122]See C. K. Barrett, "Things Sacrificed to Idols," *NTS* 11 (1964–1965): 138-53.

[123]Jon Sobrino, *Jesus the Liberator* (Maryknoll, NY: Orbis, 1993; Tunbridge Wells, UK: Burns and Oates, 1994), 145.

[124]Barth, *CD* I, 1:307.

[125]Cf. Thiselton, *1 Corinthians*, 82, 99-100; and see Kathy Ehrensberger, "To Eat or Not to Eat—Is This the Question?," in Ehrensberger et al., eds., *Decisive Meals* (London and New York: T&T Clark, 2012), 114-33.

[126]Cf. Gerd Theissen, *The Social Setting of Pauline Christianity* (Philadelphia: Fortress, 1982), 42-49.

comparison of the sets of rules in the Torah (e.g., of Ex 20–24 with Deuteronomy) indicates how flexibly God guided Israel over the centuries to reformulate rules for its life in different contexts.

While pastoral concerns thus sometimes make flexibility possible and/or necessary, sometimes theological and ethical concerns make firmness a requirement. When Paul deals in Galatians with questions about rules concerning food and the observing of days, questions that are similar to the ones that arise in Romans, he takes a tougher line; "When Cephas came to Antioch I opposed him to his face" (Gal 2:11). Perhaps the issues surfaced there in a way that seemed more radically to imperil the gospel.

Disciplined

The material either side of 1 Corinthians 7:1–11:1 likewise deals with questions that demand a firm stance. The congregation doesn't have the job of judging outsiders, but it's responsible for judging its own members. Where individuals then deliberately maintain their waywardness, a congregation is to exclude them in order to bring them to their senses and destroy their fleshly stance, so as to win them back and rescue them for the day of the Lord (1 Cor 5). The language recalls the way the Torah talks about being "cut off" from Israel (e.g., Gen 17:14; Ex 31:14; Lev 23:29), though as far as we know, the Israelites understood this expression to denote something God would do, not something they had to do.

Believers are to keep away from brothers and sisters who are idle, not to treat them as enemies but to admonish them (2 Thess 3:6, 14). The second exhortation shows that the first doesn't mean refusing to have anything to do with them; it perhaps implies dissociating yourself from their behavior. The moment when someone has been driven to grief is then the moment for forgiveness (2 Cor 2:5-11). The Scriptures are realistic about the commitment of congregations. They are holy, but they are sinful. Like the individual, the church is *simul justus et peccator*.[127] Congregations are responsible to themselves and to God for discipline and restoration. But "discipline is to be exercised in the service of mercy."[128]

---

[127]Moltmann, *Church in the Power of the Spirit*, 22; on this phrase, see further the paragraphs headed "Doing the Right Thing" and "It Bought Them Back So They Can Serve Another Master" in sections 5.2 and 5.5 above.

[128]Cf. Dietrich Bonhoeffer, *Discipleship* (repr., Minneapolis: Fortress, 2003), 271.

The setting of 1 Corinthians 13 between 1 Corinthians 12 and 14 and in the context of the letter as a whole suggests a link between love and congregational order, congregational discipline and self-discipline.[129] Love means I discipline myself with regard to the way I exercise my charisms because my concern is the congregation's upbuilding, not my self-expression. It means the congregation as a whole disciplines itself in this connection; believers in general cannot simply leave this discipline to the leadership. People speaking in tongues or prophesying are to do so in a disciplined fashion (1 Cor 14:27-32). Again, there is no indication that it is the leadership's task to enforce discipline (perhaps the leaders are the problem!). Indeed, the task of leaders is to "facilitate rather than control the manifestations of the Spirit."[130]

Be alert, then, stand firm in the faith, be brave, be strong; everything of yours should happen in love, Paul goes on (1 Cor 16:13-16). The first of these imperatives parallels a number of New Testament exhortations to wake up— exhortations addressed to believers, who could easily fall back into the sleepiness of the rest of the world.[131]

The opening four imperatives also correspond to ones in Joshua and relate to entering into the fulfillment of God's promises, though the addition of "in the faith" recalls the ease with which Israel compromised with Canaanite faith. Paul adds that "the person who does not love the Lord is to be *anathema.*" *Anathema* is the Septuagint's translation of *ḥērem* in Joshua, the word for "devoting" something to God by destroying it. This declaration then leads into the Aramaic prayer, "*Marana tha,*" "our Lord, come" (1 Cor 16:22), implicitly a plea that God may come and do the final destroying. The words thus "sum up covenant curse and covenant blessing."[132] Paul also asks that God's *anathema* may come on anyone who preaches a gospel other than the one he preached and the Galatians accepted (Gal 1:9).

Joshua and the Israelites had to combine firmness in relation to the Canaanites (Josh 6) and themselves (Josh 7; 24) with grace and mercy when firmness was inappropriate (Josh 2). Paul's addition to the earlier four imperatives about everything happening in love corresponds to his concern in

---

[129]Thiselton, *1 Corinthians*, 235.
[130]Amos Yong, *Renewing Christian Theology* (Waco, TX: Baylor University Press, 2014), 76.
[131]Cf. Barth, *CD* IV, 2:555.
[132]Thiselton, *1 Corinthians*, 302.

this letter and the particular needs of the Corinthians. There is huge potential for things to go wrong in the faith within the congregation through assimilation to the culture. They need to stand firm in relation to their culture and also thus in relation to one another, exercising discipline when that is needed. Yet even that standing firm must be done in love.

Paul is committed to being both caring and frank (cf. 2 Cor 1:12–2:4). Love and firmness are a significant pairing. The Scriptures commend love, compassion, patience, peaceableness, forgiveness, caring for enemies and faithfulness. They also commend passion and disgust. Even anger has a place (Eph 4:26): "the question, then, is not whether anger is legitimate or important" but "what we become angry about and . . . toward what ends our anger is directed."[133]

---

[133]Jones, *Embodying Forgiveness*, 247.

8

GOD'S TRIUMPH

✠

This study of biblical theology has interwoven narrative and discursive forms, in light of the way the Scriptures do so. It has thus considered things that are always true about God, about the world, about humanity and about God's people; it has also considered events such as creation, God's getting involved with Israel and the coming of Jesus. We close with what God still intends to do, considered in light of what he has done.

8.1 THE FULFILLMENT OF GOD'S INTENT

Both Testaments locate crucial events in the past, see these events as affecting the present, but also look forward. The Bible "sets out to speak of human life in the context of a vision of universal, cosmic history . . . from the creation of the world to its consummation, [and] of the nations which make up the one human family. . . . The Bible is universal history."[1] Biblical faith involves past, present and future, the Beginning, the Now and the End. It relates to action that God took, to action that God is taking and that God expects of humanity, and also to action that God intends in bringing about the fulfillment of his purpose. It comes in the form of indicative verbs, imperative verbs, then more indicative verbs.[2] God is "the one who is, and who was, and who is coming" (Rev 1:4; cf. Rev 1:8; 4:8); he thus speaks of the future not only in terms of his being or of his becoming but of his coming,[3]

[1]Lesslie Newbigin, *The Gospel in a Pluralist Society* (Grand Rapids: Eerdmans; London: SPCK, 1989), 89.

[2]J. Christiaan Beker, *Paul the Apostle* (repr., Philadelphia: Fortress, 1984), 277-78.

[3]Jürgen Moltmann, *The Coming of God* (London: SCM Press; Minneapolis: Fortress, 1996), 23.

and he speaks of "coming" with reference to himself, not merely with reference to the Anointed One (contrast John the Baptizer's question, Mt 11:3).

God Will Reign

God is sovereign in the world, taking sovereign initiatives in it and setting bounds to its waywardness. He is in control of the world in the sense of not letting human exercise of power, or natural forces, or other supernatural forces get totally out of hand; the beast "*was allowed* to make war on the saints and conquer them, and *was allowed* authority over every tribe, people, language, and nation" (Rev 13:7). In the full sense, however, God's reign or Jesus' reign belongs to the future. God will bring in the coming age and will rule at the End.

The fact that God intends to reign is good news. Escaping from slavery in the south to freedom in the north, or escaping from a country ruled by oppression to a country characterized by the rule of law, means moving from something like death to something more like life. Good government and full life can be closely related, and eternal life is closely related to God's reign. Eternal life is the life of the new age, and the new age is the age in which God reigns.

So the Scriptures can bring into close relationship talk of God's reign or realm and talk of true life. Jesus can put alongside each other the declaration that "It's better for you to go into life maimed than to go off to Gehenna with two hands" and the declaration that "It's better for you to go into God's realm with one eye than to be thrown into Gehenna with two eyes" (Mk 9:43, 47). A wealthy person asks him about eternal life, and he observes that it's hard for a wealthy person to gain entry to God's realm; the disciples comment that it's difficult to be saved, and Jesus promises that people who have given up things for him and for the good news will receive eternal life in the coming age (Mk 10:17-31). Without being born from above, a person cannot enter God's realm, but anyone who believes in God has eternal life rather than having God's anger rest on him (Jn 3:5, 36). As Jesus declares that God's reign is present now, so he declares that the life of the coming age can be enjoyed now. Eternal life is the life of the new age, life in the realm where God reigns.

It might be an exaggeration to say that "the triumph of God" is "the coherent theme of Paul's gospel" or simply that "Paul's thought is motivated by the future consummation as God's goal with history and creation,"[4] but these themes are indeed key to his thought, and not just to Paul's. Indeed, the Scriptures talk more about God's fulfillment of his purpose than about our forgiveness. They talk more theologically than anthropologically or psychologically. Whether we go along with them depends on whether "we happen to be more interested in ourselves than in God or in the fate of his creation."[5] A related principle is that neither grace nor theology can be sin-centered. God's grace is not simply the answer to human depravity; it antedates human depravity. Indeed, "sin itself can arise and take shape as sin only as sin against the grace of God, and it can be known only with the knowledge of grace. And 'the grace of God alone remains eternally.'"[6]

Objective Hope

The fact that God intends to fulfill his purpose does have implications for his people. Our sin meant that we lost God's glory (Rom 3:23). We couldn't fulfill our human vocation to exercise sovereignty in the world, and we couldn't expect our humanity to be transformed so that we live forever. And God's sending Jesus and our trusting in Jesus not only put things right between us and God; it opened up the "expectation of God's glory" (Rom 5:2). Even if we are outwardly persecuted we are inwardly renewed, which means our persecution is generating for us eternal honor, and therefore our persecution does not discourage us (2 Cor 4:16-18; cf. Rom 5:1-11). The certainty that God's triumph will come is an encouragement in affliction, a stimulus to faithful living, and a reason to focus on what will matter in the new age (e.g., Rom 8:18-25; 1 Cor 6:9-10; 7:25-35; Gal 5:21).[7] It means that God is "the God of hope" (Rom 15:13).

When Paul spells out the implications of his prayer for people to know (about) God, he first asks that they may know the hope to which God has called them, and he then explicates that prayer in terms of their knowing

---

[4]Beker, *Paul the Apostle*, ix, 176.

[5]Krister Stendahl, *Paul Among Jews and Gentiles and Other Essays* (Philadelphia: Fortress, 1976), 24; cf. Anthony C. Thiselton, *Thiselton on Hermeneutics* (Grand Rapids and Cambridge, UK: Eerdmans, 2006), 93.

[6]Barth, *CD* III, 2:37; cf. Otto Weber, *Foundations of Dogmatics* (Grand Rapids: Eerdmans, 1981), 1:556. I do not know why the final clause appears in quotation marks.

[7]Cf. John G. Gager, "Functional Diversity in Paul's Use of End-Time Language," *JBL* 89 (1970): 325-37.

"the glory of what God has done in entering into possession of his people"[8] (Eph 1:18). His subsequent prayer for them to know the extent of God's power (Eph 1:19-20) relates to this awareness. God has the power to take them to their destiny. God's raising and exalting Jesus means they can be sure that other powers cannot prevent it, because that action of God in relation to Jesus shows God's power.

We *were* dead in connection with our waywardness; we had no hope. We were "children of wrath." The phrase parallels expressions such as "children of death" to denote people who deserve death, people on their way to death (e.g., 1 Sam 26:16; 2 Sam 12:5).[9] We were people "by nature deserving of wrath" (TNIV). But God "made us alive along with the Anointed One" and "raised us up through the Anointed One, Jesus" (Eph 2:1-6). Whereas we were dead in the sense of hopeless (Eph 2:12), now we have hope, and we are alive.

"Hope" thus here refers not to a feeling of hopefulness but to the actual fact that God will send the Anointed One and will implement his purpose. It denotes objective hope. But objective hope issues in subjective hope, "the freedom for the future and the openness towards it which the man of faith has because he has turned over his anxiety about himself and his future to God in obedience."[10] Anxiety, after all, is "sin in respect of time, a failure to allow the promise of God's good future to illuminate the time given us now for action."[11]

Isaiah 12 closes Isaiah's first great portrayal of the danger and the hope of Judah with a song for them to sing on the day of fulfillment. Providing them with this song is another way of inviting them to live in hope. If they yield to the song, they're involved in praising God for fulfilling his promises before the fulfillment happens. Isaiah is presupposing the way the First Testament sees answers to prayer as commonly coming in two stages: first God says he has heard and undertaken to act, then he acts. Praise then likewise

---

[8]Andrew T. Lincoln, *Ephesians* (Dallas: Word, 1990), 60.

[9]Cf. T. K. Abbott, *A Critical and Exegetical Commentary on the Epistles to the Ephesians and to the Colossians* (Edinburgh: T&T Clark; New York: Scribner, 1897), 45.

[10]Rudolf Bultmann, *Theology of the New Testament* (repr., Waco, TX: Baylor University Press, 2007), 1:320.

[11]Oliver O'Donovan, *Finding and Seeking* (Grand Rapids and Cambridge, UK: Eerdmans, 2014), 173.

comes in two stages: we praise God first for the hearing and the undertaking, then for the act. In Isaiah 12, the act has not yet happened, but the praise can begin. Wherever the people are, they are invited to see that they've "come this far by faith" (as the hymn puts it) and that they can continue in hope, not because their faith or hope is big but because the God they trust and hope in is big. It fits that the last clause in Isaiah 1–12 is a declaration about "Israel's holy one."

While biblical hope presupposes "a perceived gap between what God has promised and what has so far come about,"[12] the gap between promise and fulfillment is not the ultimate ground of hope. Behind the promises in which we hope is the fact that God formulated a purpose back at the Beginning. Perhaps God's promise to himself is the ultimate ground of human hope. Or one might combine reference to God's purpose and his promise, as Moses did more than once in pointing out that God can hardly give up on his project with Israel (e.g., Ex 32:11-13). God could hardly let waywardness, oppression and death have the last word, though there could be various facets to his response to these realities.

Subjective Hope

"The Christian faith is repeatedly characterized by 1 Peter as 'hope.'"[13] Indeed, "the life which is characterized by the indwelling of the Spirit of God, which is a life in which God's law is established, is a life characterized by hope."[14] Living in hope is inherent in biblical faith, but "hope that is seen is not hope" (Rom 8:24), which means that living in hope necessarily involves living with tension and discontent. In connection with that reality, "the Spirit helps us in our weakness." When we do not know how to pray, as we labor and struggle to live in accordance with the Spirit rather than with the lower nature, the Spirit intercedes for us with groans that are even deeper and louder and more agonized than our own. "Weak in confidence, weak in understanding, weak in endurance, our sickened agency is restored, our ill-conceived undertakings are given good effect."[15] And the one whom the

---

[12]Anthony C. Thiselton, *The Hermeneutics of Doctrine* (Grand Rapids: Eerdmans, 2007), 541.

[13]Eduard Lohse, *Theological Ethics of the New Testament* (Minneapolis: Fortress, 1991), 179.

[14]C. E. B. Cranfield, *A Critical and Exegetical Commentary on the Epistle to the Romans* (Edinburgh: T&T Clark, 1975), 404.

[15]O'Donovan, *Finding and Seeking*, 1.

Spirit addresses (whose Spirit this is) understands those groans and can therefore respond to them (Rom 8:26-27).

The fact that such a cry emerges from people's lips is thus not a sign that something is wrong but a sign that something is right. The tension people feel as they want to do the right thing but are also inclined to follow the inclinations of the lower nature is not an indication that they are in danger of falling back into slavery. Paradoxically, the tension that makes them cry "Father!" is a sign that the Spirit of Jesus is at work in them, an indication that they are Jesus' brothers and sisters and are on the way to sharing in his inheritance. It means they are sharing in the agonized longing of the whole creation, which itself also yearns to be set free from its slavery and to share their freedom.

This dynamic means that God can take the apparently relentless, hopeless, futile struggle in which they are involved and turn it into something purposeful and positive. It is set in the context of God's having determined to make them like their brother (Rom 8:28-30). They are assailed by pressures (*pathēmata*) from within and without (Rom 7:5; 8:18). But the struggle is worthwhile, and the idea that it might end in anything other than the victory of the Spirit over the lower nature is a nonstarter. "If God is for us, who is against us?" (Rom 8:31). Whoever it is, it doesn't matter. God is committed to taking us to our destiny. It's no use our great enemies (flesh, Torah, sin, death) accusing us of anything, because Jesus has paid them their due on our behalf. None of them can separate us from Jesus' love.

The same is true of other enemies that might assail us. Hope also enables us to live with other people in the present. We know that God brought about our salvation in a way that involved people's perversity and stupidity and turned it into the means of achieving that salvation. We take that achievement as typical of the way God works, and we know that we can therefore expect God to do it again and again to make it part of the achievement of his ultimate purpose.

Greek and Latin writers list obstacles that beset the way of virtue.[16] Paul's younger contemporary Epictetus declares that "neither death nor exile, nor pain, nor anything of this kind is the cause of our doing, or not doing, any

---

[16]See Rudolf Bultmann, *Der Stil des paulinischen Predigt und die kynisch-stoische Diatribe* (Göttingen: Vandenhoeck, 1910); cf. Cranfield, *Romans*, 434-35.

action; but our opinions and principles. . . . Who is unconquerable?" His answer is, the person whom nothing disconcerts. "What, if he be tried by popular fame, calumny, praise, death? He is able to overcome them all."[17] Paul does not share the conviction that wise people can triumph over these obstacles through being cool and collected. He knows we need another form of insight in order to do so (Rom 8:31-39). He can face the fact that Epictetus's theory doesn't work because he knows that Jesus has negotiated these obstacles, defeated them and mapped out the way for us to do so. The obstacles are like opponents barring our way, but Jesus has disarmed them, we can see that they've been disarmed, and we thus have answers to give them when they challenge us.

There are two forms of hopelessness, that of anticipating the fulfillment or that of giving up hope. Both "cancel the wayfaring character of hope. They rebel against the patience in which hope trusts in the God of the promise."[18] God is the God of hope for Israel, and the God of hope for the church.

Eschatology

In discussions of the triumph of God and the hope of God's people, the words *eschatological* and *apocalyptic* are often used. While my quotations from scholars will occasionally include these words, in my own formulation of points I shall avoid using them.

J. Christiaan Beker notes "the degree of multivalence and chaos that in recent theology adheres to 'eschatology'—a concept that denotes everything from existential finality and transcendent reality to 'life after death.'"[19] Eschatology

1. can refer to the destiny of the individual, the people of God, the world as a whole and the cosmos;

2. may think in terms of an End after which there will be nothing, or in terms of historical experience giving way to an era of timeless blessing, or in terms of our era of flawed history and experience giving way to a new, wholesome era of history and experience;

---

[17] *The Moral Discourses of Epictetus* (London: Dent; New York: Dutton, 1910), 1.11, 18 (pp. 28, 41).
[18] Cf. Jürgen Moltmann, *Theology of Hope* (London: SCM Press; New York: Harper, 1967), 23; cf. Thiselton, *Hermeneutics of Doctrine*, 541.
[19] Beker, *Paul the Apostle*, xiv; cf. Beker, *Paul's Apocalyptic Gospel* (Philadelphia: Fortress, 1982), 14.

3. can involve the belief that God is putting his ultimate purpose into effect now, through events that can be seen in the world, so that it is already being actualized or realized, or the belief that God will do so at some time in the future by means that we cannot at the moment see;

4. usually implies a radical distinction between this age and a coming age, but can see the coming of this new age as gradual or as involving a dramatic transformation, reversal or discontinuity;

5. and can imply a future that is imminent or one that is far away.[20]

I am puzzled by Bruce Chilton's comment that the word *eschatological* is "easily defined," though on his next page he notes that there is dispute about its meaning.[21] The problematic nature of the word finds expression in the use by some writers of the expression "final eschatology,"[22] which ought to be a magnificent redundancy.

Eschatology sounds like a technical term, which as such would have a definable meaning, but it isn't.[23] Indeed, behind the terminological point there is a substantial one. Paul, for instance, "seems for the most part to have been willing to leave the different aspects of his eschatological expectation uncorrelated." In contrast to the systematic way he has thought through the process whereby God brought about our restoration, as he describes it in Romans, the picture of the future is "rather 'bitty' and fragmented."[24] He doesn't make very clear the interrelation of judgment, second coming, final victory and resurrection. How much more unsystematic, then, is the impression one gains from the New Testament as a whole, and then from the Scriptures as a whole. It is one of the ways in which they show "a sublime indifference to what appear to us today as momentous issues."[25]

---

[20]I adapt this analysis from John Goldingay, *Isaiah 56–66* (London and New York: Bloomsbury, 2013), 527.

[21]Bruce Chilton, *Pure Kingdom* (London: SPCK; Grand Rapids: Eerdmans, 1995), x, 1.

[22]E.g., N. T. Wright, *Paul and the Faithfulness of God* (Minneapolis: Fortress; London: SPCK, 2013), 936.

[23]Jörg Frey studies the history of the terminological problem in "New Testament Eschatology," in Jan G. van der Watt, ed., *Eschatology of the New Testament and Some Related Documents* (Tübingen: Mohr, 2011), 3-32.

[24]James D. G. Dunn, *The Theology of Paul the Apostle* (Grand Rapids and Cambridge, UK: Eerdmans, 1998), 308, 309.

[25]Ralph P. Martin, *Philippians* (repr., London: Marshall; Grand Rapids: Eerdmans, 1980), 76.

Apocalyptic

The problematic status of the word *eschatology* makes Beker prefer to speak in terms of apocalyptic, but he seems not to notice an irony when he goes on to comment that apocalyptic, too, "has always been a very 'foggy' notion in biblical scholarship."[26] He himself defines apocalyptic as centrally involving

- historical dualism
- universal-cosmic scope
- imminent expectation of the end of the world[27]

This definition further discourages use of the term, since only in carefully defined if not severely qualified senses could one say that either Testament affirms historical dualism, universal-cosmic scope and imminent expectation of the end of the world.

Elsewhere, apocalyptic has been said to involve

1. an understanding of history as structured according to a divinely determined pattern of crisis, judgment and vindication; and
2. the revelation of divine mysteries concerning what is above, below, behind and in front.[28]

To that definition I would say one has to add

3. the use of exotic imagery to portray these mysteries.

In everyday usage, however, *apocalyptic* commonly suggests terrible destruction, disaster and gloom. In extraordinary contrast, J. H. Yoder simply asserts, "The point that apocalyptic makes . . . is that people who bear crosses are working with the grain of the universe."[29]

A scholar who emphasizes apocalyptic speaks of "Paul's understanding of the word 'apocalyptic.'"[30] But *apocalyptic* is an English word, and it has no

---

[26]Beker, *Paul the Apostle*, xv.

[27]Ibid., xv, 136.

[28]For these two, see the discussion in Andrew Chester, *Future Hope and Present Reality* (Tübingen: Mohr, 2012), 1:81-90. Christopher Rowland, in *The Open Heaven* (London: SPCK; New York: Crossroad, 1982), puts the emphasis on the second feature, the revelatory aspect suggested by the word's etymology rather than on the content of the revelation.

[29]J. H. Yoder, "Armaments and Eschatology," *Studies in Christian Ethics* 1 (1988): 43-61 (on 58); cf. Stanley Hauerwas, *With the Grain of the Universe* (Grand Rapids: Baker, 2001), 4.

[30]Michael J. Gorman, *Reading Paul* (Eugene, OR: Cascade, 2008), 64.

Greek equivalent that Paul could have used. When Paul uses the verb *apokalyptō* and the noun *apokalypsis*, they don't refer to apocalyptic in any of the common uses of that English word. There is no such thing as Paul's understanding of apocalyptic. The Scriptures do not talk about "apocalyptic" any more than about "eschatology," and most scholarly use of either term must be misleading because it is contradicted by other scholarly use.

Once again, behind the terminological point there is a substantial one, related to the substantial point about eschatology. The further the scriptural writers move away from their present, the more figurative they become. God did not give them much hard information about the future, as he did not give them much hard information about the past beyond what they could discover for themselves. We cannot work out from the various scriptural descriptions of creation what we would have seen if we'd been present, and we cannot work out what we will see on the Day of the Lord from the various scriptural descriptions of it. With regard to the Beginning and the End, God gives us accounts in pictures and images, which have the virtue of being instructive, edifying and intelligible as long as we don't treat them as sources for information they don't provide.

8.2 A NEW AGE AND A NEW WORLD

While the sharp antitheses implied in some uses of the words *eschatology* and *apocalyptic* are misleading, the Scriptures do work with antitheses between this age and the age to come, and between this world and the world to come. They also presuppose related antitheses, between this age and the age that is lost, and between this world and the world that is lost. In each case there is overlap between the ages and the worlds. God has brought in the new age, which brings the implementing of his original intention for the world, promises its final implementing, and makes it possible to live in expectancy because we already experience something of that new age.

New World

Biblical theology ends with God creating a new heaven and a new earth (Rev 21–22). Why would God do so? While there was clearly something wrong with the inhabitants of the original heaven and earth, was there something wrong with the heaven and earth themselves? If so, what was it, and wherein lies the newness of the new ones? Answering the last question helps to answer the others. The first hint lies in the absence of sea in the new cosmos (Rev 21:2). In the Scriptures, the sea is often the embodiment or symbol of tumultuous power asserted against God. The four grotesque animals that stood for the four superpowers, the oppressors of God's people, emerged from the sea (Dan 7:3). Further, in the new world there will be no more murderers, spiritists, perverts and the like (Rev 21:8).

A new heaven and earth are needed, then, because the present heaven and earth are affected by resistance to God and by the oppression of people. The present earth is defiled by its inhabitants' activities (Is 24:5). The new heaven and earth will be ones where righteousness dwells (2 Pet 3:13), in two respects. Human righteousness will dwell there; more fundamentally, so will God's righteousness, the righteousness that denotes "God's reestablishing his sovereignty over the world."[31] That notion brings with it the implication that God's sovereignty means his faithfulness, his *mišpāṭ ûṣĕdāqâ* or faithful exercise of authority. The key motifs of "apocalyptic" are "anchored in the even-more-central motif of the faithfulness of God."[32]

In the new world God will wipe away all tears and abolish death; there will be no more mourning, crying or pain (Rev 21:4). Whereas the present world is characterized by conflict and war, by persecution and martyrdom, these will be abolished in the new world. Revelation may also assume the abolition of suffering through illness and of death through old age, but the suffering on which it focuses is those humanly caused kinds of suffering, which are also the focus in scriptures that inspired Revelation (see Is 25:6-10; Dan 11:33–12:3).

In the new world there will be no temple (Rev 21:22). God had never intended that there should be a temple. He liked being on the move, and he could speak, act and be present anywhere (2 Sam 7), and God's spirit had been present and active in Israel as a whole, not just in a particular place. But David wanted to build a temple, and God gave in to his idea. God subsequently sought to undo this development by making his Spirit also

---

[31]Martinus C. de Boer, "Paul's Mythologizing Program in Romans 5–8," in Beverly Roberts Gaventa, ed., *Apocalyptic Paul* (Waco, TX: Baylor University Press, 2013), 1-20 (on 6), summarizing Ernst Käsemann, *New Testament Questions of Today* (London: SCM Press; Philadelphia: Westminster, 1969), 168-82.

[32]Beker, *Paul the Apostle*, xv. Cf. Käsemann, *New Testament Questions of Today*, 180.

present in the congregation of believers, but we have noted how in due course these congregations, too, felt the need of sanctuaries, and they built churches and cathedrals. In the new world, the temple is "the Lord God Almighty and the Lamb."

In the new world there will be a new city, a holy city, a new Jerusalem. As the present earth is one defiled by its inhabitants, so the present Jerusalem is one trampled by the nations. There would be nothing wrong in itself with Gentiles being there; Gentiles as such had never been banned from Jerusalem. The problem is that these are unbelieving and oppressive Gentiles. The city is one where believers get martyred, one that is spiritually called Sodom and Egypt; it is the city where Jesus was crucified (Rev 11:8). The vision of Revelation also knows of another great and powerful city, one that is whore-like (Rev 18:10); that imperial city, too, will be destroyed and replaced.

The close association of the new Jerusalem and the new heaven and earth follows the collocation of these images in Isaiah 65:17-25. That prophecy's opening reference to creating a new heavens and a new earth could make one think in terms of a new physical cosmos, but the prophecy immediately goes on to speak of creating Jerusalem as a joy. The new creation *is* the new Jerusalem. The prophecy's subsequent description of this new Jerusalem fits with that inference. It pictures life in the new city in terms that will indeed be taken up in Revelation. There won't be weeping or crying there; babies won't die in infancy (a revolutionary promise in a premodern society), and old people won't fail to live out their days (without their being compromised by Alzheimers, one might add); people will build houses and live in them, and plant orchards and eat their fruit, rather than have them destroyed by invaders and rather than failing to live long enough to enjoy them. Even the animate world will live in harmony.

New Earth

Revelation "had not lost faith in history as the sphere of divine redemption."[33] It "brings the story of God with his people and the world to its grand finale. . . . It anticipates a great ending, a world in which the leaves of the trees are for the healing of the nations, where God wipes away every tear

---

[33]Cf. Rowland, *Open Heaven*, 435.

from every eye, where human beings dwell together in harmony with each other and with their God, worshiping God alone."[34] It will be "the greatest of Sabbaths; a Sabbath that has no evening. . . . There we shall have leisure to be still, and we shall see that he is God."[35]

The impression one gains from Revelation 21–22 and from Isaiah 65 is that the triumph of God takes place in a material new heavens and earth. It is the picture one would have expected on the basis of Genesis. The consummation does not take place in a nonphysical world. That inference fits the fact that the people who will live in the new Jerusalem are people with resurrected bodies, not people who are simply spirits. Their bodies will be spiritual in the sense of Spirit dominated, but as bodies they will need to be somewhere material. "Heaven is important but it is not the end of the world."[36]

The New Testament does see believers as given great blessings in Jesus in the heavens, but they have those already (e.g., Eph 1:3). They do have an inheritance kept safe for them in the heavens (1 Pet 1:3-5). In the heavens they have a house that belongs to the new age, a house that will be given to them after they surrender the house they presently inhabit (2 Cor 5:1-5). Their citizenship is in the heavens, from which Jesus will come to transform their lowly bodies to make them like his glorious body (Phil 3:20-21). They are looking for a heavenly country, but it is a heavenly *country*, where God has prepared a *city* for them (Heb 11:13-16). At the end of Revelation, the holy city comes out of heaven to earth (Rev 21:1-2). There is an intrinsic link between what God is doing and preparing for believers in heaven now and what he will do for them in the new world, but their destiny is a heaven on earth.

It's been said that believers from the fourth century on understood their churches to be outposts, embassies of the New Jerusalem on earth. Their physical beauty and glory was offered to God in praise and to their communities to give a vision of the Homeland, the New Jerusalem scheduled for the

---

[34]Marianne Meye Thompson, "Reading What Is Written in the Book of Life," in Richard B. Hays and Stefan Alkier, eds., *Revelation and the Politics of Apocalyptic Interpretation* (Waco, TX: Baylor University Press, 2012), 155-71 (on 171).

[35]Augustine, *City of God* 22.30.

[36]N. T. Wright, "Revelation and Christian Hope," in Hays and Alkier, *Revelation and the Politics of Apocalyptic Interpretation*, 105-24 (on 106).

end of time. On Sunday, Christians worshipped on home territory. There they were refreshed and restored. There they learned the principles of the New Jerusalem. There they learned God's structure for a healthy culture, a healthy world. When they left, they sought to put those principles into practice. They built almshouses for the poor, hospitals for the sick, schools for the ignorant, and beautiful churches filled with art and music to bear witness to the glory and the beauty of God and our eventual home.[37]

"The basic idea which influenced the form of the medieval cathedral down to its smallest details was that of the earthly copy of the glorious heavenly city." Such buildings were fashioned "to create a visible image of the nature of the church" as "man's heavenly home into which he may even now in the present enter."[38] The church building "reestablishes what had been in paradise and what will be in the Kingdom of God."[39]

New Life

John says of the divine mind/message, "What came into being through it/ him was life" (Jn 1:3-4). But much that came into being through the mind/ message at the Beginning had life only temporarily. God's intention had been that humanity should enjoy lasting life by eating from the life tree, but that intention was not realized.

Through the rest of the First Testament it is as if people have forgotten that God ever had this intention. A positive result is that the First Testament takes this life really seriously. There is no danger of its falling into the trap of thinking that "this world is not my home, I'm just a-passing through." But through Jesus, God's original intention can be realized. People start enjoying eternal life, the life of the age to come, in this life. Even now one can be "a sharer in the glory that is going to be revealed" (1 Pet 5:1).[40]

It's said that Jesus exercises a "preferential option for the poor." If we assume the usual meaning of the word *poor*, there is little evidence that he

---

[37]Roberta Green Ahmanson, "Dreams Become Reality," *Books and Culture* 21, no. 1 (2015): 18-20 (on 18).

[38]Mathias Rissi, *The Future of the World* (London: SCM Press; Naperville, IL: Allenson, 1972), 41.

[39]Leonid Ouspensky (*Theology of the Icon* [Crestwood, NY: St. Vladimir's Seminary Press, 1992], 26) attributes this statement to seventh-century theologian Maximus the Confessor in "*Mystagogy*, chs. 8-21, PG 91: 672," but this reference seems to be incorrect, and I have not been able to find the words that he quotes.

[40]Some translations have "will share," but there are no future-tense verbs in the context.

did so. There is more to the comment if we redefine the poor as the down-trodden and oppressed, the people who do not count, the "non-persons."[41] Solidarity with them is then set over against solidarity with the state or its organs. It is a solidarity with the powerless and the silenced rather than the powerful.[42]

For Jesus, it is the Jewish people as a whole who are the poor and powerless, and he indeed identifies with them. He does also exercise a preferential option for the sick and the demonized. The Gospels tell story after story about his healing and exorcising; he has a hard time resisting a sick or demonized person. His action then anticipates resurrection day. The End will be "not the triumph of destruction and nothingness but the *healing of the world*."[43] His preferential option will operate in fullness.

Our present life as believers is characterized by conflict and struggle. What wretched people we are! We need to be rescued from our present bodily existence that is afflicted by sin and is on its way to death. And we will be rescued (Rom 7:24-25). Even now, as another strange aspect of our conflictedness, while we are distraught at how things are we can at the same time be at peace and thankful because we know that the situation is temporary. The promise is not that God is going to rescue us from our bodily existence; rather our bodily existence is to be transformed. The day of resurrection will come. Our body will be redeemed (Rom 8:23). While we still have to experience death, the Spirit of God who raised Jesus from death is involved with us, which means that God will give life to our mortal bodies through that same Spirit's association with us (Rom 8:10-11).

When the Scriptures speak of the end coming (e.g., Mk 13:7), they do not refer to an end after which there will be nothing, but to the beginning of something new, like "final" exams that lead into "commencement," the

---

[41]So Gustavo Gutiérrez, *Essential Writings* (Maryknoll, NY: Orbis, 1996), 144-45; Gutiérrez, *A Theology of Liberation* (Maryknoll, NY: Orbis, 1973; London: SCM Press, 1974), 301; cf. Gutiérrez, "Option for the Poor," in Jon Sobrino and Igancio Ellacuría, eds., *Mysterium Liberationis* (Maryknoll, NY: Orbis, 1993), 235-50 = *Systematic Theology* (Maryknoll, NY: Orbis, 1996), 22-37.

[42]So Tinyiko Maluleke, "Black Theology as Public Discourse," www.religion.uct.ac.za/sites /default/files/image_tool/images/113/Institutes/Religion_in_Public_Life_ME_1999/Concep_Pa pers/Tinyiko_Maluleke.pdf. Quoted in Gerald O. West, "Liberation Hermeneutics After Liberation," in Alejandro F. Botta and Pablo R. Andiñach, eds., *The Bible and the Hermeneutics of Liberation* (Atlanta: SBL, 2009), 13-38 (on 23).

[43]Rissi, *Future of the World*, 17.

beginning of the life for which people have been preparing. When the Twelve sit on their thrones judging Israel's twelve clans (Mt 19:28), it will not be a one-time final judgment but their having the ongoing role of exercising authority and helping the community come to decisions on tricky questions. Everything is made new, Jesus is enthroned, they are ruling: it belongs to an ongoing future age.

Two Arcs

Both Isaiah 65 and Revelation 21–22 constitute the end of arcs that begin in Genesis 1. Both look back to the way God originally created "the heavens and the earth." Both imply the awareness that God's creation purpose did not find fulfillment. Humanity did not subdue earth's creatures as God commissioned but gave in to an idea from one of these creatures. In succeeding chapters of Genesis, conflict, pain and warfare follow. Isaiah and Revelation both promise the triumph of God and the triumph of God's original plan.

Yet the Scriptures also indicate that the route whereby God's purpose finds fulfillment is more complex than might by implied by talk of arcs. The journey from departure point to destination makes several stops on the way. The kangaroo hop from starting point to finishing point involves a series of leaps. The nature of history is to be essentially shifting and irregular, and the nature of God's activity in it is to be intermittent and punctiliar. Wars and disasters and also times of blessing and advancement are recurrent rather than continuous (Eccles 3:1-15 notes the puzzling aspect to this fact). The story of God's fulfilling his purpose is a journey on which the stops along the way matter, even though these are also stops along a way that is going somewhere. The stages in the story that links Genesis, Isaiah and Revelation cohere with the beginning and ending of these arcs.

Following on the troubled story of earth's beginnings, Genesis 12–50 relates how God declares the intention to kick-start another approach to fulfilling the original purpose. God promises Abraham land, increase and blessing, the realities of which the creation story spoke. The promises apply immediately to Abraham and his kin group but make explicit that all nations are to find the same blessing through their fulfillment for this kin group.

For some of Abraham's descendants, the promise starts becoming reality in the story that follows. Jacob's family becomes a numerous people in Egypt.

Then by delivering Israel from Egypt and taking them into Canaan, Yahweh brings about a further stage in the implementing of his promise. Israel moves from the age of promise to the age of fulfillment, and the book of Joshua affirms that all God's promises have been fulfilled. Yet it also makes explicit that the old age continues. God has not made it possible for Israel to possess the entire country, and they are people who make mistakes. In the time of the Judges the story takes significant steps backwards.

Saul, David and Solomon mark another transition from an old age, in which everyone did what was right in their own eyes and in which Israel was assailed by the Philistines and other foes, into a new age in which kings can do something about such questions. But again the old age continues into the new age, and again the story takes steps backward when Israel splits into two nations and experiences reversals and moral and religious erosion.

The hope of real fulfillment remains alive and comes to be conceptualized as "Yahweh's Day." By Amos's time, Yahweh's Day is an established hope in Israel, an expectation of a time when Yahweh's purpose will be fulfilled and Israel will know fullness of blessing. Amos turns this idea upside down in transforming Yahweh's Day into an occasion of gloom and judgment for Israel, not just for other peoples (Amos 5:18-20). Because of Ephraim's faithlessness, Yahweh's Day will be darkness, not light; trouble, not blessing. The people will be decimated and the land lost. The threat comes true in the successive catastrophes of Ephraim's fall to Assyria and Judah's fall to Babylon. Yes, the dark version of Yahweh's Day has arrived (Lam 1:12; 2:1, 21, 22).

Yet the idea of such a day of fulfillment and blessing was not wrong, and later Scriptures endorse it. Even while people are grieving over that dark reality, Ezekiel is promising that God will restore his people. We have noted that Ezekiel's promises constitute restatements of those promises that go back to Abraham, as supplemented by the promises to David about his line and about the temple and city.[44] Ezekiel pictures God bringing back to life the nation that feels like a corpse and that arguably is a corpse.

The restoration of the community after the exile constitutes a partial fulfillment of the promise of a new age. But prophets such as Haggai, Zechariah

---

[44]See the paragraphs headed "Visionary" in section 2.2 above.

and Malachi, and the story told in Ezra–Nehemiah, show how the old age once again continues. It is in this context that Isaiah 65 makes its promise of a new heavens and a new earth, one embodied in a new Jerusalem. It thereby indicates both that Yahweh's original purpose is still not fulfilled and that it will be fulfilled.

Yet nothing much happens in that connection over the next several centuries. In the context of the great persecution by Antiochus Epiphanes during the 160s, the visions in Daniel again promise that the new age is about to begin, and these visions are proved true by a deliverance that confounds all the odds. The Jerusalem community gets another new start. Yet once again the old age continues.

The triumph of God will come only when the arc finds completion, when the original heavens and earth reach their destiny in the new heavens and the new earth.

The New Age

The coming of Jesus brings the most far-reaching introduction of the new age. A first glance might make one infer that the New Testament simply relates the actual arrival of the new day to which the First Testament looks forward. The fullness of time has come (Gal 4:4). "The climax of the divine drama" is here.[45] "The decisive eschatological climax has already come in the death and resurrection of Jesus."[46] Jesus "gave himself for our sins so that he might remove us from the present evil age" (Gal 1:4).

The New Testament thus begins by tracing the background of Jesus' birth in a line that runs from Abraham to David, from David to the exile and from the exile to Jesus (Mt 1:1-17). His coming means the climax of that sequence of promises to Abraham, promises to David and promises in the context of exile. Gabriel tells Mary that her son will take David's throne and reign over the household of Jacob forever (Lk 1:33). Simeon realizes that his eyes have seen the deliverance for Israel that God has prepared in the sight of all nations, a light for revelation to the Gentiles and the glory of Israel (Lk 2:29-32). While Jesus' execution looked like another mighty step backwards, his resurrection reverses that impression. It leads to the pouring out of the Holy Spirit

---

[45]Gorman, *Reading Paul*, 58.
[46]James D. G. Dunn, "In Search of Common Ground," in Dunn, ed., *Paul and the Mosaic Law* (Tübingen: Mohr, 1996), 309-34 (on 328).

on the believing community, which constitutes the fulfillment of that promise to Abraham (Gal 3:14).

Thus John's vision of a new heaven and a new earth pictures the new Jerusalem coming down out of heaven from God (Rev 21:2). While John may be seeing something that is wholly future, it fits the way the Scriptures elsewhere speak if we rather understand him to be seeing something that is happening now in the life of the congregation and the world. This is "a future which interpenetrates and informs the present," a reality "in the anticipatory experience of the church." The new Jerusalem "descends out of heaven from God not only before and after the millennium, but wherever the martyr wins his crown" (Rev 3:12; 19:7; 21:2, 10).[47] It fits with the idea that the Day of Yahweh or the new age is not only something coming in the future. The Day of Yahweh happens now; the new age has already started.

Jesus' coming, his execution, his resurrection and his pouring out of the Spirit have initiated it. Yes, the new age has come, overcoming the "radical disjunction between the present age and the age to come":[48] between this age and the coming age (*erchomenos*; Mk 10:30) or this age and the future age (*mellōn*; Mt 12:32; Eph 1:21) or this age and that age (Lk 20:34-35). The New Testament makes other references simply to "this age" (Lk 16:8; 1 Cor 1:20; 2:6, 8; 3:18; 2 Cor 4:4), "the present age" (Gal 1:4), "the now age"(2 Tim 4:10; Tit 2:12), "the future" (*to mellōn*; 1 Tim 6:19), "the end of the age" (Mt 13:39-40, 49; 28:20), "the coming ages" (*eperchomenos*; Eph 2:7) and "the end of the ages" (1 Cor 10:11).[49]

Yet these references make clear that the new age also remains future and that "this age" continues. After Jesus' resurrection, Peter in his second sermon speaks of a time still to come when God will bring about the

---

[47]G. B. Caird, *A Commentary on the Revelation of St. John the Divine* (London: Black; New York: Harper, 1966), 263, 301. Caird was my first and best teacher in New Testament theology, and I am proud to have attended the same high school in Birmingham, England, as Caird and as B. F. Westcott, J. B. Lightfoot and C. F. Evans (I know of no famous Old Testament scholars who went there, though).

[48]Gorman, *Reading Paul*, 58.

[49]J. Christiaan Beker comments that Paul does not talk in terms of this age and the age to come (*Paul the Apostle*, 145); the observation is true only on a fairly minimalist understanding of what counts as Paul, but in any case (as Beker goes on to note), the language occurs elsewhere in the New Testament.

restoration (*apokatastasis*) of everything in accordance with the Prophets' promises (Acts 3:21-22); it remains future. Whereas creation groans because it is in bondage to decay, it will reach its destiny and share in the freedom and splendor of God's children (Rom 8:19-23); it has not yet reached that point. Freedom belongs in the future as well as in the present. Redemption can refer to what Jesus has already achieved by his death (Rom 3:24; 1 Cor 1:30; Col 1:14; Heb 9:15); it can also refer to something that lies in the future (Lk 21:28; Eph 1:14; 4:30).

The New Testament's account of the life and experience of the congregations it describes, in Acts, in the Epistles and in Revelation, makes clear that the old age continues there. Its account thus coheres with the First Testament pattern of promise and partial fulfillment, of the arrival of the new age but the persistence of the old age. Whereas Jesus' resurrection means he is exalted as Lord, it is "the beginning of the resurrection":[50] the period after his resurrection and after Pentecost is one in which the ages overlap and stand in tension. Raising us from death to life with Jesus will demonstrate the riches of God's grace in the coming ages (Eph 2:7). While it is real and partly visible now, it will then be more clearly manifest. At the moment we need gifts such as prophecy and tongues, but "then" we will know as fully as we have been known (cf. Jer 31:34). Eternal life is to know God (Jn 17:3); at the moment we do know but in fragmentary ways (the postmodern insight is right about the fragmentary nature of our knowledge, even though it is true knowledge).

The Past Age, the Present Age, the Coming Age

In a dark sense, an overlap between ages begins when the first human beings are told that they will die on the day they eat from the good-and-bad-knowledge tree rather than the life tree. While they do not die at that point, their lives are spoiled, and they do die nine hundred years or so later. There is a radical disjunction between Eden and life east of Eden. Their action leads to a transition from one age to another, a transition from a good first age to what can now be called the present age.

The Scriptures do not indicate that creation's purpose was fulfilled in any way at the Beginning. It does not give any indication that for a while

---

[50]George Eldon Ladd, *A Theology of the New Testament* (Grand Rapids: Eerdmans, 1974), 332 (rev. ed., 368).

humanity lived in a good relationship with God, with one another or with the world. For all we know, humanity's temptation and disobedience happened five minutes after creation.

But there is an overlap between the age of creation and the present age. While unguardedly we may describe the first human beings' relationship with God as being broken through sin, actually they are not out of relationship with God (see, e.g., Gen 4:1, 4, 23), though the relationship is not what it was intended to be. The move is not simply from light into darkness but from light into light mingled with darkness.

As there is an overlap between the creation age and the present age, there is an overlap between the coming age and the present age. There is a real initiating of the new age, but the old age continues. The old has passed away, the new has come (2 Cor 5:17; 6:2); but the life of the congregation to which Paul writes those words shows particularly clearly that things are more complicated than the words sound. In isolation, Paul's statement is an exaggeration or oversimplification parallel to Joshua's declaration that all God's promises have been fulfilled. Both Paul and Joshua show that they recognize this fact by the other statements that they make.

In due course God will resolve the tension between the ages. Sovereignty over the world has become the sovereignty of God and of the Anointed One through Jesus' execution and resurrection (Rev 11:15); it will become complete at the End. "To live during the overlap of the ages is to live in a time of great fulfillment and yet also great anticipation."[51]

The pattern within both Testaments helps one make sense of the passing of two thousand years since Jesus, during which the old age has been alive and well in the church as well as in the world. As Abraham and his family saw a partial realization of their promises but in some ways things went backwards, and as they sometimes brought trouble rather than blessing to people, so the church sees a partial realization of God's promises but also sees things going backwards, and sometimes brings people trouble rather than blessing. We live in the present age, but the past age overlaps with this present age; and we live in the present age, but the coming age overlaps with this present age.

---

[51]Gorman, *Reading Paul*, 63.

An engaged couple continue to live as single people, but they experience something of the commitment, security, love and closeness that will be more thoroughly characteristic of their married state. As a result of Jesus' death and resurrection, it is possible to live in the age to come as well as in this age, and the church experiences something of the freedom from self-centeredness and from suffering that will characterize the world to come. We are on our way to completion (*teleiōsis*) or sanctification. Our reaching completion is guaranteed because Jesus has already got there and has thereby defeated the power of death (Heb 2:9-10). He is thus the one who brings our faith to completion (Heb 12:2).

Heaven and earth as a whole are affected by the relationship between the two ages. In the present age Jesus has not put down all his enemies, in heaven or on earth, but the age to come will be characterized by a unity of commitment to God in heaven and on earth. Pending this consummation, when God will be "all in all" (1 Cor 15:25-28), both this world and the heavenly world are affected by rebellion against God. Jesus' death and resurrection brought about a victory over the rebellious powers in the heavenly realm that anticipates the final consummation. Jesus has broken the power of the rulers "of this age." Yet paradoxically, this introduces or magnifies tension in the relationship of believers with heavenly realities.

We pray for God's name to be hallowed, for God's reign to be a reality, and for God's will to be done, "as in heaven also on earth" (Mt 6:9-10). Maybe the implication is that God's will is done in heaven now, but the New Testament elsewhere raises a question about that inference. Either way, our task is to urge God to bring about that earthly hallowing, reigning and obedience.

Abolitionist Theodore Parker declared his faith that the arc of the moral universe "bends towards justice,"[52] and Martin Luther King and Barack Obama have repeated his conviction. The Scriptures give no hint that the situation in the world will improve over time, and no suggestion that efforts by disciples to further God's kingdom will be effective in that connection. The most they might seek and hope for is some holding back of the forces of deception and oppression. Any statement of faith in the arc of the moral universe has to be a statement of faith in God.

---

[52]Theodore Parker, *Ten Sermons of Religion*, 48, repr. in *The Collected Works of Theodore Parker*, vol. 2 (London: Trübner, 1879).

Expectancy

"The day is almost here" (Rom 13:12). Maybe Paul expected that the Day would come in his lifetime, but wisely he does not say so. The fact that the Day would be chronologically more than nineteen hundred years distant from his day does not undermine his line of reasoning when he speaks about it. His argument is not explicitly christological, and it may be implicitly theological, as is the case in most of Romans 12–16. He is saying the same thing that the Prophets said when they spoke in light of the certain coming of Yahweh's Day. God has decided that the Day is coming; therefore its coming is as good as here. And God's people should live in light of that fact. Indeed, there is little in what Paul says that a Jew who did not believe in Jesus would dispute. In speaking in terms of two ages, this age and the age to come, the New Testament speaks in a similar way to other strands of Second Temple Judaism.[53] And in speaking of fulfillment now while also needing to recognize that God has much more to do, Paul speaks in the same way as Joshua.

Obviously Paul's readers are nearer to that day than they were when they first came to believe in Jesus (Rom 13:11). The fact that the day is coming means they should not live as if it were night, when sleep is appropriate and when carousing, immorality and infighting are more common than they are in daylight. Believers can wear the clothes of people who belong in the darkness (go about looking and behaving like them). Or they can wear the protective armor of people who belong in the light and want to be visibly identified with the right side in the final battle between God and the forces of evil. The protective armor consists in the lifestyle Jesus went in for; we are destined to share his image, and it is thus appropriate for us to start manifesting it now (Rom 13:12-14; cf. Rom 8:29). The lifestyle will be the one Paul has been describing: ministering for the benefit of others rather than oneself, hating evil, being generous and hospitable, sharing in the joys and sorrows of other people.

At the end of a gargantuan chapter on the resurrection, Paul does not draw the inference that his readers can now sit back and relax because they know God has a great future for them. Rather he urges them therefore to

---

[53]See Richard N. Longenecker, *Galatians* (Dallas: Word, 1990), 8-9.

abound in the Lord's work because their labor is not in vain (1 Cor 15:58).[54] Looking forward to the End and to Jesus' appearing does not make people lose concern for this world and this life. If anything, it adds urgency to the pursuit of love and mutual service. After all, "the end of history was only a mission away."[55] It also generates a tolerance of ambiguity and a longing for the time when creation's groaning and longing will be fulfilled. And it "excludes all possibility of compromising the radical demands of discipleship."[56]

"Existence in faith . . . is a movement between 'no longer' and 'not yet.'"[57] It involves the decision of faith because people have to keep putting the past behind them and because the future remains future even though with Jesus it has already occurred. Knowledge is significant for the exercise and development of this faith—especially knowing the significance of what Jesus did.

There is thus a trust that relates to the final consummation of God's purpose and also a trust that relates to the lot of individuals. It is the latter trust that is tested and affirmed in different ways in the Psalms and in Job and Ecclesiastes. Faith or trust is thus not simply a mental attitude or an act that initiates our relationship with God but a stance that we keep taking in different situations that confront us. Each time we are faced by some need or challenge, we approach it in trust. We live our fleshly lives by trust in the Son of God (Gal 2:20). And trust then expresses itself in love (Gal 5:6). Such is the form that life takes when we are living between "no longer" and "not yet." And it takes individual form in the exercise of the gifts of grace God gives us.

Hopefulness

"Trust is the substantiation of things that are hoped for and the proof for things that are not seen." It means being certain about things that are present but that one cannot see, and being confident about things that are certain but are not present (Heb 11:1; a long list of examples then illustrates its dynamic). Trust operating in connection with the future is thus hope or expectancy. We do not have to make anything happen; we can wait for

---

[54]Cf. N. T. Wright, *Surprised by Hope* (London: SPCK, 2007; New York: HarperOne, 2008), 192.
[55]Dunn, *Theology of Paul the Apostle*, 311, 312.
[56]Richard B. Hays, *The Moral Vision of the New Testament* (San Francisco: Harper, 1996), 21-27, 87.
[57]Bultmann, *Theology of the New Testament*, 1:322, and pages 322-27 for what follows.

it expectantly.[58] The followers of Jesus are people who "anticipate the revelation of our Lord Jesus" (1 Cor 1:7). They "can't wait" for it. There may be some irony about Paul's comment, if the Corinthians are actually so thrilled with what God is doing now that in reality they are not so anticipating.[59] In an odd way they resemble modern Christians, for whom Jesus' coming is a doctrine we nominally accept rather than an event for which we cannot wait.

In contrast, the Colossians' trust in Jesus and their love for all the saints are realities "through the hope stored up for them in the heavens" (Col 1:5). They know that God's purpose for the world will be achieved and that they are going to see it; this fact is motivation for life now, particularly in contexts where things in the world look hopeless and believers cannot do anything about them. The reason they believe and love is then not that as a consequence they will be granted what they hope for; rather, the fact that they will see what they hope for provides the warrant for the exercise of trust and love now. And joy is a fruit of the Spirit because it also issues from the knowledge that God's purpose is going to be brought to completion. I'm about to die, and that could seem to shatter everything, Jesus says. Trust God and trust me[60] that this is going to make things work out; it's not going to stop them working out (Jn 14:1).

Waiting is the attitude of hope. The Israelites were to be people who waited for God—continually (Hos 12:6 [MT 7]). Hopefulness was to be a feature of the life of Israel, of the individual, and of the world. It is a prominent motif in Proverbs and Job, even if Job spends much time wondering whether hope is possible. Hope for the world emerges from the fact that God has undertaken to keep it in being despite its rebelliousness.[61] Thus hope is not an attitude that human beings summon up from inside themselves but an attitude that responds rationally to facts about God: that God has a long-standing purpose for his people, that he is characterized by grace and

---

[58]Barth, *CD* IV, 3, ii:667, 668.

[59]Cf. Anthony C. Thiselton, "Realized Eschatology at Corinth," *New Testament Studies* 24 (1978): 510-26.

[60]Or perhaps "you trust God and you trust me" or "you trust God; trust me too"; it will make little difference to Jesus' point.

[61]Cf. Walther Zimmerli, *Man and His Hope in the Old Testament* (London: SCM Press; Naperville, IL: Allenson, 1971), in dialogue with Ernst Bloch, *The Principle of Hope*, 3 vols. (Oxford: Blackwell; Cambridge, MA: MIT Press, 1986).

compassion, that he is his people's *gō'ēl*, like the senior member of a family who is willing to use his resources to restore the needy people in the family.

Israel's waywardness means they get into in a mess that they cannot get out of, but God is horrified at the darkness he sees in their experience, and he promises that light is going to dawn in that darkness and then shine brightly upon them. Although he has abandoned his people and his city, he intends to return; they are, after all, his people and his city, and he intends to redeem his property. He's the divine king, and he intends to exercise his authority as king. He's baring his arm, ready to act. He's like someone who has left an unfaithful spouse, but he intends to come back, and the very act of doing so will be the act that has the potential to draw them back to faithfulness and to change them. He's like the physician who knows how to heal someone who is wounded, like an ally who intends to reaffirm the covenant relationship with a party that has betrayed a covenant, like a king who can pardon a rebel. With such acts he can win them into abandoning their alternative objects of hope, trust and worship, and thus banish faithlessness from them and reestablish faithfulness, make their minds pliable instead of rigid and inspire them now to produce the fruit that he had looked for from the beginning.[62]

The knowledge that God is not finished with the world and with us is an important feature of First Testament spirituality. Christians can speak as if Jesus simply fulfilled the First Testament's expectations, which makes it seem to imply that God is now done. After another two thousand years, one would have to ask, "Is that all there is?" for the world and for the community of people that believes in Jesus and for individual believers. The Scriptures invite us into a sure and certain hope that this is not all there is for the world.[63]

8.3 BETWEEN THE END AND THE END

"The end" in the New Testament most often designates the whole period from Jesus to the End that remains still future. But the way the New Testament speaks corresponds to the First Testament dynamic whereby

---

[62]See further *OTT* 2:350-94.
[63]See further *OTT* 3:99-116, with the reference to Kornelis H. Miskotte, *When the Gods Are Silent* (London: Collins; New York: Harper, 1967), 283-88.

prophets declare that the end is near, and an end comes, but it is not *the* End, though it is an interim embodiment of it. "The Biblical writers . . . regularly used end-of-the-world language metaphorically to refer to that which they knew was not the end of the world."[64] Whether or not they did realize that the end of which they spoke would not be the End, such an understanding of the significance of their language fits the way their words find fulfillment. The Day of Yahweh is a day that will come at the End but also a day that happens from time to time. The fall of Jerusalem is that day happening, yet it leaves the End still to come. The End will involve the final fall of the superpower, and in the meantime believers must stand firm in relation to it and even be prepared to recognize that accepting martyrdom may be the way they contribute to its downfall.

The Recurrent Day of Yahweh

When Jesus speaks of "that day" (e.g., Lk 10:12; 21:34), he takes up the expectations of First Testament prophets; Revelation then takes up his prophecy as well as the work of those prophets. Jesus spells out the implications of his prophecy about "that day" in light of First Testament prophecies, in which "that day" is a significant theme. Yahweh's Day receives embodiment in particular events, but after these events, history continues. It turns out to be not the final catastrophe that one might have expected in light of the Prophets' words. *The* End does not come, though *an* end does come.

The fall of Jerusalem in 587 BC is the great example. It is the moment when "you brought about the day you proclaimed" (Lam 1:21), "the day of Yahweh's anger" (Lam 2:22; cf. Lam 1:7, 12; 2:1, 21). The Prophets, Jesus, Revelation and other New Testament writers talk in terms of final destruction and final consummation, and it does not come, but their warnings and promises receive interim fulfillments.

So God's wrath is a reality of the present, and it will be a reality of the future; it is expressed in ongoing history and at the End. The promise that God will reverse such catastrophes and restore Israel on "that day" also finds recurrent fulfillment (e.g., Is 49:8); this fulfillment, too, is not the final consummation of blessing. "The day of the Lord . . . is both an historical

---

[64]George B. Caird, *The Language and Imagery of the Bible* (London: Duckworth; Philadelphia: Westminster, 1980), 256; cf. Thiselton, *Hermeneutics of Doctrine*, 550.

visitation of God and an eschatological act."[65] A frightening possibility then arises. As we assume that the final consummation of blessing will be not worth comparing with the blessing we experience now, perhaps the final expression of wrath will also vastly outclass any experience of wrath that we experience now.[66]

One reason why the catastrophe is never final is that it combines what we might call judgment or punishment with what we might call chastisement or correction. While the Scriptures do not give the impression that judgment is always an expression of love, calamity can be an expression of God's mercy as well as of God's wrath. The catastrophe of which the Prophets speak always leaves in existence some leftovers (a "remnant"), and the same is true in respect of Jesus' declarations about calamity coming on his people. Revelation talks in terms of a total destruction, but it wouldn't be surprising if the same pattern continued. God's bark is usually worse than his bite, like that of a mother toward her children.

In one of his most extensive pieces of teaching (Mt 24; Mk 13; Lk 22), Jesus gives a frightening description of catastrophes that are to come on the earth. He begins by declaring that the entire temple complex will be destroyed. In theory it might be "just one of those things," the kind of catastrophe that a superpower sometimes brings about. But he has already declared that God will bring disaster on his people because of the rebelliousness that comes to a climax with their failing to recognize him, and this warning in itself would imply that the coming disaster is God's act of judgment.

In part his vision is fulfilled in the fall of Jerusalem in AD 70, but the fact that I am writing this book and you are reading it indicates that it was not wholly fulfilled then. With hindsight we can see pointers in Jesus' description toward a distinction between the events that are soon to take place and the events associated with "that day or hour" (Mk 13:32). Indeed, there has turned out to be quite a sharp chronological disjunction between the fall of Jerusalem and "that day or hour," though Jesus' own words in Mark 13, at least, do not make that disjunction very explicit. In light of the

---

[65]George Eldon Ladd, *The Gospel of the Kingdom* (Grand Rapids: Eerdmans; Exeter, UK: Paternoster, 1959), 36.
[66]I owe this suggestion to Kathleen Scott Goldingay.

way things turned out, we can see that events associated with the Roman destruction of Jerusalem in AD 70 belong to the events that are soon to take place, but this horrifying event was not the End. The End would still lie in the future.

The Fall of Jerusalem and the End

When Jesus speaks in a way that doesn't make a clear distinction between events associated with the coming destruction of the temple and the final consummation of God's purpose, which is still future in the twenty-first century, he speaks like other Prophets, and his prophecy portrays catastrophe, judgment and salvation in a way that takes up elements in those earlier Prophets.

Luke's version of the prophecy makes the distinction more explicit. The desolating of Jerusalem will mean that "the days of redress" have come on the city (Lk 21:22).[67] While the expression "days of redress" corresponds most closely to Hosea's words about a time of punishment for Ephraim (Hos 9:7), it also recalls Jesus' earlier reference to Isaiah 61:1-2 (see Lk 4:18-19). There, the prophet was sent "to proclaim the year of Yahweh's acceptance, the day of our God's redress." In Isaiah the two expressions are in parallelism: restoring Israel and putting down its overlords are two sides of a coin. When Jesus declares that he is taking up and fulfilling (filling out) the commission in Isaiah, he stops after "to proclaim the year of Yahweh's acceptance," which is the period of his ministry. It is not a time of redress for his people or for their overlords. That time will come when the temple is destroyed. It is the event that will bring about "the fulfilling of everything that is written" (Lk 21:22), the phrase that makes one think of the words about redress in Isaiah 61 that Jesus omitted earlier, which are the other part of the "everything."

The disciples have two reactions to Jesus' declaration about the temple's destruction. They want to know when it will come, and they want to know what will be the sign that it is imminent (Mk 13:4). Typically, Jesus insists on reframing the conversation. He will not and cannot respond to the question about timing. The pattern recurs when his disciples ask him after his resurrection whether a restoration of sovereignty to Israel is about to come; his

---

[67]Some translations have "days of vengeance," but this gives a misleading impression.

response is to sidestep the question (Acts 1:6-8). By implication, that restoration will come, but he's not going to talk about when.

In Mark 13, he comes to the matter of a sign only rather later—if what he then offers is indeed "signs." Initially he talks about when the events will not happen and what will not be the signs. People will come in his name and say "I am the one" and will deceive many into believing them. It might be possible to deceive in this way without literally speaking in the name of Jesus; it would count if you were simply projecting yourself as the one who will solve all the world's problems, as if you were "the messianic savior."[68] There will be "wars and reports of wars," earthquakes and famines. Disciples are to expect persecution, arrest and unparalleled distress but to see these experiences as a way the gospel will come to reach the nations. While there is always a temptation to be compliant crowds, false prophets, inconsistent disciples and stupid builders (Mt 7:13-27), here it is the pressure of persecution that leads to apostasy.

Paul, too, speaks of apostasy or religious rebellion (*apostasia*) that has to take place before the Lord's Day comes (2 Thess 2:3). He expects events to follow the pattern of the earlier "apostasy" during the Maccabean crisis (see 1 Maccabees 1–2). It is through many afflictions that we must enter God's realm (Acts 14:22). The pattern also follows the earlier dynamic of the fall of Ephraim and of Judah, where the apostasy resulted in part from politico-religious pressure. "The form of the cross is projected across the picture of world history."[69]

While pain can be simply pain, it can be the sign or even the means of new life. The realities of which Jesus speaks do not herald the End, though they are the beginning of labor pains. But labor can go on for days rather than hours. The pains are a sign that birth is coming but not that it is actually imminent. Wars and natural disasters are not meaningless, nor are they a sign that God is absent. They are a paradoxical guarantee that birth will come, but they are not a sign that it is about to happen. When disciples find themselves overwhelmed by disaster, the appropriate response is neither exaggerated anticipation nor despair nor alarm. They can be calm.

---

[68]M. Eugene Boring, "The Gospel of Matthew," in *The New Interpreter's Bible*, Leander E. Keck et al., eds. (Nashville: Abingdon, 1995), 8:87-505 (on 442).
[69]Lesslie Newbigin, *The Open Secret* (Grand Rapids: Eerdmans; London: SPCK, 1978), 41.

Signs of the End

Alongside persecution and deception will be a religious outrage (Mk 13:14-23), a sacrilege of the kind that happened through Antiochus Epiphanes: the disciples will see "the desolating atrocity standing where it ought not." Jesus takes up an image from Daniel 7–12, where it refers to some scandalous religious object or act introduced into the temple in the Maccabean crisis by the Seleucid ruler of Jerusalem, an image or a form of worship that stood in horrifying conflict with the Torah. Something of this kind will happen again.

Then it will be the moment to run. It will herald a time of terrible affliction. The disciples may at least have confidence that God will not allow the elimination of his chosen people and will therefore not let this distress go on. The crisis will be terrible, but it will be short. It will again be a time to be wary of imposters who claim to be the Anointed One and of prophets who perform signs and miracles of a kind that could even deceive God's chosen people. The signs of the End will be horrifying and extraordinary.

Paul similarly declares that the coming of the Lord's Day has to follow the revealing of "the lawless man," someone who "will oppose and exalt himself over everything that is called God or is an object of worship, so as to seat himself in God's temple" (2 Thess 2:3-4). The language once again takes up the description of Antiochus Epiphanes, who illustrates the kind of person the lawless man will be. He will use signs and wonders to deceive people, and they will perish because they let themselves be deceived. It is a process in which God is involved, as he "sends them a deceptive power that makes them trust in the lie" (2 Thess 2:12). At the moment something holds him back.

Augustine comments that he has no clue what Paul is referring to,[70] and understanding has not moved forward since Augustine's day. The likely reason why things are not clearer is that Paul is working forward from what the Scriptures have said. The same is true of Daniel's visions themselves, of Jesus' prophecy and of Revelation. It is inevitable that there should be the troubles and the horrors that Jesus and Paul describe, but what literal form they will take is another question. Paul's reserve also means we can see his comment fulfilled in the self-assertion of other entities that would otherwise deify themselves.

---

[70]*City of God* 20.19.

Fortunately "the lawless man" is "the person doomed to destruction." When Jesus appears, he will overthrow him by the breath of his mouth, the authoritative word that was the means of creation (Ps 33:6) but can also be the means of destruction (Is 11:4), and he will overpower him by his splendor (2 Thess 2:8).

It makes sense to associate with this picture that emerges from the words of Jesus and Paul the talk in Revelation of a period before the End during which Satan is released—and to associate with it much else in the visions in Revelation. John sees an angel seizing hold of "the dragon, that ancient serpent, who is the devil, or Satan," and imprisoning him for a thousand years (Rev 20:1-3). The "thousand years" will not be a literal figure; elsewhere in the Scriptures a thousand is not a literal number, and Revelation is the last place one expect literalness. The expression suggests a very long time by human standards, though not by God's standards (2 Pet 3:8).

The immediate context does not make clear whether these thousand years will begin at some point in the future or whether they begin with Jesus, but the first idea would imply that Satan is still totally free and able to do as he likes, which clashes with the fact that Jesus has won the victory over him (e.g., Rev 12:7-12). Jesus' ministry, death and resurrection brought about the downfall of Satan: "Now is the judgment of this world. Now the ruler of this world will be thrown out, and when I am lifted up from the earth, I will draw all people to myself" (Jn 12:31-32). During this "thousand-year" period, for which dispensationalism's term "the church age" is quite appropriate, the gospel is preached to the nations, so they are no longer subject to Satan's deceit. But at the end of the church age Satan is released for a short time, as a prelude to the very End, to deceive the nations again and orchestrate a last great attempt to destroy God's people. Yet this liberation will be merely the strategic preliminary and means to the final destruction of all that opposes God.

The Fall of Rome

The political element to this picture links with the way the leader of a superpower turns himself into God (Is 14:3-23; Ezek 28:1-19).[71] Through his agency

---

[71]These prophecies presuppose a myth about a supernatural being who tries to make himself into the top god, but they are not themselves about a fall of Satan; they use this myth to portray the fall of the kings of Babylon and Tyre.

demonic forces exercise overwhelming power and influence (Rev 13). Imperial power rivals God and enables it to kill people who resist. It embraces a deceptiveness that allies with its power, and it provides persuasive evidence that it should be heeded. Yet a voice from heaven declares that people who "die in the Lord" are blessed, and it seems to be they who have "overcome the beast and its image" (Rev 14:13; 15:2). Is the implication that the beast's overcoming them backfires because it is the way it brings about their overcoming of it?

While this domination is a prevailing reality in the time to which Daniel and Revelation speak, it is not always a reality. In the biblical story as a whole, the degree of oppression exercised by imperial powers varies, as is also true in world history. In the twenty-first century, much of the world may see itself as under the domination of the West and Russia, and see them as under the domination of the deceptiveness of the second beast (Rev 13). China or Islamic powers may follow. The challenge to God's people is to manifest the insight to see what is going on and simply to stand firm.

In Revelation Jesus elaborates the prophecy in Mark 13. Once again he implies the distinction between a final Day of the Lord's wrath and a day of the Lord's wrath that happens in history and is succeeded by further history. The events that herald the End but are not the End include wars of conquest, civil wars, famine, slaughter, martyrdom, a great earthquake and a panicked declaration by powerful and rich people and by ordinary people and slaves alike that this is "the great day of their wrath," the wrath of the one who sits on the throne and the lamb (Rev 6:17). So the events bring something like the End. Notwithstanding the fact that Jesus is Lord and that this is the age of the Spirit, this time is the time of "the cross-bearing church."[72] Through this time God makes sure of preserving the people of Israel and preserving an innumerable throng from all the nations (Rev 7).

The events involve terrible natural disaster and slaughter, apparently designed to bring people to repentance; but they fail to do so (Rev 8–9). They parallel the epidemics in Egypt and the ones referred to in Amos. The disasters are released by two witnesses (Rev 11), unidentified figures whose role and power corresponds to those of Moses and Elijah as well as to Joshua

---

[72]G. C. Berkouwer, *The Return of Christ* (Grand Rapids: Eerdmans, 1972), 121.

and Zerubbabel. They are killed but then resuscitated, after another earth-quake, whose survivors do give glory to God. Once again this development leads into something like the End, as "the kingship of this world has become the kingship of our Lord and of his Anointed, and he will reign as king forever and ever" (Rev 11:15).

In due course, imperial Rome itself, the latest embodiment of Babylon, must fall. Rome has fallen in the vision (Rev 17:1–19:5), but the fall did not happen in New Testament times. Indeed, we might wonder when Rome did fall, or even whether it did. It never became a haunt for unclean spirits and birds, any more than Babylon itself did when it fell to Persia. But in some sense Rome must fall because its great economic activity makes it rather like a whore. It must fall because of the way it has led the nations astray as local rulers and ruling classes in the different provinces have profited through their association with Rome and through the economic activity that Roman rule and Roman security made possible. It must fall because of its self-indulgence and its confidence that it will be in power forever, as if it were God. It must fall because of the false worship it encourages and inspires. And it must fall because it killed saints and apostles and prophets and or-dinary people (Rev 18:24). It will fall at the hands of the beast itself, whose action is inspired by God (Rev 17:16-17). Its sins mean that God's people must have nothing to do with it. Its fall is reason for great praise to God for its just judgment.

The Role of the Martyrs

Through this period between the resurrection of Jesus and the resur-rection of God's people, in heaven a vast company worships the Lord God Almighty and the Lamb (Rev 4–5), and the congregation on earth, which is also located in heaven in its spirit and in the Spirit, joins in that worship. Further, during this period the martyrs have a special position (Rev 20:4-6). They will not enjoy new physical life until all other believers do, but in the meantime, whereas believers in general stay dead, the martyrs are given new spiritual life, so that they can share in reigning with Jesus. By their martyrdom they have already shared in Jesus' own witnessing to death and thus in witnessing to the world and seeking to draw it to acknowledge God. Punishing the nations is not very effective in achieving this end; martyrdom with its confidence in Jesus' giving victory over death is more effective.[73]

The backfire on Rome happened in the centuries that followed John's day. Rome sought to destroy the growing church in an awareness that the Christian movement placed a question mark by the superpower's entire significance, beliefs and ideology, but the willingness of its members to go to their martyrdom was one of the factors that led to the gospel's victory. Perhaps the answer to the question when or whether Rome fell is that its conversion into an empire that acknowledged Jesus constituted its fall and/ or excused it from experiencing the kind of fulfillment of John's vision that otherwise threatened it. Ironically, however, when Rome gave in and embraced the gospel, it was then able to domesticate it; the Christian Roman Empire was *not* the fifth empire of which Daniel spoke.

When the lion-lamb opens the scroll, this action releases four forms of death and destruction (Rev 6:1-8). John doesn't say that they are punishments or that they affect only the wicked or that the sealing of the 144,000 (Rev 7) exempts them, though the calamities are held back until their sealing is complete. But the imposition of death and destruction is a response to the martyrs' pleas for redress and to the pleas of believers in general (Rev 6:9-11; 8:3-5; cf. Rev 19:2). They presuppose a context in which believers have no real power to take redress, though such contexts can stimulate people who are powerless to take desperate action even if it is suicidal. The prophecy thus also inhibits people from taking redress for themselves; they are to rely on God's promises. The conviction that aggression and forcefulness belong to God is what makes it possible for human beings to forgo violence.[74]

The fall of Babylon and of the beast is the harvest of God's wrath (Rev 14:14-20). The prospect of the seven epidemics issues in the praise of those who are victorious over the beast, who sing the song of Moses and of the lamb: it is a song appropriately comparable to the one Moses composed in connection with Yahweh's victory over Egypt. The putting down of evil is like the bloody victory of a great warrior with his heavenly armies (Rev 19:11-21). The victory is won over the armies of the nations, and over

---

[73]Cf. Richard Bauckham, *The Theology of the Book of Revelation* (Cambridge and New York: Cambridge University Press, 1993), 87-88.

[74]Cf. Miroslav Volf, *Exclusion and Embrace* (Nashville: Abingdon, 1996), 302-3.

the nations themselves, and over the beast. But the act of praise at this victory is also comparable to the "eternal gospel" proclaimed to the whole earth (Rev 15:1-4; cf. Rev 14:1-7).

It's possible to evade God's judgment, by submitting to it. Conversion means a turning to God that promises deliverance from the coming wrath (1 Thess 1:10). The reason Paul is proud of the gospel is that it is the power of God for deliverance (Rom 1:16). On the basis of people's trust, the gospel rescues them from the judgment that would otherwise overwhelm them at the End. God's *dikaiosynē* or uprightness is revealed in it: that is, it is an expression of God's uprightness in relation to the Jewish people but also in relation to the world (to the Jew first but also to the Greek). That uprightness works on the basis of trust, a trust that sets up the relationship that then entails uprightness on God's part. And it transfers. A responsive trust establishes an upright relationship on the human side and thus makes it possible for the person who enters into this relationship of trust to live rather than be consumed by God's wrath: the person who is upright through trust will live (Rom 1:17).[75]

8.4 JESUS' APPEARING

The triumph of God and the fulfillment of his purpose are tied up with the appearing of Jesus. Insofar as his appearing is an inevitable corollary of his resurrection, it is near. It could happen any moment. If we die before it happens, our death is simply a kind of sleep, secure in a comfortable hotel room. At the End, those who are alive and those who have died will together receive their resurrection bodies.

The Coming of the Man
The New Testament does not speak in terms of Jesus' "second coming," but it has no other single technical term for this event.[76] Its nearest is its talk of Jesus' *parousia*, his appearing or coming or arriving (1 Thess 2:19; 3:13; 4:15; 5:23; 2 Thess 1:1, 8; cf. 1 Cor 15:23). The term suggests the appearing of a god

---

[75]As well as Hab 2:4; Ps 98:2-3; and passages such as Is 50:7-8; 51:4-5; 52:10 lie behind Rom 1:16-17. Paul has simply "faith[fulness]," not "his faithfulness," with the Hebrew, or "my faithfulness," with the Greek; both apply, as is spelled out in *ek pisteōs eis pistin.* See Richard B. Hays, *Echoes of Scripture in the Letters of Paul* (New Haven, CT, and London: Yale University Press, 1989), 36-41.

[76]Cf. Joseph Plevnik, *Paul and the Parousia* (Peabody, MA: Hendrickson, 1997), 3-44.

or the presence of someone who has been absent, as when a king puts in an appearance in some part of his realm to assert his authority there. The Jesus who has been physically absent will now be present.[77] Unusually for Paul, *parousia* is a word without biblical overtones.[78] Jesus' coming will be his revelation (*apocalypsis*; 1 Cor 1:7), his manifestation (*epiphaneia*; 1 Tim 6:14; 2 Tim 4:1, 8).[79] He will "come" (Rom 11:26; 1 Cor 4:5; 11:26; 16:22). The "day of Yahweh" becomes the "day of our Lord Jesus, the Anointed One" (1 Cor 1:8). "The grace of God has appeared," but we live waiting for the "appearing" of Jesus (Tit 2:11-13).[80]

In his own talk about the future, Jesus declares that following the period of distress will come events of another order (Mk 13:24-27): the cosmos will shake, as Isaiah said (Is 13:10; 34:4), and people will see the Man coming on the clouds, as Daniel said (Dan 7:13). He will come in great glory to gather his chosen people, who are scattered all over the world, as Moses and the Prophets had promised (e.g., Deut 30:6; Zech 2:6 [MT 10]). There will be no doubt about what is happening when it happens; there is no need to fear being deceived.

The coming of the Man will cause the nations to mourn (Mt 24:30). Is this mourning a sign of fruitful repentance (like the mourning in Zech 12:10 whose description is picked up in Rev 1:7)? Or is it parallel to the fruitless weeping and gnashing of teeth of which Jesus often speaks? The ambiguity reflects Jesus' focus on the world's recognition of what is happening rather than on the significance of the mourning for the people who do the recognizing. It is the obverse of Jerusalem's own recognition, "Praised be the one who comes in the name of the Lord" (Mt 23:39), which might be glad and fruitful or wrested and fruitless.

When Luke's version of Jesus' prophecy makes explicit the distinction between the fall of Jerusalem and the final day, it presumably reflects the fact that by his day it's clear that the fall of Jerusalem was not the End. On one hand, Jesus says in Luke's version, "there will be great distress in the land and

---

[77]See, e.g., Wright, *Surprised by Hope*, 128-36.

[78]Cf. Wright, *Paul and the Faithfulness of God*, 1082.

[79]George Eldon Ladd (*The Blessed Hope* [Grand Rapids: Eerdmans, 1956], 63-69) notes the significance of the New Testament use of these three words for theories about the great tribulation, the rapture and the resurrection.

[80]Cf. Gorman, *Reading Paul*, 61-62.

wrath on this people," as a result of which "Jerusalem will be trodden by Gentiles, until the times of the Gentiles are filled up." On the other hand, "that day" is one that will come on the whole earth "like a trap" (Lk 21:23-24, 34-35; cf. Is 24:17). Given that it is only with the benefit of hindsight that one can make the distinction between an interim Day of Yahweh and a final Day of Yahweh, people who go through the great catastrophe go through it as if it is the End.

Its Inevitability

The prospect of Jesus' appearing or coming is integrally related to the fact of his resurrection. The recipients of Paul's earliest surviving letters were people who had "turned to God from idols, to serve the living and true God, and to await his son from the heavens whom he raised from the dead" (1 Thess 1:10). The gospel "embraces the confession of 'belief in God' and 'belief in Jesus Christ who is to come.'"[81] His resurrection looks forward to his appearing. So the community of people who believe in Jesus is also the community of people who are looking for his coming, and much of the New Testament's vision for it is shaped by this awareness.

Jesus' resurrection is not an isolated event or merely the sign and means of his present exaltation or the guarantee of the individual believer's resurrection. It is the beginning of that final resurrection. "The death and resurrection of Christ have opened up a new future for the world. This future climaxes in the reign of God as that event that will bring the created order to its glorious destiny according to God's promises."[82]

The assurance that Jesus will appear soon and/or that nothing can stop his appearing tomorrow derives from the knowledge that God doesn't need to do anything else before bringing in the triumphant achievement of his purpose for the world. Nothing else could be needed after his raising Jesus from death. The resurrection is the initiating of something; the appearing and the final resurrection will be the completing of it. That fact is bound up in Jesus' being the firstfruits of the final resurrection (1 Cor 15:20, 23). After Jesus' resurrection, nothing else needs to happen before the final resurrection of the dead.[83]

---

[81]Edward Schillebeeckx, *Christ* (New York: Crossroad; London: SCM Press, 1980), 115.
[82]Beker, *Paul's Apocalyptic Gospel*, 29.
[83]Cf. Beker, *Paul the Apostle*, 46, 145.

John knows of a scroll on which an account of coming events is written, which only the lion-lamb can open (Rev 5). It is his suffering and triumph that establish how things will turn out. They will happen not merely because they are predetermined but because God has thus predetermined them and revealed them in anticipation. There is an intrinsic link between Jesus' death and resurrection and these events. Opening the scroll signifies both that they will happen and that Jesus can tell us that they will happen.

John weeps because the church's persecution will continue if no one opens the scroll; there will be no resolution. The lion-lamb's triumph means there will be resolution; hence the enthusiasm of the ones who carry the saints' prayers, and the promise that the church will reign, not suffer forever. Jesus' death and resurrection make the End both possible and certain; it will be the outworking of the significance of those events.

So Jesus and the New Testament writers knew that the End would come. But they "refused to allow the sense of nearness to be turned into a belief that the End would definitely come within a certain number of years."[84] History sees recurrent embodiments of the dynamic of this mercy, such as are described in Revelation 6–9. God allows, even brings about, wars and other disasters, seeking to draw the world to repentance; the logic of disaster is the same as that in Amos or Isaiah. But precisely because it has this aim, God constrains the disasters and protects the people of God from being overwhelmed by them.

At this End, God "will send the one appointed for you, the Anointed One, Jesus. Heaven must receive him until the times for the restoration of everything, of which God spoke by the mouth of his holy prophets long ago" (Acts 3:20-21). The new age will come in fullness, and Jesus' Lordship will be manifest. The Scriptures' warnings about wrath and disaster are set in the context of a more encouraging Beginning and End (Gen 1; Mt 1–2; Rev 19–22). A corollary of the fall of Rome is the celebration of the marriage of Jesus and his people; perhaps the implication is that the believing community has been betrothed to Jesus since his execution and resurrection, but now the actual marriage takes place.

---

[84]A. L. Moore, *The Parousia in the New Testament* (Leiden: Brill, 1966), 207; cf. Thiselton, *Hermeneutics of Doctrine*, 570.

Its Nearness

In Acts Peter could give the impression that the time for "the restoration of everything" is imminent, though the small print could also imply that its arrival was dependent on his fellow Jews changing their stance to Jesus and turning to God (Acts 3:17-21). On the whole, that change didn't happen, and the restoration didn't arrive, and in any case other parts of the New Testament convey a more somber impression.

An implication is that believers have to keep alert for the actual End. While Jesus does not offer pointers toward the possibility that it may be two thousand years in the future, he does suggest that its timing is not fixed. He doesn't want his disciples to assume it will not come in their day. He wants them to stay alert, watching for it. His aspiration is in keeping with his not knowing when "that day or hour" will come (Mk 13:32). "The believer is called to an attitude that does not *reckon* but constantly *reckons with* the coming of the Lord."[85]

Revelation declares that people are blessed if they read out, listen to and take to heart God's revelation about what is to come, because the time is near (Rev 1:3). "I'm coming quickly," Jesus says, more than once (Rev 22:7, 12, 20). Yet elsewhere Revelation implies a longer time frame, particularly in its talk of a thousand years (Rev 20), and Jesus also bids his disciples, "Keep watch; you don't know the day or hour" (Mt 25:13). The promise that Jesus will come soon is a promise that he will definitely come and that there is nothing to stop him, except perhaps God's own mercy.[86] He is coming with the clouds, and the people who pierced him will see him; that is when all the peoples will mourn because of him (Rev 1:7).

Although Paul has a lot to say about Jesus' coming in his earliest letters, to the Thessalonians, and much less to say about this theme in his later letters, this difference may simply reflect circumstantial factors in the situations to which he writes rather than a change in his thinking. He has not moved away from expecting Jesus to come soon, nor does he suggest a

---

[85]Berkouwer, *Return of Christ*, 124.
[86]Perhaps every day is the End Day and God in his grace decides, instead of implementing what he has planned, to allow another day to give us another chance and invents a new world (one with a grace extension) instead of the one in which we are all condemned (Kathleen Scott Goldingay).

sense that the coming has been delayed. He continues to speak of the day being at hand (Rom 13:12) and of the Lord being near (Phil 4:5).

A further factor underlying the unclarity over the sense in which Jesus' appearing is near is that dynamic relationship between the final Day and the interim fulfillments of God's declarations. This interrelationship helps interpretation of the sense in which "the time is near" (Rev 1:3; cf. Rev 1:1; 22:10, 12), a nearness so real that John should not seal up his book as Daniel was to seal his (Rev 22:10). Revelation presents itself as a message from God that has direct application to readers in John's day. It does not simply refer to an End of all things that is at least two millennia away, or reveal how history is to unfold over the centuries.

The believing community thus waits for Jesus' coming. But "if this is a time of waiting, it is a period of divine waiting, to which human waiting must correspond." God waits to bring about that End, perhaps because of his desire to give humanity time to repent (cf. Lk 13:6-9; 1 Pet 3:20).[87] One implication of the New Testament writers' reluctance to set a time for Jesus' appearing may be that "they reckoned with the grace motif" and knew that the time for repentance and faith could not be limited by human beings; "the provision of God's mercy could not be measured nor forecast."[88]

Conversely, because God is prepared to wait almost forever for people to repent, it's possible for people to speed the coming of God's day (2 Pet 3:8-12). In the meantime, then, and in the short term, there is an interaction between God's plans and human responses. Thus some of Jesus' statements about the future (notably Mk 9:1; 13) give the impression of a much shorter time frame than the two millennia that have elapsed since he made them. God's purpose is put into effect in interaction with the actions of people such as the disciples, the Jewish people and the Romans, not to say subsequent peoples.

Jesus says that everything will happen within the lifetime of the present generation, but he goes on to add that no one can know when things will happen; it's therefore up to the disciples to remain alert (Mk 13:28-37). Perhaps he did mean that the lifetime of the present generation set the

---

[87]Berkouwer, *Return of Christ*, 84.
[88]Moore, *Parousia in the New Testament*, 208; cf. Thiselton, *Hermeneutics of Doctrine*, 570.

bounds for the final events to come, and God subsequently had a change of mind about the timing, or perhaps the day or hour that no one can know lies beyond that framework, or perhaps Jesus avoids adjudicating over these alternatives.

Sleep

When Jesus comes, he will transform his people's lowly bodies to make them like his glorious body (Phil 3:20-21). But what about people who die before Jesus comes?

There's nothing to be feared about death because dying is simply an extreme form of going to sleep. That's true within the First Testament, but it's even more true after Jesus because believers now sleep "through" Jesus (*dia*; 1 Thess 4:13-14); they die on the basis of a relationship with Jesus.[89] They sleep "in [relationship with]" Jesus,[90] which links with hoping "in" Jesus (1 Cor 15:18-19). Whereas Jesus died, believers really just fall asleep (1 Cor 15:3, 6; cf. Acts 7:59). Such falling asleep can be an attractive prospect, not least for someone under as much pressure as Paul (not to say someone in prison). The prospect of relaxing safely in the company of Jesus, away from the body but at home with the Lord (2 Cor 5:6, 8), means that dying is gain; it means being with Jesus (Phil 1:23).[91] "The faithful immediately after death are . . . in the presence and keeping of the Lord," but in addition, "their state after death is elsewhere described as a sleep from which they will arise" (1 Cor 15:51-52). "The one mode of representation must be qualified by the other."[92]

It's a common Christian assumption that believers go to heaven when they die, but it's hard to find Scriptures that support that assumption. Indeed, J. Richard Middleton tells us that for some years he has been offering people money if they can point to a scriptural passage that makes this statement, and he still has his money.[93] We do not go to heaven when we die; we are

---

[89]See F. F. Bruce's discussion of the expression, *1 & 2 Thessalonians* (Waco, TX: Word, 1982), 98.

[90]As it happens, Paul uses the expressions "in" the Lord Jesus and "through" the Lord Jesus with similar meaning in 1 Thess 4:1-2 (James Everett Frame, *A Critical and Exegetical Commentary on the Epistles of St. Paul to the Thessalonians* [repr., Edinburgh: T&T Clark, 1975], 169).

[91]Against N. T. Wright, *The Resurrection of the Son of God* (London: SPCK; Minneapolis: Fortress, 2003), 216, 226.

[92]J. B. Lightfoot, *Saint Paul's Epistle to the Philippians* (repr., Grand Rapids: Zondervan, 1965), 93.

[93]See J. Richard Middleton, *A New Heaven and a New Earth* (Grand Rapids: Baker, 2014), 14.

there now, and we will continue to be there.[94] When we die, we go to sleep, and in due course we will be raised to a new bodily life in the New Jerusalem.[95] Dying means beginning a sleep that may last a long time, though it may seem a short sleep to us, as happens with sleep.

Given that some believers will still be alive but some will have died when Jesus appears, first there will be a loud command, and the ones who have died will get up (1 Thess 4:13-18). The dynamics recall Jesus' raising of Lazarus; a powerful voice like that of Jesus is capable of raising a dead person (Jn 11). When that raising has happened, the dead and the living will be in the same position. Paul does not say that God will bring the dead believers with Jesus (as translations imply) but that he will *lead* them with Jesus (*agō*), so that all can together be scooped up to meet Jesus in the air by the clouds or into the clouds. The clouds are not merely a mode of transport but a sign of the presence of God, which is real but veiled.[96] In itself this statement could imply that we will be there in the clouds forever, but that slightly odd idea does not fit well with other passages, and more likely the air is simply the location of the meeting. The whole company of believers is then in a position together to accompany Jesus to earth.[97] Whether we are awake or asleep (alive or dead) when Jesus comes, we will then live with him (1 Thess 5:10).

Admittedly, there is an unpleasant aspect to the prospect of dying; it's like your tent being blown over so that you're exposed to the elements. But you know it will be okay, because God is going to provide you with another tent. Indeed, it will be a better one, so you're actually inclined to look forward to losing your present one in order to receive it, and the presence of the Spirit within you, the firstfruits and guarantee of that event, makes you even more inclined to look forward in that way (2 Cor 5:1-10).

Paul's words could imply he is thinking that we receive our new tent as soon as the old one blows over, which would be a different view from the

---

[94]See the paragraphs headed "New Earth" in section 8.2 above.

[95]Testimony to the correctness of this view is indicated by the weakness of Markus Bockmuehl's arguments against it in "Did St. Paul Go to Heaven When He Died?," in Nicholas Perrin and Richard B. Hays, eds., *Jesus, Paul and the People of God* (Downers Grove, IL: InterVarsity Press, 2011), 211-31; see also N. T. Wright's "Response to Markus Bockmuehl," 231-34; and his *For All the Saints?* (London: SPCK, 2003; Harrisburg, PA: Morehouse, 2004).

[96]Bruce, *1 & 2 Thessalonians*, 102.

[97]Cf. Wright, *Resurrection of the Son of God*, 217-18.

one in 1 Corinthians 15.[98] Yet he doesn't quite say so; his words don't undo the impression he gives elsewhere that everyone will receive their resurrection body on resurrection day. In the meantime, after dying we will all sleep, in a strange bodiless state and waiting for our resurrection body, but secure with Jesus until we all appear together before his judgment seat.

Paul thus does not imply a dualistic view that sees the body as a dispensable container for the real person. "Life-after-death requires embodiment—that is, re-embodiment."[99] He does imply that the person is distinguishable from the body and capable of a form of existence separate from it. But in due course we shall receive our new, spiritual body—not a nonphysical body but "a body animated by the Spirit of the living God."[100]

Welcome to the Hotel California

The sleep image fits with First Testament depictions of people having or regaining some consciousness after death. Samuel can be awoken and drawn into making an appearance among the living, though he is not too pleased at the disturbance (1 Sam 28). His story and the story of Moses appearing at Jesus' transfiguration raise the question, "Can't [God] just as well make them sleep on and off (or for as long as he wishes)?"[101] The martyrs are able to pray (Rev 6:9-11), though they may be a special case.[102] Jesus speaks of the God of Abraham, Isaac and Jacob as the God of the living, and Luke's version adds that "all live to him" (Lk 20:38). For Luther, there's no reason to be afraid of death. It's just like a nap on the sofa.[103] "We shall sleep, until he comes and knocks on the little grave and says, 'Dr. Martin, get up!' Then I shall get up in a moment and I shall be eternally merry with him."[104]

---

[98]See Margaret E. Thrall, *A Critical and Exegetical Commentary on the Second Epistle to the Corinthians* (Edinburgh: T&T Clark, 1994), 1:356-400.

[99]Joel B. Green, *Body, Soul and Human Life* (Grand Rapids: Baker; Milton Keynes, UK: Paternoster, 2008), 179.

[100]Wright, *Resurrection of the Son of God*, 354.

[101]Martin Luther, letter to Nicholas von Amsdorf (January 13, 1522), *Letters I*, LW 48 (Philadelphia: Fortress, 1963), 360-61; and see his comment on 1 Pet 3:8-10 in *The Catholic Epistles*, LW 30 (St. Louis: Concordia, 1967), 196-97.

[102]See the paragraphs headed "The Role of the Martyrs" in section 8.2 above.

[103]See the sermon on Mt 9:18-26 in *Sermons of Martin Luther* (repr., Grand Rapids: Baker [1989]), 5:344-62 (on 359).

[104]Martin Luther, "Predigt am 16. Sonntag nach Trinitatis (im Hause)," on Lk 7:11-17, in *Werke*, Weimarer Ausgabe 37 (Weimar: Hermann Böhlaus Nachfolger, 1910), 149-51 (on 151); cf. Jürgen Moltmann, *The Coming of God* (London: SCM Press; Minneapolis: Fortress, 1996), 101.

Jesus' resurrection means that death thus has no power; it's simply the gate to resurrection.[105]

"In my Father's house are many rooms. . . . I'm going to prepare a place for you." Then "I will come back and take you to myself, so that where I am, you may also be" (Jn 14:1-3). Like any king, God has a palace, his palace being in the heavens. Like any palace, it's a place where God's staff live along with God, and also the place where staff meetings take place; in this sense it's more like the White House than Buckingham Palace. Occasionally human beings are admitted to it. Prophets go there to join in staff meetings; Enoch and Elijah apparently go there.

Jesus picks up this scriptural image and riffs on it. Like any palace, God's palace has an extraordinary number of rooms. What is also extraordinary is that ordinary people can go and live there. There are enough rooms for everyone; they are open to everyone, not just people such as Enoch and Elijah, and people can have a semipermanent room of their own, not just temporary access for a meeting. It's possible because Jesus introduces them. He does so at the cost of dying for them. Hence he prefaces that declaration about the rooms by affirming that they should not be troubled about the fact that he is about to die. He has to go that way in order to prepare a place for them in the palace (Jn 14:1). Dying is his way to the Father, and his dying is the only way they will get there. He himself is thus the way there (Jn 14:6). And he is the truth, the true and reliable way to the Father. Other ways don't work; this one is infallible. Show other tickets, and you'll discover they are forgeries; show this ticket, and you're in. And he is thus the life; he's the way to find a lasting place in the Father's house.

All this is not to say whether or not in this palace you will come across any Canaanites, Muslims, Buddhists, Jews who have not believed in Jesus, atheists or agnostics. Perhaps you will, perhaps you won't; the Scriptures don't address that question. It's people who've met Jesus who have chance to recognize that he is the way and to go that way. Maybe others stumble across it. And maybe people who've met Jesus and then decided that he's not the way are unlikely to get to the place where this way leads. The Scriptures'

---

[105]Moltmann, *Coming of God*, 101.

point is that anyone you do come across in the palace will be there because Jesus died for them.

The rooms are *monai*, places where you rest when you are on a journey. To use another image, when believers die, they go to Paradise (Lk 23:43), a tranquil park, where the dead rest until resurrection day.[106] Although death will not be immediately succeeded by resurrection, the promise that "nothing will separate us from the love of Christ . . . holds for death as well. It will bring about no separation between Christ and us."[107]

"At the point where we shall be at our end, it is not merely death but God Himself who awaits us." It could be a frightening fact. "But the God who awaits us in death and as the Lord of death is the gracious God. He is the God who is for man."[108]

Resurrection

Death is natural and inevitable; it's innate in human existence. Life after death or new life or resurrection life is not innate in us or natural or inevitable. It's purely God's gift. It's not just a logical requirement of the working out of God's fairness to his people, and in particular to faithful people who didn't deserve to be martyred—the idea that may lie behind the Pharisees' belief in resurrection. It's not just an ungrounded hope on the part of people who can't face the idea that death might be the end. It's a prospect interwoven with Jesus' resurrection (cf. 1 Cor 15:1-11). It's not an irrelevance, as if the survival of the spirit is all we need; it's necessary for our forgiveness and for the completion of God's cosmic project (cf. 1 Cor 15:12-34). It's not a logical impossibility or something that you can't prove from the Torah, as Mark reports the Sadducees to have thought (Mk 12:18-27): God can make it a possibility, and it is a logical inference from the Torah (cf. 1 Cor 15:35-44).

Jesus' ability to restore someone from near death or from thirty-eight years of near-lifelessness (Jn 4:43–5:40) is a sign of his capacity to give new life. While one thing that is new about Jesus is that his ministry is significant for the Gentile world as well as the Jewish world, his coming is significant for

---

[106]But for the more traditional understanding of this passage, see Green, *Body, Soul and Human Life*, 163-64.
[107]Herman Ridderbos, *Paul: An Outline of His Theology* (Grand Rapids: Eerdmans, 1975), 508.
[108]Barth, *CD* III, 2:608, 609.

the Jewish world in that the life of the new age is now open to Jews because of him. Jesus will heal from illness, but he will also raise from death (Jn 5:21). He will not only resuscitate people to a life that will eventually come to an end again but will make it possible for people to pass from death to life in such a way that death will not be able to claim them again. Jesus will raise to eternal life even the long-dead. It is an indication that God has granted the Son to have life in himself. He "will transfigure our lowly body so that it is conformed to his glorious body" (Phil 3:21).

When Jesus sees people's grief at Lazarus's death, it troubles him deeply (Jn 11:33). Lazarus's being apparently young or middle-aged highlights the point. While Jesus might feel that there is something scandalous about anyone's death, the First Testament feels in particular that it's scandalous when death comes before its time. Jesus' troubled reaction is not particularly a sign of his humanity; he is embodying God's reaction to death, and perhaps particularly God's reaction to early death. His weeping is likewise an indication of the disturbance that Lazarus's death causes to him, and it further expresses God's reaction to its reality.

Martha "knows" that her brother will rise again at the last day. Perhaps she shares the faith of the Pharisees; perhaps it's her own bold venture of faith in God. "I am resurrection and life," says Jesus. The person who believes in him is the one who will live, even though dying first, and who will never die again (Jn 11:24-26). Jesus thus adjusts Martha's confession in two ways. First, he's the one through whom resurrection comes about. He is "the firstborn from the dead" (Rev 1:5); others will follow. After his resurrection dead people came to life and appeared in Jerusalem (Mt 27:52-53). Second, this being the case, his being present now means that resurrection (or at least resuscitation) does not have to wait; it can happen now. Jesus thus "revealed the resurrection."[109]

The coming climax of our story will be our resurrection. Given that Jesus' resurrection has already happened, the coming climax of his story will be his appearing. The former has the emphasis in 1 Corinthians, the latter in 1 Thessalonians.[110] The latter responds to the question whether people who die

---

[109]John of Damascus, *Exposition of the Orthodox Faith* 4.27.

[110]Cf. Karl P. Donfried, "The Theology of 1 Thessalonians," in Donfried and I. Howard Marshall, *The Theology of the Shorter Pauline Letters* (Cambridge and New York: Cambridge University

before Jesus' appearing lose out in relation to people who are still alive. The former responds to questions raised by death itself.

8.5 JUDGMENT

As the exalted Lord, Jesus is also judge, and the dark side to God's triumph is judgment. God "has set a day when he is going to judge the world with justice by a man whom he appointed, giving assurance to everyone by raising him from the dead people" (Acts 17:31). Resurrection day will be good news only for people who have done good; people who have done evil will also rise, but in order to be finally condemned (Jn 5:29). Resurrection happens to everyone at the end, but it may not be a good experience. Judgment is a theme that grows in prominence as the Scripture unfolds. It begins with the people of God. It involves an objective wrath and a subjective wrath. And it both delivers the oppressed and puts down evil.

Jesus the Judge

One of the first things we learn about Jesus is that he is to fulfill a God-like role in bringing judgment. John baptizes people with water in connection with their repentance; Jesus will baptize them with the Holy Spirit and with fire, burning up the chaff from his threshing floor with unquenchable fire (Mt 3:11-12). "You unbelieving and twisted generation! How long shall I be with you? How long shall I put up with you?" (Mt 17:17).

We use the word *judgment* to denote both the issuing of the judge's final verdict and the implementing of the punishment on the people he declares guilty, though the former leads into the latter, and the two cannot be neatly kept apart. Jesus both declares the punishment and implements it. Further, in the Scriptures both the declaration and the implementing of judgment link with deliverance. John hears the sound of a great crowd in heaven saying, "Hallelujah! The deliverance, glory, and power of our God, because his judgments are true and just!" (Rev 19:1-2). Judgment links with deliverance because it means the people of God are rescued from the powers of evil that oppress them. It also means that truth is affirmed and vindicated.

Press, 1993), 1-79, on 34, following Gerd Lüdemann, "The Hope of the Early Paul," *Perspectives in Religious Studies* 7 (1980): 195-201.

One reason why judgment is the business of a king is that it is a king's job to put down evil and deliver the oppressed. "Judgment by God is in the Bible a function of His action as King. And to this day, when the due sense of God's kingship goes, the sense of judgment goes with it." It is then striking that "many who think and speak much of the kingdom of God are yet averse to the idea of judgment."[111] God's acts of judgment are manifestations of power; they are also true and just. All those facts are reason for a shout of praise. "God's coming judgment is a good thing, something to be celebrated, longed for, yearned over."[112]

Thus Paul assures the Thessalonians, who are growing in faith, love and tenacity, that it will be just in God's sight to pay back trouble to the people who trouble them, and relief to the Thessalonians themselves as people who are troubled, "at the revelation of Jesus from heaven with his powerful angels, in blazing fire." He will then give judgment to people who do not acknowledge God and do not obey the gospel. The congregation's persecutors "will receive judgment, eternal destruction from the Lord's presence and from his strong splendor, when he comes to be glorified among his holy people and to be marveled at among the people who trust" (2 Thess 1:3-10).

God is "the one who repays the persecutors with persecution" as well as "the one who gives rest to the persecuted."[113] For the victims of violence, the perspective from which Revelation is written, the coming wrath of God and of Jesus is not bad news, an event from which one needs deliverance, but good news and the promise of liberation. "The wrath of God is also the wrath of the Lamb, that is, definitely also the wrath of the Redeemer"; the Lamb is the sufferers' shepherd, and God wipes away every tear from their eyes (Rev 6:16-17; 7:17).[114]

Compared with the images of judgment, of Jesus' return and of resurrection, the picture of "a *hell* of punishment and destruction . . . has possibly

---

[111]P. T. Forsyth, *The Justification of God* (London: Duckworth, 1916; New York: Scribner's, 1917), 180, 182.

[112]Wright, *Surprised by Hope*, 137.

[113]Karl P. Donfried, "The Theology of 2 Thessalonians," in Donfried and Marshall, *Theology of the Shorter Pauline Letters*, 81-113 (on 91).

[114]Reinhard Feldmeier and Hermann Spieckermann, *God of the Living* (Waco, TX: Baylor University Press, 2011), 359-60.

retained more power than all the rest in the modern imagination, while it has also been put to more abuse and misuse."[115]

Judgment's Deepening Shadow

One would not have predicted much of what Jesus does, though with hindsight it all makes sense. Whereas in John his first act is to turn water into wine at a wedding (perhaps huge amounts of it), he then assaults and upbraids people who are helping worshipers in the temple by selling them the animals they need for sacrifices (Jn 2:13-22); they are the people whose services Mary will have used when she brought the sacrifice to mark his birth (Lk 2:22-24). In both connections he acts like Elijah and Elisha, two of Israel's more extravagant and unpredictable prophets, neither of them men you wanted to get the wrong side of. "How dare you turn my Father's house into a market?"

His action reminded the disciples of a line from a psalm (one of the psalms that Christians are most unhappy about), "passion for your house consumes me" (Ps 69:9 [MT 10]). "He did not attempt to avoid violence in search of a peaceable existence. He rather entered actively into the situation of violence, and even exacerbated the conflict. Driving out demons involved convulsions for the possessed, and the preaching and practice of the kingdom generally brought not 'peace,' but 'a sword.'"[116]

In the New Testament, judgment is

> a shadow which for darkness has increased rather than decreased in comparison with the Old Testament parallels. How can it be otherwise, in view of the New Testament's central view of the cross of Christ, in which the early Christian community saw involved the mystery of man's sin against God and the mystery of the execution of God's punishment upon sinful man—and saw involved in both mysteries the hiddenness of God in its completed reality? Now for the first time and from this standpoint the accusation against man becomes fundamental and comprehensive. Now for the first time and at this point the threat of judgment becomes the threat of eternal judgment. Now for the first time and from this standpoint the meeting of a holy God with sinful man, to which the Old Testament bears witness, ceases to have the appearance

---

[115]James W. McClendon, *Systematic Theology: Doctrine* (Nashville: Abingdon, 1994), 85.
[116]Richard A. Horsley, *Jesus and the Spiral of Violence* (repr., Philadelphia: Fortress, 1993), 319.

of a rather unsatisfactory attempt at pædagogy, and acquires instead an ultimate seriousness.[117]

The wrath of God indeed has increasing focus as the Scriptures unfold. The pattern is especially clear in the Greek and English order of the Scriptures. God's wrath is a relatively minor theme through the narrative and poetic books. It is a more prominent one in the Prophets, which end with the word *ḥērem*, the word for devoting things by destroying them. Within a couple of pages of its beginning, the New Testament is giving a warning about wrath coming (Mt 3:7). Later Jesus speaks of people going to eternal punishment or eternal life in accordance with the way they have treated his brothers and sisters (Mt 25:31-46).

Jesus' aim in coming was not to bring judgment (Jn 3:17; 12:47), but he knew that his coming had that effect, and in this sense he did come to bring judgment (Jn 9:39). "I do not judge anyone. But if I judge, my judgment is true" (Jn 8:15-16). "If life is what is promised to those who accept the revelation of Jesus, judgement is what is promised to those who do not."[118]

The judgment is decided now, though it will not take effect until later. People will bring condemnation on themselves by their reaction to him. He is the embodiment of light, so their rejection of him indicates that they choose darkness (Jn 3:18-19). His execution brings this process to a head; it is the means of salvation and of judgment: "The Jews passed judgement on themselves by casting out the man born blind" (Jn 9:39), and "the world by crucifying Jesus passed judgement on itself."[119]

Judgment Begins with God's Household

Jesus again speaks like the Prophets and like John the Baptizer in declaring that the judgment threatened on the nations is about to fall on God's own people. He describes members of that people being thrown into darkness, where there is weeping and gnashing of teeth (Mt 22:13); "horror stories,"

---

[117]Barth, *CD* I, 2:109.

[118]John Ashton, *Understanding the Fourth Gospel* (Oxford and New York: Oxford University Press, 1991), 220 (2nd ed., 405).

[119]C. K. Barrett, *The Gospel According to John* (London: SPCK, 1962), 355.

such parables have been called.[120] Both Testaments speak of judgment in connection with the people of God more than with the nations. The people of God will be dealt with on the basis of the life they have lived (Rom 2:5-16). Paul is not referring here to the world in general but to the people of God and to the kind of Gentiles who seek glory, honor and immortality by persisting in doing good (Rom 2:7); we might think of people such as Rahab and Ruth. (The question how God deals with unbelieving Gentiles in general, maybe people who have not heard the gospel but who live good lives, is not his concern.)

If they are lucky, believers experience judgment in their own being now, which gives them opportunity to learn from being disciplined (1 Cor 11:29-32). If they deliberately carry on sinning after they have received the knowledge of the truth, there is no longer any sacrifice for sin that remains but only a fearful expectation of judgment and of raging fire that is going to consume God's opponents. After all, if people died for disobeying Moses' Torah, how much severer will be the punishment for people who have trampled the Son of God underfoot. God is then the one who takes redress (as it says in Deut 32:35-36), and it is a dreadful thing to fall into the hands of the living God (Heb 10:26-31).

Gentile believers are therefore unwise to take a superior stance in relation to Jews who were thrown out by God because of their unbelief; we can get thrown out if we don't stand firm in God's kindness (Rom 11:22). Believers who still live in accordance with the lower nature will not get access to God's realm (Gal 5:21). Paul's language about judgment on the Thessalonians' persecutors reflects the description of God's judgment in Isaiah (see Is 2:10, 11, 17, 19, 21) and elsewhere, but the Thessalonian believers themselves are exempt from such judgment only insofar as they continue to be people of faith, love and perseverance (2 Thess 1:3-5).

Having a clear conscience is no guarantee of the result of the final judgment. When he comes, Jesus will bring to light things that are hidden in darkness—that is, the purposes of our hearts, which may be hidden even from us. In the meantime, it's not our business to judge one another (1 Cor 4:4-5). "We must all appear before the seat of the Anointed One, so

---

[120]Luise Schottroff, "The Kingdom of God Is Not Like You Were Made to Believe," in Botta and Andiñach, *Bible and the Hermeneutics of Liberation*, 169-79 (on 170).

that each person may receive the recompense for what he has done while in the body, whether good or bad" (2 Cor 5:10). That principle applies specifically to people involved in ministry (1 Cor 3:10-15).

Revelation expounds the theme further. As a letter addressed to seven congregations, it implicitly addresses the whole church, as its incorporation into the Scriptures implies. Yet the church feels ambivalent about it, not least because of this stress on God's wrath. It's possible for sensitive souls to be troubled by the New Testament's talk of judgment, particularly the judgment of believers. Such people need to be given the reassurance that people who are troubled in this way are not the people who are actually threatened by that judgment. On the other hand, while Revelation sees God's wrath as good news for oppressed congregations as long as they remain faithful, the threat it constitutes to imperial-style powers suggests that there is wisdom in our ambivalence about it as Western readers.

Wrath

As "God's 'grace' is not a quality, not His timeless kindliness," so "what the gospel brings is not enlightenment as to God's hitherto misunderstood nature as if till now He had been wrongly conceived as wrathful and ought henceforth to be regarded as gracious. . . . Now, as then, '*God's Wrath*' pours out 'against all ungodliness and wickedness of men' (Rom. 1:18)." The unrepentant are still storing up wrath for themselves on the day of wrath when God's righteous judgment will be revealed (Rom 2:5). "'To inflict wrath' belongs inherently to God's 'faithfulness,' 'truthfulness,' and judicial 'justice' (Rom. 3:3-6). God continues to be the Judge, and Christian faith in God's grace does not consist in the conviction that God's wrath doesn't exist or that there is no impending judgment (II Cor. 5:10), but in the conviction of being rescued from God's wrath" (Rom 5:9; 1 Thess 1:10; 5:9). God's wrath is here "an occurrence, viz. *the judgment of God*," and the revelation of God's wrath is not the passing on of some information about it but "its becoming effective," both now (see Rom 1:18-32) and on a coming day.[121]

As judge, Jesus is a figure of authority whose eyes are fiery, his voice overwhelming and his word sword-like (Rev 1:13-16). He is destined to rule the world with an iron rod (Rev 12:5). He is "the lion of the clan of Judah, the

---

[121]Bultmann, *Theology of the New Testament*, 1:288.

root of David"; "the root and the offspring of David, the bright morning star" (Rev 5:5; 22:16: the two declarations bring together images from Gen 49:9; Num 24:17; Is 11:1, 10). He will "tread the winepress of the angry fury of God the all-powerful," in keeping with his role as the Davidic king (see Ps 2:9; Is 11:4-5; 63:1-2). "With justice he judges and makes war. . . . He is clothed in a robe dipped [or spattered] in blood. . . . From his mouth comes a sharp sword so that he can strike down the nations with it. He will shepherd them with an iron rod" (Rev 19:11-15).

He also declares that congregations that stand firm in opposition to idolatry will share in this shepherding with the iron rod and in shattering the nations like pottery (Rev 2:26-27), though for them as for him the exercise of such violence in God's name comes from the other side of martyrdom.[122]

While reference to God's wrath can simply allude to the event of judgment, it can also signify the emotion that may lie behind this judgment. God's wrath has both a subjective and an objective aspect. Subjectively, it suggests an anger that God feels as a person; objectively, it is a way of referring to the punishment or judgment itself, and it then need not imply an anger that is felt. The two aspects denote wrath as God experiences it and wrath as its victims experience it.

Psalms that look as if they are referring to the wrath that God feels may actually be referring to the wrath people experience (that is, the affliction). These psalms may not imply that Yahweh is actually angry, but they do indicate that Yahweh is treating people in the way you do if you are angry; the psalms' problem may then be that people are not aware of anything that God needs to be angry about. The First Testament can speak of great fury falling on Israel without identifying whose wrath it was (2 Kings 3:27). In this connection, wrath is more a matter of effect than of affect.[123]

In keeping with the negative implications of the idea of "the day of Yahweh" in Amos and Lamentations, in the New Testament this day becomes not only the "day of our Lord Jesus, the Anointed One" but the "great day" of the wrath of God and of the lamb (Rev 6:16-17). The "great ordeal" it

---

[122]On this theme in Revelation, see Matthew J. Street, *Here Comes the Judge* (London and New York: T&T Clark, 2012).

[123]Cf. Stephen H. Travis, *Christ and the Judgment of God* (Basingstoke: Marshall, 1986), 33 (2nd ed., 54).

implies (Rev 7:14) points to the need for the faithful God to keep believers firm to the end as people with no charges against them (*anenklētos*) on that day (1 Cor 2:8). God's having called us into the fellowship of his Son is a basis for hope in this connection. Given that there is wrath to come, it's just as well that Jesus can rescue us from it (Rom 5:9-10).

The Abolition of Evil

While God's acts of judgment manifest God's glory because they rescue the oppressed, they also do so because they treat the powers of evil themselves in a proper punitive way. The release of Satan at the end of the thousand years leads to a last great battle and to his being thrown into the lake of burning sulfur to join the beast. The last declaring of judgment follows (Rev 20:7-15). Possibly this court is one where only the guilty appear, essentially to receive their sentence; it seems to have been long established who are the people who belong to God, and it's rather late for declarations about that question. On the assumption that the lake of burning sulfur is the same as the "lake of fire," death and Hades then join Satan, as do all those whose names are not in the book of life.

It doesn't look as if judgment is simply a paradoxical expression of love.[124] More likely it's an insistence on a clean universe, though one might argue that this is the same thing. The movie *Dogma* tells the story of two angels whose job was to be agents of judgment but who were thrown out of heaven because they wouldn't do their job. They then think they've found a loophole in Roman Catholic dogma that will enable them to get back into heaven without needing to repent. But God couldn't allow that to happen. It would compromise, stain, spoil and imperil the very fabric of reality. So God comes to earth, gets beaten up and eventually wins the repentance of at least one of the angels.

The day of the Lord is "primarily a day of *judgment*" not simply in the sense of "condemnation" but in the sense that it will be "the time when everything gets sorted out, when everything that needs putting right is put right."[125] Judgment is "the dark side of hope."[126]

---

[124]See further the paragraphs under "But Wrathful and Not Acquitting" in section 1.1 above.
[125]Wright, *Paul and the Faithfulness of God*, 1080.
[126]Stephen H. Travis, *I Believe in the Second Coming of Jesus* (London: Hodder; Grand Rapids: Eerdmans, 1982), 184.

This is still a rather negative note on which to close. Surely it can't be right to end a study of biblical theology in this negative way? Yet it's how Isaiah ends. It's how the First Testament ends (in the Christian order—the Jewish order is more encouraging).[127] It's how the New Testament ends. And it's how the Sermon on the Mount ends. The point is to encourage people to make sure they don't get swallowed up by God's wrath. It's meant to be scary. Jesus says,

> Everyone who hears these words of mine and doesn't act on them will be comparable to a stupid man who built his house on sand. Rain fell down, floods came, and winds blew and beat against that house, and it fell down. Its fall was great. (Mt 7:26-27)

So I'll leave it that way.

---

[127]It's also customary in the synagogue to repeat the penultimate verse of Isaiah and of Malachi so as to end the reading of these books on a note of hope rather than of gloom (see Goldingay, *Isaiah 56–66*, 524; Eileen M. Schuller, "The Book of Malachi," in *New Interpreter's Bible*, 7:841-77 [on 876]).

WORKS CONSULTED

Abbott, T. K. *A Critical and Exegetical Commentary on the Epistles to the Ephesians and to the Colossians*. Edinburgh: T&T Clark; New York: Scribner, 1897.

Abelard, Peter. *Commentary on the Epistle to the Romans*. Washington, DC: Catholic University of America Press, 2011.

Ahmanson, Roberta Green. "Dreams Become Reality." *Books and Culture* 21, no. 1 (2015): 18-20.

Allen, Leslie C. *A Theological Approach to the Old Testament*. Eugene, OR: Wipf and Stock, 2014.

Anderson, Ray S. *Historical Transcendence and the Reality of God*. Grand Rapids: Eerdmans, 1975.

Anselm of Canterbury. *Why God Became Man and The Virgin Conception and Original Sin*. Reprint, Albany, NY: Magi, 1969.

Ashton, John, ed. *The Interpretation of John*. 2nd ed. Edinburgh: T&T Clark, 1997.

———. *Understanding the Fourth Gospel*. Oxford and New York: Oxford University Press, 1991. 2nd ed., 2007.

Athanasius. *The Letters of Saint Athanasius Concerning the Holy Spirit*. London: Epworth, 1951.

Augustine of Hippo. *The City of God*. Reprint, London and New York: Penguin, 1984.

———. *On Free Will*. In *Augustine: Earlier Writings*, edited and translated by John H. S. Burleigh, 102-217. Philadelphia: Westminster; London: SCM Press, 1953.

———. *On Grace and Free Will*. NPNF 1, 5:435-65.

———. *On Nature and Grace*. NPNF 1, 5:115-51.

Aulén, Gustaf. *Christus Victor*. London: SPCK, 1931.

Badenas, Robert. *Christ the End of the Law*. Sheffield: JSOT, 1985.

Balla, Peter. *Challenges to New Testament Theology*. Tübingen: Mohr, 1997.

Banks, Robert. *Paul's Idea of Community*. Grand Rapids: Eerdmans, 1980. Rev. ed., Peabody, MA: Hendrickson, 1994.

Barr, James. "*Abba* Isn't 'Daddy.'" *Journal of Theological Studies* 39 (1988): 28-47.

———. *The Bible in the Modern World*. London: SCM Press; New York: Harper, 1973.

Barrett, C. K. *A Commentary on the Second Epistle to the Corinthians.* London: Black; New York: Harper, 1973.

———. *The Gospel According to St John.* London: SPCK, 1962.

———. "Things Sacrificed to Idols." *NTS* 11 (1964–1965): 138-53.

Barrett, Rob. *Disloyalty and Destruction.* London and New York: T&T Clark, 2009.

Barth, Christoph F. *Introduction to the Psalms.* New York: Scribner's; Oxford: Blackwell, 1966.

Barth, Karl. *The Christian Life: Church Dogmatics IV/4: Lecture Fragments.* Grand Rapids: Eerdmans, 1981.

———. *Church Dogmatics.* 13 vols. Edinburgh: T&T Clark, 1936–1969.

Barth, Markus. *Ephesians.* 2 vols. Garden City, NY: Doubleday, 1974.

Barton, John. *Ethics in Ancient Israel.* Oxford and New York: Oxford University Press, 2014.

Barton, Stephen C., ed. *Holiness.* London and New York: T&T Clark, 2003.

———. *Where Shall Wisdom Be Found?* Edinburgh: T&T Clark, 1999.

Bassler, Jouette M. *1 Timothy, 2 Timothy, Titus.* Nashville: Abingdon, 1996.

Bauckham, Richard. *The Climax of Prophecy.* Edinburgh: T&T Clark, 1993.

———. *God Crucified.* Carlisle, UK: Paternoster, 1998; Grand Rapids: Eerdmans, 1999. 2nd ed., *Jesus and the God of Israel.* Milton Keynes, UK: Paternoster, 2008; Grand Rapids: Eerdmans, 2009.

———. *Jesus and the Eyewitnesses.* Grand Rapids: Eerdmans, 2006.

———. *The Testimony of the Beloved Disciple.* Grand Rapids: Baker, 2007.

———. *The Theology of the Book of Revelation.* Cambridge and New York: Cambridge University Press, 1993.

Bauckham, Richard, Daniel Driver, Trevor Hart and Nathan MacDonald, eds. *The Epistle to the Hebrews and Christian Theology.* Grand Rapids and Cambridge, UK: Eerdmans, 2009.

Bauckham, Richard, and Carl Mosser, eds. *The Gospel of John and Christian Theology.* Grand Rapids and Cambridge, UK: Eerdmans, 2008.

Bavinck, Herman. *Reformed Dogmatics.* 4 vols. Grand Rapids: Baker, 2003–2008.

Beale, G. K. *The Temple and the Church's Mission.* Leicester, UK: Inter-Varsity Press; Downers Grove, IL: InterVarsity Press, 2004.

Beilby, James K., and Paul Rhodes Eddy, eds. *Justification: Five Views.* Downers Grove, IL: InterVarsity Press, 2011.

Beker, J. Christiaan. *Paul the Apostle.* Reprint, Philadelphia: Fortress, 1984.

Bennett, Thomas A. "The Cross as the Labor of God." PhD diss., Fuller Theological Seminary, 2015. Forthcoming. Waco, TX: Baylor University Press, 2017.

Berkhof, H. *Christ and the Powers*. Scottdale, PA: Herald, 1962.

Berkouwer, G. C. *The Church*. Grand Rapids: Eerdmans, 1976.

———. *Man: The Image of God*. Grand Rapids: Eerdmans, 1962.

———. *The Providence of God*. Grand Rapids: Eerdmans, 1952.

———. *The Return of Christ*. Grand Rapids: Eerdmans, 1972.

———. *Sin*. Grand Rapids: Eerdmans, 1971.

———. *The Work of Christ*. Grand Rapids: Eerdmans, 1965.

Berlin, Isaiah. *The Proper Study of Mankind*. New York: Farrar, Straus, Giroux; London: Chatto, 1997.

Best, Ernest. *One Body in Christ*. London: SPCK, 1955.

Betz, Hans Dieter. *Galatians*. Philadelphia: Fortress, 1979.

———. *The Sermon on the Mount*. Minneapolis: Fortress, 1995.

Bieringer, Reimund, and Didier Pollefeyt, eds. *Paul and Judaism*. London and New York: T&T Clark, 2012.

Bieringer, R., Didier Pollefeyt and Frederique Vandecasteele-Vanneuville, eds. *Anti-Judaism and the Fourth Gospel*. Assen: Van Gorcum, 2001.

Black, C. Clifton. "The First, Second, and Third Letters of John." In *The New Interpreter's Bible*, Leander E. Keck et al., eds., 12:363-469. Nashville: Abingdon, 1998.

Black, David Alan. *Paul, Apostle of Weakness*. New York: Lang, 1984.

Bloch, Ernst. *The Principle of Hope*. 3 vols. Oxford: Blackwell; Cambridge, MA: MIT Press, 1986.

Blomberg, Craig L. *Neither Poverty nor Riches*. Downers Grove, IL: InterVarsity Press; Leicester, UK: Inter-Varsity Press, 2000.

Bloom, Harold. *Jesus and Yahweh*. New York: Riverhead, 2005.

Boda, Mark J., and Jamie Novotny, eds. *From the Foundations to the Crenellations*. Münster: Ugarit-Verlag, 2010.

Boff, Leonardo. *Jesus Christ Liberator*. Maryknoll, NY: Orbis, 1978.

Bonhoeffer, Dietrich. *Discipleship*. Reprint, Minneapolis: Fortress, 2003.

Boring, M. Eugene. "The Gospel of Matthew." In *The New Interpreter's Bible*, Leander E. Keck et al., eds., 8:87-505. Nashville: Abingdon, 1995.

———. "The Theology of Revelation." *Interpretation* 40 (1986): 257-69.

Bornkamm, Günther. *Paul*. New York: Harper; London: Hodder, 1971.

Botta, Alejandro F., and Pablo R. Andiñach, eds. *The Bible and the Hermeneutics of Liberation*. Atlanta: SBL, 2009.

Bousset, W. *Jesus*. New York: Putnam; London: Williams and Norgate, 1906.

Boyarin, Daniel. *A Radical Jew*. Berkeley and London: University of California Press, 1994.

Brower, Kent E., and Andy Johnson, eds. *Holiness and Ecclesiology in the New Testament*. Grand Rapids and Cambridge, UK: Eerdmans, 2007.

Brown, Nicholas C. R. "For the Nation: Jesus, the Restoration of Israel and Articulating a Christian Ethic of Territorial Governance." PhD diss., Fuller Theological Seminary, 2015.

Brown, Peter R. L. *The Body and Society*. New York: Columbia University Press, 1988; London: Faber, 1989.

Brown, Raymond F. *The Gospel According to John*. Garden City, NY: Doubleday, 1966; London: Chapman, 1971.

Bruce, F. F. *The Epistle to the Hebrews*. Grand Rapids: Eerdmans, 1964; London: Marshall, 1965.

———. *1 & 2 Thessalonians*. Waco, TX: Word, 1982.

Brueggemann, Walter. *Israel's Praise*. Philadelphia: Fortress, 1988.

Bruner, Frederick Dale. *A Theology of the Holy Spirit*. Grand Rapids: Eerdmans, 1970.

Bryan, Steven M. *Jesus and Israel's Traditions of Judgement and Restoration*. Cambridge and New York: Cambridge University Press, 2002.

Buber, Martin. *Two Types of Faith*. London: Routledge; New York: Macmillan, 1951.

Bultmann, Rudolf. *Existence and Faith*. New York: Meridian, 1960; London: Hodder, 1961.

———. *The Gospel of John*. Oxford: Blackwell; Philadelphia: Westminster, 1971.

———. *Primitive Christianity in Its Contemporary Setting*. London and New York: Thames and Hudson, 1956.

———. "Das Problem der Ethik bei Paulus." *Zeitschrift für die neutestamentliche Wissenschaft und die Kunde der älteren Kirche* 23 (1924): 123-40.

———. *Der Stil des paulinischen Predigt und die kynisch-stoische Diatribe*. Göttingen: Vandenhoeck, 1910.

———. *Theology of the New Testament*. Reprint, Waco, TX: Baylor University Press, 2007.

Buntain, D. N. *The Holy Ghost and Fire*. Springfield, MO: Gospel Publishing House, 1956.

Burggraeve, Roger, and Marc Vervenne. *Swords into Plowshares*. Louvain: Peeters; Grand Rapids: Eerdmans, 1991.

Burridge, Richard A. *Imitating Jesus*. Grand Rapids and Cambridge, UK: Eerdmans, 2007.

Byrne, Peter, and Leslie Houlden, eds. *Companion Encyclopedia of Theology*. London and New York: Routledge, 1995.

Caird, George B. *A Commentary on the Revelation of St. John the Divine.* London: Black; New York: Harper, 1966.

———. *The Language and Imagery of the Bible.* London: Duckworth; Philadelphia: Westminster, 1980.

Calvin, John. *The Catechism of the Church of Geneva.* Hartford, CT: Sheldon and Goodwin, 1815.

———. *Commentaries on the Epistle of Paul the Apostle to the Romans.* Reprint, Grand Rapids: Eerdmans, 1947.

———. *Commentaries on the Epistles of Paul to the Galatians and Ephesians.* Reprint, Grand Rapids: Eerdmans, 1948.

———. *Institutes of the Christian Religion.* 2 vols. Philadelphia: Westminster, 1960; London: SCM Press, 1961.

———. *The Second Epistle of Paul the Apostle to the Corinthians and the Epistles to Timothy, Titus and Philemon.* Edinburgh: Oliver and Boyd, 1964.

Campbell, Douglas A. *The Deliverance of God.* Grand Rapids: Eerdmans, 2009.

Caputo, John D., and Michael J. Scanlon, eds. *God, the Gift, and Postmodernism.* Bloomington: Indiana University Press, 1999.

Carlyle, Thomas, ed. *Oliver Cromwell's Letters and Speeches.* 5 vols. New York: Scribner, 1871–1872.

Casey, Maurice. "Where Wright Is Wrong." *JSNT* 69 (1998): 95-103.

Cassiodorus. *Explanation of the Psalms.* 3 vols. Reprint, New York: Paulist, 1990, 1990, 1991.

Charlesworth, James H., ed. *The Messiah.* Minneapolis: Fortress, 1992.

Chester, Andrew. *Future Hope and Present Reality.* Volume 1. Tübingen: Mohr, 2012.

Childs, Brevard S. *Biblical Theology in Crisis.* Philadelphia: Westminster, 1970.

———. *Biblical Theology of the Old and New Testaments.* London: SCM Press, 1992; Minneapolis: Fortress, 1993.

———. *Old Testament Theology in a Canonical Context.* London: SCM Press, 1985; Philadelphia: Fortress, 1986.

Chilton, Bruce D. *God in Strength.* Freistadt: Plöchl, 1979.

———, ed. *The Kingdom of God in the Teaching of Jesus.* London: SPCK; Philadelphia: Fortress, 1984.

———. *Pure Kingdom.* London: SPCK; Grand Rapids: Eerdmans, 1995.

Chilton, Bruce D., and J. I. H. McDonald. *Jesus and the Ethics of the Kingdom.* London: SPCK, 1987; Grand Rapids: Eerdmans, 1988.

Cochrane, Arthur C. *The Church's Confession Under Hitler.* Reprint, Pittsburgh: Pickwick, 1976.

Cole, Graham A. *The God Who Became Human*. Downers Grove, IL: InterVarsity Press; Nottingham, UK: Inter-Varsity Press, 2013.

Cousar, Charles B. *A Theology of the Cross*. Minneapolis: Fortress, 1990.

Craigie, Peter C. *The Problem of War in the Old Testament*. Grand Rapids: Eerdmans, 1978.

Cranfield, C. E. B. *A Critical and Exegetical Commentary on the Epistle to the Romans*. 2 vols. Edinburgh: T&T Clark, 1975, 1979.

Crossan, John Dominic. *God and Empire*. San Francisco: Harper, 2007.

Crump, David. *Knocking on Heaven's Door*. Grand Rapids: Baker, 2006.

Dahl, Nils A. *The Crucified Messiah and Other Essays*. Minneapolis: Augsburg, 1974.

———. *Studies in Paul*. Minneapolis: Augsburg, 1977.

Das, A. Andrew, and Frank J. Matera, eds. *The Forgotten God*. Paul J. Achtemeier Festschrift. Louisville and London: Westminster John Knox, 2002.

Davidson, A. B. *The Theology of the Old Testament*. Edinburgh: T&T Clark; New York: Scribner's, 1904.

Davies, Margaret. *Matthew*. Sheffield: Sheffield Academic Press, 1993.

Davies, W. D. *Paul and Rabbinic Judaism*. 2nd ed. Reprint, New York: Harper; London: SPCK, 1962.

de Boer, Martinus C. "Paul's Mythologizing Program in Romans 5–8." In Beverly Roberts Gaventa, ed., *Apocalyptic Paul*, 1-20. Waco, TX: Baylor University Press, 2013.

Denney, James. *The Death of Christ*. London: Hodder and Stoughton; New York: Armstrong, 1902.

Donaldson, T. L. "The 'Curse of the Law' and the Inclusion of the Gentiles." *NTS* 32 (1986): 94-112.

Donfried, Karl P., and I. Howard Marshall. *The Theology of the Shorter Pauline Letters*. Cambridge and New York: Cambridge University Press, 1993.

Dulles, Avery. *Models of the Church*. 2nd ed. Dublin: Gill and Macmillan, 1988.

Dunn, James D. G. *Baptism in the Holy Spirit*. London: SCM Press; Naperville, IL: Allenson, 1970.

———. *The Christ and the Spirit*. 2 vols. Edinburgh: T&T Clark; Grand Rapids: Eerdmans, 1998.

———. *Christology in the Making*. London: SCM Press; Philadelphia: Westminster, 1980. 2nd ed., London: SCM Press; Grand Rapids: Eerdmans, 1989.

———. *Did the First Christians Worship Jesus?* Louisville: Westminster John Knox; London: SPCK, 2010.

———. *The New Perspective on Paul*. Tübingen: Mohr, 2005.

————. *The Partings of the Ways.* London: SCM Press; Philadelphia: Trinity Press International, 1991.

————, ed. *Paul and the Mosaic Law.* Tübingen: Mohr, 1996; Grand Rapids: Eerdmans, 2001.

————. *Romans.* 2 vols. Dallas: Word, 1988.

————. *The Theology of Paul the Apostle.* Grand Rapids and Cambridge, UK: Eerdmans, 1998.

————. *Unity and Diversity in the New Testament.* London: SCM Press; Philadelphia: Westminster, 1977. 2nd ed., 1990.

Ebeling, Gerhard. *Word and Faith.* Philadelphia: Fortress; London: SCM Press, 1963.

Ehrensberger, Kathy, et al., eds. *Decisive Meals.* London and New York: T&T Clark, 2012.

Eisen, Robert. *The Peace and Violence of Judaism.* Oxford and New York: Oxford University Press, 2011.

Elliott, Neil. *The Arrogance of Nations.* Minneapolis: Fortress, 2008.

Ellul, Jacques. *The Politics of God and the Politics of Man.* Grand Rapids: Eerdmans, 1972.

Epictetus. *The Moral Discourses of Epictetus.* London: Dent; New York: Dutton, 1910.

Fee, Gordon D. *The First Epistle to the Corinthians.* Grand Rapids: Eerdmans, 1987.

————. *God's Empowering Presence.* Peabody, MA: Hendrickson, 1994.

Feldmeier, Reinhard, and Hermann Spieckermann. *God of the Living.* Waco, TX: Baylor University Press, 2011.

Forsyth, P. T. *The Justification of God.* London: Duckworth, 1916; New York: Scribner's, 1917.

Frame, James Everett. *A Critical and Exegetical Commentary on the Epistles of St. Paul to the Thessalonians.* Reprint, Edinburgh: T&T Clark, 1975.

France, R. T. *The Gospel of Matthew.* Grand Rapids and Cambridge, UK: Eerdmans, 2007.

Fredriksen, Paula, and Adele Reinhartz, eds. *Jesus, Judaism, and Christian Anti-Judaism.* Louisville: Westminster John Knox, 2002.

Frydrych, Tomáš. *Living Under the Sun.* Leiden and Boston: Brill, 2002.

Fung, Ronald Y. K. *The Epistle to the Galatians.* Grand Rapids: Eerdmans, 1988.

Gager, John G. "Functional Diversity in Paul's Use of End-Time Language." *JBL* 89 (1970): 325-37.

Gaventa, Beverly Roberts. "The Cosmic Power of Sin in Paul's Letter to the Romans." *Interpretation* 58 (2004): 229-40.

Girard, René. *Violence and the Sacred*. Baltimore and London: Johns Hopkins University Press, 1977.

Goldingay, John. *Daniel*. Dallas: Word, 1989.

———. *Do We Need the New Testament?* Downers Grove, IL: InterVarsity Press, 2015.

———. *Isaiah 56–66*. London and New York: Bloomsbury, 2013.

———. *Key Questions About Biblical Interpretation*. Grand Rapids: Baker, 2011.

———. *Key Questions About Christian Faith*. Grand Rapids: Baker, 2010.

———. *The Message of Isaiah 40–55*. London and New York: T&T Clark, 2005.

———. *Models for Scripture*. Grand Rapids: Eerdmans; Carlisle, UK: Paternoster, 1994.

———. *Old Testament Theology*. 3 vols. Downers Grove, IL: InterVarsity Press; Milton Keynes, UK: Paternoster, 2003, 2006, 2009.

———. *Theological Diversity and the Authority of the Old Testament*. Grand Rapids: Eerdmans, 1987; Carlisle, UK: Paternoster, 1995.

Gordon, Robert P. *Hebrews*. Sheffield: Sheffield Academic Press, 2000.

Gorman, Michael J. *Cruciformity*. Grand Rapids and Cambridge, UK: Eerdmans, 2001.

———. *Inhabiting the Cruciform God*. Grand Rapids and Cambridge, UK: Eerdmans, 2009.

———. *Reading Paul*. Eugene, OR: Cascade, 2008.

Goshen-Gottstein, Alon. "God the Father in Rabbinic Judaism and Christianity." *Journal of Ecumenical Studies* 38 (2000–2001): 471-504.

Green, Joel B. *Body, Soul and Human Life*. Grand Rapids: Baker; Milton Keynes, UK: Paternoster, 2008.

Green, Joel B., and Mark D. Baker. *Recovering the Scandal of the Cross*. Downers Grove, IL: InterVarsity Press, 2000.

Gregory, Andrew F., and C. Kavin Rowe, eds. *Rethinking the Unity and Reception of Luke and Acts*. Columbia: University of South Carolina Press, 2010.

Greimas, A. G. *Structural Semantics*. Lincoln: University of Nebraska Press, 1983.

Guelich, Robert A., ed. *Unity and Diversity in New Testament Theology*. G. E. Ladd Festschrift. Grand Rapids: Eerdmans, 1978.

Gunkel, Hermann. *The Influence of the Holy Spirit*. Philadelphia: Fortress, 1979.

Gunton, Colin E. *The Actuality of Atonement*. Edinburgh: T&T Clark; Grand Rapids: Eerdmans, 1989.

Gutiérrez, Gustavo. *Essential Writings*. Maryknoll, NY: Orbis, 1996.

———. *A Theology of Liberation*. Maryknoll, NY: Orbis, 1973; London: SCM Press, 1974.

Hafemann, Scott J., ed. *Biblical Theology*. Downers Grove, IL: InterVarsity Press; Leicester, UK: Inter-Varsity Press, 2002.

——. *The God of Promise and the Life of Faith*. Wheaton, IL: Crossway, 2001.

Harris, Murray J. *Slave of Christ*. Downers Grove, IL: InterVarsity Press; Leicester, UK: Inter-Varsity Press, 2001.

Hart, T. A., and D. P. Thimell, eds. *Christ in Our Place*. J. Torrance Festschrift. Exeter, UK: Paternoster; Allison Park, PA: Pickwick, 1990.

Harvey, Anthony E. *Strenuous Commands*. London: SCM Press; Philadelphia: Trinity Press International, 1990.

Harvie, Timothy. "God as a Field of Force." *Heythrop Journal* 52 (2011): 250-59.

Hauerwas, Stanley. *A Community of Character*. Notre Dame, IN, and London: University of Notre Dame Press, 1981.

——. *With the Grain of the Universe*. Grand Rapids: Baker, 2001.

Hawk, Dan. *Every Promise Fulfilled: Contesting Plots in Joshua*. Louisville: Westminster John Knox, 1991.

Hawthorne, Gerald F. *Philippians*. Waco, TX: Word, 1983.

Hays, J. Daniel. *From Every People and Nation*. Downers Grove, IL: InterVarsity Press; Nottingham, UK: Inter-Varsity Press, 2003.

Hays, Richard B. *Echoes of Scripture in the Letters of Paul*. New Haven, CT, and London: Yale University Press, 1989.

——. *The Moral Vision of the New Testament*. San Francisco: Harper, 1996.

Hays, Richard B., and Stefan Alkier, eds. *Revelation and the Politics of Apocalyptic Interpretation*. Waco, TX: Baylor University Press, 2012.

Heiler, Friedrich. *Prayer*. London and New York: Oxford University Press, 1932.

Heim, S. Mark. *Saved from Sacrifice*. Grand Rapids and Cambridge, UK: Eerdmans, 2006.

Hengel, Martin. *The Son of God*. London: SCM Press; Philadelphia: Fortress, 1976.

——. *Studies in Early Christology*. Edinburgh: T&T Clark, 1995.

Hill, Charles E., and Frank A. James III, eds. *The Glory of the Atonement*. Roger Nicole Festschrift. Downers Grove, IL: InterVarsity Press, 2004.

Hooker, M. D., and S. G. Wilson, eds. *Paul and Paulinism*. C. K. Barrett Festschrift. London: SPCK, 1982.

Horsley, Richard A. *In the Shadow of Empire*. Louisville and London: Westminster John Knox, 2008.

——. *Jesus and the Spiral of Violence*. Reprint, Philadelphia: Fortress, 1993.

Hubbard, David A. "The Wisdom Movement and Israel's Covenant Faith." *Tyndale Bulletin* 17 (1966): 3-34.

Hui, Archie. "The Spirit of Prophecy and Pauline Pneumatology." *Tyndale Bulletin* 50 (1999): 93-115.

Hurtado, Larry. *At the Origins of Christian Worship*. Carlisle, UK: Paternoster, 1999; Grand Rapids: Eerdmans, 2000.

———. *God in New Testament Theology*. Nashville: Abingdon, 2010.

———. *How on Earth Did Jesus Become God?* Grand Rapids and Cambridge, UK: Eerdmans, 2005.

———. *Lord Jesus Christ: Devotion to Jesus in Earliest Christianity*. Grand Rapids and Cambridge, UK: Eerdmans, 2003.

———. *One God, One Lord*. Philadelphia: Fortress; London: SCM Press, 1988. 2nd ed., Edinburgh: T&T Clark, 1998.

Irenaeus of Lyons. *Against Heresies*. *Ante-Nicene Fathers* 1:307-567.

Irons, Charles Lee. *The Righteousness of God*. Tübingen: Mohr, 2015.

Jackson, Bernard S. "Legalism." *Journal of Jewish Studies* 30 (1979): 1-22.

Jeffery, Steve, Michael Ovey and Andrew Sach. *Pierced for Our Transgressions*. Nottingham, UK: Inter-Varsity Press; Wheaton, IL: Crossway, 2007.

John of Damascus. *Exposition of the Orthodox Faith*. NPNF 2, 9 (second part), 1-101.

Johnson, Luke T. "The New Testament's Anti-Jewish Slander and the Conventions of Ancient Polemic." *JBL* 108 (1989): 419-41.

Jones, L. Gregory. *Embodying Forgiveness*. Grand Rapids: Eerdmans, 1995.

Kalimi, Isaac, ed. *Jewish Bible Theology*. Winona Lake, IN: Eisenbrauns, 2012.

Kaminski, Carol M. *Was Noah Good?* London and New York: T&T Clark, 2014.

Kaminsky, Joel. "Did Election Imply the Mistreatment of Non-Israelites?" *Harvard Theological Review* 96 (2003): 397-425.

Kärkkäinen, Veli-Matti. *Toward a Pneumatological Theology*. Lanham, MD: University Press of America, 2002.

Käsemann, Ernst. *Essays on New Testament Themes*. London: SCM Press, 1964.

———. *New Testament Questions of Today*. London: SCM Press; Philadelphia: Westminster, 1969.

———. *The Testament of Jesus*. London: SCM Press; Philadelphia: Fortress, 1968.

Kazen, Thomas. *Emotions in Biblical Law*. Sheffield: Sheffield Phoenix, 2011.

Keck, Leander E. *Paul and His Letters*. Philadelphia: Fortress, 1979. Rev. ed., 1988.

Keener, Craig S. "'Brood of Vipers.'" *JSNT* 28 (2005): 3-11.

Kierkegaard, Søren. *The Present Age, and Of the Difference Between a Genius and an Apostle*. Reprint, New York: Harper 1962.

Kilner, John F. "Humanity in God's Image." *Journal of the Evangelical Theological Society* 53 (2010): 601-17.

Kim, Seyoon. *Christ and Caesar*. Grand Rapids: Eerdmans, 2009.

Kimel, Alvin F., ed. *Speaking the Christian God*. Grand Rapids: Eerdmans; Leominster, UK: Gracewing, 1992.

Kirk, J. R. Daniel. *Jesus Have I Loved, but Paul?* Grand Rapids: Baker, 2011.

———. "The Sufficiency of the Cross." *Scottish Bulletin of Evangelical Theology* 24 (2006): 36-64, 133-54.

Knowles, Michael P. *The Unfolding Mystery of the Divine Name*. Downers Grove, IL: InterVarsity Press, 2012.

Köhler, Ludwig. *Old Testament Theology*. London: Lutterworth, 1957; Philadelphia: Westminster, 1958.

Kramer, Werner. *Christ, Lord, Son of God*. London: SCM Press; Naperville, IL: Allenson, 1966.

Krans, Jan, Bert Jan Lietaert Peerbolte, Peter-Ben Smit and Arie Zwiep, eds. *Paul, John, and Apocalyptic Eschatology*. Martinus C. de Boer Festschrift. Leiden and Boston: Brill, 2013.

Küng, Hans. *Does God Exist?* Garden City, NY: Doubleday; London: Collins, 1980.

———. *On Being a Christian*. Garden City, NY: Doubleday, 1976; London: Collins, 1977.

Künneth, Walter. *The Theology of the Resurrection*. London: SCM Press; St. Louis: Concordia, 1965.

Ladd, George Eldon. *The Blessed Hope*. Grand Rapids: Eerdmans, 1956.

———. *The Gospel of the Kingdom*. Grand Rapids: Eerdmans; [Exeter, UK:] Paternoster, 1959.

———. *A Theology of the New Testament*. Grand Rapids: Eerdmans, 1974. Rev. ed., edited by Donald A. Hagner, Grand Rapids: Eerdmans, 1993.

Lane, Anthony N. S., ed. *The Unseen World*. Carlisle, UK: Paternoster; Grand Rapids: Baker, 1996.

Laniak, Timothy S. *Shepherds After My Own Heart*. Downers Grove, IL: InterVarsity Press; Leicester, UK: Inter-Varsity Press, 2006.

Lapsley, Jacqueline E. "Shame and Self-Knowledge." In *The Book of Ezekiel*, ed. Margaret S. Odell and John T. Strong, 143-73. Atlanta: Scholars Press, 2000.

Larsson, Tord. *God in the Fourth Gospel*. Stockholm: Almqvuist, 2001.

Leivestad, Ragnar. "Exit the Apocalyptic Son of Man." *NTS* 18 (1971–1972): 243-67.

Levenson, Jon D. *Creation and the Persistence of Evil*. Reissued, Princeton, NJ, and Chichester, UK: Princeton University Press, 1994.

———. *The Death and Resurrection of the Beloved Son*. New Haven, CT, and London: Yale University Press, 1993.

————. *The Hebrew Bible, the Old Testament, and Historical Criticism.* Louisville: Westminster John Knox, 1993.

Levering, Matthew. *Jesus and the Demise of Death.* Waco, TX: Baylor University Press, 2012.

Levine, Baruch A. *In Pursuit of Meaning.* 2 vols. Winona Lake, IN: Eisenbrauns, 2011.

Levison, John R. *Filled with the Spirit.* Grand Rapids and Cambridge, UK: Eerdmans, 2009.

Lightfoot, J. B. *Saint Paul's Epistle to the Philippians.* Reprint, Grand Rapids: Zondervan, 1965.

Lightfoot, R. H. *St. John's Gospel.* Oxford and New York: Oxford University Press, 1956.

Lincoln, Andrew T. *Born of a Virgin?* London: SPCK; Grand Rapids: Eerdmans, 2013.

————. *Ephesians.* Dallas: Word, 1990.

————. "Liberation from the Powers." In M. Daniel Carroll R. et al., eds., *The Bible in Human Society*, 335-54. John Rogerson Festschrift. Sheffield: Sheffield Academic Press, 1995.

————. *Truth on Trial.* Peabody, MA: Hendrickson, 2000.

Lindars, Barnabas. *The Theology of the Letter to the Hebrews.* Cambridge and New York: Cambridge University Press, 1991.

Lindbeck, George A. *The Church in a Postliberal Age.* Edited by James J. Buckley. Grand Rapids: Eerdmans, 2004.

Lohfink, Gerhard. *Jesus and Community.* Philadelphia: Fortress, 1984.

Lohse, Eduard. *Colossians and Philemon.* Philadelphia: Fortress, 1971.

————. *Theological Ethics of the New Testament.* Minneapolis: Fortress, 1991.

Lombard, Peter. *The Sentences Book 3.* Toronto: Pontifical Institute of Mediaeval Studies, 2008.

Longenecker, Bruce W., and Mikael C. Parsons, eds. *Beyond Bultmann.* Waco, TX: Baylor University Press, 2014.

Longenecker, Richard N. *Galatians.* Dallas: Word, 1990.

Löning, Karl, and Erich Zenger. *To Begin with, God Created. . . .* Collegeville, MN: Liturgical, 2000.

Lüdemann, Gerd. "The Hope of the Early Paul." *Perspectives in Religious Studies* 7 (1980): 195-201.

————. *Paulus und das Judentum.* Munich: Kaiser, 1983.

Luther, Martin. *Large Catechism.* Reprint, St. Louis: Concordia, 1988.

————. *Lectures on Galatians 1535 Chapters 1–4.* LW 26. St. Louis: Concordia, 1963.

————. *Lectures on Romans.* LW 25. St. Louis: Concordia, 1972.

———. *Letters I.* LW 48. Philadelphia: Fortress, 1963.

———. *Sermons on the Gospel of St. John Chapters 1–4.* LW 22. St. Louis: Concordia, 1957.

———. *Sermons on the Gospel of St. John Chapters 6–8.* LW 23. St. Louis: Concordia, 1959.

———. *Small Catechism.* Reprint, St. Louis: Concordia, 1965.

———. *Werke: Kritische Gesamtausgabe.* 61 vols. Weimar: Hermann Böhlaus Nachfolger, 1883–1983.

Lyotard, Jean-François. *The Postmodern Condition.* Manchester: Manchester University Press; Minneapolis: University of Minnesota Press, 1984.

MacDonald, Nathan. *Deuteronomy and the Meaning of "Monotheism."* Tübingen: Mohr, 2003.

———. "The Origin of 'Monotheism.'" In Wendy North and Loren T. Stuckenbruck, eds., *Early Jewish and Christian Monotheism,* 204-15. London and New York: Continuum, 2004.

MacKinnon, D. M. "Subjective and Objective Conceptions of Atonement." In F. G. Healey, ed., *Prospect for Theology,* 169-82. H. H. Farmer Festschrift. Welwyn, UK: Nisbet, 1966.

Maluleke, Tinyiko. "Black Theology as Public Discourse." www.religion.uct.ac.za /sites/default/files/image_tool/images/113/Institutes/Religion_in_Public_Life _ME_1999/Concep_Papers/Tinyiko_Maluleke.pdf.

Marguerat, Daniel. "Paul the Mystic." In Jan Krans et al., eds., *Paul, John, and Apocalyptic Eschatology,* 76-93. Martinus C. de Boer Festschrift. Leiden and Boston: Brill, 2013.

Marshall, Christopher D. *Beyond Retribution.* Grand Rapids and Cambridge, UK: Eerdmans, 2001.

Marshall, I. Howard. *New Testament Theology.* Downers Grove, IL: InterVarsity Press; Nottingham, UK: Inter-Varsity Press, 2004.

Martin, Dale B. *The Corinthian Body.* New Haven, CT: Yale University Press, 1995.

———. *Slavery as Salvation.* New Haven, CT, and London: Yale University Press, 1990.

Martin, Ralph P. *2 Corinthians.* Waco, TX: Word, 1986.

———. *Philippians.* Reprint, London: Marshall; Grand Rapids: Eerdmans, 1980.

———. *Reconciliation.* London: Marshall; Atlanta: John Knox, 1981. Rev. ed., Eugene, OR: Wipf and Stock, 1989.

Matlock, R. B. *Unveiling the Apocalyptic Paul.* Sheffield: Sheffield Academic Press, 1996.

Mauser, Ulrich. "One God Alone." *Princeton Seminary Bulletin* 12 (1991): 255-65.

McClendon, James W. *Systematic Theology: Doctrine.* Nashville: Abingdon, 1994.

————. *Systematic Theology: Ethics*. Nashville: Abingdon, 1986.

McClendon, James W., with Nancey Murphy. *Systematic Theology: Witness*. Nashville: Abingdon, 2000.

McCue, James F. "*Simul iustus et peccator* in Augustine, Aquinas, and Luther." *Journal of the American Academy of Religion* 48 (1980): 81-96.

McFarland, Ian A. *In Adam's Fall*. Chichester, UK, and Malden, MA: Wiley-Blackwell, 2010.

McKnight, Scot. *Jesus and His Death*. Waco, TX: Baylor University Press, 2005.

————. *A New Vision for Israel*. Grand Rapids and Cambridge, UK: Eerdmans, 1999.

McKnight, Scot, and Joseph B. Modica, eds. *Jesus Is Lord, Caesar Is Not*. Downers Grove, IL: InterVarsity Press, 2013.

Meeks, Wayne A. *The First Urban Christians*. 2nd ed. New Haven, CT, and London: Yale University Press, 2003.

Meier, John P. *A Marginal Jew*. 3 vols. New York: Doubleday, 1991, 1994, 2001.

Mekilta de-Rabbi Ishmael. Philadelphia: JPS, 1933.

Melanchthon, Philip. *Letters I*. Philadelphia: Fortress, 1963.

Mendenhall, G. E. "The Monarchy." *Interpretation* 29 (1975): 155-70.

Michaels, J. Ramsey. *Revelation*. Downers Grove, IL: InterVarsity Press; Leicester, UK: Inter-Varsity Press, 1997.

Middleton, J. Richard. *The Liberating Image*. Grand Rapids: Brazos, 2005.

————. *A New Heaven and a New Earth*. Grand Rapids: Baker, 2014.

Miles, Jack. *God: A Biography*. New York and London: Simon and Schuster, 1995.

Mills, C. Wright. *White Collar*. New York: Oxford University Press, 1951.

Miskotte, Kornelis H. *When the Gods Are Silent*. London: Collins; New York: Harper, 1967.

Moberly, Elizabeth R. *Suffering, Innocent and Guilty*. London: SPCK, 1978.

Moberly, R. W. L. "How Appropriate Is 'Monotheism' as a Category for Biblical Interpretation?" In Wendy North and Loren T. Stuckenbruck, eds., *Early Jewish and Christian Monotheism*, 216-34. London and New York: Continuum, 2004.

Moltmann, Jürgen. *The Church in the Power of the Spirit*. London: SCM Press; New York: Harper, 1977.

————. *The Coming of God*. London: SCM Press; Minneapolis: Fortress, 1996.

————. *God in Creation*. London: SCM Press; San Francisco: Harper, 1985.

————. *History and the Triune God*. London: SCM Press, 1991; New York: Crossroad, 1992.

————. *On Human Dignity*. London: SCM Press; Philadelphia: Fortress, 1984.

————. *The Spirit of Life*. London: SCM Press; Minneapolis: Fortress, 1992.

------. *Theology of Hope*. London: SCM Press; New York: Harper, 1967.

------. *The Trinity and the Kingdom of God*. London: SCM Press; New York: Harper, 1981.

------. *The Way of Jesus Christ*. [San Francisco:] HarperCollins; London: SCM Press, 1990.

Moore, A. L. *The Parousia in the New Testament*. Leiden: Brill, 1966.

Morris, Leon. *The Apostolic Preaching of the Cross*. London: Tyndale; Grand Rapids: Eerdmans, 1955. 3rd ed., 1965.

Motyer, J. A. "Covenant and Promise." *Evangel: The British Evangelical Review* 1, no. 1 (1983): 2-4.

Moule, C. F. D. "The Individualism of the Fourth Gospel." *Novum Testamentum* 5 (1962): 171-90.

Moxnes, Halvor. *Theology in Conflict*. Leiden: Brill, 1980.

Munck, Johannes. *Paul and the Salvation of Mankind*. London: SCM Press; Richmond: John Knox, 1959.

Newbigin, Lesslie. *A Faith for This One World?* New York: Harper; London: SCM Press, 1961.

------. *The Gospel in a Pluralist Society*. Grand Rapids: Eerdmans; London: SPCK, 1989.

------. *The Open Secret*. Grand Rapids: Eerdmans; London: SPCK, 1978.

Newman, Carey C., ed. *Jesus and the Restoration of Israel*. Downers Grove, IL: InterVarsity Press; Carlisle, UK: Paternoster, 1999.

Newman, Carey C., James R. Davila, and Gladys S. Lewis, eds. *The Jewish Roots of Christological Monotheism*. Leiden and Boston: Brill, 1999.

Neyrey, Jerome H. *Render to God*. Minneapolis: Fortress, 2004.

Niebuhr, H. Richard. *Christ and Culture*. Reprint, San Francisco: Harper, 2001.

Niehaus, Jeffrey J. *Ancient Near Eastern Themes in Biblical Theology*. Grand Rapids: Kregel, 2008.

Nietzsche, Friedrich. *Twilight of the Idols and The Anti-Christ*. London and New York: Penguin, 1968.

North, Wendy, and Loren T. Stuckenbruck, eds. *Early Jewish and Christian Monotheism*. London and New York: Continuum, 2004.

Noth, Martin. *The Laws in the Pentateuch and Other Studies*. Edinburgh: Oliver and Boyd, 1966; Philadelphia: Fortress, 1967.

Nygren, Anders. *Agape and Eros*. London: SPCK, 1953.

Oakes, Peter. *Philippians*. Cambridge and New York: Cambridge University Press, 2001.

O'Brien, Peter Thomas. *Introductory Thanksgivings in the Letters of Paul*. Leiden: Brill, 1977.

O'Day, Gail R. "The Gospel of John." In Leander E. Keck et al., eds., *The New Interpreter's Bible*, 9:491-871. Nashville: Abingdon, 1995.

Odell, Margaret S., and John T. Strong, eds. *The Book of Ezekiel*. Atlanta: Scholars Press, 2000.

O'Donovan, Oliver. *Finding and Seeking*. Grand Rapids and Cambridge, UK: Eerdmans, 2014.

———. *Self, World, and Time*. Grand Rapids and Cambridge, UK: Eerdmans, 2013.

Origen. *Homilies on Genesis and Exodus*. Washington, DC: Catholic University of America Press, 1982.

Otto, Rudolf. *The Kingdom of God and the Son of Man*. Reprint, London: Lutterworth, 1951.

Ouspensky, Leonid. *Theology of the Icon*. Crestwood, NY: St Vladimir's Seminary Press, 1992.

Owens, Mark. *As It Was in the Beginning: An Intertextual Analysis of New Creation in Galatians, 2 Corinthians, and Ephesians*. Eugene, OR: Wipf and Stock, 2016.

Packer, J. I. *Knowing God*. London: Hodder; Downers Grove, IL: InterVarsity Press, 1973.

Pannenberg, Wolfhart. *Jesus—God and Man*. Philadelphia: Westminster; London: SCM Press, 1968.

Parker, Theodore. *Ten Sermons of Religion*. Reprinted in *The Collected Works of Theodore Parker*, vol. 2. London: Trübner, 1879.

Penchansky, David. *Twilight of the Gods*. Louisville: Westminster John Knox, 2005.

Perdue, Leo, and others. *Families in Ancient Israel*. Louisville: Westminster John Knox, 1997.

Perrin, Nicholas, and Richard B. Hays, eds. *Jesus, Paul and the People of God*. Downers Grove, IL: InterVarsity Press, 2011.

Peterson, Eugene H. *Working the Angles*. Grand Rapids: Eerdmans, 1987. Reset, 1993.

Philo of Alexandria. "Concerning the Cherubim"; "Concerning the Confusion of Tongues"; and "Concerning Dreams." In *Philo with an English Translation*, by F. H. Colson and G. H. Whitaker. 11 vols. Cambridge, MA: Harvard University Press; London: Heinemann, 1929–1943.

Piper, John. *Future Grace*. Sisters, OR: Multnomah, 1995.

Pitre, Brant. *Jesus, the Tribulation, and the End of the Exile*. Tübingen: Mohr; Grand Rapids: Baker, 2005.

Plevnik, Joseph. *Paul and the Parousia*. Peabody, MA: Hendrickson, 1997.

Pope, Alexander. *The Complete Poetical Works of Alexander Pope*. Boston: Houghton Mifflin, 1903.

Porter, Barbara N., ed. *One God or Many?* Chebeague, ME: Casco Bay Assyriological Institute, 2000.

Räisänen, Heikki. *Beyond New Testament Theology*. London: SCM Press; Philadelphia: Trinity Press International, 1990.

Rashdall, Hastings. *The Idea of Atonement in Christian Theology*. London: Macmillan, 1919.

Reicke, Bo. "The Law and This World According to Paul." *JBL* 70 (1951): 259-76.

Reid, J. K. S. *Our Life in Christ*. London: SCM Press, 1963.

Richardson, Alan. *An Introduction to the Theology of the New Testament*. London: SCM Press; New York: Harper, 1958.

Ricoeur, Paul. *Essays on Biblical Interpretation*. Philadelphia: Fortress, 1980; London: SPCK, 1981.

Ridderbos, Herman. *Paul: An Outline of His Theology*. Grand Rapids: Eerdmans, 1975.

Rieger, Joerg. *Christ and Empire*. Minneapolis: Fortress, 2007.

Rissi, Mathias. *The Future of the World*. London: SCM Press; Naperville, IL: Allenson, 1972.

Robinson, J. Armitage. *St. Paul's Epistle to the Ephesians*. 2nd ed. London: James Clarke, [?1904].

Rodd, Cyril S. *Glimpses of a Strange Land*. Edinburgh: T&T Clark, 2001.

Rogerson, J. W., and John Vincent. *The City in Biblical Perspective*. London and Oakville, CT: Equinox, 2009.

Rosner, Brian S. *Paul and the Law*. Nottingham, UK: Inter-Varsity Press; Downers Grove, IL: InterVarsity Press, 2013.

Rowland, Christopher. *The Open Heaven*. London: SPCK; New York: Crossroad, 1982.

Sanders, E. P. *Paul and Palestinian Judaism*. London: SCM Press; Philadelphia: Fortress, 1977.

———. *Paul, the Law, and the Jewish People*. London: SCM Press; Philadelphia: Fortress, 1983.

Schaeffer, Francis A. *The God Who Is There*. London: Hodder; Chicago: InterVarsity Press, 1968.

———. *He Is There and He Is Not Silent*. Rev. ed. Wheaton, IL: Tyndale House, 2001.

Scharen, Christian. *Faith as a Way of Life*. Grand Rapids and Cambridge, UK: Eerdmans, 2008.

Schillebeeckx, Edward. *Christ*. New York: Crossroad; London: SCM Press, 1980.

———. *The Church with a Human Face*. New York: Crossroad; London: SCM Press, 1985.

———. *Jesus*. New York: Crossroad; London: Collins, 1979.

Schlink, Edmund. *The Coming Christ and the Coming Church*. Edinburgh: Oliver and Boyd, 1967; Philadelphia: Fortress, 1968.

Schluter, Michael, and John Ashcroft, eds. *Jubilee Manifesto*. Leicester, UK: Inter-Varsity Press, 2005.

Schnackenburg, Rudolf. *Baptism in the Thought of St. Paul*. Oxford: Blackwell; New York: Herder, 1964.

———. *God's Rule and Kingdom*. Freiburg: Herder; Montreal: Palm, 1963.

Schneiders, Sandra M. "The Lamb of God and the Forgiveness of Sin(s) in the Fourth Gospel." *Catholic Biblical Quarterly* 73 (2011): 1-29.

Schuller, Eileen M. "The Book of Malachi." In *The New Interpreter's Bible*, Leander E. Keck et al., eds., 7:841-77. Nashville: Abingdon, 1996.

Schüssler Fiorenza, Elizabeth. *The Book of Revelation: Justice and Judgment*. 2nd ed. Philadelphia: Fortress, 1998.

———. *The Power of the Word*. Minneapolis: Fortress, 2007.

Schütz, John Howard. *Paul and the Anatomy of Apostolic Authority*. London and New York: Cambridge University Press, 1975.

Schwartz, Daniel R., and Zeev Weiss, eds. *Was 70 CE a Watershed in Jewish History?* Leiden and Boston: Brill, 2012.

Schweizer, Eduard. *The Holy Spirit*. Philadelphia: Fortress, 1980.

Seeley, David. *The Noble Death*. Sheffield: JSOT, 1989.

Segal, Alan F. *Two Powers in Heaven*. Leiden: Brill, 1977.

Seligman, Adam B. *Modernity's Wager*. Princeton, NJ, and Oxford: Princeton University Press, 2000.

Shriver, Donald W. *An Ethic for Enemies*. New York: Oxford University Press, 1995.

Smail, Thomas A. *The Forgotten Father*. London: Hodder, 1980; Grand Rapids: Eerdmans, 1981.

———. *Once and for All*. London: DLT, 1998; Eugene, OR: Wipf and Stock, 2006.

Smart, James D. *The Strange Silence of the Bible in the Church*. Philadelphia: Westminster; London: SCM Press, 1970.

Smith, D. Moody. *The Theology of the Gospel of John*. Cambridge and New York: Cambridge University Press, 1995.

Sobrino, Jon. *Jesus the Liberator*. Maryknoll, NY: Orbis, 1993; Tunbridge Wells, UK: Burns and Oates, 1994.

Sobrino, Jon, and Ignacio Ellacuría, eds. *Mysterium Liberationis*. Maryknoll, NY: Orbis, 1993. Abridged ed., *Systematic Theology*. Maryknoll, NY: Orbis, 1996.

Sommer, Benjamin D. *The Bodies of God and the World of Ancient Israel*. Cambridge and New York: Cambridge University Press, 2009.

Spurgeon, C. H. "The Immutability of God." *The New Park Street Pulpit*. www .spurgeon.org/sermons/0001.htm.

Stendahl, Krister. *Paul Among Jews and Gentiles and Other Essays*. Philadelphia: Fortress, 1976.

Streett, Matthew J. *Here Comes the Judge*. London and New York: T&T Clark, 2012.

Sun, Henry T. C., and Keith L. Eades, eds. *Problems in Biblical Theology*. Rolf Knierim Festschrift. Grand Rapids and Cambridge, UK: Eerdmans, 1997.

Swing, Albert Temple. *The Theology of Albrecht Ritschl*. New York and London: Longmans, Green, 1901.

Thattayil, Benny. *In Spirit and Truth*. Louvain: Peeters, 2007.

Theissen, Gerd. *The Social Setting of Pauline Christianity*. Philadelphia: Fortress, 1982.

Thielman, Frank. *From Plight to Solution*. Leiden and New York: Brill, 1989.

———. *Paul and the Law*. Downers Grove, IL: InterVarsity Press, 1994.

Thiselton, Anthony C. *1 Corinthians*. Grand Rapids and Cambridge, UK: Eerdmans, 2006.

———. *The Hermeneutics of Doctrine*. Grand Rapids and Cambridge, UK: Eerdmans, 2007.

———. "Realized Eschatology at Corinth." *NTS* 24 (1978): 510-26.

———. *Thiselton on Hermeneutics*. Grand Rapids and Cambridge, UK: Eerdmans, 2006.

Thomas, Heath A., Jeremy Evans and Paul Copan, eds. *Holy War in the Bible*. Downers Grove, IL: InterVarsity Press, 2013.

Thompson, Marianne Meye. *The God of the Gospel of John*. Grand Rapids and Cambridge, UK: Eerdmans, 2001.

———. *The Promise of the Father*. Louisville: Westminster John Knox, 2000.

Thrall, Margaret E. *A Critical and Exegetical Commentary on the Second Epistle to the Corinthians*. Edinburgh: T&T Clark, 1994.

Torrance, T. F. *Calvin's Doctrine of Man*. New ed. Grand Rapids: Eerdmans, 1957.

———. "The Divine Vocation and Destiny of Israel in World History." In *The Witness of the Jews to God*, ed. David W. Torrance, 85-104. Edinburgh: Handsel, 1982.

Travis, Stephen H. *Christ and the Judgment of God*. Basingstoke, UK: Marshall, 1986. 2nd ed., *Christ and the Judgement of God*. Milton Keynes, UK: Paternoster; Peabody, MA: Hendrickson, 2009.

———. *I Believe in the Second Coming of Jesus*. London: Hodder; Grand Rapids: Eerdmans, 1982.

Troeltsch, Ernst. *The Social Teaching of the Christian Churches*. London: George Allen; New York: Macmillan, 1931.

Turner, Max. *The Holy Spirit and Spiritual Gifts in the New Testament Church and Today*. Rev. ed. Carlisle, UK: Paternoster; Peabody, MA: Hendrickson, 1998.

———. *Power from on High*. Corrected ed. Sheffield: Sheffield Academic Press, 2000.

Van der Watt, Jan G., ed. *Eschatology of the New Testament and Some Related Documents*. Tübingen: Mohr, 2011.

Verhey, Allen. *The Great Reversal*. Grand Rapids: Eerdmans, 1984.

Volf, Miroslav. *Against the Tide*. Grand Rapids: Eerdmans, 2010.

———. *Captive to the Word of God*. Grand Rapids and Cambridge, UK: Eerdmans, 2010.

———. *Exclusion and Embrace*. Nashville: Abingdon, 1996.

von Harnack, Adolf. *The Mission and Expansion of Christianity in the First Three Centuries*. London: Williams and Norgate; New York: Putnam, 1908.

von Rad, Gerhard. *Old Testament Theology*. 2 vols. Edinburgh: Oliver and Boyd; New York: Harper, 1962, 1965.

Wagner, J. Ross. *Heralds of the Good News: Isaiah and Paul "in Concert" in the Letter to the Romans*. Leiden and Boston: Brill, 2002.

Ware, Kallistos. *The Inner Kingdom*. Crestwood, NY: St Vladimir's Seminary Press, 2001.

Watson, Francis. *Text and Truth*. Edinburgh: T&T Clark; Grand Rapids: Eerdmans, 1997.

———. *Text, Church and World*. Edinburgh: T&T Clark; Grand Rapids: Eerdmans, 1994.

Weber, Otto. *Foundations of Dogmatics*. 2 vols. Grand Rapids: Eerdmans, 1981, 1983.

Wedderburn, A. J. M. "Some Observations on Paul's Use of the Phrases 'In Christ' and 'With Christ.'" *JSNT* 25 (1985): 83-97.

Weinfeld, Moshe. *Social Justice in Ancient Israel and in the Ancient Near East*. Philadelphia: Fortress, 1995.

Welker, Michael. *God the Spirit*. Minneapolis: Fortress, 1994.

Wenham, David. *Paul: Follower of Jesus or Founder of Christianity?* Grand Rapids and Cambridge, UK: Eerdmans, 1995.

Wenham, G. J. "The Religion of the Patriarchs." In A. R. Millard and D. J. Wiseman, eds., *Essays on the Patriarchal Narratives*. Leicester, UK: Inter-Varsity Press, 1980; Winona Lake, IN: Eisenbrauns, 1983.

West, Gerald O. "Liberation Hermeneutics After Liberation." In Alejandro F. Botta and Pablo R. Andiñach, eds., *The Bible and the Hermeneutics of Liberation*, 13-38. Atlanta: SBL, 2009.

Westerholm, Stephen. *Israel's Law and the Church's Faith*. Grand Rapids: Eerdmans, 1988.

Westermann, Claus. *The Praise of God in the Psalms*. Richmond: John Knox, 1965; London: Epworth, 1966. Rev. ed., *Praise and Lament in the Psalms*. Atlanta: John Knox; Edinburgh: T&T Clark, 1981.

Whale, J. S. *Victor and Victim*. Cambridge and New York: Cambridge University Press, 1960.

White, Vernon. *Atonement and Incarnation*. Cambridge and New York: Cambridge University Press, 1991.

Whybray, R. Norman. *The Good Life in the Old Testament*. Edinburgh: T&T Clark, 2002.

Wiedemann, Thomas. *Greek and Roman Slavery*. Reprint, London and New York: Routledge, 2005.

Wiesel, Elie. *From the Kingdom of Memory*. New York: Summit, 1990.

Wikenhauser, Alfred. *Pauline Mysticism*. New York: Herder, 1959.

Williams, James G. *The Girard Reader*. New York: Crossroad, 1996.

Wilson, R. McL. *A Critical and Exegetical Commentary on Colossians and Philemon*. London and New York: T&T Clark, 2005.

Windisch, Hans. "Das problem des paulinischen Imperativs." *Zeitschrift für die neutestamentliche Wissenschaft und die Kunde der älteren Kirchen* 23 (1924): 265-81.

———. *Taufe und Sünde im ältesten Christentum*. Tübingen: Mohr, 1908.

Wink, Walter. *Engaging the Powers*. Minneapolis: Fortress, 1992.

———. *Naming the Powers*. Philadelphia: Fortress, 1984.

———. *Unmasking the Powers*. Philadelphia: Fortress, 1986.

Witherington, Ben, III. *The Christology of Jesus*. Minneapolis: Fortress, 1990.

Woodhead, Linda. "Love and Justice." *Studies in Christian Ethics* 5 (1992): 44-61.

Wrede, William. *The Messianic Secret*. London: Clarke; Greenwood, SC: Attic, 1971.

Wright, Christopher J. H. *God's People in God's Land*. Exeter, UK: Paternoster; Grand Rapids: Eerdmans, 1990.

———. *The Mission of God*. Downers Grove, IL: InterVarsity Press; Nottingham, UK: Inter-Varsity Press, 2006.

Wright, N. T. *Christian Origins and the Question of God*. Minneapolis: Fortress, 1992.

———. *The Climax of the Covenant*. Edinburgh: T&T Clark, 1991; Minneapolis: Fortress, 1992.

——. *For All the Saints?* London: SPCK, 2003; Harrisburg, PA: Morehouse, 2004.

——. *Jesus and the Victory of God.* Minneapolis: Fortress; London: SPCK, 1996.

——. *Justification.* London: SPCK; Downers Grove, IL: InterVarsity Press, 2009.

——. "The Letter to the Romans." In Leander E. Keck et al., eds., *The New Interpreter's Bible*, 10:393-770. Nashville: Abingdon, 2002.

——. *The New Testament and the People of God.* Minneapolis: Fortress; London: SPCK, 1992.

——. *Paul and the Faithfulness of God.* Minneapolis: Fortress; London: SPCK, 2013.

——. *The Resurrection of the Son of God.* London: SPCK; Minneapolis: Fortress, 2003.

——. *Surprised by Hope.* London: SPCK, 2007; New York: HarperOne, 2008.

——. "Theology, History and Jesus." *JSNT* 69 (1998): 105-12.

Yinger, Kent. "Defining Legalism." *Andrews University Seminary Studies* 46 (2008): 91-108.

——. *Paul, Judaism and Judgment According to Deeds.* Cambridge and New York: Cambridge University Press, 1999.

Yoder, John Howard. "Armaments and Eschatology." *Studies in Christian Ethics* 1 (1988): 43-61.

——. *For the Nations.* Grand Rapids and Cambridge, UK: Eerdmans, 1997.

——. *The Politics of Jesus.* 2nd ed. Grand Rapids: Eerdmans; Carlisle, UK: Paternoster, 1993.

——. *The Priestly Kingdom.* Notre Dame, IN: University of Notre Dame Press, 1984.

Yong, Amos. *Renewing Christian Theology.* Waco, TX: Baylor University Press, 2014.

Young, Frances M. *Sacrifice and the Death of Christ.* London: SPCK, 1975.

Zimmerli, Walther. *Man and His Hope in the Old Testament.* London: SCM Press; Naperville, IL: Allenson, 1971.

——. *Old Testament Theology in Outline.* Richmond: John Knox; Edinburgh: T&T Clark, 1978.

NAME INDEX

SUBJECT INDEX

and impurity, 321, 462, 499
and Israel, 161, 271, 286, 427, 434
and Jesus, 186, 207, 335, 347, 349, 379, 407,
    422, 424, 515, 544, 584
and mind, 377, 420, 451
and sin, 212, 336
and soul, 176, 185, 188-91, 277, 411
and spirit, 64, 192, 214, 357
and the Spirit, 194, 397
and unity, 374, 495, 498
Buddhists, 547
Caesar, 172, 275, 355-56, 450
Caiaphas, 44, 259
charis, 22, 117, 316, 424, 470
charism, 182, 423, 484, 375
    and congregation, 369, 423-29
    and love, 485, 488, 501
    and unity, 489-90, 496
charisma, 316, 375, 424, 430, 479
christos, 285
church, 63, 80, 110, 113, 116, 183, 200, 214, 284,
    365, 368, 369, 390, 425, 426, 429, 430, 460,
    482, 490, 500, 509, 524, 535, 537, 555
    and authority, 353, 369, 432
    and the Bible, 13, 17
    and Christ, 264-65, 272
    the early, 97, 330
    and Gentiles and Jews, 128, 130, 248-49,
        257-58, 264, 376, 396, 429
    and God, 264-65, 318, 371
    history, 436, 488
    and Israel, 264-66, 271-74, 430
    and Jesus, 103, 108, 264, 291
    and Paul, 432, 434
    and persecution, 51, 541
    and Peter, 105-6, 284
    and prayer, 121, 478
    and purpose, 270, 341, 464
    and rebellion, 402, 404, 419
    and the Spirit, 63, 97, 243, 245, 401
    and unity, 235, 373-75, 497
    and women, 436, 463
    and the world, 50, 200, 202, 317, 367, 371,
        403, 413, 490, 515-16, 521, 523
    and worship, 121, 148, 465-67
    See also congregation
circumcision, 193, 217, 378, 389, 393
    and Jesus, 393, 443, 459
    and promise, 93, 221
    and sacramental signs, 381, 391-93
    and the Torah, 443, 458
commitment, 85, 97, 181, 192, 262, 269, 345, 351,
    368, 370, 384, 435, 460, 467, 481-88, 524

and congregation, 371, 378, 500, 412
covenant, 92, 114, 220, 347-48
    and faithfulness, 20, 88, 93
    and God, 32, 59, 69, 79, 114, 122, 141, 199,
        221, 226, 245, 284, 307, 311-12, 318, 336,
        377, 402, 472, 474
    to God, 35, 56, 123, 125, 197, 217, 405, 447,
        451-53, 463, 524
    and grace, 22, 26, 114, 117, 303, 418-19
    and Israel, 163, 413
    mutual, 37, 38, 41, 80, 117, 167, 225, 282
    personal, 42, 160, 473
    and restoration, 362, 389
    or steadfast love, 21, 22, 171
    and the Torah, 333, 422, 441
Communion, the, 368-69
communion, 65, 294, 316, 388
compassion, 30, 52, 90, 490, 528
    and believers, 338, 358, 492, 502
    and Jesus, 192, 290
    and sacrifice, 418-19
condemnation, 245, 315, 343, 553, 557
congregation, 36, 53, 129, 161, 179, 186, 187, 198,
    254, 337, 393, 460, 470, 500, 522, 556
    and city, 160, 271
    and family, 185, 487, 491-92
    as God's children, 361-79
    and God's insight, 110-11, 120
    and God's presence, 62, 80
    and Israel, 273, 448
    and judgment, 500, 555
    and love, 481, 484-85, 488, 493-94, 501-2
    and martyr, 110, 536, 551
    and prayer, 474-76
    and revelation, 94, 98, 101-2
    the servants of, 423-38
    and the Spirit, 61, 396, 513
    and the Torah, 442, 446-47
    and unity, 105, 489-90, 495-98
    and the world, 403, 470, 521
    and worship, 464, 468-69
    See also church
cosmos, 19, 20, 57, 134, 135, 138, 139, 141, 370,
    509, 513, 514, 539
    See also *kosmos*
covenant, 41, 61, 115, 226, 450, 460, 307, 313,
    317, 372, 453, 501
    and Abraham, 334, 391
    and baptism, 126, 392
    and circumcision, 221, 443
    and commitment, 92-93, 114
    and community, 268, 366

SCRIPTURE INDEX